THE BUSINESS OF JUDGING

The Business of Judging

Selected Essays and Speeches

TOM BINGHAM

Senior Law Lord

OXFORD

UNIVERSITY PRESS

OXFORD

UNIVERSITY PRESS

Great Clarendon Street, Oxford OX2 6DP

Oxford University Press is a department of the University of Oxford.
It furthers the University's objective of excellence in research, scholarship,
and education by publishing worldwide in

Oxford New York

Athens Auckland Bangkok Bogotá Buenos Aires Calcutta
Cape Town Chennai Dar es Salaam Delhi Florence Hong Kong Istanbul
Karachi Kuala Lumpur Madrid Melbourne Mexico City Mumbai
Nairobi Paris São Paulo Singapore Taipei Tokyo Toronto Warsaw

with associated companies in Berlin Ibadan

Oxford is a registered trade mark of Oxford University Press
in the UK and in certain other countries

Published in the United States
by Oxford University Press Inc., New York

British Library Cataloguing in Publication Data

Data available

Library of Congress Cataloging in Publication Data
Bingham, T. H. (Thomas Henry), 1933–
The business of judging: selected essays and speeches/Tom Bingham.
p. cm.
Includes bibliographical references and index.
1. Judicial process—Great Britain. 2. Law—Great Britain. I. Title.
KD358.B55 2000   340—dc21   00–037328
ISBN 0–19–829912–5

1 3 5 7 9 10 8 6 4 2

Typeset in Times by
Cambrian Typesetters, Frimley, Surrey

Printed in Great Britain
on acid-free paper by
Biddles Ltd., Guildford and King's Lynn

Preface and Acknowledgements

For about the last twenty years my working life has been devoted to the work of a judge: hearing evidence as a trial judge, listening to legal argument, considering the effect of previously decided cases, making up my mind which party should win and which should lose, composing and delivering judgments; and performing the administrative and public duties which fall to the lot of a judge. Looking at the five or so hours for which a judge sits in court each day, people sometimes imagine that judges have a rather light workload. But this takes no account of the work which a judge has to do before he takes his seat in court, and after the court has risen. Most judges would regard the work they do as important and rewarding, but also as exacting, mind-stretching, and time-consuming. There is not much time left over for activities outside the line of duty.

Juges are, however, often invited to give lectures on subjects with a legal slant, or contribute papers for legal conferences, or write essays on legal topics, or address issues concerned, in one way or another, with the administration of the law. Many of these invitations have to be declined, but some are accepted, because the suggested topic is of interest or importance, or because the audience is one the judge wishes to address, or because the request comes from someone who is hard to refuse.

This book contains a sample of the lectures, addresses, speeches, and papers I have given, made, or written since 1985. They are not the result of deep scholarly research or profound original thought. With more time, I could no doubt have improved them. But I have, for better or worse, resisted the temptation to improve them retrospectively. Save for the correction of one or two factual errors, they are as given or published. I have not updated the references. This inevitably means that there are some things which, if I were writing or speaking today, I would probably not say, or would put rather differently; that I sometimes make very much the same point on different occasions; and that I look forward to the future when now, with the passage of time, we have the benefit of knowing what, in the event, has happened. I can only hope that these blemishes will not deprive the contents of any interest there may be in the contemporaneous response of one senior judge to what seemed to him to be topics of concern, interest, and importance.

I have many debts of gratitude. Some are acknowledged in the text. I am in particular, grateful to Sally Phillips, the Supreme Court Librarian, and her staff, for their prompt and willing response to my pleas for written materials; to my personal secretaries Veronica Seymour and Naomi Bannister, who bore the brunt of word-processing the texts; to Ross Cranston QC, MP (then a professor of law, now Solicitor-General), who first suggested publication; to Nick Chibnall, my private secretary, who gave immense help in the task of selection; to the Delegates of the Oxford University Press for agreeing to publish and John Louth for seeing the volume through the press; and above all to my wife, into whose holidays (as well as mine) the composition of these pieces inevitably intruded.

January 2000   TOM BINGHAM

Contents

PART I:
THE BUSINESS OF JUDGING

The judge's job at a civil trial, it is often said, is first of all to decide what happened (in legal jargon, 'find the facts'), then to identify the relevant rules or principles of law, and then to apply the law to the facts as he has found them. Broadly speaking, this is true, although in some cases there is no dispute about the facts and the only argument is about the law; and sometimes (in practice, more often) there is little or no argument about the law and the real argument between the parties is about the facts; and sometimes, after the judge has decided what happened and what the applicable law provides, the real problem is what order the judge should make, how he should 'exercise his discretion'. If a case goes to appeal the argument is normally about the correctness of the judge's ruling on the law and much more rarely about his decision on the facts.

The first of the three papers in this section concerns the first of the judge's tasks, the making of a decision on what happened (a role performed by the jury in a serious criminal trial). This is a very important function, since the parties to a civil action *know* if the judge's decision is wrong on the primary facts, and the public at large expect judges to be right when they decide that this or that did or did not happen. But judges are not, on appointment, invested with some magical gift of second sight; they are not clairvoyants; they were not there when the disputed events took place. They did not see the road accident, or witness the explosion of the factory boiler, or sit in on the negotiation of the contract. All they can do, coming to the case well after the disputed events, is to try to piece the story together and attempt, on the basis of all available evidence produced in court, to reach a sound factual conclusion. The first paper considers how judges set about this task.

The second paper concerns the judge's role in developing, or making, the law, in cases when the legal rule or principle to be applied to the facts is not clear or is seriously out of date or fails to cover the facts. This paper was given at a conference in Auckland, New Zealand, in honour of Lord Cooke of Thorndon, a great judge who had for ten years (1986–96) been President of the Court of Appeal of New Zealand (and a judge of the court for ten years before that). Lord Cooke was (and is, for he continues to sit as a judge, although now mostly in London), a very learned and scholarly judge but also a very bold, forward-looking and liberal one. So this conference to celebrate his judicial achievement seemed a good opportunity to consider whether judges do 'make' law, and whether they should and, if so, how they set about it.

The third paper addresses a more elusive problem: the exercise of the judge's discretion. If a judge concludes that one person has suffered injury or loss through the negligence or breach of contract of another, he will give judgment for the injured party and calculate the appropriate damages; he cannot exercise his discretion to deny the injured party appropriate compensation. But all judicial decisions are not so clear-cut. In some situations the judge has a choice between one course and another; there are points and arguments each way; it is a question of weighing and balancing. It may make all the difference to the parties how he decides; and appellate courts are very reluctant to disturb decisions of this kind. So this area, grey though it may be, gives rise to difficult and anxious problems.

1

The Judge as Juror: The Judicial Determination of Factual Issues*

In the hierarchy of legal skills, pride of place is given, and quite rightly, to the great exponents of legal principle, those (whether academic or judicial) who weave disparate threads of authority into coherent doctrine or plant the flag of legal principle in hitherto untrodden factual territory. In comparison with these mandarin arts, the judicial determination of factual issues occupies a somewhat lowly place, an activity of its nature ephemeral, uncreative and particular. In short, a task appropriately left in criminal cases to the legally unqualified lay juror.

But reference to the criminal juror perhaps gives one pause for thought. His obstinate survival into modern times is, after all, at least in part, a reflection of public belief that where guilt and innocence depend on them factual decisions are too important to be left to judges. To the civil litigant also, whose case will almost always be tried by a judge sitting alone without a jury,[1] findings of fact are likely to be crucial. This is because, first, most cases turn largely, if not entirely, on the facts; as Justice Cardozo observed:

Lawsuits are rare and catastrophic experiences for the vast majority of men, and even when the catastrophe ensues, the controversy relates most often not to the law, but to the facts.[2]

And secondly it is so because factual findings once made at first instance are very hard to dislodge on appeal,[3] for reasons to which I will return. Of the litigants who each year tramp out of the law courts muttering darkly of a bad day for British (never, curiously, English) justice, I strongly suspect that a large majority have been outraged not by a decision against them on the law but by a factual decision which they know or believe or claim to be wrong. To the judge, resolution of factual issues is (I think) frequently more difficult and more exacting than the deciding of pure points of law. In deciding the facts, the judge knows that no authority, no historical enquiry and (save on expert issues) no process of ratiocination will help him. He is dependent, for better or worse, on his own unaided judgment. And he is uneasily aware that his evaluation of the reliability and credibility of oral evidence may very

---

* Reprinted from *Current Legal Problems*, vol. 38 (London: Stevens & Sons Ltd, 1985), 1–27. © Stevens & Sons Limited 1985.
    [1] s. 6(1) of the Administration of Justice (Miscellaneous Provisions) Act 1933 is in practice little used save in libel cases.
    [2] Benjamin Cardozo, *The Nature of the Judicial Process* (Yale, 1921), 128–9.
    [3] See, e.g. *Hontestroom (Owners) v Sagaporack (Owners)* [1927] AC 37; *Powell* v. *Streatham Manor Nursing Home* [1935] AC 243; *Onassis v Vergottis* [1968] 2 Lloyd's Rep. 403.

well prove final. So it is, I hope, worth considering what his factual task involves, and how he sets about it.

The judge's role in determining what happened at some time in the past is not of course peculiar to him. Historians, auditors, accident investigators of all kinds, loss adjusters and doctors are among those who, to a greater or lesser extent, may be called on to perform a similar function. But there are three features of the judge's role which will not all apply to these other investigations. First, he is always presented with conflicting versions of the events in question: if there is no effective dispute there is nothing for him to decide. Secondly, his determination necessarily takes place subject to the formality and restraints (evidential and otherwise) attendant upon proceedings in court. Thirdly, his determination has a direct practical effect upon people's lives in terms of their pockets, activities or reputations.

Some would draw attention to a further difference. The common law judge, it is often said, unlike his counterpart in a civil law system and unlike the other investigators I have mentioned, is not concerned with establishing the truth of what did or did not happen on a given occasion in the past but merely with deciding, as between adversaries, whether or not the party upon whom the burden of proof lies has discharged it to the required degree of probability. The Court of Appeal has said that 'The due administration of justice does not always depend on eliciting the truth. It often depends on the burden of proof.'[4] This may be unreservedly accepted, and it is of course true that the judge's independent power to remedy deficiencies in the evidence in civil cases is extremely limited.[5] The Court of Appeal has none the less defined the English judge's object as being, 'above all . . . to find out the truth, and to do justice according to law', and as being, 'at the end to make up his mind where the truth lies'.[6] This, I respectfully suggest, accords with the reality of what occurs in an English civil trial of any substance where factual issues are important. The mills of civil litigation may grind slowly, yet they grind exceeding small. By the time both parties have explored every point which they think may help them or damage their adversary not much remains obscure, and it is not (I think) a common complaint of judges at the end of such a case that the material submitted has been inadequate in quantity. While the burden of proof always exists, few substantial cases turn upon it and in making his factual findings the judge is usually expressing his considered judgment as to what in truth occurred. The crucial difference between him and his civil law counterpart is not, surely, in their respective objectives but in the means which have been evolved under the two systems for achieving the objective common to both, the ascertainment of the truth. 'In practice,' as Lord Devlin

---

[4] *Air Canada* v. *Secretary of State for Trade* [1983] 2 AC 394 at p. 411, *per* Lord Denning M.R.
[5] *Re Enoch and Zaretsky, Rock & Cos Arbitration* [1910] 1 KB 327.
[6] *Jones v National Coal Board* [1957] 2 QB 55 at pp. 63, 64 *per* Denning LJ, these references forming part of a passage described by Lord Devlin in *The Judge* at p. 56 as 'a classic account of the judge's function in the adversary system'.

observed, referring to the two systems, 'there is not, at any rate in the civil case, all that much difference.'[7]

Let me then turn to the central questions. Faced with a conflict of evidence on an issue substantially effecting the outcome of an action, often knowing that a decision this way or that will have momentous consequences on the parties' lives or fortunes, how can and should the judge set about his task of resolving it? How is he to resolve which witness is honest and which dishonest, which reliable and which unreliable? How, as between competing experts in a field not his own, is a judge to determine where the truth lies? Is our existing way of resolving expert conflicts the best way? I shall begin by considering the resolution of issues of primary fact, the choice between first-hand eye-witnesses. Then I shall turn to expert evidence.

The normal first step in resolving issues of primary fact is, I feel sure, to add to what is common ground between the parties (which the pleadings in the action should have identified, but often do not) such facts as are shown to be incontrovertible. In many cases, letters or minutes written well before there was any breath of dispute between the parties may throw a very clear light on their knowledge and intentions at a particular time. In other cases, evidence of tyre marks, debris or where vehicles ended up may be crucial. To attach importance to matters such as these, which are independent of human recollection, is so obvious and standard a practice, and in some cases so inevitable, that no prolonged discussion is called for. It is nonetheless worth bearing in mind, when vexatious conflicts of oral testimony arise, that these fall to be judged against the background not only of what the parties agree to have happened but also of what plainly did happen, even though the parties do not agree.

The most compendious statement known to me of the judicial process involved in assessing the credibility of an oral witness is to be found in the dissenting speech of Lord Pearce in the House of Lords in *Onassis v Vergottis*.[8] In this he touches on so many of the matters which I wish to mention that I may perhaps be forgiven for citing the relevant passage in full:

'Credibility' involves wider problems than mere 'demeanour' which is mostly concerned with whether the witness appears to be telling the truth as he now believes it to be. Credibility covers the following problems. First, is the witness a truthful or untruthful person? Secondly, is he, though a truthful person, telling something less than the truth on this issue, or, though an untruthful person, telling the truth on this issue? Thirdly, though he is a truthful person telling the truth as he sees it, did he register the intentions of the conversation correctly and, if so, has his memory correctly retained them? Also, has his recollection been subsequently altered by unconscious bias or wishful thinking or by overmuch discussion of it with others? Witnesses, especially those who are emotional, who think that they are morally in the right, tend very easily and unconsciously to conjure up a legal right that did not exist. It is a truism, often used in accident cases, that with every day

---

[7] *The Judge, supra,* p. 60.
[8] [1968] 2 Lloyd's Rep. 403 at p. 431.

that passes the memory becomes fainter and the imagination becomes more active. For that reason a witness, however honest, rarely persuades a Judge that his present recollection is preferable to that which was taken down in writing immediately after the accident occurred. Therefore, contemporary documents are always of the utmost importance. And lastly, although the honest witness believes he heard or saw this or that, is it so improbable that it is on balance more likely that he was mistaken? On this point it is essential that the balance of probability is put correctly into the scales in weighing the credibility of a witness. And motive is one aspect of probability. All these problems compendiously are entailed when a Judge assesses the credibility of a witness; they are all part of one judicial process. And in the process contemporary documents and admitted or incontrovertible facts and probabilities must play their proper part.

Every judge is familiar with cases in which the conflict between the accounts of different witnesses is so gross as to be inexplicable save on the basis that one or some of the witnesses are deliberately giving evidence which they know to be untrue. There are, no doubt, witnesses who follow the guidance of the Good Soldier Šveyk that 'The main thing is always to say in court what isn't true,'[9] as a matter of principle, but more often dishonest evidence is likely to be prompted by the hope of gain, the desire to avert blame or criticism, or misplaced loyalty to one or other of the parties. The main tests needed to determine whether a witness is lying or not are, I think, the following, although their relative importance will vary widely from case to case:[10]

(1) the consistency of the witness's evidence with what is agreed, or clearly shown by other evidence, to have occurred;
(2) the internal consistency of the witness's evidence;
(3) consistency with what the witness has said or deposed on other occasions;
(4) the credit of the witness in relation to matters not germane to the litigation;
(5) the demeanour of the witness.

The first three of these tests may in general be regarded as giving a useful pointer to where the truth lies. If a witness's evidence conflicts with what is clearly shown to have occurred, or is internally self-contradictory, or conflicts with what the witness has previously said, it may usually be regarded as suspect. It may only be unreliable, and not dishonest, but the nature of the case may effectively rule out that possibility.

The fourth test is perhaps more arguable. Much time is spent, particularly in criminal but also in civil cases where the honesty of witnesses is in issue, cross-examining as to credit, that is, in cross-examining witnesses on matters not germane to the action itself in order to show that they are dishonest witnesses whose evidence on matters which are germane to the action should be rejected. The underlying theory is that if a witness is willing to lie or can be shown to have

<hr />

[9] *The Good Soldier Šveyk* (Penguin edn. 1983), 382.
[10] For this, as for much of the ensuing discussion, I acknowledge my debt to the Hon. Sir Richard Eggleston QC *Evidence, Proof and Probability* (1978), 155.

acted dishonestly in one matter, he will be willing to lie or act dishonestly in another. As the Latin maxim put it, *falsus in uno, falsus in omnibus*. The practice of many advocates would suggest that the reliability of the principle is beyond doubt. And no doubt to any witness who from earliest youth, like Matilda's aunt, 'had kept a Strict Regard for Truth', the telling of any lie, large or small, on a matter relevant or irrelevant, would be unthinkable. There must nonetheless be many other witnesses who regard questions concerning their previous career or personal history or habits as an unwarranted intrusion into their privacy, in no way bearing on the substance of their testimony and undeserving of an honest answer. Or the truth may, for reasons right or wrong, be thought to be embarrassing. Let me give one very familiar example. A husband and wife both witness an event the subject of an action tried years later. Some months before the trial both give statements to the lawyers for the party wishing to call them. Both are in due course called to give evidence and are asked by cross-examining counsel whether their evidence has been the subject of discussion between them. Much more often than not, in my experience, the witness vehemently denies that there has been any discussion at all. It usually does not matter whether there has been discussion or not, but counsel who has obtained such an answer habitually points to the extreme unlikelihood of its being true and urges that the whole of the witness's evidence should be treated as suspect. Sometimes, taken in conjunction with other grounds for suspicion, this indication may be significant. I have on occasion relied on it.[11] But I very strongly suspect that many witnesses, not being untruthful people, infer from the asking of the question that any discussion of their evidence with their spouse will be criticised as improper; so, to avoid such public criticism, they deny that such discussion occurred, contrary to the very strong probability that most unestranged husbands will discuss with their wives matters which involve and concern them both. Equally, I strongly suspect that many honest witnesses, who would do their very best to ensure that the substance of their evidence was reliable and accurate, would nonetheless be willing to prevaricate, or if necessary lie, when asked why they lost their previous job or how their first marriage came to break up. Cross-examination as to credit is often, no doubt, a valuable and revealing exercise, but the fruits of even a successful cross-examination need to be appraised with some care.

And so to demeanour, an important subject because it is the trial judge's opportunity to observe the demeanour of the witness and from that to judge his or her credibility, which is traditionally relied on to give the judge's findings of fact their rare degree of inviolability. Lord Loreburn reflected such thinking when he said in *Kinloch v Young*:[12]

Now, your Lordships have very frequently drawn attention to the exceptional value of the opinion of the judge of first instance, where the decision rests upon oral evidence. It is

---

[11] e.g. *The Zinovia* [1984] 2 Lloyd's Rep. 264 at pp. 278–9.
[12] [1911] S.C. (H.L.) 1 at p. 4.

absolutely necessary no doubt not to admit finality for any decision of a judge of first instance, and it is impossible to define or even to outline the circumstances in which his opinion on such matters ought to be overruled, but there is such infinite variety of circumstances for consideration which must or may arise, and it may be that there has been misapprehension, or that there has been miscarriage at the trial. But this House and other Courts of appeal have always to remember that the judge of first instance had had the opportunity of watching the demeanour of witnesses—that he observes, as we cannot observe, the drift and conduct of the case; and also that he has impressed upon him by hearing every word the scope and nature of the evidence in a way that is denied to any Court of appeal. Even the most minute study by a Court of appeal fails to produce the same vivid appreciation of what the witnesses say or what they omit to say.

Lord Pearce, in his speech from which I have already quoted, makes the same point:

One thing is clear, not so much as a rule of law but rather as a working rule of common sense. A trial Judge has, except on rare occasions, a very great advantage over an appellate Court; evidence of a witness heard and seen has a very great advantage over a transcript of that evidence; and a Court of Appeal should never interfere unless it is satisfied both that the judgment ought not to stand and that the divergence of view between the trial Judge and the Court of Appeal has not been occasioned by any demeanour of the witnesses or truer atmosphere of the trial (which may have eluded an appellate Court) or by any other of those advantages which the trial Judge possesses.[13]

What, then is meant by the demeanour of the witness in this context? The answer is: his conduct, manner, bearing, behaviour, delivery, inflexion; in short, anything which characterises his mode of giving evidence but does not appear in a transcript of what he actually said. In *Clarke v Edinburgh Tramways*[14] Lord Shaw put it in this way:

witnesses without any conscious bias towards a conclusion may have in their demeanour, in their manner, in their hesitation, in the nuance of their expressions, in even the turns of the eyelid, left an impression upon the man who saw and heard them which can never be reproduced in the printed page.

Lord Justice Ormrod recently emphasized the importance of demeanour as a pointer to the truth. Referring to our system of oral trial, he said:

As a method of communication, it is very complex, involving not only what is actually said, but how it is said. Inflections in both questions and answers may be highly significant, and demeanour, not only of the witness, but of others in court may be revealing.[15]

I have a hunch, which I cannot begin to justify, that in days of yore trial judges rather prided themselves on and had considerable confidence in their ability to

---

[13] [1968] 2 Lloyd's Rep. 403 at p. 431.
[14] [1919] S.C. (H.L.) 35 at p. 36.
[15] *Judges and the Process of Judging (Jubilee Lectures*, Holdsworth Club Presidential Address 7/3/80).

discern the honesty of a witness from the showing which he made in the witness box. Be that as it may, the current tendency is (I think) on the whole to distrust the demeanour of a witness as a reliable pointer to his honesty. Let me quote passages from the extra-judicial utterances of three very experienced trial judges. First, Lord Devlin:

The great virtue of the English trial is usually said to be the opportunity it gives to the judge to tell from the demeanour of the witness whether or not he is telling the truth. I think that this is overrated. It is the tableau that constitutes the big advantage, the text with illustrations, rather than the demeanour of a particular witness.[16]

Second, Mr. Justice MacKenna, in a passage which Lord Devlin later adopted as his own:

I question whether the respect given to our findings of fact based on the demeanour of the witness is always deserved. I doubt my own ability, and sometimes that of other judges, to discern from a witness's demeanour, or the tone of his voice, whether he is telling the truth. He speaks hesitantly. Is it the mark of a cautious man, whose statements are for that reason to be respected, or is he taking time to fabricate? Is the emphatic witness putting on an act to deceive me, or is he speaking from the fullness of his heart, knowing that he is right? Is he likely to be more truthful if he looks me straight in the face than if he casts his eyes on the ground, perhaps from shyness or a natural timidity? For my part I rely on these considerations as little as I can help.[17]

Third, Lord Justice Browne:

So the main job of the judge of first instance is to decide the facts. How does he do it? When there is a conflict of evidence between witnesses, some judges believe that they can tell whether a witness is telling the truth by looking at him and listening to him. I seldom believed that. . . .[18]

To these powerful voices may be added two from Australia, suggesting that a loss of faith in the value of demeanour is not a purely local phenomenon. The Hon. Sir Richard Eggleston, QC wrote in 1978:

Many judges think they can tell from the demeanour of a witness when he is lying, but in the course of my practice at the Bar there were several occasions on which witnesses, whom I firmly believed to be honest and to be telling the truth, displayed evident signs of embarrassment and discomfort in the witness-box, sufficient to make them appear to be lying. I am therefore very sceptical of such claims. A more complicated case in which demeanour was deceptive was that of a man whom I knew well, who was employed as a book-keeper on a sheep station. When called upon to tell a social lie, he was covered with blushes and showed every sign of acute embarrassment. He always spent much more than his salary and was believed to have wealthy parents, but so transparent did he appear to be that it did not occur to anyone to question his honesty until a query came from head office

---

[16] *The Judge*, 63.
[17] 'Discretion', The Irish Jurist, vol. IX (new series), 1 at p. 10.
[18] 'Judicial Reflections', *Current Legal Problems* (1982), 5.

about the accounts, when he asked for the afternoon off, and was found dead some distance away. He had been systematically defrauding his employers for years, and almost everything he had told his associates about himself was fiction.[19]

And lastly, an advocate's view from Mr A. M. Gleeson, QC.:

Reasons for judgment which are replete with pointed references to the great advantage which the trial judge has had in making the personal acquaintance of the witnesses seem nowadays to be treated by appellate courts with a healthy measure of scepticism. What might be called the Pinocchio theory, according to which dishonesty on the part of a witness manifests itself in a manner that does not appear on the record but is readily discernible by anyone physically present, seems to be losing popularity.[20]

Seeing that we have so great a cloud of witnesses, any additional observations by me are plainly unnecessary. But I shall of course make some. There are, I feel sure, occasions on which a witness leaves a judge with a profound conviction that he is, or is not, telling the truth. This may not derive from anything he has said or failed to say but may be based ultimately on impression. As such it is probably impossible to explain or justify in rational terms. Whether his conviction was soundly based the judge is unlikely ever to know, so that he has little or no check on the accuracy of his own impressions, but if an impression is strong enough he will be unable in conscience to deliver a judgment which does not give effect to it. A firm judgment of this kind formed by one whose judgment is supposed to be his stock in trade is, I think, not lightly to be overridden. I would furthermore suggest that many judges, with years of forensic experience behind them, are likely to have developed some skill at recognizing certain types of rogue, particularly if the type is one they have met before. But subject to those qualifications I ally myself with the doubters. The cases which vex a judge are not those in which he is profoundly convinced of a witness's honesty or dishonesty. In those cases, whether his conclusion is right or wrong, the decision for him is easy. The anxious cases are those, which arise not infrequently, where two crucial witnesses are in direct conflict in such a way that one must be lying, but both appear equally plausible or implausible. In this situation I share the misgivings of those who question the value of demeanour—even of inflexion, or the turn of an eyelid—as a guide. To Mr Justice MacKenna's percipient remarks I would simply add three addenda:

First, the ability to tell a coherent, plausible and assured story, embellished with snippets of circumstantial detail and laced with occasional shots of life-like forgetfulness, is very likely to impress any tribunal of fact. But it is also the hallmark of the confidence trickster down the ages.

Secondly, there is (I think) a tendency for professional lawyers, seeing themselves as the lead players in the forensic drama, to overlook how unnerving an experience the giving of evidence is for a witness who has never testified before.

---

[19] *Evidence, Proof and Probability* (1978), 163.
[20] 'Judging the Judges', *Australian Law Journal*, vol. 53 (July 1979), 344.

The architecture of the Law Courts in the Strand, with its blend of the ecclesiastical (in the entrance hall) and the custodial (in many of the upper corridors), and the lay-out of the courts themselves, with the witness raised up and isolated like a lone climber on a peak in the Dolomites, might almost have been designed to maximize his unease. It would rarely, in my view, be safe to draw any inference from the fact that a witness seemed nervous and ill-at-ease; and if he did not it could well be because he had taken a tranquilliser to fortify himself for the ordeal, so that his apparent calmness would be equally lacking in significance.

Thirdly, however little insight a judge may gain from the demeanour of a witness of his own nationality when giving evidence, he must gain even less when (as happens in almost every commercial action and many other actions also) the witness belongs to some other nationality and is giving evidence either in English as his second or third language, or through an interpreter. Such matters as inflexion become wholly irrelevant; delivery and hesitancy scarcely less so. Lord Justice Scrutton once observed: 'I have never yet seen a witness who was giving evidence through an interpreter as to whom I could decide whether he was telling the truth or not.'[21] If a Turk shows signs of anger when accused of lying, is that to be interpreted as the bluster of a man caught out in a deceit or the reaction of an honest man to an insult? If a Greek, similarly challenged, becomes rhetorical and voluble and offers to swear to the truth of what he has said on the lives of his children, what (if any) significance should be attached to that? If a Japanese witness, accused of forging a document, becomes sullen, resentful and hostile, does this suggest that he has done so or that he has not? I can only ask these questions. I cannot answer them. And if the answer be given that it all depends on the impression made by the particular witness in the particular case that is in my view no answer. The enigma usually remains. To rely on demeanour is in most cases to attach importance to deviations from a norm when there is in truth no norm.

There are of course occasions when the simple language used by a witness, reproduced on the printed page, may be ambiguous although its meaning is, to anyone who hears the answer, apparent. For example, a witness may assent to a suggestion of cross-examining counsel with a shrug of the shoulders to indicate that though theoretically possible the suggestion is in practical terms absurd, or the assent may come after a long pause and in a manner indicating full acceptance. But responsible counsel do not allow a case to proceed on the basis of a single answer without making sure that the witness's position is clearly established, and were they to do so the judge would intervene to ensure that there was no room for doubt. The occasions on which the flavour of a witness's evidence is more accurately derived from the inflexion attached to a single answer, or his demeanour when giving it, than from the gist of a series of answers must, I suggest, be few.

---

[21] *Compania Naviera Martiartu of Bilbao v Royal Exchange Assurance Corporation* (1922) 13 Ll. L. Rep. 83 at p. 97.

If these doubts concerning the significance of demeanour are justified, certain consequences logically follow. An appellate court, reading the transcript of the evidence given, could decide the facts as well as the trial judge. There need be no bias in favour of the judge's factual conclusions. There could on an appeal be a complete re-hearing, on fact as well as law. The result would be to increase very substantially the burden on the appellate courts, to delay the *finis litium* which is held to be in the public interest, to increase uncertainty (because a litigant could never be sure on what version of the facts a point of law was to be decided) and to increase the already frightening cost of litigation. These are, without doubt, ills to be avoided if possible, and it would in my view be a respectable rule that every litigant should be entitled to a full contest on the facts at one level only and that the facts should be open to review thereafter only if some glaring and manifest error could be demonstrated. This is not, I think, very different from the substance of the present practice, but that practice might perhaps be better justified on that ground than by reference to the peculiar advantage enjoyed by the judge who has seen and heard the witnesses.

Before finally leaving the subject of demeanour—to which I have already, probably, devoted too much time—perhaps I may briefly digress to recount a somewhat remarkable cautionary tale. In *La Compania Martiartu of Bilbao v Royal Exchange Assurance Corporation*,[22] the owners of the steamship *Arnus*, which had been lost at sea off the coast of Brittany, sued the defendant insurers upon a time policy issued on the hull and machinery of the vessel, alleging that the loss was caused by perils of the sea. The insurers denied a loss by perils of the sea and alleged that the vessel had been wilfully cast away—scuttled—by those on board with the knowledge and consent of the owners. After a trial lasting five days (which contrasts with the four comparable cases tried since 1960, none of which lasted less than forty) the learned trial judge reserved judgment. When he gave judgment eight days later, he referred to powerful evidence in favour of scuttling but concluded on balance that the vessel had sunk as a result of striking a piece of floating wreckage. The crucial factor in the owners' favour was the evidence of the second mate:

If I do not believe the second mate it is quite clear this vessel was scuttled. I have to make up my mind whether in fact, when he says he saw this floating mass there was this mass or not. I was from the first and am still deeply impressed with the second mate's evidence. He gave his evidence in commission and repeated it here. I was impressed with his demeanour and frankness. . . . He gave his evidence quite fairly and frankly, and with great reticence. In my judgment that was a witness of truth. . . The main reason why I decide in favour of the owners is that I accept the evidence of the second mate. . . .[23]

The learned judge had apparently formed the view that his decision, being based almost entirely upon facts, was not open to review, and indeed spoke of it with what was later described as 'some degree of sanguineness' as practically

---

[22] (1922) 11 Ll. L. Rep. 186.   [23] Ibid., at pp. 188–9.

unappealable.[24] No doubt his conclusion founded on the demeanour of the second mate fortified that belief. But he proved to be mistaken. A finding of scuttling, made by the Court of Appeal, was upheld by the House of Lords. The task of the appellate courts was made easier when it emerged that the second mate, although he had testified on commission, had never attended the trial or given evidence at all and had (as Lord Birkenhead put it) 'enjoyed therefore small opportunity of exhibiting either his demeanour or his frankness'.[25]

If too much attention has over the years been paid to the demeanour of the witness in guiding the trial judge to the truth, too little has perhaps been paid to probability. I do not use that word in any mathematical or philosophical sense, but simply as indicating in a general way that one thing may be regarded as more likely to have happened than another, with the result that the judge will reject the evidence in favour of the less likely. I think most judges give weight to this factor in reaching their factual conclusions. Mr Justice MacKenna, in the paper from which I have already quoted, has said that he habitually did:

When I have done my best to separate the true from the false by these more or less object-ive tests, I say which story seems to me the more probable, the plaintiff's or the defend-ant's, and if I cannot say which, I decide the case, as the law requires me to do, in the defendant's favour.[26]

Lord Justice Browne spoke to rather similar effect, also in the paper previously quoted:

Sometimes one has to rely on probabilities and on circumstantial evidence; which I always thought was less unreliable than oral evidence. But the judge's own opinion about prob-abilities can be dangerous, being based on his own, perhaps limited, experience. Like all motorists, I thought I could see what the probabilities of a motor accident were, but I was quite incapable of judging the probabilities of a factory accident.[27]

In choosing between witnesses on the basis of probability, a judge must of course bear in mind that the improbable account may nonetheless be the true one. The improbable is, by definition, as I think Lord Devlin once observed, that which may happen, and obvious injustice could result if a story told in evidence were too readily rejected simply because it was bizarre, surprising or unprecedented. The most striking illustration of this which I know of, although given by Wigmore,[28] is one for which I am indebted to Sir Richard Eggleston:[29]

A woman living in Lancester, Massachusetts, on the hill that leads to the gaol, was consid-ered to be suffering from hallucinations, because of her complaint that the head of her late

24 (1924) 19 L1. L. Rep. 95.
25 Ibid., at pp. 95–6.
26 'Discretion', The Irish Jurist, vol. IX (new series), 1 at p. 10.
27 'Judicial Reflections', *Current Legal Problems* (1982), 6.
28 J. H. Wigmore, *The Science of Judicial Proof* (3rd edn.) (Boston, 1937), 443–5.
29 *Evidence, Proof and Probability*, 164.

husband (a negro) had rolled down the steps into her kitchen and had been retrieved by the devil wearing a black cloak. In fact, the devil was an eminent scientist, who had been making a study of the heads of criminals, and had, on the night in question, been carrying the head of a negro who had died at the gaol; he dropped the head in the street and it rolled down the steps of the old woman's house. As the removal of the head was not strictly lawful, he had wrapped his cloak round his face and calling out 'Where's my head? Give me my head!,' gone to retrieve it, confident that he would not be recognized.

American fact is stranger than English fiction. A second note of caution must also be sounded. An English judge may have, or think that he has, a shrewd idea how a Lloyd's broker, or a Bristol wholesaler, or a Norfolk farmer, might react in some situation which is canvassed in the course of a case but he may, and I think should, feel very much more uncertain about the reactions of a Nigerian merchant, or an Indian ship's engineer, or a Jugoslav banker. Or even, to take a more homely example, a Sikh shopkeeper trading in Bradford. No judge worth his salt could possibly assume that men of different nationalities, educations, trades, experience, creeds and temperaments would act as he might think he would have done or even—which may be quite different—in accordance with his concept of what a reasonable man would have done.

None the less, and despite these important disclaimers, I think that in practice judges do attach enormous importance to the sheer likelihood or unlikelihood of an event having happened as a witness testifies in deciding whether to accept his account or not. If, for example, a witness who is shown to have been a meticulous diarist, log-keeper, letter-writer or note-taker testifies to the happening of an event which he claims to have been of importance to him at the time but of which he made no record, then in the absence of some convincing explanation the court is likely to infer that the event did not occur at all, or that if it did occur the witness did not know of it, or that if it did and he did know of it the event did not then strike him as important. This is no more than ordinary common sense. Examples could be multiplied, but perhaps I can give one from my recent experience.[30] A seaman who was due to fly out to join a new ship went to the airport with his wife and children and there met a First Officer bound for the same ship. There being some delay before the aircraft took off, they all (according to the seaman-witness's evidence) had a meal together in a public restaurant at the airport. The witness's wife commented on the heat in India, where the ship was sailing, whereupon the First Officer told the witness and his wife not to worry about the heat, because he proposed to run the ship aground before she reached India in order to earn extra over-time. It was not suggested that the First Officer had ever met the witness's wife before, or that the witness and the First Officer (although they were acquainted) had ever discussed a crime of this character before or that the witness's children (although very young) were out of earshot. As it happened, there were other strong reasons for doubting the honesty of this witness, and in

---

[30] *The Zinovia* [1984] 2 Lloyd's Rep. 264 at p. 281.

addition he did not make a favourable impression as a person, nor did his evidence accord closely with his earlier statements. But I should, dealing with a foreigner and with statements taken either through interpreters or in very different circumstances, have been unhappy to rely on these last points alone. As it was the story struck me as so highly improbable—although not, of course, impossible—that I would, if necessary, have rejected it on grounds of sheer unlikelihood alone. It is, I think, a common occurrence for a judge to find, after using his imagination to place himself in the position of the witness and in the context of the case as a whole, that an account given in evidence is one that he simply cannot swallow. While this is not a very scientific test nor is it in my view, if carefully and imaginatively applied, any the worse for that.

Different views have been expressed of the frequency with which judges encounter deliberately untruthful witnesses. Sir Richard Eggleston took a rather gloomy view:

In my experience, judges tend to overrate the propensity of witnesses to tell the truth. Since judges regard breach of the obligation imposed by the oath as a serious crime, as indeed it is, they tend to think that witnesses will be as overawed as those who impose the sanction of an oath think they ought to be. In fact, I do not think many people feel any sense of wrongdoing when they swear falsely, so long as they can persuade themselves that they are doing it in a good cause.[31]

One must certainly accept that of the thousands who take the oath each year it would be a tiny minority who would be constrained thereby to tell the truth for fear of spiritual penalty. But Lord Justice Browne expressed a more generous opinion—not, I feel sure, accounted for by the difference of national jurisdiction:

I think that in civil cases (unlike criminal cases) the witnesses are seldom lying deliberately. But I am very sceptical about the reliability of oral evidence. Observation and memory are fallible, and the human capacity for honestly believing something which bears no relation to what really happened is unlimited.[32]

I respectfully agree although, regrettably, somewhat less wholeheartedly than I should have done some years ago.

The tests used by judges to determine whether witnesses although honest are reliable or unreliable are, I think, essentially those used to determine whether they are honest or dishonest: inconsistency, self-contradiction, demeanour, probability and so on. But so long as there is any realistic chance of a witness being honestly mistaken rather than deliberately dishonest a judge will no doubt hold him to be so, not so much out of charity as out of a cautious reluctance to brand anyone a liar (and perjurer) unless he is plainly shown to be such. There are three sources of unreliability commonly referred to by judges when rejecting the evidence of honest witnesses.

---

[31] *Evidence, Proof and Probability*, 159.
[32] 'Judicial Reflections', *Current Legal Problems 1982*, 5.

The first source of unreliability, arising principally when the evidence relates to an accident or incident occurring over a very short space of time, is where the witness although present at the scene and in a position to see what happened does not in truth see, or in any event register mentally, exactly what did happen. Most of those who witness events of this kind are in the position of casual watchers of football on television, denied a commentary or a slow-motion replay: they see that a goal is scored; they know which side has scored it; they may (just) be able to identify the player who scored it; but they could not to save their lives give an accurate description of the moves and passes which led up to it. As witnesses so regularly say, 'It all happened so quickly, it was over in a flash.' There is of course a minority of accurate and very perceptive observers, although I doubt if there would be many even of that select band who could with any pretence of accuracy answer the sort of question habitually asked in motor accident cases: 'Had you reached the second telegraph pole on the left in photograph number 3 when you first saw the oncoming vehicle?'

Work done by psychologists on the operation of the human memory throws a very interesting sidelight on this point.[33] There is good reason to accept that with a significant number of witnesses, exposure to later misinformation gives rise to an inaccurate recollection as a result of supplementation or alteration. An account of this was recently given by Elizabeth Loftus, of the University of Washington, in a paper presented to the Royal Society:[34]

In a typical experiment, subjects see a complex event and are then asked a series of questions which exposes them to post-event information. Typically some of the questions are designed to present misleading information, that is, to suggest the existence of an object or detail that did not in fat exist. Thus, in one study, subjects who had just watched a film of an automobile accident were asked, 'How fast was the white sports car going when it passed the barn while travelling along the country road?' Whereas no barn existed. The subjects were substantially more likely to later 'recall' having seen the non-existent barn than were the subjects who had not been asked the misleading questions.

The scope for quite unintentional distortion of a witness's recollection by police or enquiry agents or solicitors taking pre-trial statements is obvious. The same psychological testing suggested a number of other interesting conclusions, potentially significant to litigation: that once the memory is altered in this way, it is difficult to retrieve the original memory; that there is a tendency to reject misinformation if it comes from a source which the subject regards as biased or other than independent; that a warning against possible misinformation has an effect if given before the feeding of the misinformation but not after; that the longer the interval between the original event and the misinformation, the greater the chance of distortion; that misinformation is less likely to be rejected the less prominently

---

[33] I am indebted to Gillian Butler, of The Warneford Hospital, Oxford for her expert guidance through this, to me, unknown terrain.

[34] *Misfortunes of Memory*, paper presented at meeting of the Royal Society in January 1983.

it features in the question put to the subject; and that exposure to an incident of extreme and ugly violence tends to limit a subject's recollection and also render him more vulnerable to later misinformation. I am not of course competent to discuss these conclusions, but they do perhaps go some way towards showing that the judges' habitual caution in accepting evidence of this kind reflects an approach justified by science as well as common sense.

The second source of unreliability is loss of recollection. It is an unfortunate but inescapable fact that most factual issues come to be determined, at any rate in the High Court, several years after the material events occurred. It is almost axiomatic that a witness cannot recall an event which happened several years ago as clearly and accurately as one that happened the day before. As it is often put, recollections fade with the passage of time. I do not doubt the essential truth of this proposition, although there is (I believe) a school of thought which holds that memories, once stored in the human mind, last for ever, the only problem being one of retrieval.[35] But I would add two comments:

First, it is often assumed—or appears to be assumed—that recollection fades in a more or less constant way, such that if loss of recollection were plotted against time the result would be a straight line. Thus judges sometimes speak as if a lapse of time, no matter how long after an event, must deprive a witness of some significant recollection of it. As Lord Pearce put it, 'with every day that passes the memory becomes fainter. . . .'[36] Taken very literally this is no doubt true, but I have often wondered whether loss of recollection, particularly of rather ordinary events not regarded as very striking or noteworthy at the time, does not occur in the main early on—say, the first six months or a year—with relatively little loss thereafter of what remains at the end of that period. I am reassured to find that the results of psychological investigation tend to confirm this hunch.[37] Although related to an entirely different subject matter (the retention of nonsense syllables) and a time scale altogether inappropriate to the sort of event with which litigation is likely to be concerned, these investigations appear to show a very high rate of loss immediately following the event and then no more than a minimal loss. If this pattern applied generally, it would strongly justify the attention habitually paid to the date when a witness made his first statement, that being identified as the same at which his recollection crystallized.

Secondly, I strongly suspect that recollection fades in a selective and not in a uniform way: in other words, that the circumstantial detail falls away or becomes blurred while recollection of the crucial and striking features of the event (as perceived by the witness) survive. This is suggesting no more than what is perhaps obvious, that the dominant impression lasts longest. My own experience suggests to me that the crucial features of any real emergency in which one has been personally involved remain clear for a very long time, if not indefinitely.

---

[35] Ibid. [36] See note 8, *supra.*
[37] Alan D. Baddaley, *The Psychology of Memory* (Harper & Row, New York, 1976).

Psychologists would not, I think, challenge that view, but tests reported by F. C. Bartlett as long ago as 1932[38] tended to show that the loss of recollection by subjects of the test asked to reproduce a narrative after a lapse of time followed a systematic pattern: as one would expect, the summary given became shorter and details were omitted, but omitted also were features which did not fit in with the subject's prior expectations, and there was a tendency to introduce material to explain incongruous features of the original narrative; certain detail might become dominant; words and names would be changed so as to become more familiar; and sometimes even the order of events would change. In a platitude, the memory plays funny tricks.

The third source of unreliability which I would mention is wishful thinking. I have already quoted passages in which Lord Pearce and Lord Justice Browne refer to this. Many other similar citations could be made. There can be few trial judges who have not at some time said something to this effect: 'X testified that so and so happened. I am sure that X was being entirely truthful in giving this evidence. I am also sure that so and so did not happen. In my judgment X has, over the years, erroneously but quite genuinely persuaded himself that so and so happened as he described.' This approach has philosophical support; Nietzsche observed:

'I did this,' says my memory, 'I cannot have done this' says my pride, and remains inexorable. In the end memory yields.

I certainly do not challenge that such wishful thinking, usually a process of unconscious self-exoneration, occurs. But I do a little question how often, in normal (unhallucinated) people, it does so. One cannot usefully make a clinical experiment upon oneself, because that which one has wishfully persuaded oneself to be true is (if the theory is sound) indistinguishable to oneself from the truth. I must, however confess a personal belief that the effect of time is often quite the opposite: acts or omissions which at the time one persuades oneself are in every way proper and justifiable become, in retrospect, embarrassingly obvious as grounds of criticism. Perhaps it all depends on the individual. The consensus appears to be that this is not an uncommon phenomenon, and if, as I have suggested, the memory is vulnerable to misinformation from without, it is perhaps to be expected that the urgings of the subconscious will be no less efficacious.

When one turns from witnesses of primary fact to witnesses expressing expert opinions, the problem is different. Expert witnesses may be and often are partisan, argumentative, and lacking in objectivity, but they are not dishonest. I have only ever encountered one clear instance of an expert witness consciously and deliberately attempting to mislead a tribunal. But the problem remains: how is a judge, faced with conflicting opinions of two or more experts, to choose between them? Manner and demeanour give no assistance here, and it is surely a truism

---

[38] F. C. Bartlett, *Remembering* (Cambridge, 1932).

that the more truly learned a man is the more ready he is likely to be to admit ignorance and acknowledge inability to provide a perfect solution. It is often the superficial expert or the charlatan who offers the most confident and comprehensive answer. Nor can the choice be based on comparison of the experts' respective qualifications. Frequently, the experts' qualifications are broadly comparable. Where they are not, the choice usually lies between one expert whose career has been devoted to the amassing of postgraduate degrees to the virtual exclusion of practical experience in the field and another with no formal qualifications but a lifetime of experience in handling the commodity or operation in question. There is in truth no easy way out, no short cut. The only safe way in which a judge can choose between the opinions of experts is on the basis of what they have actually said, both in any reports they have submitted and in the course of forensic questioning. This is as it should be. But it does, I think, raise a problem.

For a judge to prefer the opinion of one expert to another he must understand what they have both said and form a reasoned basis for his preference. Usually this gives rise to no problem. The conflict of expert opinion may relate to an issue which is not particularly complex, or it may arise in a field of which the judge has previous experience or which he has studied at a level which at least enables him to understand the concepts to which the experts refer and the language they use. But this is by no means always so. The more advanced and experimental a technology the more risk there is of mishap, and legal proceedings do on occasion involve issues arising at or near the frontier of the technology involved. And it would not be at all unusual for one judge in the course of his career to be confronted by highly technical problems arising in the field of (and I give examples largely at random) chemical engineering, metallurgy, soil mechanics, brain surgery, naval architecture, computer technology, nuclear radiation, oil refining, navigation, mining engineering, combustion, and the international currency markets. No single man, however sophisticated his education or eclectic his interests or broad his experience, could hope to be familiar with all these fields, and as society becomes more complex and science more specialized, so the role of the amateur is diminished and the problem of assimilation and comprehension becomes greater. There are in my view times when the ability of judges to understand the effect of evidence given sufficiently to make an informed judgment is taxed to the very utmost, and I can imagine it being exceeded. There is, I think, an anomaly here. If an aircraft crashes or a factory blows up with serious loss of life, or if a major scandal rocks the financial world, a judge or a leading practitioner may well be appointed to investigate the matter and determine what happened. He would, however, be sure to have the assistance as fellow members of his tribunal or as assessors of two or three experts skilled in the disciplines involved in the inquiry. Yet if the same or a similar issue arose in the course of ordinary litigation the judge would be expected to cope with the problem as best he could on his own.

Many would argue that there is no anomaly. They would point out that in an action, unlike an inquiry, there are competing sides, and the clash of adversarial debate will highlight the substantial strengths and weaknesses of the expert opinions on each side so as to enable the judge to make a reasoned choice between them. The official investigation does not have the benefit of the same adversarial debate. Moreover, they would add, advocates are not themselves endowed by nature with knowledge of these esoteric sciences, and if they can master them sufficiently to present the case the judge should be able to master them sufficiently to decide it. There is of course force in these points, but I think that there is at least a partial answer to each. In the first place, while it is true that an official inquiry is inquisitorial in approach, it invariably works out in practice that different parties end up in an adversarial relationship to at least some others. This may owe something to the background and training of English lawyers, but I think it owes more to the obvious desire of parties to shift blame from themselves to others or at least to implicate others in a shared blame. In addition, there are often insurance considerations and potential claims lurking in the wings. So in the end the difference between the inquiry and the action is not very great. Secondly, while judges have the opportunity to study experts' reports and hear them questioned, they do not have the great advantage which advocates enjoy of prolonged, informal discussion with experts so that the rudiments of the subject, starting if necessary from first principles, can be methodically and even laboriously explained. The constraints of presentation in court make this in practice very difficult, if not impossible, to achieve with the judge as pupil, and even if achievable involves the parties in very great expense. In the small minority of cases in which problems of this kind arise, might it not be desirable for a judge to sit with the assistance of an expert assessor or for an independent expert to be appointed to assist the court?

Lest this question should be thought to be tainted by any element of originality, let me hasten to make clear that an omniscient legislature has anticipated it. Section 70(1) of the Supreme Court Act 1981 (based on section 98 of the Judicature Act 1925) provides:

In any cause or matter before the High Court the court may, if it thinks it expedient to do so, call in the aid of one or more assessors specially qualified, and hear and dispose of the cause or matter wholly or partially with their assistance.

The costs of any such assessor are to be determined by the court and form part of the costs of the proceedings. The same section makes provision for the appointment of scientific advisers to assist the Patents Court, but the remuneration of such advisers come out of public funds.

The Rules of the Supreme Court reflect these statutory provisions. They provide for trial by a judge or official referee with the assistance of assessors as one of the permissible modes of trial.[39] Such trial is to take place in such manner

---

[39] R.S.C., Ord. 33, r. 2.

and on such terms as the court may direct.[40] They also make provision, on the application of any party, for appointment by the court of an independent expert or experts to act as a court expert and inquire into and report on any question of fact or opinion not involving questions of law or construction.[41] Such expert is if possible to be a person agreed between the parties but is, in default of agreement, to be nominated by the court. The Rules regulate the rights of the parties to cross-examine the court expert and to call their own experts on points covered by his report.

In admiralty proceedings there are special, and perhaps more familiar, provisions. The Rules of the Supreme Court here provide for an order to be made on the summons for directions whether the trial is to be without assessors or with one or more assessors, whether Elder Brethren of Trinity House, nautical assessors or other assessors,[42] and if the action is to be tried with assessors the court may on the application of any party make an order for the inspection of the ship by the assessors.[43] A special code also exists in patent proceedings under the 1949 and 1977 Acts. The court may at any time and on or without the application of any party appoint an independent scientific adviser to assist the court either by sitting with the judge at the trial or hearing of the proceedings or by inquiring and reporting on any question of fact or of opinion not involving a question of law or of construction.[44] The court nominates the scientific adviser and settles his instructions.

One might have thought that considerable use would be made of these provisions. In *Waddle v Wallsend Shipping Company Ltd*.[45] for example, a fatal accidents claim arising out of the unexplained sinking of a vessel which had been the subject of a wreck inquiry, Mr Justice Devlin felt himself at something of a disadvantage sitting alone to determine issues on which the Wreck Commissioner had had expert assistance. He said:[46]

A Wreck Inquiry has already taken place before a Wreck Commissioner assisted by two naval architects and a ship's captain as assessors. Frequent references have been made during the course of the trial before me to the evidence given at the Inquiry. The report has not been tendered and I have not been told what conclusion was reached about the cause of the loss. I think this is strictly correct; the report is not admissible and the parties are entitled to have the matter considered and determined afresh. At the same time, I think it unfortunate that an application was not made before this trial began that it should take place with assessors. That would have happened, I imagine, as a matter of course if it had been tried in the Admiralty Division, and a Judge of that Division has himself considerable experience in this class of case. I considered at the outset of the trial whether I should myself make an order in the matter, but it would have involved postponement, the date of the trial had been fixed for some time past, and many witnesses were in attendance. It will not be very satisfactory if I arrive at a different result from that reached by a very experienced Commissioner assisted by skilled assessors, but I have to do my best to arrive independently at the right conclusion.

---

[40] R.S.C., Ord. 33, r. 6.   [41] R.S.C., Ord. 40.   [42] R.S.C., Ord. 75, r. 25(2).
[43] R.S.C., Ord. 75, r. 28.   [44] R.S.C., Ord. 104, r. 11.   [45] [1952] 2 Lloyd's Rep. 105.
[46] Ibid. at p. 131.

Profiting from his experience in that case, the judge did in the following year appoint an assessor. In *Esso Petroleum Co. Ltd. v Southport Corporation*,[47] he began his judgment as follows:

In this case questions of seamanship and navigation arise and, acting under the Judicature Act, 1925, s. 98 and R.S.C., Ord. 35, r. 43, I have appointed one of the Elder Brethren of Trinity House to act as an assessor and to advise me upon them. In *Waddle v Wallsend Shipping Co. Ltd.* I called attention to what seemed to me the undesirability of having questions of this sort tried by a judge of the Queen's Bench Division sitting without assistance. The practice of sitting with the Elder Brethren is always followed in the Admiralty Division, and if it is not followed in this Division as well it is bound to lead to the belief that the result will not be as satisfactory as it should be. I have therefore been advised by an Elder Brother, Commodore Hubbard, R.D., R.N.R., before arriving at my conclusions in this case, but I have not had his assistance during the hearing. I hesitated in this case, as I did in *Waddle v Wallsend Shipping Co. Ltd.*, to adjourn the trial so that an assessor might be present because of the inconvenience to the parties and their solicitors and counsel. But I doubt whether I shall in any similar case in the future allow these considerations to deter me again.

On an appeal to the House of Lords the Lord Chancellor approved these observations:

If a judge comes to the conclusion that the case is one in which he would profit by the presence of an assessor, it is manifestly more satisfactory that this assistance should be available during the trial than after its completion.[48]

Despite these observations, the use of the provisions I have mentioned has in recent years and with only limited exceptions been slight. I have myself never known of a Queen's Bench action tried with assessors, and enquiries do not suggest my experience (or lack of it) to be untypical. Appeals against orders for the taxation of costs are heard with assessors but are scarcely in point. The only Queen's Bench judge whom I know to have proposed appointing an assessor was unable in the event to do so and was pleased at the end of the case that he had not. The Senior Queen's Bench Master tells me that he has never in seventeen years known of a court expert being appointed in that Division and nor have any of his staff. The present Admiralty Judge does sit with an Elder Brother as assessor in collision cases, but has never done so in any other class of case (although he did once propose to do so in a case which settled). The Patent Judges have on occasions, in cases involving advanced technologies such as computers and colour television, appointed a scientific adviser, usually because the parties wanted it, but these occasions have been few. By and large the judges have dealt with cases on their own.

The general neglect of assessors can be fairly readily explained. By and large counsel show great skill in presenting even very complex factual issues in a way which enables judges to grasp them. And finding a suitable assessor may be very hard. In a practical or fast-moving-field those who are most readily available—a

---

[47] [1956] AC 218 at p. 223.   [48] Ibid., at p. 238.

retired civil servant, perhaps, or academic—may be unable to give the sort of help which is really needed, while those with the best up-to-date practical knowledge may be unable to spare the time. An assessor must in addition be manifestly disinterested and this also can cause problems: in a case involving two of the Big Seven oil companies, for example, it would not be easy to find an experienced oil man who had not been employed by either of them, or been refused employment by either or been involved in close dealings or negotiations with either. The neglect of court experts is also explicable. The chances and changes of litigation are formidable enough as it is, but parties do at least feel able (sometimes, as it turns out, mistakenly) to rely with confidence on their expert saying what he has committed himself to say. They are naturally reluctant to forgo this assurance for an independent expert whom they do not engage, do not directly pay, cannot decline to call if his opinion is entirely hostile and cannot, perhaps, cross-examine so effectively.

In both cases there are, I think, other reasons. One may be that in the absence of a docket system of the kind familiar to American judges it is very unusual for the judge who is ultimately going to try the case to be in charge of the interlocutory proceedings from the start. If he were, it might be easier for unusual plans to be laid in good time before the trial for the expeditious and effective determination of expert issues. More fundamentally, the general neglect of assessors and court experts surely owes much to the temperamental reluctance of English lawyers, judges, and practitioners alike, to depart at all from the traditional, adversarial format of English proceedings. An assessor is an expert, not open to cross-examination by the parties, whose professional beliefs and interpretation of the evidence may have an important influence on the judge. A court expert is independent of either party, and for that very reason liable to carry special weight with the court. Both procedures encroach a little on the principle that truth and justice are born of the clash of warring parties before an independent and uninformed tribunal, and for that reason are viewed with suspicion.

Many would regard the professional neglect of these procedures as the surest proof of their worthlessness: 'The market knows best.' Maybe so. But we live at a time when the length and expense of trials are the subject of urgent public concern, when technologies become daily more complex and when (for professional and social reasons) the number of lawyers with any specialised expertise outside the law steadily diminishes. It could not plausibly be argued that the elucidation of complex technical issues could not be more quickly and economically achieved between judge and assessor out of court than by the laborious processes of question and answer in court, even allowing for the submission of written reports. The assessor will not decide the case. The responsibility of arriving at a judicial conclusion remains that of the judge alone.[49] As Viscount Simon said in *Richardson v Redpath Brown & Co. Ltd.*:[50]

---

[49] *The City of Berlin* [1908] P. 110 at p. 118; *The Koning Willem II* [1908] P. 125 at p. 137.

[50] [1944] AC 62 at p. 70.

He is an expert available for the judge to consult if the judge requires assistance in understanding the effect and meaning of technical evidence. He may, in proper cases, suggest to the judge questions which the judge himself might put to an expert witness with a view to testing the witness's view or to making plain his meaning. The judge may consult him in case of need as to the proper technical inference to be drawn from proved facts, or as to the extent of the difference between apparently contradictory conclusions in the expert field.

Where expert reports can be wholly or largely agreed before the hearing, no problem of course arises. But a court expert would then harm neither party. His report would identify the common ground between the parties. There are, however, many trials in which days and days of expensive time are spent in establishing that experts whose initial reports appeared to be in fundamental conflict were not in truth so deeply divided after all. There should, in any field in which an expert is entitled to testify at all, be a corpus of knowledge and experience accepted by most orthodox practitioners,[51] and a court expert would at least clarify where the essential conflict lay. It is moreover not uncommon in arbitration, particularly where some of those involved are not exclusively reared in the Anglo-American tradition, to hive off time-consuming factual issues for investigation and report by an independent expert, thereby saving days or weeks of hearing time. A court procedure does exist for reference of a factual issue to a special referee,[52] but this procedure (like the others I have mentioned) is rarely used and merely provides another mode of trial. The time has come, I suggest, when our traditional beliefs might profitably be re-examined. Almost every procedural change which is nowadays made dilutes to some extent the pure water of adversarial litigation by requiring earlier disclosure and reducing the element of surprise. The civil law procedures of the continent and elsewhere are no longer dismissed with chauvinistic scorn, even if we continue to regard our own as on the whole superior.[53] Perhaps we have something to learn. However good the results which the judges now achieve, it may be that a more flexible approach to procedure in this field would achieve even better results, or the same results more quickly and more cheaply. In the law, as in religion, there is a growing awareness that the route to the desired end may be a multi-line highway, not a monorail.

On this point, as on others, I offer no final solution but only questions. Perhaps I may end with the quotation from Holt C.J. with which Lord Denning concluded his famous speech in *Rahimtoola v The Nizam of Hyderabad*:[54]

I have stirred these points, which wiser heads in time may settle.

---

[51] Kenny, 'The Expert in Court' (1983) 99 LQR 197 at p. 205.   [52] R.S.C., Ord. 3.
[53] See, for example, *The El Amria* [1981] 2 Lloyd's rep. 119 at p. 126 *per* Brandon LJ; *Amin Rashid Shipping Corporation v Kuwait Insurance Co.* [1984] 1 AC 50 at p. 67, *per* Lord Diplock.
[54] [1958] AC 379.

2

The Judge as Lawmaker: An English Perspective*

The role of Judges as lawmakers has over the years been the subject of much discussion. There appear, broadly speaking, to be four schools of thought on the subject.

The first school would hold that Judges have no role as lawmakers: their function is to declare the law, not to decide what it should be. The business of law making is, on this view, exclusively a matter for Parliament. The most prominent standard-bearer of this school, at any rate in England in relatively recent times, was Lord Simonds. Responding to an invitation by Lord Denning to overrule the English rule on privity of contract, he said:[1]

To that invitation I readily respond. For to me heterodoxy, or, as some might say, heresy, is not the more attractive because it is dignified by the name of reform. Nor will I easily be led by an undiscerning zeal for some abstract kind of justice to ignore our first duty, which is to administer justice according to law, the law which is established for us by Act of Parliament or the binding authority of precedent. The law is developed by the application of old principles to new circumstances. Therein lies its genius. Its reform by the abrogation of those principles is the task not of the Courts of law but of Parliament.

Even better known is his description of Lord Denning's plea for a purposive approach to statutory interpretation as 'a naked usurpation of the legislative function under the thin disguise of interpretation'.[2] But Lord Simonds, even if he spoke more memorably than most, was not a lone voice. In 1951, Lord Jowitt, the Lord Chancellor, when asked in Australia what the House of Lords would do if there was an appeal in the recently decided case of *Candler v Crane Christmas & Co*,[3] replied:[4]

We should regard it as our duty to expound what we believe the law to be and we should loyally follow the decisions of the House of Lords if we found there was some decision which we thought was in point. It is not really a question of being a bold or a timorous soul; it is a much simpler question than that. You know there was a time when the earth was void and without form, but after these hundreds of years the law of England, the common law, has at any rate got some measure of form to it. We are really no longer in the

---

* Reprinted from Paul Rishworth (ed.), *The Struggle for Simplicity in the Law: Essays for Lord Cooke of Thorndon* (Wellington: Butterworths, 1997), pp. 3–12.
[1] *Scruttons v Midland Silicones Ltd* [1962] AC 446, 467–9.
[2] *Magor and St Mellons Rural District Council v Newport Corporation* [1952] AC 189, 191.
[3] [1951] 2 KB 164.
[4] See M. Zander *The Law-Making Process* (4th edn, 1994), 347.

position of Lord Mansfield who used to consider a problem and expound it ex aequa et bona—what the law ought to be . . . I do most humbly suggest to some of the speakers today that the problem is not to consider what social and political conditions do today require; that is to confuse the task of the lawyer with the task of the legislator. It is quite possible that the law has produced a result which does not accord with the requirements of today. If so, put it right by legislation, but do not expect every lawyer, in addition to all his other problems, to act as Lord Mansfield did, and decide what the law ought to be. He is far better employed if he puts himself to the much simpler task of deciding what the law is.

On this view, Judges are what Montesquieu called 'the mere mouthpieces of the law'.[5] As Lord Wright put it, the Judges proceed 'from case to case, like the ancient Mediterranean mariners, hugging the coast from point to point and avoiding the dangers of the open sea of system or science'.[6] It is a role which has attracted distinguished support. Lord Devlin, for example, wrote:[7]

In the course of their work Judges quite often disassociate themselves from the law. They would like to decide otherwise, they hint, but the law does not permit. They emphasise that it is as binding upon them as it is upon litigants. If a Judge leaves the law and makes his own decisions, even if in substance they are just, he loses the protection of the law and sacrifices the appearance of impartiality which is given by adherence to the law. He expresses himself personally to the dissatisfied litigant and exposes himself to criticism. But if the stroke is inflicted by the law, it leaves no sense of individual justice; the losing party is not a victim who has been singled out; it is the same for every body, he says. And how many a defeated litigant has salved his wounds with the thought that the law is an ass! So I am not distressed by the fact that at least nine-tenths of the judiciary spends its life submerged in the disinterested application of known law.

If the army of judicial camp-followers who would once have adhered to the declaratory view of their function has by and large melted away, the view nonetheless retains support among some lay bodies. For example, a business group in New Zealand, opposing the abolition of appeals to the Privy Council from New Zealand, recently submitted:[8]

However, it may be noted that the sovereignty argument for abolition wrongly assumes (as do some Judges) that judicial decision making is of great political and constitutional significance. In fact, Judges are at most only interstitial law-makers, that is they fill in narrow spaces left in the laws enacted by parliament. To invoke a wider role on 'sovereignty' grounds is to endorse the concept of a law-making rather than a law-interpreting role for Judges. Being unelected, Judges should not assume a law-making role, which is properly the province of parliament. With our sovereign legislature, it is always open to reverse judicial decisions by legislation if that is supported by a majority in Parliament. The proper role of the Courts should be seen within that context.

---

[5] *Esprit de Lois* XI, 6.
[6] 'The Study of Law' (1938) 54 LQR 185, 186.
[7] *The Judge* (1981), 4.
[8] New Zealand Business Roundtable *Appeals to the Privy Council* 1995, para 1.9.

A somewhat similar view, although qualified later on in the same passage, was expressed by the Chief Justice of New South Wales:[9]

Fourthly, it is expected of Judges that they will apply neutral and general principles to the resolution of individual disputes; they have no mandate to act as ad hoc legislators who, by decree, determine an appropriate outcome on a case-by-case basis.

The second school acknowledges that Judges do make law, but urges that this role should be so far as possible covert and imperceptible to the general public. It is a school which might not deserve to be singled out for special mention were it not for the eminence of the support which it has attracted. Lord Radcliffe wrote:[10]

If Judges prefer to adopt the formula—for that is what it is—that they merely declare the law and do not make it, they do no more than show themselves wise men in practice. Their analysis may be weak, but their perception of the nature of law is sound. Men's respect for it will be the greater, the more imperceptible its development.

And, some years later, Lord Radcliffe returned to the subject:[11]

I think that the Judge needs to be particularly circumspect in the use of his power to declare the law, not because the principles adopted by Parliament are more satisfactory or more enlightened than those which would commend themselves to his mind but because it is unacceptable constitutionally that there should be two independent sources of law-making at work at the same time.

Lord Scarman, somewhat more obliquely, made the same point:[12]

Great Judges are in their different ways judicial activists. But the Constitution's separation of powers, or more accurately functions, must be observed if judicial independence is not to be put at risk. For, if people and Parliament come to think that the judicial power is to be confined by nothing other than the Judge's sense of what is right (or, as Selden put it, by the length of the Chancellor's foot), confidence in the judicial system will be replaced by fear of it becoming uncertain and arbitrary in its application. Society will then be ready for Parliament to cut the power of the Judges. Their power to do justice will become more restricted by law than it need be, or is today.

The third school, to which most modern common law Judges belong, acknowledges that Judges do make law, and regards this as an entirely proper judicial function, provided it is exercised within certain limits. So general is the acceptance of this approach today that citation is scarcely necessary. But one recalls that in his famous lecture to the Society of Public Teachers of Law on the 'Judge as Lawmaker' Lord Reid in 1972 said:[13] 'We must accept the fact that for better or for worse Judges do make law, and tackle the question how do they approach their task and how should they approach it.'

---

[9] A. M. Gleeson, 'Individualised Justice—the Holy Grail' 69 ALJ 421, 432.

[10] *Law and its Compass*, (1960), 39.

[11] *Not in Feather Beds* (1968), 216.

[12] *Duport Steels Ltd v Sirs* [1980] 1 All ER 529, 551.

[13] (1972) 12 Jnl Soc Public Teachers of Law, 22.

Speaking judicially, the New Zealand Court of Appeal adopted much the same line:[14] 'While accepting that it is inevitably the duty of the Court to extend the scope of common law review if justice so requires, we are not satisfied that in this field justice does so require, at any rate at present. . . .' The limits within which this lawmaking role should be pursued are considered below.

The fourth school not only acknowledges a lawmaking role for the Judges, but glories in that role and asserts a right to pursue it wherever established law impedes the doing of justice in an individual case. The most obvious proponent of this school, whose name will instantly spring to the lips of all lawyers, is Lord Denning, who may indeed be said to have no peer in this respect. Indeed, viewing his judicial career in retrospect, he can be seen to have adopted an agenda of reform, as he himself has expressly claimed. This activity would seem to fall within Lord Devlin's definition of dynamic or creative lawmaking, by which he meant 'the use of the law to generate change in the consensus'[15] of opinion upon a given topic within society.

It is not surprising that the first, declaratory, school has little judicial support today. This may owe something to the clash of personalities between Lord Simonds and Lord Denning, the haughty figure of Simonds being less endearing than the warm personality of Denning, and the mandarin prose of Simonds being a little strong for most modern stomachs, particularly when compared with the apparently simple and highly imitable prose style of Denning. But the reasons for rejecting the declaratory view are more fundamental than that. The declaratory approach is radically inconsistent with the subjective experience of Judges, particularly appellate Judges, of the role which they fulfil day by day. They know from experience that the cases which come before them do not in the main turn on sections of statutes which are clear and unambiguous in their meaning. They know from experience also that the cases they have to decide involve points which are not the subject of previous decisions, or are the subject of conflicting decisions, or raise questions of statutory interpretation which apparently involve genuine lacunae or ambiguities. They know, and the higher the Court the more right they are, that decisions involve issues of policy. Lord Denning was among the first to acknowledge this obvious truth in *Dutton* v. *Bognor Regis UDC*:[16]

It seems to me that it is a question of policy which we, as Judges, have to decide. The time has come when, in cases of new import, we should decide them according to the reason of the thing. In previous times, when faced with a new problem, the Judges have not openly asked themselves the question: what is the best policy for the law to adopt? But the question has always been there in the background. It has been concealed behind such questions as: Was the defendant under any duty to the plaintiff? Was the relationship between them sufficiently proximate? Was the injury direct or indirect? Was it foreseeable, or not? Was it too remote? And so forth. Nowadays, we direct ourselves to considerations of policy. . . .

---

[14] *Burt v Governor-General of New Zealand* [1992] 3 NZLR 672, 683.
[15] *The Judge*, 2.   [16] [1972] 1 QB 373, 397.

Lord Cooke of Thorndon has spoken in similar vein:[17]

From the point of view of an appellate Judge hearing cases day by day it seems more than a decade since the pretence of legal formalism was abandoned and much more open emphasis began to be placed on working out a philosophical approach—to use a somewhat pompous term to describe conscious value judgments. . . . Direct debate of policy considerations, and with an eye to interests transcending those of the immediate parties, has become commonplace. Without exaggeration it may be said to be regular fare in the Court of Appeal.

The truth is that Judges cannot adhere to the declaratory principle even if they would. Take, for example, the authority perhaps most familiar to common lawyers world-wide: *Donoghue v Stevenson*.[18] No one could fail to recognize that narrow 3–2 decision as having made law, and most would have little doubt that it made good law. But if the majority had been the other way the decision would still have made law. Such a decision might not have stood the test of time, and one would incline to see it as a bad decision. But until reversed or modified such a decision would have precluded a successful action by a plaintiff in a similar position in England and Scotland and in those parts of the Commonwealth which then followed House of Lords decisions. A negative decision would, no doubt, have been less innovative, and therefore the subject of less comment and development, than the decision actually made. But it would have placed a highly authoritative roadblock in the path of a plaintiff and so would have made law. The same is true whenever a Court, on legal or policy grounds, declines to grant relief. Even if it be true, as Lord Goff has attractively suggested, that statements of the law are no more than working hypotheses,[19] it remains true also that an authoritative statement of the law on a point not the subject of an existing authoritative statement makes new law.

The inadequacy of the declaratory principle as an explanation of the judicial role is even more evident when one looks at the objective record of what Judges have done. In England, the last quarter century has seen fundamental, Judge-made changes in the law relating to public interest immunity; sovereign immunity; forum non conveniens; restitution; tax avoidance schemes; pre-emptive interlocutory remedies; the currency in which judgment may be given; and, pre-eminently, judicial review. Other examples could be given. Attention could also be drawn to the creative, if somewhat erratic, approach of the English Courts to questions of negligence where the victim has suffered economic loss.[20] In New Zealand the creative role of the Judges has been even more evident. It has been well described by Lord Cooke, and has been shown to include distinctive developments in the

---

[17] 'The New Zealand National Legal Identity' (1987) 3 Cant LR 171.
[18] [1932] AC 562.
[19] 'Judge, Jurist and Legislature' [1987] Denning LJ 79, 80.
[20] For an interesting survey, see Goldsmith, 'The Retreat from the Retreat from Anns?', paper delivered to the 11th Commonwealth Law Conference, Vancouver, August 1996.

fields of crime, family law, real property, personal property, contract, employment and, not least, the law of tort. Lord Cooke has claimed for New Zealand 'a distinct national legal identity'.[21] That this is no idle boast has been accepted by the Privy Council itself:[22]

But in the present case the Judges in the New Zealand Court of Appeal were consciously departing from English case law on the ground that conditions in New Zealand are different. Were they entitled to do so? The answer must surely be 'Yes'. The ability of the common law to adapt itself to the differing circumstances of the countries in which it has taken root, is not a weakness, but one of its great strengths. Were it not so, the common law would not have flourished as it has, with all the common law countries learning from each other.

In 1988 Lord Cooke said:[23]

The stage has now been reached in which in virtually every major field of law New Zealand law is radically, or at least very considerably, different from English law. In many respects Australian or Canadian legal experience and ideas are now more relevant for us, as we work out our legal destiny.

To the extent that this is so, it is so as a result of conscious decision-making by the Judges.

It would be very hard to reconcile the House of Lords' Practice Statement of 1966 with the declaratory principle in its purest form. It would also be hard to see how, if this principle were adopted, it could be useful to discuss the amendment of English procedure so as to permit prospective overruling of previous decisions, so as to lay down a principle to govern future cases but not the case before the Court.

The second, 'do good by stealth', approach to the judicial function no doubt has a considerable measure of practical wisdom to support it. But most Judges, and their critics, would today think it generally preferable, for better or worse, to be open about what they are doing. Lord Cooke has said:[24]

I am against hidden policy factors. Major premises should not be inarticulate, although they do not need constant restatement. A just decision is surely more likely if the Judge recognises a responsibility to be frank.

Professor Atiyah, too, has powerfully argued against judicial illusionism.[25]

If, as is accepted, it is generally incumbent on a Judge to give reasons for his decision, then it must surely follow that such reasons should be full and genuine. This duty is sometimes perhaps more honoured in the breach than in the observance. One cannot resist the suspicion that on occasion a duty of care is denied

---

[21] Cooke, 'The New Zealand National Identity' (1987) 3 Cant LR 171, 180.
[22] *Invercargill City Council v Hamlin* [1996] 1 NZLR 513, 519–520.
[23] 'Fundamentals' [1988] NZLJ 158.
[24] 'Fairness' (1989) 19 VUWLR 421.
[25] 'Judges and Policy' (1980) 15 Israel LR 346.

because the Court apprehends that, if a duty were held to exist, insurance would be impossible or prohibitively expensive to obtain in future. But such a reason is rarely explicitly stated, probably because the Court has had no evidence before it of what the insurance position might be if a duty of care were held to exist. It is, surely, an abnegation of the judicial role if a Judge allows himself to be influenced in his decision by considerations to which he does not allude.

Adherents of the third, currently majoritarian, school would acknowledge that a range of different road signs may in different situations be appropriate, ranging from 'No entry' and 'Stop' to 'Give way' and 'Slow'. The debate is as to which of these injunctions applies in differing circumstances, and with what degree of compulsion. There are, however, various situations in which most Judges, even of the reformist, majoritarian tendency, would regard one or other of these signs as apposite. Such situations would include the following:

(1) Where reasonable and right-minded citizens have legitimately ordered their affairs on the basis of a certain understanding of the law. As Lord Reid put it:[26]

And there is another sphere where we have got to be very careful. People rely on the certainty of the law in settling their affairs, in particular in making contracts or settlements. It would be very wrong if Judges were to disregard or innovate on what can fairly be regarded as settled law in matters of this kind.

(2) Where, although a rule of law is seen to be defective, its amendment calls for a detailed legislative code, with qualifications, exceptions and safeguards which cannot feasibly be introduced by judicial decisions. Such cases call for a rule of judicial abstinence, particularly where wise and effective reform of the law calls for research and consultation of a kind which no Court of law is fitted to undertake.

(3) Where the question involves an issue of current social policy on which there is no consensus within the community. As Lord Reid again put it:[27]

When public opinion is sharply divided on any question—whether or not the division is on party lines—no Judge ought in my view to lean to one side or the other if that can possibly be avoided. But sometimes we get a case where that is very difficult to avoid. Then I think we must play safe. We must decide the case on the preponderance of existing authority. Parliament is the right place to settle issues which the ordinary man regards as controversial. On many questions he will say: 'That is the lawyers' job, let them get on with it.' But on others he will say: 'I ought to have my say in this. I am not going to accept dictation from the lawyers.' Family law is a good example. It is not for Judges to say what changes should be made on big issues.

(4) Where an issue is the subject of current legislative activity. If Parliament is actually engaged in deciding what the rule should be in a given legal situation, the Courts are generally wise to await the outcome of that deliberation rather than to

---

[26] (1972) 12 Jnl Soc Public Teachers of Law 22, 23.   [27] Ibid. 23.

pre-empt the result by judicial decision. Lord Radcliffe thought the Judges should walk warily in fields where Parliament regularly legislated or had recently done so.[28] Cardozo thought the Judge should 'legislate only between gaps. He fills the open spaces in the law'.[29]

(5) where the issue arises in a field far removed from ordinary judicial experience. This is really another way of saying that whereas the Judges may properly mould what is sometimes called lawyers' law, they should be very slow to lay down far-reaching rules in fields outside their experience. They should be alert to recognize their own limitations.

Even where a Judge recognizes that a change in the law is called for, he is well advised to walk circumspectly. On the whole, the law advances in small steps, not by giant bounds. Many Judges will seek to adopt the approach of Bacon, in his declaration that 'The work which I propound tendeth to pruning and grafting the law, and not to ploughing up and planting it again'.

The fourth (Denning) approach to judicial lawmaking is perhaps open to four objections, at any rate when pursued by anyone other than Lord Denning. The first objection is that if Judges make too free with existing law, or are too neglectful of precedent, the law becomes reprehensibly uncertain and unpredictable. It is often said, rightly, that legal certainty is a chimera. So it is. But that is no reason for rejecting any attempt to achieve a measure of certainty where possible. Again, it is appropriate to quote Lord Reid:[30]

People want two inconsistent things; that the law shall be certain, and that it shall be just and shall move with the times. It is our business to keep both objectives in view. Rigid adherence to precedent will not do. And paying lip service to precedent while admitting fine distinctions gives us the worst of both worlds. On the other hand too much flexibility leads to intolerable uncertainty.

It is a question of balance.

The second objection to this approach is that too much depends on the temperament and predilections of the individual judge. As Samuel Johnson, one of the wisest legal commentators of all time, put it:[31]

To permit a law to be modified at discretion is to leave the community without law. It is to withdraw the direction of that public wisdom by which the deficiencies of private understanding are to be supplied.

The same point has been made, rather more recently, by the Chief Justice of New South Wales:[32]

The greater the scope for the exercise of individual discretion and the application of

---

[28] *Not in Feather Beds*, 216.
[29] B. Cardozo, *The Nature of the Judicial Process* (1921).
[30] (1972) 12 Jnl Soc Public Teachers of Law 22, 26.
[31] Boswell, *Life of Johnson* (Oxford, 1976), 496.
[32] Gleeson, 'Individualised Justice—The Holy Grail' (1995) 69 ALJ 421, 431–2.

subjective value-judgments, the less will be the assurance, essential for public confidence, that the outcome of the case depends as little as humanly possible upon the identity of the Judges who decide them. This is not to suggest that the law was ever capable of working in a fashion that is unaffected by the views and attitudes of individuals. But, other things being equal, the object ought to be to minimise the effect of this element of the system, not to maximise it.

The third objection to this approach is that a Judge who works to a predetermined agenda necessarily deprives himself of the capacity to respond to the merits of the particular case as it unfolds before him. Where, as in time is bound to be the case, the Judge's agenda is known, the trial process is to some extent subverted, since the advocate on one side will know that he has to overcome an obstacle, not necessarily inherent in the case itself, but arising out of preconceived views held by the Judge.

The fourth objection is that Judges are not, by and large, fitted to be law reformers. This is a point well made by Lord Devlin:[33]

The disinterested application of the law calls for many virtues, such as balance, patience, courtesy, and detachment, which leave little room for the ardour of the creative reformer. I do not mean that there should be demarcation or that Judges should down tools whenever they meet a defect in the law. I shall consider later to what extent in such a situation a Judge should be activist. But I am quite convinced that there should be no judicial dynamics.

He added, with reference to social reform:[34]

If Judges were men endowed for such a task they would not truly be Judges. In every society there is a division between rulers and ruled. The first mark of a free and orderly society is that the boundaries between the two should be guarded and trespasses from one side or the other independently and impartially determined. The keepers of these boundaries cannot also be among the outriders. The Judges are the keepers of the law and the qualities they need for that task are not those of the creative lawmaker. The creative lawmaker is the squire of the social reformer and the quality they both need is enthusiasm. But enthusiasm is rarely consistent with impartiality and never with the appearance of it.

Although Judges bind themselves to do right to all manner of people, they are to do so according to the laws and usages of the realm and not according to their own personal conceptions of what is wise or just.

It would seem that Judges of the third, majoritarian, school should be described as activists within Lord Devlin's definition:[35]

By activist law making I mean the business of keeping pace with change in the consensus. Dynamic or creative law making is the use of the law to generate change in the consensus.

Lord Cooke, however, has shown some distaste for the label 'activist', which he described in an obituary of Lord Diplock as 'a term of dubious import but often

---

[33] *The Judge*, 5. [34] Ibid. 17. [35] Ibid. 2.

having a connotation of trendy'.[36] He was anxious to make plain that a paper which he delivered on 'Fundamentals' was not intended as an incitement to judicial activism.[37] When an Associate-Professor described the New Zealand Courts, and particularly the Court of Appeal, as activist from the late 1970s or early 1980s,[38] Lord Cooke does not appear to have regarded this as a compliment.[39] In 1992, he described 'activist' as 'a misleading expression, as Judges cannot initiate action'.[40] But the opposite of active is passive, and the opposite of activism is inertia. No informed commentator could accuse Lord Cooke of being a passive Judge, nor suggest that his record is one of inertia. He has himself acknowledged that:[41]

The inevitable duty of the Courts is to make law and that is what all of us do every day. Doubtless some make more than others, but it could not seriously be contended that Judges at any level are merely applying black-and-white rules.

In the law, nothing is the work of one Court or one man; and it would be invidious for anyone, particularly an extra-terrestrial commentator, to seek to allocate praise. But if it be true, as it plainly is, that the common law in New Zealand has developed along distinctive lines peculiarly suited to the culture and customs of the people (not least the Maori people), and if it be true, as again it plainly is, that the common law as developed in New Zealand commands high respect throughout the entire common law world, no commentator, whether indigenous or extraterrestrial, could fail to recognise the immense contribution, wise and scholarly as it has been, of Lord Cooke as lawmaker.

---

[36] [1985] NZLJ 352.   [37] [1988] NZLJ 158, 164.

[38] W. C. Hodge, 'Lions under the Throne', in B. Gray and B. McLintock (eds.), *Courts and Policy: Checking the Balance* (1994), 91, 108.

[39] Foreword to *Courts and Policy: Checking the Balance*, pp. x–xi.

[40] 'Employment and Accountability: The Quest for Administrative Justice' [1992] Commonwealth Law Bulletin 1326, 1331.

[41] 'Dynamics of the Common Law', *9th Commonwealth Law Conference* 1990, 1, 4.

3

The Discretion of the Judge*

A judge of my acquaintance once told me that when, in the course of trying a case, he encountered any problem of unusual difficulty, it was his practice to glower at counsel in his most forbidding manner and demand 'Is this not a matter within my discretion?' On counsel agreeing that it was—which it seems they readily did—he would sink back in his chair with relief, relaxed in the knowledge that no matter what he decided his decision would be immune from successful challenge on appeal.

The complaisance of counsel may seem surprising, given the consequence for their clients of a decision being regarded as discretionary. But judges and practitioners have, I think, habitually used the expression 'judicial discretion' in a variety of senses, and academic writers have used it in a different sense again. This lack of consensus is also surprising. Since at latest 1581,[1] authoritative voices on both sides of the Atlantic, Coke,[2] Mansfield,[3] and Marshall[4] among them, have urged that the discretionary powers of judges and justices be strictly limited and controlled by the law to avoid the arbitrariness of an unpredictable personal decision. Right down to this century, strong language has been used. 'To remit the maintenance of constitutional right to the region of judicial discretion', said Lord Shaw of Dunfermline in 1913, 'is to shift the foundations of freedom from the rock to the sand'.[5] Or as Justice William Douglas put it, 'Absolute discretion, like corruption, marks the beginning of the end of liberty.'[6] Lord Simon of Glaisdale expressed the traditional view when he said, speaking on the judicial discretion to admit or exclude evidence, 'And if it comes to the forensic crunch . . . it must be law, not discretion, which is in command.'[7]

Any lack of certainty as to what judicial discretion is may also be thought undesirable. For if, as these warnings suggest, judicial discretions are dangerous as capable of leading to arbitrariness, it is as well judges should be quite clear when they are exercising a discretion and when not, and if the exercise of a discretion is a barrier (whether or not surmountable) to an appeal then appellate judges should similarly recognize when the barrier exists and when it does not.

I am vividly aware that he who defines invites scholarly refutation, and to

---

* The Royal Bank of Scotland Lecture, Oxford University delivered on 17 May 1990, [1990] Denning Law Journal 27.
[1] Lambarde, *Eirenarcha*, 58.   [2] *Prohibitions del Roy* (1607) Co. Rep. 63, at 64–5.
[3] *R v Wilkes* (1779) 4 Burr. 2527, at 2539.
[4] *Osborn v The Bank of the United States* (1824) 22 U.S. 738, at 866.
[5] *Scott v Scott* [1913] A.C. 417, at p.477.
[6] *State of New York v United States* (1951) 342 US 822, at 884.
[7] *D. v NSPCC* [1978] A.C. 171, at 239 G.

attempt the task in this forum may reasonably be thought foolhardy. I shall none the less proffer a definition, and briefly defend it. On the assumption that my definition is broadly acceptable, I shall then suggest that the role of judicial discretion is now narrowly confined. I shall further suggest, with appropriate apologies to Mr Dunning, as he then was, that its role has decreased, is decreasing and need not in general be much further diminished. The dragon of arbitrary discretion has not been slain, but it has been domesticated and put on a short leash.

According to my definition, an issue falls within a judge's discretion if, being governed by no rule of law, its resolution depends on the individual judge's assessment (within such boundaries as have been laid down) of what it is fair and just to do in the particular case. He has no discretion in making his findings of fact. He has no discretion in his rulings on the law. But when, having made any necessary finding of fact and any necessary ruling of law, he has to choose between different courses of action, orders, penalties or remedies he then exercises a discretion. It is only when he reaches the stage of asking himself what is the fair and just thing to do or order in the instant case that he embarks on the exercise of a discretion.

I believe this definition to be broadly consistent with the usage adopted in statutes. There are of course numerous statues which confer a discretion on the court, describing it as such; many of these relate to the award of costs, the imposition of criminal penalties and the exercise of procedural powers, all of them pre-eminently discretionary fields. To some examples I shall return. But often a discretion is conferred although not so described: 'may, in accordance with the rules of court, extend any such period to such extent and on such conditions as it thinks fit . . .';[8] 'may order that such party be at liberty to inspect and take copies of any entries in a banker's book . . .';[9] 'may . . . as it thinks fit', 'may . . . as the court thinks just'; 'may impose such other condition as it thinks fit';[10] 'On an application under this section the court may make or refuse to make the declaration asked for . . .';[11] and so on, almost *ad infinitum*. A discretion is conferred whichever form of words is used.

While my exploration of the statute book is far from comprehensive, I have encountered only two provisions which are inconsistent with my suggested definition. The first is in section 2 of Fox's Libel Act 1792 which provides 'That, on every such trial, the Court or Judge before whom such indictment or information shall be tried, shall, according to their or his Discretion, give their or his Opinion and Directions to the Jury on the Matter in Issue between the King and the Defendant or Defendants, in like manner as in other Criminal Cases.' I would have to admit that the direction which a judge gives to a criminal jury on the law is not now a matter of discretion within my definition. But the next section uses the term in my sense: it provides that nothing shall 'prevent the Jury from find-

---

[8] Maritime Conventions Act 1911, s. 8. [9] Bankers' Book Evidence Act 1879, s. 7.
[10] Housing Act 1988, s. 9(1)(2)(3). [11] Local Government Finance Act 1982, s. 19.

ing a Special Verdict, in their Discretion, as in other Criminal Cases'. The second exception occurs in section 25 of the Children and Young Persons Act 1933, the product of an age happily innocent of teenage pop-stars and tennis prodigies. It forbids anyone having the custody of a person under 18 to cause or permit such person to go abroad for the purpose of singing, playing, performing or being exhibited for profit without a licence from a police magistrate. The magistrate may vary or revoke such a licence 'for any cause which he, in his discretion, considers sufficient'.[12] Now I would have no quarrel if the magistrate were given power in his discretion to vary or revoke for sufficient cause, and that may be what the sub-section means, but I could not accept that a cause could be sufficient simply because the magistrate considered it so. The sub-section may, however, only be intended to provide that the police magistrate's judgment on sufficiency should be final, not an unusual provision when decisions are entrusted to administrators. These exceptions may scratch the paintwork of my definition; they do not, I think, hole it below the water-line.

It might be thought unnecessary to stress that the judge has no discretion in making findings of fact. But judges do sometimes describe fact-finding as discretionary. That learned and accurate judge, the late Sir Brian MacKenna (who resembled Gibbon in nothing save his account of what he owed the University of Oxford), referred to 'the judge's other great discretionary power, that of finding the facts when he tries a case alone'.[13] Lord Brightman referred to the existence or non-existence of a fact as being left to the judgment and discretion of a public body.[14] Justice Barak of the Israel Supreme Court has written 'The first area of judicial discretion deals with deciding the facts.'[15] Now it is one thing to say that the responsibility of finding the facts is entrusted to a particular person or body, be he judge, arbitrator, official or public authority, and that such finding is to be treated as conclusive or virtually so. But it is quite another to describe that function as discretionary. It is, I suggest, nothing of the kind. In finding the facts the judge's job is to consider all the conflicting evidence this way and that and decide as best he can where the truth lies. It is very much the task performed, for instance, by the historian or the journalist as part of his stock in trade. The judge is of course constricted by formalities and rules of evidence which do not afflict them. On the other hand, he has powers of compelling testimony which they would envy. It is none the less essentially the same function. Yet to say of a historian or a journalist that he exercised a discretion in reaching conclusions of fact would, I suggest, be regarded as libellous. The judge must exercise judgment, not discretion, in finding the facts, and it is usually the most difficult and often the most exacting task which the civil trial judge has to undertake. It calls for a degree of rigour which is disguised by references to choosing between competing

---

[12] S. 25 (5)(a).   [13] 'Discretion', *The Irish Jurist*, vol. IX (new series) 1, at 9.
[14] *R v Hillingdon London Borough Council ex p. Pulhofer* [1986] A.C. 484, at 518.
[15] *Judicial Discretion* (1989), at 13.

accounts of a disputed event or preferring the evidence of one witness to that of another, and to speak of discretion in this context is to open the door to potentially dangerous habits of thought. It can lead to such absurdities as assessing expert evidence on the demeanour of the expert or such errors as finding a fact to be established because it has been denied by a witness held to be unreliable. It can encourage excessive reliance on the judge's hunch and intuition, neither of them an invariably safe basis for decision.[16] The judge must decide, in as objective a manner as the materials permit, which version of a disputed event (if either) he accepts as the more convincing; once he has done so he has no choice, whether that conclusion makes the overall resolution of the case more difficult or less so. When reference is made to the trial judge's discretion to decide the facts, what is really meant is that appellate courts will usually be reluctant to interfere with his findings because he, having seen and heard the witnesses, is in a better position to decide whose evidence is reliable than anyone else. In cases turning largely on oral evidence, this is doubtless very often true: the trial judge's immediate contact with the witnesses and the unfolding drama of litigation gives him insights denied to those who come later. It is the advantage which the journalist on the scene at the time enjoys over the historian. And even if the judge may be wrong, no one else can be sure of being right. But it is well, even in this class of case, to preserve a measure of scepticism. As Lord Wilberforce has recently observed:

English judges entertain the belief that they can tell if a man—or even a woman—is speaking the truth. This is a Palladium: and it has comforting consequences: 'The judge saw the witness in the box—observed his demeanour'. 'He was disbelieved by the judge—or the jury'. 'We (the appeal court) cannot interfere'. But there is not much scientific basis for this. Such studies, as I know of, show that liars are believed as often as truth-tellers are disbelieved. And one can test it with multiple tribunals—e.g. arbitrations, whether all British or from different nations. I can give several instances where exactly opposite views as to credibility were confidently given by members of such tribunals—a fact which encourages people to avoid oral evidence before them. Indeed, one often finds foreign arbitrators irritated with the English style of examination and cross-examination—it is not a good way of getting at the truth or persuading the tribunal.[17]

Further, the very immediacy of the trial judge's impressions can sometimes cloud his judgment. There are, I think, more cases than is generally acknowledged, particularly those largely independent on documentary or expert evidence, in which the insights of the trial judge are less reliable than the more detached reflection of an appellate court as those of the journalist sometimes are than those of the historian. I fear I have digressed, but I would wish firmly to exclude the notion of discretion from the very important area of factual decision.

In boldly asserting that a judge does not exercise discretion in giving his rulings on the law I have, I appreciate, side-stepped a very high level philosophical debate

---

[16] And see *Current Legal Problems* (1985) 1, at 7.
[17] 5 Arbitration International (1989), at 349.

conducted by Professors Hart, Dworkin, MacCormick, Raz, and others.[18] I fear that my offering on the sergeant directed to take his five most experienced men on patrol would be of small value anyway, but it is plain that decisions on the law fall well outside my definition of judicial discretion. This is not in any way to criticise the usage of others; the English language is a rich pasture open to all. But on this point at least I think I can rely on the invariable usage of the practising profession in this country. It is a distinction regularly drawn when leave is sought to appeal against an interlocutory decision, the judge's usual practice being to grant leave if he has decided a question of law and to refuse it if he conceives himself to have exercised a discretion. There may well be uncertainty where discretion begins and ends but there is unanimity that it falls short of legal rulings. I would, however, offer one observation prompted by the philosophical debate. There are occasions when judges *think* that they are required to elect between different legal solutions and, in effect, create new law. Usually, even in cases that turn on the law, the question is whether the given case falls within an established principle or which of two established principles governs it. But there are occasions when existing lines of authority fall short of the given case and the question is whether they should be extended to cover it. *Donoghue v Stevenson*[19] is perhaps the most obvious example; hence, no doubt, the divergence of opinion in that case. There are other, rarer, occasions when a problem seems to occur in an authoritative desert, where the usual aids—principle, precedent, *dicta* and the opinions of learned authors—are virtually absent. The judge cannot then simply extend the line on an existing graph of authority because there is none. It is surely true that when judges buttress their conclusions with references to public policy, commercial good sense, certainty, good industrial relations and so on it is because they are conscious of making a choice and are, quite properly, concerned to justify the choice that they have made.

The role of discretion in the balancing exercises which the courts are, it seems increasingly, invited to carry out is not altogether easy to determine. For instance, in balancing the public interest in withholding official documents against the public interest in the administration of justice,[20] or in weighing the competing public interests in disclosure and non-disclosure,[21] or for and against publication[22] or in the maintenance of confidence against disclosure,[23] or between maintaining professional confidences and protecting the public against possible violence,[24] is the judge exercising a discretion and if so to what extent? Some would, I think, regard this exercise as largely if not wholly discretionary.[25] But I

---

[18] See, e.g., H. L. A. Hart, *The Concept of Law* (1961); R. Dworkin, *Taking Rights Seriously* (1977); N. MacCormick, *Legal Reasoning and Legal Theory* (1978); J. Raz, *The Authority of Law* (1979); A. Barak, *Judicial Discretion* (1989).   [19] [1932] AC 562.
[20] *Conway v Rimmer* [1968] AC 910, at 952 A..   [21] *D. v NSPCC* [1978] AC 171, at p.219C.
[22] *British Steel Corporation Ltd. v Granada Television Ltd.* [1981] AC 1096, at 1202 C.
[23] *A.G. v Guardian Newspapers* (No. 2) [1990] AC 109, at 282.
[24] *W. v Egdell* [1990] 2 WLR 471, at 491 A.
[25] e.g. Barak, *Judicial Discretion* (1989), at p. 68.

do not think the factors to be put into the scales are the subject matter of discretion. They are matters established, or held to be established, by evidence, or more rarely matters of which judicial notice may be taken. Discretion has nothing to do with that, as I have already suggested. In the English *Spycatcher*[26] litigation, for instance, detailed evidence was adduced to show why publication would damage national security; the trial judge discounted most of this, but in doing so he was not, at least in my terms, exercising a discretion. In assessing the weight to be given to various factors for and against any decision, much must of course turn on the judgment of the individual assessor, and for this reason an appeal court will be slow to interfere with a value judgment on which reasonable minds could differ. Strictly, however, I think it is probably only at the last stage of striking a balance and granting or refusing relief that one moves into the realm of pure discretion. For this view, I hope I may enlist the aid of Lord Diplock. In *Birkett v James*,[27] speaking of interlocutory decisions, he said:

They are decisions which involve balancing against one another a variety of relevant considerations upon which opinions of individual judges may reasonably differ as to their relative weight in a particular case. That is why they are said to involve the exercise by the judge of his 'discretion'. . . when leave is granted, an appellate court ought not to substitute its own 'discretion' for that of the judge merely because its members would themselves have regarded the balance as tipped against the way in which he had decided the matter . . .

That may sound like somewhat doubtful aid. But on both occasions when Lord Diplock, a stickler for accurate usage, spoke of discretion in that passage he put the expression in inverted commas, to indicate, as I infer, that he was not referring to an exercise of discretion properly so called.

The role of judicial discretion today is, I suggest, subject to one exception, fairly narrowly confined. For that proposition I summon up the weighty support of Sir Wilfred Greene MR:

In all discretionary remedies it is well known and settled that in certain circumstances—I will not say in all of them, but in a great many of them—the Court, although nominally it has a discretion, if it is to act according to the ordinary principles upon which judicial discretion is exercised, must exercise that discretion in a particular way, and if a judge at a trial refuses to do so, then the Court of Appeal will set the matter right.[28]

That was said 50 years ago, but it is even truer today, as can (I think) be demonstrated by reference to the areas in which discretion is most obviously exercised.

I start with the award of costs. A series of statutes entrusts this to the discretion of the court or arbitrator.[29] Notably, section 51 of the Supreme Court Act

---

[26] *A.G. v Guardian Newspapers* (No. 2) [1990] AC 109.
[27] [1978] AC 297, 317 D.
[28] *R v Stafford Justices* [1940] 2 K.B. 33, at 43.
[29] e.g. Arbitration Act 1950, s. 18; Magistrates Courts Act 1980, s. 64; Highways Act 1980, s. 209; County Courts Act 1984, s. 45; Agricultural Holdings Act 1986, Sched. 11, para 23.

1981 provides that costs shall be in the discretion of the court which 'shall have full power to determine by whom and to what extent the costs are to be paid'. So special is this discretion that rights of appeal are specifically restricted,[30] and its width has been recently emphasised by the House of Lords.[31] It is nevertheless universally recognized as the primary principle governing courts and arbitrators in the exercise of their discretion that costs should follow the event[32] and to depart from that rule without showing sufficient reason is to raise a rebuttable presumption of error.[33] It is of course necessary to identify the event, which in a tangle of claims and cross-claims may not be straightforward, but a party's entitlement to receive costs or responsibility to pay them is first to be judged by reference to his success or failure in the litigation.[34] This primary principle may not be applied in its full rigour, for example where a party's conduct in the litigation[35] justifies a departure or where the successful party recovers less than had earlier been offered or paid into court,[36] but a well-established body of authority[37] shows that a judge is by no means free to indulge his personal whims or prejudices when awarding costs. The reality is revealed by the traditional exchange between the court and counsel for the unsuccessful party when the victor asks for costs. 'You can't resist that, can you, Mr X?' to which the answer, much more often than not, is 'No' although, at least in the Court of Appeal, he usually adds 'But I have an application to make.' A discretion exists, but within a compass which is well understood and has, I think, shrunk over the years.

The field Sir Wilfred Greene had in mind in the passage quoted was that of remedies, and it is elementary that equitable remedies are discretionary and not a matter of right. But over a century has now passed since Lord Blackburn said:[38]

The jurisdiction of the Court of Equity to enforce the specific performance, or to grant an injunction to prevent the breach of a covenant, is no doubt a discretionary jurisdiction, but I perfectly agree with the view expressed by your Lordships that the discretion is not one to be exercised according to the fancy of whoever is to exercise the jurisdiction of Equity, but is a discretion to be exercised according to the rules which have been established by a long series of decisions, and which are now settled to be the proper guide to Judges in Courts of Equity.

Even earlier Lord Kingsdown had said:[39]

The rule I take to be clearly this: if a Plaintiff applies for an injunction to restrain a violation of a common law right, if either the existence of the right or the fact of its violation

---

[30] Supreme Court Act 1981, s. 18(1)(f).
[31] *Aiden Shipping Co. Ltd. v Interbulk Ltd.* [1986] AC 965, at 975, 979 D.
[32] *The Erich Schroeder* [1984] 1 Lloyd's Rep. 192, at 194.
[33] *Tramountana Armadora SA v Atlantic Shipping Co. SA* [1978] 1 Lloyd's Rep. 391, at 394.
[34] *Archital Luxfer Ltd. v Henry Boot Construction Ltd.* [1981] 1 Lloyd's Rep. 642, at 650.
[35] Ibid., at 650; *Video Box Office Ltd. v GST Holdings Ltd.,* [1990] *The Independent,* 27 April.
[36] *The Ios 1* [1987] 1 Lloyd's Rep. 321.
[37] See *Supreme Court Practice* (1988), vol 1, 62/2/10 et seq.
[38] *Doherty v Allman* (1878) 3 App. Cas. 709, at 728.
[39] *Imperial Gas Light & Coke Co. v Broadbent* (1859) 7 HLC 600, at 612. See also *Fullwood v Fullwood* (1878) Ch. D. 176, at 179.

be disputed, he must establish the right at law; but when he has established his right at law, I apprehend that unless there be something special in the case, he is entitled as of course to an injunction to prevent the recurrence of that violation.

The circumstances which may deprive a plaintiff of his remedy are well established: there is no likelihood of repetition; damages will be an adequate remedy; the plaintiff has acquiesced in the defendant's conduct; the plaintiff's conduct has disentitled him from seeking relief; and so on. Whether these impediments exist may involve an exercise of judgment, or findings of fact which an appeal court may be slow to disturb, but will not involve an exercise of discretion. If they do not exist, whether the remedy be injunction or any other equitable remedy, there is virtually no ground for refusing relief. If they do, an exercise of discretion will be called for but usually within a strictly confined area and it will be readily reviewable. The recently developed field of Mareva injunctions illustrates the point very clearly: the conditions for granting such an injunction have been clearly laid down;[40] where the affidavit evidence shows the conditions to be met, the judge is almost bound to grant relief. Many a judge, instinctively reluctant to grant this draconian relief, has in practice found it almost impossible on a reasonably well-prepared application to find grounds for refusing to do so.

At this point the well-informed schoolboy would doubtless interject that remedies in public law at least must be truly discretionary, because the judges are always saying so. He would be right. They are. And the judges are right too. It is therefore possible, as Professor Wade says,[41] 'that the court may find some act to be unlawful but nevertheless decline to intervene'. But there is a wide gap between the rhetoric and the reality. The constraints of time and the limitations of my own research do not enable me to discuss the subject in detail or pronounce with authority. I have, however, a very strong hunch that in the decade since the Crown Office List became a boom town there would turn out to be no more than a handful of cases in which excess or abuse of power had been established but a remedy refused. In these few cases, the reason for the refusal of relief would (I suspect) usually turn out to be that the applicant had disentitled himself to relief by his own conduct, that the illegality was of a technical nature,[42] that delay in application had made relief futile or impracticable, or that the public authority was willing to give effect to the decision without the formality of an order against it. The much trumpeted principle that an applicant for judicial review must first exhaust his other remedies[43] does not seem often in practice to have led to a denial of relief.

In the procedural field at least one might expect the judge, as master of proceedings in his court, to exercise an almost unfettered discretion. Many

---

[40] See Gee, *Mareva Injunctions & Anton Piller Relief*, 2nd edn. (1990), at 10–11.
[41] Wade, *Administrative Law* 6th edn. (1988), 709.
[42] e.g. *R v Governors of Bacon's School, ex p. ILEA* [1990] *The Independent*, 29 March.
[43] Wade, *supra* n. 41, at 714.

statutes and rules of court confer apparently wide discretions, but each is quickly confined between banks of practice and authority. The court may extend the validity of a writ, says the rule;[44] but only for good reason say the cases,[45] which also give guidance on what may and may not be a good reason.[46] If certain conditions are satisfied, the court may order the plaintiff to give such security for the defendant's costs as it thinks just if having regard to all the circumstances of the case it thinks it just to do so;[47] but the principles on which the discretion is exercised are in general so well understood that contests save as to amount are relatively unusual.[48] The court may stay an action on grounds of *forum non conveniens*, but authoritative guidance on the exercise of the discretion is now found in *The Spiliada*.[49] If certain conditions are satisfied, the court may if it thinks fit make an order for interim payment of such amount as it thinks just;[50] but experience shows the mortality rate among such orders to be high.[51] The court may, if of opinion that in the circumstances of the case undue hardship would otherwise be caused, and on such terms if any as the justice of the case may require, extend the time for commencing arbitration proceedings;[52] but the judge called upon to exercise this jurisdiction is well advised to have regard to the guidance given by Mr Justice Brandon in *The Jocelyn*[53] which earned the approval of Lord Justice Brandon in *The Aspen Trader*.[54] Perhaps no clearer example of how practice develops can be found than in section 69 of the Supreme Court Act 1981 which requires certain specified causes of action to be tried by a jury and provides that any other action shall be tried without a jury 'unless the court in its discretion orders it to be tried with a jury'. Here, one might think, was a generously framed discretion, capable of being exercised in favour of jury trial for a difficult personal injury case. So, it would seem, the master and the judge thought in *Ward v James*,[55] decided under the section's predecessor. Yet, said Lord Denning MR:[56]

it is of the first importance that some guidance should be given—else you would find one judge ordering a jury, the next refusing it, and no one would know where he stood. It might make all the difference to the ultimate result of the case. This would give rise to much dissatisfaction. It is an essential attribute of justice in a community that similar decisions should be given in similar cases, and this applies as much to mode of trial as anything else. The only way of achieving this is for the courts to set out the considerations which should guide the judges in the normal exercise of their discretion. And that is what has been done in scores of cases where a discretion has been entrusted to the judges.

---

[44] RSC O. 6 r. 8(2).

[45] In particular, *Kleinwort Benson Ltd. v Barbrak Ltd.* [1987] AC 597.

[46] See generally, Supreme Court Practice 1988, 6th Cum. Supp., p. 9, para. 6/8/3.

[47] RSC O. 23 r. 1(1).

[48] The advent of the European Community has, however, raised new questions: *Porzelack KG v Porzelack (UK) Ltd.* [1987] 1 WLR 420; *De Bry v Fitzgerald* [1990] 1 All E.R. 560.

[49] [1987] AC 460.   [50] RSC O. 29 r. 11, 12.

[51] See, e.g., *British & Commonwealth Holdings p.l.c. v Quadrex Holdings Inc.* [1989] QB 842.

[52] Arbitration Act 1950, s. 27.

[53] [1977] 2 Lloyd's Rep. 121.   [54] [1981] 1 Lloyd's Rep. 273.

[55] [1966] 1 QB 273.   [56] Ibid., at 293.

So guidance was given, and jury trials save in the specified cases have vanished from the civil scene, it would seem likely for ever.[57]

Recent experience prompts me to mention an example, drawn from quite a different field, of an apparently wide discretion legislated almost out of existence by judicial decision and finally overtaken by statute itself. Section 30 of the Law of Property Act 1925 permits the trustee in bankruptcy of a bankrupt husband to apply to the court for an order that property owned jointly by husband and wife be sold, and the court may make such order as it thinks fit. This again would have seemed to give the court a very wide discretion to do what seemed right to reflect the respective interests of the creditors on the one hand and the wife and children on the other. But a long line of cases held that the trustee was ordinarily entitled to an order for sale in the absence of 'very special circumstances' or 'good reasons' or 'a substantial case of hardship' or, finally, 'exceptional circumstances'.[58] And now the opportunity to question whether a test of exceptional circumstances does not unreasonably constrict the language of the Act has passed, for it has been woven into the 1986 Insolvency Act.[59]

I suppose most of us would today regard the criminal trial as the real sanctuary of judicial discretion. This has a large measure of truth, although even an experienced criminal judge, on reading Rosemary Pattenden's book *The Judge, Discretion and the Criminal Trial*, would (I think) be surprised at the wealth of his (or her) endowment.[60] The reason is not far to seek; during the trial the court's management decisions are to a large extent immune from challenge; and once the trial is over, all but the most obviously wrong exercises of discretion tend to be superseded by the verdict of the jury. Pattenden, however, observes[61] that over the course of this century the attitude of the courts has changed and the court's reluctance to interfere with an exercise of discretion has waned.

A glance at the more recent case law—quite apart from the recent decision concerning the Irish conspirators to murder Mr Tom King—bears her out.[62] Thus over the last few months alone the court has interfered with discretionary decisions to allow committal proceedings to continue,[63] not to stop a case going to the jury,[64] not to discharge a jury,[65] to accede to a jury's request to be supplied with scales,[66] to interrupt excessively,[67] not to direct the jury that previous convictions

---

[57] My own personal impression is confirmed by the experience of Master Warren QC, the Senior Master of the Queen's Bench Division, who knows of no such case since *Ward v James* except *Hodges v Harland & Wolff Ltd.* [1965] 1 All ER 1086, decided some 3 weeks later. And see, most recently *Singh v London Underground Ltd.* [1990] *The Independent*, 25 April.

[58] *Re Holliday* [1981] Ch 405, at 419 G, 420 B, E 415 F, 424 C, 425 H; *Re Lowrie* [1981] 3 All ER 353, at 355 j.   [59] S. 356 (5).

[60] Op. cit., Appendix, at 183.   [61] Op. cit., at 21, 22.

[62] *R v Cullen and Others* [1990] *The Independent*, 1 May.

[63] *R v Sunderland Magistrates Court, ex p. Z.* [1989] Crim. L.R. 56.

[64] *R v Morley* [1989] Crim.L.R. 566.   [65] *R v. Jaquith, Emode* [1989] Crim.L.R. 563.

[66] *R v Stewart Sappleton* [1989] Crim.L.R. 653.

[67] *R v Renshaw* [1989] Crim.L.R. 811.

for dishonesty were relevant only to credibility[68] and, on many occasions, to admit admissible but prejudicial evidence. One recalls that twenty years ago the Court of Appeal (Criminal Division) declined to interfere when a chairman of quarter sessions had on repeated occasions during a defendant's case observed in a loud voice 'Oh, God', and then laid his head across his arm and made groaning and sighing noises. Counsel had not, the Court held, been positively and actively obstructed in the doing of his work and the chairman's conduct, if it might be regarded as discourteous and as showing signs of impatience, disparaged only the defendant's counsel, not his case.[69] I do not think this decision was found convincing even at the time, at any rate by advocates with personal experience of the chairman in question, but I am quite confident that the judge's discretion to conduct a criminal trial as he wishes would today be much more rigorously scrutinized.

The accelerating tendency towards a narrowing of discretion is nowhere better illustrated than in the field of sentencing. As long ago as 1361 justices of the peace were empowered to punish offenders 'according to that which to them shall seem best to do by their discretions and good advisement',[70] and in later centuries the sentencing discretion was often described in statutes as such.[71] Interestingly, in view of the new (and to my mind obnoxious) American practice of prescribing maximum and minimum penalties within a very narrow band, one may note that the Slave Trade Act 1824 imposed as the penalty for dealing in slaves, transportation for a term not exceeding 14 years or hard labour for a term not exceeding 5 years nor less than 3 years at the discretion of the court. The practice of prescribing minimum sentences did not, happily, catch on. It does, however, seem almost incredible, looking back, that there should for so many centuries have been no effective judicial means of challenging the exercise of the sentencing discretion on the ground that a penalty, though lawful, was excessive. The first statutory step towards controlling the discretion of course came with the establishment of the Court of Criminal Appeal in 1907, which could substitute such sentence as it thought should have been passed at the trial (whether more or less severe).[72] But the Court got off to a slow start: such was the respect felt for the sentencer's discretion that in 1908, when the Act was in operation for nine months, only 14 sentences were reduced[73]—roughly the tally today on an average week-day morning. It might be objected that giving a right of appeal against sentence was merely to substitute the discretion of three judges for that of one, but any appellate court is in particular constrained to build up a body of precedent and seek to achieve a reasonable level of consistency, so that the clear result was progressively to narrow the sentencer's discretion. But I think it is really only in relatively recent times that the judge's discretion in passing sentence has been

---

[68] *R v Prince* [1990] Crim.L.R. 49.
[69] *R v Hircock, Farmer, Leggett* [1970] 1 QB 67.   [70] Justices of the Peace Act 1361.
[71] e.g. Offences against the Person Act 1861; Foreign Enlistment Act 1870.
[72] The Criminal Appeal Act 1907, s. 4(3).
[73] Holdsworth, *History of English Law*, vol. I, at 218.

subjected to the degree of discipline familiar in other fields. To this a number of causes have contributed. One, without doubt, has been the entry into the field of distinguished academic analysts, particularly Dr David Thomas, but also others. Linked with that is the systematic reporting of decisions on sentence. Another cause is the work of the Criminal Division itself. When, twenty years ago, Widgery LJ spoke of the well-known duty of the Criminal Division 'to lay down principles and guidelines to assist sentencers of all grades in the application of the discretion which the imposition of sentence requires',[74] he was speaking no less than the truth. But it is over the last decade that, for the first time, a serious attempt has been made to provide detailed guidance on sentencing in a systematic, rational and explicit way. One thinks of the landmark decisions in such fields as rape,[75] the importation of drugs,[76] theft in breach of trust,[77] serious disorder,[78] killing by dangerous driving,[79] and others. For years it was customary to challenge sentences as being wrong in principle but it was often far from easy to identify any principle. The introduction of principle into this field will, I think, be seen as the enduring and in many ways personal achievement of the present Lord Chief Justice. This is a development to be whole-heartedly welcomed. Without explicit guidelines there can be no informed public debate on sentencing practice, and the appropriate punishment of offenders against society is a proper matter for consideration by society (if for purposes of argument one assumes there to be such a thing). Such consideration is no more an encroachment on the judges' independence than the prescription of maximum penalties by statute, which has always of course been accepted. It is absurd to suppose that the judges could properly have a sentencing policy of their own independently of the society of which they form part. Another cause contributing to the narrowing of discretion has been vocal public dissatisfaction with a sentencing regime which has been frequently portrayed, on occasion fairly, as arbitrary, even whimsical, and inadequately controlled. This dissatisfaction has not in the main arisen from sentences seen as unduly severe, which have after all been amenable to review on appeal, and the cases show that the Criminal Division has been willing (often to the fury of sentencers) to make quite minor adjustments of sentence when it felt that justice required them. The real clamour has concerned sentences seen as unduly lenient and the new power to refer such sentences to the Court[80] must be understood both as a response to that body of opinion and as a guarantee of the judicial guidelines. The upshot of all these developments is certainly not that the sentencer has lost his discretion. He has not. The guideline cases are only guidelines. The fact of two cases and the personal circumstances of two defendants are never the same. The primary responsibility of passing the appropriate sentence remains with the

---

[74] *R v Newsome and Browne* (1970) 54 Cr. App. Rep. 485, at 490.
[75] *R v Billam* (1986) Cr. App. R. (S) 48.
[76] *R v Aramah* (1982) 4 Cr. App. R. (S) 407; *R v Martinez* (1984) 6 Cr. App. R.(S) 364.
[77] *R v Barrick* (1985) 81 Cr. App. R. 78.   [78] *R v Keys* (1986) 8 Cr. App. R. (S) 444.
[79] *R v Boswell* (1984) 6 Cr. App. R. (S) 257.   [80] Criminal Justice Act 1988, s. 36(1).

sentencer, whose decision in the vast majority of cases is never the subject of appeal. But I think it is undoubtedly true that this discretion has become much more judicial in the sense that it is exercised in a much more structured framework and is subject to much narrower constraints and is much more readily reviewable than it ever used to be.

In a quite different corner of the criminal field, I think we have a golden opportunity to observe the organic development of a somewhat novel discretion in something approaching laboratory conditions. The criminal judge has long enjoyed a discretion to exclude evidence of which the prejudicial effect is thought likely to outweigh the probative value. But the Police and Criminal Evidence Act 1984 moved the goalposts: it provided for the issuing of codes governing such matters as the questioning of suspects,[81] provided that the codes should be taken into account in determining any question in proceedings to which they were relevant,[82] gave suspects a right under section 58 (albeit qualified) to take legal advice and (relevant for present purposes) conferred a discretion on the court under section 78(1) to 'refuse to allow evidence on which the prosecution proposes to rely to be given if it appears to the court that, having regard to all the circumstances, including the circumstances in which the evidence was obtained, the admission of the evidence would have such an adverse effect on the fairness of the proceedings that the court ought not to admit it'. How was this discretion to be exercised? As was observed in a recent case, with some degree of understatement, 'When the Act came into force the effect which the Courts would give to this section was in doubt.'[83] One view, although not to crudely put, was that the proceedings did not become unfair if evidence was admitted which led to the conviction of a guilty defendant, whether or not a breach of the non-binding codes had occurred. This was not much different from the approach previously taken to breaches of the Judges' Rules. The other view was that since Parliament had intended a defendant to enjoy certain safeguards the proceedings became unfair if he was denied them and was convicted as a result. Plainly the risk existed that different judges would adopt highly divergent practices, with the unacceptable consequence that a decision of possibly crucial importance to the criminal defendant would turn on the predilections of the individual decision-maker. One could not, I think, claim that any wholly coherent approach to this very wide discretion has yet been formulated, but if one looks at the cases where section 58 or the codes have been breached and reliance is placed on section 78, in the relatively very short period since the 1 January 1986 when the section came into force, the elements of such an approach may perhaps be discerned. It has been repeatedly stated that a breach of section 58 or the codes does not of itself require evidence of a confession to be excluded,[84] but there has nevertheless been a

---

[81] S. 66.   [82] S. 67(11).
[83] *R v Keenan* (1989) 90 Cr. App. R. 1, at p. 6.
[84] *R v Keenan* (1989) 90 Cr. App. R. 1, at p. 12; *R v Walsh* [1989] Crim.L.R. 822, at 823; *R v Matthews* [1990] Crim.L.R. 190.

growing and possibly even exaggerated tendency to exclude. In the cases where evidence has been held to be rightly admitted, despite breaches, the reason has been given that the defendant was well aware of his rights and access to a solicitor would not have improved his position[85] or more generally that in all the circumstances of the particular case the breaches did not affect the fairness of the proceedings.[86] But in most of the cases where breaches have been established evidence has been excluded or it has been held that it should have been. The right to legal advice has been described as fundamental.[87] In a case where there had been wholesale breaches it was said that to admit the evidence would be to condone flouting of the provisions designed to protect against confessions which were not genuine.[88] But it is now clear that in the ordinary way evidence will only be excluded if the breaches are significant and substantial[89] and the crucial consideration has usually been whether, because of the breaches, the defendant gave answers he might not have given[90] or has otherwise been prejudiced in resisting the charge.[91] It may be that the pendulum has swung too far towards exclusion upon breaches being shown, without adequate consideration of the effect on the fairness of the proceedings which the Act requires.[92] My point, however, is that within about five years of the Act coming into force one sees a discretion drawn in very wide terms being defined and regulated so that the lines upon which judges should exercise it are likely quite soon to become clear and well understood. While prediction is hazardous, the general shape of the rule seems likely to be that the judge should ordinarily exclude prosecution evidence if there have been significant and substantial breaches of section 58 or the codes and the defendant has as a result given damaging answers which he would not otherwise have given or has been substantially prejudiced in resisting the charge. If this were the broad shape of the rule, difficult borderline cases would no doubt arise, but in the great mass of cases it would be obvious to judges and practitioners how the discretion should and would be exercised. One would also expect that as the consequences of failure to comply with these highly detailed provisions were increasingly born in upon police forces, the incidence of significant and substantial breaches would sharply decline.

---

[85] *R v Alladice* (1988) 87 Cr. App. R. 380; *R v Dunford* [1990] *The Independent*, 30 March.

[86] *R v Waters* [1989] Crim.L.R. 62; *R v Matthews* [1990] Crim.L.R. 190.

[87] *R v Samuel* [1988] Q.B. 615, at 630; *R v Beycan* [1990] Crim.L.R. 185, at 186.

[88] *R v Ismail* [1990] Crim.L.R. 109, at 110.

[89] *R v Absolam* [1989] Cr. App. R. 232, at 337; *R v Keenan* (1990) 90 Cr. App. R. 1. at 13; *R v Matthews* [1990] Crim.L.R. 10, at 191.

[90] *R v Samuel* [1988] QB 615, at 630; *R v Absolam* (1989) 88 Cr. App. R. 332, at 337; *R v Delaney* (1989) 99 Cr. App. R. 338; *R v Quayson* [1989] Crim.L.R. 218; *R v Walsh* [1989] Crim.L.R. 822; *R v Beycan* [1990] Crim.L.R. 190.

[91] *R v Parris* (1989) 89 Cr. App. R. 68; *R v Keenan* (1990) 90 Cr. App. R.I; *R v Fennelley* [1989] Crim.L.R. 142; *R v Britton* [1989] Crim.L.R. 144; *R v Ladlow* [1989] Crim.L.R. 219.

[92] *R v Williams* [1989] Crim.L.R. 66; *R v Fogah* [1989] Crim.L.R. 141.

Perhaps the last real stronghold of almost unreviewable discretion is where the care and custody of children are concerned. This is not because demonstrable errors in the judge's balancing exercise in this field will not be corrected: authority shows that they can and should.[93] It is because, first and most importantly, the evidence is likely to be entirely oral and the issue is likely to turn on the judge's assessment of the personal qualities and motives of the competing parents and other members of the extended family whose capacity as carers is in question. In the absence of some striking mis-judgment it will be almost impossible to show that his conclusion is wrong. And the judge's discretionary decision enjoys a rare inviolability, secondly, because there is in this field usually no satisfactory solution and it is thus impossible for an appellate court to be confident that its view of the less unsatisfactory solution, if different from that of the judge, is superior.[94] The result is, that since the House of Lords endorsed this general approach in *G v G*,[95] challenges by the aggrieved parent to the trial judge's exercise of discretion have almost always failed. It is not perhaps very happy that an unfettered right of appeal should be effectively abrogated by judicial decision, nor that, in a field where judicial decisions have a unique capacity to cause lasting misery, the trial judge's decision should be effectively final. On the other hand, it would be very hard indeed to suggest any guideline to govern the exercise of this discretion which was not either so obvious or so heavily qualified as to be futile. It would seem that in this limited field, for better or worse, reliance must be placed on the trial judge to show the wisdom, sensitivity and insight of Solomon, although lacking the latter's extra-judicial powers.

May I, in conclusion, touch—much too briefly—on the important issues raised by Professor Atiyah and Professor Treitel in their inaugural lectures respectively twelve and ten years ago?[96] Atiyah, it will be recalled, drew attention to the movement over the last century from clear, sharp-edged principles beloved of our Victorian forbears to judgmental discretionary rules thought to be better fitted for dispensing individualized *ad hoc* justice case by case. Treitel considered this development further with particular reference to the law of contract, showing how certain old rules had been diversified and qualified to cater for hard cases, but suggesting that in the contractual field discretions had not, on the whole, up to then operated so as to create an unacceptable degree of uncertainty. Now certain of the instances discussed by the professors are certainly discretions within my suggested meaning: for example, the rules relating to matrimonial property[97] or the provision in section 49(2) of the Law of Property Act 1925 enabling the court to order the return of a deposit paid under a contract for the sale of land.[98] But

---

[93] *Re F (a minor) (Wardship: appeal)* [1976] Fam. 238; *G. v G.* [1985] 2 All E.R. 225.

[94] *Clarke-Hunt v Newcombe* (1982) 4 FLR 482, at 488; *G. v G., supra* n. 93, at 228 b.

[95] *Supra,* n. 93.

[96] P. S. Atiyah, *From Principles to Pragmatism*, 17 Feb. 1978; G. H. Treitel, *Doctrine and Discretion in the Law of Contract*, 7 March 1980.

[97] Atiyah, op. cit., at 11.　　　　　　　　　　　　　　　[98] Treitel, op. cit., at 15.

other instances, although posing judgmental tests, do not involve the exercise of
any discretion in my sense: for example, the pervading test of reasonableness in
the law of tort,[99] the closest connection test in determining the proper law of a
contract,[100] the test of merchantability now contained in section 14(6) of the Sale
of Goods Act 1979,[101] any test based on the intention of the parties,[102] the new
test of common law duress,[103] or departure from the rule that damages for breach
of contract are invariably to be assessed by reference to the time of breach.[104]
None of these permits the judge to apply a simple rule of thumb test. Most require
evidence followed by an exercise of judgment, the correctness of which may give
rise to differences of opinion. I share to the full the professors' distrust of undirected and unreviewable discretions, but most of the powers they discuss are not,
I think, undirected nor, even more importantly, are they unreviewable. We may
perhaps take comfort in the fact that even the New Zealand Illegal Contracts Act
1970, which may fairly be regarded as the ultimate in conferment of wide, unde-
fined discretions, is now said,[105] despite gloomy earlier prognostications,[106] to
have produced a coherent body of decisions. So I, with Treitel, would view the
present situation, if not with complacency, at least with a reasonable degree of
optimism and confidence.[107]

It is, I think, a deeply rooted instinct of any responsible body, whether a
company, a college, a club, a body of trustees, a trade union or anything else,
however wide its powers, to endeavour to act with a reasonable measure of
consistency. So the tendency to subject a wide discretion to more or less restrictive rules is not a specifically legal phenomenon. Nor, certainly, is it an English
phenomenon: a discretion conferred by the New Zealand Matrimonial Property
Act 1963 was so mechanically applied by the judges as, in the views of some, to
subvert the object of the legislation altogether.[108]

But it is, as shown by that example and others I have discussed, a very marked
feature of judicial practice. I do not, therefore, think that whether discretion is
understood in my sense or as embracing also the judgmental open-textured rules
discussed by the professors there is in general any ground for concern that arbitrary uncontrolled discretion is likely to run riot at the expense of clear discernible
principle. Nor do I think that any approach less responsive to the circumstances
of particular cases would in general be acceptable to the public as consumers of
the judicial product in an age when the public is more inclined to see the law as
an ass than as the embodiment of everything that's excellent. But this is, I am

---

[99] Atiyah, op. cit., at 11.   [100] Ibid., at 13.   [101] Ibid., at 14.
[102] Treitel, op. cit., at 4.   [103] Ibid., at 5.   [104] Ibid., at 9.
[105] A. Beck, 'Illegality and the Court's Discretion: The New Zealand Illegal Contracts Act in
Action', (1989) 13 NZULR 389.
[106] M. P. Furmston, 'The Illegal Contracts Act 1970—An English View', 1972, 5 NZULR 151.
[107] Op. cit., at 20.
[108] See Markesinis, 'Comparative Law—A Subject in Search of an Audience', (1990) 53 MLR 1,
at 12–13.

conscious, a predictable view from one on the bureaucratic side of the counter. After all, the Lord Chancellor of former days no doubt considered the length of his foot a very convenient, reliable and serviceable measure, happily free of what would now be called resource implications.

PART II:
JUDGES IN SOCIETY

In many countries judges have, over the centuries, tended to occupy a privileged position. In the past this owed much to their power, their wealth and, perhaps, their social standing. In modern democratic societies judges continue to occupy a privileged position, but for quite different reasons. Now the privilege springs from public recognition that democratic government and society as a whole can only function fairly and properly within a framework of laws, justly and fairly administered by men and women who have no obligation save to justice itself. Thus judges must not be liable to disciplinary sanctions, or premature retirement, because their decisions do not find favour with the powers that be, or with any powerful vested interest, or with prevailing public opinion. They must be truly independent.

This does not of course mean that judges are licensed to do exactly as they like. Quite the opposite. Because society grants the judges, for the greater good of the public, certain important privileges, it is entitled to, and does, expect of the judges very high standards of propriety, integrity, assiduity and personal conduct.

These papers address these complementary aspects of the judicial role. The first, an inaugural annual lecture to the Judicial Studies Board, seeks to explore what judicial independence (a familiar expression) really means and involves. The second, an address to the Society of Public Teachers of Law, considers the ethical rules by which judicial conduct is, and should be, governed. Both are topics of continuing and, some would say, steadily increasing relevance in a changing world.

1

*Judicial Independence**

It is a truth universally acknowledged that the constitution of a modern democracy governed by the rule of law must effectively guarantee judicial independence. So many eminent authorities have stated this principle and there has been so little challenge to it, that no extensive citation is called for. It is enough to recall that in 1994 the United Nations Commission on Human Rights recorded that it was:

Convinced that an independent and impartial judiciary and an independent legal profession are essential pre-requisites for the protection of human rights and for ensuring that there is no discrimination in the administration of justice.[1]

The Commission went on to appoint a Special Rapporteur to monitor and investigate alleged violations of judicial and legal professional independence worldwide, and to study topical questions central to a full understanding of the independence of the judiciary.[2]

In his most recent report of 1 March 1996 the Special Rapporteur summarized the results of his worldwide investigation, and with reference to the United Kingdom wrote:

The Special Rapporteur notes with grave concern recent media reports in the United Kingdom of comments by ministers and/or highly placed government personalities on recent decisions of the courts on judicial review of administrative decisions of the Home Secretary. The Chairman of the House of Commons Home Affairs Select Committee was reported to have warned that if the judges did not exercise self-restraint, 'it is inevitable that we shall statutorily have to restrict judicial review'. The controversy continued and reportedly prompted the former Master of the Rolls, Lord Donaldson, who was said to have accused the Government of launching a concerted attack on the independence of [the] judiciary, to have said, 'any government which seeks to make itself immune to an independent review of whether its actions are lawful or unlawful is potentially despotic.' The Special Rapporteur will be monitoring developments in the United Kingdom concerning this controversy. That such a controversy could arise over this very issue in a country which cradled the common law and judicial independence is hard to believe.[3]

The need to guarantee judicial independence is accordingly one which we should treat very seriously, not only for the health of our own country but because of the extent to which our own conduct is still seen by other countries, to an extent which may perhaps surprise us, as a model.

---

* Judicial Studies Board Annual Lecture given on 5 November 1996. © Crown Copyright 1996. All rights reserved.
[1] *Commonwealth Law Bulletin* (July 1994), at 957.   [2] Ibid. at 958.
[3] At p. 54.

Given the centrality of this constitutional principle, one might expect to find much detailed analysis of what it means, in theory and in practice, in this country. But, as Professor Robert Stevens has written:

While there is widespread consensus on the obvious importance of the independence of the judiciary, the literature on it is meagre, and the concept itself has never been fully unpacked. Unpacking is a process worth engaging in.[4]

There have, very broadly speaking, been two approaches. One concentrates on the independence of individual judges in their day to day work of judging. This approach was well summarized by the present Lord Chancellor, Lord Mackay of Clashfern, in a lecture on 6 March 1991 when, referring to the judges, he said:

Their function is to decide cases and in so doing they must be given full independence of action, free from any influence. But in order to preserve their independence the judges must have some control or influence over the administrative penumbra immediately surrounding the judicial process. If judges were not, for example, in control of the listing of cases to be heard in the courts it might be open to an unscrupulous executive to seek to influence the outcome of cases (including those to which public authorities were a party) by ensuring that they were listed before judges thought to be sympathetic to a point of view, or simply by delaying the hearing of the case if that seemed to advantage the public authority concerned.[5]

Thus, on this approach, judges would enjoy full independence in their task of judging, and also in what the Lord Chancellor called 'the administrative penumbra immediately surrounding the judicial process', of which he gave listing as a very good example.

The alternative approach treats the independence of the judge to decide individual cases free from any extraneous influence, and to exercise control or influence over the administrative penumbra immediately surrounding the judicial process, as no more than a part (albeit an important part) of what judicial independence means. On this approach what matters is not only the independence of individual judges but the independence of the judiciary as a separate arm of government. This is the approach which Lord Browne-Wilkinson, as Vice Chancellor, persuasively advocated in his F. A. Mann Lecture, *The Independence of the Judiciary in the 1980s*.[6] On this approach the judges should, with a large measure of independence, control not only the delivery of the final judicial product (the judgment) but also the administrative infrastructure on which the delivery and enforcement of that product depend. The high watermark of that approach may perhaps be found in an article written by Sir Francis Purchas in September 1994, when he wrote:

---

[4] *The Independence of the Judiciary. The view from the Lord Chancellor's Office.* Professor Robert Stevens, 1993 at p. 3. This is a very interesting book, to which I am much indebted.

[5] See Purchas, 'What is Happening to Judicial Independence', *New Law Journal* 30 Sept. 1994 at 1306, 1308.

[6] [1988] Public Law 44.

Constitutional independence will not be achieved if the funding of the administration of justice remains subject to the influences of the political market place. Subject to the ultimate supervision of Parliament, the Judiciary should be allowed to advise what is and what is not a necessary expense to ensure that adequate justice is available to the citizen and to protect him from unwarranted intrusion into his liberty by the executive.[7]

Even in countries where the judges enjoy a very much larger measure of administrative control than they do here (one thinks, for instance, of the United States and Australia), I doubt whether this ambitious requirement comes anywhere close to being met. Nor, perhaps, should it. As professional judges we naturally, and rightly, put a very high premium on the provision of an efficient and adequately funded legal system, which we regard as a prerequisite to administering justice. But even we cannot overlook the existence of other pressing claims on finite national resources. We would all recognize the defence of the realm as a vital national priority, but I suspect that we would shrink from giving the chiefs of staff *carte blanche* to demand all the resources which they judged necessary for that end. We would all, probably, recognize the provision of good educational opportunities at all levels as a pressing social necessity, but might even so hesitate to give educational institutions all the money which they sought. We would all regard the health of the people as a vital national concern, but could scarcely contemplate the demands of health service professionals being met in full, without rigorous democratic control. I do not myself find these choices, even in theory, offensive; but in any event they must surely, in the real world, be inevitable. As the Chief Justice of British Columbia put it in a recent paper:

I subscribe to the view that there are other constitutional principles, besides judicial independence, that must be recognized and respected. One principle, possibly equal in importance to judicial independence, is the right of the legislature to decide how public money is to be spent. Thus, I do not support the view that the judiciary should write its own cheque, and I have come to realize that it is, in fact, salutary that the judiciary should not have that power. If mistakes are to be made in budgeting or funding operations, it is better that they be made by someone other than the judiciary.[8]

At least in this country judicial independence cannot be rested on any classical doctrine of the separation of powers. That is not because of the anomalous roles of the Lord Chancellor, the Law Officers and the Law Lords, but for more fundamental reasons. Judges are, after all, appointed by the executive—and even under the American constitution, which enshrines the separation of power doctrine in perhaps its purest form, appointments to the federal judiciary involve both other arms of government. After appointment, judges sit in courts provided by the state, they have offices provided, heated and lighted by the state, they have clerks paid by the state, they use books and computers mostly provided by the

---

[7] Purchas, op. cit. at 1324.

[8] The Hon Chief Justice Allan McEachern, *Judicial Independence*, paper delivered to the 11th Commonwealth Law Conference, Vancouver (August 1996).

state, they are themselves paid by the state. In all these respects the position of the judges is not very different from that of any other employee of the state. But plainly the position of the judge is, and certainly should be, categorically different from that of other employees of the government. To pinpoint where those differences lie it may perhaps be most fruitful, in the manner of the common law, to eschew statements of general principle and consider particular incidents of the judicial role.

It is convenient to begin at the beginning, with appointment of judges. Since these are effectively made by the executive, in the person of either the Lord Chancellor or the Prime Minister, the opportunity plainly exists to pack the judicial bench with appointees of a certain political persuasion or known social views. This would not be regarded as an abuse in some other countries, such as notably the United States, nor would it always have been regarded as an abuse here. But I think there is no doubt that such a policy, if it were now to be adopted here, would be regarded as an abuse, and I cannot think that it would be long before a different appointments procedure were introduced. There is, I would suggest, virtually no evidence of appointments since 1945 made otherwise than on the basis of perceived merit, and at no time has this been truer than during the last decade. If, without intolerable complacency, one is entitled to regard this as a happy and constitutionally acceptable state of affairs, one may reasonably ask how it has been achieved. I would point to three things. The first is the pool from which candidates for judicial office are selected: whether barristers or solicitors, they have been private practitioners reared in a professional tradition which prizes the exercise of an independent individual judgment above all else. I would point, secondly to the greatly increased difficulty of conducting a legal practice so as to achieve a level of success which would qualify the candidate for judicial appointment while at the same time pursuing a parallel career in politics: the result is that appointments from the ranks of active politicians are now a rarity. Thirdly, I would point to the great care which successive Lord Chancellors have shown in, and the integrity with which they have approached, their task of, appointing judges. From time to time fears have been expressed that judicial appointments might be, or had in effect been, handed over to the Lord Chancellor's Permanent Secretary. In opposing the proposal that there should be a Ministry of Justice, Lord Hewart in 1929 suggested that this was 'an effort to hand over the appointment of Judges to the Permanent Secretary of the Lord Chancellor's Office'.[9] Stevens indeed suggests that when Sir Claude Schuster was Permanent Secretary 'the views of the Permanent Secretary were inevitably seen by Bench and Bar as close to decisive'.[10] I feel bound to say, on the basis of my own experience, that whatever the position may have been in the past, the Permanent Secretary does not now seek to wield influence of that kind. The role of officials in the department is to collate, not to dictate; to gather and marshal opinions on the merits of

---

[9] Stevens, op. cit. at 31.   [10] Ibid. at 42.

possible candidates, but not to decide who should be appointed and who should not.

The key to the successful making of appointments must, I would suggest, lie in an assumption shared by appointor, appointee and the public at large that those appointed should be capable of discharging their judicial duties, so far as humanly possible, with impartiality. Impartiality and independence may not, even in this context, be synonyms, but there is a very close blood-tie between them: for a judge who is truly impartial, deciding each case on its merits as they appear to him (or, of course, her), is of necessity independent.

What really matters, of course, is that judges should enjoy complete independence while serving as such. The protection accorded to the judges of the higher courts, that they enjoy office during good behaviour and are removable only by an address of both Houses of Parliament, has over the centuries proved an effective constitutional guarantee, since no English judge has been so removed. This has not in practice meant, at any rate in recent years, that judges who through no fault of their own have become mentally or physically unfit to perform their duties have remained in office. It has proved possible to arrange consensual retirements in such cases. But it has meant that no judge, when giving judgment or deciding what judgment to give, need concern himself with the acceptability of his decision to the powers that be.

An experienced circuit judge has recently argued with some heat that the constitutional protection accorded to judges of the High Court should be extended to circuit judges also.[11] I can see considerable theoretical force in this argument. The jurisdiction of the County Court has been extended to such an extent, and the weight of cases heard by circuit judges in the Crown Court is now often such, that it is hard to justify different treatment of the circuit bench. But the threat to the circuit bench is perhaps more theoretical than real. The only circuit judge known to me to have been dismissed in recent times would plainly have been removed by the Act of Settlement procedure had he been a judge of the High Court and had he not chosen to resign in order to forestall that process. There is no case in which the decisions of a circuit judge have led to dismissal or (so far as I know) threatened dismissal. Lord Chancellors have, as it seems to me, been notably reticent in exercising their powers of dismissal. Whatever the constitutional anomaly, I cannot see the present situation as giving rise to practical grounds for concern. There are, of course, other and subtler ways in which the executive could, if so minded, seek to undermine the independence of individual judges. One would be by denying promotion to any judge whose decisions were thought to be politically unfavourable. In the past this would not have been a problem: the High Court Bench was very small; the Court of Appeal was even smaller; and appointments to the Court of Appeal or the House of Lords were frequently made on

---

[11] His Honour Judge Harold Wilson, 'The County Court Judge in Limbo', *New Law Journal* 21 Oct. 1994, at 1454.

political grounds. So a judge appointed to the High Court bench would have no lively thought or expectation of proceeding further, and promotions from the County Court bench or the circuit bench to that of the High Court have always been relatively rare. With an increased number of Law Lords and a very greatly enlarged Court of Appeal, the situation has plainly changed. This has led some commentators to suggest that the hope of promotion, or fear of non-promotion, has affected judicial decision-making. Writing in *The Commonwealth Law Bulletin* in October 1994, Professor Antony Allott wrote:

Promotion from the stipendiary bench to the circuit bench is now more frequent. Similarly, one may be promoted either from practice or from a circuit judgeship to the High Court bench. Once a High Court judge, one may hope to receive further promotion to membership of the Court of Appeal or to headship of a Division. The implication offered that, since there is little gain in pay, there is little motivation to seek promotion, is largely false. Honour and standing are at least as effective spurs as cash. As a judge of whatever grade, one can hardly, if ambitious, avoid looking over one's shoulder at the consequences of adopting a particular style or trend of decisions on one's future career as judge.[12]

In similar vein, Stevens has suggested that over the last 30 years or so the myth that there was no career judiciary in England had weakened, and suggested that

the prospect of promotion [had] sullied the purity of the relationship between the Judiciary and the executive. . . .[13]

While there were in his view other factors at work, this was also a factor.

If any judge were to trim or tailor his judicial decision in order to ingratiate himself with, or avoid offending, any member of the executive who he thought would be influential in deciding on his future promotion, or even any other member of the judiciary whom he thought might be consulted, I would myself regard such conduct as a flagrant violation of judicial duty and I would be equally critical of anyone knowingly influenced by such conduct. But suggestions of the kind quoted, although easy to make, are very hard, if not impossible, to verify. I can only express the firm belief (coupled, if need be, with the fervent hope) that considerations of this kind simply do not intrude into a judge's process of decision making at all. I can imagine no more conclusive objection to promotion than the suspicion that they might have done.

Most of us, I suspect, can call to mind one instance in which it seems likely that a judge, otherwise obviously fitted for preferment, was denied such preferment because his judicial decisions and pronouncements had excited the hostility of an incoming government. Whether this is so or not cannot be decided with confidence until the 30-year rule has operated and the relevant records made available for public scrutiny. If the suspicion turns out to be well-founded, the

---

[12] Independence of the Judiciary in Commonwealth Countries: Problems and Provisions, *The Commonwealth Law Bulletin* (Oct. 1994), at 1435.

[13] Stevens, op. cit. at 169.

incident must represent a serious blot on the record of those responsible. Our consolation must be that it is very hard to think of any other comparable incident, at any rate in recent times.

Any mention of judicial independence must eventually prompt the question: independent of what? The most obvious answer is, of course, independent of government. I find it impossible to think of any way in which judges, in their decision making role, should not be independent of government. But they should also be independent of the legislature, save in its law-making capacity. Judges should not defer to expressions of parliamentary opinion, or decide cases with a view either to earning parliamentary approbation or avoiding parliamentary censure. They must also, plainly, ensure that their impartiality is not undermined by any other association, whether professional, commercial, personal or whatever.

Sir Derek Oulton, writing in 1994, suggested that by independence is meant not only independence from improper pressure by the executive, litigants and particular pressure groups but also independence from improper pressure from the media. He wrote:

One of the most dramatic changes that has taken place over the past thirty years or so has been the increasing freedom felt by newspapers, in particular, to attack judges with a vigour (and one could use a much stronger expression) that was formerly quite unknown. The same applies to Members of Parliament, particularly of the House of Commons. There must be a limit to the well-known breadth of judicial backs. The law of contempt used to be employed to prevent this, and Stevens shows interestingly that in 1899 the Privy Council described such use of the law as 'obsolete', only to have it invented, or re-invented, by the Court of Appeal the following year, in order to prevent press criticism of the extrovert Mr Justice Darling. But the judicial committee understandably regarded it as anachronistic even at the turn of the century, and its use has steadily declined since then.[14]

Save perhaps in the case of jury trial, the law of contempt has no significant contribution to make: first, because of the presumption that a judge sitting alone will not be influenced in the decision he makes by comment in the press; secondly, because such comment often follows the decision and therefore cannot affect it; and thirdly, because such comment is often directed as much to what the judge says (not always fully or accurately reported) as to what the judge decides. In any event, the right of the press to comment on matters of public interest is all but sacrosanct. I am not for my part sure that media attacks on the judges have much to do with judicial independence; but one could wish that those who set out to destroy judicial reputations, with the harassment that almost always accompanies such attacks, gave more thought than is evident to the public interest which they are likely to injure.

The rule that judges must be politically neutral is not only, as I would suggest,

---

[14] *Journal of Law and Society*, vol. 21, no. 4, Dec. 1994 at 569.

an aspect, and a very important aspect, of their duty to be and appear to be impartial; it is also part of the price of their independence. The point was very well put by Sir Hartley Shawcross as Attorney General in 1950 when he declared that it was:

a most important principle of our constitutional practice that judges do not comment on the policy of Parliament, but administer the law, good or bad, as they find it. It is a traditional doctrine on which the independence of the judiciary rests. If once that doctrine were departed from, and judges permitted themselves to ventilate from the Bench the views they might hold on the policy of the legislature, it would be quite impossible to maintain the rule that the conduct of judges is not open to criticism or question.[15]

Another author has made a rather similar point but in a more hostile way:

The British judiciary prides itself on its independence . . . But this independence has been part of a tacit agreement between judges and politicians. Politicians normally do not meddle with the judiciary even when they could. Ministers do not pressure the Lord Chancellor to award judgeships to the party faithful. Party leaders never remove judges and only alter any statute dealing with the courts after extensive consultations. For their part the judges restrict their scope of authority to private law matters, avoiding the 'political thicket'. Most judges have seemed aware that treading too closely to questions of public policy could propel them into an unwinnable battle with the majority at Westminster. English judges traded range of authority for degree of authority in a narrow field, independence for a reduced role on the public stage. . .[16]

It is indeed obvious that if judges were to ventilate personal criticisms of government policy unnecessary for the decision of the case before them, it would only be a matter of time (and not a very long time) before those who were the subject of criticism replied in kind. It is undesirable, and plainly damaging to the independence of the judges, if they become protagonists in a debate in which they have no constitutional right to participate. This duty of restraint does not in any way inhibit the duty which occasionally falls on judges to quash decisions made by ministers or officials as unlawful, nor from giving their reasons for such decisions. Nor has this duty of self restraint been understood to prevent some senior judges from giving expression to their views, or the views of the judiciary, on questions directly pertaining to the administration of justice. It would be absurd if those judges who are members of the Upper House were precluded from offering the benefits of their wisdom and experience on issues directly related to their professional expertise. Valuable though the contributions of retired judges often are, it would be a loss if those still active in the practice of the law were denied the opportunity to contribute. It should not in practice prove too difficult to discern where legitimate observations on the administration of justice end and political controversy begins. Lord Denning's Hamlyn lectures *Freedom under the*

---

[15] See Stevens, op. cit. at 79 fn 4.
[16] J. T. Waltman, *The Courts of England* in *The Political Role of Law Courts in Modern Democracies* (1988) at 117–18.

Law, although the subject of objection by Lord Jowitt,[17] and Lord Taylor's recent observations on sentencing practice, fell on the right side of the line; letters written by Mr Justice Stephen criticising the Government's policy on India,[18] Lord Hewart's famous book *The New Despotism* and the letter written to *The Times* by Mr Justice Lloyd-Jacob about the hydrogen bomb, one might feel, fell on the wrong side of the line.

Although the Lord Chancellor has no power to penalize judges of the Supreme Court in any way, and no power to penalize judges of the lower courts save by dismissal, Lord Chancellors have on occasion taken it upon themselves to rebuke and reprimand judges whose extra-judicial conduct has given ground for complaint. I imagine Lord Chancellors do this in their role as the formal head of the judiciary rather than in their role as a member of the executive. As it now operates, the practice seems to me unobjectionable provided—and I regard the proviso as fundamental—that such rebuke or reprimand does not relate in any way to a judge's decisions made as such. It would seem to me to subvert the independence which judges are entitled to enjoy if the Lord Chancellor, save when sitting in an appellate capacity, were to base any personal criticism of a judge on the decisions which he had given. I think that this is an area in which, perhaps, the rules have become somewhat clearer. It would, I think, be surprising to find a modern Lord Chancellor writing to a Law Lord asking him to amend the proposed terms of a dissenting speech in a case to which the Lord Chancellor was not himself a party, as Lord Simon did to Lord Atkin in relation to *Liversidge v Anderson*.[19] I would also (although in this case no question of a rebuke was involved) be very surprised to receive from the Lord Chancellor a letter in terms such as those of a letter written by Lord Jowitt to Lord Goddard as Lord Chief Justice in 1947:

I do sincerely hope that the judges will not be lenient to these bandits [who] carry arms [to] shoot at the police. . . . I may be written down as a Colonel Blimp, but you know I do take the view, which I think you share, that we have got rather soft and woolly when dealing with really serious crime.[20]

As Stevens points out, this was two years before sentence was passed and carried out on Derek Bentley. It must be a consolation to modern judges to learn that Lord Goddard and his Queen's Bench colleagues after the War were regarded by the administration of the day as soft and woolly in dealing with really serious crime.

In many countries, the participation of serving judges in commissions, enquiries and committees not devoted to law reform or the administration of justice is regarded as inconsistent with the independence of the judiciary. In this

---

[17] See Stevens, op. cit. at 93.
[18] See K. J. M. Smith, *James Fitzjames Stephen* (1988), 145.
[19] See Heuston, *Lives of the Lord Chancellors, 1940–70* (1987), at 59.
[20] See Stevens, op. cit. at 95.

country a different view has been taken; a judge or a senior silk has more often than not been thought the most suitable person to lead or chair such exercises, at any rate where they do not relate to the legal system or the legal profession. A broadly similar view has been taken in New Zealand. Lord Cooke of Thorndon has written:

> In some quarters it has been said that after the recent controversies Judges may not be willing to accept appointment to commissions of inquiry. There are even suggestions that to do so is inconsistent with the judicial role. I must beg to differ. Wherever judicial qualities are called for—that is to say, typically a calm and objective factual judgment of evidence—in my opinion a Judge should be willing to serve. The essential corollary is a judicial approach.[21]

We have tended in this country to take the same view for the same reasons. So long as the final report when delivered is accepted by the government, it is hard to see how any threat to the independence of the judiciary is involved, at any rate where the report commands broad public acceptance also. The situation plainly becomes more difficult when a report is rejected by the government, as the Macmillan Government rejected Mr Justice Devlin's report on Central Africa, or when a report is the subject of acute political controversy and hostile publicity before publication, as was the case with Sir Richard Scott's recent report on Arms to Iraq, or when a major recommendation is instantly rejected, like Lord Cullen's recommendation on handguns, or when a report is regarded as unpersuasive by significant sections of opinion, as proved to be the case with Lord Widgery's report on 'Bloody Sunday'. To date, I think that the standing of the judges involved and the quality of the reports produced have almost always won for such reports a degree of acceptance denied to those who reject or criticise them. But I think that this is an area in which great caution is needed. The reputation which judges generally enjoy for impartiality and skill in arriving at the truth is a priceless asset, not to be lightly squandered. As Lord Devlin himself observed:

> In our own country the reputation of the judiciary for independence and impartiality is a national asset of such richness that one government after another tries to plunder it.[22]

Stevens also has suggested that, in the new climate of today, judges should be far less willing to accept extra-judicial chores.[23]

The connection between judicial salaries and judicial independence may not be immediately obvious. But Robert Stevens in his valuable book on *The Independence of the Judiciary*[24] devotes considerable space to recording exchanges between the judges and the Lord Chancellor's Office on this subject,

---

[21] *The Courts and Public Controversy* Sir Robin Cooke, Otago Law Review [1983] vol. 5, no. 3, 357, at 365.

[22] Patrick Devlin, *The Judge*, 9.

[23] Hardwicke Lecture, 21 May 1966, *Judges, Politics, Politicians and the Confusing Role of the Judiciary*.

[24] Op. cit.

presumably because he sees the subjects as linked. The Commonwealth Secretariat has recently appointed a working group to study

the comparative level of remuneration received by members of the judiciary vis-à-vis other national holders of public office, the method of determination of that remuneration, and the process of adjustment of the level so determined over time.

The view that a link exists is, it appears, one shared by the Law Society, which in 1992 made a submission summarized in these terms:

The question of salaries constitutes one of the Society's major concerns so far as judicial independence is concerned. The opening up of a 'dispiriting chasm' between the relatively low salaries of those seated on the nation's benches and the much more remunerative incomes of the leading practitioners on court floors below them has been the chief subject of apprehension. The disparity of the incomes of those who judge and those whose arguments are judged by them has become shameful, the Society submits.[25]

If that quotation occasions any surprise, I should allay it by making clear that the Law Society in question was that of New South Wales. The point, however, must be the same. In Ireland the constitution has been held to require that judges should receive salaries and pension benefits which are appropriate quite apart from any recruitment considerations:

Otherwise, the essential independence of judges would be undermined.[26]

In India the level of judicial remuneration is specified in the Constitution and the level of allowances cannot be varied to the disadvantage of the judge after appointment.[27] Under Article III of the Constitution of the United States judicial compensation cannot be reduced while a judge remains in office. Professor Friedland was surely right when he wrote:

There is of course, a close connection between judicial salaries and judicial independence . . . if a judge's salary is dependent on the whim of the government, the judge will not have the independence we desire in our judiciary. If salaries could be arbitrarily raised or lowered in individual cases, or even collectively, the government would have a strong measure of control over the judiciary. As Alexander Hamilton stated: 'In the general course of human nature, a power over a man's subsistence amounts to a power over his will.'[28]

There is also, perhaps, another and subtler link between independence and remuneration. In most societies, and subject to obvious exceptions, there is some perceived relationship between what someone earns and the status or prestige which he enjoys. Financial rewards are not, of course, everything, but nor are they nothing. Unless, therefore, the rewards of judicial office (with or without other benefits) are sufficient to attract the ablest candidates to accept appointment,

---

[25] *Commonwealth Law Bulletin*, (July 1992), 1043.
[26] *McMenamin v Ireland* [1994] 21 LRM 368, at 377.
[27] Article 125, Constitution of India.
[28] A *Place Apart: Judicial Independence and Accountability in Canada* May 1995, at 53.

albeit with some financial sacrifice, the ranks of the judiciary must be filled by the second best, those who (under our system) have failed to make it in private practice, and there would be an inevitable lowering in the standing and reputation of the judiciary and a sea change in the relationship between advocate and judge. There would also, I suggest, be a loss of those qualities of confidence and courage on which the assertion of true independence not infrequently depends, because these qualities tend to be the product of professional success, not the hallmark of professional mediocrity. This is not mere speculation: one need only look at some other countries with a career judiciary, in which those opting for a judicial career are by and large the weaker candidates, to see that the judiciary which results lacks the authority and standing which we very largely take for granted.

I think that our history since the early nineteenth century bears out this analysis. It is true that the salary of £5,500 awarded to High Court judges in 1825 was reduced in 1832 to £5,000. But this was, by the standards of the day, an enormous salary, equivalent in modern terms to about £250,000 and not of course subject to taxation at modern rates. By the time this salary was eventually increased in 1954, after remaining at the same level for 122 years, it had ceased to be a princely and had indeed become an inadequate salary. Since then, however, salaries have been raised at fairly regular intervals, and have been maintained at a level roughly comparable with that of the most senior public servants. Stevens points out that in 1992 Law Lords were paid appreciably more than justices of the Supreme Court of the United States.[29] This is plainly a somewhat misleading comparison, since I assume it takes no account of benefits (such as the provision of legal assistance and transport) enjoyed by Supreme Court justices but not by all Law Lords. It nonetheless suggests that maintenance of a strong and independent judiciary is recognised to depend, at least to some extent, on the payment of a reasonable salary; and I believe it to be true that British judges are on the whole more generously rewarded than their European counterparts (except in Germany). Different countries of course have different traditions. Our own tradition does, however, depend on the willingness of the most successful practitioners, at the height of their careers, to accept appointment to the judicial bench, and I gravely doubt whether that tradition can be maintained if what the New South Wales Law Society called a 'dispiriting chasm' becomes too deep.

At a Conference held at Victoria Falls in August 1994, the Magistrates and Judges of the Commonwealth adopted a proclamation of which Article 3 was to the following effect:

Provision of formal and informal instruction for judges and magistrates in the performance of their duties, in their responsibilities as independent adjudicators, and in the laws and procedures which they are required to apply is an essential element in a modern and fair legal system.[30]

---

[29] Stevens, op. cit. at 167.
[30] *Commonwealth Law Bulletin* (Oct. 1994), at 1365.

The Conference went on to refer to a new body, the Commonwealth Judicial Education Institute, one of whose purposes was to promote the independence of the judiciary in the Commonwealth through the provision of appropriate judicial education at all levels. There is nothing here which would, or certainly which should, provoke any reservation in the mind of an English judge and we have given our full support to the Institute, which performs an indispensable role, particularly in relation to the smaller and poorer members of the Commonwealth. But judicial education is not only for others. Although it is not very long since the need for judicial education and training in this country came to be recognized, I doubt whether anyone now questions the potential benefits to be gained. Such programmes no longer need to be disguised as 'judicial studies' to make them acceptable. Indeed, one of the most potent concerns provoked by Lord Woolf's proposals is whether adequate funds will be forthcoming to provide the training for which the new procedures will call. It is, however, as I would suggest, essential, if judicial education is to promote the end of judicial independence, that control of the content and form of such education should rest squarely in the hands of the judges themselves, and such agencies as they may employ, as it now does. It is obvious that if control of the education and training of judges did not rest in the hands of the judges themselves, but in those of the executive, it would become possible for judicial independence to be subverted and not promoted. It would, in short, become possible for the state to instruct judges how they should decide cases, a result which would be entirely unacceptable. Concerns along these lines were expressed in the debates on the Police and Magistrates' Court Act 1994, and appropriate amendments made. The Judicial Studies Board discharges an ever more important function; but it has no function more important than the protection of judicial autonomy in this field. I hope that the recent appointment of the Lord Chief Justice as patron of the Board will be seen as a small but symbolic way of recognizing that principle.

For better or worse, British judges do not control the financing and administration of the court system. If there were ever a chance of their doing so, which I doubt, it was lost when the Courts Act 1971 converted the Lord Chancellor's Department from a small secretariat into a department of state employing some 10,000 civil servants. It cannot be suggested that the relationship between the administration and the judges over the last quarter century has been in all respects an easy one. Many judges have resented what they perceived as an administration breathing down their necks, treating them as pawns on a bureaucratic chess board. Decisions directly bearing on the performance of judicial functions and the efficiency of court administration have on occasions been made without consultation and for ill-conceived reasons. While high standards of public administration are as necessary in this field as in any other, management concepts quite inappropriate to the unique function of administering justice have been wrongly allowed to intrude. There has been difficulty and dispute on the frontier, not alleviated by doubt about where the frontier is or should be. It would be utopian to suppose that these tensions will disappear. They may even increase. But there are two hopeful signs. The first is a written instruction given by the Lord Chancellor to the Chief Executive of the Court Service Agency in November 1994 headed 'Consultation with the Judiciary'. In his second paragraph he wrote:

I consider it particularly important that you should continue to foster good relations with all members of the judiciary. I shall require you to ensure that both you and your staff work closely with the Lord Chief Justice and the other Heads of Division, the Senior Presiding Judge, Presiding Judges and representatives of the Circuit and District Benches and other judicial officers, as appropriate, to ensure that all parties are enabled to carry out their responsibilities in the management of the courts and the administration of justice.

He went on to require the Chief Executive to discuss with the judiciary his plans for dealing with any major in-year change in resource allocation which might materially affect the performance of the Court Service before putting his plans to the Lord Chancellor. This is the second hopeful sign. The Judges' Council has established a sub-committee on resources under the chairmanship of the Senior Presiding Judge and with a membership comprising both judges and administrators (including the Chief Executive) to act as the forum for effective and continuing consultation. I very much doubt if any comparable machinery has ever before existed.

It seems on the whole unlikely that any challenge to judicial independence in this country will be by way of frontal assault. The principle is too widely accepted, too scrupulously observed, too long-established for that. The threat is more likely to be of insidious erosion, of gradual (almost imperceptible) encroachment. Such a process we must be vigilant to detect and vigorous, if need be, to resist. But my own, perhaps unduly complacent, view is that we can at present give reassurance to the United Nations' Special Rapporteur. In the country which cradled judicial independence the infant is alive, and well, and even— on occasion— kicking.

2

*Judicial Ethics**

Judicial ethics, the subject I have been asked to address in this chapter, appears to have been largely neglected in this country in recent years—by the judiciary, by the practising profession, and, less surprisingly, by academics.

No doubt this relative neglect is, up to a point, reassuring. It reflects the fact that we have in this country been spared the scandals which have given life to the subject in the United States over many years and in Australia more recently. It is indeed a striking fact that in nearly three centuries since the Act of Settlement made the superior judges irremovable save on an address by both Houses of Parliament no English High Court judge has been so removed. The practice of appointing judges from a small pool of candidates, sharing a common professional background, and known personally or by professional repute to those making and advising on appointments, has enabled much to be taken for granted. Apart from the Kilmuir Rules, which were very limited in their scope and have now been to some extent relaxed, I know of no recent attempt to state the rules which govern, or should govern, the conduct of judges, and it is of interest that, in writing the letter to the Director-General of the BBC in which the Rules were set out, Lord Kilmuir referred to 'the important qualification that, as you are already aware, the Lord Chancellor has no sort of disciplinary jurisdiction over Her Majesty's Judges'.

A moderate degree of reassurance should not, however, spill over into complacency. Though the occasions are, I feel sure, infrequent, none of us knows how often, or on what grounds, judges of the higher courts have been informally nudged or encouraged into retirement. The Lord Chancellor is of course empowered to dismiss circuit judges, district judges, magistrates, and justices, but the principles upon which he acts may not be entirely clear. The enlargement of the pool from which judges are recruited, welcome though this is, must increase the possibility of error and may mean that less can be taken for granted. Above all, whether the judges like it or not—and of course they do not—we live in a time when the judicial role and judicial performance are the subject of increasingly critical public scrutiny. No reader even of the quality press would be tempted to think that the judges were beyond reproach. If, as I think most of us present would hold, the administration of justice is one of the cardinal functions of civil society, and if for that purpose the judges are entrusted, as they are, with wide and sometimes unreviewable powers, it is surely a matter of some moment to consider the

* First published in R. Cranston (ed.), *Legal Ethics and Professional Responsibility* (Oxford: Clarendon Press, 1995), 35–51.

principles of conduct by which judges are, or consider themselves to be, bound. I am accordingly grateful to the Society for causing me to think about this subject in a more coherent way than I have had occasion to do before.[1]

Before venturing further, I should perhaps enter five caveats. First, the views I express are my own personal views, which I have not discussed with anyone. They do not carry the imprimatur of the Lord Chancellor who, as head of the judiciary, must be regarded as the ultimate, or at least the penultimate, arbiter of these matters. I do not doubt that some of my observations would provoke dissent from some of my professional colleagues. Secondly, I should make clear that my opinions have the inherent vulnerability of all opinions formed without discussion, argument, or application to specific instances. I could well imagine that situations would arise which would cause me to modify or depart from what I now think, and no doubt the passage of time and changing circumstances would anyway call at least for modification. Thirdly, it is obvious that any rules in a field of this kind must cover a wide spectrum of conduct. There are of course some acts—like acceptance of a gift from a current litigant, or conviction of conspiracy to pervert the course of justice—which would without question call for immediate removal or dismissal. There is other conduct—like using official writing paper to conduct an argument with one's insurers—which most judges would regard as 'a bit off' or 'not done' but which could not attract any sanction. Between these extremes would lie a wide range of conduct to which the appropriate response would depend on questions of degree. If it were shown, for instance, that a judge had on an isolated occasion behaved in court in an intemperate, overbearing, or unjudicial way, or fallen asleep, or neglected his duties, he might expect to be rebuked by any appellate court before which the case came or a senior judge would make an opportunity to have a quiet word. That would in all probability be that. But it might be different if a judge's unacceptable conduct in court, or somnolence, or neglect were shown to be habitual and of such an order as reasonably to undermine confidence in his ability to do justice. Fourthly, I have not attempted to cover all aspects of this subject. Despite the length of this address, there are significant areas of the subject which I shall not attempt to cover. And fifthly, I hope it will not be thought sexist if I refer to individual, hypothetical judges as 'he'. It is cumbersome to repeat 'he or she' and I am too pedantic to be happy using 'they' or 'their' after a singular noun. The alternative stratagem of saying 'she' seems inappropriate, since I know of no case where the conduct of a female judge has given serious ground for complaint.

I take as my starting point a passage in an address given by Sir Owen Dixon to law students in the University of Melbourne when professional conduct was first introduced into the curriculum of the university law school in 1953. He said:

---

[1] I am in particular grateful for being introduced to *Judicial Ethics in Australia* by the Hon Mr Justice Thomas of the Supreme Court of Queensland, a most interesting and informative work on which I have drawn heavily.

To be a good lawyer is difficult. To master the law is impossible. But I should have thought that the first rule of conduct for counsel, the first and paramount ethical rule, was to do his best to acquire such a knowledge of the law that he really knows what he is doing when he stands between his client and the court and advises for or against entering the temple of justice.[2]

If applied to judges, the passage plainly calls for some modification, but the essential point seems to me apposite: it is a judge's professional duty to do what he reasonably can to equip himself to discharge his judicial duties with a high degree of competence. Sir Owen went on to say that acquiring such knowledge of the law meant hard work for a long time, and he added: 'It is harder work than in London because counsel here do not specialise. In England it is otherwise and a man may pass his life very comfortably as an expert in an extremely narrow field.'[3]

There is a relevance to judges in this passage also, and for them there are twin dangers. Some judges, particularly circuit judges, may pass their lives very comfortably as experts trying criminal cases. The temptation for them, after a time and in run of the mill cases, is that of over-familiarity, leading to ill-prepared, impromptu, ill-organised, diffuse, and unnecessarily lengthy jury directions. The Crown Court Study, recently made for the Runciman Royal Commission, suggests that to a remarkable and very creditable extent this temptation is resisted. Appellate judges are subject to a different temptation. Almost all of them spend much of their time dealing with areas of the law with which they have no close familiarity. The temptation then is in effect to cede decision of the appeal to the member of the court who is so familiar. This, plainly, is a dereliction of judicial duty. The litigant is entitled to the considered judgment, if not the considered judgments, of all members of the court, not just one. So Sir Owen's observations, suitably adapted, seem to me the right place to start. It is also perhaps appropriate to bear in mind Professor Dworkin's recent observations on judicial integrity and the need to give, so far as possible, adequately reasoned decisions.[4] It must be possible to improve on the performance of a High Court judge to whom I once addressed submissions which he gave no reason for rejecting beyond saying 'Well, I'm sorry, but I don't agree.'

Just as the Ten Commandments of the Old Testament were subsumed in the New by 'the first and great commandment . . . and the second . . . like unto it, namely this', so (as it seems to me) much of what would go into a detailed code of judicial conduct if we had one is embraced by the judicial oath to 'do right to all manner of people after the laws and usages of this realm, without fear or favour, affection or ill will'. This is language not only noble in its simplicity but also rich in content, and I think some phrases may usefully be highlighted.

The judge's obligation is to do justice 'after the laws and usages of this realm'.

---

[2] *Jesting Pilate*, 131.   [3] Ibid.
[4] *Life's Dominion* (1993), 144–7.

In other words, he must apply the law, not his own personal predilection, reflecting the wisdom of Samuel Johnson's observation: 'To permit a law to be modified at discretion is to leave the community without law. It is to withdraw the direction of that public wisdom by which the deficiencies of private understanding are to be supplied.'[5]

This obligation does not, in the field of non-statutory law, deprive the judge of all power to innovate, and to develop the law, an almost inevitable activity when he faces a situation to which existing authority does not apply. But it does in my view restrict the judges' authority to engage in what might be called wholesale judicial legislation. I will give an example. In an unreported decision on very strong facts, the Court of Appeal recently held that there was no enforceable right to privacy in English law.[6] In so holding the Court had regard not only to authority, judicial and academic, but also to the public concern directed to this subject over thirty years, reflected in reports by the Younger Committee and JUSTICE, in a series of unsuccessful Private Members' Bills, and in the deliberations (not then concluded) of the Calcutt Committee. The Court has been criticised for excessive timidity, in failing to grasp a nettle which other organs of government appeared strikingly unwilling to handle, and for failing to lay down the foundations of a law of privacy. I do not myself accept the validity of this criticism, unsurprisingly since I was a party to the decision. It seems to me a very good example of the sort of task judges may not properly take it upon themselves to discharge.

When one turns to statute law and subordinate legislation, the judge's duty to apply the law by seeking conscientiously to give fair and full effect to the intention of the legislation is obvious. This is not simply a rule of construction but a constitutional duty, a duty which judges assume as part of the price of their independence. It is also in my opinion an ethical duty, in the sense that a judge who knowingly and deliberately neglected to give effect to the plain effect of a statute would be acting improperly. Having said that I must, no doubt surprisingly, confess to having done so, in one context. Perhaps I may elaborate, since I hope the example will show that ethical duties, even constitutional duties, are not always as straightforward as might be thought.

The context I have in mind is the Bail Act 1976. That Act was founded on the praiseworthy premise that prospective defendants who may be innocent and whom it is unnecessary to keep in prison should not be imprisoned during what may be a lengthy period until they are tried. Thus the general rule in section 4 of the Act is that a person shall be granted bail unless certain conditions apply, and in the case of imprisonable offences those conditions relate to the risk that the defendant will fail to surrender to custody, commit an offence while on bail, or interfere with witnesses, or that his own safety or welfare may be damaged by the

---

[5] Boswell, *Life of Johnson* (1976), 496.
[6] *Kaye v Robertson*, 23 Feb. 1990; see App. 1 to the Calcutt Report.

grant of bail. So far so good. It is the wording of paragraph 2 of the relevant schedule[7] which causes trouble:

The defendant need not be granted bail if the court is satisfied that there are substantial grounds for believing that the defendant, if released on bail (whether subject to conditions or not) would—

fail to surrender to custody, commit an offence, and so on. The difficulty arises because the court must do more than form an opinion that one or other consequence will or may follow if bail is refused; the court must be satisfied, an obviously more exacting state of intellectual conviction. Moreover, the court must be satisfied on substantial grounds, so hunch or personal apprehension is not enough if (as not infrequently happens) no ground of substance is presented to the court. The court's right to refuse bail is not, however, conditional on its being satisfied that there are substantial grounds for believing that the defendant may, if released on bail, do one or other of the proscribed things; the court must be satisfied that there are substantial grounds for believing that if granted bail the defendant would do one or other of the proscribed things, a very difficult test to satisfy in relation to anything as unpredictable as the future conduct of an unknown human being over a shortish time period. The dilemma presented by this provision was not in my view cured by paragraph 9 of the schedule, which required the court in taking these decisions to have regard so far as appeared to it to be relevant to the nature and seriousness of the offence charged, the probable penalty, the defendant's character, antecedents and community ties, the defendant's previous behaviour on bail, and the strength of the evidence against him. It is not very easy to relate this paragraph to paragraph 2, which I have quoted: the rigorous conditions of paragraph 2 are either satisfied or they are not, and if they are not it will only be in a minority of cases that paragraph 9 will make good the deficiency. The fact that a defendant has a long criminal record does not of itself enable the court to be satisfied that there are substantial grounds for believing that he will commit an offence if granted bail, and the fact that a defendant has a house and assets abroad, in Northern Cyprus or elsewhere, does not of itself enable the court to be satisfied that there are substantial grounds for believing that he will fail to surrender to custody if granted bail, although in each case the court will recognize a risk. An amendment to the Act has eased but not in my view cured this problem. In cases where I could not conscientiously say (to myself) that the conditions of paragraph 2 were satisfied, but in which I have felt grave apprehension that a defendant's release involved a real danger to the public, I have on occasion refused bail. I suspect other judges have done the same. It is highly regrettable that courts should be subject to this dilemma. On the repeated occasions when judges or justices have been vilified and hounded for releasing on bail a defendant who commits other offences or absconds, I have never been aware of any acknowledgement, in parliament or the press, of the stringent duty which this Act has imposed upon the courts.

---

[7] Para. 2 of Part 1 of Schedule 1 of the Act.

The judge's duty to administer justice 'without fear or favour, affection or ill will' plainly covers a very wide range of ethical duties. If one were to attempt a modern paraphrase, it might perhaps be that a judge must free himself of prejudice and partiality and so conduct himself, in court and out of it, as to give no ground for doubting his ability and willingness to decide cases coming before him solely on their legal and factual merits as they appear to him in the exercise of an objective, independent, and impartial judgment. This again calls for some elaboration.

Perhaps the most obvious reflection of this principle is the clear rule that a judge must have no pecuniary interest in the outcome of any litigation before him and should not be financially beholden to any litigant appearing before him. In *Dimes v Grand Junction Canal Company*[8] an order of the Lord Chancellor was set aside because he had a substantial interest in the company, even though he was only affirming a decision of the Vice-Chancellor and was not in any way influenced by his interest. This was, as it seems to me, a very strong decision, but I have no doubt that it would be followed today on similar facts although I do not think a judge would stand down on account of a share-holding in a litigant company, or perhaps even disclose it,[9] unless the share-holding and the action were such that the outcome could have a more than negligible effect on his fortune. That accords with an occasion in the Court of Appeal when, at the outset of a very lengthy and obviously tedious patent appeal, one member of the court disclosed that he held shares in one of the litigant companies. 'If my Brother thinks,' said (Charles) Russell LJ, presiding, 'that he can escape from this case on a ground as tenuous as that, he is in error.'

The rule against acceptance of gifts from litigants or potential litigants is clear and obvious. But it is not quite absolute. Both the Lord Chief Justice and the Master of the Rolls receive annual gifts of a quarter of roebuck from the Royal Parks (on payment of a nominal delivery charge) and until recently, received a shirt-length of cloth from the Corporation of London. If not sanctioned by immemorial custom, these gifts would no doubt be questionable. It is of interest that Lord Chief Justice Hale, in the much more venal age of Charles II, 'not only refused the customary perquisites like the venison for the justices on circuit, but insisted on paying more than the regular price for his domestic supplies'.[10]

No attempt has ever been made in this country, so far as I know, to define the

---

[8] (1852) 3 HLC 758; 10 ER 301.

[9] On reading this passage a very senior retired judge observed that he would personally disclose any share-holding of which he was aware. He had found himself severely criticised in the press for hearing a case without disclosing that he held shares in a part-owner of a litigant company. The share-holding had in fact been very small, and the judge had been unaware of it since his investments were managed on a discretionary basis by brokers. He then took steps, however, to put all his shares into the name of his brokers' nominee company. This would be effective to avert unfair criticism of this kind, but would not displace the need to disclose any significant share-holding, however held, of which the judge was aware.

[10] Bond, 'The Growth of Judicial Ethics', (1925) 10 Mass. Law Quarterly 1 at p.13.

sources from which a judge may properly receive money in addition to his judicial salary. There can, plainly, be no objection to his receiving the proceeds of ordinary investments, or the rents of any property the judge may own, or the earnings of any estate the judge may be fortunate enough to have. It has not been thought inconsistent with judicial office to be a member of Lloyd's, although it is now (I think) some years since judges sitting in the Commercial Court thought it proper to maintain their membership, an exemption for which they are, no doubt, grateful. I do not think it would be generally regarded as improper for a judge to accept a modest honorarium for a lecture or address which he had given, although most would perhaps decline or ask that the sum be paid to charity; a gift of wine or a book a judge might, properly in my view, accept, but the identity of the donor and the value of the gift would plainly affect his decision.

In his letter to the Director-General, Lord Kilmuir (ironically perhaps, in view of the furore later caused by his acceptance of company directorships while drawing the not ungenerous pension of a former Lord Chancellor) observed that 'in no circumstances, of course, should a Judge take a fee in connection with a broadcast'. This is a rule which I think most, if not all, judges would observe in relation to any radio or television broadcast or any newspaper article. This seems to be a good rule. But there is to my knowledge no similar rule or practice in relation to the proceeds of any legal treatise, novel, play, or other literary work which a judge may publish. It is possible to see a distinction between the two situations, but it is not very obvious. Probably, however, this is an area better left to judges' recognition that they must do nothing which could or could appear to compromise their judicial integrity than to any attempt at formulation of detailed rules.

All the major common law jurisdictions would, I am sure, regard it as unacceptable for a serving judge to engage in any capacity in any commercial enterprise (save for the very limited, and now unusual, exception of managing his own estate). Happily perhaps, most of us would not be tempted to emulate the Illinois judge who moonlighted as a construction worker.[11] But beyond that rule there is a surprising diversity of view. The Canons of Judicial Conduct promulgated by the American Bar Association bluntly provide that 'A judge should not act as an arbitrator or mediator.' Here, section 3 of the Administration of Justice Act 1970 expressly provides for Commercial Judges to act as arbitrators. They do not of course receive any personal benefit, since the fees payable (shortly to be increased) are prescribed and are payable to the Treasury. It may be the lack of any similar mechanism which explains the American rule. In Australia and, I think, the United States, it would be questionable whether a serving judge should serve as chairman of a sporting body. Here, judges have certainly served in such capacities, and I do not think this would be regarded as in any way objectionable unless the appointment were likely to involve the judge in controversy or the body were likely to be involved in litigation. The American Canons provide that

[11] *Re Daley* 2 Ill. Cts. Com 38 (1983).

A judge should not solicit funds for any educational, religious, charitable, fraternal or civic organisation, or use or permit the use of the prestige of his office for that purpose, but he may be listed as an officer, director, or trustee of such an organisation.

In this country, a judge would undoubtedly be expected to exercise considerable discretion about the bodies with which he allowed himself to be associated, avoiding involvement in any campaigning organization of even a non-political kind, and would be scrupulous not to exploit his judicial office for the purpose of attracting funds. But subject to those caveats, English judges would not feel themselves precluded from soliciting funds for charitable causes, and I can think of a number who have done so. Again, the American Canons provide that

A judge should not accept appointment to a governmental committee, commission, or other position that is concerned with issues of fact or policy or matters other than the improvement of the law, the legal system, or the administration of justice.

In Australia, the desirability of such a rule has been the subject of active debate. In Victoria, there has been long standing disapproval of judges serving on royal commissions. In Queensland the judges have held that they should not do so.[12] Strong and well-argued opinions have been expressed on both sides.[13] The contrast with this country, where very many judges at all levels have served as royal commissioners or conducted inquiries and investigations, is very marked. One need only instance Lord Scarman, who perhaps holds the record, with his inquiries into disturbances in Red Lion Square, Northern Ireland, and Brixton, and into the Grunwick labour dispute. It is scarcely an exaggeration to say that among senior judges 'my inquiry' is the equivalent, in other circles, of 'my operation'. But we do well to recognize that those in the United States and Australia who take the contrary view have a serious point. It is in my opinion consistent with judicial office for a judge to serve in these capacities if the reason for his appointment is the need to harness to the task in question the special skills which a judge should possess: characteristically, the ability to dissect and analyse evidence, appraise witnesses, exercise a fair and balanced judgment, write a clear and coherent report, and so on. If, however, that is not the reason for his appointment—if, more particularly, it were sought to lend the respectability of his office or reputation to some political end not otherwise acceptable to the public—it would in my opinion be the clear duty of the judge to decline to serve. In general, we seem in this country to have been able to operate within more liberal constraints than have been found to be appropriate elsewhere. So long as this liberality can be maintained, it is in my view desirable that it should be: justice is not a cloistered virtue, and it is in general desirable that judges should have acquaintances and experience outside the monastery.

It is now regarded in this country as a cardinal feature of judicial impartiality

---

[12] Thomas, op. cit., 54–5.

[13] 'Judges as Royal Commissioners and Chairman of Non-Judicial Tribunals', Australian Institute of Judicial Administration Incorporated (1986).

that the judge should be a political eunuch. If he was ever a member of any political party or organization, he must sever all ties on appointment. Thereafter he must do nothing which could give rise to any suggestion of political partisanship. A colleague once told me that he had never, since appointment, even cast his vote, although he did somewhat undermine the effect of this by adding that since he lived in Chelsea there was anyway no need.

It is perhaps worth pausing briefly to reflect how recent this tradition is. Well after the Act of Settlement, Lord Chief Justices as well as Lord Chancellors were known to sit in the cabinet.[14] Lord Stowell combined his judicial role in the Admiralty Court with a very active parliamentary role, concerned with the same measures on which he thereafter ruled as a judge.[15] Lord Romilly, the last member of my Inn to hold my office, held it while a member of the House of Commons. Sir James Stephen, while serving as a Queen's Bench puisne, contributed very lengthy letters to *The Times* attacking the government's policy on Ireland.[16] Lord Hewart, plainly, did not regard the office of Lord Chief Justice as any bar to participation in the political controversies of the day. Only in what, legally speaking, must be regarded as very recent times have the senior judicial offices ceased to be the preserve of the law officers of the day who wanted them. If my memory serves, Lord Hailsham on his first appointment as Lord Chancellor in 1970 announced an intention to increase the number of appointments to the bench from the ranks of serving members of parliament, an intention he did not, happily, implement to any significant extent.

It is also perhaps worth pausing briefly to reflect how different is the position here from that in the United States, with whose legal system we tend to think our own has so much in common. A rule of total and universal political neutrality would of course be inconceivable in a country where many members of the state judiciaries are elected and accordingly campaign for election on a platform. It is furthermore accepted that appointments to the higher, especially the highest, federal judiciary are made with what are essentially political considerations in mind, even though presidential hopes are often confounded. And there is a long tradition of active political activity by members of the Supreme Court. Brandeis was a major architect of Woodrow Wilson's legislative programme. During the Second World War Frankfurter conferred almost daily with Roosevelt about strategies and policies, and assisted in drafting some of the president's speeches. Fortas advised Lyndon Johnson on topics including the Vietnam War, steel price increases, and strategy for averting transport strikes. But this gave rise to criticism, as did some of Warren Burger's activity as chief justice.[17] So it may be that even in the United States there is some movement in our direction.

---

[14] e.g. Lord Mansfield, who was also Chancellor of the Exchequer, and Lord Ellenborough.

[15] H. J. Bourguignon, *Sir William Scott Lord Stowell* (1987), 271.

[16] K. J. M. Smith, *James Fitzjames Stephen* (1988), 153.

[17] Edwards, 'Judicial Misconduct and Politics in the Federal System: A Proposal for Revising the Judicial Councils Act' (1987) 75 Calif.LR.

Here, the rule is clear and (subject to the anomalous position of the Lord Chancellor) absolute. The Law Lords sit on the cross-benches and do not, by tradition, become involved in political controversy unrelated to the administration of justice. Perhaps the only remaining problem, and that a minor one, concerns the position of judges' spouses. When almost all judges were men and wives were expected to subordinate their personal interests to their husbands', the unwritten rule was that judges' wives should adopt the same position of strict neutrality as their husbands. But the unwillingness of wives to be treated as appendages of their husbands, recognition that there need be no identity of view between husband and wife on political any more than other issues, and—I fear it must be admitted—the increasing appointment of women to the bench, with the result that it is the husband not the wife who is expected to give up office as member of parliament or county councillor, will, I feel sure, lead to acceptance that conventional political activities of the spouse will not taint the judge provided the judge remains resolutely aloof.

The Kilmuir Rules undoubtedly had the effect of discouraging almost to the point of prohibiting contacts between judges and the media. The reason which he gave—that 'So long as a Judge keeps silent his reputation for wisdom and impartiality remains unassailable' —was not entirely flattering but contained a hard nugget of truth. As is well known, this rule (if one can call it such) has been relaxed somewhat by the present Lord Chancellor, for reasons which are in my opinion sound. If judges are fit to judge they should be able to exercise a reasonable judgment on whether to speak to the media and what to say if they do. Issues do, perhaps increasingly, arise on which it is desirable that the voice of the professional judiciary should be heard and it is unfortunate if the only audible voice is that of those retired judges most forward in offering their opinions. There is also, I suppose, a faint hope that the more grotesque caricatures of the modern judiciary will lose credibility if the public generally has a better idea of what judges are actually like. But there has now been enough experience of the new and more liberal regime to indicate the very real damage which would be done if judges did not exercise their new freedom with the greatest circumspection. It is vital that the occasions on which and the conditions under which judges contribute to public discussion are closely considered. I would whole-heartedly endorse the view more than once advanced by Mr Bernard Levin that judges should not be tempted to pontificate or offer opinions on subjects outside their professional field.[18] Nor should they, save on issues directly related to the administration of justice, and then with considerable discretion, be drawn into criticising government policy. When such issues do arise—one thinks recently of cutbacks in legal aid, the Administration of Justice Act 1992, and the number of judges—it is probably desirable that public comment should be left to the Lord Chief Justice, who by tradition enjoys a seat in the House of Lords, presumably to give him an appropriate public forum in which to discuss such matters.

[18] *The Times*, 28 Feb. 1986 and 17 Aug. 1993.

In his most interesting book on 'Judicial Ethics in Australia', Mr Justice Thomas of the Queensland Supreme Court addresses a topic never to my knowledge expressly addressed here, the social constraints to which a judge is subject. He suggests[19] that 'a judge should not have particularly close contact with anyone who regularly appears in his court' and also says[20] 'I should be very surprised if there is still any general expectation that judges should never go into a public bar.' On the first point, any English rule would have to take account of the Inns of Court, which inevitably bring judges and senior practitioners at the Bar into close contact. This is, no doubt, a source of strength, but there are potential dangers, to which judges should be alert. I can certainly think of one judge whose continuing contact with members of his old chambers was so close and frequent as to raise disquieting questions in the minds of those appearing against them before him. On the second point, as a very general proposition, I think most judges would be inclined to agree. But I would be very surprised if any judge were to be seen in a public house within about a mile of the Law Courts in the Strand or, perhaps, any court in which the judge was sitting. On a third point I have no doubt that there would be general agreement: that while a judge need not necessarily conduct his private life in accordance with the highest standards of morality he must at least do so in such a way as to avert the possibility of scandal and to demonstrate respect for the law he is appointed to serve; one could well imagine that infractions of the law which were in the past regarded as relatively venial—driving when over the prescribed limit of alcohol is the most obvious example—might in future cause much more acute concern.

If, as happens from time to time, proceedings are issued against a judge as a result of something done or not done in his judicial capacity, the standard practice is to hand any papers to the Treasury Solicitor who will take the necessary steps to have the action dismissed. If it were necessary for a judge to issue proceedings to defend his judicial reputation (an almost unheard of event), I think it would again be appropriate to invoke the help and follow the advice of the Treasury Solicitor. A judge who did not follow this course would not, I think, expect to be reimbursed out of the public purse for any expenditure he incurred. Only in the most extreme or unusual circumstances does any judge go to law in relation to a private matter: this is no doubt in part because of the somewhat invidious spectacle this would present to the public, but it is also in part because judges know, better than anyone, how uncertain the outcome of litigation is liable to be.

I fear I have occupied much of your time without having, as yet, even got the judge into court. It is perhaps difficult to improve on rules for his own personal guidance which Chief Justice Hale devised for himself in the 1660s:[21]

4. That in the execution of justice, I carefully lay aside my own passions, and not give way to them however provoked.

[19] At 44.   [20] At 42.   [21] Thomas, op. cit. App B, 203.

5. That I be wholly intent upon the business I am about, remitting all other cares and thoughts as unseasonable and interruptions.
6. That I suffer not myself to be prepossessed with any judgment at all, till the whole business and both parties be heard.
7. That I never engage myself in the beginning of any cause, but reserve myself unprejudiced till the whole be heard.

This is, literally, a counsel of perfection. It is a truism that all human beings, judges included, are to some extent creatures of their upbringing, education and experience. They inevitably hold views, entertain preferences and are subject to prejudices. But it is plainly their duty to lay these aside and approach cases in an impartial and objective way so far as possible, and to give the appearance of doing so.

There can, I think, be no doubt that much judicial behaviour was tolerated in the past which would be regarded as simply unacceptable today. Connoisseurs will doubtless savour, as I do, the account of 'The Origin of the Commercial Court' contributed by Lord Justice MacKinnon to the *Law Quarterly Review* in 1944:[22]

Mr Justice J. C. Lawrance was a stupid man, a very ill-equipped lawyer and a bad judge. He was not the worst judge I have appeared before: that distinction I would assign to Mr Justice Ridley. Ridley had much better brains than Lawrance, but he had a perverse instinct for unfairness that Lawrance could never approach.

Examples of past judicial misbehaviour spring readily to mind. There was the occasion when Norman Birkett, appearing as a young man for a plaintiff who he thought had won, rose after his opponent's closing speech and said 'I don't know if your Lordship wishes to hear me?' 'No,' said the judge, so Birkett sat down and listened with horror while the judge delivered judgment against his client. At the end he rose and protested: 'But your Lordship said you didn't wish to hear me.' 'I didn't,' replied the judge, 'and I still don't.' One recalls the notorious partisanship of Lord Hewart.[23] One recalls the judge who, on receiving the assurance of a witness wishing to affirm that he had no religious belief, observed 'And no morals either.' One recalls the appeal which succeeded against Hallett J because the judge's interruptions had been such as to make the conduct of both parties' cases impossible.[24] One recalls, much more recently, the criminal case in which a chairman of quarter sessions (unobjectionably, as was held on appeal) on repeated occasions during a defendant's case observed in a loud voice 'Oh, God' and laid his head across his arm and made groaning and sighing noises.[25] It cannot, unfortunately, be said that such aberrations never recur, and of course they were always exceptional. But I have no doubt that the modern judiciary would, as it should, regard itself as the servant of the public, not its master; would

---

[22] 60 LQR 324.   [23] C. P. Harvey, *The Advocate's Devil* (1958), 32.
[24] *Jones v National Coal Board* [1957] 2 QB 55.
[25] *R v Hircock, Farmer, Leggett* [1970] 1 QB 67.

recognize that the dignity of judicial office is enhanced and not reduced by the display of ordinary good manners; and would recognize that the appearance of justice is almost as important as its substance, if indeed the two are separable. There is much force in Sir Robert Megarry's observation that the most important person in court is not the judge or the advocate or the witness but the litigant who is going to lose.[26]

The judge's duty to be, and appear to be, completely impartial during the conduct of a case is so fundamental, so pervasive and—I must admit—so obvious that I would not be justified in wearying you with examples. But there are a number of situations which perhaps deserve mention.

First, disqualification. It is the judge's duty to disqualify himself if, pecuniary interest altogether apart, he is for any reason unable to try a case on its objective merits or might reasonably appear to be so. This can give rise to very difficult questions.[27] In the ordinary way English practice would not require a judge to stand down because he had previously decided cases against a particular party, or even because he had previously rejected the evidence of a particular material witness. But the consistency of the previous adverse decisions or the terms in which the evidence had been rejected might be such as to raise a question, however wrongly, about the judge's ability to approach a case with the necessary objectivity. In such a case the judge may prefer to stand down. The Court of Appeal has, however, emphasised very recently that a charge of bias or apparent bias is not to be lightly made.[28]

Secondly, it is quite clear that a judge should not make disparaging comments about the parties in any case he is currently trying. An extreme example of such conduct came before the Criminal Division of the Court of Appeal in the recent and notorious case of *R v Batth*.[29] In that case the then Recorder of London, while presiding over a trial in which a Sikh defendant was accused of murder, was reported in a daily newspaper to have made an after-dinner speech at the Mansion House in which, referring to the case he was hearing at the time, he made mention of 'murderous Sikhs'. It was found, not surprisingly, that in the absence of any convincing contradiction of the report, it raised an appearance of bias and the court commented on 'the extreme unwisdom of any Judge making remarks outside the court in public about a case which he is currently trying'. In an even more recent civil case,[30] the Civil Division of the Court of Appeal held that 'total abstinence from comment on a current case, in public or in private, should be the rule'.

Thirdly, while it is inherent in the appellate system that judges will disagree, and it is on occasion necessary for an appellate court to express criticism, sometimes

---

[26] 'Judges and Judging', Child & Co Lecture, 3 Mar. 1977, 5.
[27] See, e.g., *Australian National Industries Ltd v Spedley Securities Ltd* (1992) 26 NSW LR 411.
[28] *Arab Monetary Fund v Hashim*, unreported.
[29] Unreported, 9 Apr. 1990.
[30] *Arab Monetary Fund v Hashim*, unreported.

very strong criticism, of a judge's conduct, the language used on such occasions should be measured, temperate, dignified, and so far as possible polite. Such situations should never degenerate into personal vendetta. Happily, I can think of no recent parallel to the occasion on which Scrutton LJ gratuitously criticized the knowledge claimed by McCardie J, a bachelor, of women's underwear, an attack to which McCardie J responded by refusing to make his notes of judgment available to any Court of Appeal of which Scrutton LJ was a member.[31] When Lord Maugham wrote to *The Times* criticizing Lord Atkin's dissenting judgment in *Liversidge v Anderson*[32] Atkin rightly forbore to reply. I cannot think any judge would now feel justified in writing to a periodical to criticize a judgment of the Lord Chief Justice, as Sir James Stephen did in 1884 fiercely attacking Lord Coleridge's judgment in a blasphemy case.[33] The convention is now settled that differences of this kind are not aired in the press.

Fourthly, it is plainly improper for a judge to court publicity or seek public acclaim or newspaper headlines. There is still much force in the old aphorism that the best judge is he whose name is unknown to average readers of the *Daily Mail*. Chief Justice Hale three centuries ago was fully alive to this point. His 'Things necessary to be continually had in remembrance' included

11. That popular or court applause or distaste, have no influence into any thing I do in point of distribution of justice.
12. Not to be solicitous what men say or think, so long as I keep myself exactly according to the rule of justice.

Modern practice would, I think, endorse that approach fully, subject to two qualifications. In passing sentence in a difficult case, a criminal judge is often wise to take account, among many other considerations, of how a proposed sentence will be perceived by the public at large, or the community to which the defendant belongs, or the victim. This is not a surrender to the clamour of the mob; it is realistic recognition that a sentence widely seen as unjustifiably lenient may ultimately be damaging to the defendant himself and even, unless and until corrected, to the administration of criminal justice. In the civil field also, cases arise which are of public concern: it may then not be enough for the court to reach the right decision; it may be necessary also to give reasons for the decision in terms which the public can understand.

Fifthly, there has, particularly in the United States, been some debate about the *ex parte* communications a judge may properly have when preparing his judgment.[34] The view there seems to be that a judge may consult with other judges but not with any law teacher. It is without doubt fundamental that a judge should not decide a case on a point which has not been raised in argument without giving

---

[31] Thomas, op. cit. 18–19.   [32] [1942] AC 206.
[33] K. J. M. Smith, *James Fitzjames Stephen*, 171.
[34] ABA Canons of Judicial Conduct, Canon 3A(4); 'Judicial Ethics: The less-often asked questions', Andrew L. Kaufman, (1989) Washington Law Review, vol. 64, 851.

notice to the parties and allowing them an opportunity to make submissions. That is a rule which arbitrators are expected to observe and so are judges. But subject to that, English practice would not in my view frown on a judge who sought to clear his mind or test his views by discussing the matter with a colleague or a law teacher. Difficulties could arise if the discussion were with an appellate judge who was thereafter called upon to decide an appeal against the decision, but in a case raising some issue of judicial or sentencing policy I do not think consultation with an appellate judge would be thought improper provided the trial judge did not cede the responsibility for decision which was properly his.

Sixthly, modern practice requires expeditious delivery of reserved judgments. The press of other commitments, the incidence of vacations, and the occasional unavailability (in multi-judge courts) of all members may lead to some delay between hearing and judgment but (save at the highest level) this should be measured at most in weeks and not in months. I do not think any delay beyond that is regarded as tolerable save perhaps in very special circumstances.

Seventhly, judges (being human) do not like being reversed on appeal, although some dislike it more than others. But it is the judge's clear duty to do nothing to obstruct any arguable appeal, whether by making findings of fact more conclusive than the evidence warrants in the expectation that the appellate court will be unable to interfere, by passing an unduly lenient sentence in the hope of deterring an appeal against conviction, by refusing leave or a certificate in any case where such is necessary and justified, or in any other way. Whatever the cost to his *amour propre* the judge must, so far as possible, remain detached and not seek to deprive a litigant of rights which the legal system confers.

In this context the question has arisen whether and to what extent it is permissible for a judge to edit a transcript of what he said. Authority makes plain that editing a transcript of a direction to a jury is not permitted.[35] This is in my view right, since in such cases much may turn on the precise terms in which the jury is directed; in civil cases more latitude is permitted, since that is generally not so. It is common practice to correct errors and infelicities of grammar and style in the transcript of an *extempore* judgment. But that latitude does not extend to alterations in the substance or sense of what was said, to the adding of new points or the rectifying of omissions not mentioned at the time. Still less does it sanction the wholesale rewriting of the judgment, using the transcript as little more than a draft.

Eighthly and lastly under this head, the overwhelming consensus of judicial opinion would in my view discourage or condemn attempts by judges, whether from the bench or otherwise, to answer public criticism of their decisions. Lord Cockburn burned his fingers when he entered the lists in defence of his decision in *R v Bedingfield*[36] over a century ago. Other judges who have attempted to

---

[35] *R v Klucznski* [1973] 1 WLR 1230.
[36] (1879) 14 Cox CC 341.

answer criticisms, particularly of criminal sentences, from the bench have tended to cut sorry and rather unconvincing figures. Judges are almost always better advised to remain silent, leaving the wisdom or unwisdom of any decision to be judged by the appellate courts, by academic commentators, and by public opinion.

On the closing stages of the judge's official journey I have only three brief points to make. First, and whatever the position before the appointment of Fisher J in 1968, it is now in my view clear that a judge may not properly retire (save of course on grounds of ill health or incapacity) before serving a minimum period of 15 years. The Lord Chancellor makes plain to prospective appointees that elevation to the bench is a one-way street and judges are morally obliged to honour that commitment. Secondly, the judge may after retirement pursue any avocation, public or private, not inappropriate for a retired judge. This may certainly include acting as an arbitrator or giving expert opinions on the law in the capacity of a retired judge. But thirdly, and here the contrast with both the United States and Australia is stark, a retired judge may not return to the practice of law. There are in my opinion a number of sound practical reasons which strongly support that rule. There is also, I think, a formal reason: that on becoming a judge a practitioner ceases to be a barrister or a solicitor (whether he remains on the roll or not) and becomes solely a judge, with the result that on retirement he lacks any qualification to practise. I would for my part be very sorry to see that rule eroded.[37]

[37] This is a slightly modified version of a lecture given at the SPTL Annual Conference on 8 Sept. 1993.

PART III
THE WIDER WORLD

Most laws, in this or any other country, are made and applied within the boundaries of the nation-state. As long ago as 1106 the Abbot of St Denis declared that 'It is not right that the English should be governed by the French, nor the French by the English.' Nor, in practice, is this feasible. Different countries have, over the centuries, developed distinctively different legal systems. In making laws, any legislature will usually seek to work with, rather than against, the grain of public opinion: it would, for example, be very surprising if our Parliament were to make criminal a kind of conduct which was regarded by the mass of the population as wholly unobjectionable.

In the modern world, however, nation-states cannot live, legally, like hermits, even if they wish to do so. To some extent they never could. And just as the English have been, over the centuries, great traders, great importers and exporters of goods and services, so they have of ideas, including legal ideas. The first of these two papers was a lecture given in honour of Dr F. A. Mann, an outstandingly erudite lawyer and scholar who came to this country from Nazi Germany, bringing with him not only an acute intellect but also a deep knowledge of legal systems other than our own. The paper considers whether English law is as 'splendidly isolated' as English lawyers have tended to suppose, and looks forward to an increasingly internationalist future.

The second paper, written for a colloquium of Indian and British lawyers, considers the position of minorities. When a population is roughly homogeneous, and there is a broad consensus of public opinion, the legislator's task is relatively straightforward. But what of those minorities who, for reasons of race, religion, tradition, or cultural background, hold beliefs and follow practices different from the majority? Should the law oblige a Sikh to discard his turban in favour of a crash helmet or a hard hat or a wig when riding a motor cycle or working on a building site or appearing as a barrister in court? Or should the law respect the imperatives of Sikhism? The law must be fair to all, not just to the dominant majority. This paper seeks to address these difficult and sensitive issues.

The third paper in this section is a speech delivered in New Delhi on 26 November 1999 at a celebration held to mark the jubilee of the Supreme Court of India. It was a celebration worthy of the occasion, attended by the Vice President, the Prime Minister, the Chief Justice and the Minister of Justice of India, together with the Justices of the Supreme Court and many other judges, lawyers and people prominent in Indian public life. The legal links between India and the United Kingdom remain remarkably strong, both at the personal level and the professional. It was an opportunity to touch on the British legal legacy to India, but also on the strides which the Indian courts, particularly the Supreme Court, have taken over the past half-century.

1

'There is a World Elsewhere': The Changing Perspectives of English Law*

I. INTRODUCTION

Looking back over the past through the wrong end of the telescope, one has the impression—which detailed reference to the law reports would doubtless disprove—that at certain times different types of cause have dominated the work of the courts. Thus, I tend to think of the typical eighteenth-century case as involving an improvident heir seeking to sell his expectancy, that of the nine-teenth as involving a disputed will, that of the early twentieth as involving some society fracas, a libel perhaps or an argument whether the countess gave her priceless jewels to the defendant or only lent them. Perhaps these impressions owe something to literature, although in the latter case one would have to admit that Trollope got there first. In more recent times one's impression, although still quite inaccurate no doubt, becomes more clearly focused. Thus, in the 1950s much time seems to have been spent on sensitive and difficult problems arising out of the Rent Acts. In the 1960s, as the expectations of a consumer society began to grow, it was the turn of hire purchase to loom large. The 1970s were the decade of employment, with relations between employer and employee (no longer master and servant), industrial action, wage freezes and pay norms ruling the roost—a decade that saw the birth and death of the National Industrial Relations Court and the Industrial Arbitration Board and their rebirth as the Employment Appeal Tribunal and the Central Arbitration Committee. The 1980s, surely, will be remembered as the decade when judicial review came of age. I use the metaphor deliberately to acknowledge that judicial review did not, of course, spring fully armed into mature life. Its growing points can be traced back, through a series of justly famed decisions well known to us all, to the old prerogative writs for which we demonstrate our continuing affection by barbarously mispronoun-cing their names.

What, then, of the 1990s? By what, if anything, will be the present decade be remembered? There are several candidates. It could, for instance, be the decade of the consumer, when the commuter will be compensated for the late arrival of his train and the patient for the delayed replacement of her hip. Or we might see the first stirrings of constitutional tension between the Parliament in Westminster

* Based on the F. A. Mann Lecture given on 21 November 1991. First published in *The International and Comparative Law Quarterly* (1992), vol. 41, 513–29.

and devolved assemblies in Scotland, Wales, Northern Ireland and the English regions. Or a more sharply focused and long overdue attention to human rights, arising perhaps from incorporation of the European Convention. My own prognosis, offered partly in hope and partly in expectation, is that the 1990s will be remembered as the time when England—and I emphasize *England*—ceased to be a legal island, bounded to the north by the Tweed, and joined, or more accurately rejoined, the mainstream of European legal tradition, at least as an associate member; the time when, as Francis Jacobs recently put it, English lawyers ceased to regard Europe as somewhere else.

In 1831 Savigny wrote to his English translator of his pain that England 'in all other branches of knowledge actively communicating with the rest of the world, should, in jurisprudence alone, have remained divided from the rest of the world, as if by a Chinese wall'. This was never, I think, quite true, but I think there was perhaps a period in the middle years of this century when it was truer than it ever had been before or has been since.

The foundation of this Chinese wall—if that is not a contradiction in terms— lay, I think, in an unquestioning belief in the superiority of the common law and its institutions, at least in England. In so far as comparisons were drawn with what went on elsewhere, they were to England's advantage. When I started in practice, it was an almost universal article of faith that English law and legal institutions were without peer in the world, with very little to be usefully learned from others (save, on occasion, the High Court of Australia). It was this spirit, proud, confident and self-reliant, which Lord Denning reflected in the dictum:[1]

No one who comes to these courts asking for justice should come in vain . . . The right to come here is not confined to Englishmen. It extends to any friendly foreigner. He can seek the aid of our courts if he desires to do so. You may call this 'forum-shopping' if you please, but if the forum is England, it is a good place to shop in, both for the quality of the goods and the speed of service.

It would of course be a travesty to cast Lord Denning as the Castlereagh of his times, and I do not. He was, as many will gratefully remember, the most open-minded of judges, always ready to beg, borrow or invent what seemed useful for his purpose. Thus in several of the changes I shall mention, as in so much else during his long reign, Lord Denning played a leading, often a decisive, part. His dictum in *The Atlantic Star* which I have quoted none the less attracts attention not as a flag planted on the mountain top but as a relic marking the highest point the tide ever reached. Like John Bright's attributed claim that 'England is and always will be the workshop of the world', which in spirit it somewhat resembles, this observation was parting company with the facts even as Lord Denning spoke. For already—I allow myself a cocktail of metaphors—the ice-cap was breaking up, new windows were opening, new trails were being blazed and a new spirit of

---

[1] *The Atlantic Star* [1973] QB 364, 382.

exploration was abroad in the land. It is on these encouraging portents that I base my prognosis. I should, however, make clear that in criticizing, and celebrating the demise of, the Little England heresy, I would wish quite emphatically to plead not guilty to the alternative heresy of assuming or believing that everything is done better elsewhere, that English law and institutions are in some fundamental way inferior or defective. English lawyers need no persuasion of the strengths and virtues of the common law and of the English legal system, and this would be a most inappropriate occasion to argue the contrary. A conviction that they are the embodiment of a very great deal that is excellent is not, however, inconsistent with recognition that valuable lessons can be learned from the experience of others. To what, then, can I point to suggest a new dawn of internationalism in the English legal world?

II. STAYING ENGLISH ACTIONS

I take my first example from the very field which gave rise to Lord Denning's dictum: the staying of an English action brought against a defendant served in England in order that the action may proceed elsewhere. Since 1935, it will be recalled, the rule applied in the English courts was that formulated by Scott LJ in *St Pierre v South American Stores (Gath & Chaves) Limited*:[2]

In order to justify a stay two conditions must be satisfied, one positive and the other nega-tive: (*a*) the defendant must satisfy the Court that the continuance of the action would work an injustice because it would be oppressive or vexatious to him or would be an abuse of the process of the Court in some other way; and (*b*) the stay must not cause an injustice to the plaintiff.

Two things are notable about this rule. The first is that it made the defendant's task in seeking a stay well-nigh impossible in other than the most extreme case. Beneath the high-flown denunciation of driving plaintiffs from the judgment seat, there lay, I think, a more basic assumption that anyone, plaintiff or defendant, was extremely fortunate to litigate in England rather than elsewhere and should not lightly be denied the privilege. As Lord Reid observed in disavowing Lord Denning's observation, 'with all respect, that seems to me to recall the good old days, the passing of which many may regret, when inhabitants of this island felt an innate superiority over those unfortunate enough to belong to other races'.[3]

The second, and even more notable, feature of the rule is that it wholly ignored what instinct suggests and authority now confirms to have been a much prefer-able rule firmly established in Scotland. As early as 1866, in a case concerning a contract to supply munitions to the Confederacy, the question put in the Court of Session was whether justice could be more appropriately administered elsewhere

---

[2] [1936] 1 KB 382, 398.   [3] *The Atlantic Star* [1974] AC 436, 453.

and the Lord Justice-Clerk said: 'The contention involved in such a plea is rather that for the interests of all the parties, and for the ends of justice, the cause may more suitably be tried elsewhere.'[4]

A few years later, a widow living in Leith sued a railway company for the death of her husband at Middlesbrough, founding jurisdiction in Scotland by the arrest of goods because the railway company ran a small branch line through Kelso. The Lord Justice-Clerk said:

Whether jurisdiction in any case exists . . . is one question; whether, in the circumstances, this is the best and most suitable forum for trying the case is another and different question . . . The Court has in several cases refused to compel defenders resident abroad to answer in this Court where from the nature of the question to be tried it is more consonant to the ends of justice that it should be tried in another forum equally competent.

Lord Young added:

I am myself very favourable to the Court taking a large and liberal view of such questions as we have here—that is to say, where, although jurisdiction does exist, it appears that it is not convenient nor fitting for the interests of the parties to entertain any individual case, then I think the Court should not listen to any such appeal as the pursuer makes here.

So the Court declined jurisdiction, accepting that the effect might, for financial reasons, be to deprive 'a poor widow, living in Leith' of any remedy.[5]

Both these cases were before Lord Kinnear's formulation of principle in *Sim v Robinow*,[6] which was applied by English and Scottish judges when the issue was raised in a Scottish appeal to the House of Lords in 1926. Lord Sumner framed the question as 'whether the forum in question, or the other forum, is the one in which justice will be the better done'. Lord Dunedin said:[7]

I think the fallacy of Mr Macmillan's argument consisted in this, that he construed the words 'for the ends of justice' as if it must necessarily be shown that the defenders would be subject to actual injury unless the plea was upheld. I am not deciding, so far as I am concerned, that the case could not be tried at Dumbarton. I am only deciding that I think it could be better tried in France.

And the stream of Scottish authority continued. In 1930, for instance, the Lord Justice-Clerk said:[8]

The question is, where can the case best be tried? Having regard to the interests of the parties and to the ends of justice, can it be more appropriately tried in Scotland or in Spain? . . . I find it impossible to affirm, on a review of the pleadings on both sides, that the appropriate Court for the trial of an action arising out of a collision off the Spanish coast between two foreign vessels, in which most of the evidence will be Spanish, is the Sheriff Court of Dumbarton.

---

[4] *Clements v Macaulay* (1966) 4 Macph. 583, 592.
[5] *Williamson v N.E. Railway* (1884) 11 R. 596, 598, 599.
[6] (1892) 19 R. 665, 668.
[7] *Société du Gaz* 1926 SC 13, 23, 18.
[8] *Sheaf Steamship Co. v Compania Transmediterranea* 1930 SC 660, 667.

Eventually, as we know—in no small part due to the work of Lord Goff, both as advocate and judge, and the wisdom of Lord Diplock—the Scottish rule was adopted in England. But it took three appeals to the House of Lords to put the law where, one feels, it should always have been and might have been had English lawyers of the time been willing to look north of the border and acknowledge that acceptance of jurisdiction by the English court is not necessarily an unmixed blessing for all concerned.[9]

III. THE LAW OF SOVEREIGN IMMUNITY

For my next instance of a new and refreshing willingness to acknowledge the existence of a world elsewhere I turn to the law of sovereign immunity—a subject to which I think I may claim to have made roughly the same contribution as Napoleon made to the battle of Waterloo. One can pick up the story in 1938, when Lord Atkin said in *The Cristina*:[10]

The foundation for the application to set aside the writ and arrest of the ship is to be found in two propositions of international law engrafted into our domestic law which seem to me to be well established and to be beyond dispute. The first is that the courts of a country will not implead a foreign sovereign, that is, they will not by their process make him against his will a party to legal proceedings whether the proceedings involve process against his person or seek to recover from him specific property or damages. The second is that they will not by their process, whether the sovereign is a party to the proceedings or not, seize or detain property which is his or of which he is in possession or control.

Given that sovereign immunity is a doctrine of public international law, which in this field the English court recognizes and applies, Lord Atkin's pronouncement was somewhat remarkable, because he spoke in authoritative terms which, however appropriate to other pronouncements of the House of Lords, could scarcely be appropriate in applying the law of nations, which is liable to change. And the pronouncement was remarkable also because, by 1938, most nations had in large measure moved from the absolute theory—if, indeed, that had ever held sway generally—to the restrictive theory of sovereign immunity. But *The Cristina*, and in particular Lord Atkin's statement of principle, were naturally understood to lay down the English law on the subject. The first step back from the limb on which English law thus found itself came with *The Philippine Admiral*,[11] in which, goaded by Lord Simon of Glaisdale, the Privy Council held that the absolute doctrine did not apply to actions *in rem*, such as that was. The hearing did, however, involve an extensive, if not exhaustive, citation of authority on actions *in personam* as well as *in rem*, and the Privy Council acknowledged

---

[9] *The Atlantic Star* [1974] AC 436; *MacShannon v Rockware Glass Ltd* [1978] AC 795; *The Spiliada* [1987] AC 460.

[10] [1938] AC 485, 490.　　　　　　　　　　　　　　　　　　　　　[11] [1977] AC 373.

the weight of English authority affirming the absolute rule in actions *in personam*. Giving the Board's advice, Lord Cross said:[12]

The rule that no action in personam can be brought against a foreign sovereign on a commercial contract has been regularly accepted by the Court of Appeal in England, and was assumed to be the law even by Lord Maugham in *The Cristina*. It is no doubt open to the House of Lords to decide otherwise but it may fairly be said to be at the least unlikely that it would do so, and counsel for the respondent did not suggest that the Board should cast any doubt on the rule.

This was, one can now see, an illogical resting place, since an action *in rem* depends on the existence of an underlying personal claim and there is no very convincing reason that the law should be different depending on the type of claim. This was the opinion very robustly expressed by the Court of Appeal a very short time later in *Trendtex v Central Bank of Nigeria*. Lord Denning called retention of the absolute rule for claims *in personam* an 'indefensible anomaly' and roundly declared:[13]

I see no reason why we should wait for the House of Lords to make the change . . . We can and should state our view as to those rules and apply them as we think best, leaving it to the House to reverse us if we are wrong.

It yet remained to be seen whether, when the question reached the House of Lords, the House would adhere to the distinction favoured by the Privy Council in *The Philippine Admiral* or adopt the Court of Appeal's root and branch solution in *Trendtex*. There was not long to wait until the answer was given in the *I Congreso del Partido*.[14] The dramatic facts of that case, turning on relations between Cuba and the Pinochet regime which came to power in Chile on the ousting of Señor Allende, raised questions to which I thought at the time and still think the answer was not obvious. And in giving judgment their Lordships did not speak with one voice. But on the central issue, whether the absolute or the restrictive theory of sovereign immunity should apply to personal actions, there was a clear and unanimous preference for the latter. In this instance, as with *forum conveniens*, it took three actions for English law finally to escape from the unsatisfactory corner in which it had boxed itself. But again there was in the end a welcome recognition that singularity is not necessarily a virtue, that other nations had adopted a better rule and that English law could usefully profit from their experience and jurisprudence.

IV. ACCESSION TO THE EUROPEAN COMMUNITY

If I am right in suggesting that there was during much of the first half of this century a prevailing mood of introversion among the English legal community,

---

[12] At p. 402G.
[13] [1977] QB 529, 557.   [14] [1983] 1 AC 244.

one might have expected British accession to the European Community to provoke a grudging, jealous and restrictive acceptance of the legal consequences of membership. That has, after all, been the general popular reaction to membership (partly, I have always thought, because the Community's Civil Service is housed in one big building instead of several small ones, and partly because of the widely held belief that on the continent of Europe a defendant is presumed to be guilty unless he establishes his innocence). And I do not think England's record is without blemish. We have, for example, been very slow to recognize that Community law is not just another legal subject—like divorce, defamation or death duties—which a competent lawyer can pick up if he needs to, but 'a coherent system of law; a system governed by common principles, subject to its own principles of interpretation, which are very different from those of English law, and a system of which the component parts are closely interrelated'.[15] There is more than a grain of truth in David Pannick's recent observation:[16]

It is a national disgrace that there should continue to be widespread ignorance of Community law two decades after Britain joined the European Community. Few lawyers, and only a handful of judges, would claim that they have even a rudimentary appreciation of the nature and content of the principles of Community law.

At a time when some leading American law schools are considering a four-year course, with one year spent in Europe, it seems strange that English universities, with the benefit of the Erasmus scheme, have been so slow to take the plunge. There may also on occasion have been reluctance to regard the European Court of Justice as a proper court. I recall an occasion, many years ago now, when the United Kingdom had been ordered by that Court to stop paying a certain subsidy 'forthwith', and I was asked by the Attorney-General of the day to advise what 'forthwith' meant, because the minister wanted to go on paying the subsidy for three months. I advised that it meant exactly the same as if a Queen's Bench judge had said it (not then appreciating, I'm afraid, that ministers were immune from liability in contempt). More substantially, the initial response to the new procedure of reference under Article 177 of the Treaty of Rome was, I suggest, disappointingly negative. It is true that in *Bulmer v Bollinger* Lord Denning spoke in stirring terms of the new European legal order: 'when we come to matters with a European element, the Treaty is like an incoming tide. It flows into the estuaries and up the rivers. It cannot be held back.'[17] But when it came to the small print of the decision the message was much less *communautaire*. Emphasis was laid on the complete discretion of the English judge to decide a Community law point himself if he wished: 'He can say "it will be too costly", or "it will take too long to get an answer" or "I am well able to decide it myself." If he does decide it

---

[15] F. G. Jacobs, 'Preparing English Lawyers for Europe'. Ver Heyden de Lancey Lecture, Council of Legal Education, 23 May 1991.
[16] *The Times*, 6 Aug. 1991.
[17] [1974] Ch. 401, 418. See also *MacShannon v Rockware Glass* [1977] 1 WLR 376, 380.

himself, the European court cannot interfere.' The answer might be obvious. References caused expense and delay. The European Court should not be over-burdened. English judges should not shirk their responsibility to decide.[18] Happily, as I think, a more enlightened approach to references—by which I mean an approach more loyal to the spirit of the Treaty—has now prevailed.[19]

These blemishes should not, I think, obscure a fact of much more striking significance. The supremacy of Community law has been accepted by the English courts with a readiness and applied with a loyalty which, if equalled in one or two other member States, has probably been exceeded in none. One can point to a series of decisions, particularly in the House of Lords, which show not merely a resigned acceptance of Community law as king but something much closer to an enthusiastic embrace.

Not all member States can claim as much. In 1974 the German Federal Constitutional Court reserved to itself the control over violations of constitutional rights in Community law so long as there was no bill of constitutional rights passed by the European Parliament.[20] In 1985 another court expressed its suspicion that in a certain judgment the European Court of Justice had violated the principle of due process of law, the principle that a case be heard by the competent court, and the principle that judicial power is subject to law.[21] In certain fields, particularly the constitutional, the French juridical system has resisted the incorporation of Community law. Much the same is true of Italy, of which it has been said: 'More than in the other member states, the question of the primacy of Community law has been the object in Italy of great doctrinal debates and intense jurisprudential activity.'[22]

This picture is interestingly reflected in a review published by the European Commission in recent years, at the instance of the Parliament, drawing attention to decisions of national courts which do not adequately implement the law of the Community. Sometimes the comment is quite mild: 'At the very least, it must be said that the decisions of the Court of Justice do not permit the categorical conclusions drawn by the Belgian Conseil d'État.[23] Sometimes the comment is stronger. Thus a decision of the French Conseil d'État in 1986 is described as 'clearly contrary to a decision of the Court of Justice',[24] and two decisions of the same court in 1987 were described as misapplications of the *acte clair* theory.[25] A decision of the French Cour de Cassation in 1986 led to the initiation of infringement proceedings against France.[26] In 1989 a decision of the French Conseil d'État

---

[18] [1974] Ch. 401, 420, 423, 424.

[19] *R v Royal Pharmaceutical Society of GB, ex p. Association of Pharmaceutical Importers* [1987] 3 CMLR 939.

[20] BVerfG (Federal Constitutional Court) 29.5.1974. BVerfGE 37, 271 (280). The Court has mean-while reversed its position and will no longer review secondary EC law against the German constitu-tion: BVerfG 22.10.1986, BVerfGE 73, 339 (387).

[21] Ibid. See also Rudiger Stolz, "La primauté du droit communautaire en Allemagne" (Nov.–Dec. 1990) 6(6) Rev. fr. de dr. admin. 957.   [22] Di Bucci, ibid.

[23] (1987) O.J. C338/33 (16 Dec.).   [24] Idem. C338/34.

[25] (1988) O.J. C310/44 (5 Dec.).   [26] (1989) O.J. C330/53 (30 Dec.).

prompted the acerbic comment: 'The ignorance of the principle of the primacy of Community law (in this case the Treaty itself, no less) is manifest.'[27]

But France was not alone in the dock. Of the Italian Consiglio di Stato the Commission said:[28]

The position is, therefore, that the . . . Consiglio di Stato omitted to make a reference to the Court of Justice for a preliminary ruling despite the fact that all the parties to the action had advanced arguments based on Community law and despite its being expressly requested by the Italian Government to refer to the Court a question on the interpretation of Article 92 of the Treaty. In addition, it misinterpreted the Court's pronouncements on the Community rules on State aids and proved incapable of resolving correctly, along the lines set out both by the Court of Justice and by the Italian Constitutional Court in its landmark judgment in Case 170/1984 *Granital*, conflicts between domestic and Community law. As in its Judgment No. 504 of 6 May 1980 concerning the effects of a direction in the domestic legal order, the Consiglio di Stato persists in refusing to recognise the direct effect of the acts of the Community institutions in national law.

In the reports which I have seen, extending over the last four years, the United Kingdom has escaped such headmasterly rebuke, save on one occasion when a procedural decision of the High Court was criticized.[29]

Now if I am right in claiming for English courts an unusual degree of legal rectitude, a number of obvious explanations suggest themselves. One is that, having no constitutional court, England has escaped problems which have vexed the French, the Germans and the Italians. Another is that British judges are so enured to unquestioning application of Acts of Parliament that effect is dutifully given to Community law because that is what the 1972 Act requires. Another may perhaps be a sporting tradition that whatever the rules of the game they should be followed. But I question whether any of these quite explains the general readiness with which the courts have embraced the law of the Community. It is not hard to think of other fields in which they have been much less ready to enter into the spirit of legislation. Perhaps one can, here again, trace the influence of a growing belief that legal isolation is not necessarily splendid and that there are benefits in rejoining the European community of nations.

V. PUBLIC AND PRIVATE LAW

From Europe perhaps I may turn to public law. The distinction between public and private law is not of course a new one, nor is it an import from Europe. As Lord Mackenzie-Stuart had pointed out, Article XVIII of the Act of Union between England and Scotland 1707 explicitly provided that the new UK Parliament should leave unaltered the law of Scotland:[30]

[27] Idem. C330/54.   [28] Ibid.
[29] (1988) OJ C310/44 (5 Dec.).
[30] 'Recent Developments in English Administration Law—the Impact of Europe?', in *Du Droit international au droit d l'integration* (liber amicorum Pierre Pescatore, 1987).

With this difference betwixt the laws concerning publick right, policy and civil government, and those which concern private right, that the laws which concern publick right, policy and civil government, may be made the same throughout the whole United Kingdom; but that no alteration be made in laws which concern private right, except for evident utility of the subjects within Scotland.

Perhaps the Scots, once again, were ahead of the game. The distinction was not unknown in England either. In 1872, and again in 1922, candidates in the Final Honour School of Jurisprudence at Oxford were invited to explain the true nature of the distinction between public and private law, although it is not entirely clear to me what answer they were expected to give.[31] But what, surely, is clear beyond argument is that the last few years have seen a rather minor and esoteric branch of the law, ordinarily occupying the Lord Chief Justice and two puisnes for an hour or two now and then, burgeon into a major field of litigious activity. No doubt it was always untrue to claim that England had no administrative law. The prerogative writs had ancient roots, and were capable of vigorous flowering, as when the creation of the county courts gave the old writ of prohibition a new lease of life.[32] But there was really nothing in the previous history to prepare us for the explosion of activity which has occurred.

Whether and to what extent England's practical embrace of the distinction between public and private law is attributable to external influences may be debatable. A very distinguished authority, the late Sir Otto Kahn-Freund, attributed the change at least in part to the educational function of European community law.[33] But even if the whole board is not imported, some of the pieces on the board surely are. The most obvious example is the concept of the legitimate expectation of which it has been said (again by Lord Mackenzie-Stuart):[34]

The concept of recognising that a failure to respect legitimate expectations may give rise, in public law, to a remedy is a novelty in English law and lacks discernible English parentage. To find the true ancestry one does not have to look far across the Channel.

A further, equally obvious, example is the nascent doctrine of proportionality, born in Germany, adopted by France and the European Community and recognized by Lord Diplock as a possible recruit to the list of established grounds for reviewing administrative decisions.[35] This import has been greeted with some

---

[31] F. H. Lawson, *The Oxford Law School 1850-1965*, 192, 224.

[32] Morgan Lloyd, *A Treatise on the Law of Prohibition* (1849).

[33] Sir Otto Kahn-Freund, 'Common and Civil Law—Imaginary and Real Obstacles to Assimilation', in Mauro Cappelletti (Ed.), *New Perspectives for a Common Law of Europe* (1978), 137.

[34] Op. cit. *supra* n.30. Lord Denning's references in *Schmidt v Home Secretary* [1969] Ch. 149 and *Breen v AEU* [1971] 2 QB 175 may not amount to parentage.

[35] *Council of Civil Service Unions v Minister for the Civil Service* [1985] AC 374, 410. See also Jowell and Lester, 'Proportionality: Neither Novel nor Dangerous' (1988) Current Legal Problems (Special Issue): New Directions in Judicial Review.

caution, even overt hostility,[36] and one can see why. To some considerable extent, as has been suggested, proportionality no doubt overlaps with the established ground of reasonableness,[37] from which it is said to derive:[38] if an administrative act is not proportionate to the public end to be achieved it can be attacked as unreasonable. But Lord Diplock's equation of unreasonableness with irrationality, and his definition of irrationality as meaning that a decision is so outrageous in its defiance of logic or of accepted moral standards that no sensible person who had applied his mind to the question could have arrived at it,[39] confines unreasonableness within very tight limits. The same is true of Lord Scarman's requirement that the consequences of a decision must be so absurd that the decision-maker must have taken leave of his senses.[40] Continental lawyers would not, I think, confine the concept of proportionality so strictly, and once a judge begins to ask whether an administrative decision was disproportionate to the public end intended to be achieved he is perhaps beginning to enter the administrator's mind rather than simply reviewing the process by which the decision was reached. He will of course allow the administrator a generous margin of appreciation, but he is perhaps, consciously or unconsciously, edging closer to the merits of the decision. I feel it would be worth a modest investment in proportionality as a growth stock.

VI. *MAREVA* INJUNCTIONS

For my next example I take the *Mareva* injunctions.[41]

In 1968 the Payne Committee on the Enforcement of Judgment Debts reported.[42] Its report included these paragraphs:

1250. Under section 45 of the Judicature Act 1925 the court has a wide power to grant an injunction in all cases in which it appears to the court to be just or convenient so to do, but these words do not confer an arbitrary or unfettered discretion on the court and the power is used to protect a plaintiff against the infringement or threatened infringement of his legal rights. A legal right must, however, be established.

1251. It is, we think, clear that at the present time an injunction under this section would not be granted to restrain a debtor from disposing of assets or removing them from the jurisdiction.

---

[36] *Allied Dunbar (Frank Weisinger) Ltd. v Frank Weisinger, The Times,* 17 Nov. 1987; *R v Home Secretary, ex p. Brind* [1991] 1 All ER 720.

[37] Professor Neville Brown, "General Principles of Law and the English Legal System" in Cappelletti, op. cit. *supra* n. 33, 178.

[38] By Mr Paul Craig.

[39] *Council of Civil Service Unions, supra* n. 35, at 410.

[40] *R v Secretary of State for the Environment, ex p. Notts CC* [1986] AC 240.

[41] I gratefully acknowledge the help I have received on this topic from Mr Steven Gee.

[42] Cmnd. 3909.

The Committee recommended that the court should have power before or after judgment to restrain a debtor from disposing of property or transferring it out of the jurisdiction with the intention of defeating his creditors.[43] The Committee made no reference to the old City of London procedure of foreign attachment.

Nor, in contrast with the admirable (and by then already developing) practice of the Law Commission, does it appear to have made any comparative study of procedure elsewhere. Had it done so, it would have found a close analogy to foreign attachment in France, originating as a customary procedure in Orléans but later, as *saisie foraine*, embodied in the Civil Code and available where a debtor had neither domicile nor residence in the municipality where the creditor resided.[44] It would also have learned that in 1955 the French had extended the remedy of *saisie conservatoire*, a summary pre-judgment procedure for freezing the assets of an alleged debtor, so as to make the remedy available in any case.

The English law mirrored the progress of the French. The early cases on *Mareva* injunctions, like *saisie foraine*, were limited to foreign defendants. Section 37 of the Supreme Court Act 1981 removed that limitation, and there resulted a procedure which was essentially one of *saisie conservatoire*.

Now I do not know what was in the mind of counsel who made the early applications for *Mareva* injunctions. It is possible that American authority made a contribution.[45] But it seems clear that Lord Denning had the French practice in mind from an early stage. In *Nippon Yusen Kaisha v Karageorgis* he said: 'We know, of course, that the practice on the continent of Europe is different . . . It seems to me that the time has come when we should revise our practice.'[46] *Saisie conservatoire* was mentioned in argument in the *Pertamina* case,[47] and Lord Denning in his judgment in that case mentioned both *saisie conservatoire* (with which he was already familiar from other cases)[48] and the City of London procedure of foreign attachment.[49] Lord Diplock referred to *saisie conservatoire* again in *The Siskina*.[50] So I hope it is fair to see the Payne Committee's request being met, not by legislation, but by the willingness of imaginative judges to borrow procedures readily available elsewhere.

VII. PROCEDURAL CHANGES

Perhaps in passing I can touch very briefly on parallel changes in procedure. What could have seemed stranger to the continental lawyer than the rule that one could cite the work of a dead jurist but not a living one? That one could cite *Byles*

---

[43] Idem. Para. 1260.

[44] Peter Herzog, *Civil Procedure in France* (1967), 199; Civil Code, Arts. 822-5.

[45] *Ownley-Morgan* 256 U.S. 94 (1921); see Lord Denning MR in *Pertamina, infra* n. 47, at 658.

[46] [1975] 1 WLR, 1093, 1094–1095.   [47] [1978] QB 644, 650G.

[48] *Ionian Bank v Couvreur* [1969] 1 WLR 781.

[49] [1978] QB 644, 657-8.   [50] [1979] AC 210 at 233.

on Bills but not a similarly alliterative work on money?—although of course we all did, there being no alternative and the pretence that the text was part of one's argument being more than ordinarily implausible. How the rule would have coped with works of joint authorship such as Goff and Jones or Mustill and Boyd, had fatal misfortune afflicted one member of the partnership, I do not know. But the rule seems simply to have been dropped *sub silentio*, surviving if at all only as a ghost occasionally glimpsed in the Chancery Division. Whether continental practice played a part in the demise of that rule I rather doubt, and I do not know if the Scots accept a similar constraint, but both continental and American practice as well as the economic facts of life have surely contributed to a much more profound change, away from fully oral exposition and towards a more written procedure. In a recent case I saw the written submissions of one party, headed as such. They ran to some 30-odd pages and about 50 paragraphs; they also had something over 100 footnotes, in lower-case type at the foot of the page, some of them simple references, some of them adding to the factual narrative and discussing the authorities in a little detail. There is really very little difference between such a document and an American brief or a submission to the European Court—indeed it could be said that England has captured the worst of both worlds, by accepting written submissions without very significantly shortening oral argument. I do, however, think that if a judge of (say) the immediate post-war period were to return to the courts today, whether at first instance or on appeal, he would feel himself to be in an environment that would feel quite strange and, as he might think, un-English.

VIII. WHY THE INCREASED INTERNATIONALISM?

If my basic proposition is correct, and recent years have seen a more international outlook and a growing willingness to learn from others, one cannot escape the question why this should be so. One obvious answer is that membership of the European Community has brought us into closer contact with continental and Scottish lawyers. Another is the growing importance of international conventions, not only on transport by sea, air and land but in fields as diverse as international sale of goods, arbitration and many others. Another, I think, is the growth of international commercial practice: English commercial practitioners are well used to arguing cases governed by laws other than their own and in the course of doing so discover that the common law, as it has developed in England, is not the sole repository of legal wisdom.

Perhaps I may mention two less obvious but, as I think, potent causes. The first is the settlement in England, before and after the Second World War, of very distinguished legal scholars, particularly from Germany, bringing with them a rich legal culture with which, to our lasting benefit, they fertilized our own. None of us would have difficulty compiling a short-list, and at the top of it there would undoubtedly appear the name of Dr Francis Mann, who combined the highest of scholarly gifts with the more pragmatic qualities of the successful practitioner. To an unusual degree he was able to combine a scholar's quest for the truth with a practitioner's devotion to the interests of his client, proving himself almost equally formidable with the pen and the sword—implements which, indeed, in his hands, shared a number of important characteristics. We may all take pride in the fact that his respect for the common law and its institutions was not, as with most of us, born of ignorance but was rooted in a knowledge both wide and deep of continental practice and jurisprudence. It is appropriate to acknowledge here the great debt which the profession of the law in his adopted country owes to this great man.

The second cause I would mention is the work of the comparatists. Patiently but persistently they have laboured over the years to expose, for the caricatures they mostly are, the common lawyer's image of civil law and practice and the civil lawyer's image of common law and practice, demonstrating in the process that whatever the differences of nomenclature, procedure and reasoning the solutions reached turn out to be remarkably similar. If, as I think, the message of the comparatists is attracting more attention than heretofore, it is perhaps because of a welcome and growing tendency to abandon the comparison of large and rhetorical statements of principle and concentrate instead on the more detailed treatment of individual cases. Professor Markesinis's work on the *German Law of Torts* is a shining example of the modern approach.

In showing a new receptiveness to the experience and learning of others, the English courts are not, I think, establishing a new tradition but reverting to an old and preferable one. I can point to the reception of continental commercial law in England in the eighteenth century; to Lord Lindley, who studied Roman law at Bonn and translated Thibaut's *Jurisprudence*; to Pollock, who dedicated his *Treatise* in 1875 to Lindley, as having taught the author 'to turn from the formless confusion of textbooks and the dry bones of students' manuals to the immortal work of Savigny'; to Maitland's translation of Gierke, and his description of the German Civil Code as 'the most carefully considered statement of a nation's law that the world has ever seen';[51] to the observation of Best J in 1822 that the authority of Pothier's *Treatise on the Law of Obligations* was 'the highest that can be had, next to a decision of a court of justice in this country'.[52] I can point to the celebrated speech of Francis Hargrave in the great case of the slave *Somersett*,[53] ranging as it did not only over such English authorities as Blackstone, Coke, Glanville and Fitzherbert, but also over authorities such as Justinian, Grotius, Puffendorf, Bynkershoek and Stair, and practice among the Jews, the Greeks, the Romans and the ancient Germans, with appropriate reference to Spain, Portugal,

---

[51] Maitland's Translator's Introduction, *Political Theories of the Middle Age*, by Otto Gierke (1990), p. xvii.
[52] *Cox v Troy* (1822) 5 B. & All. 474, 480; 106 ER 1264.
[53] 20 S.T. 1; (1772) Lofft 1.

America, Holland, Scotland, France, Poland, Russia, and Turkey. I can point to that great flower of common law jurisprudence, Baron Alderson's formulation in *Hadley v Baxendale*[54] of the rule governing the measure of damages in contract, and confidently trace the unacknowledged ancestry of that rule to the American author Theodore Sedgwick, whose *Treatise on the Measure of Damages* was published in New York in 1847 and was itself based on the Napoleonic Code; from the Code the rule laid down can be traced back through Pothier, French authorities of the sixteenth and seventeenth centuries, medieval doctors of the law and Justinian to the classical Roman jurists.[55] So when Lord Diplock borrowed from the French Civil Code to distinguish between unilateral and synallagmatic contracts, and when (as seems likely) he borrowed from Pothier to distinguish between primary and secondary contractual obligations, he was aligning himself with an old and honourable tradition.[56]

IX. CONCLUSION

It would doubtless be impossible, even if it were desirable, to recreate the world evoked by Professor Stein in which it was possible for a student of law in any European country to enrol at any university and hear lectures in the same language on the same topics, in which a general legal culture prevailed in universities from Aberdeen to Prague, with even the universities of Oxford and Cambridge no exception.[57] But it is surely true that the divide between the common law and the civil law is narrowing and not continuing to widen, as common law countries pay more attention to codification and civil law judges become more consciously activist.[58] An Italian scholar recently wrote:[59]

The basic rules of natural justice and substantive fairness have a tradition which is admittedly older and firmer in England than in most Continental nations. Indeed, whereas the greatness of the Civil Law has lain, historically, primarily in the areas of private and commercial law, the strength of the English Common Law has been essentially in the law concerning the status of the individual vis-à-vis authority.

If this is so (and I believe that several continental languages have no close equivalent to the English word 'fair') there is surely a good prospect, if not of marriage, at least of enjoyable courtship. We should not expect too much too quickly. Lord Devlin observed: 'No doubt judges, like any other body of elderly men who have

---

[54] (1854) 9 W., H. & G. 341; 156 ER 145.

[55] I have gratefully relied on some unpublished notes, 'The Rule in *Hadley v Baxendale*; Some Notes on Ancestry', prepared by Professor Bernard Rudden.

[56] (1990) 10 Ox. J. Legal Studies 288.

[57] Peter Stein, 'Law after 1992'. *The Cambridge Review*, Oct. 1990, 101.

[58] John Merryman. 'On the Convergence (and Divergence) of the Civil Law and the Common Law', in Cappelletti, op. cit. *supra* n. 33, at 199.

[59] Mauro Cappelletti, idem, p. 10.

lived on the whole unadventurous lives, tend to be old-fashioned in their ideas.'[60]
But the elderly gentlemen have been stirring, and it may be that, emboldened by
their successes so far, they may seek more foreign adventures in the 1990s and
beyond. It is, after all, a good deal more exciting than hire purchase and the Rent
Acts.

[60] 'Judges and Lawmakers' (1976) 39 MLR 1.

2

Law in a Pluralist Society

In his much-discussed book *A Theory of Justice* John Rawls suggested that the relative justness of various societies could be tested by asking which society one would choose to belong to if ignorant what position one would occupy within it. In most plural societies some roles are a good deal pleasanter than others. One might, for example, steer clear of an otherwise attractive society such as fifth-century Athens in case one were a slave. As the late Paul Sieghart observed, 'the ultimate measure of whether a society can properly be called civilized is how it treats those who are near the bottom of its human heap . . .'[1]

There are many groups which may in different societies be subjected, to a greater or lesser extent, to disadvantage: racial, ethnic, religious, or linguistic minorities; women; children; homosexuals; refugees; gypsies; prisoners; the mentally ill or deficient; the diseased; and so on. For reasons of space this paper will be confined to the first group—racial, ethnic, religious, and linguistic minorities. In doing so it is convenient to speak of 'minorities', while recognizing that the group so disadvantaged need not be a minority (e.g. the black populations of South Africa or, formerly, Rhodesia) and that a group may, although a minority of the population as a whole, be a majority in its own heartland (as, for example, the Catholic nationalist population in parts of Northern Ireland, the Sikhs in the Punjab or the Tamils in parts of Sri Lanka).

The law ordinarily plays a crucial role in regulating relations between the majority and the minorities under discussion. There are, speaking very broadly, three ways in which the law may be used.

A. DOMINATION

The law may, first, be used to entrench the dominance of the majority and secure its continuing monopoly of power and influence.[2] Various devices may be used to disenfranchise, or weaken the electoral position of, the minority, as in Sri Lanka,[3] South Africa, Rhodesia (until it became Zimbabwe), the southern states of the United States (until the 1950s), Northern Ireland (until 1969), or Malaysia. The law may also be used to give one community the lion's share of wealth and economic influence at the expense of another, as it was in most of the countries

---

[1] *Human Rights in the United Kingdom* (1988), ed. Sieghart.
[2] Palley, *Constitutional Law and Minorities*, MRG Report No. 36.
[3] Schwarz, *The Tamils of Sri Lanka*, MRG Report No. 25.

just mentioned and has been, to the detriment of the Asian trading community, in parts of East Africa. The law may be similarly used in the cultural sphere, particularly by adoption of a single official language with which the majority are and the minority are generally not familiar, as in Malaysia, Burma, Thailand, Iran, and Sri Lanka. In all these cases the law is used in a manner inconsistent with the principles which should underlie a liberal democracy.

B. AUTONOMY

The law may, secondly, be used not to ensure the subjection of the minority but to recognise its existence as a distinct entity, seeking to avoid conflict by according the minority its own rights and institutions and as much autonomy as the political situation permits. Segregation can of course be an instrument of oppression, as notoriously in the case of *apartheid*, but what is more relevant under this head is a benign application of the law, designed to make a virtue of diversity and not to suppress it. The world contains many examples of the law being successfully used in this way. In Switzerland, where many citizens believe themselves to be members of a minority, the federal form adopted, giving great autonomy to the cantons and reflecting an extreme commitment to the democratic process, has proved very successful in minimizing internal conflict.[4] The entrenched constitutional autonomy and economic rights granted by Italy to the South Tyrol have largely solved a seriously divisive problem which had previously led to terrorist violence.[5]

The measures taken by Finland in 1921 to preserve the language and rights of the Swedish minority have been described as 'the best treatment of a minority group by a host nation anywhere in the world'.[6] In an attempt to solve a very long running linguistic conflict Belgium has revised its constitution so that there are at the federal level three communities (Flemish, French and German-speaking) and three regions (Flemish, Brussels, and Walloon).[7] In many countries (such as India, Cyprus, New Zealand, Fiji) separate electoral rolls and separate blocs of seats in the legislature have been employed to ensure fair representation of minorities. In others (such as Switzerland and Canada) there have been conventions governing the ethno-linguistic composition of the cabinet or provisions (as formerly in Lebanon under the Lebanese National Pact of 1943) for the allocation of cabinet posts on a confessional basis.[8]

The objection to laws providing for autonomy or benign separation of a minority

---

[4] Steinberg, *Switzerland*, in *Co-existence in some plural European Societies*, MRG Report No. 72.

[5] Alcock, *South Tyrol*, ibid.

[6] *The Swedish Community in Finland*, ibid., at 10.

[7] Bossuyt, *Belgium,* ibid.

[8] Palley, op. cit.

is not so much legal as political. No state wants to see itself dismembered. There is accordingly an understandable reluctance to grant anything approaching full autonomy to a minority which might wish to secede or separate itself altogether from the state of which it forms part. This has no doubt influenced the Indian response to the Sikhs[9] and the Nagas.[10] It also throws light on the contrasting experience of the United Kingdom in Scotland and Northern Ireland. Scotland has long enjoyed a high degree of autonomy, with its own church, its own laws, legal system and courts, its own currency, its own civil service, its own secretary of state, its own professional institutions and its own educational system. Northern Ireland, between 1922 and 1972 had an even greater degree of autonomy, with its own parliament and executive responsible for most governmental powers other than income tax, defence, and foreign affairs. The unionist majority, however, believed, not without reason, that the aim of the nationalist minority was not to promote the success of Northern Ireland as a political sub-division of the UK but to secede from the UK and destroy Northern Ireland as a political entity. The result was that power was not shared with the minority, against which there was discrimination on an institutionalized basis. The result has been the introduction of direct rule from London and the virtual extinction of Northern Ireland's local autonomy. The problem of how power can be safely shared with a minority whose loyalty to the state cannot be relied upon remains (in Northern Ireland) unsolved.

C. INTEGRATION

The third broad approach is sometimes labelled, not altogether happily, assimilationist or integrationist. The essence of this approach is a guarantee that all citizens, whether of the majority or the minority, shall be treated equally and that minorities shall not be the subject of adverse discrimination. The underlying hope is that, with the passage of time, education and growing familiarity, racial, religious, and linguistic differences will cease to be divisive and the bonds of common citizenship will be gradually strengthened. It is this broad approach which, with some exceptions, the law of the United Kingdom adopts. But the labels are not entirely apt because, as the Home Secretary pointed out in 1966, the integration sought is 'not . . . a flattening process of assimilation but . . . equal opportunity coupled with cultural diversity in an atmosphere of mutual tolerance'.[11]

This approach has a solid foundation in international law.[12] The Universal

---

[9] Shackle, *The Sikhs*, MRG Report No. 65.

[10] Maxwell, *India, The Nagas and the North East*, MRG Report No. 17.

[11] See Peter Sanders, Chief Executive of the Commission for Racial Equality, in letter to *The Independent*, 28 August 1990.

[12] See generally Fawcett, *The International Protection of Minorities*, MRG Report No. 41, and Thornberry, *Minorities and Human Rights Law*, MRG Report No. 73.

Declaration of Human Rights, adopted by the General Assembly of the United Nations in December 1948, declared in Article 1 that 'All human beings are born free and equal in dignity and rights' and in Article 2 that 'Everyone is entitled to all the rights and freedoms set forth in this Declaration without any distinction of any kind such as race, colour, sex, language, religion, political or other opinion, national or social origin, property, birth or other status.' The later UN Covenants[13] and the European Convention of Human Rights repeat this prohibition of discrimination and pledge the contracting states to take all necessary steps to give effect to it for all their inhabitants and to provide them with effective remedies for breach. The UN Civil and Political Rights Covenant further provides, in Article 27:

In those States in which ethnic, religious or linguistic minorities exist, persons belonging to such minorities shall not be denied the right in community with other members of their group, to enjoy their own culture, to profess and practise their own religion, or to use their own language.

Between 1948 and 1972 some twenty-five constitutions gave express effect to the Universal Declaration.[14] The Indian Constitution, in Article 15, prohibited discrimination on the grounds of religion, race, caste, sex, or place of birth. The United Kingdom, lacking a written constitution and perhaps suspicious of general principles has, although bound by all these conventions, incorporated them into its domestic law in a cautious, piecemeal and partial manner. It is convenient briefly to consider the law of the United Kingdom under the three heads of race (using that expression in its broadest sense to embrace all questions of colour, nationality, and ethnic or national origins), religion and language, although there is some unavoidable overlap between the first two heads.

(1) *Race*

The British tend to think that (differences between England, Wales, Scotland, and Northern Ireland apart) their society was racially relatively homogeneous until large-scale immigration from the New Commonwealth began in the 1950s onwards. This was never true: from the earliest times there have been successive waves of settlers culminating, in the first half of the present century, in large-scale settlement of Jews seeking to escape pogroms in Eastern Europe and Nazi persecution.[15] The greatest mark has however been made by post-war immigrants from Jamaica and the West Indies, the Indian sub-continent, Cyprus, Malta, Hong Kong, West Africa, East Africa, Vietnam, Iran, and Sri Lanka. In the result the British have been described as 'clearly among the most ethnically composite of the Europeans'.[16]

---

[13] Civil and Political Rights Covenant and the Economic Social and Cultural Rights Covenant.
[14] Thornberry, op. cit. 9.
[15] On this and many of the topics which follow I am deeply indebted to Dr S. M. Poulter's illuminating work *English Law and Ethnic Minority Customs* (1986).
[16] J. Giepel, *The Europeans: An Ethnohistorical Survey* (1969), 163–4.

In 1962 an Act was passed to restrict immigration into the country and in 1965 a White Paper *Immigration from the Commonwealth* was published, having two declared aims: to reduce further the number of Commonwealth immigrants to enter Britain; and to promote better race relations and help achieve the integration of those already settled. These latter aims were reflected in the Race Relations Act 1965. The Act sought to achieve these aims by amicable persuasion, not coercion. It has been said to have contained 'probably the most reluctant enforcement mechanism that could be devised by the mind of man'.[17] In the three years the Act was in force no case ever reached the courts.[18] A further Race Relations Act (and a further Immigration Act) were enacted in 1968, and then the Act now in force, the Race Relations Act 1976. This Act is very far-reaching in its scope, applying to almost every imaginable transaction, service and facility.[19] For purposes of the Act a person discriminates against another if (put very summarily) he treats him less favourably than others on racial rounds or imposes unjustifiable requirements with which that other, on racial grounds, is unable or less well able than others to comply.[20] Complaints arising from employment are pursued before industrial tribunals, other complaints in the County Court.[21] In either case damages may be awarded, including compensation for injury to feelings.[22] In a recent case arising from discrimination against a convicted prisoner by the prison authorities the Court of Appeal increased the damages awarded from £50 to £500.[23] The Race Relations Act is reinforced by provisions, now found in the Public Order Act 1986, imposing criminal penalties on those convicted of inciting racial hatred.[24]

During very roughly the same period the United States enacted the Civil Rights Acts of 1964 and 1968 and The Voting Rights Act 1965 to achieve somewhat similar ends. These Acts were tougher than their British counterparts and affirmative action was taken to promote the interests of the black minority in a way not duplicated in Britain. But the background problem was interestingly different. The Untied States was dealing with a long-settled black population against which a complex body of discriminatory laws had been built up; the concern in the UK arose in the main from a recent immigrant population which was the subject of no formal discrimination. Again, the United States Acts followed a decade (or rather longer) of radical Supreme Court decision-making which undermined the constitutional basis of segregation;[25] in the UK the 1965 Act represented the first tentative step in the field, taken at a time when there were doubts, conscientiously held, whether the intrusion of law into this delicate field might not do more harm than good. There can be little doubt that the intervention of the law has proved salutary in the United States.[26]

---

[17] Claiborne, *Race and Law in Britain and the United States*, MRG Report No. 22, 11.
[18] Ibid. 11.   [19] ss. 4, 17, 20, 21, 25, 29.
[20] s. 1.   [21] ss. 54, 57.   [22] ss. 57(4), 56(1)(b).
[23] *Alexander v Home Office* [1988] ICR 685.   [24] ss. 17–29.
[25] Ibid. 6–8.   [26] Ibid. 14–15.

Since the purpose of the Race Relations Act in the UK is to educate public opinion and modify public conduct, no crude tally of legal decisions can indicate with any reliability whether the legislation is achieving its object or not. But some legal decisions none the less deserve brief mention as illustrating the strengths and weaknesses of the Act.

The most celebrated decision is *Mandla v Dowell Lee*, [27] a case in which a Sikh boy was denied admission to a private school because he and his father insisted on his wearing a turban, which the headmaster would not accept. The Court of Appeal held[28] (contrary to the undoubted intentions of those who framed the Act) that Sikhs were not a racial group and so were not protected by the Act. The House of Lords reversed this ruling. In doing so it acknowledged that the boy could physically comply with the requirement of not wearing a turban (which is not of course one of the five symbols of Sikhism) but held that 'can comply' in the Act should be read as 'can consistently with the customs and cultural conditions of the racial group comply'. The House rejected the headmaster's justifications based on practical convenience and the Christian nature of the school.

This enlightened decision laid to rest a somewhat similar problem (already, perhaps, on the way to solution), the insistence of Hindu and Muslim women on keeping their legs covered, a practice unacceptable to some employers whose female staff were dressed in skirts. In *Malik v British Home Stores*[29] an industrial tribunal found for an 18-year old Muslim schoolgirl who had been refused employment because she wished to wear trousers under her skirt. In *Kingston and Richmond Health Authority v Kaur*[30] a Sikh woman was refused training as a nurse on similar grounds. The case led to a modification of the statutory instrument governing nurses' dress and a change of mind by the health authority, and the applicant was eventually allowed to train wearing grey trousers and a white tunic top.[31]

There have been more questionable decisions the other way. In *Singh v Rowntree Macintosh Ltd*,[32] *Panesar v Nestlé Co Ltd*[33] and *Singh v Lyons Maid Ltd*[34] Sikh men lost claims against food manufacturers who maintained a ban on beards in the interests of hygiene. In *Kuldip Singh v British Rail Engineering Ltd*[35] a Sikh employed in an engineering workshop was demoted because he refused to wear a voluntary form of protective headwear. One's reservations concerning these decisions are not as to the genuineness of the employers' interest in hygiene or safety but as to whether adequate thought was given to reconciling this interest with the cultural requirements of the Sikh community. In more obvious cases, however, the results seem plainly correct. Where, as a result of theft at a manufacturing plant, the employer required every black person seeking to enter the plant to be interrogated, it was held that this could be a detriment to

[27] [1983] 2 AC 548.
[29] (1980), unreported, Manchester.
[31] Poulter, op. cit. 263.
[33] [1980] ICR 144.
[35] *The Times*, 6 Aug. 1985, see Poulter, op. cit. 262.

[28] [1983] QB 1.
[30] [1981] IRLR 337.
[32] [1979] IRLR 199.
[34] [1975] IRLR 328.

black employees.[36] Where a Liverpool store required its employees to live outside the city centre, it was held that this amounted to indirect discrimination against black job seekers who mostly lived in the city centre.[37] Where Asian bank employees who had served overseas were denied the benefit of previous service for pension purposes (unlike, as they complained, their white counterparts) the case was allowed to proceed.[38]

The governmental agency entrusted with promoting good race relations in the UK is the Commission for Racial Equality, one of whose most important tasks is to investigate and report on suspected discriminatory practices.[39] The Commission's investigations have covered a very wide range, from medical school admissions,[40] to the allocation of council housing[41] and the employment of dustmen in Westminster.[42] The Commission also seeks to protect the interests of racial minorities when new legislative changes are proposed.[43]

While serious and disturbing racial discrimination undoubtedly remains in the UK, it is reasonable to hope that the law has helped to mitigate its worse effects. But the prohibition of discrimination is only one objective of the law; the other, as already noted, is that all citizens shall be treated equally. The general policy of UK law undoubtedly is that there shall be one law for all, irrespective of race or cultural tradition. Thus, for example, a marriage celebrated in England under the age of 16, or within the prohibited degrees of consanguinity and affinity, appears to be void even though valid by the law of the parties' domicile outside England.[44] An English marriage is necessarily monogamous, even though the personal laws of the parties may allow polygamy.[45] A father who punishes his son excessively by English standards cannot escape conviction by showing that the punishment would have been normal in his native West Indies.[46] The statutory prohibition on tattooing children makes no exception for communities in which this practice is normal and accepted.[47] A Nigerian mother who incised the cheeks of her young sons in accordance with Yoruba tradition was convicted of assault causing actual bodily harm, although the trifling nature of the incisions and the boys' eager consent earned her an absolute discharge.[48] While the circumcision of males has long been accepted, although only of ritual significance to Jews and Muslims, the circumcision of females is forbidden by statute even among

---

[36] *B L Cars Ltd v Brown* [1983] ICR 143.
[37] *Hussain v Saints Complete Home Furnishers*, Liverpool Industrial Tribunal.
[38] *Barclays Bank v Kapur* [1989] ICR 753.
[39] Race Relations Act 1976, ss. 48-51.
[40] Report into St George's Hospital Medical School (1988).
[41] Report into the allocation of council housing (1982).
[42] Report into Westminster City Council, NUPE and four named NUPE officers (1988).
[43] e.g. Response to the Home Office White Paper 'Crime, Justice and Protecting the Public'.
[44] Dicey and Morris, *The Conflict of Laws*, 11th edn. (1987), vol. 2, 636-7.
[45] Ibid. 657.   [46] *R v Derriviere* (1969) 53 Cr App Rep 637.
[47] Tattooing of Minors Act, 1969.
[48] *R v Adesanya*, *The Times*, 16 and 17 July 1974. And see Poulter, op. cit. at 150–1.

communities where it is traditionally practised.[49] It is of interest that although this prohibition is subject to a mental health exception, the Act provides that 'In determining . . . whether an operation is necessary for the mental health of a person, no account shall be taken of the effect on that person of any belief on the part of that or any other person that the operation is required as a matter of custom or ritual.'[50]

Happily, the principle of equality is not applied in blind disregard of cultural differences. Sikhs have been exempted by statute from the requirement to wear crash helmets on motor cycles,[51] even though imposition of the ordinary rule on Sikhs involved no breach of the European Convention of Human Rights.[52] In *Hirani v Hirani*[53] the Court of Appeal, on a petition for annulment of a marriage on grounds of duress, took full account of the position of a 19-year old Indian Hindu girl pressured by her family to marry a man not of her choice instead of the Muslim she wished to marry. A complaint of cruelty against a husband has been upheld even though the act in question was not that of the husband but of a member of his extended family with whom the wife was required to live.[54] A wife who, at her instigation, obtained a divorce valid in Jewish law by a *get* of the Beth-Din in London on grounds of her husband's desertion was held to be disentitled to complain of her husband's desertion thereafter.[55] In *Brett v Brett*[56] a divorced husband refused to give his wife a *get*, without which she would not be free to remarry under Jewish law; the Court of Appeal's order relieved the husband of part of his financial obligation if he delivered a *get* and in that way gave recognition to the Jewish custom. A charge of having unlawful sexual intercourse with a girl under the age of 16 will not lie where the parties were validly married in Nigeria, where they were domiciled, when the girl was 13.[57] Where an unsophisticated Muslim woman helped to unpack imported cannabis on the direction of her brother-in-law, sentence was reduced to reflect her relative lack of criminality.[58] Where a Portuguese waiter confessed to having corruptly offered money to a driving examiner, believing that what was common practice in Portugal was common practice in England also, he was not prosecuted.[59]

(2) *Religion*

There is in the UK, in contrast with the United States,[60] no constitutional protection of religious freedom. It is not generally unlawful (save in respect of employment in

---

[49] Prohibition of Female Circumcision Act 1985.   [50] Section 2(2).
[51] Motor-Cycle Crash Helmets (Religious Exemption) Act 1976.
[52] *X v United Kingdom* (1978) 14 Decisions and Reports of the European Commission 234. And see Poulter op. cit. 284.
[53] (1983) 4 FLR 232.   [54] *Devi v Gaddu* (1974) 4 Fam. Law 159.
[55] *Joseph v Joseph* [1953] 1 WLR 1182. But see *Corbett v Corbett* [1957] 1 WLR 486.
[56] [1969] 1 All ER 1007. And see Poulter, op. cit. 109, 128.
[57] *Alhaji Mohamed v Knott* [1969] 1 QB 1. And see Poulter, op cit. 19–21, 273.
[58] *R v Bibi* [1980] 1 WLR 1193.   [59] Poulter, op. cit. 275.
[60] First amendment to the US Constitution, 1791.

Northern Ireland)[61] to discriminate against another on grounds of religion alone. The religious freedom which is enjoyed in fact is the product not of legal protection but of the removal of disabilities formerly imposed on those who were not members of the Church of England. This freedom is of relatively recent growth. The Toleration Act, 1688, despite its encouraging title, was of benefit only to protestant dissenters. Not until the last century were disabilities against Roman Catholics and Jews gradually dismantled.[62] In 1847 Baron de Rothschild, elected to Parliament for the City of London, could not take his seat because he was unable to swear allegiance 'on the true faith of a Christian'.[63] Until the 1850s only members of the Church of England could become members of Oxford University or take degrees at Cambridge.[64] Not until 1871 were lay posts in those universities thrown open to men of all creeds on equal terms.[65] From 1880 to 1886, although repeatedly elected by his constituents, Bradlaugh was prevented from taking his seat in the House of Commons because he was an avowed atheist, and the Court of Appeal aided his exclusion.[66] As late as 1974 a statute was needed to make clear that a Roman Catholic could lawfully be appointed Lord Chancellor.[67]

The lack of formal prohibitions and disabilities now means that people are in general free to worship when, where and how they please. If planning permission to build a synagogue, mosque, temple, *gudwara*, or other place of non-Christian worship were found to have been refused on grounds of religious prejudice the decision would without doubt be quashed on an application for judicial review. There is nothing to prevent the establishment of a private denominational school and there is nothing to prevent the state contributing towards Hindu and Muslim schools as it does towards Anglican, Roman Catholic, and Jewish schools. But a Muslim may not, in breach of his contract of employment, absent himself from his professional duties to comply with those of his religion,[68] nor will a Seventh Day Adventist be excused work on Saturdays unless his contract so provides.[69]

Within the state educational system the existence of religious minorities is acknowledged. Thus although pupils are required on each school day to take part in an act of collective worship,[70] which in most schools must be 'wholly or mainly of a broadly Christian character',[71] and although the national curriculum taught in state schools must provide for religious education,[72] a parent may

---

[61] Fair Employment (Northern Ireland) Act 1976.

[62] By Acts such as the Roman Catholic Relief Act, 1829; the Jewish Disabilities Removal Act 1845, the Jews Relief Act 1858 and the Qualification for Offices Abolition Act 1866.

[63] Woodward *The Age of Reform 1815-1870,* 156.   [64] Ibid. 471.

[65] University Tests Act 1871. And see generally Engel, *From Clergyman to Don* (1983).

[66] *AG v Bradlaugh* (1885) 14 QBD 667.

[67] Lord Chancellor (Tenure of Office and Discharge of Ecclesiastical Functions) Act 1974.

[68] *Ahmad v Inner London Education Authority* [1978] QB 36.

[69] *Esson v United Transport Executive* [1975] QB 36.

[70] Education Reform Act 1988, s. 6(1).   [71] Ibid., s. 7(1).

[72] Ibid., s. 2(1).

request that a child be excused from the act of worship and the education provided by the school and alternative arrangements may be made[73] (although there is currently some dissatisfaction among ethnic minority parents on this score). Deference to the beliefs or wishes of minorities may also be found, for example, in the anomalous exemption of Quakers and Jews from the general law governing the solemnisation of marriages,[74] and in the making of special provision for slaughtering animals and poultry in the manner approved by the Jewish and Muslim religions.[75]

The most striking inequality of treatment which now survives in the religious field concerns the law of blasphemy. It is an offence at common law to vilify the Christian religion, in particular if a breach of the peace is likely to result. In *Whitehouse v Lemon*[76] Lord Scarman strongly urged that the law be extended to cover all recognized religions and not Christianity alone, as was provided in the Indian Penal Code originally drafted by Lord Macaulay in 1837. The Law Commission, to which the problem was referred, was divided; a bare majority favoured abolishing the common law offence and putting nothing in its place; the minority thought that a new statutory offence should be created and that its scope should be wide enough to cover non-Christian faiths as well as Christianity.[77]

This issue has recently become highly topical following the publication in 1988 of *The Satanic Verses* by Salman Rushdie, a book understood by Muslims to be a scurrilous and deeply offensive libel on their religion. The book has led to violence and disorder in various parts of the world, including the UK, and to the pronouncement of a sentence of death on Rushdie by religious leaders in Iran, which imposes a duty on devout Muslims to assassinate the author.

The sense of outrage undoubtedly felt by devout Muslims led to an application to the Chief Metropolitan Magistrate in London for the grant of a summons against the author and publishers on grounds of blasphemous libel at common law. The grant was refused, and the applicant then sought to quash the Magistrate's decision. This application failed,[78] the Divisional Court ruling as it was bound to do that the law as it stood did not extend to religions other than Christianity. The Court did, however, say that if it were open to them to extend the law to cover religions other than Christianity they would refrain from doing so,[79] believing that to do so would pose insuperable problems and would be likely to do more harm than good.[80] The resentment of the Muslim minority was the more understandable when a film (*International Guerillas*) portraying the author in a bad light was banned in the UK, but this decision was later reversed.

---

[73] Ibid., s. 9.
[74] Marriage Act 1949, s. 26(1)(c)(d).
[75] Slaughter of Poultry Act 1967, s. 1(2); Slaughterhouses Act 1974, s. 36(3).
[76] [1979] AC 617.
[77] Report No. 145: *Offences against Religion and Public Worship* (1985).
[78] *R v Bow Street Magistrates' Court ex parte Choudhury*, unreported, 9 April 1990.
[79] Transcript, p. 22.
[80] Transcript, p. 30.

The problem of amending the law may be exaggerated, but there remains a deep division of opinion how it should be amended. Over the last two years there have been no fewer than four attempts to introduce bills, some seeking to extend the criminal law of blasphemy to protect Hinduism, Islam, Sikhism, Judaism and Buddhism as well as Christianity,[81] some seeking to abolish the offence altogether.[82] None has progressed to a second reading and the Government is proposing no change in the law because there is too little agreement whether there should be change and, if so, what the change should be. It may none the less be questioned whether it is acceptable, in a plural society such as the UK now undoubtedly is, that adherents of world religions, locally in the minority, should lack the legal protection afforded to the local majority.

(3) *Language*

The onward march of the English language within the UK has proved irresistible, extinguishing (or nearly extinguishing) such old indigenous languages as Gaelic, Manx and Cornish. The only exception is Welsh. In 1847 a government commission on education strongly favoured the suppression of the Welsh language:

The Welsh language is a vast drawback to Wales, and a manifold barrier to the moral progress and commercial prosperity of the people. It is not easy to over-estimate its evil effects . . . It dissevers the people from intercourse which would greatly advance their civilization, and bars the access of improving knowledge to their minds. As a proof of this, there is no Welsh literature worthy of the name.

The evil of the Welsh language . . . is obviously and fearfully great in courts of justice . . . It distorts the truth, favours fraud, and abets perjury, which is frequently practised in courts, and escapes detection through the loop-holes of interpretation . . . The mockery of an English trial of a Welsh criminal by a Welsh jury, addressed by counsel and judge in English, is too gross and shocking to need comment. It is nevertheless a mockery which must continue until the people are taught the English language . . .[83]

Matthew Arnold, an inspector of schools, shortly afterwards wrote in *The Times*: 'The Welsh language is the curse of Wales.'[84] But the language struggled to survive, and in 1967 the Welsh Language Act was passed by Parliament recognizing that

it is proper that the Welsh language should be freely used by those who so desire in the hearing of legal proceedings in Wales; that further provision should be made for the use of that language, with the like effect as English, in the conduct of other official or public business there; and that Wales should be distinguished from England in the interpretation of future Acts of Parliament.

---

[81] e.g. a bill introduced by Harry Greenway in March 1990.
[82] e.g. bills introduced by Tony Benn and Bob Cryer.
[83] Jan Morris, *Wales* (1982), 66.   [84] Ibid.

There are Welsh language radio and television programmes and the language has a special place, protected by statute in the curriculum of schools in Wales.[85]

No other language alternative to English enjoys such protection. The UK is bound by a European Community Directive 'to take appropriate measures to promote, in co-ordination with normal education, teaching of the mother tongue and culture of the country of origin for the children' of other Community nationals,[86] and has informally agreed that this obligation should be extended to the children of non-Community nationals.[87] It is not, however, clear that very much has been done to perform this obligation, which in any event does not avail the children of UK nationals unless they could show themselves to be the subject of less favourable treatment. In 1985 the Swann Committee did not favour the introduction of programmes of bilingual education in state schools[88] and considered that maintenance of the mother-tongue was best achieved within the ethnic communities themselves, but the Committee did favour the teaching of pupils' mother tongues as part of the general foreign language teaching in schools. The Secretary of State has authority to specify any modern foreign language as part of the national school curriculum and the means therefore exist to give effect to this recommendation.[89]

One cannot, however, disguise or conceal the dominant position of the English language in the UK today. Where a statute requires information to be provided, it has been held that the information need be provided only in English.[90] A consultation exercise has been held not to be flawed by lack of adequate interpretation for the benefit of all minority ethnic groups attending a meeting.[91] Pressure towards integration or assimilation is here perhaps seen at its strongest, motivated (one trusts) not by a desire to dominate or extinguish cultural diversity but by a belief that mastery of English is an almost essential pre-condition of personal fulfilment and success in an overwhelmingly English-speaking society.

CONCLUSIONS

The law is not, of course, omnipotent: as Professor Palley wrote:

it would be legal megalomania to imagine that legal regulation can stem powerful political, economic and social forces or massive revolutionary violence, but Law can, particularly in the long run, affect the framework in which these forces will operate, and can reinforce or weaken the claims of particular groups in society, whether these claims be political, economic, social or cultural and already enunciated or merely latent.[92]

---

[85] Education Reform Act 1988, s. 3 (1)(b), (2)(c).
[86] EEC Directive on the Education of Children of Migrant Workers 1977.
[87] Swann Committee Report, 401–2.   [88] Ibid. 406–11.
[89] Education Reform Act 1988, s. 3(2)(b).
[90] *R v Governors of Small Heath School, ex parte Birmingham City Council*, unreported.
[91] *R v Birmingham City Council, ex parte Kaur*, 10 July 1990, unreported.   [92] Op. cit. 5.

Most lawyers would probably accept the same author's description of legal rules as:

management agents for suppressing, confining, limiting, guiding, directing, standardising, integrating, adapting and changing behaviour.[93]

The challenge to politicians, lawyers and society generally is at root the same: to shape those rules so as to promote in practice the fundamental values which the United Nations covenants so ambitiously proclaim.

[93] Ibid. 3.

3

*Speech on the Jubilee of the Supreme Court of India**

Over the last 50 years, the Supreme Court of India has established itself as one of the indisputably great courts of the world. No other court in the free world exercises jurisdiction over more than a small fraction of the nearly one billion men, women, and children who form the population of India. The Golden Jubilee of this court is accordingly a matter of much more than local importance. I am greatly honoured to have this opportunity to pay tribute to its achievements over this crucial and formative period of its and the country's history.

The honour and the pleasure are all the greater for a visitor from the United Kingdom since for over two centuries, for better or worse—I hope not wholly for worse—our fortunes and histories were so closely intertwined.

The late Sir Penderel Moon—one of the last generation of British Civil Servants in India, a very intelligent man, deeply devoted to India and its peoples—strongly criticized his British fellow-countrymen for bequeathing to independent India institutions based on a British model which were, he thought, alien and unsuited to the genius of the country. In his criticism he very expressly included the legal system.[1] Although lacking his knowledge and experience of India, let alone the knowledge and experience of my present audience, I find that to be not only a disappointing judgment, but also a surprising one, which indeed I find hard to accept.

It is doubtless true that the first judge to exercise jurisdiction in Surat in the seventeenth century contributed little to world jurisprudence. He was a retired sea captain, and was removed from judicial office for refusing to pay his debts. He then enrolled as a captain of infantry but was again in trouble for an offence which (in the reticent words of those reporting it to the authorities) 'we know not well how to put into such decent terms as may become us to your Honours'.[2] It is also true that for long periods, particularly at the lower levels there was a marked lack of differentiation between the exercise of judicial and executive power. This may well have made for the effective enforcement of judicial orders, and perhaps encouraged the friendly resolution of civil disputes, but it would have offended any purist.

There are surely many things to be put on the credit side. First, I would put what seems to me to have been an enlightened approach to the application of laws

* Delivered to the Supreme Court of India in New Delhi on 26 November 1999.
[1] Moon, *Strangers in India* (1945); *Divide and Quit* (1961).
[2] Woodruff, *The Men who Ruled India*, vol. 1, 58.

foreign to India. As it was put with reference to Bombay in 1827, following some of the language of earlier provisions:

The law to be observed in the trial of suits shall be Acts of Parliament and Regulations of Government applicable to the case; in the absence of such Acts and Regulations the usage of the country in which the suit arose; if none such appears, the law of the defendant; and in the absence of any specific law and usage justice, equity and good conscience.[3]

In earlier years the expression 'justice, equity and good conscience' was, it seems, taken to refer to generally accepted notions of justice, which might or might not coincide with English law,[4] although in course of time these values were increasingly taken to be represented by the English common law, a trend reinforced by measures such as the Indian Penal Code and the Indian Evidence Act. It is, however, my impression that respect continued to be paid to local customs and traditions. Describing the magistrate of yore a Victorian versifier described him as:

> Prompt with the rifle, niggard of the pen,
> By manly deeds he won the hearts of men;
> His watchful eye each rival chieftain viewed,
> And oftener calmed than curbed the rising feud . . .
> Nor sought to substitute with ruthless hand
> The alien systems of a distant land. . . . [5]

The Judicial Committee of the Privy Council also accepted, in some cases at least, that the rules of the English common law could not be undiscriminatingly applied in a country, such as India, with old and valuable traditions of its own:

Where Englishmen establish themselves in an uninhabited or barbarous country, they carry with them not only the laws, but the sovereignty of their own State; and those who live amongst them and become members of their community become also partakers of, and subject to, the same laws.

But this was not the nature of the first settlement made in India – it was a settlement made by a few foreigners for the purpose of trade in a very populous and highly civilised country, under the Government of a powerful Mahomedan ruler, with whose sovereignty the English Crown never attempted or pretended to interfere for some centuries afterwards.[6]

So, called upon to decide whether to apply in India the English rule that goods of one who has committed suicide should be forfeited to the Crown, the Judicial Committee (agreeing with the Supreme Court at Calcutta) declined to apply it: it was recognized that suicide need not in all societies and in all circumstances be regarded as the worst of all murders but as

deriving its moral character altogether from the circumstances in which it is committed:

---

[3] See Matson 'The Common Law Abroad: English and Indigenous Laws in the British Commonwealth', (1993) 42 ICLQ 753 at 761.   [4] Ibid.

[5] Woodruff, op. cit., vol. 2, 59.

[6] *Advocate General of Bengal v Ranee Surnomoye Dossee* (1863) Moo. Ind. App. 391 at 428.

sometimes as blameable, sometimes as justifiable, sometimes as meritorious, or even an act of positive duty.[7]

I am indebted to Mr M. C. Setalvad, then the Attorney-General of India, who, in his 1960 Hamlyn Lectures, gave further instances of this same approach:

The High Courts in India have followed the same trend rejecting the principles of English law whenever they were thought unsuitable to Indian conditions. As early as 1874 the Sunday Observance Acts were held inapplicable in India. In 1875 the High Court of Bombay refused to apply the statutes against superstitious uses to Hindu religious endowments. Similarly, that court held that the rule in *Shelley's case* did not apply to a disposition by a parsee. The English rule in regard to marriage with a deceased wife's sister has been held not to extend to persons who were not by origin or domicile English. Similarly the common law rules as to survivorship, special damages in a case of imputation of unchastity to a married woman in the mofussil, have been held inapplicable to Indians.[8]

I am indebted to the same learned author for two very early but very striking statements of principles which have since become familiar, both taken from Governor Aungier of Bombay. The first, on inauguration of the Court of Judicature in Bombay in 1672, is very short:

Laws though in themselves never so wise and pious are but a dead letter and of little force except there be a due and impartial execution of them.[9]

The second is much longer, but I think deserves quotation despite its length:

The Inhabitants of this Island consist of severall Nations and Religions to wit—English, Portuguess and other Christians, moores, and jentues, but you when you sit in this seat of Justice and Judgement, must looke upon them with one single eye as I doe, without distinction of Nation or Religion, for they are all His Majesties and the Honble. Company's subjects as the English are, and have all an equall title and right to Justice and you must doe them all Justice, even the meanest person of the Island, and in particulare the Poore, the Orphan, the Widdow and the stranger, in al matters of controversy, of Common right, and Meum and Tuum; And this not only one against the other but even against myself and those who are in office under me, nay against the Honble. Company themselves when Law, Reason and Equity shal require you soe to doe, for this is your Duty and therein will you be justified, and in soe doing God will be with you to strengthen you, his Majestie and the Company will commend you and reward you, and I, in my place, shall be ready to assist, Countenance, honour and protect you to the utmost of the power Authority entrusted to me: and soe I pray God give his blessing to you.[10]

A similarly, early statement of a principle which took some time to be generally accepted is found in the instruction of Cornwallis in the 1780s:

that the collectors of revenue and their officers and indeed all the officers of Government

---

[7] Ibid., at 432–3.
[8] 'The Common Law in India', at 54–5.
[9] Quoted in ibid., at 42.
[10] Quoted, 'The Common Law in India', Hamlyn Lectures (1980) at 10.

shall be amenable to the courts for acts done in their official capacities, and that Government itself in cases in which it may be a party with its subjects in matters of property shall submit its rights to be tried in these courts under the existing laws and regulations.

As in the statement of legal principles, so in administration were ideals expressed which remain worthy of support. Despite some note of condescension in the language used, I would find it hard to quarrel with the view expressed by the Board established to administer the Punjab:

The Board desire that substantial justice should be plainly dealt out to a simple people, unused to the intricacies of legal proceedings. The aim is to avoid all technicality, circumlocution and obscurity; to simplify and abridge every rule, procedure and process. They would endeavour to form tribunals which shall not be hedged in with forms unintelligible to the vulgar and only to be interpreted by professional lawyers but which shall be open and accessible Courts of Justice where every man may plead his own cause, be confronted face to face with his opponents, may prosecute his own claim or conduct his own defence.[11]

The achievement of independence in 1947 was of course a climacteric event in the history of India. But the constitutional and legal history of India is, I think, a continuum and not a story of radical revolution. As Mr Setalvad put it:

The builders of the Indian Constitution not only drew largely from the collection of British ideas and institutions which was India's heritage from British rule, but they also took care to maintain a continuity with the Governmental system which had grown up under the British. They believed not in severing their links with the past but rather in treasuring all that had been useful and to which they had been accustomed. The structure which emerged was therefore not only basically British in its framework but took the form of an alteration and extension of what had previously existed.[12]

Thus the Constitution provided (in Article 372) for the continuance in force of existing laws, and on its inauguration the Supreme Court paid a graceful and generous tribute to the Judicial Committee of the Privy Council as

the great judicial tribunal which has so well and so ably functioned as the highest Court of appeal for about a hundred years. The great Judges who have from time to time presided over its deliberations have left a deep and ineffaceable impress on the law of the country. Our tie with the Judicial Committee of the Privy Council has now snapped. But the law laid down in their judgments will doubtless continue to mould and influence the decisions of this Court. This is inevitable because the roots of our statute law and legal forms lie deeply enmeshed in the jurisprudence of England and the decisions of the English courts.[13]

With equal generosity Justice Vivian Bose of the Supreme Court of India said in 1960:

[11] Quoted Woodruff, op. cit., vol. 1, 341.
[12] 'The Common Law in India', Hamlyn Lectures (1960) at 168.
[13] Quoted Setalvad, 'The Role of English Law in India' (1966), 56–7.

one of the greatest boons that the English conferred on India was to introduce the Rule of Law into the land and to imbed it so firmly into the lives of the people that its displacement seems unlikely in any foreseeable future . . .[14]

Having already expressed my reservations concerning the gloomy strictures of Sir Penderel Moon, I am reassured to find that the Law Commission of India, in its fourteenth report of 1958, investigating whether the system of administration of justice bequeathed to India by the British failed to accord with the pattern of Indian life and conditions, concluded that

the system which has prevailed in our country for nearly two centuries though British in its origin has grown and developed in Indian conditions and is now firmly rooted in the Indian soil. It would be disastrous and entirely destructive of our future growth to think of a radical change at this stage of the development of our country.[15]

So the legal and constitutional history of India did not end in 1947 or even in 1950. Rather it took giant strides forward, showing a sense of purpose, an energy and an imaginative willingness to innovate which must leave any British observer full of rather breathless admiration. On the occasion of this jubilee it is perhaps appropriate to mention some of the factors contributing to this great resurgence, familiar though they must be to you.

First of course one must mention the constitution of India, the cornerstone of the new Union, and an enduring monument to the wisdom, erudition and idealism of Dr Ambedkar and all others who framed this remarkable document. Unlike the British constitution, but like that of the United States, it is an entrenched constitution, and it is supreme. It is no doubt true as Mr Setalvad observed, that:

We have in truth not the supremacy of the courts but the supremacy of the Constitution.[16]

But the Supreme Court is clearly established as the guardian of the constitution and that also Mr Setalvad acknowledged:

The makers of the Indian constitution eventually chose to subject the decisions of the legislature in certain matters to a close and an impartial scrutiny by the judiciary in the fullest confidence that the judiciary would, in making their determination, be guided solely by the interests of the nation.[17]

The Preamble to the constitution, as amended in 1976, affirms the resolve of the people of India to constitute India into a Sovereign, Socialist, Secular, Democratic Republic and to secure to all its citizens justice, social economic and political, liberty of thought, expression, belief, faith and worship and equality of status and opportunity. This preamble is not, as I understand, regarded as part of the constitution itself, or as a source of substantive law.[18] But I understand that

---

[14] 'The Migration of Common Law: India', (1960) 76 LQR 59 at 63.
[15] Quoted Setalvad, 'The Role of English Law in India', (1966), 56.
[16] 'The Common Law in India', Hamlyn Lectures (1960) at 187.
[17] Ibid.   [18] Bomai's Case (1994) 3 SCC 1.

the Supreme Court has regarded the preamble as indicating the basic structure of the constitution, and has had regard to it in construing the constitution and determining those features of it which are to be regarded as basic and inviolable. It seems to me wholly admirable that a new nation, embarking on an independent future, should commit itself to a statement of the principles upon which its future development is to be founded. Wherever one is in the world, one need not look very far afield to see countries in which these basic principles have commanded little or no allegiance. I hope I may be permitted to pay respectful tribute to the way in which, over a turbulent and difficult half century, the people of India have remained almost unfailingly true to these principles.

Scarcely less striking to an English observer, although again unsurprising to an American, was the decision to place on the face of the constitution the resounding roll call of fundamental rights to be found in Part III of the constitution. It is not so much the content of these rights which impresses. Many of them would appear in any similar tabulation, and do appear in our own, belated, Human Rights Act of 1998, although certain of them, notably the abolition of untouchability and the prohibition of child labour in hazardous employments, were highly ambitious ideals. More significant, as it seems to me, was the decision of the new citizens of this nation to commit itself to these rights as the foundation of their future life together. It was an express and conscious social contract of a kind which political philosophers have had to imagine.

But of course a mere statement of rights, however admirable and idealistic in itself, is valueless unless effective means of enforcement exist. In Articles 32 and 226 of the constitution such means were unambiguously provided to the Supreme Court and the High Courts of the States. Dr Ambedkar himself fully recognized the central importance of Article 32, of which he said in the Constituent Assembly:

I am very glad that the majority of those who spoke on this article have realised the importance and significance of this article. If I was asked to name any particular article in this constitution as the most important – an article without which the Constitution would be a nullity – I could not refer to any other article except this one. It is the very essence of the Constitution and the very heart of it and I am glad that the House has realised its importance.[19]

In his R. B. Datar Memorial Lecture given in April 1999, Mr Fali Nariman described the years since 1977 as 'the best years of the court', during which, he said, 'the Court has built around itself (step by step and case by case) an almost impregnable fortress of judicial inviolability'.[20] In its role as guardian of the constitution, the Court has indeed been remarkably staunch. One of the Directive Principles of State Policy in Part IV of the constitution required the state to take steps to separate the judiciary from the executive in the public services of the

---

[19] Constituent Assembly Debates, vol. VII, 953, proceedings 9 Dec. 1948
[20] 'Fifty Years of the Supreme Court—A Balance Sheet of Performance', 3.

state, manifesting an intention that the independence of the judges should be preserved and enhanced. But this principle was given greatly added force when, in the *Second Judges' Case*[21] a majority of the Supreme Court courageously held that, having regard to the independence of the judiciary and the separation of powers, the views of the Chief Justice of India when consulted on the appointment of judges should be determinative. In this way, as Mr Nariman has pointed out,[22] effect was eventually given to the preference of Sir Patrick Spens, the last British Chief Justice of India. Whatever room for argument there may be about the correct construction of Article 124 of the Constitution, one can have no doubt that this decision does all that any decision could to ensure a politically neutral, professionally distinguished and uncorrupt judiciary. Scarcely less striking is the Court's decision in the *Keshavananda Case*[23] that, while no part of the constitution including even the fundamental rights in Part III was beyond the amending power, the basic structure of the constitution could not be abrogated even by a constitutional amendment. It seems likely that, particularly in retrospect, this decision, and the failure of an attempt to reverse it two years later, will come to be seen as a major landmark in the constitutional development of this country, rather as Magna Carta or the Petition of Right have come to be seen in ours. In the same distinguished category must surely be placed the court's decision in *Indira Gandhi v Raj Narain*[24] that judicial review and free and fair elections were fundamental features of the constitution and so beyond the reach of the amending power. You will be able to judge better than I whether Mr Nariman was justified when he wrote:

If the pernicious clauses of the Thirty-Ninth Constitutional Amendment had been upheld, Indian democracy would not have long survived.[25]

By these and other decisions the Supreme Court made sure that it was a guardian of the constitution, and of the values and principles embodied in it, not only in name but also in the cockpit where, in real life, the realities of power and authority are adjusted and settled.

All this, even if standing alone, would be memorable enough. But even more striking to a British observer—perhaps to almost any non-Indian observer—is the Court's active acceptance of responsibility for the pursuit of objects well outside the bounds of conventional litigation.[26] The basis of this activity, as explained by former Chief Justice Bhagwati, with whom it is, as I understand, particularly associated, is very clear:

The weaker sections of Indian humanity have been deprived of justice for long years: They have had no access to justice on account of their poverty, ignorance and illiteracy. They are

---

[21] *Supreme Court Advocates on Record Association case* AIR 1994 SC 268.
[22] Op. cit., at 4 n.   [23] AIR 1973 SC 1461.
[24] AIR 1975 SC 2299.   [25] Op. cit., at 12.
[26] I have received very great help from Professor G. L. Peiris, 'Public Interest Litigation in the Indian Subcontinent: Current Dimensions' (1991) 40 ICLQ 66.

not aware of the rights and benefits conferred upon them by the constitution and the law. On account of their socially and economically disadvantaged position they lack the capacity to assert their rights, and they do not have the material resources with which to enforce their social and economic entitlements and combat exploitation and injustice.[27]

The constitutional imperative of equal protection of the law could not, it seems, be left to take care of itself:

The concern shown [by the law] to the poor and the disadvantaged is much greater than that shown to the rich and well-to-do because the latter can, on account of their dominant social and economic position and large material resources, resist aggression on their rights where the poor and the deprived just do not have the capacity or the will to resist and fight.[28]

To achieve the aim of enabling the poor and the disadvantaged to enjoy their legal and constitutional rights, two things were needful. The first was to be generous in recognising the right of persons other than the immediate victim to sue, in other words to apply relatively relaxed rules of standing. In England the test has been one of 'sufficient interest' and this, not too strictly interpreted, has been found satisfactory, although in the Human Rights Act 1998, to the regret of many, it is required that the applicant be a victim of the conduct complained of.[29] It is easy to understand why, in the Indian context, a different philosophy has prevailed, encouraging any member of the public to invite the adjudication of the courts on matters of interest to the wider public.[30] While the Court has declared its unwillingness to act at the instance of

pseudo public-spirited citizens who indulge in wild and reckless allegations besmirching the character of others[31]

it has permitted grievances to be ventilated at the instance of those who, in many jurisdictions, would have difficulty crossing the threshold of the court. As Professor Peiris of the University of Colombo wrote, in an article to which I am greatly indebted:

At the core of the concern consistently shown by Indian courts for fostering public interest litigation in the conditions of contemporary life in the subcontinent, is candid recognition that, in the absence of innovative mechanisms of this nature, substantive rights central to human dignity cannot but assume an illusory character in the eyes of large sections of the population. Thus, in a case where a public interest organisation was permitted to petition the court on behalf of a group of bonded labourers working in conditions of appalling adversity in stone quarrying operations, the observation was justly made that the very existence of the circumstances which the invocation of judicial relief was intended to remove or mitigate, precluded in practice access to the courts by the persons directly affected.[32]

---

[27] *Bihar Legal Support Soc. v Chief Justice of India* [1986] 4 SCC 767, 768.
[28] Ibid., at 769.   [29] Section 7(1).
[30] *SP Gupta v Union of India* [1982] 2 SCR 365.
[31] *Chaitanya Kumar v State of Karnataka* [1986] 2 SCC 594, 606.
[32] Op. cit., see n. 26 above, at 70.

The second thing needful was to eschew a technical approach to the formalities of commencing litigation. If the poor and disadvantaged, particularly those living in remote rural areas, had been obliged to comply with the ordinary formalities attendant upon the issue of legal process, they would plainly have lacked the means and the professional assistance necessary to do so. This, as I understand, is the rationale of the rule which permits anyone alleging violation of a fundamental constitutional right to invoke the assistance of the Court simply by writing a letter to a judge. This epistolary jurisdiction has, to my knowledge, no counterpart anywhere in the world, and no doubt the effect is greatly to increase the burden on the judges called upon to decide the public interest issues thus informally raised. I cannot, however, imagine a more radical and imaginative response to an obvious social problem; and the right of any citizen to invoke the insistence, directly, of a judge of the Supreme Court seems to me to be a democratic right of the utmost value. One could not conceive of Hitler or Stalin, or other tyrants of more recent vintage, giving their citizens such a right, unless of course they could be sure that the judges were solid and reliable party members.

In seeking to protect the important constitutional rights of Indian citizens the Supreme Court has, no doubt for good reason, involved itself much more closely in the detail of administrative decision making than would be acceptable in more staid jurisdictions. The regulation of railway transport,[33] the giving of directions to a State Government when legislation should be brought into force,[34] the management of a children's home,[35] the contents of a film about communal violence at the time of partition,[36] the pollution of the Ganges[37] and the classification of a jungle as a reserve forest[38] have all engaged the attention of the Supreme Court, whose function appears to have gone beyond the ordinary bounds of legal review, at any rate as understood by English judges and lawyers.

If the court was to rule responsibly on detailed administrative questions, it plainly had to have access to reliable and objective information. This too was a challenge which the court accepted, and it led to another radical departure from what would, in the past, have been regarded as normal practice. Of the fact-finding processes which resulted, Professor Peiris has written:

It is with regard to creation and refinement of these fact-finding processes, unconventional and yet eminently suited to the purpose in hand, that Indian courts can probably be said to have made their most imaginative contribution to the strategy of social action litigation. Without doubt the strengths—and pitfalls—of this dimension of their work possess a significance which far transcends the particular setting of societal conditions in the subcontinent.[39]

---

[33] *Dr P Nalla Thampy v Union of India* [1983] 4 SCC 598.
[34] *Sheela Barse v Union of India* [1986] 3 SCC 596.
[35] *Sheela Barse v Secretary Children's Aid Society* 1987 3 SCC 50.
[36] *Chotolal v Union of India* 1988 1 SCC 668.
[37] *MC. Mehta v Union of India* 1987 4 SCC 463.
[38] *Banwasi Seva Ashram v State of Uttar Pradesh* 1986 4 SCC 753.   [39] Op. cit., at 77.

The Professor gives examples: the appointment of committees of experts to report on the ecological and environmental effect of quarrying and mining in the Mussoorie Hills in one case[40] and the radiation levels of milk and dairy products in another,[41] the appointment of a commission to visit lands on which a depressed community were being encouraged to settle,[42] the appointment of Commissioners (and later a director of the Indian Institution of Technology) to investigate a complaint made, allegedly by bonded labourers working in quarries in Faridabad.[43] To ensure that human rights violations did not persist for want of exposure, the Court has been willing to order extensive disclosure and also to arm petitioners with extensive investigative powers: thus where a question was raised about the conditions in which children were being held in custody, far reaching orders were made requiring district judges to ascertain the conditions prevailing in their localities, and the petitioner was specifically empowered to visit jails, children's homes, observation homes, borstal schools and all institutions providing accommodation for delinquent children in every part of the country.[44]

There appears to be no doubt that the Court has on occasion been drawn into laying down very detailed and specific administrative requirements. One example given by Professor Peiris relates to a mental hospital in Bihar where the court specified the allowance to be made for food per patient per day, revoked the limit put on the expenditure of drugs by the hospital authorities, ordered that all patients should be provided with blankets and mattresses within 15 days, ordered that the sanitary facilities be improved and directed that arrangements be made for the supply of drinking water.[45] Another example relates to a protective home for girls run by the Government Uttar Pradesh, in which case directions were given covering the width of the road giving access to a building, the partitioning of the interior, precautions to prevent the accumulation of rain water, the installation of exhaust fans and mosquito nets, the provision of gas in the kitchen, access to a telephone and the rewiring of the building.[46] In a third case the court laid down appropriate standards for admission to private professional education in medical and engineering colleges.[47] One can well understand, in each case, why the measures specified were regarded as necessary to give effect to the very basic rights which the constitution was framed to protect. Dr Ambedkar and the fathers of the constitution might, perhaps, have been surprised that it was left to the Court rather than to a political organ of the State to take action along these lines, but if they had doubted whether any political organ of the State would take

---

[40] *Rural Litigation & Entitlement Kendra v State of Uttar Pradesh* [1986] (Supp.) SCC 517.
[41] *Dr Shiv Rao Shanta Rao Wangla v Union of India* 1988 1 SCC 452.
[42] *Kutti Padmarao v State of Andhra Pradesh* [1986] Supp. SCC 574.
[43] *Bandhua Mukti Morcha v Union of India* 1984 3 SCC 161.
[44] *Sheela Barse v Union of India* 1986 3 SCC 596.
[45] *Rakash Chand Narain v State of Bihar* [1986] (Supp.) SCC 576.
[46] *Dr Upendra Baxi v State of Uttar Pradesh* [1986] 4 SCC 106.
[47] *Unnikrishan v State of Andhra Pradesh* 1993 1 SCC 645.

the necessary action they would surely much have preferred that it should have been taken by the Court, than that it should not be taken at all.

All courts, and particularly all supreme courts, have to be mindful of their relationship with the other arms of Government. Modern democratic States, like the solar system, function best if major constellations follow their pre-ordained paths. The Supreme Court of India has been sensitive to these considerations. Thus when a High Court in effect directed a State to legislate to prevent ragging of college students, the Supreme Court regarded this as no part of the High Court's business.[48] The same answer was given where a High Court ordered a public works department to complete a public road.[49] When retired defence personnel sought to claim preferential access to residential facilities in a strategic tract of territory in an area adjacent to the boundary with Burma and China the court observed:

The matter appears to have political overtones and, in the absence of adequate material placed before the court, we do not think it would be appropriate for us to go into the matter and dispose of it as an ordinary dispute.[50]

The court has recognized that there are some issues which simply do not lend themselves to judicial determination.[51] It has also acknowledged that it is the apex court of the country to which resort should only be, and can only be, exceptional,[52] and it has accepted a general need to concentrate on cases in which legal injury or wrong has been done to a class of individuals rather than to a single person.[53]

It is unfashionable nowadays for any public body, looking back on its past, to express pride or pleasure in its achievements. The ever-critical media prefer apologies for past errors, admissions of past failure, acknowledgement of continuing, unsolved problems, warnings against complacency and calls to face the future with renewed energy and ambition. All these have their place. But I hope that I, as a British visitor, may be allowed to violate these conventions on this occasion. Building on the foundations it inherited, the Supreme Court has established itself as a central organ of the Indian Republic and fashioned a body of jurisprudence which is new without being revolutionary and wisely directed to serving the needs of the people of India. I leave the last word to the President of the Bar Association of India who, of all people, is well placed to pass judgment:

I believe that the Judges of the nineties and the Judges of today are somehow more important than the Judges of yesteryears simply because they have been called upon to discharge

---

[48] *State of Himachal Pradesh v A Parent of A Student of Medical College, Simla* [1985] 3 SCC 169.
[49] *State of Himachal Pradesh v Umed Ram Sharma* 1986 2 SCC 68.
[50] *Assam Rifles Multi-Purpose Co-operative Society Ltd. v Union of India* [1987] 2 SCC 638, 639.
[51] *Vincent Parikulangara v Union of India* 1987 2 SCC 165.
[52] *Bihar Legal Support Society v Chief Justice of India* [1986] 4 SCC 767.
[53] *SP Gupta v Union of India* [1981] (Supp.) SCC 87.

and have readily assumed, far greater responsibilities than their predecessors ever did. Over recent years 'judging' is no longer what it used to be. Judges have now a dominant role in society—and because of this they are more often criticised for what they do and what they say—and yet today, the highest Judiciary is also held in highest public esteem. This may sound paradoxical, but it is not. The public turns to the Judiciary, and ultimately to the highest Judiciary, more and more for the resolution of its problems—more than it ever did in the past.[54]

---

[54] Nariman, op. cit., at 27.

PART IV
HUMAN RIGHTS

There is probably nothing which matters more to any of us during our lives on earth than that we should be properly and fairly treated as human beings. We do not want to be arbitrarily executed or locked up or beaten up or tortured. If we have the misfortune to find ourselves involved in a trial in court, we want the trial to be fairly conducted. We want to be free to say and write and believe and do what we want, and meet (or not meet) who we like, so long as we do no harm to anyone else. We do not want unnecessary interference in our affairs. The problem is: how are these beneficial results most effectively achieved?

One answer, given by a number of very distinguished people over many years, was by making the European Convention on Human Rights a part of the statute law applied by British judges trying cases and giving judgments in the United Kingdom; in other words, by formally incorporating the Convention into our law. But this was an answer spurned, again over many years, by the two main political parties which (with some vocal dissidents) actively opposed the notion of incorporation. The first of these papers, delivered as a lecture in March 1993, rehearsed the arguments in favour of incorporation; the day before, as it happened, the late John Smith had signalled a change in Labour Party policy. Now, as we know, that change has been given legislative effect.

The second of these papers is devoted to one aspect of human rights: the right to privacy. This is a particularly sensitive issue, because while we are probably sympathetic to an individual's desire to keep his or her affairs private we also respect and cherish the right and duty of the media to inform, disclose, and on occasions expose. Should a line be drawn between the right to privacy and the right to free expression? and if so where? and who is to draw it? Such questions are easy to ask, but hard to answer.

When the third paper was given, as the Earl Grey Lecture at the University of Newcastle in January 1998, change was afoot. A bill to incorporate the Convention (or most of it) was before Parliament. So this paper, again supporting incorporation, looks at our national experience as a defendant in the European Court of Human Rights at Strasbourg, and considers how, under the Convention, tensions between the right to privacy and the right to free expression might be resolved.

The fact that we in Britain have not, up to now, had the benefit of any detailed statutory Bill of Rights has not of course meant that human rights in this country have lacked all legal protection. It has meant that the task of protecting citizens' human rights has fallen, in a rather piecemeal way, to other parts of the law. One of these is what English lawyers call the law of tort. Continental lawyers refer to the law of delict. It means the same thing. Broadly speaking, the law of tort or delict comprises that part of the law where the claim for injury or damage (or apprehended injury or damage) forms the only legal bond between the parties— in obvious contrast to a legal bond based on marriage, parenthood, entitlement under a will or intestacy or trust, or by virtue of owning shares, for example. Professor John Fleming was an internationally renowned scholar, specializing in the law of tort, and on his retirement a volume of essays was published in his honour (although unhappily he died before it was published). The fourth paper in this section is a contribution to that volume. It seeks to explore the contribution made by the law of tort to the protection of human rights.

1

The European Convention on Human Rights: Time to Incorporate*

I would confidently hope that human rights, the subject of this lecture, qualifies as a suitable subject for a Denning Lecture, and I am reassured to know that the argument I shall be advancing is one which Lord Denning, after some initial hesitation, came to support.[1] For there is no task more central to the purpose of a modern democracy, or more central to the judicial function, than that of seeking to protect, within the law, the basic human rights of the citizen, against invasion by other citizens or by the state itself. I hope this point is too obvious to need labouring. But I cannot resist two quotations. The first is from an Italian lawyer, who wrote (perhaps significantly) during the 1930s that

the State finds its highest expression in protecting rights, and therefore should be grateful to the citizen who, in demanding justice, gives it the opportunity to defend justice, which after all is the basic *raison d'être* of the State.[2]

The second quotation is from the agreed statement issued at the end of an international conference on human rights, over which the Lord Chancellor presided, held in Oxford in September 1992:

In democratic societies fundamental human rights and freedoms are more than paper aspirations. They form part of the law. And it is the special province of judges to see to it that the law's undertakings are realised in the daily life of the people.[3]

When, as sometimes happens, one right conflicts with another (the right of free expression, for instance, with the right to privacy) then the judge has, so far as the law allows, to reconcile the two.

I would suggest that the ability of English judges to protect human rights in this country and reconcile conflicting rights in the manner indicated is inhibited by the failure of successive governments over many years to incorporate into United Kingdom law the European Convention on Human Rights and Fundamental Freedoms. But I should like, in the manner of the modern fast bowler, to take a rather lengthy run up to that question, making some preliminary observations about the constitution.

---

* The Denning Lecture of the Bar Association for Commerce, Finance, and Industry, delivered at the Middle Temple on 2 March 1993. Reprinted from *The Law Quarterly Review* (July 1993), 390–400. © Sweet & Maxwell, London.

[1] Anthony Lester, QC, 'Fundamental Rights: The United Kingdom Isolated?' [1984] PL 63, 83.

[2] Piero Calamandrei, *Eulogy of Judges* (1992).

[3] Balliol Statement of 1992, 23 September 1992, para. 6.

Lord Hailsham, I think, once observed that judges are usually illiterate in constitutional matters. I should therefore preface my observations with a health warning. But I shall not talk a great deal of rubbish on this particular subject because I shall not say a great deal about it at all.

Most of us, I suspect, were reared on a fairly straightforward Diceyan concept of the constitution. The centrepiece of this was of course a sovereign parliament, able to do anything except make a man a woman or a woman a man. The executive was another arm of government, but not a separate arm since it was controlled by ministers who were of necessity members of one or other house of parliament. The third horse of the troika was the judiciary, separate from legislature and executive save for the anomalous position of the Lord Chancellor and (in theory, not in practice) the Law Lords, and bound to interpret and apply the law of the land including of course the law made by Parliament. Over all, as the ultimate source of power and authority, was the Crown.

On this view the protection of human rights would have been seen as first and foremost the business of Parliament: if a government were to propose or permit any derogation from fundamental human rights, then it could expect to be restrained and even voted down in Parliament.

Much of this picture remains accurate. But constitutional organs, like constellations, wax and wane and change position relative to each other and the present century has seen such changes in our constitutional arrangements. Most striking has been the increase in the size and power of the executive, in particular the Prime Minister, the cabinet and ministers. Almost equally striking has been the weakening of parliamentary influence on the conduct of governments. For this there are no doubt many explanations, but the decline of the truly independent member, the doctrine of the electoral mandate, the tightening of party discipline and the less deferential attitude of constituency parties are probably among them. At the same time Parliament, in practice if not in theory, has ceded a part of its sovereignty; for the first time ever a secular body beyond the mountains can bindingly declare Acts of Parliament to be unlawful. And the increase of executive power has been matched by a degree of judicial review unthinkable even a few years ago.

Where does all this leave the protection of human rights? Not in a very satisfactory position, I would suggest. The elective dictatorship of the majority means that, by and large, the government of the day can get its way, even if its majority is small. If its programme or its practice involves some derogation from human rights Parliament cannot be relied on to correct this. Nor can the judges. If the derogation springs from a statute, they must faithfully apply the statute. If it is a result of administrative practice, there may well be no basis upon which they can interfere. There is no higher law, no frame of reference, to which they can properly appeal. None of this matters very much if human rights themselves are not thought to matter very much. But if the protection of its citizens' fundamental rights is genuinely seen as an important function of civil society, then it does matter. In saying this I do not suggest—and I must stress this—that the present government or any of its predecessors has acted with wilful or cynical disregard of fundamental human rights. I would adopt and apply by analogy what Samuel Johnson said about truth: 'It is more from carelessness about truth than from intentional lying that there is so much falsehood in the world.' What I do suggest is that a government intent on implementing a programme may overlook the human rights aspects of its policies and that, if a government of more sinister intent were to gain power, we should be defenceless. There would not, certainly, be much the judges could do about it. This would seem regrettable to those who, like me, would see the judges as properly playing an important part in this field.

Two factors give the question a special immediacy. The first of these is the parliamentary timetable. The pressure on parliamentary time is such that measures to remedy violations of human rights will not, in the ordinary way, find a place in the queue. They will not have featured in the party manifesto. They will not win elections. They command no political priority. If anyone doubts this, I would refer to the thirty-eight reports of the Law Commission which currently await implementation. These reports, produced at quite considerable public expense, represent clear, well-argued and compelling proposals for improving the law; only two of the thirty-eight have been specifically rejected by the government of the day; they gather dust not because their value is doubted but because there is inadequate parliamentary time to enact them. So anyone who sees Parliament as a reliable guardian of human rights in practice is, I suggest, guilty of wishful thinking.

The second factor which gives the question a special immediacy is of quite a different nature. It is the increasingly heterogeneous nature of our society and the increasingly assertive stance of minorities. The inhabitants of these islands have never, of course, sprung from a pure common stock: Jutes, Angles, Saxons, Vikings, Normans, Huguenots, and Jewish refugees from various parts of Europe are among those who have over the centuries blended with the native Celt and the indigenous Gael. But it is probably true that post-war immigration, particularly from the Indian sub-continent and the West Indies, has made us a more heterogeneous people than we have ever been. And it is surely true that some of these more recent citizens have shown less willingness to be submerged in the prevailing British way of life, and more desire to preserve their own traditions of language, custom and religion, than most of their predecessors have been inclined to do. There is at the same time a general lessening of deference towards authority, a growing unwillingness to accept the say-so of the teacher, the local government officer or the man from the ministry. So it seems reasonable to predict a growing number of cases—not only involving the ethnic minorities, but very often involving some minority—in which prevailing practice, perhaps of very long standing, will be said to infringe the human rights of some smaller group or some individual. As it stands, our courts are not well-fitted to mediate in these situations.

Those who share my view that the situation is unsatisfactory may well ask whether it is none the less inevitable, one of those inescapable blemishes which must exist in an imperfect world. I would say not. In the European Convention an instrument lies ready to hand which, if not providing an ideal solution, none the less offers a clear improvement on the present position.

I hope I may be permitted to touch on the history of the Convention, as I shall now call it, with apologies to those already very familiar with these points and with gratitude to Anthony Lester, QC from whose work most of them are drawn.[4]

First, the Convention was not (as might have been thought) the ethereal brain-child of some continental professor. It was in large part prepared by British lawyers and in particular by that most terrestrial of politicians, the late Lord Kilmuir.[5] Its main protagonists in the early stages were Churchill, Macmillan and John Foster, with Liberal and some Labour support.

Secondly, during the ante-natal stages of the Convention the focus of discussion was not the substance of the rights themselves, which was thought to be rather obvious, but the means of enforcement, a matter of some understandable difficulty.

Thirdly, despite the British contribution to siring the Convention, the United Kingdom's ratification of it was fraught with dissension. Although supported by Ernest Bevin, the Foreign Secretary, ratification was strongly opposed by the Chancellor of the Exchequer (Cripps), the Colonial Secretary (Griffiths) and, in particular, the Lord Chancellor (Jowitt), who reported to a colleague that the cabinet

were not prepared to encourage our European friends to jeopardise our whole system of law, which we have laboriously built up over the centuries, in favour of some half-baked scheme to be administered by some unknown court.[6]

He also described the proposed Commission on Human Rights as 'a sort of Court of Star Chamber'. Sir Hartley Shawcross, the Attorney-General, was similarly of the view that

we should firmly set our faces against the right of individual petition which seems to me to be wholly opposed to the theory of responsible Government.

Only at Bevin's insistence did the United Kingdom continue to support the Convention, and then only on the clear understanding that the United Kingdom Government could not accept the right of individual petition and the proposed European Court of Human Rights, nor various amendments which had been proposed.

Fourthly, subject to these reservations the United Kingdom did sign the Convention and, on 8 March 1951, (the day before Bevin's replacement by

---

[4] Lester op. cit. *supra*, n. 1, at 46.

[5] R. F. V. Heuston, *Lives of the Lord Chancellors, 1940–1970* (1987), 166.

[6] Interestingly, however, Jowitt does seem to have assumed that the Convention would have to be incorporated into domestic law: Lester, op. cit. *supra*, n. 1 at 53.

Herbert Morrison), became the first state to ratify. But with no incorporation into United Kingdom law, no right of individual petition and no recognition of the compulsory jurisdiction of the Strasbourg Court, the Convention was—to the United Kingdom—a hobbled horse. And when in October 1951 a Conservative government was returned to power, nothing was done to fulfil the ambitions of the Convention's founding fathers. When the Minister of State for Foreign Affairs was asked in 1958 what was the good of ratifying the Convention if one did not accept its application he answered:

As I understand it, if one subscribes to a Convention one then sees that the laws of one's country are in conformity with the Convention, and the individual cases are then tried under the laws of one's own country.[7]

But he might of course have added that the laws of one's own country may not necessarily conform with the Convention until the citizen has been put to the trouble and expense of going to Strasbourg to procure that result.

Fifthly, it was not until December 1965—after, but not immediately after, the election of a Labour government—that the decision was made to accept for a limited period the right of individual petition to the Commission and the compulsory jurisdiction of the Court. This momentous decision, so recently thought to jeopardize our whole system of law laboriously built up over centuries, and to undermine responsible government, was apparently taken without discussion by the Cabinet or any Cabinet committee.[8]

Sixthly, the years since that decision was taken have seen publication of a report by the Northern Ireland Standing Advisory Commission on Human Rights and a Lords Select Committee Report, both recommending incorporation, and two Bills having that object have completed all stages in the Lords. Support has come from such distinguished and politically divers quarters as Lord Hailsham, Lord Gardiner, Lord Scarman and Lord Jenkins of Hillhead.

Meanwhile, seventhly and lastly, on an ever-lengthening list of occasions, many of them well-publicized, the Commission or the Court have found the United Kingdom to be in breach of its obligations under the Convention. Her Majesty's Government has, as one would expect, responded appropriately by taking steps to cure the default and pay compensation where indicated. These breaches have been established on individual petition by the aggrieved citizens, who before applying are obliged to exhaust their remedies here. The whole process is one which takes a very long time and costs a great deal of money. And the problem is getting worse. On 12 October 1992, the Strasbourg Court gave judgment in four cases. In those cases, the total length of time which proceedings took before the Commission and the Court was four years and six months, six years and eight months, six years and nine months, and seven years and one

---

[7] Ibid., at 59.   [8] Ibid., at 60.

month.[9] The Strasbourg machine is becoming overwhelmed by the burdens placed upon it. But despite unremitting argument over the last few years that the Convention should be incorporated into English law so as to make its provisions enforceable, like every other law, by judges sitting in this country, no governmental move has been made in that direction.

Since incorporation would seem, at first blush, to be a simple and obvious way not only of honouring the United Kingdom's international obligations but also of giving direct and relatively inexpensive protection to its citizens, one would suppose that very powerful reasons must exist for not taking this step. It is indeed true that over the years a number of arguments against incorporation have been powerfully and persistently put. I shall review what I believe to be the more important of these arguments.

Constitutional experts point out, first of all, that the unwritten British constitution, unlike virtually every written constitution, has no means of entrenching, that is of giving a higher or trump-like status, to a law of this kind. Therefore, it is said, what one sovereign Parliament enacts another sovereign Parliament may override: thus a government minded to undermine human rights could revoke the incorporation of the Convention and leave the citizen no better off than he is now, and perhaps worse. I would give this argument beta for ingenuity and gamma, or perhaps omega, for political nous. It is true that in theory any Act of Parliament may be repealed. Thus theoretically the legislation extending the vote to the adult population, or giving the vote to women, or allowing married women to own property in their own right, or forbidding cruel and unusual punishment, or safeguarding the independence of the judges, or providing for our adhesion to the European Community, could be revoked at the whim of a temporary parliamentary majority. But absent something approaching a revolution in our society such repeal would be unthinkable. Why? Because whatever their theoretical status constitutional measures of this kind are in practice regarded as enjoying a peculiar sanctity buttressed by overwhelming public support. If incorporated, the Convention would take its place at the head of this favoured list. There is a second reason why formal entrenchment is not necessary. Suppose the statute of incorporation were to provide that subject to any express abrogation or derogation in any later statute the rights specified in the Convention were to be fully recognized and enforced in the United Kingdom according to the tenor of the Convention. That would be good enough for the judges. They would give full effect to the Convention rights unless a later statute very explicitly and specifically told them not to. But the rights protected by the Convention are not stated in absolute terms: there are provisos to cover pressing considerations of national security and such like. Save in quite extraordinary circumstances one cannot imagine any government going to Parliament with a proposal that any human right guaranteed by the

---

[9] Andrew Drzemczewski, 'The Need for a Radical Overhaul' (1993) 143 NLJ 126.

Convention be overridden. And even then (subject to any relevant derogation) the United Kingdom would in any event remain bound, in international law and also in honour, to comply with its Convention obligations. I find it hard to imagine a government going to Parliament with such a proposal. So while the argument on entrenchment has a superficial theoretical charm, it has in my opinion very little practical substance. There would be no question, as under Community law, of United Kingdom judges declaring United Kingdom statutes to be invalid. Judges would either comply with the express will of Parliament by construing all legislation in a manner consistent with the Convention. Or, in the scarcely imaginable case of an express abrogation or derogation by Parliament, the judges would give effect to that proviso also.

A second and quite different argument runs roughly along the following lines. Rulings on human rights, not least rulings on the lines of demarcation between one right and another, involve sensitive judgments important to individual citizens and to society as a whole. These are not judgments which unelected English (or perhaps British) judges are fitted to make, drawn as they are from a narrow, unrepresentative minority, the public-school and Oxbridge-educated, male, white, mostly protestant, mostly middle-class products of the Bar. They are judgments of an essentially political nature, properly to be made by democratically elected representatives of the people. I do not, unsurprisingly, agree with most of the criticisms which it is fashionable to direct at the composition of the modern judiciary, for reasons which could fill another lecture. Nor would I, again unsurprisingly, accept the charge sometimes made that protection of human rights cannot safely be entrusted to British judges: no one familiar with the development of the law in fields as divers as, for instance, the Rent Acts, the Factories Acts, labour law or judicial review could, I think, fairly accuse the judges of throwing their weight on the side of the big battalions against the small man or woman. But it is true that judgments on human rights do involve judgments about relations between the individual and the society of which the individual is part, and in that sense they can be described as political. If such questions are thought to be inappropriate for decision by judges, so be it. I do not agree, but I can understand the argument. What I simply do not understand is how it can be sensible to entrust the decision of these questions to an international panel of judges in Strasbourg—some of them drawn from societies markedly unlike our own—but not, in the first instance, to our own judges here. I am not suggesting that the final right of appeal to Strasbourg should be eliminated or in any way curtailed (which, indeed, is not something which most opponents of incorporation support). I am only suggesting that rights claimed under the Convention should, in the first place, be ruled upon by judges here before, if regrettably necessary, appeal is made to Strasbourg. The choice is not between judges and no judges; it is whether *all* matches in this field must be played away.

The proposition that judgments on questions of human rights are, in the sense indicated, political is relied on by opponents of incorporation to found a further argument. The argument is that if British judges were to rule on questions arising under the Convention they would ineluctably be drawn into political controversy with consequent damage to their reputation, constitutionally important as it is, for political neutrality. This argument, espoused by a number of senior and respected political figures, should not be lightly dismissed. But it should be examined. It cannot in my view withstand such examination for two main reasons. The first is that judges are already, on a regular and day by day basis, reviewing and often quashing decisions of ministers and government departments. They have been doing so on an increasing scale for 30 years. During that period ministers of both governing parties have fallen foul of court decisions, not once or twice but repeatedly. Some of these decisions have achieved great public notoriety. All judges are accustomed to making every effort to put aside their own personal viewpoints, and there is no reason to think that English judges are any less good at this than any others. Political controversy there has been, on occasion, a-plenty, but it has not by and large rubbed off on the judges. Why not? Because, I think, it is generally if not universally recognised that the judges have a job to do, which is not a political job, and their personal predilections have no more influence on their decisions than that of a boxing referee who is required to stop a fight. In a mature democracy like ours, this degree of understanding is not, surely, surprising, but it does in my view weaken this argument against incorporation.

There is, I suggest, a second reason why this is not a good argument. Although there are states other than the United Kingdom which have not incorporated the Convention into their domestic law, in particular the Scandinavian countries, most parties to the Convention have done so. Thus the judges of Austria, Switzerland, Italy, Belgium, Cyprus, France, Greece, Luxembourg, the Netherlands, Portugal, Spain, Turkey, Germany, Liechtenstein, and elsewhere give effect to the Convention as part of their own domestic law. If doing so involves them in political controversy damaging to their judicial rôle one would expect to find evidence of that unhappy result. There is to my knowledge no such evidence, and I do not think that those who advance this argument have ever pointed to any.

An additional argument sometimes heard is that incorporation is unnecessary since the Convention rights are already protected by the common law. The House of Lords recently held that in the field of freedom of speech there is no difference in principle between English law and Article 10 of the Convention.[10] Lord Goff of Chieveley said the same thing in one of the *Spycatcher* judgments.[11] But the House of Lords' earlier *Spycatcher* decision[12] has itself been held to have violated the Convention, as of course have other of their Lordships' decisions. If in truth the common law as it stands were giving the rights of United Kingdom citizens

---

[10] *Derbyshire County Council v Times Newspapers Ltd.* [1993] 2 WLR 449.
[11] *Att.-Gen. v Guardian Newspapers Ltd. (No. 2)* [1990] 1 AC 109 at 283–4.
[12] [1987] 1 WLR 1248.

the same protection as the Convention—across the board, not only in relation to Article 10—one might wonder why the United Kingdom's record as a Strasbourg litigant was not more favourable.

There are those who argue against incorporation on the grounds that it would give permanent form to a view of society and the human condition which, though accepted immediately post-war at the time of drafting, has no claim to eternal verity. Further, it is said, a constraint is placed on the ability of the law to develop and change as the views of society develop and change. This is, in truth, an argument against the Convention itself. But it is not a very persuasive argument, since the Convention can of course be modified to reflect changing views and values. And there is a more fundamental answer, which is to look, necessarily very briefly, at the rights which the Convention (including its First Protocol) protects.

The rights (shorn of very important qualifications) are: the right to life; the right to protection against subjection to torture or inhuman or degrading treatment or punishment; the prohibition of slavery and forced labour; the liberty and security of the person; the right to a fair trial; the prohibition of retrospective criminal legislation; the right to respect for private and family life, home and correspondence; the right to freedom of thought, conscience and religion; the right to freedom of expression; the right to freedom of peaceful assembly and association; the right to marry and found a family; the right to peaceful enjoyment of property; the right to education; the requirement that there be free elections at reasonable intervals by secret ballot; and the right to enjoy these rights and freedoms without discrimination on any ground.

Now it is obvious that the content of these rights will be held to change as social and political attitudes develop. This has demonstrably happened already. For example, punishments which were commonplace (at least in the United Kingdom) in 1950 have been held to be, and would now be very widely thought to be, degrading. Views are bound to change on what the articles of the Convention require and, not less important, what the qualifications to the articles permit. I cannot, however, for my part accept that these articles represent some transient sociological mood, some flavour of the month, the decade or the half-century. They encapsulate legal, ethical, social and democratic principles, painfully developed over 2,000 years. The risk that they may come to be regarded as modish or *passés* is one that may safely be taken.

I am conscious that I have given much time to considering the arguments against incorporation and rather less to the case in favour. This is no doubt because I regard the positive case as clear and the burden as lying on the opponents to make good their grounds of opposition. But there is one argument in favour of incorporation that I would like to mention. It is not a new argument,[13] but it is an important one, and it has recently been drawn to the House of Lords'

---

[13] See, e.g., Andrew Drzemczewski, *The European Human Rights Convention in Domestic Law* (1983), chap. 9, 229.

attention by Lord Slynn of Hadley (in his legislative, and not judicial, mode).[14] The Court of Justice has now made clear that the fundamental human rights which the Convention protects are part of the law of the Community which that court is bound to secure and enforce. Community law is, of course, part of the law of the United Kingdom. As Lord Slynn put it,

> every time the European Court recognises a principle set out in the convention as being part of Community law, it must be enforced in the United Kingdom courts in relation to Community law matters, but not in domestic law. So the convention becomes in part a part of our law through the back door because we have to apply the convention in respect of Community law matters as a part of Community law.

Drawing on his own experience as counsel appearing at Strasbourg, he felt it would be more satisfactory if the convention were to enter by the front door. It was, he said,

> quite plain that many, although perhaps not all, of the cases could be dealt with just as well and more expeditiously by our own judges here.

I end on a downbeat note. It would be naive to suppose that incorporation of the Convention would usher in the new Jerusalem. As on the morrow of a general election, however glamorous the promises of the campaign, the world would not at once feel very different. But the change would over time stifle the insidious and damaging belief that it is necessary to go abroad to obtain justice. It would restore this country to its former place as an international standard bearer of liberty and justice. It would help to reinvigorate the faith, which our eighteenth and nineteenth century forebears would not for an instant have doubted, that these were fields in which Britain was the world's teacher, not its pupil. And it would enable the judges more effectively to honour their ancient and sacred undertakings to do right to all manner of people after the laws and usages of this realm, without fear or favour, affection or ill will.

---

[14] H. L. Deb., 26 Nov. 1992, cols. 1096–8.

2

Opinion: Should There Be a Law to Protect Rights of Personal Privacy?*

In December 1890 Samuel Warren and Louis Brandeis wrote an article which has been described as the most influential article ever to appear in a legal journal. It was entitled 'The Right to Privacy' and was published in the *Harvard Law Review*.[1] In the article the authors, having touched on the development of the law to accord recognition to rights unknown in early times, wrote:

Recent inventions and business methods call attention to the next step which must be taken for the protection of the person, and for securing to the individual what Judge Cooley calls the right 'to be let alone'. Instantaneous photographs and newspaper enterprise have invaded the sacred precincts of private and domestic life; and numerous mechanical devices threaten to make good the prediction that 'what is whispered in the closet shall be proclaimed from the house-tops'. For years there has been a feeling that the law must afford some remedy for the unauthorised circulation of portraits of private persons; and the evil of the invasion of privacy by the newspapers, long keenly felt, has been but recently discussed by an able writer. . . .

Of the desirability—indeed of the necessity—of some such protection, there can, it is believed, be no doubt. The press is overstepping in every direction the obvious bounds of propriety and of decency. Gossip is no longer the resource of the idle and of the vicious, but has become a trade, which is pursued with industry as well as effrontery. To satisfy a prurient taste the details of sexual relations are spread broadcast in the columns of the daily papers. To occupy the indolent, column upon column is filled with idle gossip, which can only be procured by intrusion upon the domestic circle. The intensity and complexity of life, attendant upon advancing solitude and privacy have become more essential to the individual; but modern enterprise and invention have, through invasions upon his privacy, subjected him to mental pain and distress, far greater than could be inflicted by mere bodily injury. Nor is the harm wrought by such invasions confined to the suffering of those who may be made the subjects of journalistic or other enterprise. In this, as in other branches of commerce, the supply creates the demand. Each crop of unseemly gossip, thus harvested, becomes the seed of more, and, in direct proportion to its circulation, results in a lowering of social standards and of morality. Even gossip apparently harmless, when widely and persistently circulated, is potent for evil. It both belittles and perverts. It belittles by inverting the relative importance of things, thus dwarfing the thoughts and aspirations of a people. When personal gossip attains the dignity of print, and crowds the space available for matters of real interest to the community, what wonder that the ignorant and

* This is an annotated version of a lecture delivered to the Society of Liberal Democrat Lawyers on 21 May 1996. Reprinted from *European Human Rights Law Review*, 5 (1996), 450–62. © Sweet & Maxwell Limited, London 1996.

[1] (1890) 4 Harvard LR 194.

thoughtless mistake its relative importance. Easy of comprehension, appealing to that weak side of human nature which is never wholly cast down by the misfortunes and frailties of our neighbors, no-one can be surprised that it usurps the place of interest in brains capable of other things. Triviality destroys at once robustness of thought and delicacy of feeling. No enthusiasm can flourish, no generous impulse can survive under its blighting influence.[2]

These sentiments, by their unashamed seriousness and their deeply moral view of the improvability of man, ring strangely in modern ears. They would not, I think, have sounded strange at all to those Liberal statesmen who formed this Club in 1880 as Gladstone, still a mere stripling of 71, embarked on his second Government. That is, if true, a melancholy comment on our 'progress' over the last century, which has established the profound untruth of Tennyson's suggestion that 'We needs must love the highest when we see it.' But the article also involves a paradox: although, in arguing that a right to privacy already existed at common law the authors relied very largely on legal cases decided in England, the recognition of a right to privacy as such has been more generously accorded in almost every developed country than in our own. 'It is', as one author has recently written, 'one of the law's great ironies that, though rooted in the English law of confidence, the American "privacy" torts have failed to germinate in England.'[3]

It is not therefore surprising that the question posed in the title to this lecture has been frequently asked over the last 30–40 years. It has provoked no consensual answer. A majority of the Younger Committee, reporting in 1972,[4] advised against enactment of any general tort of invasion of privacy, preferring to deal in a piecemeal way with such deficiencies of the existing law as they believed to exist. Eighteen years later, the Calcutt Committee, which reported in 1990,[5] recommended that a tort of infringement of privacy should not at that time be introduced. In July 1995 the Government, making its response to the House of Commons National Heritage Select Committee,[6] expressed the conclusion that a case had not been made for enactment of a civil remedy for infringement of privacy.

Others have taken the opposite view. In its 1970 report *Privacy and the Law* JUSTICE recommended legislation to introduce such a right. In his *Review of Press Self-Regulation*, published in 1993,[7] Sir David Calcutt, QC recommended that the Government should now give further consideration to the introduction of a new tort of infringement of privacy. The National Heritage Committee in its Fourth Report on *Privacy and Media Intrusion* of March 1993[8] recommended

    [2] At 195–6.
    [3] Wacks, *Privacy and Press Freedom* (1995) at 48. This is a most interesting book, from which I have derived great benefit.
    [4] Report of the Committee on Privacy, Cmnd. 5012 (1972), para. 659.
    [5] Report of the Committee on Privacy and Related Matters, Cm. 1102, (1990), para. 12.5.
    [6] *Privacy and Media Intrusion—The Government's Response*, Cm. 2918 (1995), para. 4.13.
    [7] Cm. 2315 (1993) at xiii, para. 17.   [8] House of Commons, papers 294–1.

that a Protection of Privacy Bill, which would provide protection for all citizens and whose provisions similarly would apply to all citizens, should now be introduced. That appears also to have been the view of the Lord Chancellor who, launching a consultation paper on behalf of his own Department and the Scottish Office in July 1993, said:

The time has come to ensure that the law protects the privacy of everyone. This is a matter which has been the subject of cross-party study for many years, and I think it right to offer concrete proposals for reform. The way ahead now is to provide a new remedy for individuals, with appropriate defences.[9]

That was also the view of Lord Mancroft, Mr Brian Walden MP, Mr Alex Lyon MP, Mr William Cash MP, Mr John Browne MP, and Lord Stoddart, all of whom have at different times introduced Bills into Parliament in order to protect personal rights of privacy.

This diversity of response to a seemingly straightforward question justifies, if it does not compel, a reconsideration of first principles. All of us would accept that as members of a civil society we are not, and should not be, free to act in total disregard of the legitimate interests of others. We do not expect to be free to choose the side on which we drive our cars down the street. We do not claim a right to keep our neighbourhoods awake all night by making a grossly excessive noise. We accept the constraints of the criminal law. We accept, with such grace as we can muster, that we may not erect any building we want wherever we like, perhaps mindful of Ruskin's observation that 'A single villa can mar a landscape and dethrone a dynasty of hills.' These are all compromises which we accept that one citizen must necessarily make in the interests of his fellow citizens. There should surely be, however, as I would suggest, a *quid pro quo* for these necessary concessions; this is that the citizen should be entitled to preserve his autonomy as an individual, to keep his personal affairs to himself, so long as his doing so does not harm any fellow-citizen or impair the proper functioning of society. The fact that a number of individuals live together in a society does not mean that anything pertaining to any of them is necessarily fair game for all the others.

The basic human right to privacy is clearly enshrined in international treaties which the United Kingdom has bound itself to observe. Article 12 of the United Nations Declaration of Human Rights and Article 17 of the International Covenant on Civil and Political Rights provide:

(1) No one shall be subjected to arbitrary or unlawful interference with his privacy, family, home or correspondence, nor to unlawful attacks on his honour and reputation.
(2) Everyone has the right to the protection of the law against such interference or attacks.[10]

[9] See Calcutt, *Freedom of the Press: Freedom of the Press*, Child & Co Lecture, 1994, [1994] Denning Law Journal, at 9.
[10] See chap. 12, 'Privacy', in Harris and Josephs (eds.), *The International Covenant on Civil and Political Rights and United Kingdom Law*, (1995).

Article 8 of the European Convention on Human Rights declares:

(1) Everyone has the right to respect for his private and family life, his home and his correspondence.

(2) There shall be no interference by a public authority with the exercise of this right except such as is in accordance with the law and is necessary in a democratic society in the interests of national security, public safety or the economic well-being of the country, for the prevention of disorder or crime, for the protection of health or morals, or for the protection of the rights and freedoms of others.

These international treaties, being no part of our domestic law, are not instruments to which English judges can ordinarily or directly give effect. But judges have none the less, on occasion, acknowledged the importance of the right to privacy. In one case Lord Denning said: 'While freedom of expression is a fundamental human right, so also is the right of privacy.'[11] In another case Lord Scarman described the right to privacy as 'fundamental'.[12] In yet another Lord Keith of Kinkel observed that 'the right to personal privacy is clearly one which the law should in this field seek to protect'.[13]

But the situation remains that there is in this country no recognition of a general right to privacy. This contrasts with the law in many other countries: in Germany, for instance, the courts have developed far reaching safeguards of personal privacy; and in France, following and reflecting the effect of a series of cases in the courts, a law was enacted in July 1970 which simply provided that 'each person has the right to have his privacy respected'.

This does not mean that the citizen whose privacy is invaded in England is bereft of any protection. In a wide range of situations he has a remedy. If anyone intrudes on his property against his wishes, he can sue the intruder for the tort of trespass. If anyone publicises false and damaging statements about him, he can sue for defamation (provided he is rich enough and brave enough to sue without the benefit of legal aid, which is unavailable in this field). If information of a confidential character is imparted in circumstances importing an obligation of confidence, then the recipient of the information and anyone receiving it from him with knowledge of its provenance, will be prevented from using the information to the detriment of the person to whom it relates. Often the relationship of confider and confidant is governed by agreement or implied agreement, as in the case (for example) of doctor and patient, accountant and client and banker and customer. But even where there is no agreement, the courts will within wide limits restrain breaches of confidence: a former husband may restrain his ex-wife from disclosing intimate details of their married life together,[14] a woman who has in strict confidence told her friend of a lesbian relationship which she has had

---

[11] *Schering Chemicals v Falkman* [1982] QB 1 at 21C.
[12] *Morris v Beardmore* [1981] AC 446 at 464 C.
[13] *AG v Guardian Newspapers Ltd* (No. 2) [1990] 1 AC 109 at 255.
[14] *Argyll v Argyll* [1967] Ch. 302.

may restrain the friend and a newspaper from exploiting that information;[15] a criminal suspect, photographed by the police, can prevent improper use of the photograph.[16] It is plain that the courts have, in recent years, extended the remedy for breach of confidence in order to afford a measure of protection for rights of personal privacy. This is true also of the emerging tort of harassment. Earlier suggestions that there was no tort of harassment[17] have been rejected, and the Court of Appeal has recognized the need to give effective relief to unwilling victims of molestation, harassment and pestering.[18] In cases involving children, whether or not they are wards of court, the courts routinely restrict disclosure which would be damaging to the interests of the child.[19]

These common law powers are buttressed by a number of specific statutory provisions directed to the preservation of confidentiality or privacy. An obvious example is the Data Protection Act 1984, which controls the use of personal information stored on computers; anonymity is also accorded to the victims of rape and some other sexual offences;[20] and there are wide-ranging statutory powers to restrain reports of proceedings, particularly where minors are involved.[21] The state also, and very properly, treats as confidential information which it has extracted from the citizen on an assurance of confidentiality: census returns and income tax returns are good examples.

An obvious question arises. If these remedies are available, and are effective, what is the need for a statutory tort of privacy? The proponents of reform give a clear answer. It is that, however effective these remedies may be in the cases to which they apply, there are other cases in which privacy is infringed and to which they do not apply, leaving the victim without a remedy. The Younger Committee received more complaints about the activities of the press than on any other aspect of the subject of privacy, but were uncertain about the scale of the problem.[22] Later authorities have felt less doubt. Public concern about intrusions into the private lives of individuals by certain sections of the press was assumed in the terms of reference given to the Calcutt Committee,[23] which received a wide range of complaints about intrusions into privacy.[24] A member of that Committee, a working journalist and former editor of *The Times*, himself an opponent of a statutory tort of privacy, has since written critically of the tabloids' activities:

My objection is not to the gun but to its aim, the archaic obsession of the tabloids with sex. All but two of the 17 scalps that Fleet Street claims to have cut from the heads of senior Tories of late are for sexual 'misbehaviour'. The misbehaviour is usually of a sort that none

---

[15] *Stephens v Avery* [1988] Ch. 449.
[16] *Hallewell v Chief Constable of Derbyshire* [1995] 1 WLR 804.
[17] *Patel v Patel* [1988] 2 FLR 179 at 182.
[18] *Khorasandjian v Bush* [1993] QB 272; *Burris v Azadani* [1995] 1 WLR 1372.
[19] For an unusual case see *Z (A Minor)* [1996] 2 WLR 88.
[20] Sexual Offences (Amendment) Act 1976.
[21] e.g., under s. 39 of the Children and Young Persons Act 1993.
[22] See *Report*, paras. 116, 123.　　　　　　　　　　　[23] See *Report*, para. 1.1
[24] Ibid., para. 4.1.

of the journalists would recognise as such in themselves or their colleagues. No politician is hounded from office for incompetence or wasting public money. It simply does not happen. The thinnest of justifications for sexual intrusion is that the victims are 'hypocrites', that those who preach family values and back-to-basics lay themselves open to intrusion, even if they are doing nothing that impinges on their public duties. That is garbage.[25]

He added:

The revelation of the contents of private phone calls or of the personal misfortunes of relatives of the Royal Family is ethically indefensible. They are rarely 'investigative' and merely involve paying money to a snooping intermediary. They are also breaches of the code drawn up by all newspapers back in 1990.[26]

Another journalist, the editor of *The Independent* Andrew Marr, has written in similar vein:

For intrusion isn't something endured by a few famous people for the amusement of the rest of us; it has spread everywhere. A country once famous for its quiet, its privet-hedged, suburban reticence has become obsessed by toe-curlingly intimate details of the sex-lives of quite obscure people. In our papers and increasingly in broadcasting, we have become a nosy nation.

   Privacy doesn't seem to be a big issue in this country. But it should be. The common view of privacy legislation is that it would help protect the politicians and is therefore a bad thing. But a proper privacy law—one which distinguished between intrusion into sexual lives (bad) and into business dealings, (good, or at least legitimate) would help rebuild the fence between public and private life ...[27]

In his Review of Press Self-Regulation[28] Sir David Calcutt, QC considered a number of instances involving both private individuals and public figures whose privacy had been invaded by the press in ways which the Press Complaints Commission had in his judgment proved ineffective to control or prevent. Among the public figures whose private affairs had been the subject of extensive newspaper coverage were Ms Clare Short MP, Mr Paddy Ashdown MP, The Prince and Princess of Wales, Mrs Virginia Bottomley MP and Mr David Mellor MP, QC. The National Heritage Committee was at pains to emphasize that it was as much concerned about the privacy of ordinary citizens as that of public figures,[29] but it observed:

So while the Committee believes that the public does have the right to know that the Chancellor of the Exchequer had legal advice partly financed by the tax payer, it does not believe that the public has the right to know details of the Chancellor's credit card transactions. While it is a matter for argument whether the public has the right to know that a member of the royal family or a cabinet minister is involved in an adulterous affair, the

---

[25] See Wacks, op. cit., at 171.   [26] Ibid., at 172.
[27] *The Independent*, 25 April 1996, 17.   [28] Chap. 4.
[29] *Report*, para. 5.

Committee does not believe that the public has the right to know the content of such a person's intimate conversations or the details of his or her sexual activity.[30]

In its Response to the Report of the National Heritage Committee, the Government did not contest that a problem existed; instead, it pinned its hope on an improved regime of self-regulation as its preferred solution.

One case[31] will serve to illustrate the sort of situation in which the courts have held themselves to be unable to afford adequate relief to a plaintiff who plainly deserved it. The plaintiff in the case was Mr Gordon Kaye, well known for his portrayal of the café-owner René in ''Allo 'Allo'. He was driving his car during a gale in January 1990 when a piece of wood became detached from an advertisement hoarding, smashed through the windscreen of his car and struck him on the head. He suffered severe injuries to his head and brain. He was taken to a hospital where he was on a life support machine for three days. He was then in intensive care until, still very ill and heavily sedated, he was moved to a private room. His accident naturally aroused intense interest among his many fans. For fear that his recovery might be hindered if he had too many visitors, and to lessen the risk of infection, the hospital authorities placed notices at the entrance to the ward asking visitors to see a member of the staff before visiting. Mr Kaye's agent agreed with the hospital a list of people who might be permitted to visit him, and this list was pinned up outside his room. A similar notice to that outside the ward was pinned on the door of the room itself. Acting on the instructions of their editor, a journalist and photographer from a publication known as *Sunday Sport* went to the hospital. They loitered outside Mr Kaye's room until an opportunity arose to enter unseen by the hospital staff, and enter they did, ignoring the notices on the door. They greeted Mr Kaye warmly, and gave him presents. He, so heavily medicated as to be in no more than partial command of his faculties, chatted to them amicably and discussed his recovery from the accident. The photographer then proceeded to take pictures of Mr Kaye, showing the substantial scars to his head, and also of a number of cards and flowers in the room. The taking of the photographs involved the use of a flashlight, which alerted the hospital staff to what was happening. The responsible nurses attempted to persuade the journalist and the photographer to leave, which they declined to do, but eventually security staff were summoned and they were ejected. *Sunday Sport* proposed to publish the record of the interview with Mr Kaye, regarding it as a 'great old-fashioned scoop' since it was his first interview following his accident.

In seeking relief to restrain *Sunday Sport* from publishing the record of this interview, Mr Kaye (by his agent) relied on four causes of action. These were libel, trespass to the person, passing-off, and malicious falsehood. The judge at first instance, understandably critical of the newspaper's conduct, granted the relief sought. The newspaper appealed.

---

[30] *Report*, para. 7.   [31] *Kaye v Robertson* [1991] FSR 62.

The basis of Mr Kaye's claim in libel was that the public would think the worse of him for choosing to give his first post-accident interview in a newspaper of as little repute as *Sunday Sport*. The Court of Appeal felt bound to regard this as a tenuous basis on which to grant pre-emptive relief, since Mr Kaye's choice of newspaper would only become known to readers of *Sunday Sport*, and it was doubtful whether they would think the worse of him for choosing the newspaper which they read. The complaint of trespass to the person was untenable, since this is legalese for assault, and no physical contact was made with Mr Kaye at all. The suggestion that the flashing of the light represented an assault on his eyes was regarded as unpersuasive. The cause of action in passing-off, which exists to prevent one trader passing-off his goods or services as those of a better known rival in order to attract business, was plainly inapposite to this situation. The only basis upon which the Court of Appeal felt able to grant relief was malicious falsehood: this rested on the contention that Mr Kaye had a commercial interest in his first interview following his accident, and that the newspaper would misleadingly damage this commercial interest if it suggested to the public that Mr Kaye had given this interview voluntarily. The court did not therefore restrain publication of the interview, because it felt unable to do so; all it could do was restrain publication of the interview without a clear indication that it had been given involuntarily. The newspaper accordingly went ahead and published the interview, boasting of the fact that it had been obtained without Mr Kaye's consent. All three members of the court, of whom I was one, regretted that in the absence of a law protecting privacy in this country they could afford Mr Kaye no more effective relief.

This decision has been the subject of much criticism, and it is perhaps a pity both that the case had to be prepared, argued and decided within a relatively short period and that the court contained no member expert in the law of intellectual property. The court has been taken to task by various commentators for showing a regrettable lack of inventiveness and boldness.[32] It has been suggested that if the hospital had been added as a plaintiff, appropriate relief could have been obtained which was not open to Mr Kaye alone, since as a patient he lacked the necessary interest to support an action for trespass to land.[33] This may well be so, although whether authority to sue on the hospital's behalf could have been obtained in time to make an effective application for pre-emptive relief is more doubtful. Once the interview had been published, it is hard to see what damage the hospital could have shown. It has also been suggested, to my mind more ingeniously than persuasively, that the action could have successfully been based on a breach of confidence.[34] My own view is that a claim for breach of confidence could not have been successfully made, at any rate without doing impermissible violence to

---

[32] Anthony Lester, QC, 'English Judges as Lawmakers' [1993] 269 at 285.

[33] Peter Prescott, QC, '*Kaye v Robertson*—a reply' (1991) 54 MLR 451 at 452.

[34] Fenwick and Phillipson, 'Confidence and Privacy: A re-examination', in *Cambridge Law Journal* at 452.

the principles upon which that cause of action is founded: the complaint in this case was not that information obtained or imparted in confidence was about to be misused, but that Mr Kaye's privacy had been the subject of a monstrous invasion but for which the interview would never have been obtained at all.

This again is a case involving a figure well-known to the public. It is naturally such cases which attract most attention. We should not however overlook the cases, in some ways even more deserving of protection, of those who suddenly and unexpectedly find themselves thrust into the limelight of unsought publicity: close relatives of those engulfed in a national tragedy, for example, or of those who have committed notorious crimes. Sir Louis Blom-Cooper, QC recently referred to the case of a family whose son had committed suicide. After the inquest the grieving family went to a restaurant and when they left a photographer took a picture of them which appeared in the local paper.[35] At a time when they are least able to resist such pressure, people in this position may find themselves literally hounded by packs of journalists and photographers.

It was against this background that the Calcutt Committee, Sir David Calcutt himself and the National Heritage Committee recommended that certain acts should be criminal.[36] These were the placing of a surveillance device on private property without the consent of the occupant, with intent to obtain personal information; the using of a surveillance device in relation to an individual who was on private property without the consent of the individual, with intent to obtain personal information about that individual; the taking of a photograph of an individual on private property without his consent; the publishing of a recording or an intimate photograph of an individual taken without consent; the entering of private property without the consent of the lawful occupant with intent to obtain personal information; and the dealing in material obtained through eavesdropping or use of long-range cameras where the parties were aware that the material was procured through illegal means. Sir David and the National Heritage Committee also recommended that these criminal offences should be buttressed by a civil remedy, a course which the Calcutt Committee did not reject but thought unnecessary if the other components of its report were accepted and implemented.

What then, are the arguments which have been held to outweigh the apparently powerful case in favour of legislating to create a civil wrong of privacy? There are, I think, six arguments to be considered. The first and most important is that any legislation along the lines suggested would undermine the fundamental right of free expression. It is, of course, true that the right of free expression is not only a fundamental right of the individual, but is also the lifeblood of a healthy democracy. No advocate of the proposed reforms has to my knowledge failed to take account of that vital fact. Even in countries such as the United States which give greatest weight to the right of free expression, however, that right is not treated as

---

[35] *New Law Journal,* 8 March 1996, at 327.
[36] See e.g., *Report of the National Heritage Committee* at para. 52.

absolute. It is subject to derogations, however small, and (perhaps as a result of
the article from which I quoted at the outset) a right to privacy has been recognized in the United States to a significantly greater extent than it has here, even if
in practice the privacy plaintiff tends to lose.[37] The question is not whether there
should be such derogations, but about their extent. In this context it is significant
that the international treaties already mentioned, which contain very clear safeguards of the fundamental right of free speech, also recognize that there may be
derogations from that right and also protect the right to privacy. Those who
drafted and ratified these instruments cannot have regarded these rights as irre-
concilable; their conduct would otherwise have involved a degree of cynicism
which I would myself be very reluctant to impute. The simple truth is that these
two rights are readily reconcilable in principle, since the sort of conduct which
would (if the proposed reforms were implemented) become criminal or tortious
have nothing whatever to do with the right of free expression as that is properly
understood.

Secondly, it has been suggested that the right of privacy is so elusive as to
make a workable and enforceable definition incapable of achievement. The
Younger Committee[38] was daunted by this problem of definition, and the government in its negative Response of July 1995 expressed similar apprehensions.[39]
The Calcutt Committee, on the other hand, while acknowledging the difficulty of
definition, found it possible to formulate a working definition which it regarded
as satisfactory.[40] The National Heritage Committee was able to define what it
meant by invasion of privacy.[41] The Lord Chancellor's consultation paper of July
1993 stated:[42]

As foreshadowed in Chapter 1, we therefore propose a new civil wrong in the following
terms:
  • A natural person shall have a cause of action, in tort or delict, in respect of conduct
    which constitutes an infringement of his privacy, causing him substantial distress,
    provided such distress would also have been suffered by a person of ordinary sensi-
    bilities in the circumstances of the complainant.
  • A natural person's privacy shall be taken to include matters appertaining to his
    health, personal communications, and family and personal relationships, and a right
    to be free from harassment and molestation.

If, as the proponents of reform believe, the conduct which it is desirable to
prohibit is sufficiently clear, it would perhaps be strange if difficulties of definition presented more than a minor obstacle to legislation.

A third and related objection is based on the difficulty of defining the appropriate defences available to a defendant accused of or sued for infringing privacy.
In fact, there has been considerable agreement by most of those who have consid-

---

[37] 'Fundamental Issues in Privacy Law', David Anderson, *Clifford Chance Lectures*, vol. 1 (1996),
chap. 7 at 123.   [38] *Report*, paras. 57–8.
[39] *Response,* para. 3.26.   [40] *Report*, para. 3.5–3.8.
[41] Ibid., para. 48.   [42] At para. 5.22.

ered this issue on the appropriate defences, the most obvious of which would be the consent of the party whose privacy is said to have been invaded. It has also been accepted that the public interest, of which various aspects have been identified, should justify what would otherwise be unjustifiable. These difficulties have, I would suggest, been exaggerated. For example, commenting on the National Heritage Committee's recommendation that it should be a criminal offence to take a photograph of an individual who is on private property without his consent, with a view to its publication and with intent that the individual should be identifiable, the Government's Response of July 1995 observed:

> As it stands, this provision would prevent a photographer from taking a photograph of Her Majesty the Queen on the balcony of Buckingham Palace, or opening a new ward in a hospital. That would certainly be indefensible.[43]

It certainly would. But how could it possibly be suggested that the Queen did not consent to the taking of a photograph of herself on the balcony of Buckingham Palace, when the taking of such a photograph would be the main reason for her appearing on the balcony at all? And how could it be suggested that the taking of a photograph on the opening of a new ward in a hospital was not taken with her consent, when the Queen would in all probability intend that such a photograph should be taken? To describe arguments of this kind as unpersuasive would be charitable.

Fourthly, it has been suggested that the law, if enacted, would be uncertain, because of the difficulty of deciding in borderline cases whether conduct amounted to an unlawful invasion of privacy or not. There is force in this. One could well imagine cases arising in which it might indeed be very hard to determine whether a Minister's out of hours behaviour threw doubt on his fitness for office, or whether the conduct of a minor member of the Royal Family raised questions about the future of the Monarchy. There are two answers to this objection. The first is that very many cases decided in the courts do involve the drawing of lines in difficult borderline cases. That is the job which judges are employed to do. If they draw the line in the wrong place, they are subject to review in the higher courts, and ultimately to the will of Parliament. In this as in other fields, a body of case law would build up over time which would give considerable guidance as to here the line lay. The second answer is that this objection has nothing at all to do with the legitimate complaints of those whose private affairs are of no significance to the general public at all. Even if the public's right to know were given the most ample recognition, as many would feel it should be, there would remain a residue of cases in which it could not plausibly be argued that the public had a right to know. The Press Complaints Commission has itself recognised that 'public interest' is not synonymous with what interests the public.[44]

---

[43] *Response*, para. 3.14.
[44] 'Privacy Jurisprudence of the Press Complaints Commission', Blom-Cooper and Pruitt, [1994] Anglo-American Law Review 133 at 156.

The fifth argument is that the problem is best left, at any rate for any the time being, to an improved regime of self-regulation of the press. If a new regime of self-regulation is now in being, effective to eliminate the abuses which have understandably given rise to public concern in the past, that is of course a result to be unreservedly welcomed. But the public is entitled to seek reassurance: over many years it has been promised a new dawn of effective self-regulation, but the light on the eastern hills has proved strangely elusive. It is now some years since we all started drinking in the last chance saloon. Those years have, however, seen the emergence of a remodelled Press Complaints Commission, administering a code which has provisions relating to privacy, listening devices, hospitals, harassment, intrusion into grief or shock, innocent relatives and friends, interviewing or photographing children, children in sex cases, victims of crime and so on. Plainly these provisions are aimed at many of the same mischiefs as would be actionable as an invasion of privacy. Perhaps the problem is now adequately addressed. If that is so, and self-regulation proves adequately effective, that might mean that a criminal offence (even if created) led to no prosecutions and a civil tort (even if introduced) led to no claims. That would involve some waste of legislative effort, but would not otherwise be harmful. On the other hand, if privacy is indeed regarded as an important right (and that would appear to be the undoubted basis of the treaties by which this country is bound) it may properly be regarded as unsatisfactory if an aggrieved party is unable to obtain a remedy by way of injunction and damages, neither of which any non-statutory body would have power to grant, at any rate in the absence of an agreement which does not at present exist. It may also be argued, in my view with some force, that this objection overlooks the educative effect of the law. There are some fields, of which drink-driving and race relations are perhaps two, in which the existence of legislation, quite apart from the cases in which it is invoked, plays a part in educating the public mind to recognize what is and is not acceptable conduct in a modern society.

The sixth objection is that the matter is best left, not to legislation, but to the courts, to work out appropriate safeguards on a case by case basis. This is the argument favoured by those who believe that the judges should receive a large injection of testosterone to bolster their flagging fertility. The prospects for procreation are, however, discouraging. The Younger Committee in 1972 reported: 'There is no legal right to privacy as such in the law of England and Wales.'[45] In a later case Sir Robert Megarry VC said: 'I can find nothing in the authorities or contentions that have been put before me to support the plaintiff's claim based on the right of privacy.'[46] In the case of Mr Kaye, it was bluntly stated: 'It is well known that in English law there is no right to privacy, and accordingly there is no right of action for breach of a person's privacy.'[47]

---

[45] *Report*, para. 83.
[46] *Malone v Metropolitan Police Commissioners* [1979] Ch. 344 at 375 B.
[47] *Per* Glidewell LJ, at 66.

If the judges are, on a case by case basis, to extend the protection available under the existing law, it seems clear that this will be done not by introducing a law of privacy so called, but by enlarging the boundaries of existing causes of action. The process is already evident, and is becoming more explicit. As a judge recently said:

If someone with a telephoto lens were to take from a distance and with no authority a picture of another engaged in some private act, his subsequent disclosure of the photograph would, in my judgment, as surely amount to a breach of confidence as if he had found or stolen a letter or diary in which the act was recounted and proceeded to publish it. In such a case, the law would protect what might reasonably be called a right of privacy, although the name accorded to it would be breach of confidence.[48]

This is, without doubt, one way forward. It may be the best way. I have some unease about appropriating causes of action to purposes quite alien to their original object, but this is how the law has developed in other fields and it does have the advantage that rules are forged in the furnace of everyday human experience.

The lecturer who asks himself a question must answer it. So I do. Should there be a law to protect rights of personal privacy? To a very large extent the law already does protect personal privacy; but to the extent that it does not, it should. The right must be narrowly drawn, to give full effect to the right of free speech and the public's right to know. It should strike only at significant infringements, such as would cause substantial distress to an ordinarily phlegmatic person. My preference would be for legislation, which would mean that the rules which the courts applied would carry the imprimatur of democratic approval. But if, for whatever reason, legislation is not forthcoming, I think it almost inevitable that cases will arise in the courts in which the need to give relief is obvious and pressing; and when such cases do arise, I do not think the courts will be found wanting.

---

[48] *Hallewell v Chief Constable of Derbyshire* [1995] 1 WLR 804 at 807, *per* Laws J. See also 'Emergence of a Right to Privacy from within the Law of Confidence?', Ng-Loy Wee Loon, [1996] 5 EIPR 307.

3

The Way We Live Now: Human Rights in the New Millennium*

In their more elevated moments, and after dinner, lawyers are wont to apostrophize the law as the ultimate guarantor of the rights and liberties of the citizen and to portray themselves as ministers of justice, protecting the weak against the strong. As Dr Christopher Hill reminds us in his recent book *Liberty against the Law*,[1] these perceptions have not always and universally been shared. Lawyers would have been banned from Sir Thomas More's Utopia,[2] and would also have been forbidden in Gerrard Winstanley's ideal commonwealth.[3] They were in fact forbidden to practise in Massachusetts in the early days of that colony,[4] a rule which some would no doubt like to reintroduce. In a plea to Parliament to reform the laws before it was too late, William Cole in 1659 argued that 'The major part of the laws made in this nation are founded on principles of tyranny, fallacy and oppression for the benefit of those that made them.'[5] By many radicals the law was seen not as a protection of the weak against the strong, but as a means by which the strong perfected their dominion over the weak.

It was not to be expected that the great Dicey, a professor of law, would share these radical sentiments. But he did accord the law a relatively subordinate role in the protection of individual rights and freedom in our society. He saw a sovereign Parliament as the prime protection of the citizen, no doubt envisaging a Parliament of robust and independent-minded members, astute to detect and quick to remedy unjustified encroachments upon individual liberty. It is of course true that over the centuries Parliament has been responsible for many major strides towards the protection of fundamental human rights and freedoms. One thinks, for example, of the statutory protection given to the ancient writ of habeas corpus,[6] to the extension of political rights with which the name of the second Earl Grey will be forever and gloriously associated, and of a series of measures improving the protection given to criminal defendants;[7] in our own time one may instance the provision of legal aid to enable the less well-to-do to assert their legal rights as plaintiffs or defendants,[8] to the detailed provisions of the Police and Criminal Evidence Act 1984 governing the rights of suspects, the introduction of time limits to restrict the periods of time spent by defendants in prison awaiting

---

* The Earl Grey Lecture: delivered at the University of Newcastle on 29 January 1998.
[1] (1996).
[2] Op. cit. 264.   [3] Op. cit. 268, n.13.   [4] Op. cit. 268.
[5] Op. cit. 267.   [6] Habeas Corpus Amendment Act 1679.
[7] e.g. Criminal Evidence Act 1898.   [8] Legal Aid and Advice Act 1949.

trial,[9] and the measures seeking to outlaw discrimination on the grounds of sex and race.[10] It is, however, plain that the robust and independent-minded member of Parliament is rarely able to make an effective impact when faced by a determined government. Governments for their part are understandably anxious to retain the support of the electorate and accordingly concentrate on measures which will earn the gratitude of a majority of the voters. Thus Parliamentary opinion is likely to reflect the opinion of the majority and show less concern for the interests of minorities. It is accordingly possible, looking back over our history, to identify a number of groups who have been either unpopular or disregarded and whose rights and freedoms have as a result been of little or no Parliamentary interest: Jews, Roman Catholics, dissenters; vagrants, vagabonds, beggars, gypsies; married women; children; prisoners; mental patients and the disabled; immigrants of various kinds, asylum seekers, aliens; homosexuals; strikers; single mothers; paedophiles. All of these have had occasion at some time or another to feel that the defence of their rights by a sovereign Parliament was something short of whole-hearted.

In Dicey's view the second great bulwark against infringement of the rights and freedoms of the individual was the force of public opinion. We have for centuries prided ourselves, not without reason, on our attachment of freedom. Thus in the great case of *Somersett*,[11] Francis Hargrave, as counsel, was able to submit persuasively that the air of England was too pure for any slave to breathe.[12] Alexis de Tocqueville, an acute observer, believed that in England there was 'more liberty in the customs than in the laws of the people' and thought it impossible to think of the English as living under any but a free government.[13] Public opinion is, however, the opinion of the majority; it rarely reflects the views of any minority, let alone an unpopular or disregarded minority. And while public opinion is capable of being generous and tolerant it is also capable of being vengeful and intolerant. Public opinion is an unreliable source of protection to those most in need of it.

This was, of course, exactly the problem which confronted the framers of the United States constitution. On the one hand, they wanted to establish a government by, of and for the people, a government reflecting the will of the people much more directly and faithfully than any government in the Old World at that time did. On the other hand, mindful perhaps of the experiences of the earlier colonists as a persecuted minority fleeing from oppression, they wanted to

---

[9] Prosecution of Offences Act 1985, s. 22.

[10] Sex Discrimination Act 1975; Race Relations Act 1976.

[11] *R v Somersett* (1772), 20 St.Tr.1.

[12] But this famous phrase originated in the Court of Star Chambers: see Nolan and Sedley, *The Making and Remaking of the British Constitution*, (1997), at 51.

[13] Quoted in Klug, Starmer, and Weir, *The Three Pillars of Liberty. Political Rights and Freedoms in the United Kingdom* (1996), a comprehensive and provocative work to which I am much indebted. See p. 74.

provide effective protection for those who might fall foul of the popularly controlled government. The solution was to enact the first ten amendments to the United States Constitution, almost contemporaneously with adoption of the constitution itself, so that the Bill of Rights (as these amendments were called) became, as it were, a codicil to the constitution and gave to those clauses the special, entrenched status of constitutional provisions. This is not a solution which we in this country have, until recently, been tempted to follow. Our Bill of Rights in 1689 did, it is true, contain some provisions which have later appeared in many other codes of human rights, such as the familiar prohibition of cruel and unusual punishment. But our own Bill of Rights was essentially part of an overall settlement between Parliament and the Crown, and did not purport to list or afford protection to what would then have been regarded as the basic rights of the citizen.

Protection of human rights in this country has accordingly depended, to a very large extent, on Dicey's third source of protection, the ordinary law of the land. Because of the way in which the common law develops, the ordinary law of the land has not formulated a list of rights and freedoms which may not be infringed. Rather, it has proscribed certain forms of conduct as unlawful, leaving the citizen free to do anything which is not so proscribed. Thus the freedom of the citizen has essentially rested on the absence of legal prohibition, a form of negative right which Dicey believed to afford the best protection. In many respects the ordinary law of the land, in particular the law of tort, has indeed, in this negative way, afforded the citizen considerable protection. Whereas a Bill of Rights might guarantee a right to liberty and security of the person, the law of tort has proscribed a threat of unwelcome physical contact as assault, deliberate and unwelcome physical contact as battery, and confinement of a person without lawful authority as false imprisonment. Where one person owes a duty not to cause physical injury to another, he is liable to that other in negligence if he fails to take reasonable care to prevent injury. The old aphorism that an Englishman's home is his castle finds its reflection in the legal rule that it is a trespass to enter land occupied or owned by another without permission. The courts have been reasonably generous in their application of these rules. Thus they have held it to be a battery to spit in someone's face,[14] and have held that a criminal assault can be committed over the telephone.[15] It has been held that an unwanted kiss, however affectionate in intention, may be a battery.[16] While there is no recognized right of free expression, everyone is free to write or say what they like provided it is not libellous or slanderous, or in breach of confidence, or contrary to the Official Secrets Act, or calculated to incite public disorder or racial hatred, or blasphemous, or in contempt of a court order, or in breach of statute. In many respects the protection afforded in this way has been solid and effective. But the development of the law by the

---

[14] *R v Cotesworth* (1704) 6 Mod. 172. [15] *R v Ireland* [1997] 3 WLR 534.
[16] *R v Chief Constable of Devon and Cornwall, ex parte CEGB* [1982] QB 458.

courts is inevitably piecemeal and incomplete. Where faced by an Act of Parliament which is clear in its meaning, or by subordinate legislation clearly within the powers conferred by a parent Act, the courts have been powerless to protect human rights even if the statute appeared to violate them. There have moreover been obvious deficiencies in the coverage which the common law has giving. When Mr Malone complained that his telephone had been intercepted and his right to privacy in that way violated, it was held that he had no right to privacy.[17] A similar conclusion was reached when Mr Kaye, a very well-known television actor, when in hospital following a very severe accident, found himself giving an interview to newspaper journalists to which, because of his mental state following the administration of drugs, he was in no state to consent.[18] The law has been slow and hesitant in recognizing a tort of harassment, although it is now clear that obsessive stalking of one person by another can both infringe the personal security of the victim and amount to a gross invasion of privacy.[19] The law of defamation has caused widespread dissatisfaction, the media complaining that their freedom of expression is unreasonably circumscribed, and many members of the public feeling that they have no adequate redress against an irresponsible and intrusive press. In deciding the cases coming before them, the courts have of course done their best to reflect the values of society, but they have been hampered by the absence of any standard to which reference can be made when choosing, as is often necessary, between competing values.

It is no doubt understandable that the British, proud of their tradition of liberty, were disinclined to emulate the example of the French revolutionaries who at Versailles in August 1789 made their Declaration of the Rights of Man and the Citizen, and there must also have been a natural reluctance to follow the example set by the rebellious colonists in the United States. Following exposure of the enormities which had been committed before and during the Second World War, one might perhaps have expected this country to give some form of statutory recognition to the United Nations' Universal Declaration of Human Rights in 1948, but it was generally felt, not least by us, that Britain's political and legal institutions had emerged from the trauma of these years with considerable credit. Thus when the Council of Europe, an international body then comprising the United Kingdom and nine other nations, promulgated the European Convention on Human Rights and Fundamental Freedoms, we were very much to the fore, both in signing the Convention at the end of 1950 and in ratifying, the first country to do so, in March 1951. But we took no steps to incorporate the Convention into our law, and did not until 1966 allow any British citizen to pursue a complaint in the Court of Human Rights at Strasbourg.

For some time there was no significant pressure to incorporate the Convention

---

[17] *Malone v Metropolitan Police Commissioner* [1979] Ch 344.

[18] *Kaye v Robertson* [1991] FSR 62.

[19] See Birks, *Harassment and Hubris: The Right to an Equality of Respect*, John Kelly Memorial Lecture, University College, Dublin, 16 Nov. 1995.

into our law. But in time such pressure did grow. The history of this debate has been very well described by Professor Michael Zander in his book *A Bill of Rights?*,[20] and that history need not be repeated. While some prominent figures, notably Lord Scarman, Lord Wade, and Lord Lester of Herne Hill, argued strongly and persistently for incorporation, governments of both colours were adamantly opposed. The turning point came in March 1993 when the late Mr John Smith, as leader of the Labour Party, observed in a lecture:

The quickest and simplest way of achieving democratic and legal recognition of a substantial package of human rights would be by incorporating into British law the European Convention on Human Rights.[21]

From then onwards the Labour Party espoused the cause of incorporation, although the Conservative government remained strongly opposed.

The reluctance of successive governments to incorporate is on one view surprising, given the very basic nature of these rights. But it may well be that it was indeed the basic nature of these rights which fostered the view that in a country such as ours with a long and respected tradition of tolerance and respect for individual rights, no resort to the Convention was needed. It is salutary to remind oneself what these rights are: in short, the right to life; freedom from torture or inhuman and degrading treatment or punishment; freedom from slavery, servitude or forced or compulsory labour; the right to liberty and security of the person; the right to a fair trial; freedom from prosecution and punishment for offences not criminal at the time when they were done; the right to respect for private and family life, home and correspondence; freedom of thought, conscience and religion; freedom of expression; freedom of assembly and association; the right to marry and found a family; the right to an effective remedy; and the prohibition of discrimination in the enjoyment of the rights and freedoms guaranteed by the Convention. By the First Protocol, ratified by the United Kingdom but not incorporated into our law, there were further rights: to enjoyment of one's possessions; to education in conformity with one's parents' religious and philosophical convictions; and to free elections.

These rights fall in different categories. Some are absolute, in the sense that a State may not opt out of, or derogate from, them, and unqualified. For example, no State may opt out of Article 2 (the right of life), Article 3 (the right not to be subjected to torture or to inhuman or degrading treatment or punishment), the first paragraph of Article 4 (the right not to be held in slavery or servitude) and Article 7 (the right not to be held liable for a criminal offence on the ground of any act or omission which had not been criminal at the time when the act or omission took place). Other Articles are not expressed in these absolute terms, but are subject to certain limited and express qualifications. This is true of Articles 8 (the right to respect of private and family life, home and correspondence); 9 (freedom

---

[20] 4th edn. (1997), chap. 1, 1–39.   [21] Op. cit., at 33.

of thought, conscience and religion); 10 (freedom of expression); and 11 (freedom of assembly and association). I quote the full terms of the last of these Articles, Article 11, as an example:

1. Everyone has the right to freedom of peaceful assembly and to freedom of association with others, including the right to form and to join Trade Unions for the protection of his interests.

2. No restrictions should be placed on the exercise of these rights other than such as are prescribed by law and are necessary in a democratic society in the interests of national security or public safety, for the prevention of disorder or crime, for the protection of health or morals or for the protection of the rights and freedoms of others. This article shall not prevent the imposition of lawful restrictions on the exercise of these rights by members of the armed forces, or the police or of the administration of the State.

Thus, if a complaint is made that Article 11 has been violated, the first question will be whether the complainant's right to freedom of peaceful assembly or to freedom of association with others has been restricted or obstructed. This will involve considering what the right in question should, and does, mean. If it is found that the right has not been violated, then that is plainly the end of the complaint. If, however, it is found that one of these rights has in some way been restricted or obstructed, then the court is obliged to apply a three-fold test. First it must ask whether the restriction or obstruction is 'prescribed by law'. This means that it must be governed by legal rules, which are sufficiently clear and accessible to enable the individual citizen to find out what the rules are. This, generally speaking, limits the freedom of the authorities to make the rules as they go along, and to make decisions directed to a particular case.[22] Secondly, the courts must ask whether the restriction or obstruction in question falls under one of the objectives listed in the Article, which has been held to be an exhaustive list and not simply by way of illustration.[23] If the object of the restriction does fall within one of the listed headings, then the court comes to the third and most difficult question: is the restriction necessary in a democratic society? To obtain a favourable answer to this question the State whose conduct is in issue must show that the restriction fulfils a pressing social need and that it is proportionate to the aim of responding to that need. While it is not incumbent on a State to show that the restriction is indispensable, it is not enough for it to show that the restriction is reasonable. The European Court of Human Rights has imposed a strict test of necessity, relying on such concepts as pluralism, tolerance and broad-mindedness. The overriding principle is clear: since the right in question is to be regarded as fundamental, any restriction of it must be strictly justified.[24]

The belief that our sovereign Parliament, public opinion and the common law were together enough to ensure compliance with the standards embodied in the

---

[22] *Sunday Times v UK* (1979–80) 2 EHRR 245.

[23] *Golder v UK* (1975) 1 EHRR 524.

[24] *Sunday Times v UK*, above.

European Convention has not survived our acceptance of the compulsory juris-diction of the European Court of Human Rights and the right for individual citi-zens to petition that court in 1966. The court has found violations by the United Kingdom in fifty cases, a larger number than in the case of any other State save Italy: and that total takes no account of the cases which have reached the European Commission of Human Rights, and which the United Kingdom has then settled in order to prevent the matter reaching the court. There are not very many Articles which the United Kingdom has not been found to have violated. In September 1995 we were held to have violated Article 2 (the right to life) in the famous case where members of the SAS shot dead three members of an IRA active service unit on a bombing mission in Gibraltar. This was a majority deci-sion of the court, and there are many (including myself) who find the reasoning of the minority more persuasive. We have been found to have violated Article 3 (the right not to be subjected to torture or to inhuman or degrading treatment or punishment) in cases arising from interrogation techniques used in the North of Ireland (1978), birching of a juvenile offender in the Isle of Man (1978), the treat-ment of a German national whose extradition was sought by the United States to face a murder charge in a State where the death penalty was still in force (1989), protection against the risk of torture (1996) and deportation of a drug courier with AIDS (1997). We have not, to my knowledge, been held to have violated Article 4 (the right not to be held in slavery or servitude). Article 5 (the right to liberty and security of the person) has been violated in relation to mental patients (1981), the granting of parole to mentally disordered offenders serving life sentences (1987), detainees held in the North of Ireland (1988), freedom from arbitrary detention (1966) and deportation of an immigrant (1996). We have violated Article 6 (the right to a fair and public hearing within a reasonable time by an independent and impartial tribunal established by law) in relation to prisoners (1975, 1983, and 1984), children (1987 and 1995), the grant of legal aid (1984, 1990, 1994, and 1996), delay in the hearing of civil proceedings (1993 and 1997), access to legal advice (1996) and the right to a fair trial (once in 1996 and twice in 1997). We were in 1995 found to have violated the prohibition of retroactive criminal laws in Article 7, when a criminal defendant was made the subject of a retrospective confiscation order under the Drug Trafficking Act 1986. We have been held to have violated Article 8 (the right to privacy) in relation to prisoners (1975, 1983, 1984, 1988, 1990, and 1992), homosexuals (1981), the tapping of telephones (1984), the application of residence qualifications in the Channel Islands (1984), immigration (1985), the care of children (1987, 1989, and 1995) and the interception of an Assistant Chief Constable's telephone in a police head-quarters (1997). We have not to my knowledge been held to have violated Article 9, the right to freedom of thought, conscience, and religion. We have been held to have violated Article 10, relating to freedom of expression, in three cases: one (decided in 1979) when the *Sunday Times* were restrained under the law of contempt from full reporting of the Thalidomide litigation; the second (in 1995) when the award of £1.5 million damages by a libel jury to Count Tolstoy was held to be disproportionate to the aim of protecting the rights of Lord Aldington as the person libelled and the third in 1996 when a journalist had been punished for refusing to identify a source. We were found in 1981 to have violated Article 11 (the right to freedom of association) in an important case which had the effect of prohibiting Trade Union closed shops. I am aware of no violation by the United Kingdom of Article 12 (the right to marry). Breaches of Article 13 (the right to an effective remedy) were found in relation to prisoners (1983 and 1984), immigrants (1985), deportees (1996), and an Assistant Chief Constable (1997). Discriminatory treatment of immigrants, contrary to Article 14, was found in 1985. A breach of Article 2 of the First Protocol to the Convention was found in 1982 when 2 children in a State school were caned contrary to their parents' beliefs concerning the proper education and punishment of children. For a nation proud of its culture of liberty the record is not, on any showing, a happy one.

Yet throughout this period the courts have been strictly debarred from direct application of the Convention in cases coming before the British courts for the sound legal reason that the Convention formed no part of our domestic law and hence formed no part of our domestic legal system. The courts did what they properly could to side-step these difficulties. Where they found a statute to be ambiguous, they presumed that Parliament intended to legislate in conformity with the Convention and the international obligations of the United Kingdom rather than in conflict with them. Where the common law was uncertain, unclear or incomplete, the courts ruled, wherever possible, in a manner which conformed with the Convention. Where the courts were asked to construe a domestic statute enacted to fulfil a Convention obligation, they presumed that the statute was intended to meet that obligation and construed the statute accordingly. Where the courts had to exercise a discretion, they usually sought to exercise it in a way which did not violate the Convention. When the courts were called upon to decide what, in a given situation, public policy demanded, they had regard to the international obligations of the United Kingdom embodied in the Convention as a source of guidance on what British public policy required. When relying on European Community law, binding on the United Kingdom courts, the judges sometimes found themselves applying the Convention, to the extent that Community law included laws derived from the Convention.[25] In these ways the Convention made a clandestine entry into British law by the back door, being forbidden to enter by the front. But these practices, if they mitigated the problem, did not solve it. Courts continued to reach decisions, without directly considering the impact of the Convention, in full knowledge that the Convention might compel a different answer. The dilemma was well explained by Lord Justice Simon Brown in a well publicized case concerning homosexuals in the Armed Forces:

---

[25] See HL Hansard, 3 July 1996, cols. 1465–7; and see Hunt, *Using Human Rights Law in English Courts*, (1997).

If the Convention for the Protection of Human Rights and Fundamental Freedoms were part of our law and we were accordingly entitled to ask whether the policy answers a pressing social need and whether the restriction on human rights involved can be shown proportionate to its benefits, then clearly the primary judgment (subject only to a limited 'margin of appreciation') would be for us and not for others; the constitutional balance would shift. But that is not the position. In exercising merely a secondary judgment, this court is bound, even though acting in a human rights context, to act with some reticence.[26]

In short, the court was unable to consider the Convention question whether the policy of the Ministry of Defence was necessary in a democratic society, and had to confine itself to the much more limited question whether that policy was, according to a strict test prescribed by the English authorities, irrational in the sense that no reasonable body could have adopted or maintained it.

I am, as is probably clear, an unqualified supporter of incorporation. The rights specified in the Convention are rightly regarded as fundamental. If the United Kingdom binds itself by international treaty to guarantee these rights to its citizens, it makes no sense that the rights should not be enforceable in and by British courts. Resort to the European Court in Strasbourg is very time consuming (cases take years and years to reach a decision) and not inexpensive. Decisions affecting this country, and other countries, would be strengthened if there were in the first instance a decision of a British court, and if British judges had the opportunity to contribute to the developing jurisprudence on human rights. It is, I think, very damaging to public confidence in our institutions that citizens should believe, usually but not always wrongly, that there exists a superior form of justice, available in Strasbourg but not at home. This is a field in which public perceptions matter. It is important to remember that nothing will be decided by judges after incorporation which would not be decided by judges now: the difference is that whereas at present cases are decided by judges of the forty member states who have acceded to the Council of Europe or are in the process of acceding, after incorporation the Convention will in the first instance be applied by British judges who can reasonably be expected to have the best knowledge of British life and society.

If one rejects as untenable the argument that British laws and practices already comply with the Convention, so that there is no need to incorporate the Convention into our law, there are really only three arguments against incorporation. The first is that it undermines the sovereignty of Parliament. If the courts were to be empowered to strike down, disapply or overrule Acts of Parliament on the ground that they conflicted with the Convention, there might be some force in this argument, although since the courts could only derive this power from Parliament, which could at any time take it away again, the argument has theoretical weaknesses; but it is certainly true, in my opinion, that if the courts were to be so empowered there would be inevitable and damaging conflict between

---

[26] *R v Ministry of Defence ex parte Smith* [1996] QB 517 at 541.

Parliament, as the democratically elected forum of the nation, and the courts who are not democratically accountable in any ordinary sense. Wisely, however, the Bill before Parliament does not confer this power on the courts. Instead, the courts are required 'so far as it is possible to do so' to read and give effect to primary legislation and subordinate legislation in a way which is compatible with the Convention. If, and only if, the higher courts are satisfied that a provision of primary legislation is incompatible with the Convention they will make a declaration to the effect, without making any order which would invalidate or overrule the primary legislation. If that declaration is challenged, no doubt an appeal will follow. If it is accepted, then the legislation requires the government of the day to implement a fast-track procedure to rectify the incompatibility in question. In applying Convention rules so far as possible, and in declaring that in given cases they are unable to do so, the courts are in no way challenging the sovereignty of Parliament, but are giving effect to what Parliament has ordained. The final decision on how to rectify any incompatibility with the Convention rests with Parliament. It is hard to see how even the most ardent democrat could regard this process as undermining the sovereignty of Parliament.

A second argument is that the possibility of a House of Lords decision on a Convention issue being overruled at Strasbourg would deprive the House of Lords judicial committee of its status as a supreme court. It is true that at present no appeal lies from a decision of the House of Lords sitting judicially. But Parliament has never hesitated to overrule a decision of the House of Lords which it found uncongenial. And if faced with contentious matters of European Community law, the House of Lords is obliged to seek a ruling from the European Court of Justice at Luxembourg, and obliged to give effect to that ruling in making its ultimate decision; while this is not strictly an appellate process, the result is very much the same as if it were, the only difference being that it remains for the national court to pronounce the final decision. It will in my view do nothing to undermine the authority or dignity of the House of Lords as our supreme court that, in matters arising from interpretation or application of a multilateral international treaty, the final decision is accorded to the body established by that treaty as the ultimate authority on those questions. I am not aware that this argument has been advanced by any judicial member of the House of Lords.

Thirdly, it is sometimes argued that the effect of incorporation will be to politicize the judiciary. I do not myself accept that argument. It is not an effect which has been demonstrated in any of the other member states which have incorporated the Convention. But I do accept that the judges will be called upon to perform a task somewhat different from that which they have habitually performed. Perhaps I may revert to my earlier discussion of Article 11, relating to the right to free assembly and freedom of association. I do not think that the judges, guided by earlier cases on the subject, will have difficulty deciding what the content of the right is, although arguable borderline cases are bound to arise. Nor do I think they will find it hard to decide whether any restriction relied upon is 'prescribed by law' and whether it falls under one or other of the exemptions specified in the Article. But when they come to decide whether any restriction relied upon is 'necessary in a democratic society', then I think that the judges will be undertaking a task which will be, to some extent at least, novel to them. They will have to decide whether there is a pressing social need for the restriction, and whether the restriction is proportionate to the mischief against which it is directed: both of these are problems which do not ordinarily confront judges in their familiar task of deciding applications for judicial review according to the threefold tests of illegality, irrationality and procedural impropriety. The problem was very well explained by the Lord Chancellor on the 16 December 1997 in his Tom Sargant Memorial Lecture when he said, under the heading of 'The Morality of Decisions', the following:

The Courts' decisions will be based on a more overtly principled, and perhaps moral, basis. The Court will look at the positive right. It will only accept an interference with that right where a justification, allowed under the Convention, is made out. The scrutiny will not be limited to seeing if the *words* of an exception can be satisfied. The Court will need to be satisfied that the *spirit* of this exception is made out. It will need to be satisfied that the interference with the protected right *is* justified in the public interest in a free democratic society. Moreover, the Courts will in this area have to apply the Convention principle of proportionality. This means the Court will be looking *substantively* at that question. It will not be limited to a secondary review of the decision making process but at the primary question of the merits of the decision itself.

In reaching its judgment, therefore, the Court will need to expand and explain its own view of whether the conduct is legitimate. It will produce in short a decision on the *morality* of the conduct and not simply its compliance with the bare letter of the law.[27]

Discussion of the new Bill so far would suggest, I think rightly, that one of the most difficult and sensitive areas of judgment will involve reconciliation of the right to privacy guaranteed by Article 8 with the right of free expression guaranteed by Article 10. While the law has up to now afforded some protection to privacy (in actions for breach of confidence, trespass, nuisance, the new tort of harassment, defamation, malicious falsehood, and under the data protection legislation) this protection has been patchy and inadequate. But it seems very likely that difficult questions will arise on where the right to privacy ends and the right to free expression begins. The media are understandably and properly concerned that the conduct of valuable investigative journalism may be hampered or even rendered impossible. It is very difficult, and probably unwise, to offer any opinion in advance about where the line is likely to be drawn. But it may be helpful to consider a case recently decided in Germany, under German law and not under the Convention.[28] The case concerned Princess Caroline of Monaco who was

---

[27] At p. 9.
[28] I am indebted to Mrs Justice Arden, Chairman of the Law Commission, for this example, given in a lecture at King's College London on 26 November 1997, 'The Future of the Law of Privacy'.

photographed by the press having a meal at a garden restaurant in France where she sat with a male friend on what appears to have been a romantic occasion. The case concerned a provision of the German constitution which states that 'The dignity of man shall be inviolable.' German law also provides that in general pictures of a person may be distributed only with that person's consent, but if the person is a person of contemporary history his or her consent is not required 'unless legally protected interests of the person are infringed'. The Supreme Court of Germany referred to the competing public interests in information protected by freedom of the press and the complainant's right to her personality. It observed:

The protection of a person's private sphere of life has a special importance when the two interests are weighed against each other. The right to respect for one's own private sphere of life is an emanation of the general right to one's own personality, which grants every person an autonomous area of personal life within which he can develop and experience his own individuality, free from the interferences of others. The right to be left alone and 'to belong to oneself' forms part of this area . . . As a result, since 1954, the German courts have, especially in the area of civil law, given particular weight to the right to respect one's own private sphere of life, i.e. treated it as a basic right guaranteed by the constitution which includes the right to one's own image . . .[29]

The Supreme Court rejected an argument accepted in the court below that privacy stopped 'at the doorstep' and that therefore the press were entitled to take photographs of the Princess who was dining in the corner of the public restaurant. The Supreme Court held that it was enough that the Princess had 'retreated to a place of seclusion where [she wished] to be left alone, as [could] be ascertained by objective criteria, and in a specific situation, where [she], relying on the fact of seclusion, acts in a way that [she] would not have done in public. An unjustified intrusion into this area occurs where pictures of that person are published if taken secretly or by stealth'. A place of seclusion could be in a place open to the public so long as the person in question shut himself or herself off from the public. Such a place could include a garden restaurant so long as the fact that the person had shut himself or herself off from the public was reasonably obvious to third persons. The Supreme Court went on:

When weighing up the various interests involved, the information value of the events depicted plays a significant role. The greater the interest of the public in being informed, the more the protected interests of the person of contemporary history must recede in favour of the public's need for information. Conversely, the need to protect the depicted person's privacy gains in weight as the value of the information which the public obtains from the photographs decreases. In this case the photographs which show the plaintiff with Vincent Lindon in a garden restaurant contain little, if anything, of value. Here, according to the appeal court, mere prying sensationalism, and the public's wish to be entertained,

---

[29] BGH 19 Dec. 1995, BGHZ 131, 332–46.

which is to be satisfied by pictures of totally private events of the plaintiff's life, cannot be recognized as worthy of protection.

On the other hand, in the view of the court, when the Princess was in public, for example dining or shopping, there was a public interest in knowing how she behaved even if she was not performing a public function. In these situations she had not retreated to a place secluded from the general public. On this basis, it would appear that under German law a person in the position of Princess Caroline is in general entitled to privacy in respect of things done in private, or in exceptional circumstances things done in public. Those exceptional circumstances were where the complainant had made it clear that she had retreated to a place of seclusion. In that situation she was not exposed to photographers in the same way as if she had appeared normally in public. These, plainly, are exceptional circumstances which would only rarely arise. But it would seem quite clear that, for example, photographs taken of her on private property by use of a long range lens would have been held to be an objectionable invasion of her right to privacy.

Fears have been expressed that incorporation of the Convention may lead, via the guarantee of privacy in Article 8, to a new and far-reaching form of media censorship developed and administered by the courts. Unsurprisingly no doubt, I regard those fears as misplaced. In the first place, it should be noted that the media will, for the first time in British history, enjoy a guaranteed right of free expression (not an absolute right, but a guaranteed right). Secondly, I point out that in the 30 years since we accepted the compulsory jurisdiction of the Strasbourg court, and although that court has found fourteen violations of Article 8 proved against us, none of them has had anything to do with invasions of privacy by the media. But incorporation does not alter the substance of Convention rights; it simply makes those rights enforceable here. Thirdly, the Convention (understandably in view of its genesis) is an instrument designed to protect citizens against the state. So while a citizen complaining of an invasion of privacy by the media could complain that the Press Complaints Commission had given no adequate redress, it would be to the commission (assuming it to be a public body) that the citizen would primarily look.

I think it likely that in the years to come we shall see some development in the law of privacy even in actions between private citizens. The recognition given by the Convention to the social value of privacy will, I think, encourage the courts to remedy what have been widely criticized as deficiencies in the existing law. But the common law scores its runs in singles: no boundaries, let alone sixes. The common law advances—to change the analogy—like one venturing onto a frozen lake, uncertain whether the ice will bear, and proceeding in small, cautious steps, with pauses to see if disaster occurs. It seems to me at least possible that the German case I have mentioned may contain some clues as to the direction our law may take. But I cannot for my part believe there will be any threat to serious investigative journalism. It is one thing to hold that a public figure may not be photographed, against his or her wishes, when dining privately in a secluded corner of a public restaurant. It is quite another to impose any restriction on photographs or reports which may bear on the fitness of any public or responsible figure to discharge the duties of their office.

So, in this respect at least, I view the new millennium with optimism. The rights and freedoms of all our citizens will, I think, be more effectively protected than ever before. It is time, perhaps, to remind oneselves of Milton's injunction:

Let not England forget her precedence of teaching nations how to live

4

*Tort and Human Rights**

For most English lawyers of (or above) a certain age, Human Rights formed no
named or identifiable part of the legal landscape in which they grew up. They had
heard of the Declaration of the Rights of Man and the Citizen approved by the
National Constituent Assembly at Versailles in August 1789 and knew of the
rights protected by the first ten amendments to the United States Constitution, but
these were no more than historical titbits, of little or no practical significance to
the practice of the law in England. They had heard or came to hear of the
Universal Declaration on Human Rights adopted by the United Nations in 1948,
of the European Convention for the Protection of Human Rights and Fundamental
Freedoms ratified by the United Kingdom in 1951, and of the International
Covenant on Civil and Political Rights which the United Kingdom signed in 1968
and ratified in 1976; but these again were matters of mere general knowledge,
interesting but (from a professional point of view) useless. Even the most rudimentary legal education did, of course, involve some exposure to legal provisions
giving protection against (for example) unlawful detention, wrongful arrest, the
issue of general search warrants, the imposition of cruel and unusual punishments, and the right to a fair trial according to law, but in the absence of an
entrenched written constitution, or any statutory code of human rights with any
claim to be comprehensive, these provisions were not generally seen as part of a
coherent attempt to protect rights identified as being of particular importance to
the citizen as a human being and a member of society.

In the international instruments already mentioned, and in the charters and
bills of rights adopted by an ever-increasing number of countries, it has been the
practice to define (subject to appropriate qualifications) a series of different rights
identified as deserving special protection. This is no doubt necessary and desirable for drafting purposes, to avoid undue generality and complexity. But it would
seem that most if not all of the primary rights usually singled out for special
protection are related directly or indirectly to the belief that the individual citizen
should enjoy as much personal autonomy as is consistent with the reasonable
interests of other citizens and the community as a whole. In other words, the individual citizen should be left to do his or her own thing to the maximum extent
possible without impinging on the rights of others; where restraints on personal
autonomy are called for they should be the minimum needed to serve their
purpose; where penalties for anti-social conduct are called for, they should be for

* Essay first published in Peter Cane and Jane Stapleton, *The Law of Obligations: Essays in
Celebration of John Fleming* (Oxford: Clarendon Press, 1998), 1–12.

proved breaches of known rules, imposed by a fair and impartial body. The right to life; to freedom from inhuman and degrading treatment and slavery; to liberty of the person; to a fair trial before an independent and impartial tribunal within a reasonable time; to privacy; to freedom of thought, conscience, and religion; to freedom of expression; to freedom of association; to freedom to marry and found a family; to own property: all fit into this pattern. In referring to Fundamental Freedoms, as its full name does, the European Convention makes an important point: freedom from unwarranted interference with an individual citizen's right to do his or her own thing lies at the heart of what is now recognized as a discrete field of legal study known as Human Rights.

The absence in the United Kingdom of an entrenched written constitution or any comprehensive statutory code of human rights has not, of course, meant that such rights have been unprotected. But it has inevitably meant that protection, where it exists, has been piecemeal and ad hoc. Various fields of law have made their contribution to this protection: statute, constitutional law, criminal law, equity, rules of practice and procedure. But it would seem clear that it is the law of tort, to which the late Professor Fleming made such a notable and enduring contribution, which has borne the heat and burden of the battle.

To define or accurately to describe what is meant by tort law is one of the oldest and most intriguing of legal conundrums. For present purposes, however, one may perhaps borrow the definition to be found in *Street on Torts*, where the aim of the law of torts is said to be

to define the obligations on one member of society to his or her fellows, and to adjust, once it is decided that some adjustment is to be made, those losses which must inevitably result from the ever-increasing activities of those who live in a common society. The adjustment is made by providing compensation for the harm suffered by those whose interests have been invaded owing to the conduct of others.[1]

The interests protected by the law of tort, it is suggested in *Street*, include:

(1) intentional invasion of personal and proprietary interests;
(2) interests in economic relations, business and trading;
(3) interests in intellectual property;
(4) negligent interference with personal proprietary and economic interests;
(5) further protection of personal and proprietary interests;
(6) reputation;
(7) due process; and
(8) miscellaneous interests.[2]

If this definition and this breakdown are accepted, the aptness of tort law as a

---

[1] M. Brazier, *Street on Torts*, (9th edn., 1993), 1.

[2] Ibid. 5–7. And see the valuable contribution by Robert S. French, 'Statutory Modelling of Torts', to Nicholas J. Mullany (ed.), *Torts in the Nineties* (1997), a fascinating survey of the law of tort in several jurisdictions from which I have derived much benefit.

vehicle for protecting human rights can be readily recognized, for both acknowledge that the personal autonomy of A, his freedom to do his own thing, must be circumscribed at the point where his activity becomes harmful to B to the extent that the law gives B a right to complain. So, at any rate *faute de mieux*, the law of tort is a suitable vehicle for protecting human rights. But whereas an entrenched written constitution or a statutory code of rights will set out and identify the rights to be protected, with any appropriate qualifications, the law of tort operates in a quite different and negative way, by proscribing and providing remedies for certain acts and omissions judged to be unacceptable. To the extent that the law of tort proscribes all acts and omissions which undermine or encroach on the rights which a constitution or a statutory code would protect, it may give the citizen the same rights, the same personal autonomy, the same freedom from unwarranted interference, as a constitution or a code. If, as seems likely at the time of writing, the United Kingdom is at last set to incorporate the European Convention into its municipal law, it is timely and perhaps interesting to consider how effective the law, and in particular the law of tort, has been in practice in safeguarding the basic human rights and fundamental freedoms of the British citizen.

It is probably safe to assume that most citizens would in the last resort, however unheroically, value their own physical security above all else. This is recognized in the international instruments already mentioned. It is also recognized by the law of tort. If A threatens B with unwelcome physical contact, he commits the tort of assault. If he deliberately makes unwelcome physical contact with B, he commits the tort of battery. If, without lawful authority, he confines B and restricts the freedom of B to go where B wishes, he commits the tort of false imprisonment. If, owing a duty to take reasonable care not to cause physical injury to B, A fails to take such care and so causes or allows such injury to be caused to B, A is liable to B for the tort of negligence. Generally speaking, the law of tort protects the individual's right to physical autonomy.

The old adage that an Englishman's home is his castle reflects another aspect of personal autonomy, the right of the individual who is causing no harm to anyone to live peaceably in his habitation and refuse entry to all unwelcome intruders. Over the years an increasing number of public officials have won the right, in defined circumstances, to enter the castle against the wishes of the occupier, but the basic right, subject to these exceptions, survives. And that is, of course, because the law of tort proscribes unauthorized entry on to land owned or occupied by another.

True to form, neither the law of tort nor any other branch of English law provides any guarantee of the individual's right to publish (by speech or writing) what he wishes. Such a right, if it may be called such, exists only by default, by the absence of any legal objection to such publication. Various branches of the law proscribe different forms of publication: that which is libellous or slanderous; that which breaches confidence; that which discloses official secrets or is subversive or incites public disorder or racial hatred; that which is blasphemous; that which is prohibited by statute; that which breaches orders made by the court; and so on. But despite the multiplicity of grounds upon which publication may be proscribed, the citizen's freedom to publish what he wishes is in practice much more than interstitial. It conveys a truer impression to state that the British citizen may publish what he wishes with impunity in the absence of legal objection than to state that in the absence of legal objection the British Citizen may publish what he wishes with impunity.

So far this is all plain sailing through smooth water safely protected by the harbour wall. But beyond the harbour wall the condition of the sea is more taxing. There are breakers and cross-currents and sunken wrecks and uncharted waters. No survey of the efficacy of tort law in protecting human rights can respectably shirk the challenge of the open sea.

The torts of assault and battery afford adequate protection against the more crude and obvious threats or acts of physical violence. And the courts have avoided undue literalism in their approach to these torts. It was long ago held to be a battery to throw water over a person or spit in his face,[3] or to overturn a chair on which he is sitting[4] or a ladder on which he is standing.[5] It is now clear that a criminal defendant may commit an assault over the telephone,[6] and there would seem to be no good reason why a defendant sued in tort would not be similarly liable as has been held in Australia.[7] In *R v Chief Constable of Devon and Cornwall, ex parte CEGB*[8] Lord Denning MR relied on old authority in holding that 'an unwanted kiss may be a battery' and most lawyers would surely regard this as an acceptable conclusion. But the requirement that to be actionable contact must be non-consensual may, and in the past has, led to strange (and to modern eyes) unacceptable results. In *Latter v Braddell*,[9] for example, a female servant was examined by a doctor on the instructions of the employer who thought (wrongly) that the servant was pregnant. The servant submitted to the examination believing that she was obliged to do so but protested and sobbed throughout. It was held, by a majority, that the servant's reluctant obedience did not amount to a lack of consent, so her claim failed. One can only hope that the result would be different today. One could not, however, be sanguine about a plaintiff's chances of success if she invoked the tortious law of assault to complain of a friendly but unsolicited invitation to indulge in sexual relations. This might be deeply offensive to the plaintiff, but if accompanied by no threat of force and if not persisted in, and if made in the belief that the invitation would be welcome, would not at all obviously amount to an assault.[10] Even if the English law of tort embodied the rule in section 46 of the American Law Institute's *Restatement (Second) of Torts* (1965) that 'One who by extreme and outrageous conduct intentionally or

---

[3] *R v Cotesworth* (1704) 6 Mod. 172.   [4] *Hopper v Reeve* (1817) 7 Taunt. 698.
[5] *Collins v Renison* (1754) Sayer 138.   [6] *R v Ireland* [1997] 3 WLR 534.
[7] *Barton v Armstrong* [1969] 2 NSWR 451. J. Conaghan & W. Mansell, *The Wrongs of Tort* (1993), 133.   [8] [1982] QB 458.
[9] (1881) 44 LT 369.   [10] Conaghan & Mansell, n. 7 above, 137.

recklessly causes severe emotional distress to another is subject to liability for such emotional distress', it must be doubtful whether a case such as this would be covered; and it must further be doubted whether *Wilkinson v Downton*[11] or any later English authority could or would be extended so far.[12]

In its continuing tolerance of corporal punishment inflicted on children (provided it is not 'excessive', whatever that may mean), the English law of tort would be held by international and progressive opinion to have failed to acknowledge what would now be widely recognized as the rights of the child. But this is an area in which, even now, there is perhaps no consensus of domestic opinion. More significant, certainly in practical terms, are the difficulties which face plaintiffs seeking to complain as adults of sexual abuse suffered as children. There can be no doubt that such abuse, if inflicted without consent and if the subject of timeous action, can found a successful complaint of battery. But save, it seems, in Canada, there appear to have been few actions,[13] and the explanation can scarcely be the absence of grounds for complaint. In England the House of Lords in *Stubbings v Webb*[14] applied the limitation rules in a way which posed real difficulties for plaintiffs, but the European Court of Human Rights was content to accept that decision.[15] The Canadian cases, however, show that difficulty arises from the requirement that conduct must, to be a battery, be non-consensual.[16] Even where an initial act of abuse was non-consensual, courts have been willing to hold that later acts in a sustained course of abuse took place with the consent of the child. The problem may perhaps have been resolved, or at least clarified, by the decision of the Supreme Court of Canada in *Norberg v Wynrib*,[17] holding that the traditional assumption of individual autonomy and free will could not safely be made, even between adults, in the case of 'power dependent relationships' such as those of parent–child, psychotherapist–patient, physician–patient, priest–penitent, professor–student, attorney–client, and employer–employee. Unless, in a similar case, the English courts were to adopt a similar approach, the protection given by tort law to a human right of obvious importance would seem clearly defective.

The essential mischief of false imprisonment, where A without lawful authority detains B, is clear enough. But even this tort becomes a little fuzzy at the edges.[18] A surprising number of questions arise. Where an act of detention is

---

[11] [1897] 2 QB 57.

[12] Account should, however, be taken of P. B. Birks's erudite and sustained argument to the contrary in 'Harassment and Hubris: The Right to an Equality of Respect', John Maurice Kelly Memorial Lecture of 1995 (University College Dublin, 1995).

[13] See P. B. Feldthusen, 'The Canadian Experiment with the Civil Action for Sexual Battery' in Mullany, n. 2 above, 274.

[14] [1993] AC 498.   [15] (1997) 23 EHRR 213.

[16] *Madelena v Kunn* (1989) 38 BCLR (2d) 273; (1989) 61 DLR (4th) 392; *Lyth v Dagg* (1988) 46 CCLT 25.   [17] [1992] 2 SCR 226.

[18] See F. A. Trindade, 'The Modern Tort of False Imprisonment' in Mullany, n. 2 above, 229, to whose analysis I am much indebted.

established, must the plaintiff show that the detention was wrongful or the defendant show that it was not? English law, it would seem, gives the first answer,[19]
Australian law the second.[20] Is the tort established if the detention complained of
is not intentional but reckless or negligent? To this question English law gives a
negative,[21] Australian law an affirmative,[22] answer. So if A turns off the power to
a lift on Friday evening, carelessly failing to check whether any passenger is in
the lift, with the result that B spends the weekend in a stationary lift between
floors with no means of escape, his claim for damages for false imprisonment
would (it seems) fail in England but succeed in Australia. What if the restraint on
B's freedom of movement is brought about indirectly, as by an indication that
harm will follow to B, or to another close to B, if B moves from where he is? It
appears that Australian courts would give a remedy in such circumstances.[23] If A,
claiming to be an eyewitness of a serious crime, dishonestly and maliciously
identifies B to a police officer as the perpetrator, with the result that the officer,
reasonably believing the information to be reliable, arrests B, is A liable in tort
for the ensuing detention of B? Until recently, English law would again have
given a negative answer, unless A asked the officer to take B into custody.[24] But
the recent decision of the House of Lords (relating to malicious prosecution) in
Martin v Watson[25] may throw doubt on earlier authority. It seems likely that the
Australian courts would regard A's conduct as causative of the detention. If B is
lawfully ordered to serve a term of imprisonment, has he any right of complaint
against the prison authorities if his residual liberty as a prisoner is infringed or if
the conditions of his confinement fall clearly below the minimum acceptable
level? After some hesitation,[26] English law appears for the present to give a
clearly negative answer.[27] Whether this negative answer can survive incorporation of the European Convention may be doubtful; there is perhaps less room for
doubt whether it should. Must a detention, to be tortious, be total, or does A avoid
liability if he leaves B with some means of escape? The answer here must surely
turn on the acceptability, in fact, of the means of escape. A can scarcely be liable
if he locks B in a room which B is free and able to leave by an open French

[19] *Fowler v Lanning* [1959] 1 QB 426.
[20] *McHale v Watson* (1964) 111 CLR 384; *Tsouvalla v Bini* [1966] SASR 157; *Carnegie v State of Victoria*, (Supr. C. Victoria, Sept. 1989),
[21] *Letang v Cooper* [1965] 1 QB 232.
[22] *Williams v Milotin* (1957) 97 CLR 465; Trindade, n. 18 above at 252.
[23] Trindade, n. 18 above at 232; *R v Garrett* (1988) 50 SASR 392; and see *Chayton v London, New York and Paris Association of Fashion Ltd* (1962) 30 DLR (2d) 527.
[24] *Grinham v Willey* (1858) 4 H & N 496; *Pike v Waldrum and Peninsular & Oriental Steam Navigation Co.* [1952] 1 Lloyd's Rep. 431; *Davidson v Chief Constable of North Wales* [1994] 2 All ER 597.
[25] [1996] AC 74.
[26] *Middleweek v Chief Constable of Merseyside (Note)* [1992] 1 AC 179 at 186; *Weldon v Home Office* [1992] 1 AC 58 at 139.
[27] *R v Deputy Governor of Parkhurst Prison, ex p Hague* [1992] 1 AC 58; *Weldon v Home Office*, ibid.

window. But it would be otherwise if A drove off in his car with B an unwilling passenger, able to leave only by throwing himself out of the moving car. What if B, having voluntarily agreed to some restraint on his freedom of movement, seeks to revoke his agreement in breach of contract? Earlier this century it was held that B could not complain of false imprisonment if detained in accordance with the conditions of the original contract.[28] There is, however, authority in England,[29] Canada,[30] and Australia[31] that A is not entitled to detain B for non-payment of a contractual debt, and it would seem clear in principle that B should not be personally detained as security for his contractual performance. Is it necessary to establish the tort that B should know at the time that he is being detained? Both in England[32] and the United States[33] it was held or thought that it was. But doubts were expressed.[34] In the United States the rule was changed.[35] In England knowledge of the detention was authoritatively held not to be a necessary ingredient of a successful claim.[36] This view has found favour in Australia.[37] Need A, to be liable, know that he is wrongfully detaining B? Not in Australia: in *Cowell v Corrective Services Commission of New South Wales*[38] the prison authorities were held liable in false imprisonment for detaining the plaintiff beyond the period permitted by law as a result of miscalculating the remission to which he was entitled. There can be little doubt that the same result would follow in England.

It not infrequently happens, often following the end of an acquaintance or the breakdown of a relationship, that the rejected party finds it impossible to accept the finality of the rupture and reacts by bombarding the other party with oral and written communications, messages, presents, and telephone calls, or by loitering at or near the other party's home or workplace or places where they spend their leisure time. The same behaviour may of course have quite other motivations (it is an affliction to which many well-known public figures are subject) but the harmful effect on the victim may be the same, and is often serious. This is conduct which plainly infringes the personal autonomy of the victim, representing as it does an unwarrantable violation of the victim's right to be left alone. Yet the courts in England have been curiously slow to treat such conduct as tortious. In *Patel v Patel*[39] it was roundly stated that no tort of harassment existed. This view was soon rejected by the Court of Appeal in *Khorasandjian v Bush*[40] and

---

[28] *Robinson v The Balmain New Ferry Co. Ltd* [1910] AC 295; *Herd v Weardale Steel, Coal and Coke Co. Ltd* [1915] AC 67.
[29] *Sunbolf v Alford* (1838) 3 M & M 248.
[30] *Bahner v Marwest Hotel Co. Ltd* (1969) 6 DLR (3d) 322.
[31] *Gold v Healco Services (Vic) Pty Ltd*, (Supr. C. Victoria, 15 Apr. 1988).
[32] *Herring v Boyle* (1834) 1 CM & R 377.
[33] *Restatement of Torts* (1934), para 42.
[34] *Meering v Grahame-White Aviation Co. Ltd* (1919) 122 LT 44; Trindade, n. 18 above at 247.
[35] *Restatement of Torts, Second* (1965) para 35.
[36] *Murray v Ministry of Defence* [1988] 1 WLR 692.
[37] *Myer Stores Ltd v Soo* [1991] 2 VR 597.　　　　[38] (1988) 13 NSWLR 714.
[39] [1988] 2 FLR 179.　　　　[40] [1993] QB 727.

Burris v Azadani.[41] But the majority decision in the earlier of those cases, holding that a daughter living as a licensee in her mother's house could complain of
unwanted telephone calls in private nuisance, has since been disapproved by the
House of Lords.[42] The House did not, however, go on to hold that there existed
no tort of harassment. The criminal law witnessed a similar development: in *R v
Burstow*,[43] a case in which conduct of the kind described had caused the victim
to suffer psychiatric damage, the defendant was convicted of inflicting grievous
bodily harm. In the light of these developments it must be doubted whether there
was a lacuna in the law which the Protection from Harassment Act 1997 was
needed to fill.[44]

The most notable breach in the walls of the Englishman's castle came to light
with the decision, in *Malone v Metropolitan Police Commissioner*,[45] that the civil
law of England offered no protection against the official interception of telephone
communications or, by necessary analogy, postal communications. It required
resort to Strasbourg, and an Act of Parliament,[46] to remedy the deficiency. The
remedy was only partial, however, for although the Security Service was
subjected by statute[47] to strict controls and scrutiny in entering private premises
to plant electronic listening devices, the police were subject to no such control or
scrutiny, and when this obviously lawless conduct by the police came to light the
initial response of the government of the day, supported by the Opposition, was
not to outlaw such behaviour but to give it statutory sanction. Happily, in the end,
more principled counsels prevailed,[48] largely as a result of judicial criticism. Such
entry by the police was, of course, tortious, but since it was covert the victim
never became aware of it and so was unable to sue; and even if he suspected such
entry he would be likely to face insuperable problems of proof. That the law of
tort in this instance afforded inadequate protection of the citizen's basic rights
seem clear; that a constitutional guarantee would afford more effective protection
in practice is perhaps less clear.

Reviewing the law of defamation from a New South Wales perspective, the
Hon Mr Justice Dennis Mahoney has written,

The law of public defamation is seen publicly to be a failure: it does not do what it should
do and what it does it does not do in an efficient, effective and timeous way.[49]

Most commentators familiar with the English law of defamation would tend to
take a similar view, regarding this as a field in which the law of tort most obviously

---

[41] [1965] 1 WLR 1372.   [42] *Hunter v Canary Wharf Ltd* [1997] 2 WLR 684.
[43] [1997] 3 WLR 534.
[44] This statute was enacted to criminalize what is popularly known as 'stalking'. Where such
conduct caused physical or psychiatric injury it was already criminal. It was also, even in the absence
of injury, restrainable by civil injunction.
[45] [1979] Ch 344.   [46] Interception of Communications Act 1985.
[47] Security Service Act 1989.   [48] The Police Act 1997, Pt III.
[49] 'Defamation Law—A Time to Rethink', in Mullany, n. 2 above, 261.

failed to protect the rights of the citizen in the way and to the extent the citizen could reasonably expect.

While most would agree in expressing dissatisfaction, however, the grounds of dissatisfaction would be quite different. The media, and particularly the Press, criticize the English law of defamation (and perhaps, to a lesser extent, contempt) as so onerous and restrictive as to inhibit valuable investigative journalism and confine within too narrow a compass the basic right of free expression. Particular objection is taken to the rule which requires a defendant to prove the truth of a defamatory statement rather than the plaintiff its untruth, to the absence of a rule such as that laid down in *New York Times v Sullivan*[50] giving special protection to publishers of statements made about public figures, to the inadequate protection accorded to journalists' sources, to the willingness of the courts to impose restraints prior to publication, and to the disproportionate awards of damages not infrequently made by juries to successful plaintiffs.

Others, notably including those exposed to adverse or unwanted publicity in the Press, voice a different complaint: that the cost and risk of suing any major organ of the Press are such as can be contemplated, in the absence of Legal Aid, only by those who are very wealthy or very foolhardy or (preferably) both, so that in practice the law affords little or no protection to the ordinary citizen; and that the law does too little to protect the privacy of the citizen against the intrusions of a vulgar and often irresponsible Press.

Many objective observers would probably see force in both sides of this argument. It is perhaps contrary to general principle and surprising that a plaintiff who comes to court to complain of a false and defamatory statement should not have to show that the statement is false as well as defamatory, although it may be questionable how much practical difference a change in the rule would make. On the merits of the rule in *New York Times v Sullivan* there is much to be said both for and against, as evidenced by the rejection of the rule in England[51] and Canada[52] and its acceptance in Australia.[53] But the courts have resolved a long-running issue as to whether local authorities enjoyed a reputation protected by the law of defamation in favour of free speech.[54] It has long been the rule that an interlocutory injunction restraining publication should not be granted where a defendant plausibly undertakes to justify.[55] And the level of jury awards, already the subject of adverse decision in Strasbourg,[56] has in recent years become the subject of more effective control and review.[57]

---

[50] 376 US 254 (1964).

[51] *Derbyshire County Council v Times Newspapers Ltd* [1993] AC 534.

[52] *Hill v Church of Scientology of Toronto* [1995] 2 SCR 1130.

[53] *Theophanous v The Herald & Weekly Times Ltd* (1994) 182 CLR 104.

[54] *Derbyshire County Council v Times Newspapers Ltd*, above, resolving a difference between *Manchester Corporation v Williams* [1891] 1 QB 94 and *National Union of General and Municipal Workers v Gillian* [1946] KB 81 and *Bognor Regis Urban District Council v Campion* [1972] 2 QB 169.   [55] *Bonnard v Perryman* [1891] 2 Ch 269.

[56] *Tolstoy Miloslavsky v United Kingdom* (1995) 20 EHRR 442.

[57] *John & MGN Ltd* [1997] QB 586.

The problems facing a defamation plaintiff are indeed formidable, and it remains to be seen how effective a judicially inspired statutory reform which has recently been enacted proves in practice.[58] But in the view of many the most glaring failure of English tort law in this areas has been in declining to recognize the invasion of personal privacy as an independent tort. As has been pointed out before,[59] much has been done, in particular by extending and adapting equitable rules on breach of confidence, to protect the privacy of the citizen. But the Court of Appeal did hold, in the notorious case of *Kaye v Robertson*,[60] that English law recognized no right to privacy, and felt unable to grant the substantial relief it would have wished. This decision has provoked much criticism and disagreement,[61] and it seems clear that in (for instance) the United States, France, Germany, Switzerland, and Canada the plaintiff would have fared better.[62] In his thought-provoking contribution to *Torts in the Nineties*, Professor Todd has valuably drawn attention to several cases which give pause for thought.

As long ago as 1931, a Californian court held that giving publicity eight years after the event to the facts that the plaintiff had worked as a prostitute and had been tried and acquitted of murder was an actionable violation of her right to privacy.[63] In *Tucker v News Media Ownership Ltd* a New Zealand plaintiff, seeking by means of a publicity campaign to raise funds for a major operation abroad, learned that the media proposed to publish details of his previous convictions of sex offences and applied for interim injunctive relief. This he was successful in obtaining at first instance and on appeal.[64] Before trial, disclosure was made by other sources, and the injunctions were discharged, but McGechan J tentatively supported the view taken by the earlier courts.[65] In *Bradley v Wingnut Films Ltd*[66] the defendants made a horror film part of which was shot in a public cemetery and the plaintiff complained (among other things) that the inclusion of his family tombstone in the film was an unlawful invasion of his privacy. The claim failed on the facts, but Gallen J was willing to hold that the law of New Zealand recognized in principle the cause of action sued upon.

It would be very strongly arguable, to say the least, that under the English common law all three of these claims would be struck out as disclosing no course of action. The result would then necessarily be to deprive the plaintiff of relief (unless some other cause of action could be ingeniously adapted to cover the facts). Are these cases in which the plaintiff ought to be protected? That is a much

---

[58] Defamation Act 1996.

[59] Notably by D. J. Serpp in his important article 'English Judicial Recognition of a Right to Privacy', (1983) 3 OJLS 325; also by myself, 'Should there be a Law to Protect Rights of Personal Privacy?', (1996) 5 EHRLR 450.   [60] [1991] FSR 62.

[61] See, e.g., Peter Prescott QC '*Kaye v Robertson*—A Reply', (1991) 54 MLR 451, Birks, n. 12 above; Stephen Todd, 'Protection of Privacy' in Mullany, n. 2 above, 174 at 210.

[62] See Basil Markesinis, 'Our Patchy Law of Privacy—Time to do Something about it', (1990) 53 MLR 802.   [63] *Melvin v Reid* 297 P.91 (1931).

[64] High C., Wellington, 20 Oct. 1986, Jefferies J; CA, 23 Oct. 1986.

[65] [1986] 2 NZLR 716.   [66] [1993] 1 NZLR 41

more difficult question, and one to which reasonable people could give different answers. The value of free speech has been described so frequently and so eloquently as to leave no room for doubt of its importance. The international instruments mentioned at the outset also recognize a right to privacy, as would most ordinary citizens. It is, however, difficult and sensitive to determine where free speech ends, or should end, and privacy begins. Wherever the line is drawn, there will be cases clearly falling on one side of it or the other. But there will be other cases (touching, for example, on private activities of political figures unrelated to performance of their public duties, or the private lives of collateral members of the Royal Family with no realistic prospect of succession to the throne) which would be much more problematical. These are problems which, until now, the English courts have scarcely had to confront. If, as expected, the European Convention is incorporated into English law (protecting privacy in article 8 and free speech in article 10) the nettle of reconciling the two will have, it would seem, to be grasped. It must be hoped that on a case by case basis, and guided by authority and academic commentary here and elsewhere, a pattern and thence a discernible dividing line, will emerge—unless, of course, Parliament takes the initiative and lays down statutory rules to define the bounds of privacy. But it seems perhaps unlikely that statutory rules could be devised which were so clear, so comprehensive, and so easy of application that a body of case law would not build up, putting the flesh of real-life experience on the bones of the statutory skeleton.

It seems clear that the law of tort has the fertility and flexibility to protect nearly all of the most basic of human rights. But remedies may only be developed in the cases which happen to come before the courts. In the absence of any principled frame of reference judicial responses are inevitably partial and to some extent inconsistent. So perhaps the end-of-term report on the performance of the English courts in this field, on the eve of incorporation, should be: 'Has done some good work, and tried hard, and set a good example. But there are areas of weakness which call for attention. The next few terms will call for energy, imagination, an open mind, and, above all, a willingness to learn.'

PART V
PUBLIC LAW

Particularly in recent years, lawyers in this country have drawn a distinction between matters of private law (which may arise, for instance, between parties to a contract, or husband and wife, or employer and employee, or trustee and beneficiary, or trade union and member, or driver and road accident victim) and matters of public law (which arise between the individual or a private body and some body exercising public power whether it be the central government, or a minister or official, or local government, or an official regulator, or any other body exercising public functions). Criminal proceedings, of course, almost always arise between the individual and the state, but when lawyers talk of public law they have civil and not criminal proceedings in mind. Public law proceedings have a particular importance, since they provide much the most important legal means of ensuring that public and governmental power is lawfully and fairly exercised.

There are several different remedies which a claimant may seek in a public law action, several of which have old-fashioned Latin names. He may ask that a decision or order be quashed (*certiorari*). Or he may ask that the public body be ordered by the court to do something (*mandamus*) or not to do or stop doing something (prohibition). If he complains that he has been unlawfully detained, he may invoke a long-standing procedure to obtain a court decision whether he has been unlawfully detained or not (*habeas corpus*). Or he may simply ask the court to decide what the law is, where that is in dispute. The first paper in this section takes up, in the public law context, the question considered in 'The Discretion of the Judge' in section 1. If the citizen is able to show an abuse of public power, should it be open to the judge to deny a remedy, and if so in what circumstances? That is the problem.

Lord Hewart of Bury was Lord Chief Justice of England from 1922 to 1940. He had previously been Attorney-General. He felt, very strongly, that in seeking to ensure the lawful and fair exercise of public power the courts were being progressively hamstrung by legislative and bureaucratic devices intended to inhibit judicial control of administrative action. In 1929 he wrote a book, *The New Despotism*, to say so. The second paper in this section considers the origin, content and impact of this remarkable book.

Judges, like practitioners in any other field, vary in quality. Even among those who are learned, fair-minded, and conscientious, there are some who pass away leaving little of enduring value behind them and others whose qualities of intellect, imagination or courage leave a personal imprint on the law which time does not erase. This last class is, inevitably a small one, but among British judges of the twentieth century few would be more readily assured of inclusion than Lord Atkin. His contribution to several areas of the law was outstanding and enduring. But, oddly, perhaps his most famous judgment of all was given in a case in which, as one judge in a court of five, he reached a conclusion with which all four of his colleagues strongly disagreed. So, legally speaking, his judgment counted for nothing. This was his judgment in *Liversidge v Anderson*, to which the third paper in this section is devoted.

1

Should Public Law Remedies be Discretionary?*

If any of us were buttonholed in the street by an intellectually curious Martian who asked what was meant by 'the rule of law'—an expression he had observed much used in some of the more pretentious journals—our definition might be more or less incoherent. But it would, I think, include as an important element the requirement that the rights and obligations of citizens should depend on clear rules publicly stated and not on the whims, prejudices or predilections of the individual decision-maker. 'Where law ends tyranny begins.'[1] If the Martian were to ask how in the public law sphere these rights and obligations were now enforced in English law, we would with great confidence regale him with an account of judicial review, Order 53 and the boom town that the Crown Office List has become, perhaps garnished with a reference to Lord Diplock's judicial lifetime.[2] So, the Martian persists, where unlawful conduct in the public law sphere is shown to have occurred or to be threatened, according to clear rules publicly stated, relief must follow as a matter of right and not of the judge's discretion? 'Well, no, not exactly,' we reply, perhaps with a little less confidence, acknowledging that public law remedies are for the most part discretionary. Understandably puzzled, the Martian puts his final question, which I take as the title of this lecture: Should public law remedies be discretionary? To this I would answer: 'Well, yes, probably, in some cases, up to a point, provided the discretion is strictly limited and the rules for its exercise clearly understood.' Disgusted with this tortuous and heavily qualified answer, the Martian stumps off, and we may all share a sense of relief that he will not reappear.

I hope, however, that his final question is worth asking and deserves some consideration. The judge in a civil law country would not, I think, claim such a discretion. The French administrative judge can annul for *vice de forme* if an essential procedural requirement has been broken, as can the European Court under Article 173 of the EEC Treaty, and this involves a judgment whether the procedural requirement broken is in truth essential. Similarly, in evaluating the legality of *mesures de police* the French judge must make a judgment on proportionality, and the doctrine of *erreur manifeste d'appréciation* requires him to

* Revised lecture delivered to the Administrative Law Bar Association in the Parliament Chamber of the Inner Temple on 17 October 1990. Reprinted from *Public Law* (Spring 1991), 64–75. © Sweet & Maxwell, London, 1991.
[1] William Pitt. See K. C. Davis, *Discretionary Justice: A Preliminary Inquiry* (1969).
[2] *R v Inland Revenue Commissioners, ex p. National Federation of Self-Employed and Small Businesses* [1982] AC 617, 641.

assess whether the *erreur* is *manifeste*. And it may be that a civilian judge will exercise a discretion without acknowledging it as such. It is, however, my impression that a continental lawyer would raise an eyebrow at the notion that a remedy for a *proven* abuse of power should be discretionary.[3]

THE REMEDIES AND THEIR BACKGROUND

In seeking to justify the tortuous and qualified answer I have already suggested, it is perhaps worth pointing out at the start that all public law remedies are not discretionary. The clearest exception is habeas corpus, legally and historically the most important of the prerogative writs and well described by de Smith as 'the most renowned contribution of the English common law to the protection of human liberty'.[4] The governing principle here is not in doubt: 'In principle, *habeas corpus* is not a discretionary remedy: it issues *ex debito justitiae* on proper grounds being shown.'[5] Thus, in a relatively recent case, the Court of Appeal held that habeas corpus was not to be denied on grounds that there was an alternative remedy, however convenient, beneficial and effectual.[6]

The old mediaeval writ of certiorari originated in the late thirteenth century, but had a function distinct from that familiar today.[7] It was a means of removing a case from lower courts to the King's Bench, the mediaeval equivalent (as Professor Plucknett suggested) of 'Get me the file on such and such a matter.'[8] The use of certiorari to quash emerged in the mid-seventeenth century and appears to have been recognized as largely discretionary from the start. In 1657 it was said:

This Court hath authority to Quash Orders of Sessions, Presentments, Endictments etc made in inferior Courts, or before Justices of Peace or other Commissioners if there be cause, that is, if they be defective in matter or form. . . . But this Quashing is but by favour of the Court, for the Court is not tyed Ex Officio to do it, but may leave the party to plead unto them, as in many cases they use to do.[9]

But if largely discretionary, it is not clear that the remedy is or ever has been

---

[3] M. Roger Errera, Conseiller d'Etat, has helpfully commented on this paragraph and suggested that it may be slightly misleading. He advises (with reference to the analysis which I make below) that French judges exercise a discretion in respect of, for instance, standing, exhaustion of other remedies and restricted areas although not in respect of delay, acquiescence, conduct and motives, inevitability of outcome, lack of a useful purpose or adverse public consequences. Overall, he suggests, there is little distance between *politique jurisprudentielle* and judicial discretion. Perhaps there is scope here for the public law comparativist.

[4] S. A. de Smith, *Judicial Review of Administrative Action* (4th edn., by J. M. Evans, 1980), 596.

[5] R. J. Sharpe, *The Law of Habeas Corpus* (2nd edn., 1989) 58.

[6] *R v Governor of Pentonville Prison, ex p. Azam* [1974] AC 18.

[7] On this and much that follows, I am greatly indebted to E. G. Henderson, *Foundations of English Administrative Law: Certiorari and Mandamus in the Seventeenth Century* (1963).

[8] Ibid. 89.

[9] Style's *Practical Register* (1657), quoted by Henderson, *supra*, n. 7, at 107.

discretionary in all circumstances, leading de Smith to observe,'Whether the court retains any discretion where want of jurisdiction appears on the face of the proceedings has not been clearly settled.'[10] The question may be of theoretical interest only, since it is not easy to imagine the court denying the remedy in such circumstances even if a discretion did exist.

The creation of the county courts in 1846 led to a late but vigorous flowering of the old writ of prohibition[11] and to much authority on the limits of the court's discretion to deny the remedy. As Shortt wrote in 1887,

It may be doubted whether any legal question has ever given rise to so great a conflict of judicial opinion as the question—whether the grant of a prohibition is discretionary, or whether it is demandable as of right. The authority of eminent judges can be cited in support of either view; and sometimes the authority of the same judge can be adduced in favour of both views.[12]

By 1911, however, later authors found it possible to discern and lay down a clean rule:

Ordinarily the writ is to be granted ex debito justitiae.
But where the applicant has been guilty of delay, or has acquiesced in, or waived the want of jurisdiction (without excuse for such delay, acquiescence, or waiver), or has failed to discharge the onus which lies upon him to show his right to the writ—in such cases, the grant of the writ is in the discretion of the Court, Provided that if the defect of jurisdiction (however such defect arises), is apparent on the face of the proceedings, or the applicant has taken the objection in the inferior Court, the grant of the writ is ex debito justitiae, notwithstanding delay, acquiescence or waiver.[13]

It seems likely that, in part at least, this is still the law today.[14]

The remedy of mandamus has never, as I understand, been regarded as other than discretionary[15] and has been described as 'pre-eminently a discretionary remedy'.[16] It is none the less a remedy which administrative lawyers should regard with particular affection because of the case of James Bagge[17] to which its origins are traditionally traced.[18] Bagge was a capital burgess and magistrate in Plymouth but relations between him and other dignified citizens of the town were evidently somewhat strained and events came to a head when he turned *posteriorem partem corporis sui* towards the mayor, Thomas Fowens, and said 'scurrilously, contemptuously, rudely and in a high voice', 'Come and kisse' and later, 'I will make thy neck cracke'. This indelicate conduct led to his removal from

---

[10] *Supra*, n. 4, 419.
[11] Morgan Lloyd, *A Treatise on the Law of Prohibition* (1849).
[12] *Informations, Mandamus and Prohibition* (1887), 441.
[13] Curlewis & Edwards & Wrottesley, *The Law of Prohibition* (1911), 279.
[14] de Smith, *supra*, n. 4, 587; *R v Comptroller-General of Patents, ex p. Parke Davis & Co.* [1953] 1 All ER 862, 866.
[15] See, e.g., W. J. Impey, *Treatise on the Law and Practice of the Writ of Mandamus* (1826).
[16] de Smith, *supra*, n. 4, 540. [17] (1615) 11 Co.Rep. 93b at 95–7.
[18] Henderson, *supra*, n. 7, 47.

office, but despite the lack of previous authority[19] the court ordered him to be restored. The remedy, once exercised, quickly took root, and not long thereafter it was said: 'This Court hath power not only in judicial things, but also in some things which are extra-judicial . . . and this thing is peculiar to this Court, and is one of the flowers of it.'[20]

There can be no doubt but that the remedies available in this field by way of declaration and injunction are truly discretionary. So much is plain from the wording of section 31(2) of the Supreme Court Act 1981.[21] It also seems clear that the residual *quo warranto* jurisdiction under section 30 is discretionary. I do not think that the statute alters the law already referred to so far as certiorari and prohibition, still less habeas corpus, are concerned. But the result certainly is that an element of judicial discretion exists almost throughout the field. The question is: how wide and how tightly controlled is that discretion?

THE NATURE OF JUDICIAL DISCRETION

Before answering that question, I should make clear what I mean by judicial discretion. I hope I may be permitted to repeat, without now defending, a definition I have propounded elsewhere:

an issue falls within a judge's discretion if, being governed by no rule of law, its resolution depends on the individual judge's assessment (within such boundaries as have been laid down) of what it is fair and just to do in the particular case. He has no discretion in making his findings of fact. He has no discretion in his rulings on the law. But when, having made any necessary finding of fact and any necessary ruling of law, he has to choose between different courses of action, orders, penalties or remedies he then exercises a discretion. It is only when he reaches the stage of asking himself what is the fair and just thing to do or order in the instant case that he embarks on the exercise of a discretion.[22]

GROUNDS FOR THE EXERCISE OF DISCRETION

Against that background I turn to consider and comment very summarily on nine of the grounds upon which, in the exercise of his discretion, a judge may properly

---

[19] Henderson, *supra*, 72.

[20] *Awdley v Joy* (1682) Popham 176.

[21] 'A declaration may be made or an injunction granted . . . in any case where an application for judicial review, seeking that relief, has been made and the High Court considers that, having regard to—
  (a) the nature of the matters in respect of which relief may be granted by orders of mandamus, prohibition or certiorari;
  (b) the nature of the persons and bodies against whom relief may be granted by such orders; and
  (c) all the circumstances of the case,
it would be just and convenient for the declaration to be made or the injunction to be granted. . . .'

[22] 'The Discretion of the Judge': Royal Bank of Scotland Lecture, Oxford (17 May 1990), [1990] Denning Law Journal 27.

refuse a public law remedy in the case of a proven abuse of power, using that expression broadly to embrace all grounds on which such remedies might properly be granted.

(1) *Delay*

The combined effect of section 31(6) of the 1981 Act and Order 53, rule 4(1) has now been authoritatively settled:

1. An application for leave to move for judicial review must be made promptly, and in any event within three months of the decision or conduct under challenge. In some circumstances the court may hold that an application for leave made within the three month period was not made promptly.
2. Where an application is not made promptly or within the three months, there has been undue delay within section 31(6).
3. If there has been undue delay but the applicant advances good reason for the delay, the court has a discretion to extend time.
4. In exercising that discretion, the court will consider under section 31(6) whether to grant the relief sought 'would be likely to cause substantial hardship to, or substantially prejudice the rights of, any person or would be detrimental to good administration.'

If any of these results are likely to follow a grant of leave, then, even if there was good reason for the delay, the court may still refuse in its discretion to extend the time.[23]

For present purposes, it is also necessary to bear in mind that delay may well be relied on in denying leave, at which stage there will, of course, be no proven or established abuse of power.

The application of these rules may call for an exercise of discretion, but it is (I suggest) a narrow one. The question whether an applicant has applied promptly may involve an exercise of judgment, but it involves no exercise of discretion. The judge must consider all the facts and circumstances and resolve, as a fact, whether the application was made promptly. However difficult the decision, he must form a conclusion one way or the other. Having done so he has no choice. Similarly, under Order 53, rule 4(1) he has to consider whether there is good reason for extending the period. Again a review of the evidence and an exercise of judgment are called for, but this is not in my sense a discretionary exercise. If he concludes that there has been undue delay but that there are good reasons for extending the period he will consider, as section 31(6) requires, whether the grant of relief would be likely to cause substantial hardship to, or substantially prejudice the

---

[23] *R v Dairy Produce Quota Tribunal, ex p. Caswell* [1990] 2 WLR 1320, approving *R v Stratford on Avon D.C., ex p. Jackson* [1985] 1 WLR 1319. And see *R v Council of the City of Westminster, ex p. Hilditch* [1990] COD 434.

rights of, any person or would be detrimental to good administration. If on the evidence the answer is No, the court's discretion virtually disappears because there is only one way it may be effectively exercised.[24] If the answer is Yes, then a true discretion arises because the judge has to decide what is the fair thing to do, balancing the good reasons for extending time against the detriment which is likely to result. But the rules are clear and publicly stated. In most cases the outcome could be safely predicted. Any decision outside the area of appreciation reserved to the trial judge would be challengeable. There is, as it seems to me, no risk of arbitrariness, which is the real bane of uncontrolled discretion.

(2) Standing

There was in the past much discussion of standing and it was frequently said that remedies could be granted even to a stranger.[25] But the more direct the applicant's injury the greater his chances of obtaining relief and it seems that a discretion was exercised to grant or refuse relief depending (among other things) on the applicant's *locus standi*. Now the position is clarified by the requirement in section 31(3) of the 1981 Act that leave to apply for review shall not be granted unless the court considers that the applicant has a sufficient interest in the matter to which the application relates. That provision, standing alone, gives the judge little help and the question whether, on the facts of a given case, an applicant has a sufficient interest is one on which reasonable minds could form different judgments. This is a very open-textured rule, although there is a good deal of existing authority, but it is not one which gives the judge a discretion in my sense, and the organic development of the case law will no doubt, over a period, peg out the boundary—or more likely, bound-aries—on the ground. But the effect of the statutory provision is, I think, to reduce the judges' discretion, not increase it.

It would none the less seem that the 'sufficient interest' provision in section 31(3) does not apply to the residual *quo warranto* jurisdiction under section 30. In that field the court's approach to standing was in the past very relaxed. In 1915, when a citizen with no personal interest tried to challenge the membership of the Privy Council of two members born, in one case in Germany and in the other else-where outside the King's dominions, of alien parents, a challenge on grounds of standing did not succeed. Lord Reading CJ said:

[The applicant] appears to have brought this matter before the Court on purely public grounds without any private interest to serve, and it is to the public advantage that the law should be declared by judicial authority. I think the Court ought to incline to the assistance,

---

[24] Cf. *R v Stafford Justices, ex p. Stafford Corporation* [1940] 2 KB 33, 43.

[25] *R v Surrey Justices* (1870) LR 5 QB 466, 472–3; *Worthington v Jeffries* (1875) LR 10 CP 379; *Mayor of the City of London v Cox* (1866) LR 2 HL 239, 279. For a discussion of the present law, see P. Cane, 'Statutes, Standing and Representation' [1990] PL 307 and Sir Konrad Schiemann, 'Locus Standi' [1990] PL 342.

and not to the hindrance of the applicant in such a case if the Court has the power, which I think it has. . . .[26]

It seems clear that this approach could not now be taken in any case governed by section 31(3), and it may be that this restriction is to be regretted. But whether one likes the test of sufficient interest or not, there is, I suggest, nothing discretionary about it.

(3) *Acquiescence*

The court has always asserted a discretion to refuse certiorari or prohibition if the applicant knew of a tribunal's lack of jurisdiction not apparent on the record but none the less failed to take the point when it was reasonably open to him.[27] When, for example, a baker was convicted of an offence against the Bread Act 1836 by a bench which, contrary to the provisions of the Act, included a baker, his application for certiorari failed because he had not shown himself to be ignorant of his right to object when appearing before the bench.[28] It is otherwise if the applicant was ignorant at the relevant time of the point open to him, there being then no acquiescence.[29]

The common law version of the Latin maxim *vigilantibus non dormientibus jura subveniunt* might, I suppose, be 'Speak up or shut up!', an injunction which has a certain down-to-earth appeal. But we are considering acts of proven unlawfulness: excesses of jurisdiction, denials of a fair hearing and so on. I can well understand the fairness of denying costs to an applicant who could and should have objected earlier, particularly if an objection taken earlier might have obviated the need to apply. Such an applicant might also fall foul of the rules on delay. But on a prompt application by an applicant who has acquiesced, I suggest that this discretion should be rarely exercised. The baker may have had many reasons for not objecting to the constitution of the bench, even assuming he knew of his rights. The fact is that the bench was unlawfully constituted. Its decision should not have stood. The baker would seem to me to have been hard done by.

(4) *The conduct and motives of the applicant*

The court has refused relief because of an applicant's conduct or motives on many occasions, for example where he has suppressed or misrepresented material facts in presenting the application,[30] where a fireman has deliberately and foolishly

---

[26] *R v Speyer* [1916] 1 KB 595, 613.
[27] See, e.g., *Mayor of the City of London v Cox* (1866) LR 2 HL 239, 283; *Broad v Perkins* (1888) 21 QBD 533.
[28] *R v Williams, ex p. Phillips* [1914] 1 KB 608.
[29] *R v Inner London Quarter Sessions, ex p. D'Souza* [1970] 1 WLR 376.
[30] *R v Kensington Income Tax Commissioners, ex p. de Polignac* [1917] 1 KB 486.

disobeyed a direction of his superior officer instead of challenging it by an available internal procedure,[31] where the applicants' ulterior motive was to put competitors out of business,[32] where a former magistrates' clerk had acted in an obstructive, inconsistent and unreasonable way,[33] and where the court held that the litigation should never have been started.[34]

It may no doubt be reasonable to give to a court the power to deny relief to an applicant who has tried to deceive it or who has abused its process, and perhaps some other cases should be susceptible to similar treatment. But, as with acquiescence, I would wish this discretion to be (as I think it is) rarely and cautiously exercised. Lilburne, Wilkes, Bradlaugh, and Mrs Pankhurst—to name but four—would now pursue their grievances by way of judicial review. Their conduct and opinions would no doubt have been anathema to the powers that were in their day, as those of their successors might be to many of us today. But they have won the verdict of history. If an applicant who has proved an abuse of power is to be denied relief in the exercise of the court's discretion on grounds of his or her conduct or motives, the rules governing the exercise of the discretion should be narrow and perhaps more clearly defined than they are at present. It is not, surely, for the courts to spurn these who are Right unless they are a good deal more than Repulsive.[35]

(5) *Exhaustion of other remedies*

The principle that an applicant for judicial review may be denied relief if he has not exhausted other available and equally efficacious remedies is not new,[36] but it has recently received additional impetus from strongly expressed dicta in the House of Lords[37] and the Court of Appeal.[38]

There is obvious good sense in this rule at the stage of application for leave, for at that stage no unlawfulness has been established and the applicant is (one assumes) in a position to pursue the other remedy. I suspect (although others will know more about this than I) that it is usually at this stage that this discretionary bar is applied. There is also obvious good sense in the rule where the alternative remedy has already been invoked,[39] since the grant of leave would lead to duplicated proceedings with the risk of inconsistent results, or where the alternative remedy may give the applicant substantial relief on the merits as opposed to mere correction of procedural error.

[31] *Ex p. Fry* [1954] 1 WLR 730.

[32] *R v Commissioners of Customs and Excise, ex p. Cook* [1970] 1 WLR 450.

[33] *Fullbrook v Berkshire Magistrates' Courts Committee* (1970) 69 LGR 75.

[34] *Windsor and Maidenhead Royal Borough Council v Brandrose Investments Ltd.* [1983] 1 WLR 509.   [35] With apologies to Sellar and Yeatman, *1066 and All That*.

[36] *R v Smith* (1873) LR 8 QB 146; *R v Poplar Borough Council* [1922] 1 KB 72; *R v Hillingdon London Borough Council, ex p. Royco Homes Ltd.* [1974] QB 720, 728.

[37] *R v Inland Revenue Commissioners, ex p. Preston* [1985] AC 835, 852, 862.

[38] *R v Chief Constable of Merseyside, ex p. Calveley* [1986] QB 424, 433, 435.

[39] As in *R v Council of the City of Westminster, ex p. Hilditch, supra* n. 23.

It is, however, my impression that at the stage of the substantive hearing this principle is more often proclaimed than applied, and I wonder if in practice the reality quite matches the rhetoric. There are not, to my knowledge, many cases where at this stage relief has been denied on this ground to an applicant who has established an abuse of power. If so I am pleased, because I do not find the arguments in support of the principle altogether convincing. Where Parliament has established a procedure for remedying grievances, it did no doubt intend those with a grievance to use it; but Parliament can scarcely have envisaged that such persons would have been the victims of unlawful, as opposed to unjustified, treatment. It is again true that the courts have plenty to do without speedily resolving disputes where alternative procedures exist; but the courts should be the last to complain if aggrieved citizens feel that they (the courts) are best fitted to recognize and remedy the consequences of unlawful conduct.[40] It would seem to me on the whole desirable that when unlawful conduct is proved before a court of justice, it should generally be willing to say so and grant relief, whether an equally convenient, beneficial and effectual alternative remedy exists or not.

(6) *Inevitability of outcome*

Judges of the highest distinction have held that an applicant who has been unlawfully and unfairly denied a right to be heard may be denied relief if the outcome would have been no different if he had been heard.[41] Sir William Wade has referred to 'the dubious doctrine that a hearing would make no difference',[42] and in a recent case I gave six reasons for expecting (by which I really meant hoping) that such cases would be of great rarity.[43] Since the case has not been widely reported, perhaps I may repeat them here:

(i) Unless the subject of the decision has had an opportunity to put his case, it may not be easy to know what case he could or would have put if he had had the chance.

(ii) As memorably pointed out by Megarry J. in *John v Rees*,[44] experience shows that that which is confidently expected is by no means always that which happens.

(iii) It is generally desirable that decision-makers should be reasonably receptive to argument, and it would therefore be unfortunate if the complainant's position became weaker as the decision-maker's mind became more closed.

---

[40] *R v Panel on Take-overs and Mergers, ex p. Guinness plc* [1990] 1 QB 146, 177–8 (*per* Lord Donaldson MR).

[41] *Glynn v Keele University* [1971] 1 WLR 487; *Malloch v Aberdeen Corporation* [1971] 1 WLR 1579; *Cinnamond v British Airports Authority* [1980] 1 WLR 582.

[42] *Administrative Law* (6th edn., 1988), 573.

[43] *R v Chief Constable of the Thames Valley Police Forces, ex p. Cotton* [1990] IRLR 344.

[44] [1970] Ch. 345, 402.

(iv) In considering whether the complainant's representations would have made any difference to the outcome, the court may unconsciously stray from its proper province of reviewing the propriety of the decision-making process into the forbidden territory of evaluating the substantial merits of a decision.

(v) This is a field in which appearances are generally thought to matter.

(vi) Where a decision-maker is under a duty to act fairly the subject of the decision may properly be said to have a right to be heard, and rights are not to be lightly denied.

(7) *No useful purpose*

The court has exercised its discretion to refuse declarations which will serve no useful purpose,[45] or to refuse relief where the applicant has achieved the substantial result which he seeks without any order,[46] or where a public body has shown that it is doing all it honestly can to comply with its statutory duty,[47] or where an error has been substantially cured.[48] This seems to me a beneficial rule. If the court is satisfied that a public body will readily perform its duty once the court tells it what its duty is, I see no reason why it should be the subject of a coercive order. The rules that the court will not compel a party to do the impossible and will not make futile or unnecessary orders seem hard to challenge. But happily the court does not take too strict a view of futility, as when it gave leave to challenge a sentence of 42 days' imprisonment for non-payment of fines which had been served 3 years before.[49]

(8) *Adverse public consequences*

Stirring statements have been made to the effect that the court 'will not listen readily to suggestions of "chaos". . . . Even if chaos should result, still the law must be obeyed',[50] and that 'whatever inconvenience or chaos might be involved in allowing the appeal, the court would not be deterred from doing so if satisfied that the valuation officer had acted illegally'.[51] I do not, however, know of any case where relief was granted when the court actually expected chaos to result. The maxim *fiat justitia ruat coelum* may be most firmly insisted upon when relief

---

[45] *Att.-Gen. v Scott* [1905] 2 KB 160, 169; *Eastham v Newcastle United Football Club Ltd.* [1964] Ch. 413, 449.

[46] *R v Commissioner of Police of the Metropolis, ex p. Blackburn* [1968] 2 QB 118.

[47] *R v Bristol Corporation, ex p. Hendy* [1974] 1 WLR 498.

[48] *R v Secretary of State for Social Services, ex p. Association of Metropolitan Authorities* [1986] 1 WLR 1.

[49] *R v Liverpool City Justices, ex p. Lunt*, unreported, 21 July 1988, Transcript 675 of 1988, CA.

[50] *Bradbury v Enfield London Borough Council* [1967] 1 WLR 1311, 1324.

[51] *R v Paddington Valuation Officer, ex p. Peachey Property Corporation Ltd.* [1966] 1 QB 380, 419.

is to be denied on other grounds or the administrative heavens are not expected to fall. By contrast, the court has relied on adverse public consequences as an additional ground for refusing relief.[52]

I suggest that a straight clash between the rights of the individual and the wider interests of society may usually be avoided by application of the rule on promptness, since administrative chaos would often be avoided if an application were made promptly enough. But where these rules do not apply, one must face up to a choice between the high ground of purist principle and the more pragmatic, utilitarian approach which our law in practice tends to adopt. Unless predictions of administrative chaos were to become more prevalent and more persuasive than seems to be the case at present, I would incline to think that this discretion should remain on its present, apparently very limited, basis.

(9) *Restricted areas*

There have been some areas of activity into which the courts have in the past been reluctant to intrude, notably the management or conduct of a disciplined force such as the fire brigade[53] or the police force.[54] And it has been said times without number that it is not for the court to second-guess a public body or official within the area of decision accorded to it or him. The growing willingness of commercial opponents to pursue their policies by other means, namely by litigious warfare, has led to qualified declarations of judicial abstinence in this area also. I have in mind particularly the Argyll Group's application against the Monopolies Commission during the Guinness takeover of Distillers,[55] the application by Datafin against the Takeover Panel during a contested takeover battle[56] and Guinness's complaint against the Takeover Panel following the acquisition of Distillers.[57]

Had the courts declared the field of financial regulation a no-go area that would, I think, have been regrettable, but they have not done so. On the other hand, it would seem to me wise for the courts to venture into this uncharted minefield with considerable circumspection lest the cure be more damaging to the wider investing public than the disease. I would expect the developing case law

---

[52] *Flint v Att.-Gen.* [1918] 1 Ch. 216; *R v Brentwood Superintendent Registrar of Marriages, ex p. Arias* [1968] 2 QB 956; *Coney v Choyce* [1975] 1 WLR 422; *R v Monopolies and Mergers Commission, ex p. Argyll Group plc* [1986] 1 WLR 763.

[53] *Ex p. Fry* [1954] 1 WLR 730; *Buckoke v G.L.C.* [1970] 1 WLR 1092.

[54] *R v Commissioner of Police of the Metropolis, ex p. Blackburn* [1968] 2 QB 118, 136; *R v Chief Constable of Devon and Cornwall, ex p. Central Electricity Generating Board* [1982] QB 458, 472. Other well-known areas into which the courts are slow to intrude are those involving national security (e.g. the *GCHQ* case, [1985] AC 374) and operational emergency (e.g. the *Pegasus* case [1988] 1 WLR 990).

[55] *R v Monopolies and Mergers Commission, ex p. Argyll Group plc* [1968] 1 WLR 763.

[56] *R v Panel on Takeovers and Mergers, ex p. Datafin plc* [1987] QB.

[57] *R v Panel on Takeovers and Mergers, ex p. Guinness plc* [1990] 1 QB 146.

to define with greater precision the grounds on which the court will exercise its discretion to refuse relief, but for the moment perhaps the courts have got the balance about right.

CONCLUSION

So, in concluding, I would repeat my unheroic answer to the question posed in my title: 'Well, yes, probably, in some cases, up to a point, provided the discretion is strictly limited and the rules for its exercise clearly understood.' There should be no room for arbitrariness. But in the long run the administration of justice rests on public acceptance, and judicial review is more likely to command public acceptance if it is seen as a precision instrument and not a juggernaut. For, as Lord Devlin memorably observed, 'The British have no more wish to be governed by judges than they have to be judged by administrators.'[58]

[58] 'The courts and the abuse of power', *The Times*, 27 Oct. 1976.

2

*The Old Despotism**

Seventy years ago there appeared in Britain a series of newspaper articles, which in the autumn of the year were published in book form. To this book the author, perhaps drawing on his earlier career as a journalist, gave a headline-catching title: *The New Despotism.*[1] In the Richter scale of world events this publication was not, as even the most introverted lawyer would have to acknowledge, the most memorable event of 1929. But on the more specialized Richter scale which measures movements in the landscape of constitutional and administrative law, and standards of judicial conduct, a noticeable tremor was registered. For the author of *The New Despotism* was Lord Hewart of Bury, who held office as Lord Chief Justice of England, and the book was a coruscating attack on what he pejoratively called the bureaucracy, the great departments of state, whom Hewart accused of acquiring and exercising legislative and administrative powers in a manner which circumvented Parliament, excluded judicial control through the ordinary courts and undermined the rule of law.

Lord Hewart's thunderbolt did not, it is true, emerge from a blue sky. C. K. Allen, a greatly respected legal scholar, had in 1923 and 1925 published articles of which the tenor was summarized in their titles: 'Bureaucracy Triumphant'[2] and 'Bureaucracy Again'.[3] In 1928 he again criticized the vulnerability of the British citizen when confronted by the state.[4] Dr W. A. Robson of the London School of Economics wrote, in 1928:

What we now find . . . is that large judicial duties of an important character have been given, not to persons holding judicial office, not even to known and ascertainable individuals, but to vast departments of the State, huge administrative organisations employing thousands of anonymous civil servants. In some cases the responsible ministry does not itself perform the judicial function in question, but is empowered to set up and regulate the tribunal, which is to do the work. This does not affect the principle involved, however, because the vital feature of the whole arrangement is the fact that there is no appeal to the regular courts of law.[5]

Lord Justice Sankey, before becoming Lord Chancellor in 1929, had questioned whether Britain should not move towards adopting a full-blown system of administrative law.[6] Professor Morgan, in an introduction to a work on Public

---

* Lecture delivered at the Hebrew University of Jerusalem, 31 May 1999.
[1] The Rt Hon Lord Hewart of Bury: *The New Despotism* (Benn, 1929) (hereafter cited as 'ND').
[2] *Quarterly Review*, no. 477 (Oct. 1923).   [3] Ibid., no. 483 (Jan. 1925).
[4] 'Some Aspects of Administrative Law' (1929) *JSPTL* 10.
[5] W. A. Robson, *Justice and Administrative Law* (Macmillan, 1928), at 91.
[6] *Principles and Practice of the Law Today*, 17.

Authorities and Legal Liability, in 1925 had spoken of 'the growing arbitrariness of temper . . . which is in flagrant contradiction with the most elementary principles of justice'. Dr John Port shared the view that new and better safeguards of private rights were needed.[7] A Scottish practitioner, although thinking things rather better in Scotland, made a similar diagnosis:

The policy of the executive departments in invading the judicial sphere has thus been (1) to disclaim judicial methods of procedure and to substitute nothing in their place but an unlimited and indefinable discretion; (2) to assert the right to finality in judgment and so to deprive themselves voluntarily of the invaluable discipline and stimulus of having to furnish decisions which will bear the scrutiny of a court of review; and (3) to replace open publicity and reasoned judgments by the methods of obscurantism.[8]

Another Scottish authority was even more forthright:

Even to the casual observer of the development of law in this country, it is abundantly clear that every year wider powers both of law making and judgment are being exercised by our Government departments . . . Unfortunately, the province of the Judiciary has been ruthlessly invaded by Government departments, and as yet no serious attempt has been made by Parliament to stay this invasion. Everybody knows how difficult and how expensive it is for the individual—even with a good measure of right on his side—to combat successfully a Government department.[9]

Hewart himself had made no secret of his views. Addressing the American Bar Association at Buffalo in 1927 he had referred to

a marked and increasing development of bureaucratic pretensions, the essence and aim of which are to withdraw more and more matters from the jurisdiction of the court and to set them aside for purely official determination.[10]

While acknowledging a duty to be careful in what he said,[11] Hewart saw no duty to be reticent. 'I have never connived', he said in 1927:

and I never will connive, at any heresy which involves the proposition that a Chief Justice of England, summoned as he is to the House of Lords not merely to vote but also to advise, is condemned to a lifelong and compulsory silence upon the affairs and interests of the State . . . No, a Chief Justice, whatever his privations may be, is not relegated, on all occasions, to an austere and pensive silence.[12]

In replying to a toast by the Lord Mayor of London to the Judges at the Mansion House in June 1928, Hewart addressed the topic in a way that was only superficially

---

[7] E. J. Port; *Administrative Law* (Longmans, 1929).

[8] T. M. Cooper KC, 'The Limitations of the Judicial Functions of Public Authorities', *Public Administration*, July 1929, 260 at 263.

[9] Margaret H. Kidd, 'The Encroachment of Administrative Bodies on the Judicial Sphere', *Scottish Law Review*, vol. xlv (Nov. 1929), 325 at 325, 329.

[10] *Canadian Bar Review*, Jan. 1930, 'Bureaucracy and the Courts', at 77.

[11] *Essays and Observations*, (Cassell, 1930), 'Manchester Revisited', at 142.

[12] Ibid., at 142, 143.

humorous. Having dismissed criticism of the system by which cases were tried by judges travelling to the provinces of England he continued:

But perhaps at the present moment questions like these need not be regarded as definite matters of urgent public importance. If I dare to make that suggestion, it is because I seem to gather, from the usual sources of information, that the inhabitants of these islands are within measurable distance of an El Dorado where there will be no Judges at all. In those Isles of the Blest, unless all the indications are misleading, all controversial questions will be decided in the third-floor back of some or other Government Department; the decision so reached will not be open to appeal by way of case stated, mandamus, certiorari, prohibition, or otherwise by any means whatsoever; no party or other person interested will be permitted to appear or to offer evidence; the whole law will have been codified in a single interminable statute consisting of thousands of sections and millions of sub-sections, without arrangement and without punctuation; no lawyers will be tolerated except a group of advisers, departmentally appointed; any question likely to excite difference of opinion will be submitted to those advisers beforehand on hypothetical facts and behind the back of the parties; and the Lord Chancellor himself will have been exchanged for a Minister of Administration for whose office any knowledge of law, however slight, will be a statutory disqualification. Meanwhile, and until that happy day arrives, our fellow-countrymen seem somehow to think not too unkindly of judicial decisions given in open Court upon real cases by perfectly independent and impartial Judges, who are individually responsible, and who have heard both sides.[13]

In *The New Despotism* Hewart deployed his argument in eight main chapters. He concluded with two unreadable chapters, one containing excerpts from leading cases, the other listing examples taken from statutes. Chapter 1 was entitled 'The Nature of the Question', and in it Hewart went straight to a section in a recent statute dealing with rates and valuation which provided:

If any difficulty arises in connection with the application of this Act to any exceptional area, or the preparation of the first valuation list for any area, or otherwise in bringing into operation any of the provisions of this Act, the Minister may by order remove the difficulty or constitute any assessment committee, or declare any assessment committee to be duly constituted, or make any appointment, or do any other thing, which appears to him necessary or expedient for securing the due preparation of the list or for bringing the said provisions into operation, and any such order may modify the provisions of this Act so far as may appear to the Minister necessary or expedient for carrying the order into effect.[14]

The Minister was permitted to exercise these powers for a period of three and a quarter years, and any order was subject to annulment by resolution of either House of Parliament.

Objecting strongly to the conferment of power on the minister or a department to modify an Act of Parliament, Hewart was in little doubt where the fault lay:

A little inquiry will serve to show that there is now, and for some years past has been, a

---

[13] Ibid., 'His Majesty's Judges', at 122–3.
[14] Rating and Valuation Act 1925, s. 67(1).

persistent influence at work which, whatever the motives or the intentions that support it
may be thought to be, undoubtedly has the effect of placing a large and increasing field of
departmental authority and activity beyond the reach of the ordinary law.[15]

Hewart was at pains to disclaim any attack on the civil service, the excellence of
which he was happy to assume as, in a treatise on photography, one might assume
the existence of the sun.[16] But he somewhat weakened this tribute by going on to
observe that high capacity and ardent zeal never need to be so carefully watched
as when they appeared to have entered, with all their might, on a wrong road.[17]
'It does not', he said:

take a horticulturalist to perceive that, if a tree is bearing bad fruit, the more vigorously it
yields the greater will be the harvest of mischief[18]

The strategy of the new bureaucratic despotism was to give Parliament an anaes-
thetic, and thus

to subordinate Parliament, to evade the Courts, and to render the will, or the caprice, of the
Executive unfettered and supreme[19]

The core of Hewart's objection was to the granting of power to make regulations
which would have the force of statute although not requiring parliamentary
approval:

It is one thing to confer power, subject to proper restrictions, to make regulations. It is
another thing to give those regulations the force of a statute. It is one thing to make regulations which are to have no effect unless and until they are approved by Parliament. It is
another thing to make regulations, behind the back of Parliament, which come into force
without the assent or even the knowledge of Parliament. Again, it is a strong thing to place
the decision of a Minister, in a matter affecting the rights of individuals, beyond the possibility of review by the Courts of Law. And it is a strong thing to empower a Minister to
modify, by his personal or departmental order, the provisions of a statute which has been
enacted.[20]

The new despotism was the emerging practice of drafting statutes in a way which
enabled departments to make regulations having the force of statute without seeking parliamentary approval, and to make orders amending the parent Act, thus
diminishing the role of Parliament and avoiding the possibility of enquiry by the
courts, using in effect a pretence of parliamentary sovereignty to defeat the rule
of law.

In Chapter 2 Hewart explained what he meant by the Rule of Law. His
account, drawing heavily on Dicey, is unexceptional. He emphasised three principles in particular: that no one can lawfully be restrained or punished or
condemned in damages save for a violation of the law established to the satisfaction of a judge or jury in proceedings regularly instituted in one of the ordinary

---

[15] *ND*. 11.   [16] Ibid., at 13.   [17] Ibid.   [18] Ibid.   [19] Ibid., at 17.
[20] Ibid., at 19.

courts; that everyone, whatever his position, is governed by the ordinary law of the land and personally liable for anything done by him contrary to that law, being subject to the ordinary courts, civil and criminal; and that no one charged with a violation of the law may effectively plead, in any court, that his act was done in obedience to the command of any superior.[21] The characteristic features of a court, Hewart wrote, were

(1) that the judge is identified and is personally responsible for his decisions; (2) that the case, subject to rare exceptions, is conducted in public; (3) that the result is governed by the impartial application of principles which are known and established; and (4) that all parties to the controversy are fully and fairly heard.[22]

All this Hewart contrasted with

the edict, however benevolent, of some hidden authority, however capable, depending upon a process of reasoning which is not stated and the enforcement of a scheme which is not explained.[23]

In Chapter 3 Hewart considered the 'Administrative Law' prevailing in France and other European continental countries, putting the title in inverted commas to express his distaste for a system of special rules to govern the rights and obligations of servants of the State and of private individuals in relation to servants of the State.[24] It is unnecessary to summarise Hewart's account of the French system, which was based on the 'brilliant and popular exposition of Dicey' but took insufficient account of developments in France after 1872 which gave the French citizen easier, speedier and cheaper remedies against the state than were available to the British citizen.[25] Hewart did, however, acknowledge that the French *droit administratif* was a definite system of law, differing from the system applicable between private citizens, but none the less a system of true administrative law, administered by a tribunal which applied judicial methods of procedure.[26]

Modest though his tribute to the French system of administrative law, Hewart none the less contrasted it favourably with the 'Administrative Lawlessness' prevailing in Britain, which he described in Chapter IV.[27] His objection was to the vesting of power in public officials, to the exclusion of the courts, to decide questions of a judicial nature. The decision once made is provided to be final and conclusive; and although nominally conferred on the minister the decision is in practice made by

some official, of more or less standing in the department, who has no responsibility except to his official superiors.[28]

The official is anonymous and unascertainable; he is bound by no course of

---

[21] Ibid., at 26–7. [22] Ibid., at 36. [23] Ibid. [24] Ibid., at 37.
[25] C. K. Allen, 'Some Aspects of Administrative Law' (1929) JSPTL 10–13.
[26] ND. at 41–2. [27] Ibid., 43, 45. [28] Ibid., at 43.

procedure or rules of evidence; he need hold no oral hearing; the parties have no right to be heard; there are usually no reasons given for the decision.[29]

To employ the terms administrative 'law' and administrative 'justice' to such a system, or negation of system, is really grotesque. The exercise of arbitrary power is neither law nor justice, administrative or at all.[30]

Private decisions by anonymous officials responsible only to their departments, made with none of the safeguards provided by judicial decisions, were in Hewart's view 'a mere travesty of justice'.[31] When, as was common, a departmental decision was provided to be final and conclusive:

the Courts are powerless to intervene, however unjust and absurd a decision may appear to be, and even though it is obviously based on an erroneous view of the law . . . The victim is, in such a case, perfectly helpless, and entirely without remedy. He is completely at the mercy of a person who, for all he knows, may be a bureaucratic tyrant.[32]

It was sometimes provided that a ministerial decision should be preceded by a public inquiry and report.

But that provision is no real safeguard, because the person who has the power of deciding is in no way bound by the report or the recommendations of the person who holds the inquiry, and may entirely ignore the evidence which the inquiry brought to light. He can, and in practice sometimes does, give a decision wholly inconsistent with the report, the recommendations, and the evidence, which are not published or disclosed to interested parties.[33]

Lastly in Chapter 4 Hewart discharged a broadside at the conferment of power on ministers to modify the provisions of a statute, a legislative device usually referred to as the Henry VIII clause. The historical attribution implicit in this phrase is questionable;[34] but it carries a suggestion of autocratic tyranny which is what users of the phrase often wish to convey.

In Chapter 5, describing 'The System at Work', Hewart identified the legislative devices which he found objectionable, most of them already mentioned. They included powers given to ministers to repeal or vary the express provisions of an Act,[35] the exclusion of judicial control by conferring a wide and apparently unfettered discretion,[36] provisions that the decision of a minister shall be 'final and conclusive',[37] and 'not subject to appeal to any Court',[38] provisions that a rule or order once made shall take effect as if enacted in the parent statute[39] and provisions that confirmation of an order by a nominated public body shall be conclusive evidence of compliance with the requirements of the statute.[40]

Hewart found the excuses offered even by the most able of the apologists to be

----

[29] ND. at 43–4.   [30] Ibid., at 44.   [31] Ibid., at 47.   [32] Ibid., at 49–50.
[33] Ibid., at 51.
[34] ECS Wade, 'Departmental Legislation. The Civil Service Point of View' (1933) 5 Camb. LJ 77 at 79.   [35] ND. at 60.   [36] Ibid., at 63.   [37] Ibid., at 64.
[38] Ibid., at 65.   [39] Ibid., at 66.   [40] Ibid., at 69.

sometimes rather entertaining. It is said that Parliament simply has not time to do otherwise than delegate legislative power; that Parliament, even if it had the time, has not the requisite aptitude for the work; and that, after all, it is not the task of Parliament, but the task of the Executive, to govern the country.[41]

These arguments did not find favour with the author, himself a former Member of Parliament and Attorney-General. It was precisely because it was the task of the executive to govern the country that it was so dangerous to hand over to the executive the power to make the laws as well.[42] Hewart associated himself with an adaptation, proposed elsewhere, of Dunning's famous resolution of 1780 that 'The power of the Executive has increased, is increasing, and ought to be diminished.'[43]

Hewart devoted Chapter 6 to an account of subordinate legislation by departments.[44] He accepted it as

tolerably obvious that the system of delegation by Parliament of powers of legislation is within certain limits necessary, at least as regards matters of detail, because it is impossible, if only for want of time, for Parliament to deal adequately and in detail with all the matters calling, or supposed to call, for legislation.[45]

He conceded that the system, if not abused, and subject to proper safeguards, might have its uses.[46] It was the abuses that called for criticism. Valuable safeguards were in his view provided if, before powers were exercised, persons interested were given notice and the opportunity to make representations,[47] and if it were generally provided that rules should be laid before Parliament before taking effect.[48]

In Chapter 7 Hewart turned to 'The Independence of the Judiciary'. After a brief reference to the struggle between Parliament and royal despotism, he observed:

But despotism may be no less sinister, and perhaps even more mischievous, if it acts under the cloak of Parliamentary forms than when it seeks to act in direct opposition to Parliament.[49]

It was therefore

necessary also to be astute to preserve judicial independence against any assault, however insidious.[50]

The main protection against such assault was what Hewart described as 'the profoundly important office of Lord Chancellor'.[51] He bitterly opposed the suggestion that he should be replaced by a Minister of Justice.

Sooner or later, and rather sooner than later, it is to be expected that the office of Minister

---

[41] Ibid., at 74.   [42] Ibid., at 75–6.   [43] Ibid., at 77.   [44] Ibid., at 79.
[45] Ibid., at 81.   [46] Ibid., at 81–2.   [47] Ibid., at 82.   [48] Ibid., at 85 *passim*.
[49] Ibid., at 103.   [50] Ibid., at 103–4.   [51] Ibid., at 104.

of Justice would be held by somebody who, without the smallest disrespect, might be described as a mere politician.[52]

Such a person would lack the knowledge, the standing, the background and the political independence of the Lord Chancellor.[53] But the greatest danger of all was that judicial appointments would come to be made, not by a person steeped in the traditions of the law and personally acquainted with the appointees, but by the permanent officials who surround the minister.[54] Nominal responsibility would belong to one person while real authority would rest with another.[55]

Nothing could be more sinister, nothing could be more odious, than that any such division of powers should be erected into a system in the crucially important matter of making judicial appointments.[56]

Hewart then referred to a number of historical instances in which the judges had defied the wishes of the executive, and rounded off the chapter with a sustained attack on a recent legislative proposal which would, if enacted, have permitted the minister, if it appeared to him that a substantial question of law had arisen, to submit the question to the High Court which, after hearing such parties as it thought proper, would give its opinion on the question.[57] The provision had been the subject of a sustained attack by the judicial members of the House of Lords, and had in the event perished. The thrust of the criticism was succinctly expressed by one judge:

It is no part of the business of His Majesty's judges, and never has been part of their business, at any rate since the Act of Settlement, to have any advisory concern in the acts of the Administration, or to take any part in advising the Administration.[58]

In Chapter 8 Hewart turned from diagnosing the disease to proposing treatment. Posing the question 'What is to be done?',[59] he gave effectively six answers. First, the worst offending clauses in existing Acts of Parliament should be repealed or amended.[60] Secondly, the enactment of further provisions of this kind should be prevented.[61] Thirdly, each House of Parliament should establish a committee to examine every new bill to observe whether and in what respects its provisions might have the effect of increasing the power of bureaucracy.[62] Fourthly, some at least of the leading newspapers should regularly and as a matter of course examine new bills for the same purpose.[63] Fifthly, existing legislation should be amended so as to exclude exception or evasion and secure real and effective parliamentary supervision over all rules and orders.[64] Sixthly, there should be an end of all schemes to enable government departments to re-write a statute, or to invite premature opinions on hypothetical cases from the judges, or to shelter departmental decisions or orders against review by the courts.[65]

[52] ND. at 105.   [53] Ibid., at 104–7.   [54] Ibid., at 108.   [55] Ibid., at 109.
[56] Ibid.   [57] Ibid., at 119.   [58] Ibid., at 124.   [59] Ibid., at 143.
[60] Ibid., at 147.   [61] Ibid., at 147–8.   [62] Ibid., at 148.   [63] Ibid., at 149–9.
[64] Ibid., at 150.   [65] Ibid.

Reverting to earlier themes, and relying on a recent speech by the Lord Chancellor,[66] Hewart found it an irresistible conclusion that the bureaucratic system under attack was

manifestly the offspring of a well thought out plan, the object and the effect of which is to clothe the department with despotic powers.[67]

He did not regard litigation as in itself desirable,[68] but regarded the existence and activity of the ordinary courts as 'a vast system of public insurance' of compliance with the law.[69]

According to Hewart's biographer, *The New Despotism*

caused intense anger in Whitehall. . . . The Lord Chancellor's department in particular was angered at the suggestion that there was a conspiracy on the part of civil servants to create a Ministry of Justice and allow a non-legal Minister to appoint judges, with all the obvious dangers. But Hewart believed in the existence of a conspiracy, and was sure that in addition the department took every opportunity to thwart him . . .[70]

More generally, however, at least among lawyers, the book was well received.[71] Press notices were on the whole favourable.[72] Professor E. C. S. Wade, writing in the *Law Quarterly Review*, thought Hewart to be 'not alone in seeing grave peril to the working of the Constitution'.[73] But there was some comment on the style of the book. *The Solicitors' Journal* considered it

a very remarkable book, not so much because of its bitter attack on bureaucracy—the new despotism—as by reason of the high judicial position of the author.[74]

The *Scots Law Times* thought it

an unparalleled event in modern times that a judge of the Supreme Court in England should publish an elaborate and sustained attack on the recent policy of the Legislature. If the example which the Lord Chief Justice has set should be followed by some of his judicial brethren taking up the cudgels on behalf of the policy which he impugns, the resulting controversy might contribute to the mirth of nations, but would hardly add to the dignity or the public estimation of the English Bench.[75]

This reviewer thought

Lord Hewart might have done better service if he had not weakened his case by unfortunate illustrations and by a somewhat intemperate and violent use of language more suited to his former role of politician than to the judicial calm expected of a Lord Chief Justice.[76]

---

[66] ND, at 151–2.   [67] Ibid., at 154.   [68] Ibid., at 155.   [69] Ibid., at 156.
[70] R. Jackson, *The Chief: The biography of Gordon Hewart Lord Chief Justice of England 1922–40*, (Harrap, 1959), at 214. He nurtured a particular animus towards the Lord Chancellor's Permanent Secretary, Sir Claude (later Lord) Schuster, to whom he referred, unflatteringly, as 'Shyster': ibid., at 258.   [71] Ibid., at 214.
[72] See, for example, (1929) 168 LT 364–5; (1929) Sol.Jo. 291; (1929) 43 JP & LGR 710; (1929) TLS 833; (1930) Can.Bar Rev. 77–82; (1930) 39 Yale LJ 763–5.
[73] (1930) 46 LQR 107.   [74] (1929) Sol.Jo. 291.   [75] (1930) SLT 34.
[76] Ibid., at 36.

More than one reviewer described the book as an 'indictment',[77] no doubt in recognition of Hewart's combative and adversarial approach. One of the few more critical reviews was written by Dr Robson, who found it difficult to see why we should regard the discretion of a judge, who is independent and virtually irremovable except for serious misconduct, as less 'irresponsible or uncontrolled' than the decision of a civil servant, who might fairly be regarded as no less anxious to serve the public welfare, but who in the case of a serious error might be dismissed by a superior Minister responsible to Parliament.[78]

Whatever the merits or demerits of the book, and whether or not Hewart acted with propriety in writing it, the serving government took it seriously. On the day before the book appeared, a committee was established under the chairmanship of the Earl of Donoughmore,

> to consider the powers exercised by or under the direction of (or by persons or bodies appointed specially by) Ministers of the Crown by way of (a) delegated legislation and (b) judicial or quasi-judicial decision, and to report what safeguards are desirable or necessary to secure the constitutional principles of the sovereignty of Parliament and the supremacy of the Law.[79]

In the judgment of Dr Robson, an acidulous critic, the committee, although appointed by a Labour Lord Chancellor, had the membership which might have been expected from a Conservative ministry:

> Out of the 17 members originally appointed, six are eminent practising barristers or solicitors, and another two are lawyers of highly conservative views—a majority of the entire Committee. Three of the remaining members are conservative ex-ministers; and the only persons from whom progressive ideas might reasonably be expected were Sir John Anderson, Professor Laski and three labour members of Parliament. A reforming Lord Chancellor appears to be an impossibility at the present time.[80]

The committee, however, had no judicial members, and Hewart himself, although invited to give evidence, declined, replying that as the committee had read his book and he had at present nothing to add to it, he did not think he could be of further assistance to the committee.[81]

When it reported in April 1932, the Committee addressed two main topics. The first was delegated legislation.[82] The Committee regarded some delegation of legislative powers for certain purposes within certain limits and under certain safeguards as legitimate and inevitable.[83] But it regarded the prevailing practice as unsystematic and potentially dangerous.[84] Parliament should take care in the

---

[77] For example, (1930) SLT 34 AT P. 35; Robson, *The Contemporary Review* (Jan. 1930), 88 at 90.
[78] 'A Charge of Despotism', *The Contemporary Review* (January 1930) 88 at pp. 89–90.
[79] *Report of the Committee on Ministers' Powers* (Cmd. 4060, April 1932), at p.(v) (hereafter cited as *Report*).   [80] Robson, op cit., at 350.
[81] *Report* at 3. The fact that Sir Claude Schuster was a member of the Committee may have contributed to his unwillingness to appear: R. Jackson, op cit., at 215.
[82] Section II of the *Report*, at 8.   [83] Ibid., at 58.   [84] Ibid.

language it used, should clearly define the limits of the power to be delegated and should never, save on exceptional grounds, delegate power to legislate on matters of principle or to impose taxation.[85] The Committee did not regard arguments of convenience as enough, save very exceptionally, to justify use of the Henry VIII clause.[86]

It acquitted the civil service of any attempt or desire to arm itself with arbitrary power.[87] It disapproved of 'conclusive evidence' clauses,[88] and thought Parliament should be careful to preserve in all but very exceptional cases the jurisdiction of the courts to review whether a minister had acted within the scope of his delegated powers: the rule of law required that regulations should be open to challenge in the courts save where Parliament deliberately concluded that it was essential in the public interest to preclude such a challenge.[89] The Committee regarded the existing procedures in judicial review as 'archaic and in some ways cumbrous and inelastic', and suggested simpler, cheaper and more expeditious procedures.[90] It favoured improved publicity for proposed new rules, but was unwilling to absolve both Houses of Parliament from their primary responsibility to supervise delegated legislation, and proposed a standing committee of each House to scrutinise every bill and every regulation, and report to the respective Houses.[91] It recommended an improved and uniform procedure for laying regulations before Parliament.[92] The Committee was inclined to think that the drafting of delegated legislation, like primary legislation, required the knowledge, experience and skill of professional parliamentary draftsmen.[93]

The Committee then turned to the topic of judicial or quasi-judicial decisions,[94] which the Committee considered interestingly and at some length. The Committee roundly accepted the fundamental necessity of not only maintaining but strengthening the supremacy of the law, and recognised that this involved the equal subjection of all classes to regular law administered by the ordinary courts.[95] The Committee was unanimously of opinion that no considerations of administrative convenience, or executive efficiency, should be allowed to weaken the control of the courts, and that no obstacle should be placed by Parliament in the way of the subject's unimpeded access to them.[96] It defined judicial decisions as involving the application of the law of the land to the facts as ascertained, and quasi-judicial decisions as involving considerations of public policy so that, in the last resort, the decision would not be one as to the respective rights and obligations of the parties but on what it was in the public interest to do.[97] It recommended that judicial, as distinct from quasi-judicial, functions should normally be entrusted to the ordinary courts of law.[98] When, exceptionally, Parliament considered it necessary to depart from the normal course, it should entrust the judicial decision to a ministerial tribunal independent of the minister in the exercise of its

---

[85] Ibid., at 58–9, 64–5.   [86] Ibid., at 59, 61, 65.   [87] Ibid., at 59.   [88] Ibid., at 61.
[89] Ibid., at 61, 65.   [90] Ibid., at 62.   [91] Ibid., at 62–3, 66–7.   [92] Ibid., at 67.
[93] Ibid., at 70.   [94] Section III of the *Report*, at 71.   [95] *Report*, at 113–14.
[96] Ibid., at 114.   [97] Ibid.   [98] Ibid., at 115.

functions and not to the minister personally.[99] Special and exceptional reasons
would be required before judicial functions were entrusted to a minister, and even
then it should not be done if the effect was to make him a judge in a departmental cause.[100] Quasi-judicial decisions, in the Committee's view, fell naturally to
ministers and not to courts of law or ministerial tribunals, provided the minister
was not disqualified by departmental interest.[101] Before any decision was given,
judicial or quasi-judicial, each of the parties should be given the opportunity of
stating his case (not necessarily orally) and of knowing the case he had to
meet.[102] Ministers exercising judicial or quasi-judicial functions and ministerial
tribunals exercising judicial functions should give the reasons for their decisions
in a document made available to the parties.[103] Where statutory public inquiries
were held in connection with the exercise of judicial or quasi-judicial functions
by ministers, the report should be published, and only the most exceptional
circumstances and the strongest reasons of public policy should be held to justify
a departure from this rule.[104] The supervisory jurisdiction of the High Court
should be vigilantly maintained, although court procedure should be modernised,
simplified and made less expensive.[105] Any party aggrieved by the judicial decision of a minister or a ministerial tribunal should have an absolute right to appeal
to the High Court on any question of law, such appeals being subject to a uniform
and simple procedure, but there should generally, subject to some possible exceptions, be no appeal to the court from any decision on fact.[106] The Committee
roundly rejected a suggestion made by Dr Robson that a system of administrative
law and administrative judges on the French model should be established.[107] But
it supported the enactment of a Crown Proceedings Bill to improve the rights of
the citizen in litigation against the state.[108] This is a proposal which Lord Hewart
also had made,[109] and he had indeed presided over a very strong committee which
had in 1927 prepared a draft bill.[110]

The Committee's *Report* was welcomed on publication as 'a very carefully
and fully compiled document',[111] 'a document of importance',[112] 'a report of the
greatest interest and importance'[113] and even, an ambitious claim, 'one of the
most important documents in the history of our Constitutional Law'.[114] One of
the few discordant notes was struck, perhaps predictably, by Dr Robson. He did,
it is true, acknowledge that:

All things considered, the Committee has done a far better piece of work than might have
been expected in view of the unpropitious circumstances attending its birth.[115]

---

[99] *Report*, at 116.   [100] Ibid.   [101] Ibid., at 116.   [102] Ibid.   [103] Ibid.
[104] Ibid., at 116–17.   [105] Ibid., at 117.   [106] Ibid.   [107] Ibid., at 118.
[108] Ibid.   [109] ND, 162–4.
[110] *Report of the Crown Proceedings Committee*, April 1927 (Cmd. 2842).
[111] (1932) 46 JP & LGR 377.   [112] (1932) 48 LQR 307.
[113] (1932) 76 Sol.Jo. 351 at 353.   [114] (1932) SLT 169.
[115] W. A. Robson, 'The Report of the Committee on Ministers' Powers', *The Political Quarterly*
(1932), 346 at p. 351.

But he considered that the English legal system had shown the most remarkable incapacity to expand in accordance with the needs of the modern state:[116] he criticized the failure of the *Report* to make any significant contribution to the structure of the system[117] and the failure of the courts to modernize, cheapen or bring into accordance with modern needs 'a fantastic procedure which has been obsolete for at least a century'.[118] Once again, he thought, we were muddling through; but he questioned whether anyone, ever again, would say that we had no administrative law.[119]

Those who saw the Committee's *Report* as a seminal constitutional document fit to rank with Magna Carta and the Petition of Right were doomed to disappointment. The recommendations proved unacceptable to the government of the day[120] and, as put by Wade and Forsyth in their work on *Administrative Law*:

The report led to certain improvement in delegated legislation, but in other respects it was little more than an academic exercise.[121]

The verdict of Professor Keeton, writing in 1949, was even more damning:

Few reports have assembled so much wisdom whilst proving so completely useless . . . its recommendations are forgotten, even by lawyers and administrators, and in no important respect did the report influence, much less delay, the onrush of administrative power, and the supersession of the ordinary forms of law which is taking place to-day.[122]

Lord Hewart for his part took pride in his authorship of *The New Despotism*, but changed his mind over delegated legislation: as, in the early days of the 1939 war, the rudimentary foundations of the welfare state began to be laid he is said to have expressed regret that he had ever written the book.[123]

In 1940, at the age of 70, Lord Hewart retired, or was forced into retirement, a step he had intended never to take,[124] and in May 1943 he died, his last words, characteristically enough, being an imprecation against the vernal outpouring of a cuckoo.[125] His death heralded what Sir William Wade has described as a very low point in the long struggle between governmental power and the protection of individual rights:

During and after the Second World War a deep gloom settled upon administrative law, which reduced it to the lowest ebb at which it had stood for centuries. The courts and the legal profession seemed to have forgotten the achievements of their predecessors and they showed little stomach for continuing their centuries-old work of imposing law upon government. It was understandable that executive power was paramount in wartime, but it was hard to understand why, in the flood of new powers and jurisdictions that came with the welfare state, administrative law should not have been vigorously revived, just when the need for it was greatest.[126]

---

[116] Ibid., at 357.   [117] Ibid., at 360.   [118] Ibid., at 361.   [119] Ibid., at 364.
[120] Wade and Forsyth, *Administrative Law*, 7th edn. (1994) at 18.   [121] Ibid., at 18.
[122] *The Nineteenth Century and After* (1949), 230.   [123] R. Jackson, op. cit., at 216.
[124] Ibid., at 334, 335.   [125] Ibid., at 336.   [126] Wade and Forsyth, op. cit., at 18.

From that slough of despond we have, I hope, dragged ourselves. Many causes have no doubt contributed to that recovery. I think one can identify three in particular.

First, and I think most importantly, we have witnessed a return to older and more principled habits of legal thought or, as it might be more crudely put, a startling rediscovery of judicial nerve. There have, of course, been many decisions which signalled rejection of the more abject precedents of earlier years.[127] But if, in the manner of a television game, one were to seek to identify two decisions which, more than any other, showed that the courts were willing once again to recognize and discharge their historic responsibilities, my chosen candidates would be *Anisminic v Foreign Compensation Commission*[128] and *Council of Civil Service Unions v Minister for the Civil Service*.[129] In the first of these cases the House of Lords annulled a decision of the Commission despite a statutory stipulation that:

The determination by the commission of any application made to them under this Act shall not be called in question in any court of law.

The disembodied spirit of Lord Hewart must have rejoiced. In the second the House made clear that almost any exercise of public power, whatever the source of the power, is reviewable by the courts. There remain some no-go areas, such as review of the treaty-making power,[130] but they are few. Conspicuous among those whose judgments restored the rule of law in this area were Lord Denning, Lord Reid, Lord Diplock, and Lord Wilberforce. Henceforward there was much less to be gained by use of the statutory formulae to which Lord Hewart had particularly objected, since the courts were now willing, if an unlawful abuse of power were shown, to decline to give effect to such formulae.

The beneficial effect of these bold decisions would, however, have been limited but for the second of my three decisive causes: changes in the procedure for seeking judicial review, made in 1977. Apparently modest in scope, and made without statutory intervention, these procedural changes transformed judicial review from the part-time activity of the few to a mass sport for the many. In the process an old truth was demonstrated: that with courts, as with airlines, a demand only becomes evident when the means exist to meet it.

The third cause I would mention is of a different character, but no less important. By the late 1950s the use of tribunals outside the main court system, to resolve issues, disputes and objections arising from the exercise or application of public powers, had become an established feature of public life. But there remained an important and unresolved question: were these tribunals to be

---

[127] e.g., *R v Northumberland Compensation Appeal Tribunal ex parte Shaw* [1952] 1 KB 338; *Ridge v Baldwin* [1964] AC 40; *Secretary of State for Employment v ASLEF (No 2)* [1972] 2 QB 455; *Secretary of State for Education and Science v Tameside Metropolitan Borough Council* [1977] AC 1014; *Padfield v Minister of Agriculture Fisheries and Food* [1965] AC 997; *Conway v Rimmer* [1968] AC 910.   [128] [1969] 2 AC 147.   [129] [1985] AC 374.

[130] *R v Secretary of State for Foreign and Commonwealth Affairs ex parte Rees-Mogg* [1994] 1 All ER 457.

regarded as an extension of the administrative function or a variant of the judicial? A Committee on Administrative Tribunals and Enquiries was established under Sir Oliver Franks to consider the question. Its report[131] was a resounding endorsement of the judicial model. Forty years on the Committee's conclusions read well:

403. Our general conclusion regarding tribunals is that, despite the haphazard way in which they have developed, this method of decision by tribunals works on the whole reasonably well. It could, however, be greatly improved in certain respects, particularly by providing for its continuous oversight by the Lord Chancellor's Council on Tribunals and the Scottish Council on Tribunals, whose establishment we have recommended, by the application to it of consistent basic principles and by associating tribunals more closely with the higher courts.

404. Our general conclusion regarding administrative procedures involving an enquiry or hearing is that because the resultant decisions are taken by Ministers and therefore to a considerable degree by departmental processes it is essential, if public confidence is to be maintained, that the various procedures should be as open as possible . . .

406. We regard both tribunal and administrative procedures as essential to our society. But we hope that we have equally indicated our view that the administration should not use these methods of adjudication as convenient alternatives to the courts of law. We wish to emphasise that in deciding by whom adjudications involving the administration and the individual citizen should be carried out preference should be given to the ordinary courts of law rather than to a tribunal unless there are demonstrably special reasons which make a tribunal more appropriate, namely the need for cheapness, accessibility, freedom from technicality, expedition and expert knowledge of a particular subject. Similarly, preference should be given to a tribunal rather than to a Minister, and this requires that every effort should be made to express policy in the form of regulations capable of being administered by an independent tribunal. We recognise, however, that this may not always be possible and that in these cases the adjudication must be made by a Minister.

407. Where, in the light of these considerations, it is justifiable to establish a tribunal or to entrust adjudicating functions to a Minister we are convinced that an ultimate control in regard to matters of law should be exercised by the traditional courts. We are not satisfied that a sufficient case has been made out for the establishment of a separate administrative court to hear appeals from tribunals or ministerial adjudications.[132]

The Committee took as its guiding principle the need for openness, fairness and impartiality,[133] highlighting the need for tribunal members to be impartial, for procedures to give the citizen fair notice of the case he has to meet,[134] for public hearings,[135] for the giving of reasons.[136] The decision of the tribunal should not be immune from challenge in the courts:

409 (25) There should be an appeal on fact, law and merits from a tribunal at first instance to an appellate tribunal, except where the tribunal of first instance is exceptionally strong and well qualified . . .

---

[131] Cmd 218 (1957).   [132] At 89–90.   [133] At para. 402.   [134] At para. 409 (10).
[135] Ibid. (13).   [136] Ibid. (22).

(26) As a matter of general principle appeal should not lie from a tribunal to a Minister . . .

(28) No statute should contain words purporting to oust the remedies by way of certiorari, prohibition and mandamus . . .[137]

In this area also, I think, the spirit of Lord Hewart would rejoice.

A much more recent, and as yet unproven, experiment is perhaps deserving of mention. In 1992–3 the House of Lords established a Delegated Powers Scrutiny Committee. Since then the Committee has examined proposed legislation in order to see whether the grant of secondary rule-making powers to ministers is appropriate, whether the power in question is so important as to require inclusion in primary legislation, whether the purposes of the rule-making power and the principles governing the exercise of the power are sufficiently clear, and whether any proposed Henry VIII clauses are appropriate. The task of the Committee is not to comment on the merits of Bills but to monitor proposals to confer rule-making powers on ministers and recommend changes if proposals are regarded as too wide or insufficiently defined. These are early days; but the Committee's reports have commanded the respect of ministers and the House.[138] Not many people, I think, would now share Lord Hewart's belief that this would be a task reliably carried out by any newspaper.

Over the last seventy years the clarion call issued by Lord Hewart in 1929 has, I think, been answered. We have in that time witnessed the harm done by judicial abdication; but we have also, I think, come to recognise the potential dangers of excessive judicial activism. While the courts have their own important sphere of activity, so too do the executive, and good government depends on respect rather than competition between the two. It is this simple truth which, I think, the Lord Chancellor, Lord Irvine, recognized in his recent Paul Sieghart Memorial Lecture:

Crucially however, the judiciary's activist endeavour in the field of public law has been tempered with appropriate restraint. The courts have consistently accepted the limits of their role within the British State. They have appreciated that their function of providing effective protection for citizens against maladministration must be discharged in a manner which takes account of other values which society embraces, such as the democratic imperative of Parliamentary Sovereignty and the need to respect the executive's area of decision-making autonomy. In this manner it has been possible for English courts to fashion a modern régime of administrative law, without challenging the established axioms of the legal order. It is their realistic perception of the judicial role that explains the successful track record of our courts in the difficult task of balancing the competing demands of intervention and restraint.

I am inclined to agree. But if I did not agree, I should hesitate to write a book to say so; and if I did write a book, I would not seek to emulate the style of my distinguished predecessor.

---

[137] Cmd 218 (25) (26) (28).
[138] e.g., 5th Report, Select Committee on Delegated Powers and Deregulation, 13/1/99, HL Paper 17; HL Hansard, 19/1/99, col. 483 et seq.

3

*Mr Perlzweig, Mr Liversidge, and Lord Atkin**

On 29 May 1940 Mr Jack Perlzweig was arrested and taken to Brixton Prison. He remained in prison until his release in early January 1942. There is nothing very remarkable in that. Every year many men spend periods of time in Brixton Prison, often staying longer than Mr Perlzweig. But during his sojourn, under the assumed name of Robert Liversidge, he achieved the special, eponymous fame reserved for those who participate, successfully or unsuccessfully, in major lawsuits. It is as a litigant that Mr Liversidge enters the pages of English history.

In the summer of 1939 it was appreciated that war with Germany was imminent. It was clear that the government required exceptional powers to enable it to meet the expected emergency. To that end, there was introduced into Parliament the Emergency Powers (Defence) Bill. Clause 1 (2) of the Bill provided that

without prejudice to the generality of the powers conferred by the preceding subsection Defence Regulations may, so far as appears to His Majesty in Council to be necessary or expedient for any of the purposes mentioned in that subsection,

(a) make provision for the ... detention of persons whose detention appears to the Secretary of State to be expedient in the interests of the public safety or the defence of the Realm; ...

This clause was seeking to obviate an issue which had arisen during the First World War concerning the validity of Parliament's delegation to the executive of power to issue Regulations authorizing internment without trial. On 24 August 1939, when the House of Commons considered this clause in Committee, a member moved to substitute a reference to 'a judge of the High Court' for the reference to the Secretary of State, intending that the expediency of detaining persons without trial should be subject to the judgment of the court and not the executive government. This proposal was rejected by the Home Secretary of the day, Sir Samuel Hoare, but he undertook to establish an Advisory Committee and other safeguards for the liberty of the subject and on this assurance the amendment was withdrawn. The clause accordingly received the Royal Assent in the form which I have quoted. As enacted, the statute made provision for the establishment of an Advisory Committee to which persons interned could make objection, and it was the duty of the chairman of the Advisory Committee (in the event, Norman Birkett QC) to inform the objector of the grounds on which the order had been made against him and to furnish him with such particulars as were in the opinion of the chairman sufficient to enable the objector to present his case.

* Lecture delivered at the Reform Club, 16 October 1997.

Exercising his powers under the Act, the Home Secretary made the Defence (General) Regulations 1939. The relevant Regulation for present purposes was Regulation 18B, which in its original form read:

The Secretary of State, if satisfied with respect to any particular person that with a view to prevent him from acting in any manner prejudicial to the public safety or the defence of the Realm it is necessary to do so, may make an order. . . .

This wording made it plain that the judgment was one for the Secretary of State alone. It was on this ground that on 31 October 1939 Mr Dingle Foot, from the Liberal benches, attacked the form of Regulation 18B. His attack was supported by others, and the Home Secretary, by this time Sir John Anderson, failed to satisfy the critics. To save the day, the Lord Privy Seal (Sir Samuel Hoare) intervened to offer all-party consultations. As a result, an informal conference took place on 8 November 1939. Among those attending were the Home Secretary, the First Parliamentary Counsel, the Permanent Under-Secretary of the Home Office, Sir William Jowitt and Mr Dingle Foot. It is not now possible to reconstruct with any confidence the precise effect of what transpired at this meeting. It may indeed have been a somewhat unfocused discussion. Following the meeting, however, Regulation 18B of the Regulations was amended, and became law in the following terms:

If the Secretary of State has reasonable cause to believe any person to be of hostile origin or associations or to have been recently concerned in acts prejudicial to the public safety or the defence of the Realm or in the preparation or instigation of such acts and that by reason thereof it is necessary to exercise control over him, he may make an order against that person directing that he be detained.

I draw attention to the change of wording from 'the Secretary of State, if satisfied . . .' to 'If the Secretary of State has reasonable cause to believe . . .'

In the Spring and early Summer of 1940, when invasion was imminently expected, there was understandable public concern at the risk presented by those who might support or collaborate with the invader. It is therefore unsurprising that between May and August 1940 Sir John Anderson as Home Secretary made orders for the detention of 1,428 people. One of them was Mr Liversidge. On 26 May 1940 Sir John Anderson made and signed an order which began:

Whereas I have reasonable cause to believe Jack Perlzweig alias Robert Liversidge to be a person of hostile associations and that by reason thereof it is necessary to exercise control over him. . . .

Three days later Mr Liversidge was detained.

On 14 March 1941 Mr Liversidge issued a writ claiming a declaration that his detention in prison was unlawful and damages for false imprisonment. The defendants were Sir John Anderson and Mr Herbert Morrison, who had become Home Secretary in October 1940. Both parties pleaded their cases with a brevity perhaps indicative of a patriotic desire to save paper. The plaintiff simply pleaded the order and the detention and asserted that both were unlawful. The defendants simply admitted the order and put the rest of the plaintiff's case in issue. The plaintiff responded by asking for details of the grounds upon which Sir John Anderson had reasonable cause to believe Liversidge to be a person of hostile associations and upon which he had reasonable cause to believe that by reason of such hostile associations it was necessary to exercise control over the plaintiff. The defendants declined to give these details. The plaintiff accordingly applied to Master Moseley (no relation) asking that they be ordered to do so. He declined to make such an order. The plaintiff appealed. Mr Justice Tucker, sitting in chambers, also declined to make an order in the plaintiff's favour. At this stage the parties were debating a rather legalistic issue of onus: was it for the plaintiff to prove that the Secretary of State had had no reasonable cause to believe, or was it for the Secretary of State to prove that he had had reasonable cause? Both the Master and the judge held that the onus lay on the plaintiff to prove lack of reasonable cause, and so declined to order the Secretary of State to give the details requested.

In the Court of Appeal the issue between the parties changed. For the first time the real crux of the argument emerged. Was it enough to justify an order of detention that the Secretary of State, acting in good faith, thought he had reasonable cause to believe Liversidge to be a person of hostile associations and that it was therefore necessary to detain him? The defendants argued that it was, and if they were correct it meant that the court could not investigate the reasonableness of the Secretary of State's belief in any way. Or was it necessary that the Secretary of State should actually have reasonable cause to believe Liversidge to be a person of hostile associations and that by reason thereof it was necessary to detain him, so that the court could, if the lawfulness of detention were challenged, investigate whether the Secretary of State had reasonable cause for his beliefs or not? The plaintiff sought an affirmative answer to this question. In the division of opinion on this issue lies the historic importance of this case.

The Court of Appeal unanimously answered the question in favour of the defendants. Liversidge appealed to the House of Lords. The argument took place over three days in September 1941 before Viscount Maugham, a former Lord Chancellor, presiding, Lord Atkin, Lord Macmillan, Lord Wright and Lord Romer. Judgment was delivered on Monday, 3 November 1941 in the Robing Room at Westminster, the Lords having surrendered their own Chamber for use by the Commons following destruction of the House of Commons' Chamber in May 1941. Viscount Maugham was absent, having received inadequate notice of the date of judgment. His speech was read by Lord Macmillan. Having set the scene, Viscount Maugham observed that the language of the Act was such as to give power to the Secretary of State to make regulations having the effect for which the defendants contended. In this he was plainly right, and the contrary had not been argued. The question was whether that power had been exercised. That was a question of construing, namely giving the correct meaning to, the words of the Regulation. Viscount Maugham held that the House should prefer a construction which would carry into effect the plain intention of those responsible for the Regulations rather than one which would defeat that intention. While acknowledging that a phrase such as 'if AB has reasonable cause to believe' could be understood to mean 'if there is in fact reasonable cause for believing', he was quite unable to take the view that the words could only have that meaning. It seemed to him reasonably clear that if the thing to be believed was something essentially within the knowledge of AB the words might well require AB only to act on what, in good faith, he thought to be reasonable cause. There were a number of circumstances which in his judgment tended to support that conclusion. First of all, he regarded the matters in question as so clearly matters for executive discretion and nothing else that he could not believe that those responsible for the Regulations could have contemplated for a moment the possibility that the actions of the Secretary of State should be subject to the discussion, criticism or control of a judge in court. Secondly, he attached importance to the fact that the Home Secretary could act on hearsay, and thought it strange if his decision could thereafter be questioned in a court of law. Thirdly, he pointed out that the Secretary of State would often act on information of the most confidential character which could not be communicated to the person detained or disclosed in court without prejudice to the public interest. Fourthly, drawing a contrast with the position of a police constable, he thought it important that the person entrusted with these important duties was a principal Secretary of State and a member of the Government answerable to Parliament for the proper discharge of his duties. The establishment of the Advisory Committee and the absence of any express right of appeal pointed towards the Secretary of State as the final arbiter.

Viscount Maugham made reference to arguments presented for Liversidge on the different language of different Regulations, and accepted that these were of some weight. But he pointed out that Regulations did not in general receive the same attention and scrutiny as statutes; he suggested that even in statutes a change of words did not necessarily indicate a change of meaning; and he thought that the language of Regulation 18B might well have been dictated by the desirability of drawing the attention of the Secretary of State to the fact that in cases when he was considering depriving a person of his liberty for an uncertain period he should himself have considered whether there was reasonable cause for forming the belief which would justify his action. These last three points are not persuasive. Even statutory instruments must be given the meaning which they naturally bear; they cannot be given some other meaning on the assumption that they have been sloppily drafted. Where, in statutes, a change of language is used without any change of meaning being intended, that represents a defect in the drafting. It seems scarcely credible that the language was adopted to bring home to the Secretary of State the need for great care when detaining members of the public for an indefinite period without trial. Viscount Maugham was, perhaps, on stronger ground in holding that it cannot have been intended, in this dire national emergency, to subject the Secretary of State's executive decision to review in a court of law.

Lords Macmillan, Wright, and Romer all delivered speeches in which, at some length, they agreed with Viscount Maugham's conclusion. Lord Macmillan quoted an earlier case in which Lord Parker had said:

Those who are responsible for the national security must be the sole judges of what the national security requires. It would be obviously undesirable that such matters should be made the subject of evidence in a court of law or otherwise discussed in public.

Lord Wright said:

But in the constitution of this country there are no guaranteed or absolute rights. The safeguard of British liberty is in the good sense of the people and in the system of representative and responsible government which has been evolved. If extraordinary powers are here given, they are given because the emergency is extraordinary and are limited to the period of the emergency.

Lord Atkin alone reached a different conclusion. Early in his speech he said:

It is surely incapable of dispute that the words 'if A has X' constitute a condition the essence of which is the existence of X and the having of it by A. If it is a condition to a right (including a power) granted to A, whenever the right comes into dispute the tribunal whatever it may be that is charged with determining the dispute must ascertain whether the condition is fulfilled. In some cases the issue is one of fact, in others of both fact and law, but in all cases the words indicate an existing something the having of which can be ascertained. And the words do not mean and cannot mean 'if A thinks that he has'. 'If A has a broken ankle' does not mean and cannot mean 'if A thinks that he has a broken ankle'. 'If A has a right of way' does not mean and cannot mean 'if A thinks that he has a right of way'. 'Reasonable cause' for an action or a belief is just as much a positive fact capable of determination by a third party as is a broken ankle or a legal right. . . .

Lord Atkin then proceeded to show, by reference to a multitude of examples, that the requirement of reasonable cause had always in the past been understood as requiring proof of an objective fact. He then went on to consider the Regulations themselves, pointing out that in some a subjective test was posed ('If it appears to the Secretary of State . . .') and in others, such as 18B, an objective test. In holding that the test in Regulation 18B was, and was intended to be, objective, Lord Atkin relied on the amendment which had been made to the language of the Regulation. In his view there was no ambiguity at all in the language of 18B. It was not a question of substituting the decision of judges for the decision of the Minister, but of providing a power of review.

Close to the end of his speech, Lord Atkin said, in a passage which despite its length calls for citation:

I view with apprehension the attitude of judges who on a mere question of construction when face to face with claims involving the liberty of the subject show themselves more executive minded than the executive. Their function is to give words their natural meaning, not, perhaps, in war time leaning towards liberty, but following the dictum of Pollock CB in *Bowditch v Balchin*, cited with approval by my noble and learned friend Lord Wright in *Barnard v Gorman*: 'In a case in which the liberty of the subject is concerned, we cannot go beyond the natural construction of the statute.'

In this country, amid the clash of arms, the laws are not silent. They may be changed, but they speak the same language in war as in peace. It has always been one of the pillars of freedom, one of the principles of liberty for which on recent authority we are now fighting, that the judges are no respecters of persons and stand between the subject and any attempted encroachments on his liberty by the executive, alert to see that any coercive action is justified in law. In this case I have listened to arguments which might have been addressed acceptably to the Court of King's Bench in the time of Charles I.

I protest, even if I do it alone, against a strained construction put on words with the effect of giving an uncontrolled power of imprisonment to the Minister. To recapitulate: The words have only one meaning. They are used with that meaning in statements of the common law and in statutes. They have never been used in the sense now imputed to them. They are used in the Defence Regulations in the natural meaning, and, when it is intended to express the meaning now imputed to them, different and apt words are used in the regulations generally and in this regulation in particular. Even it were relevant, which it is not, there is no absurdity or no such degree of public mischief as would lead to a non-natural construction.

I know of only one authority which might justify the suggested method of construction: ' "When I use a word", Humpty Dumpty said in rather a scornful tone, "it means just what I choose it to mean, neither more nor less." "The question is," said Alice, "whether you can make words mean so many different things." "The question is," said Humpty Dumpty, "which is to be master—that's all." ' ('Through the Looking Glass', c.vi). After all this long discussion the question is whether the words 'If a man has' can mean 'If a man thinks he was.' I am of opinion that they cannot, and that the case should be decided accordingly.

Lord Atkin's reference to Alice prompted an occurrence unknown in my personal experience. Just before the weekend preceding the delivery of judgment, copies of the speeches to be delivered were seen by the Lord Chancellor, Viscount Simon, who on 31 October wrote to Lord Atkin suggesting that the Lewis Carroll reference would be wounding to his colleagues whom he was holding up to ridicule. The speech would not, Simon suggested, be weakened if the paragraph were removed. Atkin wrote a polite but unyielding reply. I am not at all surprised. It is inherent in the independence of the judges that they should be independent of each other. Even among judges sitting on the same case, points on the substance of another judgment will be made only with the utmost diffidence. It is extraordinary that such a suggestion should have been made by any one not involved in the case at all.

In believing that Atkin's colleagues would be wounded by his speech, however, Simon was right. After delivery of the speech Atkin was cold-shouldered by his colleagues. And Maugham was stung into writing a letter to *The Times* to say that he had for his part heard no argument addressed on behalf of the defendants which justified the reference to the Court of King's Bench in the time of Charles I. The Lord Chief Justice, Lord Caldecote, wrote to Atkin to express his shock at being told that when he was face to face with claims affecting the liberty of the subject he was more executive minded than the executive. Whether his sensitivity owed anything to his having, until very recently, been a member of the executive must be a matter of conjecture. Atkin wrote a friendly and reasoned, but uncompromising, answer.

The speeches of the House of Lords, and in particular Atkin's eloquent dissent, attracted wide public attention. The press was divided. The *Manchester Guardian*, the *Spectator*, and the *New Statesman* supported Atkin. The *Daily Telegraph* and *The Economist* supported the majority. So also did *The Times*, in a judicious leading article. A number of prominent churchmen, including the Bishops of Birmingham and Monmouth and the Dean of St Paul's, and a number of members of the public, wrote to Atkin expressing support. So also, and significantly, did a number of prominent practitioners, who included Cyril Radcliffe KC, Hartley Shawcross KC, F. A. Sellers KC, and Clement Davies KC, MP, the future Liberal leader. From the Judges' Lodgings in Leicester, Mr Justice Stable, who had decided an earlier case (not cited in the House of Lords) in the same way as Atkin, wrote to him and said:

I venture to think the decision of the House of Lords has reduced the stature of the Judiciary with consequences that the nation will one day bitterly regret. Bacon, I think, said the judges were the lions under the Throne, but the House of Lords has reduced us to mice squeaking under a chair in the Home Office.

A rising junior named Gerald Gardiner followed Lord Maugham's example and wrote to *The Times*. Having referred to the earlier withdrawal and amendment of Regulation 18B, he posed the question:

What is one to think of an Executive whose law officers now argue that the amended regulation means, and must have been intended to mean, precisely the same as the regulation which was withdrawn?

Lord Gardiner later told Mr Geoffrey Lewis, the author of Lord Atkin's biography, that he understood the benchers of the Inner Temple had considered disciplining him for writing this letter but had decided not to do so, perhaps on the basis that if an ex-Lord Chancellor wrote a silly letter to *The Times* he might expect a silly reply. But in truth Gardiner's point was far from silly, and deserved an answer.

The decision had a sequel in both Houses of Parliament. In the Lords, the Lord Chancellor was invited to reprove Lord Maugham for writing to *The Times* as he had done. The Lord Chancellor predictably said that he had no responsibility for the activities of judges. But Maugham took the opportunity to make a personal statement to the House. Atkin himself was not present. In the House of Commons it was moved on 26 November, with express reference of Lord Atkin's dissenting judgment, that the Regulations should be amended to provide for an appeal to an independent tribunal. This motion was strongly resisted, and the government

triumphantly defeated it without a vote. By this time Herbert Morrison had
released a large number of those detained the year before, and Liversidge himself
was released within two months or so of the House of Lords decision.

Among those who wrote to Lord Atkin to express support for his decision were
several academic lawyers, including Mr Hazel, the Principal of Jesus College
Oxford, Sir John Miles, the Warden of Merton, and C. K. Allen, the Warden of
Rhodes House. The January 1942 issue of the *Law Quarterly Review*, however,
was hostile. It opened with strong support for the majority conclusion, and in
particular the analysis of Lord Wright, from the heavyweight figure of Sir
William Holdsworth. In his opinion it was clear that the question whether a
person was of hostile origins or associations so that it was necessary to exercise
control over him raised not a justiciable but a political or administrative issue. The
editor of the *Review*, Professor Goodhart, also supported the majority, believing
that the primary importance of the case was to be found not in its constitutional
aspect but in the method of statutory interpretation adopted by the majority of the
House. Professor Goodhart placed considerable reliance on Parliament's rejection, after the decision, of the objective test favoured by Atkin, but also found it
possible to argue that there was no difference between saying that one has a
broken ankle and saying that one thinks one has a broken ankle. In the course of
his note he wrote:

It is this idea that there can be no law unless it has been pronounced by the judiciary which
in the past has hindered the rational development of administrative law in this Country. It
is to be hoped that one result of the *Liversidge Case* will be to make it clear that review by
the Courts is not essential whenever an executive officer or body had been given the power
to decide a case . . . Sir Cecil Carr in his recent book *Concerning English Administrative
Law* remarks (at page 97) that the "belief that the judges are the sole repositories of incor-
ruptibility must be a modern growth". This belief, as illustrated by Lord Atkin's speech is,
we think, an unfortunate one as it places undue emphasis on judicial review of administrative acts.

The professor considered that the majority speeches represented not only good
law but also good common sense.

The next issue of the *Review*, in April 1942, contained an eloquent rebuttal of
these views by C. K. Allen. Drawing on famous historical precedents, including
the *Ship Money* case, he wrote:

Generations of Englishmen have been brought up to regard it as one vital aspect of the
Rule of Law (for which, among other things, this country is now fighting the most crucial
war in its history) that all persons are equal before the law and that for any unjustified
infringement of the liberty of the subject the liability of a Minister of State is no whit
different from that of a policeman, or, indeed, from the meanest of the King's subjects.

In the *Modern Law Review* for July 1942 Professor G. W. Keeton wrote a
balanced assessment of the decision, placing it in its historical context. He
concluded:

Those who have greeted Lord Atkin's judgment with warm approval are not unaware of the urgent necessity for vigorous Executive action in the interests of national safety in a war such as is at present being waged, but they are also aware that 'appetite grows with that it feeds upon', and they would see in even the limited check which Lord Atkin's interpretation of Regulation 18B would impose upon the Executive a reassertion of a principle for which a number of Englishmen in recent years have rather strangely lost their enthusiasm.

In a postscript he expressed inability to follow the reasoning in Professor Goodhart's *Law Quarterly* note.

When Lord Atkin delivered his speech in *Liversidge*, he was within weeks of his 74th birthday, a reminder perhaps that judicial virtue does not necessarily wither with age. In an obituary note published in the *Law Quarterly Review* for October 1944, Lord Wright (an unrepentant member of the majority in *Liversidge*) said of that decision that 'Lord Atkin had at least shown his habitual courage and independence.' In a longer and more detailed note Professor H. C. Gutteridge KC, an old friend of Atkin, wrote:

In *Liversidge v Anderson* his sense of indignation against what he regarded as a flagrant breach of the liberty of the subject caused him to express himself with a freedom which was perhaps unwarranted by the circumstances. But, be this as it may, his speech in the House of Lords will go down to posterity as a vigorous re-assertion of the rights of the individual citizen and, as such, will find a place in the annals of the law.

In the January 1970 issue of the *Law Quarterly Review* the late Professor Heuston published a detailed and well-researched article on the decision, '*Liversidge v Anderson* in retrospect', on which later commentators (certainly including myself) have heavily drawn and depended. Heuston wrote of the 'passionate, almost wild, rhetoric of the three concluding paragraphs' of Lord Atkin's speech. He described it as 'an explosion' in Lord Atkin's mind. Professor Heuston's own conclusion was this:

Although neither side can be said to be clearly 'right' or 'wrong' it is possible to express a rational preference as between the two lines of reasoning to be found in the judgments. This author's preference is for the reasoning of the majority.

He added:

No subsequent proceedings by Liversidge have been traced, although nearly twenty-five years later Mr D. N. Pritt [his counsel on the appeal] stated the grounds for his client's internment, as they were known to him. Apparently Liversidge had been accused

  (1) of having been engaged in commercial frauds;
  (2) of having been in touch with persons who were suspected of being enemy agents; and
  (3) of being the son of a Jewish Rabbi.

If indeed these were the grounds for Anderson's belief that it was necessary to intern Liversidge, it was fortunate for the executive that the courts held that they had no power to inquire into the matter.

If these were indeed the grounds for his internment, it is no surprise that Liversidge was so quickly released after the decision. In conclusion Professor Heuston observed:

Fortunately Mr Justice Stable's gloomy prediction in 1941 that the stature of the judiciary had been reduced "to mice squeaking under a chair in the Home Office" has not been fulfilled. So although Lord Atkin's speech in *Liversidge v Anderson* may not have been "correct" within the context of that decision itself, it yet has had more profound influence on public law than the speeches of any of the majority Law Lords.

In truth, Professor Heuston underestimated the extent to which Lord Atkin's dissent had already come to be regarded as the correct view of the law. As early as *Nakkuda Ali v Jayaratne* [1951] AC 66, the reasoning of the majority was distinguished. In *Ridge v Baldwin* [1964] AC 40 Lord Reid described the decision as 'the very peculiar decision of this House'. In a series of decisions (such as *Secretary of State for Employment v ASLEF (No. 2)* [1972] 2 QB 455) the reasoning of the majority was bypassed, or the reasoning of Lord Atkin preferred. But it was not until *Inland Revenue Commissioners v Rossminster* [1980] AC 952 that the *coup de grâce* was administered. In that case Lord Diplock, with the support of the other Law Lords, said:

For my part I think the time has come to acknowledge openly that the majority of this House in *Liversidge v Anderson* were expediently and, at that time, perhaps, excusably, wrong and the dissenting speech of Lord Atkin was right.

How, then, more than half a century later, does the balance sheet stand? I have for my part no doubt at all but that Lord Atkin was correct in his essential argument on the meaning of the words used in the relevant version of Regulation 18B. There is a simple but crucial distinction between a condition which requires the existence of an objective fact (on the existence of which the court can, if necessary, rule) and the existence of a subjective belief (which requires little more than good faith and an absence of gross irrationality, which leave little room for review by the court). Lord Atkin's central legal argument was surely correct. But I think that the majority were right, in fact if not in law, in concluding that it was the subjective and not the objective test which those who framed the Regulation, and Parliament, intended. Both before the decision and after, Parliament had the opportunity to adopt the objective test, and expressly declined to do so. It seems clear that in those early and perilous years of the war, the outcome of which (we must remember) was far from certain, Parliament did not wish the effectiveness of executive action to be hampered by the toils of judicial review.

In the sense much more important than the narrow legal sense, however, Lord Atkin has been proved to be triumphantly correct. At one of the lowest moments of our national history, it was no doubt easy to feel that exceptional circumstances called for exceptional remedies, that this was no time for legal niceties, that it was expedient to intern one man that the whole nation perish not. But we are entitled to be proud that even in that extreme national emergency there was one voice, eloquent and courageous, which asserted older, nobler, more enduring values: the right of the individual against the state; the duty to govern in accordance with law; the role of the courts as guarantor of legality and individual right; the priceless gift, subject only to constraints by law established, of individual freedom. It would be hard to express these values more shortly, more simply, more memorably, than in Atkin's neatly turned Ciceronian allusion:

In this country, amid the clash of arms, the laws are not silent. They may be changed, but they speak the same language in war as in peace. It has always been one of the pillars of freedom . . . that the judges are no respecters of persons and stand between the subject and any attempted encroachments on his liberty by the executive, alert to see that any coercive action is justified in law.

PART VI
THE CONSTITUTION

We are all, as members of clubs, associations, trade unions, universities or limited companies, familiar with the sort of statutes, rules, and regulations which govern the proceedings of such bodies. They usually prescribe what offices there shall be, what powers the office-holders may exercise, how the office-holders are to be elected or appointed, how long they shall serve, how and on what grounds they may be removed, to whom they are accountable, how a member aggrieved by the conduct of the body may seek redress, and so on. Sometimes this governing instrument is called a constitution. That, at any rate, is the name given to the body of rules and conventions which govern our life as a nation. Since the life of the nation is complex and multifarious, we cannot expect our national constitution to be simple.

Nor can we expect it to be permanent. Times change, and constitutional arrangements must change with them. The constitutional arrangements of Queen Victoria's day, however appropriate then, would not be acceptable to any rational democrat today. So our national constitution must be kept under review, and points of friction eased or resolved. The first of the two papers in this section addresses the constitutional position of the courts. This paper opens by contrasting the British constitution with that of the United States. It goes on to consider what I then saw as issues of current concern affecting the constitutional role of the judges.

The second of the two papers was the inaugural Pilgrim Fathers lecture given at the University of Plymouth. This was an opportunity to think further about the differences and likenesses between our constitution and the American, some of which this paper seeks to explore.

1

*The Courts and the Constitution**

Anyone visiting the National Archives in Washington DC is likely to be struck by the sight of a long queue wending its way slowly but respectfully towards an object in a glass case. The object, treated with almost the veneration which the devout might show towards a holy relic, is the Constitution of the United States.

There are a number of obvious reasons why such a scene would not be seen here. In the first place, our constitution, although in large measure written, is not contained in any single document suitable for public exhibition. The nearest we come, perhaps, is the Great Charter of 1215, an instrument of which the significance is, interestingly, much more generally appreciated in the United States than here. But it is not a document which is easy to read, and most of its provisions carry no immediate contemporary message. Secondly, despite a plethora of statutes governing constitutional matters, it remains true that our constitution depends on convention to a greater extent than most. Even questions as potentially important as when the sovereign may refuse a dissolution of Parliament, and who the sovereign should invite to form a government if no party in the House of Commons has an overall majority, are governed by precedent and convention, not statute. One cannot queue up to gaze at a convention or a precedent. Thirdly, of course, our constitution is not entrenched, and therefore lacks the sacrosanct quality which may attach to a constitutional code which enjoys the status of a higher law.

All this may go some way to explain, but it does little to excuse, the mixture of ignorance and insouciance with which, as it seems to me, many in this country approach our own constitutional arrangements. This would not matter if the constitution were a peripheral feature of our national life. But the constitution is, after all, the body of rules and conventions which governs our life as a nation, the articles of association of United Kingdom PLC of which we are all members. Surely, therefore, it deserves more thoughtful consideration than the public seem inclined to give it.

I will give one recent, and general, example of the sort of comment which I venture to criticize. A few months ago it was being suggested that the Prince of Wales could not accede to the throne if he were to be divorced. Why not, I ask? His forebear King Henry VIII was not a noted monogamist, and King George I succeeded to the throne despite a previous divorce. It is true that the sovereign is Supreme Governor of the Church of England, which does not encourage divorce.

* Lecture delivered at King's College, London on 14 February 1996. First published in *The King's College Law Journal* (1996–7), vol. 7, 12–26.

But although the Act of Settlement requires the sovereign to be in communion with the Church of England, it does not require him or her to be a member of it, and the first two Hanoverian monarchs were German Lutherans. It is also worthy of note that the sovereign is bound by the Act of Union to preserve and maintain the Presbyterian Church of Scotland, and on visiting Scotland conventionally becomes a member of that church and so a Presbyterian. None of this suggests that the constitution requires the sovereign to carry devotion to the Church of England to the point of fanaticism. One might furthermore ask why the Prince of Wales should be debarred from succession by his participation in a process which he shares with a very large number of his adult subjects. All, of course, ultimately depends, or might depend, on the will of Parliament. Twice in the 900 years since the Norman Conquest Parliament has, by statute, altered the succession to the throne, most recently on the abdication of King Edward VIII in 1936. So Parliament may intervene, were it (very improbably) to wish to do so, but in the absence of such intervention the Prince of Wales's right to accede would be unchallengeable. Since the Queen has now, one understands, encouraged a divorce between the Prince and the Princess, it would seem clear that she (quite rightly) has no doubt on the point.

When one turns to the constitutional role and position of the courts and the judges—my topic this evening—the evidence of misunderstanding is perhaps even more profuse. I will give three examples.

1. From time to time a judge will make some observation which is, or is thought to be, foolish or ill-advised, or reaches a decision which is, or is thought to be, objectionable and wrong. It should not surprise anyone that this is so. Judges perform their duties in the public eye; most of what they say in public is not read from a prepared script, carefully composed to avoid giving hostages to fortune; and they are not immune from ordinary human error. Nor are they immune from inaccurate reporting. But when one of these episodes occurs, the response is predictable: a chorus of demands from the tabloid press and sometimes from parliamentary sources that the offending judge be dismissed or disciplined, the Lord Chancellor usually being identified as the appropriate instrument of these sanctions. Now it is of course elementary that a judge of the High Court or above can only be removed on an address both Houses of Parliament, something which has never been done in the case of any English judge in the course of nearly three centuries since this provision was enacted in the Act of Settlement 1701. Further, as Lord Kilmuir acknowledged in 1955, the Lord Chancellor has no sort of disciplinary jurisdiction over senior judges. The Lord Chancellor does, it is true, have power to remove circuit judges, but in the last quarter century he has done so only once—when a judge was convicted of smuggling—and successive Lord Chancellors are very slow to exercise this power.

Now of course these constitutional safeguards do not exist to make life easier for judges, or to protect them against the consequences of their own mistakes, or to insulate them against public criticism, whether fair or unfair, justified or not.

They exist because an independent judiciary is recognized as being an essential feature of a free, democratic society, and independence involves not only the doing and saying of things which attract public acclaim but also, on occasion, the doing and saying of things which incur public opprobrium. The moment a judge has to ask himself whether a decision may cost him his job, his independence is gone. We all look askance at other countries where judges lack, or are thought to lack, true independence. We demand of countries, formerly subject to authoritarian regimes and now seeking to join the comity of Western democratic nations, that they introduce rules to guarantee the independence of their judges. No informed person would, I think, fail to recognize the establishment of an independent judiciary as one of the major milestones in our long but successful battle against absolutism. But all these obvious truths, it would seem, count for nothing when a judge, for reasons good or bad, falls foul of popular opinion.

The newspaper-reading public may be forgiven if they overlook these obvious truths, since much reporting does little to remind them. Earlier this year an inside page of the *Mail on Sunday* carried the headline, eye-catching to any constitutionalist, 'Holiday row judge fired'. But the constitutional significance of the story somewhat faded when it was appreciated that the subject of the story was not a judge but a practising solicitor who had for some years sat in a part-time capacity as a recorder. And he had not been dismissed: his appointment had been for a series of renewable terms, following the last of which his appointment had not been renewed.

2. According to a report in the *Daily Mail*—and if it is inaccurate I can only apologize to him—a very leading solicitor recently said that the Home Secretary should summon leaders of the judiciary to warn them about over-lenient sentencing. 'He should say to the judges', said the solicitor, if the report is accurate, '"unless you impose stricter sentences we'll introduce minimum sentences".' Now the present Home Secretary practised at the Bar for a number of years with very considerable success, and he would—I have no doubt—be the first to recognize that no minister, however senior, has any right to summon a judge or tell him how to perform his judicial duties and the first to recognize also that any attempt to do so would amount to serious constitutional impropriety. If, however improbably, the Home Secretary were to summon the judges in this way, the probability is that none would answer the summons and if any did—perhaps out of curiosity—such judges would be false to their judicial oaths if they did not continue to exercise their own judgment whether that coincided with the view of the Home Secretary or not. As the Lord Chancellor recently put it in a letter to the *Daily Telegraph*,

Each judge decides the case before him or her on the facts and the law and in accordance with the judicial oath. This independence is something in which I believe absolutely and which neither the Lord Chancellor nor any other member of the Government would ever seek to challenge.

The vice in the proposal I am criticizing lies not in the risk of its implementation. That, I am sure, is nil. The vice lies in the promulgation of a view so fundamentally contrary to the rudiments of constitutional propriety.

3. In the House of Commons debate on crime on Friday, 8 December 1995 a senior government backbencher, as one item in a catalogue of suggestions which included the castration of rapists, the payment of a double Christmas bonus to old-age pensioners who could show that they had shot a burglar in the past year and the abandonment of child molesters to the violence of other prison inmates, referred to 'mad judge disease' and said that 'Perhaps judges should be paid a percentage of the fines that they impose'. Now I do not dwell on the obvious policy issue, whether such a practice would promote the government's expressed wish that more offenders should be sent to prison and for longer periods, but I do draw attention to the constitutional implications of this suggestion. How, consistently with constitutional propriety, could it be right to give judges a direct financial interest in the outcome of the decisions they make or the sentences they impose? I hope it is enough to ask the question.

I also hope that these examples, which could readily be multiplied, will be thought to justify a brief re-statement of basic principles.

Every fourth-former knows that powers exercised on behalf of the state fall under three broad heads, the legislative, the executive and the judicial. The legislature makes the law, the executive carries it out and the judiciary, in case of doubt or dispute, interprets and applies it. Life in the fourth form is pleasantly simple.

But of course it is not quite as simple as that. True, Parliament does enact new laws—3,233 pages of it in 1985—but it also has important functions in debating policy, holding ministers to account and providing a forum for the redress of grievances. True, the executive does implement the laws made by Parliament, but it also plays a crucial role in initiating almost all new legislation; ministers exercise many powers which are not conferred by Parliament and ministers also, acting under legislative authority and usually subject to parliamentary control, make laws in the form of subordinate legislation—6,518 pages of it in 1985. True again, the judges interpret and apply the laws made by Parliament. But the cases which reach the courts are not usually cases in which Parliament has made its intention clear. In such cases there is nothing to litigate about. It is when the intention of parliament is unclear, or where Parliament has failed to provide for a particular eventuality at all, that litigation ensues. The essential function of the court is then to declare the law which it infers that Parliament intended to make, or would have made if it had addressed the point at all. This is not a legislative role, but nor is it a purely interpretative role, since the court may have to do a good deal more than elicit the meaning of what Parliament has enacted. In the great expanses of English law which are largely untouched by statute, the function of the courts is, I would suggest, even less interpretative, since the legal issues which fall to be decided rarely fall squarely within the ratio of an earlier decision, unless it is sought to challenge that decision. More often cases arise on the border between one decision and another, or at the confluence of two or more competing principles or in an area where there is virtually no relevant authority. The courts have then to decide, in the light of legal principle and such authority as there is, and having regard to the apprehended practical consequences of one decision as opposed to another, what the law should be. The courts also have a role in providing a forum for the redress of grievances and in holding the executive to account, if in either case (but only if) a breach of the law is shown. So the functions of legislature, executive and judiciary are not quite as distinct as one might suppose.

Nor, in contrast with many constitutions, notably the American, does our constitution provide for any rigid separation of powers. The fact that the cabinet, as the engine of the executive, and all other ministers, are necessarily members of one or other House of the legislature is indeed the clearest possible negation of the doctrine. But between the legislature and the executive on the one hand and the judiciary on the other the separation is all but total. It was not always so. In the early years of the last century it was not unknown for the Lord Chief Justice to be a member of the cabinet, and up to the middle of that century holders of my office combined it with a seat in the House of Commons. Lord Stowell, the great admiralty judge (and, for good measure, Samuel Johnson's executor) was active both in promoting orders in council on the floor of the House of Lords and in interpreting them from the judicial bench.

I describe the separation as 'all but total' to allow for two apparent anomalies. The first is the position of the Lords of Appeal in Ordinary, who combine their judicial function with membership of the upper house of the legislature. The anomaly is mitigated, perhaps removed, by the convention that Law Lords sit on the cross benches, abjuring party allegiance and eschewing political debate. There is the potential for embarrassment when the same, or related, issues come before the House in both its legislative and judicial capacities—as happened in the recent instance of compensation for criminal injuries—but on the whole the conventions are well understood and respected. The other apparent anomaly is the office of Lord Chancellor, which involves a single person acting simultaneously as (in effect) speaker of the House of Lords, a senior member of the cabinet and head of the judiciary. Some Lord Chancellors—like Lords Kilmuir and Hailsham— reach that office as the culmination of full-blown political careers. Others—like Lords Simonds, Gardiner and the present Lord Chancellor—have been distinguished lawyers who have never held elective political office. But however political the Lord Chancellor's background, the convention is quite clear that when acting as head of the judiciary—and in that capacity deciding cases, for instance, or appointing judges—the Lord Chancellor acts without any regard at all to political considerations. I know of scarcely any suggestion that any Lord Chancellor since the war has not honoured that convention to the full. For the majority of recent Lord Chancellors who have previously served as Law Officers, whether in England or Scotland, the requirement will not be novel, since Law Officers are also accustomed to make a very wide range of decisions without regard to political considerations.

In outlining these constitutional arrangements I have made no mention of the Crown. This is a serious omission, since it is the Crown which gives our constitution its essential unity. The legislature is the Queen in Parliament. Members of the government are Her Majesty's Ministers. The judges are Her Majesty's Judges. The crown provides the essential reminder that legislature, executive and judiciary are not satellites in independent orbit but—to change the metaphor— wheels on the same coach. Writing on the constitution in 1992, Lord Hailsham observed of the monarchy

I am myself wholly persuaded that of all our institutions, this is one with which I would be least inclined to meddle.

I certainly agree. There are those who regard the sovereign's role as wholly formal, making reference to it little more than an indulgence in sentimentality. That is a point of view, and I have no doubt that in certain spheres—the giving of assent to Parliamentary Bills, for instance—her role is purely formal. But even if purely formal the monarch's role does not necessarily lack symbolic significance and the history of previous reigns tends to show that the royal right to be consulted, to advise and to warn has been exercised to greater effect than anyone appreciated at the time.

The constitutional role of the courts and the judges cannot, I think, be better expressed than in the judicial oath taken by a newly appointed or promoted judge. The judge swears to

do right to all manner of people after the laws and usages of this realm, without fear or favour, affection or ill-will.

The essential elements are all there. First, the judge must do what he (or, of course, she) holds to be right. The poet Dryden wrote of a man whose counsels were 'oft convenient, seldom just'. The judge's duty is the opposite, to do what is just, not what is convenient. But secondly, and vitally, he must do right according to the laws and usages of the realm. He is not a free agent, who can properly give vent to his own whims and predilections, or even (save within very narrow limits) give effect to his own schemes of law reform. As Samuel Johnson, sagely as always, observed:

To permit a law to be modified at discretion is to leave the community without law. It is to withdraw the direction of that public wisdom by which the deficiencies of private understanding are to be supplied.

This is by no means universally understood: many critics of judicial decisions proceed on the basis that the judges could of course have reached the decision which the critics favour if only they had been as wise, sensible and closely in touch with public opinion as the critics.

Thirdly, the judicial oath makes clear, as I have already emphasized, that in administering the law the judge must act with complete independence, seeking neither to curry favour nor to avoid any form of victimization. And fourthly, so far as humanly possible, judges must decide cases with total objectivity, having no personal interest beyond that of reaching a just and legally correct solution.

I turn now to three areas in which the position of the courts and the judges has been the subject of recent controversy. The first is judicial review, the process by which members of the public seek to challenge public law decisions made by ministers, departments, officials, local authorities and others exercising public powers. The background to the controversy is the undoubted and remarkable increase in the number of applications, which has risen from 160 in England and Wales in 1974 to nearly 3,000 in 1993.

Sometimes the judges are criticized for being too timid and asserting themselves too little. For instance, in his recent best-selling work *The State We're In*, Will Hutton wrote:

Nor has the judiciary—the third branch of government—thrown up many obstacles to a party with hegemonic ambitions. 'The judges', as Sir Ian Gilmour writes, 'were lambs under the throne'. The longstanding tradition of Britain's judiciary being more executive-minded than the executive, in Lord Atkin's famous dictum, came into its own in the 1980s with the law providing almost no refuge from the ambitions of the Conservative Party to enlarge the centralising powers of the state. The judges went along with the government's efforts to ban *Spycatcher,* and local authorities found that they had no redress for the various initiatives that curtailed their autonomy, entrenched by custom and practice but not by law.

I confess to finding this an amazing passage. Lord Atkin's famous dissenting speech in *Liversidge v Anderson* has today become the only citable speech in that case. The judges ruled against the government on *Spycatcher*, save at an interlocutory stage. I think the Prime Minister and his colleagues, to say nothing of the Treasury Solicitor, would find this description of the judges' role hard to match up with the world they live in.

Usually, the criticism is to the opposite effect, that the judges have been too active, too intrusive, altogether too big for their court shoes. I am alive to two main lines of criticism; if there are others I fear they have escaped me. The first is that the judges are using judicial review as a means of wresting power away from ministers and arrogating it to themselves. An elaboration of this is that the judges, although not democratically elected and not accountable to Parliament or the public, are using the process of judicial review to substitute their own decisions for those of the democratically elected ministers or bodies to whom such decisions were properly entrusted, thereby challenging the sovereignty of Parliament. The second is that the judges have colluded to quash decisions by ministers in the present government, in particular decisions by the Home Secretary and the department for which he is responsible. No one, I am sure, will

be surprised to hear me say that I regard these lines of criticism as wholly untenable, and merely to reject them inevitably invites the Mandy Rice-Davies retort.
So perhaps I may seek to explain why I reject them.

First, any proposition beginning 'The judges . . .' is almost bound to be false.
For it suggests an identity of thought and a uniformity of reaction which do not
in practice exist. Every lawyer and every law student knows how frequently the
Court of Appeal disagrees with the trial judge (roughly one appeal in four
succeeds), how frequently the House of Lords disagrees with the Court of Appeal,
and how frequently the members of the Court of Appeal and the House of Lords
disagree among themselves. The truth is that senior judges have grown up in a
highly individualistic profession, paid to form and express their own views and
defer to those of no one else. While they do not disagree for the sake of it, they
will not acquiesce in a proposition which they believe to be false or potentially
pernicious. The notion that this independent-minded and idiosyncratic body of
prima donnas would harbour and give effect to a common design along the lines
suggested is, I would suggest, fanciful. It is the more obviously so when one
reflects that the thirty-three judges of the Court of Appeal, who would have to be
party to such an agenda if there were one, meet as a body only once a year, at a
meeting called to decide who will man the court during the bank holidays and
vacations of the forthcoming year. There is simply no forum in which matters of
the kind now under consideration are discussed. I would accept that when, some
years ago, the government published green papers proposing changes in the delivery of legal services, there appeared to be a broad consensus of judicial opinion
opposed to the proposals. But these were proposals for structural changes in the
administration of the law, and even then there were judges who expressly disso-
ciated themselves from the common view. It is simply inconceivable to me that
judges would form a common view in advance as to how they would decide
future cases not currently before them.

My second reason for rejecting these criticisms is very important, but will take
a little longer to make good. In a democratic society governed by the rule of law
no one—literally no one—is entrusted with unfettered power. The reason is obvious: unfettered power is tyranny or despotism, both of which are inconsistent
with the rule of law. So, while the complexity of modern government leads to the
conferment of wide powers and important discretions on particular bodies and
office-holders, all such powers are conferred for a purpose which is either explicit
or implicit and no discretion is so broad as to be subject to no limit at all. Much
the same is true of non-statutory prerogative powers. Whatever the source of the
power in question, the judge's task when reduced to essentials is always the same:
to examine whether the power in question has been lawfully used. It will not have
been lawfully used if it has been used for a purpose alien to that for which the
power existed. It will not have been lawfully used if statutory conditions attaching to its exercise have not been observed. It will not have been lawfully exercised
if the decision to exercise it has been swayed by irrelevant considerations or if the

decision-maker has disregarded relevant considerations. It will not have been lawfully exercised if, in a situation where ordinary fairness required a certain procedure to be followed, and the decision was one calling for ordinary fairness, such a procedure has not been followed. It will not have been lawfully used if the decision to exercise the power was one which no one in his or her right mind could have made if properly advised in law. These are not new tests. They are, admittedly, judge-made tests. But they originated well before the recent boom in judicial review, at times when the judges were generally perceived to be overly respectful of government and, for that matter, excessively right-wing. The point I wish to emphasize, however, is that even where the judge finds one or other of these tests to be satisfied, and so quashes the decision under challenge, he does not thereby become the decision-maker. The judge's only role is to decide whether the challenged decision was lawful or not: if the challenge is upheld the consequence is not that the judge makes the decision but, almost invariably, that the decision is quashed, leaving the true decision-maker at liberty to make another decision, lawfully, whether to the same effect as the earlier decision or not. The only real exception is where a decision is condemned as perverse, such as no reasonable property-directed person could have made, in a situation where there was an effective choice between two decisions; but the threshold of perversity is, rightly, very high.

Frequently, when dealing with well-publicized cases likely to attract media attention, judges go out of their way to assert that they are in no way concerned with the policy merits of the decision under review but only with its lawfulness. I have often said this myself. I am not sure what critics of the judicial role say about this. They may perhaps regard it as a meaningless incantation; or as an unconvincing attempt to camouflage an illegitimate agenda, like a sadistic Victorian schoolmaster saying 'I don't want to do this'; or as evidence of the judges' ability to delude themselves. I can only assert that the judges mean what they say. Matters inevitably arise on which any intelligent and reasonably informed person is likely to have his or her own views. Very frequently a judge will reach a judicial decision which runs counter to those views. I would challenge the critics to identify any significant body of recent cases in which judges could be fairly accused of making decisions on other than purely and genuinely legal grounds. I think I can claim to have had my fair share of well-publicized judicial review appeals in the last year or two: compensation for criminal injuries, the banning of stag-hunting in Somerset, homosexuals in the armed forces, the penal term of mandatory life sentence prisoners, the terms of railway franchises, and others. I can assert with complete confidence that my private views have not influenced my judicial decisions, and the same is, I know, true of my colleagues.

My third point is obvious, but again important and rarely made: the judges have no control whatever over the nature or the number of applications for judicial review which members of the public, usually acting on advice, choose to make to them. Their role is purely reactive. If the first instance judge considers an application to be obviously ill-founded, he will refuse leave to pursue it: but if he considers that the application could properly succeed he has no choice but to grant leave; and if he wrongly refuses leave in a case which is arguable the odds are that the Court of Appeal will grant it. Where leave is granted and the applicant demonstrates an unlawful exercise of power, the judge has a limited discretion to refuse relief but such a discretion, like any other, must be exercised in a principled way, and a judge may not refuse relief without solid, legally defensible, reasons for doing so. On rare occasions a judge may hold an issue raised before him to be incapable of judicial decision but that is itself a judicial decision and capable of challenge like any other. Not so long ago I read an article—I forget where, or by whom—in which the author criticized a judge for having decided a particular case at all. What, I wondered, did the author think the judge should have done? Put up a notice saying 'Machine out of order?' or 'Counter closed'? Those who accuse the judges of seeking to usurp powers properly belonging elsewhere must in fairness acknowledge that the judges initiate nothing; that it is members of the public who bring cases before the judges; that the judges are duty-bound to rule on cases properly brought before them: that if a judge wrongly finds a public body to have abused its power that body has at least one and perhaps two opportunities to correct him; that the final decision almost always falls to be made by the appointed decision-maker; and that save in cases with a European dimension any judicial error, or any seriously embarrassing judicial decision, can be reversed by legislation.

I would wish, fourthly, to reject the suggestion that there is any judicial bias against the Home Office or that the Home Office is the victim of exceptional reverses in the courts. Some departments of state—I would instance, by way of example, the Treasury—are rarely, if ever, the respondent to an application for judicial review. That is probably related to the nature of the decisions which such departments make. The Home Office, being centrally involved with immigration and the administration of the penal system, makes many decisions which individual members of the public have a strong incentive to challenge. The very nature of its functions makes it inevitable that many attempts will be made, successfully or unsuccessfully, to challenge its decisions. But most of these challenges fail. Week in, week out, many attempts are made to challenge Home Office decisions, particularly in the immigration field, and the great majority do not succeed. The extensive publicity given to occasional decisions adverse to the Home Office gives a quite misleading impression of the department's fortunes as a litigant. Save on isolated occasions, little attention is given to the continuous flow of cases in which the Home Office is routinely successful.

The second area of controversy on which I would like to touch is sentencing in criminal cases. I can deal with this more shortly, since there is—I suggest—no constitutional issue involved at all. The question relates to the judges' sentencing discretion, that is, the extent to which judges should be free to exercise their own judgment as to the appropriate sentence in a given case.

In the familiar case of murder, Parliament has prescribed a sentence of life imprisonment which must be passed on all sane convicted adults: section 1(1) of the Murder (Abolition of Death Penalty) Act 1965. There has been much weighty and authoritative criticism of this rule, for understandable reasons. A doctor who deliberately administers a lethal drug to terminate the unbearable suffering of a moribund patient, and a professional gangster who shoots a policeman in the course of a robbery, are both guilty of murder under the law as it stands and the trial judge pronounces the same sentence in each case. But the quality of the criminal conduct in the two cases is quite different, and critics of the present rule contend that the law should reflect this, as the penal treatment of the defendant after conviction of course already does. Those who support the present rule reply that murder has always been regarded as a peculiarly heinous crime and that any modification of the rule would appear to blur what should be a stark and unqualified message of social condemnation. Those in favour of change counter that the effect of the existing rule is itself to blur the message of social condemnation, because it leads to the imposition of a mandatory life sentence on those whose crimes do not fall in the most heinous category and in cases where a relatively short period of imprisonment might reasonably be considered to be enough. One may take one side of this argument or the other, or a variant of either. But no one argues that Parliament was not fully entitled to legislate as it did in 1965, and if the present rule remains law it will continue to be observed. The argument is about what the penal rule should be, and the effect of a change would undoubtedly be to increase the sentencing discretion of the judge in those categories of case which no longer attracted the mandatory penalty. It cannot, however, be said that the present rule, depriving the judge of any discretion, is constitutionally objectionable, any more than the previous rule which required the judge to pass sentence of death.

Where statutes create serious criminal offences punishable by imprisonment they invariably provide for a maximum term, perhaps life, more commonly a term of years or months. This has always been so, and the effect is of course to deny the court jurisdiction to impose a longer term. To that extent, again, the discretion of the sentencing court is restricted. Cases have arisen in which judges have criticized the statutory maxima as being too low, or in which they have criticized restrictions on the imposition of custodial sentences. But this has been a penological, not a constitutional, argument. On none of these occasions that I recall has any judge ever criticized these statutory constraints as an infringement of his independence under the constitution.

The current debate about minimum sentences is, I suggest, to be viewed against this background. Minimum sentences are not entirely novel. Section 10 of the Slave Trade Act 1824 provided that those convicted of dealing in slaves, if not transported beyond the seas for up to fourteen years, should be confined and kept to hard labour for a term not exceeding five years nor less than three years. In the more mundane field of driving offences, minimum penalties are commonplace.

Where, for example, a defendant is convicted of causing death by careless driving when under the influence of drink or drugs the court must order him to be disqualified for a period of not less than twelve months. The court may for special reasons order disqualification for a shorter period, or for no period, but 'special reasons' is an expression with a clear and narrowly defined meaning and this provision confers no general discretion on any court to waive the general requirement to disqualify. What is unusual in current proposals is the intention to provide for minimum sentences in much more serious categories of case, thus restricting the discretion of the sentencing judge to impose a lesser sentence in such cases.

The rationale underlying these proposals is not hard to understand. Scarcely a day goes by without a newspaper report of stomach-turning violence. There is a clear public need that defendants convicted of serious violence should be, and be seen to be, seriously punished. The citizen is entitled to expect the legal system to protect him and there is a widespread sense of insecurity.

The grounds for disquiet are also intelligible. Since the days of the Old Testament prophets, mercy has been seen as the handmaiden of justice. Portia submitted:

And earthly power doth then show likest God's When mercy seasons justice.

Although the judges do not swear, as does the Queen in her coronation oath, to 'cause Law and Justice, in Mercy, to be executed in all my judgments', most criminal judges would regard the tempering of justice with mercy in appropriate cases as an important attribute of the judicial function. There is also, perhaps, a fear that populist clamour may be an unsure guide in a field such as this. The American experience of mandatory sentencing guidelines has not, in the view of many informed observers, been a happy one.

In this case also it is possible to favour either view, or a variant of either. There is room for rational argument whether it is desirable to restrict the judges' sentencing discretion in the way suggested or not. But even this is not a constitutional argument. As Parliament can prescribe a maximum penalty without infringing the constitutional independence of the judges, so it can prescribe a minimum. This is, in the widest sense, a political question—a question of what is beneficial for the polity—not a constitutional question.

The third controversial topic I wish to mention is incorporation of the European Convention on Human Rights. There are those—including a number of senior judges—who favour incorporation on the ground that human rights which the United Kingdom has bound itself by treaty to respect should in the first instance be safeguarded by our domestic courts here in the UK. Opponents of incorporation say that it would have the undesirable effect of drawing the judiciary into the political arena. Others again point out that the Convention is now 40 years old and argue that it is today an unsatisfactory statement of the rights which the law should protect. These are issues on which much can be, and has been, said. Most of the arguments are by now familiar, and it is perhaps unlikely that those who hold one view or the other will experience a sudden conversion.

The question I wish to pose tonight is not whether incorporation would be a good thing or a bad thing. Rather I wish to ask: would the constitutional implication of incorporation be fundamental? Would it involve an important change in the functions of the judiciary or of the judiciary's relations with the legislature or the executive? Would it undermine the sovereignty of Parliament? My answers to all these questions are that it would not.

Those answers are given on what I take to be a readily acceptable premise, that incorporation would be made effective by scheduling the Convention to an Act of Parliament, which would require that effect should be given to the Convention (subject to any relevant derogation) save in so far as any later Act might expressly require otherwise. That Act would represent the will of Parliament. So long as it stood, unrepealed, the courts would loyally give effect to it. There would be no question of striking down statutes as incompatible with the Convention: if Parliament wished to depart from the Convention, it would so provide; if it did not, the courts would strive to interpret later statutes consistently with the Convention, as in cases of doubt they already do.

This, as I understand, is what the Opposition propose. In his contribution to *Law Reform for All*, recently published, Lord Irvine of Lairg QC, Shadow Lord Chancellor, wrote:

Incorporation could easily be achieved. Parliament should pass a Human Rights Act that incorporates the rules of the Convention directly into British law, and gives citizens the right to enforce those rules in their own courts.

Although technically a British Act of Parliament cannot be 'entrenched', effective protection of the Human Rights Act from undermining by the courts would be provided by a clause that requires that any other Act that is intended to introduce laws inconsistent with the Convention must do so specifically and in express terms.

He went on:

In a democracy, Parliament decides what rights should apply, and should set them out in a manner that citizens can understand for themselves. Under these proposals, it would not be left to the discretion of the judges, or to archaeological investigations by legal and constitutional experts, to decide what protections citizens do and do not have.

I agree, only observing that the judges would still have to interpret the provisions of the Convention, pay regard to previous authority and apply the law as determined to the facts of the case. But there is nothing novel in that. Nor is there anything which should alarm any informed student of our constitution.

Constitutional arrangements, like motor cars, require periodic inspection and overhaul, so that worn-out parts may be renewed and ill-fitting parts adjusted. The fact that a constitution such as ours has been on the road for a very long time makes this attention more necessary, not less. Many commentators feel that we have of late allowed our constitutional arrangements to fall into disrepair, and talk of change is in the air. This is all to the good. Nothing should be taken for granted. Nothing is incapable of improvement. It is, however, important to distinguish between the law of the constitution as it is and speculation as to what the law of the constitution might be. At the heart of our constitution is the doctrine of Parliamentary sovereignty. Whatever political theorists, or even judges in their more speculative, off-duty, moments, may opine, that doctrine is not, as a matter of law, under threat. The courts do not question the legislative process and do their best to give full and fair effect to what Parliament enacts. Judicial review reinforces, and in no way undermines, the will of Parliament. Parliament for its part respects the function of the courts, for instance by curbing debate on issues which are awaiting judicial decision and restraining personal criticism of judges or questioning of their motives. This is part of a delicate but important constitutional balance. My plea this evening is not for an end to debate of constitutional issues, but for a more informed and enlightened approach to that debate.

2

Anglo-American Reflections *

May I begin by thanking you for asking me to give the inaugural Pilgrim Fathers Lecture? I regard it as a very great privilege and honour. And it has given me the great pleasure of visiting Plymouth. I think I have visited Plymouth, Massachusetts; I have certainly, and very recently, visited Plymouth, Michigan; but I must shamefacedly confess that I have never before visited the father and mother of all Plymouths.

Your invitation has also prompted me to enquire a little into the Pilgrim Fathers themselves. Of those who set sail from here on 6 September 1620 in the *Mayflower*, it appears that sixty-six came from London and Southampton. The core of thirty-five came from Leyden in the Netherlands. They belonged to Independent or Congregational churches originally established in Nottingham and Lincolnshire, who had in 1608 emigrated to Amsterdam to escape Anglican oppression. After a short time there they moved to Leyden. But, as the *DNB* entry on William Bradford puts it, in terms which would earn applause at a Tory party conference, 'actuated by a desire to live as Englishmen under English rule, they resolved to emigrate to some English colony. . . .' There was some debate about which, but in the end the vote went for the royal plantation in Virginia. So the party left from Leyden, picking up the additional recruits already mentioned. From Southampton the passengers travelled in two vessels, *Mayflower* and *Speedwell*. Unhappily as maritime practitioners know only too well, vessels with names like *Speedwell* fail to live up to them. So it was with *Speedwell*. After the voyage from Southampton to Plymouth she was judged to be irreparably unseaworthy and her passengers were transferred to join those already aboard the *Mayflower*. There the passengers must have endured a degree of sensory deprivation exceeding even that to be experienced in the economy cabin of a cut-price jumbo.

The level of satisfaction aboard the *Mayflower* cannot have been raised when weather conditions prevented the vessel making her landfall in Virginia and drove her to the rather less hospitable shores of Massachusetts. At this stage some of the London recruits, described at the time as 'an undesirable lot', boasted that they were not under the jurisdiction of the Virginia Company which had granted the Leyden Separatists a patent for a private plantation and 'would use their own libertie'. To establish some form of government in this unwelcome situation, the Pilgrim leaders drew up one of the earliest and one of the most remarkable of American constitutional documents. Not intended as a constitution of the new

* Inaugural Pilgrim Fathers Lecture delivered 29 October 1994.

colony, it served as such until 1691. The document, dated 11 November 1620, became known as *The Mayflower Compact*. I hope you will feel it merits quotation:

In the Name of God, Amen. We, whose names are underwritten, the Loyal Subjects of our dread Sovereign Lord King James, by the Grace of God, of Great Britain, France, and Ireland, King, Defender of the Faith etc. Having undertaken for the Glory of God, and Advancement of the Christian faith, and the Honour of our King and Country, a voyage to plant the first colony in the northern parts of Virginia; Do by these Presents, solemnly and mutually in the Presence of God and one another, covenant and combine ourselves into a civil Body Politick, for our better Ordering and Preservation, and Furtherance of the End aforesaid; And by Virtue hereof do enact, constitute, and frame such just and equal Laws, Ordinances, Acts, Constitutions, and Offices, from time to time, as shall be most meet and convenient for the general Good of the Colony; unto which we promise all due submission and Obedience . . .

And then follow 40 signatures, almost all of them very familiar English surnames like Clark and White and Fletcher and Fuller.

From this celebrated text I would draw three points, all of them—as I hope— of some importance and interest. The first is this. Later in the century and thereafter, political philosophers were to advance theories of government based on the hypothesis of a social contract, of men living in a state of nature and becoming, by agreement, members of an ordered civic society. This is what the Pilgrim Fathers, embarking on an attempt to live in what was almost literally a state of nature—and hostile nature at that—appear actually to have done. Only a minority of the *Mayflower*'s passengers, it is true, appear to have signed the compact. But for them at least the basis of citizenship was explicitly contractual.

The second point worthy of note is that the signatories of the compact chose to put their faith in a written constitution. Perhaps this does not seem surprising: every club, association or trade union, after all, has its rules. But the Pilgrim Fathers had been bred in a country in which no one had ever attempted to put on paper the rules by which the country was governed. They clearly regarded a written statement of constitutional principle, skeletal though it was, as some guarantee of peace and order.

The third point is that this constitutional declaration was a highly democratic one. It so happened that the first signatory of the compact, John Carver, was chosen as the first governor of the new colony, and when he died 6 months later he was succeeded by the second signatory, who was elected annually to serve as governor until 1656, just before his death, except for two periods of respectively 3 and 2 years when he stood down at his own request. So of course the new colony had its leaders. But these leaders were elected by the citizens, and compared with any society the Pilgrim Fathers can ever have known there was a notable absence of hierarchy.

Nothing, of course, is quite new. From the time of Edward the Confessor, it had been the practice of English kings to confirm to their subjects the rights and

liberties they would allow them to enjoy. After the Conquest the practice continued, with references (however unhistorical) to the good old times of the
Confessor. It was in particular the practice for new monarchs to make such declarations on accession, as a sort of non-election manifesto. The Great Charter of
June 1215 formed part of this series. It was not of course a statute, for there was
no Parliament. Nor was it in any way voluntary on the King's part. But it did
include a number of terms traditionally included in such declarations, and it may
not be fanciful to see such charters as a form of bargain or compact between the
ruler and the ruled. Magna Carta itself, of course, was valid only for 3 months in
the summer of 1215, was never fully executed and was annulled by a bull of Pope
Innocent in August 1215. Such is the fate of some compacts. Happily, Magna
Carta enjoyed an after-life more vigorous than most. By the time of the Pilgrim
Fathers it had come to be seen as a cornerstone of the English constitution, and
to that extent at least the English constitution was written. The democracy which
the Pilgrim Fathers imported into the government of their new colony was, again,
only novel up to a point. It found no reflection in the political life of England; but
it reflected very fully the manner in which the Independent Congregations had
ordered their church.

From these small beginnings have grown what are, I think, enduring differences between the United States and the United Kingdom. The notion of a
compact endured. The Declaration of Independence proclaimed that to secure the
rights of Life, Liberty and the pursuit of happiness 'Governments are instituted
among Men, deriving their just powers from the consent of the governed.' The
Constitution of the United States was adopted in the name of 'We the People of
the United States.' The enduring faith in a written constitution was enshrined not
only in that constitution but in the constitutions of the ever-increasing number of
constituent states. It was to become a republic of laws: in no country before or
since have the laws and lawyers occupied so central a place—and despite all the
jokes about lawyers the law itself seems to continue to command respect and
loyalty. And the Constitution itself was, and has remained, a remarkably democratic document, designed to ensure that the will of the majority shall prevail.
Even in the appointment of federal judges the voices of the people, through the
Senate, is to be heard: since 1787 about thirty out of 142 presidential nominees
for appointment to the Supreme Court have been rejected.

de Tocqueville, visiting the United States in 1831-2, made pertinent observations, consistent with what I have suggested:

However irksome an enactment may be, the citizen of the United States complies with it,
not only because it is the work of the majority, but because it is his own, and he regards it
as a contract to which he is himself a party.

In the United States, then, that numerous and turbulent multitude does not exist, who,
regarding the law as their natural enemy look upon it with fear and distrust. It is impossible, on the contrary, not to perceive that all classes display the utmost reliance upon the
legislation of their country, and are attached to it by a kind of parental affection.

The contrast with the United Kingdom is not absolute. We would justly claim that our system of government is democratic, and we are well aware that the government of the day draws its authority from the votes of the people cast at general elections. But I do not think we have the same vivid sense of 'Us the People' as the average American citizen, nor the same sense (save at times of high public protest) of governments deriving their just powers from the consent of the governed. To some extent tradition, and the role of the monarch as head of both church and state, may cloud our vision. It could also be said that our system of parliamentary representation, whatever its other virtues, is a somewhat imperfect instrument for reflecting minority opinion. Certainly we have in general shown no urge for a written constitution. This is not to say that much of our constitution is not written. Large sections of what would appear in a written constitution if we had one are to be found scattered through numerous Acts of Parliament: one could instance the succession to the Crown, the powers of the House of Lords, the union with Scotland, the government of Northern Ireland, the right of representation in Parliament, the conduct of local government, the powers of the courts, the tenure of judges, etc. The true distinction between the American constitutional settlement and our own is not, I would suggest, that theirs is written and ours is not but that theirs is entrenched and ours is not. Theirs enjoys a special status, unamendable save by a cumbersome and highly consensual procedure. Ours enjoys no special, entrenched status. It is in theory amendable by a simple parliamentary majority. The contrast is obvious. Under the US Constitution a senator, once elected to the US Senate, ordinarily serves for 6 years. That term cannot be altered without constitutional amendment. Here, a Parliament ordinarily sits for a maximum of 5 years. But in both world wars this period was extended. However improbable, it would be open to Parliament to extend the period even in peacetime.

There is a more substantial point to be made. I have already described the US Constitution as a document in which great pains were taken to ensure that the will of the majority should prevail. It was a highly majoritarian settlement. But even at the time when the Constitution was adopted there were fears about the position of minorities. It was all very well making sure that the will of the majority prevailed, but what if the power of the majority is used to oppress a minority? This was not a theoretical problem: the Pilgrim Fathers may themselves have been refugees from oppression, but they made quite effective oppressors themselves when they had the chance. The solution adopted to this problem was to agree that there should, almost at once, be amendments to the Constitution designed for the protection of minorities. It is there, in these first ten amendments, that one finds the famous clauses protecting religion, free speech, peaceable assembly and due process and forbidding, among other things, the inflicting of cruel and unusual punishments.

In prohibiting cruel and unusual punishments, the American Bill of Rights— as these amendments are usually called—of course borrowed a provision enacted, in exactly the same terms, in the English Bill of Rights 1689. But there is this difference. So long as this amendment remains a part of the US Constitution, an American court will be not only entitled but bound to override any state or federal statute properly held to be inconsistent with it. de Tocqueville wrote that 'the power vested in the American courts of justice, of pronouncing a statute to be unconstitutional, forms one of the most powerful barriers which has ever been devised against the tyranny of political assemblies'. A British judge is in a different position. If Parliament were clearly and unambiguously to enact, however improbably, that a defendant convicted of a prescribed crime should suffer mutilation, or branding, or exposure in the public pillory there would be very little a judge could do about it—except resign. He would be duty-bound to give effect to a later, specific statute in preference to an earlier, general statute. There would be no higher, entrenched, fundamental law to which he could appeal. Even if he concluded that the defendant could probably mount a successful challenge to the provision in the European Court of Human Rights in Strasbourg he would not be able to place direct reliance on the text of the Convention.

In many areas these differences of constitutional principle perhaps make little difference in practice. For all his lack of constitutional guarantees one would rather have been James Somerset in England than Dred Scott in the United States. There was not very much difference between the treatment meted out to German aliens in this country in 1940 and that enjoyed by Japanese aliens in California in 1941. In both countries the present mood seems to be one of unusual, perhaps even unprecedented, vengefulness, regarding no punishment as too severe for the serious convicted prisoner: but in the United States sentences of death are routinely carried out which British courts would hold, and have held, to be cruel and unusual.

Sometimes, too, it may fairly be said that the two countries arrive at very much the same decision by different routes. The fifth amendment to the US Constitution provides (in part):

nor shall any person be deprived of life, liberty or property, without due process of law; nor shall private property be taken for public use, without just compensation.

The English provenance of this provision is very clear. Article 39 of Magna Carta provided:

No free man shall be seized or imprisoned, or stripped of his rights or possessions, or outlawed or exiled, or deprived of his standing in any other way, nor will we proceed with force against him, or send others to do so, except by the lawful judgment of his equals or by the law of the land.

But in seeking to protect British citizens against unfairness and abuse of power, British judges have not relied on this principle, even in the later re-enactments of Magna Carta. They have instead relied on the so-called rules of natural justice, so-called because there is nothing natural about justice; on a series of maxims, many of them derived from Roman law; on doctrines of vires and authority; and, particularly in recent times, on self-made rules of procedural propriety and fairness. In the result, I would question how much difference there is.

But in one field the difference is stark. It arises from the absence in this country of anything equivalent to the first amendment prohibition on abridgement of freedom of speech and of the press. The difference is at once apparent in three areas: the very limited protection against defamation enjoyed by an American public figure; the general unwillingness of American courts to restrain forthcoming publications not yet shown to be unlawful; and the remarkable freedom of parties to litigation, whether prosecutors or defendants, plaintiffs or criminal defendants, to make statements directly bearing on the issues in a future trial. The publicity surrounding the trial of Mr O. J. Simpson is an extreme, but by no means unprecedented, example. There is, I think, no doubt about the general attachment of American citizens to this principle, although minority groups are beginning to complain that it deprives them of a protection they ought to have. But the courts appear determined to uphold the principle, to the extent of striking down statutes making it an offence to burn the Stars and Stripes, an act regarded as sacrilegious and unbearably offensive by the great mass of American citizens.

This contrast has recently been highlighted in a high-profile case proceeding in Canada, in a place some few miles from the border with the United States. In Canada the law governing comment on forthcoming proceedings is, as I understand, not unlike our own. So the Canadian newspapers are obliged to be very reticent in their comment on the case. The American newspapers are not similarly inhibited, and the case interests the public on the American side of the border as much as that on the Canadian. So one has the anomalous result that material freely available in one place is suppressed in another place only a few miles away.

I think that most British citizens not professionally involved in the media would incline to think that on the whole we have perhaps got closer to the right answer on this matter than the Americans. We would expect our political leaders, having voluntarily entered the arena, to endure the ordinary rough and tumble of political controversy. But we would not, I think, wish to deny them legal protection against false and serious defamatory publications. We would incline, I think, on the whole to allow material to be published, even though it is alleged to be defamatory, on the basis that if the complaint is made good the publisher will pay for his wrong. But if, on an application made before the date of publication, the prospective publisher is unable to show any arguable case that the material is true and cannot assert an intention to justify, I do not think most of us find it offensive that he is enjoined from publishing at all: what's said is said, and even the payment of damages cannot unsay it. On the issue of contempt, most of us would, I think, feel that judges could be relied on to ignore anything they have read in the newspaper or seen on television; but most of us would probably feel it desirable that jurors, particularly in high-profile criminal cases such as those involving the killers of James Bulger, or the Bishopsgate bombing, or the Maxwell brothers, should enter the jury box with their minds as free as possible of preconceived notions about the facts or the guilt of the accused.

Even if we regard this latter principle as in general salutary, however, we may none the less feel unease about its operation in practice. In a recent case police officers accused of serious malpractice in an IRA case were discharged because the judge held that the surrounding publicity made a fair trial impossible. I do not criticize that decision. I accept it as correct. But there is, despite the existing law, much publicity surrounding some cases. Those I have mentioned are examples. I very much doubt whether, in the modern world, such publicity can be prevented. Must we not put our faith in the capacity of jurors, once they have entered the jury box, to abide by the oath they have taken and the direction they are given to decide the case according to the evidence they hear in court? I do not myself regard that as an extravagant or naive thing to do. Most of us with any experience of criminal juries are, I think, impressed by the serious, sober and conscientious way in which jurors with rare exceptions set about their momentous task.

I do not on the whole think that the lack of a constitutional guarantee of free speech in this country leads to an objectionable abridgement of the British citizen's freedom to say and write what he likes. But I do think that on occasion the absence of anything comparable with the first amendment has unfortunate results, because the British judge is inclined to regard free speech as one right to be balanced against other competing rights and not as a right which must be protected and upheld save in the most compelling circumstances.

When I speak of unfortunate results, I have two fairly recent decisions in mind, neither of them in my view among the finest flowers of modern English jurisprudence.

The first is *Home Office v Harman* [1983] 1 AC 280. Miss Harman, it will be recalled, had conducted a case for a prisoner who complained of his treatment while in prison. A large number of documents had been disclosed by the Home Office on discovery. These documents, it was accepted, were read out loud in full in open court. Miss Harman supplied copies of some of these documents to a journalist who made use of them in an article. Miss Harman was held to have been in contempt and fined. The House of Lords by a majority upheld this finding. Now there was a case against Miss Harman. Discovery involves an invasion of privacy, judged to be necessary in the interests of justice. Every lawyer knows, or certainly should know, that documents disclosed on discovery are to be used for the purpose of the action in which they are disclosed and no other purpose. So the majority in the House of Lords, as one would expect, had a reasoned basis for their decision. But they could never, surely, have reached that decision had free speech been regarded not as one right among many but as a right demanding everything short of absolute judicial protection. These were, after all, documents which had been read in a public forum. Any reporter with the energy and the technical skill could have made a note of every word. Anyone with the necessary inclination and the necessary means could have bought a transcript. How, if free speech is in truth a right which we respect in deed as in word, could it have been judged right to hold Miss Harman liable? That question cannot in my view be answered, as Lord Diplock at the outset of his speech attempted to do, by saying that the case was '*not* about freedom of speech, freedom of the press, openness of justice or documents coming into "the public domain"'. It is not perhaps surprising that when Miss Harman appealed to the Court of Human Rights in Strasbourg, Her Majesty's Government found itself constrained to compromise: because, of course, the Convention of Human Rights does give certain rights, including free speech, a special status and permits only limited derogations.

My second example also is a majority decision of the House of Lords, this time the decision reached on 30 July 1987 in the course of the protracted *Spycatcher* litigation: [1987] 1 WLR 1248. The issue was whether certain news-papers should be restrained from publishing material taken from Peter Wright's book. By this time the book had gone on sale in the United States. Now I hold no brief for Peter Wright, the author of the book. He was wrong to act as he did, however badly he felt the Secret Intelligence Service had treated him. And I have no reason to believe that the scorn poured on his allegations by official sources was other than justified. But how, if freedom of speech and of the press are ser-iously valued in our society, can it be right to restrain publication of material freely available elsewhere and obtainable by anyone here who cared to take the trouble? In this instance again, I would suggest, the decision was one which could not have been reached had free speech been regarded not as one right among many but as a right demanding almost absolute judicial protection.

In some ways, however, the absence of entrenched constitutional guarantees may prove a blessing. In this country, as all lawyers know, it was the general prac-tice until the Administration of Justice Acts of 1920 and 1933 to try common law civil actions with a jury. Thus in a claim for damages for tort or breach of contract the judge directed the jury on the law and the jury brought in a verdict on liability and damages. In 1920 and (after a brief restoration of the old law) 1933 the law was changed. Henceforward there were to be juries as of right in actions based on defamation, malicious prosecution, false imprisonment, seduction, and breach of promise. But although a discretion remained to order jury trial in other actions, such as claims for damages for personal injuries, the discretion was in effect snuffed out by the Court of Appeal's decision in *Ward v James* [1966] 1 QB 273.

I do not think I have ever met anyone in this country who mourned the demise of the civil jury. There are those, probably including all lawyers and members of the public other than those who are or act for libel plaintiffs, who feel that the sometimes irresponsible generosity of libel juries brings the law into disrepute and that trials would be better conducted in this field as in others by a judge alone. I am not myself aware of any body of opinion hankering for a return to civil jury trial across the board. This seems to be a reform easily and beneficially effected.

In the United States such an effortless reform would not have been possible. The seventh amendment to the Constitution provides:

In Suits at common law, where the value in controversy shall exceed twenty dollars, the right of trial by jury shall be preserved, and no fact tried by a jury, shall be otherwise re-examined in any Court of the United States, than according to the rules of the common law.

We should not be very surprised at the American affection for juries, since it is (in relation to criminal juries) fully shared by the British people. When the Roskill Committee proposed that there should be no juries in serious fraud trials, the proposal proved unacceptable to public and parliamentary opinion. When the Runciman Royal Commission suggested restrictions on a defendant's existing right to demand jury trial, there were howls of protest. At least where guilt and innocence are concerned, most people would rather entrust their fortunes to the good-sense of their fellow citizens than to the narrow judgment of a professional lawyer. It is not therefore surprising that those who framed the American Bill of Rights insisted on trial by civil jury as a protection of the citizen's rights and freedom. But in the late twentieth century the scene looks rather different. The awards made in tort claims in the United States have become a national scandal, with ever vaster awards being made for ever more trivial and questionable injuries. There can be no doubt that the level of awards has an inhibiting effect on business and professional life. At the heart of the problem lies the American civil jury, making hugely inflated awards to try and ensure that after the lawyers have taken their rich pickings there is still something left for the injured plaintiff. The British option, of quietly phasing out the civil jury, is not open. The constitutional guarantee of one century may become the constitutional millstone of the next. The second amendment guarantee of the right to keep and bear arms provides another persuasive example of a guarantee one is happy to do without.

I have so far concentrated on what seem to me significant differences between the American constitutional and legal settlement and our own. I would like, in closing, to suggest two respects in which we are perhaps moving together.

I have drawn a contrast between our own doctrine of parliamentary sovereignty—the unchallengeable power of Parliament to do everything except make a woman a man or a man a woman, as Dicey put it—and the American doctrine of ultimate judicial supremacy. But Parliament is looking a little less sovereign than it did. The doctrine of unlimited parliamentary sovereignty had no counterpart in the law of Scotland before the Act of Union in 1707, and while in that Act there were certain articles which the post-Union parliament was expressly authorized to modify there were others which were stated to be fundamental and unalterable. Since the Act of Union was in effect a treaty made between two parties, the Scots Parliament and the English Parliament, which immediately thereafter ceased to exist on establishment of the British (Scots and English) Parliament, it is hard to see how the bargain could ever be modified. It is also noteworthy that in Article XVIII of the Act it is provided 'that no alteration be made in Laws which concern private Right, except for evident utility of the subjects within Scotland'. It is in my view highly questionable whether these are provisions which a parliamentary majority at Westminster could lawfully repeal. There have been several attempts since the Second World War to put the matter to the test. In the first case an injunction was sought to restrain the use by the Queen in Scotland of the title Queen Elizabeth II, the argument being that she was the only Queen Elizabeth Scotland had ever had. The second case challenged European Community restraints on Scottish fishermen: the relevant Regulations, it was said, were not for the evident utility of the subjects within Scotland. Since then there have been challenges to the poll tax, which was again argued with some plausibility to be not for the evident utility of the subjects within Scotland. In none of these cases so far has it been necessary for the Court of Session to resolve the underlying constitutional issue concerning the possible limitation of parliamentary sovereignty in relation to Scotland. But it seems perhaps unlikely that the subject will remain dormant for ever.

If one turns one's gaze away from Edinburgh and towards Luxembourg, an even more striking infringement of parliamentary sovereignty is immediately apparent. To many this truth only became clear on the decision in the case of the Spanish fishing boats, *R v Secretary of State for Transport ex parte Factortame* [1991] 1 AC 604 and [1992] AC 85. This was the case, it will be recalled, in which the European Court decision inspired the British press to new levels of verbal ingenuity. 'EC fishes in troubled waters' said *The Independent*. 'Old Spanish Customs' commented *The Times*. 'The legal bones and the stink over fish' wrote the *Guardian*. 'Court ruling fails to make a splash' opined the *Financial Times*. 'Brussels rules the waves' trumpeted the *Daily Mail*. 'Britannia waives the rules', replied *The Times*. But behind all the journalistic cleverness lay a serious point, not new to any lawyer but apparently new to wide swathes of public and political opinion: that a British statute inconsistent with Community law was to that extent unlawful and void. Not since medieval times had judges, at least in England, been obliged to ask themselves a question unimaginable to Dicey: 'Well, that may be what the statute says and means, but is it good law?' Now they were not only entitled but bound in appropriate circumstances to ask themselves that question. So they took a large step closer to the position of their American brethren, even though—in answering the question—they have the benefit, which American judges do not have, of a reference library in Luxembourg.

For my second point of rapprochement I again turn to de Tocqueville. In *Democracy in America* he wrote:

Scarcely any political question arises in the United States which is not resolved, sooner or later, into a judicial question.

The truth of that statement remains as obvious today as 150 years ago, probably more so. The battle for civil rights took place not in Congress but in the courts. The argument about abortion has become primarily a legal question. Hence the forum of debate has been different. The protections accorded to women and ethnic minorities in this country, for instance, have been the result of legislation in Parliament and in the European Community. Controversy about abortion has been focused in Parliament, not in the courts.

But there are, perhaps, signs of change. To an extent which would have surprised even our recent forebears issues now come before the courts raising for judicial decision questions of high political content. One need not delve far into the past to find examples: the legality of the treaty negotiated at Maastricht; the ordination of women to the Anglican priesthood; the amenability of a minister to the contempt jurisdiction of the court; the extent, if any, to which a minister must have regard to the effect of statutory provisions not yet brought into effect; the prerogative power to grant a free pardon; the executive power to review life sentences and parole; the Lord Chancellor's decisions affecting fees and legal aid; the ban on live broadcasting of Sinn Fein spokesmen; the decision to close Bart's Hospital casualty department; pension arrangements for part-time workers; the export of the Three Graces; and so on and so on. Now most of these challenges have failed. And there is of course no question of judges setting themselves up as self-appointed political pundits. Their role is, and is only, to review the lawfulness of acts and omissions brought before them. But the concept of lawfulness is widening, and to an extent unknown in our history the citizen is resorting to the courts to seek what is, in a sense, political redress. In this country, as in the United States, political questions are increasingly being transmuted into judicial questions.

The Pilgrim Fathers might not be altogether surprised, or dismayed. They put their trust in God, but also in 'just and equal Laws, Ordinances, Acts, Constitutions, and Offices . . . as shall be most meet and convenient for the general Good of the Colony'. They would not have wished the courts to usurp the rights of the sovereign people, but they would have wished the courts to support and protect these rights. That is perhaps the challenge which continues to face all of us engaged, in any capacity, in the legal process, as much in the land from which the Pilgrim Fathers set out as in that to which they sailed.

PART VII
THE ENGLISH CRIMINAL TRIAL

To most readers of the newspaper and watchers of television, 'the law' is thought of as the criminal law, and when reference is made to trials in court many people instinctively think of criminal trials. In fact, of course, criminal law is only one branch of the law, and criminal trials only one form of trial. But this branch of the law and the conduct of these trials are of enormous importance, since they directly affect the safety and welfare of the public. It is of great public importance that those who have committed crimes, other than the most trivial, should be apprehended, tried, and convicted; and that those who have not committed crimes should not be treated as if they had. Our tradition has long been to regard the conviction of an innocent defendant as a worse affront to justice than the acquittal of a guilty defendant, but neither outcome is satisfactory.

The first paper in this section was delivered to a foreign audience at the University of Leyden in the Netherlands. It seeks to describe the safeguards which the English system of criminal justice provides against wrongful conviction. But it also considers two then very recent cases—generally known as the Guildford Four and the Maguire Seven—in which miscarriages of justice had, or were thought to have, occurred.

When that first paper was given, the convictions of the Birmingham Six had not yet been quashed. When they were, a Royal Commission was established with the object, among others, of seeking to ensure that such miscarriages never occurred again. The second paper, also delivered to a foreign audience but this time in India, is complementary to the first. It reviews the wrongful convictions which have occurred in the past. But it also takes account of the recommendations made by the Royal Commission and shows how cases referred to the court by the Criminal Cases Review Commission (a body set up on the recommendation of the Royal Commission) had up to that time been dealt with by the courts.

When a person is suspected of committing a crime he is likely to be questioned by the police, when he may choose either to answer the police questions or to remain silent. If prosecuted, he has a right at trial to give sworn evidence on his own behalf, but he may again choose not to do so. In neither instance, whether at the police station or in court, can he be forced to speak. But a question arises: can his failure to answer the police questions or testify at trial be held against him as evidence of his guilt, and if so in what circumstances? This is a very controversial and sensitive question. The Royal Commission took one view; the government of the day took another. Professional opinion was, and remains, divided. The third paper in this section addresses this vexed topic. Many would not agree with the views expressed. It is perhaps unlikely that we have heard the last of the subject.

The fourth paper in the section (indigestible fare for an after-dinner speech) calls for enactment of a comprehensive, modern, and intelligible code of criminal law. Most countries in the world, including our former colonies, have such a code. We do not. In this speech I suggest that this omission should be made good.

1

The English Criminal Trial:
The Credits and the Debits*

The story is familiarly told that when Oliver Cromwell sat for his portrait to the great Dutch painter Peter Lely he desired the artist to 'remark all these rough-nesses, pimples, warts, and everything as you see me, otherwise I will never pay a farthing for it'.[1] To most British citizens of my generation it was a hereditary article of faith that the English criminal trial, if subject to occasional roughnesses, was notably free of anything that could be called a wart. Indeed, uniquely so, for uncritical and ill-informed comparisons were habitually drawn with what was thought to prevail everywhere else. The Americans were felt to have some of the right ideas, but to have allowed the criminal trial process to degenerate into some-thing of a circus. In continental Europe, it was confidently thought, defendants were treated as guilty until they established their innocence. Happily, through the labours of comparative lawyers such as your distinguished Director, such misleading insular assumptions in this and other legal fields have been tempered by exposure to the realities of law and practice elsewhere. The invincibility of ignorance has been challenged. And a series of shocks have in recent times caused us to ponder, not whether the English criminal trial process is subject to warts but whether in truth the disfigurements are more deep-rooted and serious—carbuncles, perhaps.[2] The old certainties have come to look much less secure. My purpose this morning is to discuss, in a practical not a formal way, how the process is *meant* to work, to consider how miscarriages (or alleged miscarriages) of justice have occurred, and to touch on possible solutions. But I fear, under this last head, I have rather meagre fare to offer. Perhaps this experienced audience will come to my aid and suggest an answer.

I would like to approach the subject by considering the roles of the leading players in the English criminal jury trial even if I cannot guarantee, like the play-wright, to list them in the order of their appearance.

First, prosecuting counsel. He is an advocate in private practice who in the ordinary way will appear sometimes to prosecute, sometimes to defend. His duty when prosecuting is, unsurprisingly, to present the prosecution case. But very

---

* This lecture was delivered at the University of Leiden on 26 October 1990 at the invitation of the Leiden Institute of Anglo-American Law. First published in Basil S. Markesinis (ed.), *The Clifford Chance Lectures*, (Oxford University Press, 1996), 91–110.

[1] Walpole's *Anecdotes of Painting*, ch. 12.

[2] The topic has been addressed by the Home Affairs Committee of the House of Commons in 1982 (1982 HC 451); by *JUSTICE* in a report later referred to; by much journalistic discussion; by at least one political party at its conference; and in learned journals.

well-established rules make it clear that it is not the duty of prosecuting counsel to obtain a conviction by all means at his command. He should not regard himself as appearing for a party. Rather, he must lay before the jury fairly and impartially the whole of the facts which comprise the case for the prosecution and see that the jury are properly instructed in the law applicable to those facts. Where he holds statements from witnesses he does not propose to call he should make them available to the defence, so that the defence can call the witnesses if they want to. If prosecuting counsel finds that a witness' oral evidence differs markedly from a written statement in his possession, he should show the statement to the defence. If a witness called by the prosecution is known to have previous convictions the defence must be informed. If the judge's direction to the jury is felt to be deficient in its treatment of the facts or the law, the prosecutor should draw the deficiency to the judge's attention. He may not seek by advocacy to influence the court in regard to sentence, and if the defendant is unrepresented he should tell the court of any mitigating circumstances.[3] Overall, he has a duty to be fair. I have indeed known judges to complain that prosecutors are so anxious to be fair that they fail to present the case against the accused with sufficient vigour.

Secondly I come to counsel for the defence. He also will be an advocate in private practice. The best account ever given of his role is, in my opinion, Samuel Johnson's, given during his tour of the Scottish Hebrides in August 1773 and recorded by James Boswell. (I digress to express regret that I cannot refer to Boswell, the greatest biographer in the English language, as an alumnus of this university. Scottish law being based on civil law principles, it was the practice for aspiring Scottish advocates in the eighteenth century to visit the continent of Europe in order to study the best European models. Thus it was that Boswell's father and grandfather studied here at the University of Leiden. When Boswell's turn came, there was anxious consideration whether he should follow in their footsteps, but in the end he went to the University of Utrecht. I hope, however, that honour will be regarded as satisfied when I record that Utrecht was preferred on social, not academic, grounds and that Boswell was no sooner installed at Utrecht than he bitterly regretted not being here at Leiden).[4] I hope that Boswell's record of Johnson's exposition, long though it is, may be felt to merit quotation:

We talked of the practice of the law. Sir William Forbes said, he thought an honest lawyer should never undertake a cause which he was satisfied was not a just one. 'Sir, (said Mr Johnson), a lawyer has no business with the justice or injustice of the cause which he undertakes, unless his client asks his opinion, and then he is bound to give it honestly. The justice of the cause is to be decided by the judge. Consider, sir; what is the purpose of courts of justice? It is, that every man may have his cause fairly tried, by men appointed to try causes. A lawyer is not to tell what he knows to be a lie: he is not to produce what he knows to be a false deed; but he is not to usurp the province of the jury and of the judge,

---

[3] See *Code of Conduct for the Bar of England and Wales*, Annex H, and Archbold, *Criminal Pleading Evidence and Practice*, 43rd edn. (1988) vol. I. paras. 4–178, 180.

[4] *Boswell in Holland* 1763–1764, ed. Pottle, 3, 9, 10, 16.

and determine what shall be the effect of evidence,—what shall be the result of legal argument. As it rarely happens that a man is fit to plead his own cause, lawyers are a class of the community, who, by study and experience, have acquired the art and power of arranging evidence, and of applying to the points at issue what the law has settled. A lawyer is to do for his client all that his client might fairly do for himself, if he could. If, by a superiority of attention, of knowledge, of skill, and a better method of communication, he has the advantage of his adversary, it is an advantage to which he is entitled. There must always be some advantage, on one side or other; and it is better that advantage should be had by talents, than by chance. If lawyers were to undertake no causes till they were sure they were just, a man might be precluded altogether from a trial of his claim, though, were it judicially examined, it might be found a very just claim.

'This', Boswell comments, 'was sound practical doctrine, and rationally repressed a too refined scrupulosity of conscience.'[5] So the duty of counsel for the defence is, within the limits prescribed by practice and propriety, to do the best he can for his client according to his instructions.

Thirdly, the defendant. He may play as large or as small a part in his trial as he chooses. (I hope it will not be regarded as sexist to cast this villain as a male.) Until 1898 he had no general right to give evidence at his own trial. There were several, somewhat illogical, reasons for this: partly it was thought that as an interested party his evidence was of no value; partly it was to protect him against incriminating himself; partly it was a reaction against the oppression of the Court of Star Chamber which had, in the seventeenth century, obliged those brought before it to answer questions on oath.[6] During the nineteenth century the defendant was given the right to make an unsworn statement from the dock—a valuable right, because it enabled him to appeal to the emotions of the jury while not exposing him to the hazards of cross-examination by counsel for the prosecution. It was, however, a right capable of abuse, and this led to its abolition in 1982.[7] Although since 1898 the defendant has been free to testify in his own defence if he wishes,[8] the choice whether to do so rests with him and his advisers. They have to balance the chances of weakening the prosecution or strengthening the defence cases against the risk that the defendant when subjected to skilful and searching questioning may make damaging admissions. It might be thought that an honest man, charged with an offence he did not commit, would leap at the opportunity to establish his innocence before the jury through his own mouth, but the defendant's right to remain silent is jealously protected. The prosecution may not comment on the defendant's failure to give evidence.[9] If the judge comments on the defendant's failure in his direction to the jury, he must be very circumspect in doing so: he must tell the jury that the defendant is fully entitled to give no

---

[5] Boswell, *Journal of a Tour to the Hebrides* (OUP, 1974), 175.
[6] Cross on *Evidence*, 7th edn. (1990), 203–4.
[7] Criminal Justice Act 1982, s. 72.
[8] Criminal Evidence Act 1898, s. 1.
[9] Criminal Evidence Act 1898, s. 1(b).

evidence, and his failure to give evidence must not be taken as evidence of guilt; stronger or less balanced comment may lead to a conviction being quashed.[10] The rule in The Netherlands and Germany is, as I understand, rather similar. So the defendant may play the role of mute observer or active participant: to advise which is often the most anxious and difficult decision the criminal defender has to make.

In turning, fourthly, to the criminal jury I am anxious to stress the central and also the extraordinary role of this body, quite different from the lay judges seen in the German criminal courts or the jurors found in the French *cours d'assises*. Unqualified by legal knowledge or forensic experience, jurors are nonetheless entrusted, in any major trial, however momentous, with the sole decision on whether the case is established against the defendant or not. The judge will instruct the jury on the relevant law, but the jury may acquit in disregard of his direction with impunity. The judge must tell the jury that its task is to decide the disputed issues of fact, ignoring any views of his which they do not accept. Any decision by the jury to acquit is final, any decision to convict (after a properly conducted trial and a correct direction on the law) is exceedingly hard to challenge. They need give no reasons for their decision. They enjoy full judicial privilege and are not accountable for anything said or done in the discharge of their office. Any attempt to influence their decision by abuse, threats or media pressure is punishable as a contempt.[11] So it is to obtain, disclose or solicit any details of the jury's deliberations after verdict, a provision which makes academic enquiry into the working of the jury system virtually impossible.[12] Lord Devlin was reflecting popular sentiment when he wrote:

So that trial by jury is more than an instrument of justice and more than one wheel of the constitution: it is the lamp that shows that freedom lives.[13]

The jury is seen as a guarantee of freedom for, as Lord Devlin also says, 'no tyrant could afford to leave a subject's freedom in the hands of twelve of his countrymen'.[14] So when, as happens from time to time, it is proposed to limit a defendant's right to choose jury trial in more minor cases, or when, as happened in 1986, it is proposed to conduct complex cases of serious fraud without a jury,[15] there is a storm of popular and parliamentary protest and the proposal founders. I stress both the finality of the jury's verdict and the very deep popular attachment to jury trial because both are directly germane to the problems I shall shortly discuss and the difficulty of finding a solution.

Fifthly, I come to the judge. He will until appointed to the judicial bench in middle age, have spent his career in private practice, almost certainly as an advocate. It is customary to speak of the judge presiding over the trial, and in the case

---

[10] See, e.g. *R v Sparrow* (1973) 57 Cr. App. R. 352.
[11] Lord Devlin, *Trial by Jury* (rev. edn. 1976), 41.
[12] Contempt of Court Act 1981, s. 8.
[13] Devlin, *op. cit.,* 164.
[14] Ibid., 164.
[15] Fraud Trials Committee Report (1986).

of a criminal trial the expression is particularly apt. For the judge takes (or should take) no part in the adversarial contest between prosecuting and defending counsel. He will have played no part at all in the investigation or preparation of the case. He will usually have had nothing whatever to do with the case until he receives the papers very shortly before the trial begins. He is above the battle. But this detachment from the fray does not mean that he has no important role to play. His function is threefold. First of all it is his duty to see that the trial is regularly conducted according to settled legal rules. Thus if, to take just one example, either party objects to the admissibility of evidence which the other party wishes to call, it is for the judge, applying the established law of evidence, to rule whether the evidence is admissible or not. Secondly, and perhaps more importantly, the judge has many discretionary powers, that is, powers which he is not required by law to exercise in a certain way but which he exercises in accordance with what justice seems to him to require, his overriding duty being to ensure a fair trial for the defendant. Some of these discretionary powers have grown up at common law, others have been conferred by statute. They are far-reaching in their scope and may have an important impact on the outcome of the trial. Thus where two or more defendants are accused jointly, the judge may order them to be tried separately if he thinks it may be unfairly prejudicial to one defendant to be tried at the same time as another. Where several charges are joined in one indictment against a defendant, the judge may order different charges to be tried separately if he is of opinion that a person may be prejudiced or embarrassed in his defence by reason of being charged with more than one offence in the same indictment.[16] Or, to take another important example, the judge may exclude evidence which is technically admissible if its prejudicial effect in blackening the conduct or character of the accused in his judgment outweighs its value in proving the case against him. This discretion, which originally grew up at common law,[17] has recently been embodied in a statute[18] which provides:

In any proceedings the court may refuse to allow evidence on which the prosecution proposes to rely to be given if it appears to the court that, having regard to all the circumstances, including the circumstances in which the evidence was obtained, the admission of the evidence would have such an adverse effect on the fairness of the proceedings that the court ought not to admit it.

A learned author has recently identified literally dozens of discretionary powers exercisable by the criminal judge.[19] I cannot of course mention them all, but I do wish to stress the range of powers available to the judge: he will exercise them constantly bearing in mind that the final decision rests with the jury, and so his concern will be to ensure that the case reaches the jury in a form fit for their fair

---

[16] Indictments Act 1915, s. 5(3).
[17] It is traceable back to *R v Christie* [1914] AC 545.
[18] Police and Criminal Evidence Act 1984, s. 78.
[19] R. Pattenden, *Judicial Discretion and Criminal Litigation*, 2nd edn. (1990).

decision. The proper exercise of these powers is often an anxious matter for the judge. He cannot simply protect the defendant against prejudice, since of course the prosecution evidence and the cross examination of defence witnesses including the defendant himself will ordinarily be prejudicial to the defendant, and the whole purpose of the prosecution is to prejudice. So the judge has to distinguish that which is unfairly prejudicial from that which is simply prejudicial, and that is not so easy.

The judge's third important role is to direct and sum up the case to the jury. So far as the law is concerned, he will instruct the jury as simply and accurately as he can on the principles of law applicable to the case. Thus he will, for example, tell the jury what mental intention must be proved before they can convict of murder, or what are the ingredients of theft. He will tell the jury to accept the law as accurately stated by him and this the jury should do although, as I have already said, if the jury choose to defy the judge's ruling on the law in order to acquit there is nothing anyone can do about it. When he turns to the facts the judge must tell the jury that all factual issues are for their decision alone. While a judge may, within limits, make his own views on the facts and the credibility of witnesses (including the defendant) clear, a resulting conviction will be quashed if he fails to emphasize that it is for the jury, not him, to decide what evidence to accept and whether guilt is established to the requisite standard. When dealing with the facts the judge's real task is to dissect and analyse the issues which the jury must decide, in the light of his ruling on the law, to help them in their task. He must also instruct them, as a matter of law, that they must not convict the defendant unless they are all (or, after a long period of deliberation and a further judicial direction, by a majority of not less than 10–2[20]) sure that he is guilty.

I shall say nothing of the judge's further function—of passing sentence on a defendant convicted by the jury—since that has no relevance to the subject of this lecture.

Lastly I should mention the Criminal Division of the Court of Appeal which is, in all save a handful of cases raising points of pure legal principle, a defendant's final court of appeal following a jury trial. The Court of Appeal's powers are statutory and the Court must allow an appeal against conviction if they think

(*a*) that the conviction should be set aside on the ground that in all the circumstances of the case it is unsafe or unsatisfactory;
(*b*) that the judgment of the court of trial should be set aside on the ground of a wrong decision of any question of law; or
(*c*) that there was a material irregularity in the course of the trial.

But the Court may dismiss the appeal, even if they think one of these conditions might be made out, if they consider that no miscarriage of justice has actually occurred.[21] The Home Secretary, acting for this purpose as if he were a minister

---

[20] Juries Act 1974, s. 17.   [21] Criminal Appeal Act 1968, s. 2.

of justice, may refer a case to the Court of Appeal for its consideration, and this is a power regularly exercised.[22] It is an important power to which I shall return. But if there has already been an unsuccessful appeal the Home Secretary will ordinarily refer a case to the Court of Appeal only if new evidence has come to light, not presented to the jury, and possibly capable of throwing doubt on the soundness of the conviction.

It is not altogether easy for me, as one bred up in this system of criminal justice, to know how this brief and impressionistic glimpse of how the system is meant to work will strike those not so conditioned. The audience may be wondering how such a system, combining the certainty which is required of the law with the flexibility needed for ensuring justice in the individual case, and rooted in the necessity to convince a jury randomly drawn from the general public of the defendant's guilt, can give rise to miscarriages of justice. Or the audience may be wondering how a system so deficient in the fundamental safeguards which a citizen is entitled to expect ever enjoyed the confidence which the British public traditionally placed in it. I must hope to have provoked, at least tentatively, the first of these reactions, for if not there will be rather less interest in what I have to say about how miscarriages have occurred and what may be done to prevent them.

I suppose a purist might argue that a miscarriage of justice occurs as much when a guilty man is acquitted as when an innocent man is convicted. It is not, however, the acquittal of the guilty which on the whole gives rise to public disquiet, and the occasional acquittal of guilty defendants is, I think, generally accepted as the price which has to be paid for observance of the beneficial principle that the defendant shall enjoy the benefit of any doubt. No doubt the courts of the Netherlands, France, Germany, and elsewhere which observe the same principle do so for the same sort of reason. By miscarriages of justice, therefore, I mean and mean only cases in which a defendant later established to be innocent or about whose guilt there is later shown to be real doubt is tried and convicted for a crime he did not commit or may well not have committed. If the wrong is corrected in the ordinary process of appeal, the case is not in my view to be regarded as a miscarriage, for the ordinary machinery of justice has correctly operated to deliver the right result. The archetypal miscarriage of justice occurs where the defendant's appeal against conviction is unsuccessful and he has served a sentence, perhaps of years, before the error or doubt becomes apparent.

It seems probable that the most fruitful source of miscarriages, in the sense I have just defined, arises from the honest but mistaken identification of a suspect as the author of a crime. Typically, a crime is committed; a witness or witnesses of the crime, most frequently the victim, has only a brief glimpse of the criminal; a suspect is arrested; the witness confidently identifies the suspect as the criminal; the jury convict; an appeal fails; it is later—perhaps much later—established, perhaps because of new evidence, perhaps because another man confesses

---

[22] Ibid., s. 17.

(demonstrably truthfully) to having committed the crime, that the convicted man could not or may not have committed it.

This is not a new problem. After years of agitation by weighty authorities, notably Sir James Fitzjames Stephen,[23] the Court of Criminal Appeal (as it was then called) was finally set up in 1907[24] as a result of public disquiet concerning the case of Adolf Beck. At a trial in 1896 ten women identified Beck as the man who had defrauded them. He was convicted and served a sentence of seven years penal servitude. In 1904 he was tried again for further offences of the same kind and five women identified Beck as the man who had defrauded them. He was again convicted. It was later proved that all fifteen witnesses, although honest and party to no conspiracy against Beck, had been mistaken. It was doubtless hoped that the Court of Criminal Appeal would be effective to prevent repetition of such miscarriages.

Unhappily, this has not proved to be so. In 1969 Laslo Virag was convicted of a shooting offence. He was convicted and his appeal failed. Only after he had been in prison for some years did it emerge that he had been wrongly convicted, another man having confessed to the crime and been found in possession of the gun from which the bullet in question had been fired. Luke Dougherty was convicted of stealing curtains from a shop in 1973. His defence was that he had been on a coach outing to the sea at the time of the crime. Two shop assistants identified him as the thief. Two others who had been on the coach trip gave evidence supporting Dougherty's defence. They were not believed by the jury, who convicted. An appeal failed. It was only later, when further statements were taken from those on the coach, that the truth of Dougherty's account became clear. The Home Secretary referred the case back to the Court of Appeal and the conviction was quashed.[25]

Shortly after the quashing of this conviction a committee under the chairmanship of Lord Devlin was established to consider evidence of identification in criminal cases. It recommended that save in exceptional circumstances convictions should not be permitted to rest on eyewitness evidence of identification alone. It wishes this requirement to be statutory. This recommendation has not been followed. Instead, the Court of Appeal in *R v Turnbull*[26] laid down detailed rules for the guidance of trial judges directing juries in eye-witness identification cases. Thus juries must be told to consider the circumstances in which the witness saw the defendant, the length of time the witness saw the defendant, the lighting conditions, the opportunity for close observation, the previous contact between the parties (if any), and so on. Above all, the jury must be told in clear terms that a mistaken witness may be a very convincing witness and that an entirely honest

---

[23] See K. J. M. Smith, *James Fitzjames Stephen* (1988).

[24] Criminal Appeal Act 1907.

[25] For information on this and other cases I am very greatly indebted to a report 'Miscarriages of Justice' published by *JUSTICE* in 1989.

[26] [1977] QB 224.

witness may none the less be mistaken. These rules fall somewhat short of Lord Devlin's recommendation, but the Court of Appeal is likely to quash a conviction if a full *Turnbull* direction is not given to the jury in a case where it should have been.

The *Turnbull* directions, again, have failed to prevent miscarriages. The case of Anthony Mycock is a good example. He was convicted in 1983 and sentenced to 5 years imprisonment for attacking a woman late at night in the course of a burglary at her home. She gave a detailed description of her assailant. Mycock did not fit this description but she identified him at a parade some weeks after the attack. The jury convicted and an appeal failed. The conviction was later quashed on a reference back to the Count by the Home Secretary after it came to light that the woman had herself sold many of the items she claimed to have been stolen in the burglary and had, immediately after the incident, identified a different man (also, curiously, called Mycock) as the culprit.

It may well be asked why, in these and perhaps other cases, the Court of Appeal did not, as its founding fathers intended, detect the error and put the matter right. In part at least the answer is to be found in the tradition, on which I have already commented, of regarding the verdict of a properly directed jury as almost sacrosanct. From the outset the Court of Criminal Appeal made it clear that its function was not to re-try cases properly left to the jury.[27] As the Lord Chief Justice put it in 1949.

Where there is evidence on which a jury can act, and there has been a proper direction to the jury, this Court cannot substitute itself for the jury and retry the case. That is not our function. If we took any other attitude it would strike at the very root of trial by jury.[28]

The judgment of the Court of Appeal when dismissing Mycock's original appeal illustrates the point very clearly. The Court held, as counsel for Mycock accepted, that the trial judge had directed the jury strictly in accordance with the *Turnbull* guidelines. He had warned the jury against the danger of relying on the identification of a single eyewitness. He had forcefully told them that a convincing witness could be mistaken. He had pointed out the discrepancies between the woman's description and Mycock's appearance. The Court of Appeal acknowledged the difficulties and dangers inherent in evidence of this sort, but held that they were overcome by a proper direction to the jury. Since the matter had been fairly left to the jury, the jury were entitled to convict and there was (the Court of Appeal held) nothing unsafe or unsatisfactory in the conviction.[29]

It would seem that present procedures provide inadequate protection. Steps to tighten police practice in identifying suspects at the investigatory stage have already been taken.[30] There is, however, as I think, force in the suggestions made

[27] *R v Williamson, The Times*, 16 May 1908.
[28] *R v McGrath* [1949] 2 All ER 495.
[29] See *JUSTICE* report, *supra*, at 87–8.
[30] Pursuant to Code of Practice D under the Police and Criminal Evidence Act 1984.

that the Devlin Committee's recommendations should be given statutory force, superseding the *Turnbull* guidelines, and that the Court of Appeal should be more ready to interfere where it has doubts about the correctness of the jury's verdict.[31]

I should mention, although I do not wish to linger on, a further serious source of miscarriages: the voluntary but false confession. The best known cases are those of Timothy Evans, who was hanged in 1950 for murdering his child and later pardoned, and the case of three young men convicted in 1972 of murdering Maxwell Confait, their convictions being later quashed. In each case the convictions rested on confessions which were made voluntarily but were false. To the ordinary person, and to the juries who tried these cases, it would seem unreasonable that anyone of sound mind should voluntarily confess to a crime he had not committed, and no doubt the incidence of such confessions is small. But a growing body of evidence[32] shows that certain people will for psychological and other reasons, in the absence of any improper pressure, threats, inducements, fraud or violence confess to crimes they have not committed. The most constructive proposals for remedying this problem are, I think, that interrogations should be video-taped so that the manner in which a confession is made may be assessed; that defendants should have an early opportunity of disavowing a confession before a judicial officer; that the truthfulness of a confession should require to be corroborated by independent evidence; and, perhaps, that a defendant's suggestibility should be accepted as a proper subject for expert evidence.[33]

These cases are in themselves serious enough, but it is not they which have in recent years and months caused our English criminal procedures to be the subject of serious questioning and concern. That has been very largely provoked by cases arising from the activities of Irish terrorists on the mainland of Britain. The setting has unfortunately become familiar enough. A bomb is placed, often in a public house, timed to explode during the evening when the public house is crowded. The bomb explodes, killing and injuring members of the public. There is a widespread reaction of public outrage. The situation is fraught with difficulty, because the responsible police forces come under the strongest pressure to bring the perpetrators of such atrocities to justice and jurors would be less than human if, despite the strongest judicial warnings, they were not tempted to reflect the sense of outrage felt by the community as a whole.

The three cases which have really excited public concern have become popularly, and sometimes officially, known as the Birmingham Six, the Guildford Four, and the Maguire Seven.

Of these three cases I put on one side the Birmingham Six, which is not to be regarded as a miscarriage of justice. The Birmingham Six were arrested, tried, and convicted following the detonation of bombs in public houses in Birmingham causing multiple deaths and injuries. Their appeal failed. Following public agitation,

---

[31] See the *Justice* report, *supra*, 74–5, paras. 6 and 13.
[32] Ibid., 27-30, paras. 3.13–3.19.   [33] Ibid., 74-5, paras. 3, 7 and 8.

including press comment and the publication of at least one book, the Home Secretary referred the case back to the Court of Appeal. A long and detailed hearing then took place before the Lord Chief Justice and two senior Lords Justices, who delivered a lengthy judgment dismissing the appeals and holding that the convictions were not unsafe or unsatisfactory. Since then new evidence has come to light and the Home Secretary has referred the case back to the Court of Appeal yet again. The further hearing has not yet taken place. There remain some sections of the public which continue to challenge the correctness of the convictions, but as matters stand the Court of Appeal's decision is that the convictions were sound and it would be quite improper of me to question the Court of Appeal's decision, which in any event I do not. I express no personal opinion one way or the other but simply record what has happened.

So I pass to the Guildford Four. On 5 October 1974 a bomb exploded in a public house in Guildford, during the evening, killing five people and injuring over fifty. Less than an hour later, another bomb exploded in another public house in Guildford, injuring eleven people. Two days later a bomb was thrown through the window of a public house in Woolwich, killing two people and injuring twenty-seven. Investigations were made by the Surrey and Metropolitan Police forces and the Guildford Four were arrested, tried and convicted of causing these explosions. The case against them rested solely on confessions which they were said to have made while in the custody of the Surrey police. The defendants disputed the truth of these confessions and denied that they were freely given but these issues were decided against them. That was for many years the end of the matter. Further investigations, however, threw doubt on these convictions, which aroused expressions of concern at the highest level,[34] and the Home Secretary referred the case back to the Court of Appeal. Three results followed. First, the prosecuting authorities accepted in the Court of Appeal that they could not seek to uphold the convictions, which were accordingly quashed last October. Secondly, Sir John May, a recently retired Lord Justice of Appeal, was appointed to inquire into the convictions of the Guildford Four and the related convictions of the Maguire Seven. And thirdly, criminal proceedings were begun against certain officers of the Surrey police.

These criminal proceedings have caused Sir John May to defer, until their conclusion, his inquiry into the case of the Guildford Four. But it is clear that the convictions were quashed because it had become clear that Surrey police officers had seriously misled the court when they gave evidence in respect of the confessions. There are, I think, two points worthy of note even at this interim stage.

First, in England the investigation of any crime up to the time a suspect is charged with an offence is exclusively in the hands of the police. Thereafter, since 1985,[35] the preparation of the case is handled by a body, the Crown Prosecution

---

[34] From, among others, Lord Devlin, Lord Scarman, and the Cardinal Archbishop of Westminster.
[35] Prosecution of Offences Act 1985.

Service, under the direction of the Director of Public Prosecutions and ultimately the Attorney General. But during the very important period when suspects are arrested and interrogated the police, although now subject to detailed statutory rules,[36] are not in any way supervised by any independent, let alone judicial, authority. This lack of supervision presents no danger if the probity of the investigating police officers and the experts they consult can be relied on without question. But it may be thought to present the gravest dangers if these police officers or experts are or even may be dishonest, unscrupulous, overzealous or willing to cut corners to ensure the conviction of a suspect of whose guilt they are, for reasons good or bad, convinced.

The second point again concerns the appellate jurisdiction. Where a defendant challenges the voluntariness and truth of a confession, the issue of voluntariness is tried by the judge alone because if the confession was involuntary evidence of it cannot be placed before the jury. If, having heard the conflicting evidence in the absence of the jury, the judge rules the confession to have been voluntary, evidence of it is placed before the jury[37] who, having in their turn heard the conflicting evidence, must decide whether the confession was truthful or not. This situation is very far from unusual, since in a significant proportion of criminal trials defendants who have made damaging confessions seek to renounce or disown them, frequently contending that they never made them at all. Save in an extreme case, or a case where the judge has fallen into legal error, the Court of Appeal judges will be very slow to reverse the trial judge's decision on voluntariness, he having enjoyed the opportunity denied to them of seeing and hearing the witnesses and forming a first-hand impression of where the truth lay. On grounds now familiar, the Court will be even slower to reverse the jury's decision on credibility where the issue has been fully and fairly laid before it. One must question whether the Court of Appeal is an effective sensor to detect miscarriages of justice involving no error of law or irregularity of procedure.

It would be rash to suggest solutions when Sir John May's inquiry into the Guildford Four has not begun. The remedies already mentioned—a requirement that confessions be corroborated, an early hearing before a judicial officer—will no doubt be considered. So, perhaps, will be a suggestion made by Lord Scarman that the investigation of offences be the subject of judicial oversight, a proposal tentatively favoured by one political party.

Sir John May has made an interim report on the case of the Maguire Seven.[38] Of the Seven, four (two parents and two children, the youngest aged 13 on arrest) belonged to the Maguire family and two more were related. The seventh was a family friend. One of the Seven was the father of one of the Guildford Four, and it was (it seems) as a result of statements said to have been made by the Guildford

---

[36] Under the Police and Criminal Evidence Act 1984.
[37] Unless the judge, in the exercise of his discretion, rules that it should not.
[38] 12 July 1990. My summary of the facts, necessarily somewhat oversimplified, is entirely based on Sir John May's report.

Four that the Seven were arrested, on the evening of 3 December 1974. All their hands and fingernails were swabbed and scraped that same night as the first step in a scientific investigation and the police took possession of a large quantity of plastic gloves found in a kitchen drawer. The personal samples and the plastic gloves were sent for examination to a government scientific laboratory where they were subjected to a testing procedure technically known as thin layer chromatography (or TLC).

The Maguire Seven stood trial at the Old Bailey on an indictment which charged each of them with having had in his or her possession or control an explosive substance, namely nitroglycerine, in circumstances giving rise to a reasonable suspicion that it was not possessed or controlled for a lawful object.[39] The trial lasted some seven weeks and they were all convicted. Their attempt to challenge these convictions in the Court of Appeal proved unsuccessful.

The prosecution case against the Seven rested in the main on the following points:

1. The samples taken from six of the Seven were shown by the TLC tests to contain small traces of nitroglycerine.
2. In the case of the seventh, Annie Maguire, although the personal samples proved negative, the gloves which were hers were shown by the TLC tests to contain small traces of nitroglycerine.
3. The TLC testing carried out was specific to identify nitroglycerine, that is, the positive results could not have been given by any other substance, whether explosive or non-explosive.
4. The finding of nitroglycerine under the fingernails of all the Seven save Annie Maguire showed that the explosive had been handled or kneaded as a baker kneads dough and could not have been the result of innocent contamination.

At the eleventh hour of the trial, when the judge was on the point of beginning to sum up, a document came to light (emanating from the laboratory which had carried out the TLC testing, and dating from before the Guildford explosions) showing that these tests as carried out did not distinguish between nitroglycerine and another explosive substance, PETN. Coming when it did, this document placed all parties in a quandary. On its face the document contradicted the third prosecution point I have summarized, although the prosecution still believed that they could show (because of the colour development of the samples) that the samples were nitroglycerine and not PETN. The defence for their part, believing the closing speeches for the defendants to have been effective, were reluctant that witnesses should be re-called for further questioning and the issues reopened afresh. Accordingly, and with the judge's agreement, the new document was placed before the jury with a short written statement agreed by all parties which concluded:

---

[39] Explosive Substances Act 1883, s. 4.

It is clear that there is no suggestion by either the prosecution or the defence that PETN was a substance either on the swabs or the gloves.

In his interim report Sir John May expressed the personal conclusion that the convictions were unsound, that the Home Secretary should refer the cases to the Court of Appeal and that the Court should be invited to set aside the convictions.[40] The cases were duly referred but the further appeals have yet to be heard by the Court.

For the purpose of Sir John May's inquiry further scientific tests were ordered to be carried out by a distinguished independent chemist. These tests showed that the TLC technique used in 1974 could not distinguish between nitroglycerine and PETN. Even more importantly, they showed that significant and detectable amounts of nitroglycerine could be picked up, and found under the fingernails, as a result of handling a contaminated object such as a towel. Plastic gloves could similarly become contaminated if they came into contact with a hand which was itself contaminated. These findings destroyed the scientific premise upon which the prosecution case had been founded, because the evidence did not suffice to show that the defendants had possessed or controlled any explosive substance, innocent contamination remaining a possibility, or that the contaminating substance was nitroglycerine rather than PETN.

In his report Sir John May criticized almost all the parties whose roles I earlier described. He implicitly criticized counsel for the prosecution and the defence for dealing with the last minute document in the way they agreed to do without recalling witnesses. He criticized the judge for giving that agreement his blessing. He criticized the prosecution for failing to make the government scientists' original notes available to the defence on their request. He criticized the judge for failing fully to appreciate and explain to the jury that the TLC testing carried out was not, as the prosecution had contended almost throughout the trial, specific to identify nitroglycerine. He also criticized the judge for allowing evidence to be given of TLC tests being carried out on a large number of members of the public, with negative results, when there was no evidence of how the tests had been conducted. He criticized the Court of Appeal for upholding the judge's direction to the jury on the significance of the last-minute document and for upholding the judge's admission of the evidence of random testing.

But the main weight of Sir John May's criticism was directed at the government scientists who appeared for the prosecution. They had known throughout, he found, that the TLC tests were not specific to nitroglycerine, but had failed to say so. They had testified that second tests were not necessary or practicable although second tests had in fact been carried out and proved negative. They had failed to disclose the results of the tests carried out during the trial. They had spoken as if with first-hand knowledge of tests which had in fact been carried out by others. Sir John concluded that if all these matters had been known to the jury

---

[40] Pp. 50–1, paras. 14.3 and 14.5.

the trial might have turned out differently. So once again one is confronted by a miscarriage of justice deriving, certainly in the main, not from defects in the trial process as such but from failure of the trial procedures to detect and neutralize error or malpractice in the preceding investigatory stages.

The cases which have given rise to concern are, relatively speaking, few in number but the results have been serious and unacceptable.[41] Many solutions have been suggested. I fear this lecture would be of even more intolerable length were I to do more than touch, and that superficially, on four of the more important.

For many years it was the practice of the Court of Appeal, in an appeal when new evidence was before it,[42] to ask itself the question whether the new evidence might have led the original jury to entertain a reasonable doubt about the guilt of the accused.[43] This of course reflected the principle I have ventured to emphasize that guilt and innocence are questions for jurors and not judges. In 1973–4 the Court of Appeal and the House of Lords adopted a new line, of asking whether the new evidence caused them to entertain a reasonable doubt about the conviction.[44] This change of front has been passionately and authoritatively criticized,[45] as many would think justly. Not only does it involve an usurpation by judges of the jurors' role, but it involves great practical problems, because although the appellate judges have heard and considered the fresh evidence, given orally, they have only the written record of the evidence originally given, so they have to compare the impression given by live witnesses against the record of what was said before, not of course knowing why the jury decided to convict or where, if anywhere, their hesitations lay. The jury might, for example, have accepted a confession as true at the original trial when, with the new evidence before them, they would not. How can the judges tell? A reversion to the former practice has much to commend it.

The second suggestion is closely linked: that the Court of Appeal should be much readier to exercise its power to order a re-trial. These powers have existed since 1964 where a conviction has been quashed following the admission of fresh evidence on appeal[46] and since 1988 on the quashing of any conviction.[47] But the power has been very sparingly exercised,[48] no doubt because of the difficulty of conducting a fair and effective trial years after the event. It may, however, be that greater readiness to order re-trials, in cases where judges have real doubts about

---

[41] One need only mention the case of *R v Cooper and McMahon* in which there were five separate appeal hearings before the Home Secretary exercised his prerogative power to release the men.

[42] Under the Criminal Appeal Act 1968, s. 23 and its predecessor section.

[43] See, e.g., *R v Parks* (1961) 46 Cr. App. R. 29.

[44] *R v Stafford & Luvaglio* [1974] AC 878.

[45] Notably by Lord Devlin, 'The Judge and the Jury: Sapping and Undermining', published in *The Judge* (1981).

[46] s. 1 Criminal Appeal Act 1964; s. 7 Criminal Appeal Act 1968.

[47] s. 43 Criminal Justice Act 1988.

[48] See P. O'Connor, 'The Court of Appeal: Re-Trials and Tribulations' [1990] Cr.L.Rev. 615 at 622.

how new evidence would have affected the jury's minds or about the soundness of the conviction, would offer a partial solution.

A more radical proposal which has attracted considerable support[49] is that there should be an independent body with the responsibility of reviewing alleged miscarriages of justice. This has been rejected by the Government as violating the constitutional principle that the administration of justice is a matter for the courts. This principle is not, however, rigidly observed, as shown by the Home Secretary's power to release convicted prisoners whose appeals have been dismissed, and the proprieties could be preserved if the tribunal were composed of members, such as members of the Judicial Committee of the Privy Council, who although judges stand (or sit) somewhat outside the ordinary court system.[50] If lay membership were thought to be important, the Privy Council could no doubt supply suitable members, although judicial hackles might predictably rise.

The most radical proposal of all is that recently adopted by the Liberal Democrats at their recent party conference that a Royal Commission be appointed

to consider the advantages and/or disadvantages of a change from the adversary system of criminal justice to the inquisitorial system as practised on the continent. . . .

Of course it may be said that there is nothing radical about considering something, and all possibilities should doubtless be considered.

But those who call for proposals to be considered often view consideration as a halfway house on the road to implementation and I would have great reservations about implementing this change. I give three brief reasons. First, I simply do not think that human institutions can be lifted out of one society which has grown up round them and adapted itself to them and transplanted into another quite different society whose other organs are not adapted to receive them. Secondly, as our system operates in our society—I make no comparison with any other system in any other society—it has great strengths which we should be slow to sacrifice. Thirdly, serious though these warts, or carbuncles, that I have described undoubtedly are, I think they can be treated by medical means. I do not think they call for heroic transplant surgery. But there I fear I reveal the invincible conservatism traditionally associated with the legal, and particularly the judicial, profession. I will plead guilty if I must.

---

[49] e.g. from the *Justice* report at 75; the Home Affairs Committee of the House of Commons; O'Connor, op. cit., at 624–6.

[50] This has been suggested informally by Lord Scarman.

2

Justice and Injustice *

Since the time of Plato's *Republic*, and perhaps even earlier, philosophers, lawyers and politicians have discussed the true meaning of justice. We can have no doubt that when our descendants approach the fourth millennium the topic will still be under active discussion. The same difficulties of principle and definition attend the concept of injustice. But there is one instance of injustice which we would all instantly recognize and condemn as such: where a person is convicted and punished for a crime that he has not, or is not shown to have, committed. If, in reasonable time, such a wrongful conviction is corrected on appeal, the legal system may be said to be working. Appellate courts exist to remedy mishaps or errors of this kind. But if a wrongful conviction is not corrected within a reasonable time on first appeal, then a gross injustice has been perpetrated. As Peter Ustinov put it:

I regard injustice, or even the risk of injustice perpetrated in the august precincts of a court of law, with calm consideration and time for reflection, as utterly repellent.[1]

So, I am sure, do we all. So repellent indeed that one is instinctively tempted to believe that such a thing cannot happen. Were we not reared on Blackstone's celebrated principle 'It is better that 10 guilty persons escape than one innocent suffer'?[2] A moment's reflection unhappily reminds one how unhistorical such a reaction would be. Any Christian is aware of a politically driven mistrial as a central historical fact of his religion. Nor is it necessary to go back two thousand years for such an example. English history is full of examples. One may instance the case of Francis Weston, accused and convicted on the flimsiest evidence of committing adultery with Queen Anne Boleyn, Henry VIII's second wife, and duly executed.[3] Or the case of Sir Walter Raleigh, convicted of treasonable conspiracy on unsubstantiated hearsay evidence, pleading in vain to be confronted by his accuser, and subjected by the Attorney General, Sir Edward Coke, to abuse as 'a monster', a 'viper', 'a spider of hell', 'the most vile and execrable Traitor that ever lived', and a 'damnable atheist'.[4] Or King Charles I, whose challenge to the jurisdiction of the court which tried him was never answered because it could not be answered.[5] One may instance Judge Jeffreys'

---

* The Sir Dorabji Tata Memorial Lecture was delivered under the auspices of the Sir Dorabji Tata Trust in New Delhi on 5 January 1999 and in Mumbai on 6 January 1999.

[1] P. Ustinov, *Dear Me*, quoted by Bob Woffinden, *Miscarriages of Justice* (1965).
[2] L. Blackstone, *Commentaries on the Laws of England*, (iv) 27.
[3] C. G. L. Du Cann, *Miscarriages of Justice* (1960), 164.
[4] Alan Wharam, *Treason: Famous English Treason Trials* (1995).
[5] C. V. Wedgwood, *The Trial of King Charles I* (1964), ch. 6.

vindictive progress through the West Country following the failure of the Duke of Monmouth's rebellion, or the execution of Admiral Byng 'pour encourager les autres'.[6] Such instances are not of course confined to English history. In France one may point to the anti-semitic prejudice which motivated the wrongful conviction of Captain Dreyfus. In the United States one may point to the xenophobic anti-Bolshevik hysteria which surrounded the convictions of Sacco and Vanzetti, promoting so distinguished a commentator as Felix Frankfurter to support the plea for a new trial.[7] Or one may point to the naked assertion of political power represented by the show trials of Stalinist Russia, the tainted justice of Nazi Germany, or the recent trial in Nigeria of Ken Saro-Wiwa.[8]

Cases of this kind represent, in one sense, the most glaring departure from any ordinary notion of institutional justice, since they lacked the basic feature of any properly conducted trial—the giving of a fair opportunity to the person accused to rebut the accusation of guilt. They were not in truth trials at all, but the abuse of legal forms to achieve a predetermined end, the conviction of the person accused. No more striking violation of legal right can be imagined. But in truth cases of this kind represent a political and not a legal problem: the problem of so educating one's citizens and organizing one's society as to ensure that political power is not held by men or women prepared to abuse it in such a way. For a lawyer it is much more worrying when a legal system not deliberately perverted for political or religious or other extraneous reasons is shown to permit and sustain the conviction of the innocent or those not shown to be guilty.

One cannot doubt that in the earlier centuries of British criminal justice many such injustices must have occurred: with private prosecutors, unrepresented defendants not permitted to testify on their own behalf, very short trials, sometimes inexpert judges and summary penalties quickly executed the scope for error must have been great. But in the absence of any court of appeal or any formal procedure to investigate unjust convictions and, importantly, in the absence of a popular press willing to campaign on behalf of those alleged to have been wrongly convicted, a public willing to support such campaigns, a legal profession willing to question the soundness of convictions and a bench willing to acknowledge the possibility of error, such injustices became part of the untold, unremembered history of the nation.

Leaving aside the high profile, politically and religiously motivated, trials of the kind I have mentioned, it is only, I think, in the last century or so that the attention of the press, the public, and the legal profession in Britain have been

---

[6] Voltaire, *Candide*, ch. 23.

[7] O. K. Fraenkel, *The Sacco-Vanzetti Case* (1931), 5–7, 20. In *In Spite of Innocence*, Professors Bedau and Radelet list 400 cases of Americans executed since 1900 whom they claim to be innocent. Doubts persist about the conviction of Richard Hauptmann in 1936 of kidnapping and murdering the infant son of Charles Lindberg, the transatlantic flying hero: see Ludovic Kennedy, *The Airman and the Carpenter* (1985).

[8] M. Birnbaum, *Injustice in Port Harcourt* (1995) 145 NLT 1757.

engaged by cases in which convicted defendants are said to have been wrongly convicted. One of the earliest such cases was Mrs Maybrick, convicted of poisoning her husband by arsenic and sentenced to death. A petition supporting a reprieve from the death penalty attracted half a million signatures, and her counsel (later a very distinguished Lord Chief Justice) believed in her innocence to his dying day.[9] The trial judge, a notable criminal lawyer in his day, had been ill for some time before the trial, which he conducted inexpertly and unfairly.[10]

Whatever the defects in Mrs Maybrick's trial, there was room for more than one view about her guilt. In the case of Adolf Beck there was none. His case was, and remains, to British lawyers, *the* classic case on the dangers of mistaken identification. In 1877 a man named Smith was accused of offences of deception practised on a number of women whose confidence he had obtained by false use of aristocratic titles. He was convicted and sentenced to penal servitude, being released in 1881. Years later, in 1895, a number of women complained of similar conduct, and several of them identified Beck, a man of Norwegian origin, as the culprit. So did a former policeman, who had himself arrested Smith years before and swore that Beck was the same man. At Beck's trial in 1896 expert handwriting evidence was called by the prosecution to prove that the handwriting of Smith and Beck was the same. The defence attempted to prove that Beck had been in Peru when Smith's writing had been done 17 years earlier, but this alibi evidence was excluded (quite wrongly) by the trial judge. Beck was convicted and sentenced to 7 years' penal servitude. In prison he was described as 'Adolf Beck, previously convicted in the name of John Smith'. He had no right of appeal. The Home Office, to whom many representations were made, were provided with positive proof that Beck was physically different from Smith, but declined to interfere. Beck served his sentence and was released in 1901. After his release, the same conduct—deceitful exploitation of women involving the use of false aristocratic titles—resumed. In 1904 Beck was again arrested, charged, tried, and convicted. But on this occasion the trial judge was uneasy about the case and adjourned sentence pending further inquiries. The press took an interest in the case. After 10 days the real criminal, Smith, was himself arrested for another offence and confessed to the crimes of which Beck had been convicted. The handwriting expert admitted his error. Beck was released and compensated, but did not long survive his release.[11]

A second much-publicized miscarriage came to the notice of the public at about the same time. This concerned George Edalji, a Birmingham solicitor and the son of an Anglican clergyman of Parsee origin. An epidemic of cattle, sheep, and horse maiming broke out near his father's vicarage in 1903, and anonymous letters were written accusing the son of disembowelling a horse. Although he had

---

[9] Du Cann, op. cit., ch. 13.

[10] Ibid., K. J. M. Smith, *James Fitzjames Stephen* (1988), 249–50.

[11] Pattenden, *English Criminal Appeals: 1844–1994* (1996), 28–30.

an alibi, and these crimes continued while he was in prison awaiting trial, George Edalji was convicted and sentenced to 7 years' imprisonment. A petition on his behalf was signed by 10,000 people, including hundreds of lawyers, but the Home Office took no action. His case was taken up by Sir Arthur Conan Doyle, the creator of Sherlock Holmes, who in two long newspaper articles attempted to show that Edalji was not guilty. An inquiry was established which found his conviction to be unsatisfactory, and after prolonged public pressure he was pardoned, although no compensation was ever paid.[12]

These disturbing cases had at least one beneficial result: the disquiet which they provoked led to pressure in the press and among the public for establishment of a court of criminal appeal which, despite the opposition of the judges, became irresistible.[13] Pressure for such a court had been exerted time and again since 1835,[14] during which period the Home Office had, by granting free pardons, acknowledged that there had been miscarriages of justice in twelve notorious cases stretching back to 1857.[15] In 1907 such a court was established, with power to allow an appeal against conviction if the court thought that the judgment of the convicting court should be set aside on the ground (among other things) that there had been a miscarriage of justice.[16]

It was of course hoped and intended that the new court would identify and prevent miscarriages of justice such as those which befell Adolf Beck and George Edalji. The court has indeed been described by an experienced and not uncritical author as 'a potent influence for good'.[17] But the court has never lacked severe critics, and the object of detecting and preventing miscarriages has proved, to say the least, elusive.[18] Between 1844 and 1905 no fewer than twenty-five unsuccessful parliamentary attempts were made to introduce a power to order a new trial of a convicted person; but no action was taken until a departmental committee recommended in 1954 that the Court of Criminal Appeal should have power to order a new trial of a convicted person where the appeal was based on fresh evidence adduced on appeal,[19] and after a delay of 10 years such a power was conferred.[20] The fresh evidence condition was removed in 1988.[21] But already by that date cases had come to light, clearly showing that the errors of identification which had led to the wrongful conviction of Adolf Beck were continuing to be made.

Two cases in particular were the subject of a penetrating analysis and report by

---

[12] Pattenden, op. cit., 30. In Scotland there was a somewhat similar miscarriage in the case of Oscar Slater: see Du Cann, op. cit., ch. 14.

[13] See particularly HL Deb. (4th series) vol. 179 cols. 1471–1484, 5 Aug. 1907. See also Pattenden, op. cit., 22 *passim*.   [14] Ibid. 6.   [15] Ibid. 13.

[16] Criminal Appeal Act 1907, s. 4(1).   [17] Du Cann, op. cit., 88.

[18] The cases of Miss Seaby, Brenda Lamb (see Du Cann, op. cit., chs. 17 and 19), Timothy Evans (see Ludovic Kennedy, *Ten Rillington Place*) and Maxwell Confait (see *Report of an Inquiry by the Hon. Sir Henry Fisher into the Circumstances leading to the Trial of 3 Persons on charges arising out of the Death of Maxwell Confait*) are proof enough of that.

[19] *Report of the Departmental Committee on New Trials in Criminal Cases* (Cmd 9150) (May 1954).

[20] Section 4, Criminal Appeal Act 1964.   [21] Section 43, Criminal Justice Act 1988.

a committee under the Chairmanship of Lord Devlin.[22] The first of these cases concerned a man named Luke Dougherty, who was convicted of stealing from a supermarket in Sunderland. In fact, he had on the day in question been a member of a coach party visiting a nearby seaside resort. He had been in the company of his partner and her four children, together with the coach driver and about forty other passengers, all of whom were available to support his account. As the committee, with some understatement, observed:

A very unusual number of things went wrong in the case of *R v Dougherty*. . . .[23]

Dougherty's alibi, notified to the prosecution in advance, was inadequately investigated. There was an improper photographic identification. There was no identification parade. The defence took inadequate steps to substantiate his alibi. There was an identification of Dougherty in the dock in a manner which has since been disapproved. The defence mistakenly refused an adjournment, offered by the judge, to enable them to call witnesses to substantiate Dougherty's alibi. The Court of Appeal wrongly decided not to admit fresh evidence on appeal to substantiate Dougherty's alibi, holding that such evidence could and should have been called at the trial. The case vividly illustrates the peril which faces a defendant if parties to the criminal process—here the police, the prosecuting authority, the defence and the Court of Appeal—fail to observe the highest standards, conscious of the paramount need to prevent an injustice such as in the event occurred.

The second case was even more disturbing. The facts were summarized by the Devlin Committee in this way:

At the Gloucestershire Assizes on 11 July 1969 Laszlo Virag was convicted of offences committed at Liverpool on 19 January 1969 and at Bristol on 23 February 1969. The offences consisted at each place of the theft of parking meter coin boxes, coupled with at Liverpool the using of a firearm to resist arrest and at Bristol the wounding of a police officer with intent to cause grievous bodily harm or to resist arrest. Mr Virag was sentenced to 3 years' imprisonment for the Liverpool offences and 7 years' for the Bristol offences consecutively, making 10 years' in all. On 5 April 1974 the Home Secretary recommended the grant of a Free Pardon to Mr Virag who was immediately released. After examination of the evidence which we summarise below we have reached the conclusion that the Bristol offences were committed not by Mr Virag but by a man known as Georges Payen; and we consider it to be probable that this man also committed the Liverpool offences.[24]

The miscarriage came to light when, after Virag's conviction, Payen was arrested for an attempted murder at Notting Hill in London. A search of his house revealed the presence of a number of items which clearly connected him with the Bristol shooting, including the gun used to fire the shots on that occasion. The prosecution case against Virag had rested very largely on the evidence of witnesses who had identified him as the perpetrator of the Liverpool and Bristol

---

[22] *Report to the Secretary of State for the Home Department of the Departmental Committee on Evidence of Identification in Criminal Cases* (HC 338) (April 1976).
[23] Ibid., para 2.63.   [24] Ibid., para 3.1.

crimes, and the Committee regarded the wrong identification as unquestionably the main cause of his wrongful conviction.[25] There were contributory causes, including a failure by the prosecution to disclose material potentially helpful to the defence, and an inadequate presentation of Virag's alibi defence; there was also a lamentable failure by the Home Office to take action for a period of two years after learning of evidence which, at the very lowest, threw grave doubt on the safety of Virag's convictions. The main significance of the case is, however, as another illustration of the perils of convictions based on eye witness identification alone. The committee recommended that juries should be directed not to convict on such evidence alone, save in exceptional circumstances.[26] This recommendation was not accepted but a stricter approach to such evidence was laid down by judicial decision.[27]

These cases were in themselves disquieting enough. But they were followed by three cases, familiarly known as the Guildford Four, the Maguire Seven, and the Birmingham Six, a trio of cases described by Lord Devlin as 'the greatest disasters that have shaken British justice in my time'.[28] All three cases concerned Irish terrorist atrocities committed on the mainland of Britain, and the understandable public outrage which such atrocities occasioned may well have played a part in the miscarriages which followed.

The Guildford Four were convicted of charges arising out of public house explosions in Guildford on 5 October 1974, and two of them were also convicted of charges arising out of an explosion in a Woolwich public house on 7 November 1974. These convictions were quashed by the Court of Appeal on a reference by the Home Secretary on 19 October 1989, and were the subject of a detailed inquiry by Sir John May, a former appeal judge.[29] The prosecution case against the Guildford Four rested solely on their confessions. There was no other evidence against them[30] and at the trial they disputed the confessions they were alleged to have made. Thus the case rested on the jury's willingness to accept the evidence of the police officers who took and witnessed the confessions as honest and reliable witnesses. In the course of investigation for purposes of the appeal in 1989, documents came to light which threw the gravest doubt on the reliability and honesty of the police officers. As Sir John May put it:

In a case in which the credibility and integrity of the police officers involved was essential in proving guilt any evidence which seriously undermined that given by the officers was plainly of the greatest importance. Had the jury known what the Crown were later to accept as being the true position they clearly should not have convicted.[31]

---

[25] Ibid., para 3.103.　　　　　　　　　　　　　　　　　　　　　[26] Ibid., para 8.4.

[27] *R v Turnbull* [1977] QB 224.

[28] *The Conscience of the Jury*, 107 LQR (1991) 398.

[29] *Return to an Address of the Honourable the House of Commons dated 30 June 1994 for a Report of the Inquiry into the Circumstances surrounding the Convictions arising out of the Bomb Attacks in Guildford and Woolwich in 1974*, 30 June 1994 (HC 449).

[30] Ibid., para 21.10.　　　　　　　　　　　　　　　　　　　　　[31] Ibid., para 21.20.

The Maguire Seven were convicted in 1976 of having in their possession an explosive subject, namely nitroglycerine, in circumstances giving rise to a reasonable suspicion that it was not possessed or controlled for a lawful object. Leave to appeal against conviction was sought but refused. The case against them rested on traces of nitroglycerine found on the defendants or their possessions. At the trial the Crown set out to prove that this contamination was the result of contact with explosives; it was therefore necessary to show that any kind of innocent contamination could be ruled out. On the evidence adduced at the appeal hearing the court was unable to exclude the possibility of innocent contamination. The convictions were therefore quashed.[32]

The convictions of the Birmingham Six arose from explosions in Birmingham which killed 21 people and wounded 162.[33] The two main pillars of the prosecution case were expert scientific evidence relied on as showing that certain of the defendants had had recent contact with nitroglycerine and police evidence of written confessions by four of the defendants and oral admissions by the other two.[34] At the second hearing of the appeal on a reference to the court by the Home Secretary, the court heard fresh evidence which at least threw doubt on the expert evidence originally relied on[35] and showed, in the absence of any explanation, that four police officers, including one senior officer, were at least guilty of deceiving the court.[36] So, amidst much public commotion, and nearly 16 years after the jury verdicts, the convictions were quashed.

As one would hope and expect, this series of decisions quashing convictions which had already led to the defendants serving very long sentences of imprisonment gave rise to profound public disquiet. On the very day that judgment was given quashing the convictions for murder of the Birmingham Six, the Home Secretary announced the establishment of a Royal Commission (of which Viscount Runciman was appointed Chairman) 'to examine the effectiveness of the criminal justice system in England and Wales in securing the conviction of those guilty of criminal offences and the acquittal of those who are innocent . . .' The Royal Commission were asked to report within two years of their formal appointment, and did so, their report being signed on 2 June 1993.[37] But during the period of their deliberations history did not stand still. On 4 June 1992 another defendant, convicted on fifteen counts arising from terrorist acts, was released. Her most serious offences were twelve murders, committed when a bomb placed on a coach carrying soldiers and their families exploded, killing twelve people. The case against her rested on scientific evidence and also on her own, very full, confessions. On appeal, both limbs of the case were found to be highly suspect.[38] The disclosure of scientific evidence was described as 'woefully deficient'. The

---

[32] *R v Maguire & Others* (1992) 94 Cr. App. R. 133.
[33] *R v McIlkenny & Others* (1991) 93 Cr. App. R. 287.
[34] Ibid., 292.   [35] Ibid., 318.   [36] Ibid.
[37] The Royal Commission on Criminal Justice, *Report*, (Cm. 2263).
[38] *R v Ward* (1993) 96 Cr. App. R 1.

scientists upon whom the prosecution relied took the law into their own hands, concealed from the prosecution, the defence and the court matters which might have changed the course of the trial, failed to reveal their actual test results and results which threw doubt upon them, suppressed some of their experimental data, misrepresented certain of their results and made witness statements designed to obstruct inquiry by the defence. At the trial they gave oral evidence which placed a false and distorted scientific picture before the jury.[39] As the court observed, 'Forensic scientists may become partisan.'[40] The second limb of the prosecution case was equally suspect. Although Judith Ward had made full confessions, apparently voluntarily,[41] and had not sought in the first instance to challenge her conviction on appeal, there was later evidence which showed her to have been suffering from a hysterical personality disorder such as might well have caused her to claim responsibility for crimes which she had not in fact committed.[42] So the case vividly illustrates the risk of a full voluntary confession which is none the less false, a possibility which lawyers, who are usually rational and rather literal-minded people, find difficult to accept. It is well to be reminded of some wise words spoken by a judge over a century ago:

I would add that for my part I always suspect these confessions, which are supposed to be the offspring of penitence and remorse, and which nevertheless are repudiated by the prisoner at the trial. It is remarkable that it is of very rare occurrence for evidence of a confession to be given when the proof of the prisoner's guilt is otherwise clear and satisfactory; but, when it is not clear and satisfactory, the prisoner is not unfrequently alleged to have been seized with the desire born of penitence and remorse to supplement it with a confession;—a desire which vanishes as soon as he appears in a court of justice.[43]

This is not, I feel sure, a uniquely English problem: Sir James Stephen, who famously contributed to the Indian Criminal Code, records an Indian policeman as saying 'It is much more agreeable to sit in the shade rubbing red pepper into the defendant's eyes in order to make him confess the crime than to go about in the hot sun looking for evidence against him that you cannot find and that may not even exist.'[44]

While the Royal Commission deliberated, further convictions unrelated to terrorism were quashed, on references to the court by the Home Secretary. In one case, convictions were found to be unsafe because of serious police malpractice and expert evidence throwing doubt on the reliability of a confession.[45] In another, a man convicted of murder many years before was released on the strength of fresh medical evidence which established that he was and always had been physically incapable of committing sexual acts very closely associated with

---

[39] *R v Ward* (1993) 96 Cr. App. R 1.　　　　　　[40] Ibid.　　　　　　[41] Ibid., 67.
[42] Ibid., 60.
[43] *R v Thompson* [1893] 2 QB 12 at 18, per Cave J.
[44] Quoted by Du Cann, op. cit., 149; and see Kirby, *Miscarriages of Justice—Our Lamentable Failure*, Child & Co. Lecture (4 June 1991), 3.
[45] *R v Raghip, Silcott and Braithwaite* (CACD, 5 Dec. 1991).

the killing.[46] In yet another the court allowed appeals by two men convicted some years before of murdering the manageress of a sex shop. Applications for leave to appeal following the trial had been refused. The court on this occasion held the police records of interviews to be 'wholly discredited', expressed scepticism about the evidence linking the defendants with the murder and considered the evidence of identification to be further weakened by fresh evidence: altogether the court found a 'formidable and overwhelming' case for allowing the appeals.[47]

The Royal Commission surveyed the whole field of investigation, interrogation, prosecution, trial and appeal and made 352 recommendations. Relevant for present purposes, and almost entirely uncontentious, was its recommendation that the Home Secretary's power to refer cases to the Court of Appeal should be removed and a new body established to consider allegations made to it that a miscarriage of justice might have occurred,[48] to ensure that any further investigation called for was launched, to supervise that investigation if conducted by the police, and, where there were reasons for supposing that a miscarriage of justice might have occurred, to refer the case to the Court of Appeal. Effect was shortly thereafter given to this recommendation by statute: the power of the Home Secretary to refer cases to the court was abolished,[49] and power was given to a new body (called The Criminal Cases Review Commission) to refer cases to the court if they considered that there was a real possibility that the conviction, verdict, finding or sentence would not be upheld.[50] On such a reference the case was to be treated as an appeal.[51]

It is devoutly to be hoped that wrongful convictions will not be recorded in the first place and the Royal Commission made numerous recommendations, supplementary to steps already taken, to achieve that end. If, despite those measures, wrongful convictions are recorded, then the primary duty of detecting and rectifying such errors must lie with the Court of Appeal. The Royal Commission has recommended that the court should be readier to disturb jury verdicts, even in the absence of erroneous legal directions by the judge or material irregularities in the trial, if the court doubts the safety of the conviction.[52] The Royal Commission has also recommended that the court should be readier to admit fresh evidence,[53] should more directly consider whether errors made by defendants' lawyers have or may have led to a miscarriage of justice,[54] and should more readily order retrials, where practicable, in cases of doubt.[55] In an ideal world there would be nothing

---

[46] *R v Kiszko* (CACD, 18 Feb. 1992).

[47] *R v Darvell & Darvell* (CACD, 31 July 1992), 12, 16, 17, 18, 23. In *R v Molloy & Ors* (CACD, 30 July 1997) the court had again to allow appeals, primarily on grounds of police malpractice.

[48] *Report*, 217 recommendations 331 and 332. It had not always been uncontentious. In its Reply to the Sixth Report from the Home Affairs Committee Session 1981-2 (HC 421) the Government in April 1983 (Cmnd. 8856) rejected the Committee's proposal that an independent review body should be established: para. 15.

[49] Criminal Appeal Act 1995, s. 3.   [50] Ibid., s.3(1).   [51] Ibid, s. 9(2)(3).

[52] *Report*, 216, recommendation 319.

[53] Ibid. 320.   [54] Ibid. 321.   [55] Ibid. 175, ch.10, para 65.

for any additional body, after the appeal stage, to do. But the melancholy history I have recited makes plain that the world in which we live is not ideal, and the successful discharge of its role by the new Criminal Cases Review Commission (which I shall call 'the Commission') is accordingly of fundamental importance if abuses of the kind I have described are to be prevented, or at least very speedily rectified, in future. It is accordingly, I hope, of some interest to review the cases so far referred to the court by the Commission.

In *R v Mattan*, a defendant of Somali origin was convicted in 1952 of murdering a shopkeeper, apparently in the course of a robbery, and thereafter executed. The linchpin of the prosecution case against him was a witness, Harold Cover, who testified that he had seen Mattan come out of the victim's house at about the time when the murder was committed. The appeal succeeded on the ground of a crucial failure by the prosecuting authority, before and at the time of the trial, to disclose material to the defence and to the jury which would greatly have weakened the identification evidence given by Cover, and would have pointed towards the involvement of another man, also of Somali origin, who, two years after Mattan's execution, was convicted of murder and found to be insane.[56]

In *R v Cook* a sentence for aggravated burglary was reduced because the sentencing judge had thought, mistakenly, that the defendant had committed a very similar offence before. Remarkably, this mistake was not pointed out to the judge at the time, nor was it relied on when seeking leave to appeal.[57]

In *R v Shahid & Others* a legal direction, correct when given, was invalidated by a change in the law: the appeal was allowed and a re-trial ordered.[58]

In *R v Nicholls*, the conviction of a man who had spent 23 years in custody on conviction of murdering a 74-year-old woman was quashed on the strength of fresh medical evidence which, contradicting the medical evidence available and given at the trial, suggested that the victim could have died from natural causes, as the defendant had always contended.[59]

In *R v Taylor*, the appellant was a 76-year-old man who had, in 1962, been sentenced to 5 years' imprisonment on conviction of an offence against the Larceny Act 1916. The court allowed his appeal, although with considerable hesitation, because he had been unrepresented at his trial, his defence had not been presented as effectively as it could have been, and he had been denied the opportunity, on a legally incorrect basis, to call a witness important to his defence.[60]

R v Bentley was a case very much better known to the general public. In 1952, Christopher Craig (then aged 16) and Derek Bentley (then aged 19) were convicted of murdering a policeman by shooting. Craig was too young to be executed, and was sentenced to be detained for life (in the event being released after 10 years). Bentley, being older, was sentenced to death, and despite public representations no reprieve was granted. The case continued to arouse widespread

[56] CACD, 24 Feb. 1998.   [57] CACD, 27 Feb. 1998.   [58] CACD, 12 May 1998.
[59] CACD, 12 June 1998.   [60] CACD, 18 June 1998.

concern, in particular because it was Craig who had fired the fatal shot and Bentley who had paid the ultimate penalty. A Royal Pardon limited to sentence granted to Bentley in 1993 did what could then be done to acknowledge the harshness of his treatment, but Bentley's conviction stood and was referred to the court by the Commission. On the hearing of the appeal criticisms were made of the evidence given by the police officers at the trial, which the court did not uphold; and fresh evidence was adduced, which did not, in the opinion of the court, add anything of importance to what was known at the trial, save in one significant respect. The appeal was, however, allowed, essentially because of an unfair and prejudicial summing up to the jury by the trial judge which had, as the Court of Appeal put it, been 'such as to deny the appellant that fair trial which is the birthright of every British citizen'.[61]

In *R v James* a wife died after taking a fatal dose of immobilon, a drug used in veterinary practice to anaesthetize horses. The defendant was a veterinary surgeon with access to the drug. He was charged with her murder, and the issue at trial was whether he had administered the fatal dose or whether she had given it to herself to commit suicide. He was convicted. Two years after the trial, there came to light for the first time a note written by the wife shortly before her death which suggested that she was expecting to die and which could be read as a suicide note. The court regarded the conviction as unsafe and quashed it.[62]

James Hester, an experienced criminal, was convicted of burgling a house. The only evidence against him was that of a 12-year-old boy who arrived home from school and disturbed the burglars. Hester denied involvement, and said that at the time of the burglary he had been playing backgammon with a friend named Danny Shortt. For reasons which remained somewhat obscure, Shortt was not called to testify at the trial or on appeal, although it was intended that he should do so. On the reference of the case to the court by the Commission, he did give evidence supporting Hester's account. A document was produced which, if genuine and contemporaneous, corroborated this account, and in one significant but not conclusive respect the account was corroborated by independent evidence. The court concluded that the conviction was unsafe and quashed it.[63]

In 1994 Michael Gilfillan was accused of murdering another man by kicking him to death. There was no doubt that the fatal injuries were caused by him, and at the trial the issues were self-defence, whether Gilfillan had the necessary intent and provocation. No issue was raised about his mental capacity. He was convicted and sentenced to imprisonment for life. Early in his sentence he was transferred to hospital and it became clear that he was very seriously deluded. When the case reached the court on a reference by the Commission the psychiatric evidence was all one way: Gilfillan was and had at the time of the killing been a paranoid schizo-phrenic whose mental state could well have diminished his responsibility for the killing. The court, having heard psychiatric evidence, quashed the conviction and

[61] CACD, 30 July 1998.   [62] CACD, 31 July 1998.   [63] CACD, 3 Dec. 1998.

ordered that Gilfillan be detained in hospital indefinitely, subject to restrictions on his release.[64] It appeared that at the time of the trial he had deliberately and with surprising success concealed his mental illness from his legal advisers and the doctors who had examined him, and had prevailed on his parents to do the same.

In *R v MacNamee* the defendant had been convicted of conspiring to cause an explosion in Hyde Park, very close to Kensington Barracks in the middle of London, which had killed four soldiers and seven horses, and caused many injuries. The evidence against the defendant rested on three fingerprints which connected him with explosive devices. Two of those fingerprints were, and remained, undisputed, although innocent explanations of them were proffered. But on appeal the third fingerprint was disputed, and it became clear that there were failures of disclosure to the defence. The court could not conclude that, in the light of this evidence, the jury would necessarily have convicted.[65]

In only one instance, so far, has an appeal arising from a reference to the court by the Commission been unsuccessful. In *R v Gerald* the defendant had been convicted of offences of violence in 1987. The case against him rested largely on statements which he had made to the police. At the trial it was not contended that evidence of those statements could not properly be given, and following the conviction no attempt was made to challenge it. The Commission referred the case to the court because there appeared to be defects in the interviewing procedure, in particular the denial of access to a solicitor, and it was suggested that if objection had been taken at the trial to evidence of these interviews the judge would have ruled against the evidence being given. On appeal the court could not resolve whether the denial of access to a solicitor had been justified, the question never having been explored at trial. But it was, in any event, unpersuaded that the trial judge would have been bound to exclude the evidence.[66]

Of the thirty-three cases referred to the court by the Commission up to 24 November 1998, these are the only cases so far decided. Case committees comprising at least three Commission members have refused to refer seventy-nine cases, and single Commissioners have refused to refer some 480 other cases.[67] It is of course early days to begin passing judgment, and I can have no way of knowing whether the Commission has been right in refusing to refer when it has. But so far as I can judge, the Commission appears to me to perform its difficult task with a high degree of professional skill, thoroughness and fair-mindedness. I think it provides, and will increasingly provide, an invaluable safeguard against injustice. But I have one, very serious, worry.

When the Commission became operational on 31 March 1997, 284 cases were

---

[64] CACD, 7 Dec. 1998.   [65] CACD, 21 Dec. 1998.   [66] CACD, 3 Nov. 1998
[67] Information supplied to the author by the Criminal Cases Review Commission.

transferred to it by the Home Office. Over the next year it received 1096 applications, and in the 7 months to the end of October 1998 a further 678, making a grand total of 2058 cases.[68] Many of these—the overwhelming majority, one trusts—will prove to have no substance. But it will not usually be possible to decide whether the cases have substance or not until they are considered in detail, and the total of cases awaiting detailed consideration has risen from 562 cases at the end of October 1997 to over 1,000 at the end of October 1998. The reason for this ominous development is clear: the Commission lacks the staff needed to consider, investigate, and reach decisions on the applications made to it with reasonable expedition. 'Ominous' is not, I think, too strong a word to use, since if a miscarriage of justice cannot be rectified at least reasonably promptly, much of the resulting damage can never be undone. It would indeed be tragic if this very hopeful initiative, taken to address a grave blemish on British national life, were to be frustrated by denial of the relatively modest means needed to do the job the Commission was set up to do.

It is perhaps difficult to devise a better definition of a miscarriage of justice than that offered by Sir John May in his Final Report on the Guildford and Woolwich bombings:[69]

Thus I suggest that a miscarriage of justice occurs when the result of criminal proceedings is one which might not have been reached had a specific failing in the criminal justice system not occurred in connection with or in the course of those proceedings. Such a failing may be one of procedure, it may be a breach by the investigating police officer of the rules of proper practice, it may be an error on the part of the trial judge or the Court of Appeal, it may be that a witness or witnesses perjured themselves, it may arise because a witness who could give relevant evidence could not be found or refused to testify, or through the passage of time has forgotten or has a muddled memory of that which he observed. It may be the result of incompetence on the part of the lawyers, or the inadequacy or inherent uncertainty of some of the rules of evidence. It may even be due to prejudice on the part of the jury.

The cases I have touched on illustrate almost all these failings.

On the strength of this long and unhappy experience it is, I think, possible to offer certain general rules, none of them novel but all of them, I would suggest, fundamental:

(1) The investigation, prosecution and trial of crime must be carried out in complete independence of the executive government.
(2) All concerned in the criminal process—whether as investigators, scientists, prosecutors, advocates, witnesses, judges or jurors—must to the greatest extent humanly possible discharge their tasks in a detached and

---

[68] Criminal Cases Review Commission, *Annual Report 1997–8*; and information supplied to the author by the Commission.
[69] HC 449, para. 21.4.

unprejudiced manner. The greater the sense of public outrage which a crime may have aroused, the greater the need for that detachment and objectivity.

(3) Miscarriages of justice will occur

    (a) in the absence of rules governing the investigation of crime and the interrogation of suspects which provide adequate safeguards to protect both suspects and defendants;

    (b) if police officers and prosecuting authorities do not at all stages act with complete integrity, in compliance with the rules and with a high degree of professional competence and thoroughness;

    (c) if the courts do not, in general, insist on compliance with rules made for the protection of suspects and defendants;

    (d) if experts involved in criminal investigations and trials do not act with complete academic integrity and high professional standards;

    (e) if material potentially helpful to a defendant is not disclosed to the defence.

(4) If the case against any defendant rests on eye-witness evidence of identification, or a confession which has been retracted or challenged, in the absence of any confirmatory evidence, it should be viewed with grave scepticism and rigorously scrutinized.

(5) Trial judges must seek to conduct criminal trials with complete even-handed fairness, applying any relevant procedural rules to ensure, so far as possible, not only that the prosecutor has a fair opportunity to prove the guilt of the accused but also that the accused has a fair opportunity to contest it.

(6) Appellate courts should be ready to exercise the full powers conferred upon them in any case where it appears that a miscarriage of justice has or may have occurred, whether or not there is fresh evidence before them and whether or not the original trial was tainted by legal misdirection or procedural irregularity.

(7) A valuable additional safeguard against miscarriages of justice is afforded by the establishment of a body, independent of government and the courts, properly staffed and adequately funded, charged to investigate cases in which a miscarriage is said to have occurred and empowered to refer to the courts cases which in its opinion deserve further consideration. As the Court of Appeal observed in *R v Mattan:*

> the Criminal Cases Review Commission is a necessary and welcome body, without whose work the injustice in this case might never have been identified.[70]

In the same case the court expressed, very pithily, the fundamental truth of this matter:

---

[70] See n. 56 above, transcript p. 18.

injustices of this kind can only be avoided if all concerned in the investigation of crime, and the presentation of criminal prosecutions, observe the very highest standards of integrity, conscientiousness and professional skill.[71]

That, above all, is the lesson to be learned if the failures of the past, with all their tragic implications for those involved, are to be avoided or at least very greatly reduced, in the millennium on which we are about to embark.

[71] Ibid. 19.

3

*Silence is Golden—or is it?**

There are, I suppose, legal topics on which more has been said and written than the right to silence, but not many; and there can be few on which differences of opinion are so wide and so persistent.

I should make plain at the outset that by 'the right to silence' I mean, adopting Lord Mustill's language:

a specific immunity . . . possessed by accused persons undergoing trial, from having adverse comment made on any failure (*a*) to answer questions before the trial, or (*b*) to give evidence at the trial.[1]

This right, if it be such, is sometimes treated as indistinguishable from the citizen's right not to incriminate himself, the well-known privilege against self-incrimination. It is, I think, something different, but related; a first cousin once removed, perhaps.

The origins of the right to silence as we know it are by no means clear. It used to be accepted, on the great authority of Wigmore, that the right developed as a common law reaction to the oppressive procedure enforced by the authorities in the prerogative courts of High Commission and Star Chamber, in which parties subjected to questioning were subject to punishment if they refused to answer the questions, or if they gave false answers, or if they admitted guilt.[2] But other scholars have traced the privilege against self-incrimination back to English criminal procedure in the Middle Ages.[3] It has also been argued that the roots of the privilege lay in Roman—canon law, only blossoming into a right recognized in English criminal courts in the late seventeenth century at the earliest.[4] At least one authority has described the privilege as a religious principle deriving from ancient Jewish thinking and exerting an indirect subterranean influence on social and legal thought in this country during the sixteenth and seventeenth centuries.[5] Happily, this is a question which, as mere practitioners, we are not called upon to resolve.

---

* Delivered to the Criminal Bar Association on 14 October 1997.

[1] *R v Director of Serious Fraud Office ex parte Smith* [1993] AC 1, 31.

[2] J. H. Wigmore, *A Treatise on Evidence* and see Greer, 'The Right to Silence: A Review of the Current Debate', 53 MLR 709 (1990).

[3] Maguire, 'The Attack of the Common Lawyers on the Oath Ex Officio', in *Essays in History and Political Thought in Honour of C. H. McIlwaine* (ed. Wittke, 1936); Levy, *Origins of the Fifth Amendment.*

[4] McNair, 'The Early Development of the Privilege against Self-Incrimination', [1990] OJLS 66.

[5] Horowitz, 'The Privilege Against Self-Incrimination: How did it Originate?' 31 Temple Law Quarterly 121 (1958).

The history of the debate over the right to silence during the last quarter of a century has often been told, but it may be worth recalling the important milestones. The story really begins in 1972 when a strikingly distinguished Criminal Law Revision Committee recommended that while the right to remain silent during questioning by the police should be preserved its exercise should not be immune from the risk that adverse inferences might be drawn from it at trial, and that if a prima facie case were made against the defendant at trial his failure to give evidence on oath should be open to adverse comment by both prosecution and trial judge.[6] Despite their eminent provenance, these proposals provoked a storm of protest in this country and they were not adopted or implemented here, although they were in Singapore. Against this background a majority of the Phillips Royal Commission on Criminal Procedure, reporting in 1981, recommended that the existing law on silence in the face of police questioning after caution should not be altered; but the Royal Commission was unanimous that the accused should retain his right to remain silent in court.[7]

There, no doubt, the controversy might have rested. A number of events conspired to ensure that it did not. One of those events was the passing of the Police and Criminal Evidence Act 1984, which gave effect to many of the recommendations of the Phillips Royal Commission and greatly tightened and improved control of police interrogations, giving a suspect a greatly strengthened right to obtain legal advice. Another was the adoption by the Republic of Ireland, in the same year, of a Criminal Justice Act which restricted the right to silence. Another was a lecture given to the Police Foundation in July 1987 by the Home Secretary, Mr Douglas Hurd, questioning whether, in the light of the procedural safeguards conferred on a suspect by PACE and the Codes adopted under it, the time had not come to reconsider the rule on silence during police questioning. Another was a speech by the Lord Chief Justice, Lord Lane, to the same effect. Another was the making of the Criminal Evidence (Northern Ireland) Order 1988 which, based on recommendations of the Criminal Law Revision Committee in Northern Ireland, introduced a regime very similar to that now in force here.[8] Another was the setting up, by Mr Hurd, of a Home Office Working Group to make recommendations not on whether the law on silence during police questioning should be changed but on the form which changes should take. The Working Group in due course recommended that the recommendations of the Criminal Law Revision Committee as to the inferences which might be drawn from silence during police questioning should be given force subject to certain additional safeguards for the suspect.[9]

These recommendations attracted much the same negative response as those of

---

[6] Eleventh Report, Cmmd. 4991, particularly paras. 28 and 110 and draft bill clauses 1 and 5.

[7] Report, Cmmd. 8092, 1981.

[8] The Order was announced on 20 Oct. 1988, enacted on 14 Nov. and came into effect on 15 Dec. HC Deb. Vol. 138, cols. 983–4, 20 Oct. 1988.

[9] Report of the Working Group on the Right of Silence, Home Office, 13 July 1989, para. 126.

the Criminal Law Revision Committee in 1972. But by this time miscarriages of justice were very much in the public eye, and opponents of change were able to suggest that the Working Group recommendations would increase the risk of such miscarriages. It was, of course, acute public concern about these miscarriages which prompted the appointment of the Runciman Royal Commission in 1991.

A majority of the Runciman Royal Commission recommended that adverse inferences should not be drawn from silence at the police station and recommended that the then current caution and trial direction should be retained.[10] The Royal Commission did, however, with only one dissentient, recommend that a duty of disclosure before trial should be laid on the defence.[11] And a majority recommended that it should be when, but only when, the prosecution case had been fully disclosed that defendants should be required to offer an answer to the charges made against them at the risk of adverse comment at trial on any new defence they might then disclose or on any departure from the defence previously disclosed.[12] The Royal Commission did not, it would seem, envisage any very radical departure from existing practice.[13] As is well known, the government lighted eagerly on the recommendation that the defence should be subject to a duty of advance disclosure, but rejected the Royal Commission's recommendations concerning silence at the police station and at trial, a course robustly criticized by Viscount Runciman when the Criminal Justice and Public Order Bill came before the House of Lords.[14] Although some significant improvements to the Bill were made during its passage through Parliament, the core of these government proposals became law, and I shall return to these provisions.

The main argument deployed in favour of change has been an essentially pragmatic one. The innocent, it is said, need no right to silence. It is criminals, and among criminals the more experienced and sophisticated, who exercise and benefit from exercise of the right. But crime is a serious business, and criminal trials are not a game. The interests of society are served by the conviction of the guilty, and the legitimate interests of suspects and defendants are now safeguarded to an extent which now calls for this adjustment to the balance between prosecution and defence.

One can understand the appeal, not least the political appeal, of this argument. But it seems very doubtful whether the premises of the argument are sound, and early experience in Singapore of the changes recommended by the Criminal Law Revision Committee in 1972 was not judged to have materially assisted the police and prosecutors there in fighting crime.[15] The changes introduced in Northern

---

[10] Report, Cmmd. 2263, recommendation 82, 195.
[11] Ibid., recommendations 132–138, 200.
[12] Ibid., recommendation 83, 195.
[13] Ibid., Ch. 4, paras. 26-7, pp. 55–6.
[14] HL Deb., 25 Apr. 1994, cols. 418–22.
[15] Meng. Heong Yeo, 'Diminishing the Right to Silence: The Singapore Experience', [1983] Crim. LR 89.

Ireland were not at first judged to be very effective,[16] although it seems that with the passage of time judges sitting without juries became more willing to draw adverse inferences from silence.[17] Most significant, however, was the research commissioned by the Runciman Royal Commission into exercise of the right during police interrogation, which showed that

(1) the right to silence is exercised in only a minority of cases;
(2) the right tends to be exercised where the potential charge is of a serious nature;
(3) there is no evidence to suggest that the right is exercised disproportionately by professional criminals;
(4) there is no evidence to show that silence in the police station leads to a greater chance of acquittal; and
(5) the majority who exercise the right plead guilty at trial or are convicted following trial.[18]

In the light of these research findings, it is scarcely surprising that a majority of the Royal Commission rejected the pragmatic argument for change.

On the other hand, some of the arguments against curtailment of the right to silence seem to me unconvincing. I do not think the citizen is deprived of his right not to incriminate himself. He is not compelled to speak. He can still exercise his right to remain silent during police questioning or at court. The only change is that exercise of the right is no longer free of risk. Similarly, it seems to me untrue to suggest that the burden of proof is reversed. The burden remains on the prosecution from beginning to end, as before. The prosecution can, however, in appropriate cases, rely on adverse inferences drawn from the silence of the defendant in discharging that burden. It is not true to suggest that defendants may be convicted of crimes simply because they have chosen to remain mum: the legislation makes plain that a conviction cannot rest on silence alone.[19]

Much the most powerful argument against change, in my view, and much the most difficult to assess, is that adverse inferences will be unfairly drawn, particularly against those who remain silent during police questioning, with the result that miscarriages of justice will multiply. This is not a risk to be lightly discounted. In the House of Lords Viscount Runciman said:

The first effect which will inevitably follow from the provisions as they stand is that there will be a significantly increased risk of wrongful convictions.

JUSTICE has consistently expressed the same fear. Since these provisions now

---

[16] Jackson, 'Curtailing the Right of Silence: lessons from Northern Ireland', [1991] Crim. LR 404.

[17] Jackson, 'Inferences from Silence: From Common Law to Common Sense', 44 NILQ 103 (1993).

[18] Leng, 'The Right to Silence in Police Interrogation: A Study of Some of the Issues Underlying the Debate', RCCJ Research Study No. 10 (1993); Allen and Cooper, 'Howard's Way—A Farewell to Freedom?' 58 MLR 364 (1995).

[19] Criminal Justice and Public Order Act 1994, s. 38(3). HL Deb. 25/4/94, col. 419.

are the law, whether we welcome them or not, it is clearly incumbent on judges and practitioners to do all in their power to ensure that this very gloomy prediction is not fulfilled.

During this long debate, I think it is true to say that judges have, on the whole, been more favourable to change than the practising profession. I suggest there are perhaps two main reasons for this.

The first is that the change brings the judicial direction on silence more closely into line with the dictates of ordinary common sense. Let me give a simple, indeed a jejune, example.

I go out into my garden. I observe a gaping hole in my neighbour's window and my 10-year-old son standing on the lawn with a cricket bat in his hand. I ask him what happened. He replies that he is not saying. Do I draw an adverse inference? Yes, I do. I am assuming that he is an unsophisticated boy who does not give the answer attributed by *Punch* many years ago to the QC's son asked the same question in similar circumstances: 'The window is not broken. If it is, I did not break it. If I did, it was an accident.' When in such a situation the judge instructs the jury that the defendant is fully entitled to withhold any answer and that his silence must not on any account be treated as indicative of guilt, the jury are likely to regard both the law and the judge as an ass and disregard the instruction. It is very undesirable that judges should be routinely required to give instructions which strike rational people as nonsensical, not least because of the doubt which must be cast on the rest of the direction. This is what Professor Rupert Cross had in mind when, in 1970, he described the right to silence as 'a sacred cow obstructing the operation of common sense'[20], and when, in 1973, he wrote that rationalization of the law

would spare the judge from talking gibberish to the jury, the conscientious magistrate from directing himself in imbecile terms and the writer on the law of evidence from drawing distinctions absurd enough to bring a blush to the most hardened academic face.[21]

The second reason why judges have, I think, inclined to favour the change is that generally speaking a criminal trial is more satisfactory if the jury hear the defendant's own account of the matters alleged against him, and hear his answers in cross-examination, described by Wigmore as 'the greatest legal engine ever invented for the discovery of truth'.[22] Notable acquittals have of course been won in cases where the defendant has declined to testify; one need only instance John Bodkin Adams, Jeremy Thorpe and O. J. Simpson. But the commonly heard accusation that criminal trials are little more than a glorified game of poker is, I

---

[20] 'The Right to Silence and The Presumption of Innocence—Sacred Cows or Safeguards?' 11 Jo. SPTL (1970), 66.

[21] 'A Very Wicked Animal Defends the 11th Report of the Criminal Law Revision Committee', [1973] Crim. LR 329 at 331. See also Heydon, 'Confessions and Silence', 7 Sydney Law Review (1974), 375 at 386.

[22] *Evidence*, para 1367.

think, harder to sustain when the jury have heard full evidence on both sides, and heard the evidence tested, and are genuinely able to match the evidence on one side against that on the other, and make an informed judgment where the truth lies. When the defendant remains silent at trial, jurors must be tempted to speculate what he would have said and what his answers would have been. So I think judges are inclined to welcome a change which lures the defendant into the witness box. And if, having testified, the defendant spends long years in prison it is probably better that he does not spend the time reflecting how much better he might have fared if only the jury had heard from him.

The terms of sections 34 to 37 of the 1994 Act are no doubt familiar to competent practitioners, and it is unnecessary to plod through them. I draw attention only to the fact that in all four sections reference is made to the drawing of such inferences as appear proper. In Northern Ireland, where these provisions originated, concern was expressed at the generality of this language, and the Standing Advisory Commission on Human Rights commissioned a report on whether there was need for statutory or appellate guidance on when inferences should and should not be drawn.[23] I am bound for my part to say that I recognize no such need, least of all for statutory guidelines. The drawing of inferences is a matter for the jury, subject of course to appropriate judicial direction. To attempt by general guidelines to indicate when inferences should and should not be drawn would be scarcely less futile than attempting to prescribe what witnesses juries should and should not believe. But it is very important indeed that juries should understand that adverse inferences should be drawn from silence when, and only when, they consider it fair to do so in all the circumstances. This of course means that they must consider very carefully any explanation, supported by evidence, why the defendant did not answer questions or testify. It is very easy to construct hypothetical situations in which one would, and would not, incline to regard silence as indicative of guilt.

Any legislation of this kind is bound to spawn a crop of decisions, and these sections have not disappointed. It would be tedious, even if it were possible, to attempt to summarize the effect of the cases decided so far. But perhaps I may draw attention to three of them, all decisions of the Criminal Division of the Court of Appeal.

R v Cowan & Others,[24] although specifically dealing with section 35 (silence at trial), is of wider significance. The following rulings are important:

(1) Section 35 is intended to alter the law and must be given full effect.
(2) The right of silence remains and is not abolished.
(3) The burden of proving guilt to the required standard remains on the prosecution throughout.

---

[23] Sixteenth Report, 1991, para. 7.29; Jackson, 'Criminal Evidence (Northern Ireland) Order 1988—Need for Statutory Guidance on Drawing Inferences from Silence?', March 1991.
[24] [1996] 1 Cr. App. R. 1.

(4) The specimen direction of the Judicial Studies Board, quoted in the judgment, is in general terms a sound guide, adapted to the particular case as necessary.

(5) The drawing of inferences is a matter for the judgment of the fact-finding tribunal.

(6) It is not open to advocates, by way of submission, to purport to give explanations of their clients' silence. As the court put it, 'It cannot be proper for a defence advocate to give the jury reasons for his client's silence at trial in the absence of evidence to support such reasons.[25]

Any advocate seeking to circumvent this rule must expect to incur judicial wrath.

R v Condron and Condron[26] dealt with section 34 (silence during police interrogation). It gives valuable guidance on procedure and timing. It approves, subject to an addition based on *R v Cowan*, the specimen direction of the Judicial Studies Board on section 34. Perhaps most importantly, it makes clear that the drawing of inferences cannot be precluded by legal advice to remain silent.

This point was taken a little further in *R v Argent*,[27] another section 34 case. That decision makes the following points:

(1) While there will be some situations in which a judge will rule against the admission of evidence of failure to answer questions, the proper course is ordinarily for a trial judge to allow evidence to be given and direct the jury carefully concerning the drawing of inferences.

(2) It is for the jury as the tribunal of fact to decide what inferences it is proper to draw.

(3) Close attention must be paid to the statutory conditions which must be met before inferences may be drawn under section 34 or, by analogy, the other sections.

(4) The reference in section 34(1) to 'the circumstances existing at the time' is to the time of the questioning, and the reference to 'the accused' means the actual accused, not a hypothetical, reasonable accused.

(5) Like so many other issues in criminal trials, this is one to be resolved by the jury in the exercise of their collective common sense, experience, and understanding of human nature.

(6) Trial judges should be slow to direct juries that they should, or should not, draw adverse inferences.

(7) Neither the Law Society by its published guidance, nor a solicitor (or barrister) by his advice, can preclude consideration by the jury of the issue which Parliament has left to the jury to determine.

---

[25] At p. 9G.   [26] [1977] 1 Cr. App. R. 185.   [27] [1977] 2 Cr. App. R. 27.

Since we are all human rights lawyers now, at any rate in embryo, it is pertinent to touch on the case of *John Murray v United Kingdom*[28] which, although deriving from Northern Ireland, has important lessons for England and Wales.

At 5.40 p.m. on 7 January 1990 Murray was arrested at 124 Carrigart Avenue, Belfast and cautioned in accordance with the formula under the Northern Irish 1988 Order. At the police station he asked to see a solicitor, but access to a solicitor was delayed for 48 hours on the authority of a senior police officer as permitted in Northern Ireland. During that 48-hour period he was repeatedly cautioned and questioned and refused to answer. When permitted to consult a solicitor he declined to answer questions on his solicitor's advice.

He was charged, with others, with conspiracy to murder and false imprisonment, and also with belonging to the Provisional IRA, and was tried before the Lord Chief Justice sitting alone. The prosecution case was that a man L, a former member of PIRA, was believed to be a police informer. He was accordingly tricked into visiting 124 Carrigart Avenue on 5 January and there held and interrogated until the police arrived at the house two days later. The Crown alleged that L was to be executed as an informer.

Evidence was given at the trial that when the police entered the house they saw Murray coming downstairs. L testified that he had been forced on pain of death to make a taped confession that he was an informer. On the evening of 7 January, he said, he heard movement and was told to take off his blindfold, which he did; he opened the door of the bedroom in which he had been held, and saw Murray at the head of the stairs; Murray told him that the police were at the door and he should go downstairs and watch television; Murray meanwhile was pulling tape out of a cassette. At the house the police found a cassette, and a tangled tape containing a confession by L of working for the police.

At the close of the prosecution case Murray was called upon to testify and warned in accordance with the Northern Irish procedure. He chose not to give or call evidence, and was convicted of aiding and abetting the unlawful imprisonment of L. A co-defendant, whose evidence the judge rejected, testified that Murray's arrival at the house had been late and innocent.

Article 3 of the 1988 Order, corresponding to section 34 of the 1994 Act, permits inferences to be drawn where proper from failure to mention facts when charged or questioned. In his reasoned decision the trial judge declined to draw any inference under this Article.

Article 4 of the 1988 Order, broadly corresponding to section 35 of the 1994 Act, permits inferences to be drawn where proper from a defendant's failure to testify at trial. The judge did on the facts draw an inference adverse to Murray under this Article.

Article 6 of the 1988 Order, corresponding to section 37 of the 1994 Act, permits inferences to be drawn where proper from a defendant's failure when

---

[28] Case 41/1994/570, 8 Feb. 1996; (1996) 22 EHRR 29.

asked to account for his presence at a particular place, here 124 Carrigart Avenue. The judge did on the facts draw an inference adverse to Murray under this Article.

Murray appealed against his conviction to the Court of Appeal in Northern Ireland contending that the judge should not have drawn the inferences that he did. The judge's decision was held to be fully justified on the facts, in common sense, and his appeals failed. In another, rather similar, case the House of Lords adopted a similar approach.[29]

In the European Court of Human Rights Murray mounted two arguments. First, he contended that there had been a violation of the right to silence and the right not to incriminate oneself contrary to Article 6, paragraphs 1 and 2 of the Convention. These provide, so far as relevant:

(1) In the determination of . . . any criminal charge against him, everyone is entitled to a fair and public hearing within a reasonable time by an independent and impartial tribunal established by law . . .
(2) Everyone charged with a criminal offence shall be presumed innocent until proved guilty according to law.

This argument was rejected by 14 votes to 5. The majority of the Court held that the right to silence was not absolute; that the silence of the accused throughout the proceeding was not necessarily neutral, and that:

Whether the drawing of adverse inferences from an accused's silence infringes Article 6 is a matter to be determined in the light of all the circumstances of the case, having particular regard to the situations where inferences may be drawn, the weight to be attached to them by the national courts in their assessment of the evidence and the degree of compulsion inherent in the situation.[30]

The Court shared the view of the Northern Irish court that on the facts the drawing of adverse inferences was a matter of common sense and was neither unreasonable nor unfair in the circumstances.[31] In the Northern Irish context, of course, the Court had the advantage of knowing what inferences the trial court had and had not drawn, and why. In an English jury trial there would be no way of knowing what inferences the jury had drawn, if any. The Court in Strasbourg would presumably have to base itself on the apparent soundness of the trial judge's direction to the jury.

Murray's second argument was that he had been wrongly denied access to a solicitor. This argument was based on Article 6.1 of the Convention, already quoted, in conjunction with paragraph 3(c), which provides:

Everyone charged with a criminal offence has the following minimum rights . . .
(c) to defend himself in person or through legal assistance of his own choosing or, if he has not sufficient means to pay for legal assistance, to be given it free when the interests of justice so require.

---

[29] *Murray v DPP* [1994] 1 WLR 1.
[30] *Murray v UK*, above, para. 47.
[31] Ibid., para. 54.

This complaint succeeded, by 12 votes to 7. In the view of the majority, fairness demanded that the accused should have the benefit of legal assistance at the outset of a police interrogation.[32] The dissenting minority, which included the very distinguished President of the Court, held that on the particular facts of this case there was no unfairness in drawing adverse inferences from Murray's silence during police questioning before he had access to his lawyer.[33] Given the sequence of events after Murray did have access to legal advice, it is very hard to see how Murray was prejudiced by the earlier questioning. But the clear message must be that it is inappropriate to draw inferences from the silence of a suspect who has asked for legal advice but been questioned before receiving it. Since one of the main arguments for curtailing the right of silence rested on the improved safeguards now available for suspects, and in particular their right to legal advice, this message should not cause undue dismay or surprise; it was because of the right to legal advice that it was thought safe to curtail the right to silence. But there is a lesson to be learned. And if, as I understand, there are a number of other challenges relating to the right of silence pending in Strasbourg, we may have a number of other lessons awaiting us.

Although many others take a contrary view, I myself think that the new provisions, carefully applied, should serve to promote the ends of justice. But this does mean that solicitors advising their clients in the police station should approach each case on its merits, and not simply advise against answering in the hope that juries will not blame defendants for doing what their solicitor advises. It does mean that defence counsel must consider, even more carefully than before, whether a client should be advised not to give evidence. It does mean that prosecutors should exercise judgment in deciding what, if any, comment to make. It does, above all, mean that trial judges must frame their jury directions with care, particularly in relation to police interrogations, drawing attention to any evidence which may serve to excuse or explain the defendant's silence. We have a common duty to ensure that these new rules do not lead to wrongful convictions; and since the reputation of the criminal justice system is, I am sure, a matter of moment to us all, we have a common interest as well.

---

[32] Ibid., para. 66.

[33] Ibid., joint partly dissenting opinion of Judges Ryssdal, Matscher, Palm, Foighel, Sir John Freeland, Wildhaber and Jungwiert, para. 9.

4

*A Criminal Code: Must We Wait for Ever?**

We are currently witnessing a degree of constitutional, institutional, procedural, and professional change of which we have not in combination seen the like for 350 years. One need only mention such expressions as Devolution, House of Lords reform, Human Rights, Freedom of Information, Woolf, Modernization of Justice for the seismic nature of the current changes to be appreciated. They are, one can have no doubt, changes intended to meet the needs, hopes, and expectations of citizens of this modern plural democracy governed as it is by the rule of law. But there is one feature of such a democracy which, I fear, we shall still lack: something enjoyed by our former colonies, and almost all the great countries of the world; something which has the support of the present government, as of its predecessor; something which we have in the past come tantalisingly close to achieving. I refer to enactment of a clear, authoritative, comprehensive, accessible, modern, written statement of our criminal law. In short, a criminal code.

The plea for such a code cannot, I fear, startle by its novelty. In 1818 both Houses of Parliament petitioned the Prince Regent asking him to establish a Law Commission to consolidate the statute law of England. In 1831 a Commission was set up to inquire into the possibility of codifying the criminal law. The Commission produced its first report in 1835 and seven further reports over the next 10 years, culminating in a Criminal Law Code Bill which was referred to a Select Committee and then dropped. In 1879 a Royal Commission under the eminent chairmanship of Lord Blackburn recommended the adoption of a draft criminal code containing over 550 clauses. Between 1844 and 1882 Lord Brougham and others made no fewer than eight separate parliamentary attempts to secure enactment of such a code. All ended in failure. And then the campaign flagged until, in 1965, the Law Commission was established and charged by Parliament to review the law of England and Wales 'with a view to its systematic development and reform, including in particular the codification of [the] law . . . and generally the simplification and modernization of the law'. The criminal law was an obvious—*the* obvious—candidate for codification. So a Criminal Code team was set up, notably including Professor Sir John Smith, whom most would gladly hail as the outstanding criminal lawyer of our time. A code was produced and published in 1985; it was revised and expanded in 1989. It has very largely withstood the appraisal and criticism to which it has been properly subjected, and has in general commanded respect and support. But the code has not been

---

* Delivered at a dinner for HM judges at the Mansion House, London on 22 July 1998. Part of the text was first published in the *Criminal Law Review* (1998), 694–6. © Sweet & Maxwell 1998.

enacted, not for want of confidence in its objects or its contents, but for lack of parliamentary time, a powerful but not, surely, an insuperable obstacle. The Law Commission has tried, with indifferent success, to achieve what it can on a partial, piecemeal basis. But this is a far cry from a comprehensive code containing a general statement of principles, and defences, and offences, and penalties, and procedure and evidence, accessible to every citizen.

The arguments in favour of codification are what they have always been. First, it would bring clarity and accessibility to the law. As the Attorney-General put it in the House of Commons 119 years ago:

Surely, it is a desirable thing that anybody who may want to know the law on a particular subject should be able to turn to a chapter of the Code, and there find the law he is in search of explained in a few intelligible and well-constructed sentences; nor would he have to enter upon a long examination of *Russell on Crimes*, or *Archbold*, and other text-books, because he would have a succinct and clear statement before him.[1]

Secondly, a code would bring coherence to this branch of the law. Sir John Smith has expressed his general disbelief in codes—a disbelief which I for my part share—but he continued:

The criminal law is entirely different. It is incoherent and inconsistent. State almost any general principle and you find one or more leading cases which contradict it. It is littered with distinctions which have no basis in reason but are mere historical accidents. I am in favour of codification of the criminal law because I see no other way of reducing a chaotic system to order, of eliminating irrational distinctions and of making the law reasonably comprehensible, accessible and certain. These are all practical objects. Irrational distinctions mean injustice. A is treated differently from B when there is no rational ground for treating him differently; and this is not justice.[2]

Sir John has entertained generations of students, practitioners and judges by highlighting the anomalies in our present law. As the present chairman of the Law Commission has herself said, the cure now can only be achieved by codification; it cannot be provided by the courts alone.

Thirdly, a code would bring greater certainty to the law, and in this of all fields the law should be so far as possible certain. The arguments for incremental development of the law, persuasive elsewhere, have no application here. It is not just that a defendant should be held punishable for an act which would not have been thought criminal when he did it; and if he is held not liable for conduct which would at that time have been thought criminal, the almost inevitable consequence is that others have been unjustly punished. Incorporation of the European Convention reinforces the need for certainty if the principle of legality is to be observed. Even the most breathless admirer of the common law must regard it as a reproach that after 700 years of judicial decision-making our highest tribunal

---

[1] *Hansard*, HC (series 3) vol. 245, col. 316 (3 April 1879).
[2] *Codification of the Criminal Law*, Child & Co. Lecture (1986).

should have been called upon time and again in recent years to consider the mental ingredients of murder, the oldest and most serious of crimes.

The task is not beyond us. Writing in 1966 of the Indian Criminal Code, devised by Macaulay and Stephen among others, an Indian author said:

The Code has been very successful. It has stood the test of time very well. A proof of its intrinsic worth and merit may be found in the fact that during the last century that it has been in force it has not been found necessary to amend it except only a very few times, and substantially the Code subsists as it was enacted in 1860.[3]

For 25 Canadian dollars the Canadian citizens can buy a small paperback which contains a comprehensive and comprehensible statement of everything he, and the policeman, and the judge, need to know about the substantive criminal law, evidence, procedure and sentencing in Canada.

And so I could go on. But I shall exercise the judicial quality of mercy. I leave the last word to Lord Campbell, a predecessor not only of mine but of the Lord Chancellor, speaking in 1845:

There was not a country of the Continent that had not its criminal law reduced into form, and published for the benefit of those who were either to administer or to obey it. There was now no reason why the people of this Empire should not enjoy the same advantage; and he trusted that this just reproach upon our legislation would soon be wiped away, and that a criminal code would be prepared for Great Britain.[4]

One hopes that parliamentary time may yet be found to achieve something that has eluded our predecessors but would, I think, come to be recognized as an important milestone in our legal and public life.

[3] M. P. Iain, *Outlines of Indian Legal History* (2nd edn., 1966), xxiv, 'Codification of Law', 655–6.
[4] *Hansard*, HC (series 3) vol. 82, col. 1087 (25 July 1845).

PART VIII
CRIME AND PUNISHMENT

Concern about crime is as old as society itself. But in recent years, in many countries throughout the world, that concern has greatly intensified. Levels of crime have risen. Many of the crimes committed are seen as more depraved than in days past. Old questions have been asked, here and elsewhere, with a new urgency: how can crime best be prevented? how can criminals be deterred? how can the commission of crime be most effectively punished? how and when is a balance to be struck between the punishment of the criminal and his rehabilitation? There are no simple answers to these questions.

The first paper in this section considers the problems and dilemmas which confront the judge when he has to decide what sentence to impose on an offender and explains, in general terms, the current English approach to sentencing.

The second paper is addressed to the special problem of the young offender. The risk of course is that children and adolescents committing not very serious crimes may grow up into experienced criminals committing much more serious crimes. Prevention is better than cure; but cure where possible is preferable to most of the alternatives. The problem is not an academic one, since more and worse crimes seem now to be committed by ever younger offenders.

In almost all cases of serious crime the judge, informed of all relevant circumstances concerning the crime and the offender decides what sentence to impose, usually subject to a maximum fixed by statute. If the offender considers the judge's sentence to be too severe, he can seek to appeal against it. If the Attorney-General considers it to be unduly lenient he may, in many but not all cases, ask the court to increase the sentence. But the sentencing is carried out by judges. The most notable exception is in the case of murder. Then the only sentence which the judge may impose is one of life imprisonment. It then falls to the Home Secretary, a serving politician and member of the executive, to decide whether the offender should spend the rest of his life in prison and, if not, the minimum term the offender should serve before conditional release. The third paper in this section criticizes in principle the rule which requires a life sentence to be imposed in all cases, regardless of the facts, and the role of the executive in deciding how long a criminal should stay in prison.

In 1996 the government of the day introduced a bill which, subject to some amendment, in due course became the Crime (Sentences) Act 1997. Some of the proposals embodied in that bill had attracted strong criticism from a number of senior judges, notably including the Lord Chief Justice, Lord Taylor of Gosforth, and others. When the Bill reached the House of Lords, I (having succeeded Lord

Taylor) criticized three provisions of the Bill. The first object of my criticism was a proposal to shorten remission and abolish parole for prisoners serving determinate sentences. These provisions were duly enacted; but they were never brought into force and have since been repealed. The second object of my criticism was a provision requiring the imposition of an automatic life sentence on a second conviction of certain serious sexual and violent offences. This provision was enacted, subject to amendment, and has been brought into force. Thirdly, I criticized clauses which required judges to impose mandatory minimum sentences on repeat burglars and drug dealers. These clauses were enacted and have also been brought into force. The basis of my objection in these last two instances was that the provisions restricted the discretion of the judge to impose whatever sentence he regarded as just on the facts of the particular case. Once a provision is enacted, it is of course the duty of the judges to give effect to the will of Parliament, whatever their personal reservations, although they must, in future, seek to interpret statutory provisions conformably with the European Convention on Human Rights. The fourth item in this section is the speech which I made in the House of Lords on 27 January 1997.

1

*The Sentence of the Court**

The past few years have witnessed a vigorous debate on the sentencing of criminal defendants. The debate has raged in countries as far apart as the United States, Australia and the Netherlands. It has burned with particular brilliancy in this country.[1] The existence of this debate is not something which judges or magistrates should deprecate. The maintenance of peace, order and security is one of the oldest functions of civil society. The imposition of penal sanctions on those who have infringed the rules by which a society has bound itself are a matter of legitimate interest to the members of that society. In modern societies such as ours, this is a task entrusted to judges and magistrates, who act in this capacity as the medium through which society visits such sanctions on transgressors.

So the existence of this debate is a healthy phenomenon in a democratic society. It is, however, desirable that the debate should be reasonably informed, that is, that the participants should have some understanding of the practice and principles involved. It is also desirable that the debate should be based on fact, not fiction; that the debate should be largely concerned with general levels of sentence rather than with individual sentences which may on occasion be aberrant; and that the debate should not be fuelled by tendentious or inaccurate reporting. Perhaps most importantly of all, it is desirable that the debate should be apolitical. There is plenty of room for genuine differences of opinion on these difficult and important questions. But we all have the same aims. It is unfortunate if these matters should become the staple of party political controversy.

It follows from what I have said of the judges' role in society that I do not consider it would be right, even if it were possible, for judges to ignore the opinion of the public. They do not live the lives of hermits; they are in and of the world; and they are inevitably alive to the opinions of their fellow-citizens. The judges are also conscious that the gift of infallibility is not conferred on them, along among mortals. So when differences of opinion arise on issues of sentencing between the judges and an identifiable body of public opinion, the judges are bound to reflect whether it may be that the public are right and they are wrong. In two instances which occur to me, rape and killing by dangerous driving, I think it is true that public opinion (reinforced in the latter case by legislation) brought home to the judges that they had on occasion failed in their sentences to reflect the seriousness with which society regarded these offences.

* Delivered to the Police Foundation at the Merchant Taylor's Hall, London on 10 July 1997. First published as a booklet by the Prison Reform Trust and The Police Foundation. © Lord Bingham of Cornhill, The Prison Reform Trust and The Police Foundation (1997), 19–34.
  [1] See, generally, Rutherford, *Transforming Criminal Policy* (1996).

Given the temper of our society in the last 5 years, I do not find it surprising that the prison population should have increased by 50 per cent, reflecting the more ready resort to custody by sentencers and an increase in the length of sentences imposed. The tenor of political rhetoric has strongly favoured the imposition of severe sentences; this rhetoric has been faithfully reflected in certain elements of the media; and judges accused of passing lenient sentences have found themselves routinely castigated in some newspapers. Against this background judges have, understandably, sought to avoid the unwelcome experience of passing sentences which the Attorney-General has sought leave to refer to the Court of Appeal as unduly lenient. So we have the extraordinary paradox, that judges and magistrates have been roundly criticized for over-lenient sentencing during a period when they have been sending more defendants to prison for longer periods than at any time in the last 40 years. The increase in the prison population is not explained by any recent increase in sentencing powers, and I have no doubt that it is related to the pressure of public opinion. This is not necessarily wrong in a general sense, if indeed levels of sentence were too low. But judges do well to remember that public and political opinion are volatile. It is but a few years since judges were widely and frequently reproached for imposing sentences of unnecessary severity. They should take care not to be blown hither and thither by every wind of political or penal fashion. And in determining sentence in any given case the judge should close his or her ears to public and media clamour concerning that case. As the House of Lords very recently pointed out, there is a distinction

between public concern of a general nature with regard to, for example, the prevalence of certain types of offence, and the need that those who commit such offences should be duly punished; and public clamour that a particular offender whose case is under consideration should be singled out for severe punishment.[2]

As another Law Lord added in the same case:

Plainly a sentencing judge must ignore a newspaper campaign designed to encourage him to increase a particular sentence. It would be an abdication of the rule of law for a judge to take into account such matters.[3]

The purposes of criminal sentencing have traditionally been said to be retribution, deterrence and rehabilitation. To these there may now perhaps be added: incapacitation (i.e. putting it out of the power of the offender to commit further offences) and the maintenance of public confidence. It is obvious that the different sentences available to the courts serve these purposes in very different measures. For example, a sentence of imprisonment is very largely retributive, punitive, although it will prevent the offender committing further offences while

---

[2] *Per* Lord Goff, *R v Secretary of State for the Home Department, ex parte V and T.* 12 June 1997 at 20.

[3] *Per* Lord Steyn, ibid., at 61.

imprisoned and may deter others from offending. A sentence of imprisonment is not usually passed with a view to rehabilitating the offender, even if in a minority of cases it has that effect.

By contrast, a hospital order made in a case of a mentally disordered offender is purely rehabilitative; there is no element of retribution or deterrence, and the element of incapacitation is largely incidental. A probation order, similarly, is intended to rehabilitate. A combination order, which places an offender under the supervision of a probation officer and also obliges him to perform a number of hours' community service, is intended both to rehabilitate the offender and also to contain a punitive element, protecting the public from harm caused by the offender and preventing the commission by the offender of further offences.

Although easy enough to describe, these purposes of criminal sentencing are less easy to analyse and apply. Retribution is perhaps the most difficult. It is not immediately obvious why the fact that A has caused loss or suffering to B should justify the deliberate causing of loss or suffering to A, when this may be of no advantage to B. Carlyle was in no doubt about the answer:

'Revenge' my friends! revenge, and the natural hatred of scoundrels and the ineradicable tendency to . . . pay them what they had merited: this is forever more intrinsically a correct, and even a divine, feeling in the mind of every man.[4]

Dr Johnson took a different view:

Since revenge for its own sake cannot be justified, it will follow that the natural justice of punishment, as of every other act of man to man, must depend solely on its utility, and that its only lawful end is some good more than equivalent to the evil which it necessarily produces.[5]

Some have justified the retributive element in sentences by a theory of atonement or expiation, the paying of a debt by the criminal to society. In a sense, however, the theory underlying retribution may be of less importance than the fundamental, if primitive, instinct which it represents. The feeling that anyone who has committed a grave crime should be appropriately punished is one that is too basic and too universal to be ignored. Unless effect were given to it, public confidence in the administration of criminal justice would undoubtedly suffer.

Incapacitation expresses a basic truth that while an offender is confined within a penal institution he cannot commit offences, at any rate offences against any one outside that institution. The downside of course is that in all but a handful of the most extreme cases the period of incapacitation is temporary. The offender will at some point re-enter society. And he may, as a result of his experience in confinement, be an even more dangerous criminal than he had been before.

---

[4] *Latter Day Pamphlets* (1872), at 66–7, quoted by J. Hostettler, *The Politics of Punishment* (1993), 131.

[5] Robert Chambers: *Vinerian Lectures on the English Law*, Part II, Lecture I, attributed to Johnson.

Research findings show that the effect of incapacitation on general levels of crime is very small.[6]

The effect of deterrence may be personal to an offender, by deterring him from re-offending; or it may be more general, by its effect on those other than the defendant who might be deterred from offending by the example of his sentence. But these again are not entirely straightforward concepts. It is often hoped and believed that an offender's first taste of imprisonment may deter him from doing anything which might lead to a repetition of the experience, but plainly this is an effect which tends to diminish each time he is imprisoned. It may perhaps be that general deterrence operates most effectively at an almost unconscious level: we might all be tempted to falsify our tax returns but for a general recognition that such a course could lead to public exposure and humiliation. But it is probably unwise to place excessive reliance on the deterrent effect of sentences. There is cogent and authoritative research which discounts the effect of the death penalty in deterring murder. And it seems quite clear that many crimes are committed on impulse, or by those under the influence of drink or drugs, or by the feckless and the unintelligent, with little or no thought given to the consequences of the action taken.[7] So long as those detected and apprehended represent only a tiny fraction of those who commit crimes, deterrence is likely to remain a somewhat blunt instrument.

Mention of rehabilitation often provokes differing reactions. To the tabloid tendency it tends to be seen as an ineffective way of enabling offenders to escape the punishment they really deserve. To penal reformers it will seem obvious that many offenders now subject to sentences of imprisonment could with advantage undergo courses of treatment in the community designed to address the underlying problems which give rise to their offending. There is an inevitable tension in many cases between the interests of the offender, viewed in isolation, and the perceived need to protect society. But the reformers would of course retort that there is, in the medium or longer term, no better way to protect society than by diverting an offender from a life of crime.

There is surely much force in this argument. I have recently urged that the strongest possible support should be given to agencies, whether public or private, whether national or local, which seek to identify and assist potential delinquents before they are drawn into a destructive cycle of offending. Whether the issue is viewed in human, social or financial terms, this must make sense. The prevalence of drug and alcohol addiction among the young, at ever younger ages, and the undoubted link between these addictions and the commission of crime, make the effective treatment of addiction a high national priority. There are, of course, other schemes with a proven record of success in rehabilitating offenders. Sherborne House, run by the Inner London Probation Service in Bermondsey, is

---

[6] Tarling, *Analysing Offending: Data, Models and Interpretations* (HMSO, 1993).
[7] Home Office White Paper, 1990, *Crime, Justice and Protecting the Public*.

one such. Participants attend the programme for $4^1/_2$ days per week for 6 hours per day for 10 weeks, and are obliged to admit and face up to the reality of their offending and to appreciate the effect of their crimes on their victims. Those who take part do not, I understand, find this an easy or enjoyable thing to do. Some drop out, unable to do it at all. But for those who can and do bring themselves to do it, it seems clear that the experience is salutary and the risk of re-offending reduced. There is evidence to suggest that community programmes, properly attuned to particular offenders, can reduce re-offending by 10–16 per cent when compared with custody. This is a saving well worth making.

It is obviously desirable that long-term prisoners serving sentences for sexual or violent offences, or offences related to drug or alcohol addiction, should while in prison receive any treatment which can be given to cure, mitigate or control the propensity or the addiction which led to the offending. Courses exist for that purpose in many prisons; they are to be welcomed; and their effect can only be beneficial. But I do not think most knowledgeable observers would make ambitious claims for the rehabilitative effect of imprisonment. The régime in almost any prison is to some extent repressive; the environment is not therapeutic; and if the prison population continues to rise the difficulty of providing rehabilitative treatment to all who might benefit from it is likely to grow even more acute.

The first task of the sentencing judge is to take note of the precise crime for which the defendant falls to be sentenced, whether on his own admission or on conviction. This is blindingly obvious, but it is also fundamental. For the general practice of the criminal law is to focus on the intention and state of mind of the offender and to treat most seriously those crimes where the offender's intention and state of mind are the most vicious. The most obvious illustration is provided by the contrast between sections 18 and 20 of the Offences Against the Person Act 1861. Under both sections it is an offence to wound or cause or inflict grievous bodily harm. But under section 18 the offence is only committed where there is an intent to do grievous bodily harm, and the maximum penalty is imprisonment for life. Under section 20 no intention to cause grievous bodily harm is charged, and the maximum penalty is imprisonment for 5 years. A similar contrast exists in the case of arson. Under one subsection of the Criminal Damage Act 1971 it is an offence to destroy or damage premises by setting fire to them with the intention of destroying or damaging the property or being reckless as to such result. Under another subsection it is an offence recklessly or intentionally to destroy or damage premises by setting fire to them, but with the additional intention of endangering life. While the maximum penalty in each case is the same, the criminality involved in the latter case is quite clearly greater.

There are, however, exceptions to the general rule that the intention or state of mind of the offender governs, as a matter of law, the gravity of the offence. There are some offences of strict liability, where all that need be proved is that the offender intended to do the prohibited act; these are mostly offences of a regulatory nature, and do not include the most serious offences. But there are other offences of a much more serious nature where the commission of the crime depends not on the offender's intention or state of mind but on the consequences of his conduct: manslaughter and causing death by dangerous driving are the most significant examples.

Two examples will illustrate the sentencing dilemmas which can arise:

1. A stabs B with a knife intending to cause him very serious, disabling injury. By a freak of fortune or a miracle of medical science B escapes serious injury and makes a full recovery.

   C unlawfully punches D on the jaw. He does not intend to cause him serious injury and the blow is not one which would ordinarily cause anything other than trivial bruising. But D accidentally stumbles backwards, falls and hits his head on a marble fireplace, with fatal results.

   On these facts A is guilty of wounding with intent to cause grievous bodily harm. C is guilty of manslaughter. In each case the maximum sentence is life imprisonment. Which of the two is morally the more culpable? Surely A, because his intentions were the more vicious. Which is legally the more culpable? This is much more difficult. C has unlawfully caused the death of another human being, a result for which he must accept responsibility. But it would be very unjust if his sentence did not take account of the fact that this was a result he neither intended nor foresaw.

2. E, deliberately and knowingly, drives his car very dangerously over a long distance. But providentially, and no thanks to him, there is no collision and no damage or injury is caused. He is guilty of dangerous driving. The maximum penalty is two years' imprisonment.

   F also drives dangerously, but much less dangerously than E and over a shorter distance. His dangerous driving causes an accident in which a passenger, or another driver, or a pedestrian or a cyclist, is killed. He is guilty of causing death by dangerous driving, an offence subject (as a result of recent legislation) to a maximum penalty of 10 years' imprisonment.

   Which of the two, E or F, is morally the more culpable? If anything, E, since on the hypothetical facts assumed his driving was more dangerous and more sustained. But in the eyes of the law F is to be treated as the more culpable, since Parliament has made clear its intention, recognized in the decided cases, that the fatal outcome should attract a more severe sentence. This is a legitimate reflection of the public outrage aroused by fatalities of this kind. But the sentencer has to ensure that the penal consequences are not altogether disproportionate to the criminality of the conduct penalised.

Both these dilemmas are, I hope, helpful to explain a recurring source of public concern. Time and again the grieving relatives of a victim unlawfully and tragically killed in circumstances such as I have described inveigh against the injustice of a system which deprives the perpetrator of his liberty for 2, 3, 5, or 7 years, as the case may be, when their child, or brother or sister, or spouse, has lost his or her life forever. Such feelings are understandable, and must attract sympathy. But they betray a basic misunderstanding. It is not, as the courts have repeatedly pointed out, the function of the sentencing judge to attempt to construct an equation between the value of a human life and a period of months or years in custody. The judge's task is to impose such punishment as is appropriate for the crime committed in all the circumstances. Among those circumstances, the fact that another human being has died through the criminal conduct of the defendant must loom large. But the court must also pay close regard to the nature and quality of the criminal conduct actually involved.

Having considered the nature and circumstances of the crime the sentencing judge will consider the personal circumstances of the offender. Statute recognizes that when imposing a custodial sentence a court may take account of such matters as, in the opinion of the court, are relevant in mitigation of sentence.[8] The matters which may, in a proper case, mitigate the seriousness of an offence or the severity of a sentence are legion. They may, depending on all the facts, include such matters as: uncharacteristic behaviour under the influence of drink or drugs; the voluntary payment of compensation; lapse of time since commission of the offences; the consequences of conviction or sentence; responsibility for dependents; youth or old age; emotional stress; financial need, illness or disability; assistance to the police; provocation. In the generality of cases, however, the two most potent grounds of mitigation are likely to be an early plea of guilty to the charge and a previous good character. An early plea of guilty carries weight partly because it spares the victim the anxiety of awaiting trial and the trauma of giving evidence, partly because it obviates the risk of unjustified acquittal and partly because it reduces the cost and delay of the trial process. But it carries weight also because it does, in many cases, involve a genuine acceptance of responsibility for the crime, which may well be the first step towards rehabilitating the offender. And where an early plea is tendered there is frequently reliable evidence of remorse. A much-respected academic authority, Professor Andrew Ashworth QC, has recently thrown a little cold water on the notion of remorse, and chided the judges for attaching importance to it.[9] I do not agree with the professor. There are in my experience a significant number of cases in which an offender is personally devastated by the consequences of what he has done. In such cases it may be reasonable to hope that the risk of re-offending will be greatly reduced.

Good character is a more variable factor. Sometimes it counts for very little: for example, in the case of couriers bringing drugs into the country, often recruited for the task because of their lack of any previous involvement with the authorities.[10] But usually it weighs in favour of an offender that he has not

---

[8] Criminal Justice Act 1991, section 28(1).

[9] Eve Saville Memorial Lecture, 21 May 1997, *Sentencing in the '80s and '90s: The Struggle for Power.*

[10] *R v Aramah* (1982) 4 Cr. App. R. (S)407.

committed any crime, or any crime of the kind in question, before. This surely accords with common sense. A single transgression gives room to hope that the transgressor may learn his lesson; persistence in wrongdoing shows that he has not learned it. This does not however mean that in the case of repeat offences each sentence need necessarily be more severe than was imposed the time before. There comes a point, at least in the case of minor offences, when any increase would cease to be proportionate to the gravity of the offence. It is not, for example, easy to imagine a court imposing the maximum term of seven years' imprisonment on a casual shoplifter, even if the offence had been committed (as it often has been) on many occasions.

To speak of 'the typical offender' is, plainly, to generalize. But research findings confirm what many practitioners from their own experience would assert, that the personal profile of the typical offender can be drawn with considerable accuracy and particularity. He is usually male, and often of low intelligence, and addicted to drugs or alcohol, frequently from an early age. His family history will often include parental conflict and separation; a lack of parental supervision; harsh or erratic discipline; and evidence of emotional, physical or sexual abuse. At school he will have achieved no qualification of any kind, and will probably have been aggressive and troublesome, often leading to his exclusion or to truancy. The background will be one of poverty, poor housing, instability, association with delinquent peers and unemployment. These considerations do not of course excuse or justify crime. For everyone who offends there are others subject to the same disabilities who do not. We are, in terms of the famous limerick, buses not trams.[11] But these considerations do help to explain the commission of crime, and those who urge the imposition of ever more severe sentences as a solution to the great and growing problem of crime should pause to ask whether they are treating the symptoms rather than the disease.

In recent years greatly increased attention has been paid to the victims of crime. This is welcome. In the past there was a tendency to treat the victim as if he or she had a walk-on part in the criminal process, whereas in truth the role of the victim is central. But there is, again, misunderstanding here. In April of this year the *Daily Telegraph* reported that the then Home Secretary proposed to give victims of crime a louder voice in the criminal justice system. 'At present', said the report, 'when a defendant pleads guilty to a violent offence, the judge may not be informed of the full impact of the crime on the victim.' This could lead the uninformed to suppose that it had not in the past been the practice to give the court this information. Such an impression would be quite false. It has always

---

[11] 'There once was a man who said, 'Damn!'
It is borne in upon me I am
An engine that moves
In predestinate grooves,
I'm not even a bus, I'm a tram'.
Hare, 1905.

been the practice for prosecutors to tell the court, if it did not emerge in evidence, that the victim of a violent attack had as a result been off work for six months, or was permanently disabled, or that the elderly victim of a burglary had been so shaken by the experience as to move house or be frightened of living alone, as the case may be. These are matters directly relevant to the seriousness of the offence, and they should be before the sentencing court. But it would be quite another matter, and plainly contrary to the interests of justice, in my opinion, to accord the victim any significant say in determining the appropriate level of sentence. Victims are, by virtue of their position as such, ill-placed to make that balanced and impartial judgment of a case which is the hallmark of a properly-functioning judicial tribunal. The passing of sentence must be governed by reason and guided by precedent, not coloured by emotion or a desire for revenge.

Since any judicial officer in passing sentence exercises authority conferred by the public for the benefit of the public the sentencer must always have regard to the wider public interest. It is important to maintain public confidence in the justice and effectiveness of the sentencing process. If, for instance, informed public opinion perceives that the sentences which are imposed fail to match the gravity of the crimes committed, then the public will be tempted to take the law into their own hands and resort to private vengeance. This is a form of civic breakdown. As Samuel Johnson wrote:

The right of private vengeance . . . is a principle so opposite to quiet, order, and security that every nation may be considered as more civilized and every government as nearer to perfection in proportion as it is more effectually repressed and extinguished.[12]

'The *public security*', he added, 'is the principal end of public punishment.'[13] But he also, in his famous argument against excessive and indiscriminate resort to the capital penalty, pointed to the dangers of undue severity:

To equal robbery with murder is to reduce murder to robbery, to confound in common minds the gradations of iniquity, and incite the commission of a greater crime to prevent the detection of a less. If only murder were punished with death, very few robbers would stain their hands in blood; but when by the last act of cruelty no new danger is incurred, and greater security may be obtained, upon what principle shall we bid them forbear?[14]

Where the law itself requires what is seen as excessive severity, the tendency is to evade the law. Lord Campbell—not, admittedly, the most reliable of biographers—gives an example:

[While] trying a prisoner at the Old Bailey on a charge of stealing in a dwelling house to the value of forty shillings, when this was a capital offence, Lord Mansfield advised the jury to find a gold trinket, the subject of the indictment, to be of less value. The prosecutor exclaimed, with indignation, 'Under forty shillings, my Lord! Why, the fashion alone,

---

[12] Robert Chambers, *Vinerian Lectures*, attributed to Johnson. [13] Ibid.
[14] Rambler No. 114, *Capital Punishment.*

cost me more than double the sum'. Lord Mansfield calmly observed, 'God forbid, gentle-men, we should hang a man for *fashion*'s sake!'.[15]

Difficult and taxing though the task of sentencing often is, there are some funda-mental principles.

First, statute requires what common justice in any event dictates, that in the generality of cases a custodial sentence shall be for such term (not exceeding the statutory maximum) as in the opinion of the court is commensurate with the seri-ousness of the offence or offences and associated offences for which the offender is to be sentenced.[16] In assessing the seriousness of any offence the court is now, once again, permitted to take into account any previous convictions of the offender and any failure of his to respond to previous sentences.[17] But the court may, as already noted, take into account such matters as, in the opinion of the court, are relevant in mitigation of sentence.[18] And in determining what sentence to pass on an offender who has pleaded guilty to an offence a court must take into account the stage in the proceedings at which the defendant indicated his inten-tion to plead guilty (the earlier the indication, the better for the defendant) and the circumstances in which the indication was given. Despite these rules the sentencer must always, in the case of all serious crimes other than murder, exer-cise a subjective judgment. At any rate until recently, this was thought to promote the ends of justice.[19] A Home Office White Paper of 1990 declared:

It is not the Government's intention that Parliament should bind the courts with strict legislative guidelines. The courts have shown great skill in the way they sentence excep-tional cases. The courts will properly continue to have the wide discretion they need if they are to deal justly with the great variety of crimes which come before them. The Government rejects a rigid statutory framework, on the lines of those introduced in the United States, or a system of minimum or mandatory sentences for certain offences. This would make it more difficult to sentence justly in exceptional cases.[20]

The most common ground of appeal against sentence is that the sentence passed was wrong in principle or manifestly excessive, but this is a field in which prin-ciples are notoriously hard to identify. The facts of individual cases and the circumstances of individual offenders are so infinitely variable that undue constriction of the sentencer's powers must lead to the imposition of unjust sentences in some cases.

It is, none the less, important to acknowledge—and this is my second point—that inconsistency may itself be a form of injustice. It is generally desirable that cases which are broadly similar should be treated similarly and cases which are broadly different should be treated differently. As Aristotle observed, 'True equal-ity exists in the treatment of unequal things unequally.' To this end the Court of

---

[15] Campbell, *Lives of the Chief Justices*, vol. II at 569.
[16] Criminal Justice Act 1991, sections 2(2)(a) and 31(2).   [17] Ibid, section 29.
[18] Ibid, section 28.   [19] Criminal Justice and Public Order Act 1994, S. 48.
[20] *Crime, Justice and Protecting the Public*, para 2.16.

Appeal has, in a series of guideline cases, indicated the brackets within which sentences for given offences should ordinarily be expected to lie. Decisions of this kind apply to a number of offences, including causing death by dangerous driving, public order offences, kidnapping, rape, incest, unlawful sexual intercourse, buggery, living on immoral earnings, theft in breach of trust, robbery, explosive offences, obscene publications and drugs.[21] Even where there are no guideline cases, a wealth of appellate decisions give pointers towards the appropriate level of sentence in a given case. Where there is no guideline case it is normally because the circumstances of a given offence vary so widely that any guidance would be so general as to be meaningless. But the Court of Appeal has been criticized for failing, in recent years, to give guidance in such commonly recurring offences as manslaughter, many kinds of theft and deception, and the government propose in forthcoming legislation to impose a duty on the Court of Appeal to provide guidance on levels of sentence. This is, without doubt, an important function of the Court, developed with great skill and insight under the leadership of Lord Lane. We must seek to rise to the challenge, for while the preservation of discretion in this field is important there is no room for arbitrariness or whimsy. It is, however, pertinent to observe that in most of the leading cases in which guidance on levels of sentence has been given the effect has been to increase the general level of sentencing. At a time when the prison population is rising sharply this is an effect to be noted. It has also, in practice, proved easier to raise the general level of sentences than to lower it.

Thirdly, it is a cardinal rule enshrined in statute of which we must never lose sight, that an offender willing to serve a community sentence must not be sentenced to imprisonment or detention unless his crime or crimes are so serious that only a sentence of this kind can be justified or the offence is of a violent or sexual nature such that only a sentence of this kind is adequate to protect the public against serious harm caused by him. The rationale of the rule is not far to seek. For the state to deprive a citizen of his liberty is a gross invasion of his ordinary rights as a human being. As already observed, imprisonment is not ordinarily a therapeutic experience; it can have a devastating effect on individuals and families; it can, and with depressing regularity does, lead to suicide; it confronts the offender with great difficulty in obtaining a job and re-establishing his life on release. As the Home Office said in its 1990 White Paper:

---

[21] See, for example, *R v Boswell* (1984) 6 Cr. App. R. (S) 257; *Attorney General's References Nos. 14 & 24 of 1993* (1993) 15 Cr. App. R. (S) 640; *R v Keys* (1986) 8 Cr. App. R. (S) 444; *R v Spence & Thomas* (1983) 5 Cr. App. R. (S) 413; *R v Billam* (1986) 8 Cr. App. R. (S) 48; *Attorney General's Ref. No. 1 of 1989* (1989) 11 Cr. App. R. (S) 409; *R v Taylor* (1977) 64 Cr. App. R. 183; *R v Willis* (1974) 60 Cr. App. R. 136; *R v Farrugia* (1979) 69 Cr. App. R. 108; *R v Barrick* (1985) 7 Cr. App. R. (S) 142; *R v Turner* (1975) 61 Cr. App. R. 67; *R v Daly* (1981) 3 Cr. App. R. (S) 340; *R v Byrne* (1975) 62 Cr. App. R. 159; *R v Noov & Schyff* (1982) 4 Cr. App. R. (S) 308; *R v Aramah* (1982) 76 Cr. App. R. 190; 4 Cr. App. R. (S) 407; *R v Bilinski* (1987) 9 Cr. App. R. (S) 360.

however much prison staff try to inject a positive purpose into the regime, as they do, prison is a society which requires virtually no sense of personal responsibility from prisoners. Normal social or working habits do not fit. The opportunity to learn from other prisoners is pervasive. For most offenders, imprisonment has to be justified in terms of public protection, denunciation and retribution. Otherwise it can be an expensive way of making bad people worse. The prospects of reforming offenders are usually much better if they stay in the community, provided the public is properly protected.

There are, of course, cases in which sentences of custody are, as it is often put, inevitable. But such sentences are improper save where they truly are necessary.

In the public mind, I think that custody is generally seen as the only truly retributive or punitive sentence. Anyone who commits a crime of any seriousness and is not sentenced to custody is generally perceived to have got away with it. This is very unfortunate, because of the inherent drawbacks of imprisonment, which I have just mentioned; because the efficacy of imprisonment is in many cases open to question; because the cost of imprisoning offenders is very high, and inevitably absorbs resources which would otherwise be available for schools, hospitals and other facilities of more obvious benefit to the public than prisons; and because the prison system is already bursting at the seams. It is the more unfortunate because there exists another sentence—community service—which is intended to punish, and intended to provide an alternative to custody in cases which would otherwise demand a sentence of custody. There will always, of course, be serious offenders, in whose cases nothing but custody would provide adequate punishment for them or adequate protection of the public. But it is highly desirable that the sentence should be one of community service in any case where such a sentence would provide adequate punishment and protection.

To that end, there are, I think, three steps which need to be taken with some urgency. The first is to ensure that a sentence of community service does require, invariably, the performance of the specified number of hours of serious and exacting work. I do not think the work required need (or should) be degrading, humiliating or particularly unpleasant; but it does seem to me important that the unforgiving hour should be filled with 60 minutes' work of rigorous and demanding work, done punctually and to an acceptable standard. I do not doubt that most existing programmes already meet these criteria; but every time a story appears suggesting that these criteria are not met, the credibility of the penalty tends to be seriously weakened.

The second task is to convince sentencers that community service is a serious punishment. Many magistrates and judges are no doubt familiar with the work programmes in their areas, and are already convinced. But there may be some who are sceptical, and tend to see community service as a soft option; to the extent that they do, avoidable sentences of custody are likely to be passed.

The third task, in some ways perhaps the most important of all, is to convince the public that community service is not a soft option. So long as it is perceived to be so, while the present vengeful mood of the public endures, courts will hesitate to make such orders in cases where the interest of the public is engaged. There is, I think, an educative job to be done here, and it is not a job which can be left to the courts. It is not for them to mould or guide public opinion. This is an essentially political task, as was recognized a few years ago when the thrust of government argument was, very clearly and explicitly, in favour of community penalties and against resort to custody save where it was truly and obviously necessary.

How, violent and sexual offences apart, do the courts judge whether an offence is so serious that only a custodial sentence can be justified? The answer given by authority is: when the offence is of such a kind that right thinking members of the public, knowing all the facts, would feel that justice had not been done by the passing of any sentence other than a custodial one.[22] This answer has attracted some criticism. Who are these right-thinking members of the public? And how does the judge know what they would think?[23] There is force in these criticisms. It seems inconceivable that a sentencer would attribute to right-thinking members of the public any view he did not himself share. So the formula does little more than reflect the judge's subjective judgment that justice would not be done by the passing of any non-custodial sentence. The Court of Appeal has been criticized for failing to give judges more help in identifying the custodial threshold, and given the importance of doing so it is a task which it would be highly desirable to accomplish if it were possible. I must, however, confess that to my mind the difficulty of accomplishing this task is formidable.

I cannot attempt to summarize these somewhat discursive and far from comprehensive remarks. I am conscious of asking more questions than providing answers. But answers are needed. I recently added my voice to others who have urged the case for a Royal Commission on crime and punishment, or at least a revival of the Advisory Council on the Penal System, disbanded in 1980.[24] I repeat the hope which I then expressed, that the beginning of a new Parliament may be recognized as the ideal moment for such an initiative. The decisions which I have been discussing have a profound effect on people's lives. We owe it to them to ensure that such decisions are as sound as human wisdom, fortified by human experience and intelligence, can make them.

---

[22] *R v Bradbourne* (1985) 7 Cr. App. R. (S) 180; *R v Cox* (1993) 14 Cr. App. R. (S) 479.
[23] Professor Andrew Ashworth QC, op. cit.
[24] Address to the Prison Reform Trust, 25 June 1997.

2

*Justice for the Young**

In a judgment twice quoted with approval by the House of Lords,[1] an Australian judge sitting in the Supreme Court of Victoria said:

'No civilised society' says Professor Colin Howard in his book entitled *Criminal Law*, 4th ed. (1982), page 343, 'regards children as accountable for their actions to the same extent as adults.' . . . The wisdom of protecting young children against the full rigour of the criminal law is beyond argument. The difficulty lies in determining when and under what circumstances that protection should be removed.[2]

This view of a child's responsibility has not always prevailed. As Professor Radzinowicz and Professor Hood have pointed out:

The concept of the young offender, with all that it implies for penal policy, is a Victorian creation. Until well into the nineteenth century there were no differentiations accorded to age in the method of bringing offenders to trial, in the form of trial itself, in the punishments that could be imposed nor, generally, in the way in which they were enforced.

It is true that no child under seven could be convicted of a felony. And it is also true that those between 7 and 14 were held to be *doli incapax* unless it were proved that they had acted with malice. But that proof was frequently forthcoming, even for the vast number of crimes carrying the death sentence. Children were not only sentenced to death, in a few cases they actually suffered death. Anyone over 14 was an adult as far as the criminal law was concerned.[3]

But even before the end of the eighteenth century, philanthropic attempts were made to mitigate the rigour of the law. The Marine Society tried to save teenage boys from a life of crime by training them for the sea. The Philanthropic Society tried to reform outcast children and bring them back into the stream of law-abiding citizens.[4] And some enlightened judges, magistrates and reformers tried to redeem young offenders from a life of crime.[5] Transportation, however, remained the standard punishment for offences of any seriousness, and although in time young offenders were confined in hulks, superannuated warships moored at Chatham and Portsmouth, instead of being physically transported, the conditions

* Delivered as the Prison Reform Trust Annual lecture on 25 June1997. First published as a booklet by The Prison Reform Trust and The Police Foundation. © Lord Bingham of Cornhill, The Prison Reform Trust, and The Police Foundation.

[1] *C (A Minor) v DPP* [1996] AC 1, 40 C-D; *R v Secretary of State for the Home Department ex parte Venables and Thompson*, 12 June 1997, 63.

[2] *R (A Child) v Whitty* (1993) 66 A Crim.R 462.

[3] *A History of English Criminal Law*, Vol 5 (1986), p.133. As succeeding footnotes show, my debt to this work is very great.　　　[4] Ibid. 133, 134.　　　[5] Ibid. 135, 136.

in which they were held were such as to make this a very questionable change for the better.[6]

In 1835 it was decided to establish a government penitentiary for young offenders sentenced to transportation, and in due course a disused barracks at Parkhurst was chosen as the site. The institution was duly established by the Parkhurst Act 1838, and survived as, in effect, a prison for young offenders until the experiment was eventually ended in 1864.[7] Meanwhile, attention was directed to a system of agricultural reform schools which had grown up in Europe, particularly a German scheme established at Horn near Hamburg and a French scheme at Mettray, near Tours. It was in imitation of these models that the Philanthropic Society in 1849 established a farm school at Redhill in Surrey, which was reported to be a striking success.[8]

In 1847 a House of Lords Select Committee, under the influence of Lord Brougham, enquired into the treatment of juvenile offenders. The judges were consulted, and even answered a questionnaire. The great majority favoured imprisonment with hard labour and whipping rather than transportation. They were much more doubtful about the value of reformatories, some of them regarding it as wrong that the commission of crime should be rewarded by an education and training which the offender would not otherwise have enjoyed.[9] Interestingly, this Committee was the first to recommend that, wherever possible, part of the cost of convicting and punishing juvenile offenders should be legally chargeable to their parents.[10]

Despite the doubts of the judges, an Act was passed in 1854 to establish reformatory schools, and an Act to set up industrial schools followed in 1857.[11] Under the Education Act 1876, day industrial schools and special schools for truants were established.[12]

Some of the sentences imposed at this time make disturbing reading. The Home Secretary of the day was, it is true, moved to rebuke a magistrate who sentenced a 12 year-old girl to 14 days' imprisonment followed by four years' detention in a reformatory for doing wilful damage to a geranium plant growing in front of almshouses in Spalding, Lincolnshire.[13] But other sentences appear to have caused no public concern; for example, a boy of 12 who stole one bottle of beer, having no previous convictions, who was sentenced to one calendar month's imprisonment and five years in a reformatory; or four boys aged 8 to 12 whose crime was described as 'not much above the gravity of orchard robbing' who were sentenced to '10 days with such hard labour as they are capable of performing, six strokes of a birch rod, and five years in a reformatory'.[14]

A Royal Commission in 1884 felt that major strides had been taken towards the elimination of juvenile crime.[15]

---

[6] Ibid. 142.   [7] Ibid. 148, 155.   [8] Ibid. 160.   [9] Ibid. 173, 174.
[10] Ibid. 210.   [11] Ibid. 177, 178.   [12] Ibid. 181.   [13] Ibid. 184.
[14] Ibid. 184.   [15] Ibid. 225.

The Gladstone Committee of 1895 was less confident.[16] By this time penal reformers were directing attention to the Elmira Reformatory established in the State of New York in 1876, built on an ambitious scale and resembling a college or a hospital rather than a prison, which housed 1,400 young inmates.[17] It was decided to replicate this American model here, but the great Mother Country of the Empire had more modest ideas, and the English experiment began with eight selected young prisoners at Bedford prison.[18] This proved so successful that a year later part of Borstal convict prison in Kent was set aside for a special class of youths chosen from London prisons who had received sentences of at least six months.[19] Thus began what was, for over half a century, regarded as one of the outstanding successes of the English penal system. In 1914 the Lord Chancellor described with obvious approval the regime under which the inmates, having got up at 5:00am, performed gymnastics before breakfast and observed, 'it is an early hour; but it is found that the process of reformation is assisted by early rising'.[20]

By the beginning of this century it was accepted that young offenders formed a distinct category of offenders for whom special arrangements were necessary. The Children Act 1908 was a major reforming measure which reflected this change of attitude to young offenders. Thus it abolished the use of prisons for offenders under 14; it abolished penal servitude for those subject to the Act; and it permitted imprisonment for those between 14 and 16 only exceptionally. Section 103 formally abolished the sentence of death against a child or young person. There was instead substituted, for young offenders convicted of murder, the sentence of detention during His Majesty's Pleasure. In its original form the Bill was much more radical, it would, for example, have raised the age of criminal responsibility to 14, and relieved children of 14 to 16 from criminal liability save in extreme cases.[21] But the Act was a major step forward and, following a lead given by Birmingham and ten other county boroughs, for the first time formally established courts specifically concerned with the trial and sentencing of juveniles.[22] Combined with the Probation of Offenders Act 1907, it gave a new direction to the treatment of juvenile offenders. It is, however, noteworthy that within ten years a distinguished metropolitan magistrate was moved to criticise the procedures of the new juvenile courts as cumbersome, solemn, far too complicated for children to understand and excessively legalistic.[23]

It would be excessively tedious, even if it were possible within the reasonable confines of a lecture, to attempt to chart the constantly changing rules governing the treatment of young offenders which have, at one time or another, been in force since 1908. It is, however, pertinent to mention section 44(1) of the Children and Young Persons Act 1933, which has served as a guiding principle for most of this century, and which remains in force. It provides:

[16] Ibid. 376.   [17] Ibid. 378.   [18] Ibid. 384.   [19] Ibid. 384.
[20] Ibid. 394.   [21] Ibid. 631.   [22] Ibid. 630.   [23] Ibid. 632.

Every court in dealing with a child or young person who is brought before it, either as an offender or otherwise, shall have regard to the welfare of the child or young person and shall in a proper case take steps for removing him from undesirable surroundings, and for securing that proper provision is made for his education and training.

This enactment followed the report of a Departmental Committee on the Treatment of Young Offenders in 1927 which described the Children Act 1908 as 'a notable piece of legislation, enshrining as it did in almost every section the principle that a young offender shall receive different treatment from an adult . . .'[24] This principle would appear to give effect to the obligation of the United Kingdom as a party to the United Nations Convention of the Rights of the Child 1989, which among other things provides:

Article 3 (i): In all actions concerning children, whether undertaken by public or private social welfare institutions, courts of law, administrative authorities or legislative bodies, the best interests of the child shall be a primary consideration.

Article 40 (i) states:

Parties recognize the right of every child alleged as, accused of, or recognized as having infringed the penal law to be treated in a manner consistent with the promotion of the child's sense of dignity and worth, which reinforces the child's respect for the human rights and fundamental freedoms of others and which takes into account the child's age and the desirability of promoting the child's reintegration and the child's assuming a constructive role in society.

In 1960 the Ingleby Committee in its Report on Children and Young Persons strongly endorsed the policy of differentiating between the sentencing of adult and juvenile offenders. The Report observed that originally the principle of equality before the law meant that children were hanged, transported or imprisoned on the same principles as applied to adults; but the Report stated in categorical terms that the conception of a standard or ordinary punishment applicable to everyone, child or adult, had gone.[25]

As recently as 1991, when the Criminal Justice Act of that year was passed, the system of juvenile justice was, I think, seen as a story of success. From around 8,000 custodial orders passed per annum at the beginning of the 1980s, the number had fallen to fewer than 2,000 at the end. From more than 6,000 criminal care orders in the mid 1970s, the figure had declined to about 600 in 1988. Pride was taken in the decline in custodial sentences passed on juveniles and the fact that there had been no explosion of crime as a result.[26] But within a very short time the picture was seen somewhat differently. It was hard to come by reliable figures. Whereas the Home Office and the Standing Committee for Youth Justice

---

. [24] Cmnd. 2831, p. 8.

[25] Cmnd. 1191, paras 53(d) and 58.

[26] See Rob Allen, *Policy and Responsibility for Young Offenders— Lessons and Prospects*, 9 March 1995.

suggested that the number of known young offenders had fallen, others, including the Association of Chief Police Officers, did not accept that the problem had lessened, and suggested that there were other explanations for any apparent fall.[27] One thing cannot be doubted. Whatever the figures might show, the perception of the public, fed by lurid media coverage of certain high profile crimes committed by the young, was that juvenile crime was a significant and growing problem with young offenders committing ever more serious crimes at ever younger ages. It is only necessary to recall the tragic case of Jamie Bulger, the recent gang rape by teenagers of an Austrian tourist and, most recently, the alleged rape of a nine-year old year girl by ten-year old boys in a primary school. There have been recurring tales of young offenders committing hundreds of burglaries, seemingly with impunity, or even being rewarded with exotic holidays funded by the taxpayer. The 1994 British Crime Survey found that 25 per cent of those whose opinions were sampled were worried by 'teenagers hanging about'.[28] It is now widely believed that a significant number of teenagers are dangerous, out of control and a menace to society.

Against this background, it is not surprising that the system of youth justice as it now exists should have been the subject of close scrutiny. The results are not encouraging.

It has become clear, first, that the system is very slow. A young offender will usually appear in court on about four different occasions, and adjournments (for a variety of reasons) are frequent.[29] The Audit Commission, in an authoritative study, found that the average delay between arrest and disposal varied from 70 to 170 days in the sample courts which they studied.[30] Home Office statistics for 1994 gave an average time from commission of the offence to completion of proceedings in the youth court of 132 days.[31] There is a wide and justified opinion that, particularly when dealing with children, it is important for the sentence to follow hard on the heels of the offence, and that objective is not, currently, being met.

Secondly, the prosecution process was found to be only partly effective. A CPS survey in the West Midlands found that one in four prosecutions of young offenders was discontinued or dismissed;[32] the Criminal Statistics for 1994 showed that 31 per cent of youth court proceedings were discontinued or withdrawn, and a further 7 per cent dismissed.[33] And, of course prosecutions could only be brought against the minority of offenders who were detected and caught.

Thirdly, it appeared that there were wide disparities between different police

---

[27] Home Affairs Committee, *Sixth Report, Juvenile Offenders*, Vol. II, July 1993, p. 63.

[28] *Preventing Children Offending*, Home Office, March 1997, p. 5.

[29] *Misspent Youth: Young People and Crime*, Audit Commission, 1996, p. 29.

[30] Ibid. 29.

[31] Jack Straw and Alun Michael, *Tackling Youth Crime: Reforming Youth Justice*, May 1996, p. 5.

[32] *Misspent Youth: Young People and Crime*, Audit Commission, 1996, p. 25.

[33] Ibid. 25.

areas in use of the caution. For offenders aged 17, the caution was used for 11 per cent of cases in some areas and for up to 58 per cent in others.[34]

Fourthly, the length of the prosecution process had the result that in a significant minority of cases further offences were committed by the offender while on bail.[35] Since youth courts tried, in compliance with earlier judicial guidance, to deal with all outstanding cases concerning a youth offender on the same occasion, so as to take a comprehensive overall view of the gravity of the offending and the appropriate disposal, the unfortunate effect was to delay still further the date on which the offender came to be sentenced.

Fifthly, the system was perceived to be failing to deal with a body of persistent juvenile offenders. There was persuasive evidence that a small minority of young offenders were responsible for a very large proportion of juvenile crime.[36] It was even more disturbing that the evidence suggested an increase in offending by girls, and also an increase in the peak age of known offending by boys.[37] The Audit Commission was rightly concerned at evidence that young males were failing to grow out of their offending habits, as earlier evidence suggested that they tended to do.[38]

Sixthly, it was plain that the prosecution process was very expensive. The Audit Commission investigated the cost to all public services in processing and dealing with young offenders and estimated the total cost to be £1 billion per year broken down between the police, legal aid, the prosecution service and the cost of the courts, social services, probation and custody. When account is taken of the direct cost of the effects of crime as well as the cost of dealing with it, the figures become very large indeed.[39]

In his report entitled *Review of Delay in the Criminal Justice System*, Mr Martin Narey quoted a metropolitan stipendiary magistrate as suggesting that:

the single largest contribution to youth crime reduction would be the abolition of the Youth Court in its present form, and a complete rewriting of the principles on which it is currently based.[40]

In a thoughtful paper which he has since prepared to explain his observation, the magistrate in question (Mr Geoffrey Wicks) has deplored what he sees as an increasing tendency for young offenders, encouraged by their lawyers, to plead not guilty to charges against them in the hope of securing acquittal on technical or spurious grounds, leading to formal and adversarial proceedings little different from those involving adults and greatly delaying the time at which, if at all, constructive steps can be taken to address the offender's real needs.

---

[34] Home Affairs Committee, *Sixth Report, Juvenile Offenders*, Vol. II, July 1993, p. 14.
[35] *Misspent Youth: Young People and Crime*, Audit Commission, 1996, p. 30.
[36] *Preventing Children Offending*, Home Office, March 1997, p. 9.
[37] Jack Straw and Alun Michael, *Tackling Youth Crime: Reforming Youth Justice*, May 1996, p. 3.
[38] *Misspent Youth: Young People and Crime*, Audit Commission, 1996, p. 12.
[39] Ibid. 6, 7.
[40] *Review of Delay in the Criminal Justice System*, Home Office, February 1997, p. 43.

This is a complaint made, as I have already pointed out, 70 years ago. But that does not mean it is invalid; and anything which can *fairly* be done to prevent young offenders 'playing the system' should be done. There is force in Mr Wicks' suggestion that those under 15 years of age should be dealt with in principle outside the criminal justice system, with only a residue of hard cases having possibly to come within a system which contains punitive elements. This might, however; be easier to achieve if the age of criminal responsibility in this country were higher. Our present age of 10 is lower than in most European countries, comparing with 12 in the Netherlands, Greece and Turkey; 13 in France; 14 in Germany and Italy; 15 in Denmark, Norway and Sweden; and 18 in Belgium and Luxembourg.

I do not propose to review the forms of sentence available to the courts when dealing with young offenders. These are familiar in general if not in intricate detail. All of these forms of sentence, properly used, have a value, not excluding the most severe sentences provided by section 53 of the Children and Young Persons Act 1933. It would be hard to argue with any pretence of plausibility that there does not exist a small core of serious young offenders for whom nothing but a severely punitive sentence can be regarded as appropriate.

By the time teenagers appear before the courts as persistent or serious offenders, however, the opportunity to divert them into more constructive and satisfying ways of life may well have been lost. That is why, in my opinion, every encouragement and support should be given to schemes aimed to save offenders from being irretrievably sucked into the criminal process. There are many such schemes, but perhaps I may mention seven as examples of what can be done.

1. The Dalston Youth Project, on which the Audit Commission reported.[41] It caters for young people aged 15 to 19, most of whom have offended and many of whom have been excluded from school. They are referred by the police, youth workers, social workers and schools. After an initial meeting, the most vulnerable are selected to go on a residential course, which is a mixture of out-door challenge, reflection on past behaviour and the setting of goals. On return home, participants are matched with a mentor whom they meet weekly. The group as a whole meets monthly and a range of educational programmes is offered, including courses in literacy and numeracy. Assistance is given in qualifying for and obtaining employment. Early results suggest a high rate of success. At £3,000 per participant, the cost is high, until it is compared with the cost of prosecution and incarceration.

2. The Milton Keynes Retail Theft Initiative, on which the Home Office reported in March 1997.[42] This is directed towards young shoplifters, to

---

[41] *Misspent Youth: Young People and Crime*, Audit Commission, 1996, p. 41.
[42] *Preventing Children Offending*, Home Office, March 1997, p. 7.

educate them to appreciate that shoplifting is not a victimless crime, to understand the consequences of their actions and to resist temptation in future. A formal caution is given on completion of the scheme. Attendance is voluntary. Home Office research found a re-offending rate of 3 per cent during the period of study, compared with a rate of 35 per cent for first-time offenders dealt with in other ways.

3. The Ilderton Motor Project, on which David Utting reported in 1996.[43] This project, launched in 1974, is the oldest of many such projects in England and Wales. The aim is to inculcate awareness of the dangers of illegal, unskilled driving while enabling the young to pursue a constructive and legitimate interest in cars. The majority of those referred, by social workers and probation officers, have been involved in motor crime and cautioned, although not convicted. Participants are expected to attend at least eight evening sessions per month to learn car mechanics, maintenance and restoration. For those who attend regularly, the carrot of attending 'banger' race meetings is offered. An evaluation of the programme by the Inner London Probation Service, which funds staff salaries, found that a sample of 30 participants were significantly less likely to re-offend in the following three years than a matched sample with similar histories of car crime.

4. Youth at Risk, on which David Utting also reported.[44] This scheme works with local authorities and the probation service to provide a 12 month programme to help damaged and difficult young people to accept responsibility and change their lives. The target age group is 15 to 20 years, and referrals come from schools, social services, probation and other agencies. In the Sutton 3 programme, out of 25 young people, 18 were persistent or serious offenders, 21 had a recent history of violence and 21 had a current alcohol and/or drug problem. Participation is voluntary. The programme involves a week-long intensive residential course, involving out-door activities, and small group sessions and plenary workshops led by trained leaders and supported by qualified psychotherapists and agency staff. One of the techniques used is intended to enable participants to recognize the unsatisfactory nature of their lives and come to terms with painful past experiences. After the residential course, there is a nine month follow-up period when the group meets weekly, but participants also remain in frequent contact with their individual mentor who is known as a 'committed partner'. The follow-up period is designed to support the participant in achieving the goals and commitments set at the end of the residential programme and specific topics are addressed such as anger management,

---

[43] David Utting, *Reducing criminality among young people: a sample of relevant programmes in the U.K.*, 1996, pp. 58, 59.
[44] Ibid. 75–79.

substance abuse, problem-solving and advice on careers. While some of those who attended the programme continued to offend, 17 out of 25 who had previously been unemployed or failing to attend school (whether because of truancy or exclusion) were either employed or attending school or college. There is again reason to hope that schemes such as this will significantly reduce the rate of recidivism.

5. The Northamptonshire Diversion Unit is made up of 29 staff formed from the police, probation, social, education and health services.[45] After referral by the police, an offender is allocated to a staff member who visits the offender to discuss the offence (assuming it is admitted) and to determine what reparation he or she is able and willing to offer. Contact is then made with the victim to discuss reparation and whether the victim wishes to meet the offender. A two part action plan is then drafted: to resolve the particular offence and to prevent further offending. After approval by the team, this plan is forwarded to the police for agreement. The police decide whether to caution and trigger the plan or prosecute. An independent assessment concluded that the scheme appeared to reduce offending. In particular, it appeared that a very high percentage of the compensation negotiated had actually been paid. Furthermore, a high percentage of victims were satisfied or very satisfied with the outcome, and only a small minority dissatisfied. The multi-agency approach was found to be effective, with each discipline making a valid and important contribution.

6. The HALT Scheme operates in Holland.[46] It was started in the 1980s and there are now 70 schemes covering about half the local authorities in that country. In The Hague, the police may refer offenders aged under 18 to the scheme if the cost of the offence is low, the offender admits guilt, the offender is willing to participate and the offender has not attended on a scheme twice already. A HALT worker writes to the offender and the offender's parents offering the choice of HALT or prosecution and inviting them to a meeting. Eighty five per cent accept this invitation. There are ten discussions with the offender concerning reparation and the reasons for the offending behaviour. At that stage the victim is contacted to consider reparation. A proposal is then devised consisting of work, relevant to the victim and the offence if possible, the payment of compensation and perhaps an educational component. Compensation for the victim and shaming of the offender are regarded as important elements in the scheme; for example, offenders cleaning graffiti will wear distinctive clothes. In The Hague, one-third of young offenders are referred to the HALT Scheme, and some 95 per cent successfully complete the programme, the remainder being referred back for prosecution. Follow-up studies show that only half as many HALT

[45] *Misspent Youth: Young People and Crime*, Audit Commission, 1996, p. 46.
[46] Ibid. 47.

participants in The Hague re-offend as of those who are prosecuted. The comparison is not, however, of like with like, since it is plainly the less serious offenders who are referred to the HALT Scheme.

7. The Multi-Agency At-Risk Youth Committee (MAARY-C) established in the County of Los Angeles.[47] Prompted by the research finding that 16 per cent of Los Angeles County's first-time youthful offenders accounted for 67 per cent of subsequent arrests, the Los Angeles County Probation Department established this scheme, designed and based in the community and intended to identify and help potential members of this 16 per cent core of the youthful recidivist population before they entered the criminal justice system. Although the Probation Department acts as the lead authority, many other agencies, public and private are involved. The scheme provides a powerful example of the efficacy of joint agency collaboration, and relies on information held by or supplied to the Probation Department to identify those most at risk. A range of programmes is available to provide drug education, advice on parenting, help in obtaining employment, advice on housing and financial problems and so on. The programme is supported by all political parties and is beginning to show hopeful results.

The last example highlights a very important fact: that, while the interplay of the factors which predispose to youthful offending is variable and hard to predict, the factors themselves are well-known and generally accepted. Some of these factors are personal. The rate of offending is much higher among males than females; among those who are hyper-active and impulsive; among those of low intelligence; and among those who abuse drugs or alcohol or both. I strongly suspect that a greatly increased number of very young children now abuse drugs or alcohol or both. Some of the risk factors relate to the family: poor parental supervision; harsh or erratic discipline; conflict between the parents; weak bonds within the family; separation from one or other parent; criminal conduct by a parent or sibling; parental neglect or abuse. Some of the factors relate to schooling; the typical picture is of low attainment and aggressive and troublesome behaviour at school, often (and increasingly) leading to exclusion, and of course truancy. Some of the factors are of a more general, social kind. They include poverty; poor housing; unstable living conditions; association with other young delinquents, often in an area where criminal activity among the young is rife and involvement with the authorities is seen a rite of passage; lack of any occupation, employment or recreation. Many of these factors are, of course, interrelated and some are symptomatic of others. It is accepted that a young person exposed to multiple risk factors has an increased chance of becoming a persistent offender. Where offending begins at a young age, the risk of a settled pattern of delinquency is correspondingly greater.

[47] MAARY-C 16% Program, 1996.

Since the root causes of juvenile crime are to be found in these intractable predisposing factors, it must follow that the public interest is best served by effectively addressing these problems, which (if it can be done) will save the victims of crime much needless misery, will enable the young offenders themselves to live constructive and fulfilling lives and will relieve the public purse of a large part of the cost of handling young criminals, many of whom will in time (if nothing effective is done) become older and even more expensive and harmful criminals. It is in truth only by measures such as these that we can treat the underlying disease rather than attempt to ameliorate or mask the symptoms. Happily, there are a significant number of organizations which have exactly this object, many of them enjoying the financial support and sponsorship of the Home Office.

There are, for example, a number of organizations which seek to educate parents in the handling of their children. One example is Parent Network, a national organization started in 1986. It runs programmes throughout the country, sometimes privately, sometimes through local authorities. Emphasis is placed on setting boundaries and disciplining children in a consistent and non-violent way. A drawback of the scheme is that most participants appear to be white and middle class, with more mothers attending than fathers, and it may be doubted whether these programmes reach the constituency most in need of help. Another scheme, imported from the United States and known as Parents as Teachers UK, is offered in a few primary schools and offers help to any parent of a child aged three or under. A further example is Home-Start, which is now 20 years old and has a network of 180 home visiting schemes. It works alongside the statutory health and social services to help families with problems such as post-natal stress, domestic violence and suspected child abuse, as well as money problems and behavioural problems with children. Yet another example is Family Nurturing Network, based in Oxfordshire and particularly aimed at parents with significant difficulties in parenting, including parents who are at risk of abusing or neglecting their children.

In the educational field there are similar schemes. One is High/Scope UK, another American initiative directed to the involvement of parents and children in pre-school education. A long term evaluation of a similar scheme in the United States, based on a programme run for poor black children, showed a marked improvement in those subject to the programme as compared with the control sample. The Dorset Healthy Alliance Project is an experimental project, sponsored by the Home Office and intended to promote closer parent-school links while tackling a range of behavioural problems, including disruptive behaviour, truancy and bullying. A scheme based at a primary school on a disadvantaged estate in Bournmouth is still subject to evaluation. Cities in Schools (UK) works with young people with school attendance and behavioural problems including non-attendance and exclusion. Since 1993, 75 projects have been established across the UK. The principal programmes are directed towards those whose education has in effect broken down, and are intended to fill the educational gap, reintegrate the participants into mainstream education and prevent offending.

There have been other schemes designed to provide activity or recreation. The Runcorn Youth Action Project ran for three years in 1993–1996, and was designed to engage the young inhabitants of a socially disadvantaged estate, particularly including the rowdiest of these young, in a range of constructive activities, including dance workshops, an arts week, an after school club for younger pupils, conservation work and the establishment of health groups. An evaluation by Crime Concern concluded that the project had succeeded in engaging many young people who were outside the reach of existing provision. There was no evidence of the reduction in recorded crime but there was a very large reduction in complaints of rowdy behaviour. The Millwall Community Sports Scheme covers a range of activities offered by Millwall Football Club, which has one of the longest-established 'Football in the Community' initiatives. It offers sports sessions in local schools, and gives persistent secondary school non-attenders the opportunity to spend one day in the week at the club for a combination of educational, sporting and crime prevention activities. The Kickstart programme offers a year-long course to unemployed, poorly qualified school-leavers for 16 hours per week, divided between receiving basic education at college, pursuing their sports interests and assisting with the community scheme in schools. Internal monitoring showed that for 1994–1995, at least ten of the 15 truants on the truancy project thereafter returned to full-time education; 60 per cent of students on the Kickstart project in 1994–1995 gained an NVLQ level one, and 80 per cent went on to further education. There are of course, numerous organizations devoted to the provision of education in the avoidance of drug and alcohol abuse.

I end by offering five not very startling conclusions:

1. There is a small but identifiable core of young offenders whose criminal conduct is such as to call for serious punitive sentences. Nothing else will afford the public adequate protection, or satisfy the public that grossly anti-social behaviour is adequately punished. But we should not lose sight of the human suffering so often involved. In his recent book *Hidden Agendas*, the former Director General of the Prison Service reminds us of the cruel reality:

They often start young. I well remember walking into a cell at Onley Young Offender Institution near Rugby. A boy in his early teens was sitting under the harsh glare of a ceiling strip light. A partially completed jigsaw puzzle on the table in front of him was in danger of floating away as the tears streamed down his childish face. A fatherly prison officer had his arm round his shoulder, trying to comfort him as he cried for his mother. How, I wondered, could such a vulnerable looking boy be in prison. The officer supplied the answer: a succession of burglaries.[48]

2. Steps to expedite, improve and make more effective the procedures in the youth justice system are to be welcomed and supported, provided always that the

---

[48] Derek Lewis, *Hidden Agendas: Politics, Law and Disorder*, 1997, p. 54.

legitimate interests of the defendant and the independence of the magistracy and the judiciary are adequately safeguarded.

3. The youth justice system—meaning thereby the police, the Crown Prosecution Service and the courts—cannot on its own solve the problem of juvenile crime.

4. Nor can the problem be effectively addressed by any other agency on its own. Salvation lies in the active collaboration of all agencies involved directly or indirectly in the causes and consequences of juvenile offending, including the police and probation services, social services, the health and education authorities and other agencies public and private. It is vital that lines of functional demarcation do not impede effective and harmonious co-operation.

5. While the advice and support, financial and otherwise, of the central government is invaluable, there is great strength in local, community-based schemes directed at the root causes of young offending. It is members of local communities who are the victims of crime; they best know the identity of the wrong-doers and the problem families; they are best placed to take effective preventative action before the destructive cycle of offending and court appearances begins.

One last thought. In a pamphlet published by the Prison Reform Trust in January of this year, Sir Louis Blom-Cooper QC and Professor Seán McConville persuasively argued the case for appointment of a Royal Commission on Crime and Punishment to conduct a comprehensive review of crime and the responses to crime.[49] They were not primarily concerned with youth justice, but that is so important a part of the whole picture that any Royal Commission would be bound to give it close attention.

I hope this proposal will be seriously considered. No one can be confident that we have all the answers, or even most of them, to the important and intractable problems which exist in this area of our national life. The beginning of a new Parliament is the ideal moment for such an initiative, which need not lead to inactivity pending its conclusions.

Alternatively, as has been urged in other quarters, notably by Lord Ackner, the Advisory Council on the Penal System, set up in 1966 and later disbanded, might be revived.[50] If such a Royal Commission or a revived Advisory Council were able, with the benefit of intensive world-wide research and consultation, to reach authoritative conclusions which commanded the respect of public and professional opinion, and if those conclusions were given legislative effect, this Parliament would earn an assured and honourable place in the history of this country.

---

[49] *A Case for a Royal Commission on Crime and Punishment*, Prison Reform Trust, 1997.
[50] *H.L. Debs.*, 9 June 1997, c. 812.

I should like to express my gratitude to Ms Ann Backhouse for her invaluable research assistance in the preparation of this lecture.

3

*The Mandatory Life Sentence for Murder**

It is a cardinal principle of morality, justice, and democratic government that an offender guilty of crime should be sentenced by the court to such penalty as his crime merits, taking account of all the circumstances including the nature of the crime, the circumstances of the offender, the effect of the crime on the victim and the victim's family, the need to prevent the offender from re-offending and deter others from offending in the same way, and the need to protect the public. Authorities such as More, Coke, Bacon, and Clarendon recognized the need for a right balance between crime and punishment.[1] A French author in 1898 entitled his work 'L'Individualisation de la Peine',[2] the fashioning of the penalty to the needs of the individual case. Parliament has recognized the principle when enacting, in 1991, that a custodial sentence should save in special circumstances be for such term (not exceeding the permitted maximum) as in the opinion of the court is commensurate with the seriousness of the offence.[3] I doubt if there is anyone in this knowledgeable and experienced audience who would question the validity of this principle. Indeed, I doubt if anyone who was not an anarchist, a fascist, or a revolutionary would wish to do so.

But in the case of murder this principle has, quite deliberately, been cast aside. Parliament has enacted that a person convicted of murder shall be sentenced to imprisonment for life.[4] So, in the case of an adult offender convicted of murder, one sentence and one sentence only can be passed, whatever the nature of the crime, however strong the mitigating circumstances, whatever the position of the offender, the victim and the victim's family, however minimal the need to prevent the offender from re-offending or to deter others from offending in the same way, however negligible, on the particular facts, the need to protect the public. The penalty, far from being individualized, is generalized to the ultimate degree. In practice, of course, our sentencing regime is not as undiscriminating as this statement, accurate though it is, might suggest. For the sentence pronounced by the court is a formula, not a meaningless formula, but a formula which gives no real clue to the offender, to the victim, to the media or to the public at large, what in practical terms—that is, in years to be served in prison—the sentence means. That is decided later. But it is not decided by a judge, an experienced professional, immune from all extraneous pressures, weighing all aspects of the particular

---

* Newsam Memorial Lecture delivered on 13 March 1998 at the Police Staff College, Bramshill.
[1] Radzinowicz, *A History of English Criminal Law*, vol. I, 259.
[2] Saleilles, op. cit.
[3] Criminal Justice Act 1991, s. 2 (2)(a).
[4] Murder (Abolition of Death Penalty) Act 1965 s. 1(1).

offence and the particular offender, drawing on his experience and that of his colleagues, giving detailed reasons in open court, and imposing a term of years or a minimum term of years which, if too severe, can be challenged on appeal by the offender[5] and, if too lenient, can be challenged on application by the Attorney-General.[6] It is decided, behind closed doors, by the holder for the time being of the political office of Home Secretary or, in most cases, his subordinate ministers, with no right for the offender to appeal against the decision and no right for the Attorney-General to make application. For the past 15 years successive Home Secretaries have chosen, quite voluntarily, to invite the trial judge and the Lord Chief Justice to offer advice on the term, the punitive, or 'tariff', term as it is colloquially if unfortunately called;[7] but the Home Secretary is free to reject this advice in favour of a longer or shorter term, and unless he does so he need give no reasons for his unappealable decision. Thus the real punishment to be undergone by the murderer subject to a mandatory life sentence is decided not by a judge sitting in open court and subject to all the constraints which bind anyone performing that function, but by a member of the government subject only to such constraints as the courts have, by a series of recent decisions,[8] imposed upon him. It is not easy to imagine a more complete contrast with the practice which obtains in sentencing all other classes of offender.

Although convicted murderers are the only mandatory life sentence prisoners, the only offenders on whom the judge is required by law to impose a sentence of life imprisonment, they are not the only prisoners sentenced to imprisonment for life. There are others, a minority but a significant minority of the lifer population, who have committed crimes carrying a maximum of life imprisonment in whose cases the trial judge, in the exercise of his discretion or judgment, has imposed a sentence of life imprisonment although not obliged by law to do so. Case law prescribes the conditions in which such a sentence may be imposed,[9] and if the sentencing judge finds those conditions satisfied he may impose a life sentence if he concludes that the interests of justice require him to do so. If he does, the sentencing regime is quite different from that which I have just described. The sentencing judge, in almost all cases, specifies in open court the 'relevant part'[10]—that is, the minimum term to be served in prison before the offender has any prospect of release save on compassionate grounds—and his reasoned decision, given in open court, will be challengeable on grounds of excessive severity

---

[5] Criminal Appeal Act 1968, s. 9.

[6] Criminal Justice Act 1988, s. 36.

[7] I agree with Lord Windlesham's description of this as a 'crude and ugly word': 'Life Sentences: The Paradox of Indeterminacy'. [1989] Crim. LR 244 at 251.

[8] *R v Secretary of State for the Home Department, ex parte Doody* [1994] 1 AC 531; *R v Secretary of State for the Home Department ex parte Venables and Thompson* [1997] 3 WLR 23; *R v Secretary of State for the Home Department ex parte Pierson* [1997] 3 WLR 492.

[9] See notably *R v Hodgson* 52 Cr. App. R 113, but also *Attorney-General's Reference (No. 32 of 1996) (R v Whittaker)* [1997] 1 Cr. App. R(S) 261.

[10] Crime (Sentences) Act 1997, s. 28 (5).

or undue leniency. But when that specified term has been served, the offender will not be automatically released. Underlying the decision to impose a discretionary life sentence of this kind will always be an apprehension that the offender may be a continuing danger to the public for an indefinite term. So, when the determinate term has been served an expert independent body, the Parole Board, will judge whether it is safe to release the offender, and depending on its judgment the offender will, or will not for the time being, be released. At no stage of the process has any minister or other representative of the executive any influence on the period for which the offender is detained. This regime applies to all discretionary life sentence prisoners, whether adult or under age; and it also applies, although only in part, to under-age murderers subject to mandatory life sentences.[11] So it is only adult murderers who are fully subject to special and extra-ordinary treatment.

Many of us, in a rather instinctive way, tend to think of murder as something different, a crime apart. Our religious heritage reminds us of the sixth commandment and the mark of Cain. Our cultural heritage includes many works in which murder was the central event: one need only instance plays such as *Hamlet*, *Macbeth*, *Othello*, and *Julius Caesar* (three political assassinations and one *crime passionnel*); or novels such as *Crime and Punishment*. On a more popular level we witness an unending flow of books, plays, and films based on the commission and detection of murder. Scarcely a day passes (or so it seems) without reports in the media of some new and horrifying killing. The names of some murderers are burned on our minds, and their crimes are part of our national experience. So it is not altogether surprising that we think of murder as different. Despite the final abolition of the death penalty in this country, and despite their familiarity, the expressions 'murder' and 'murderer' have a chilling connotation all of their own.

Reactions of this kind, even if easily explained, do not however relieve us of the need to enquire, in an objective and rational way, whether there are good reasons to depart, in the case of adult murderers, from principles which govern the sentencing of all other offenders. Ministers and officials play no part in deciding the sentences to be served by those convicted of torturing and abusing children, or conspiring to commit terrorist offences which may lead to multiple deaths, or importing hard drugs which may blight countless lives, all of them crimes of the utmost seriousness; it has never to my knowledge been suggested that they should; and it would be contrary to constitutional principle if they did. So I pose the question: Why should adult murderers, alone, be treated differently? I shall try to state fairly what I understand to be the main reasons advanced by those who support the existing practice. It will, I suggest, become clear that these reasons will not withstand searching scrutiny.

The first, and much the most prominent, argument advanced by supporters of the existing practice is that murder, the deliberate taking by one person of the life

[11] Following *Hussain v UK* [1996] 22 EHRR 1; Crime (Sentences) Act 1997, s. 28(1)(b).

of another, is a crime of so uniquely heinous a character that it can only adequately be punished, irrespective of any other fact or circumstance, in all cases, by the most severe punishment permitted by law, now life imprisonment. No other penalty, it is said, would mark the revulsion with which society regards the crime of murder.[12] The answer to this point is that it is at best a quarter-truth, both factually and legally.

It is of course true that some murders plumb the depths of imaginable human, or more properly sub-human, depravity and involve a degree of sadistic or callous violence which is almost impossible to describe. A number of such cases are well known to us all, and to the public at large; and we could all add additional examples from our own professional experience. Murders of this character are, however, a very small fraction of the murders committed year by year, most of which occur in a domestic or emotional context, the product of sudden anger, often fuelled by drink, or obsession rather than planning or the hope of gain. It must always be a serious thing and attract a criminal penalty deliberately to take another human life but there are many murders which cannot fairly be regarded as uniquely heinous and which, if they arouse public revulsion, must also arouse the sympathy of any reasonably imaginative observer.

Let me give six examples, and lest it be thought that I am inventing unrealistic examples to support my argument I take them from the Report of the Royal Commission on Capital Punishment 1949-53.[13]

Case 1. A man struck his brother in the groin with a knife after an altercation about payment for drinks. They had been drinking but were not drunk, and had previously been close friends. The offender made frantic efforts to obtain help for the victim, who none the less died.

Case 2. A man killed his fiancée because she persisted in going out with another man on the two evenings each week when she did not go out with him. He was a man of good character and was said to be of even temper and quiet disposition.

Case 3. A man killed his sweetheart who was pregnant by him but whom he had not enough money to marry. He was worried on this account and also because he thought he had infected her with syphilis. He said that he had contemplated suicide; that on the night of the crime he had told her that they could not marry but could not bring himself to tell her the reason; and that when she began to cry he lost all control of himself. He could not explain the crime.

Case 4. A woman gassed her son, aged 30, a hopeless imbecile, who had to be attended to like a baby. She had been told that she must enter a hospital immediately to undergo an operation. She at first said that she could not have the operation because there was no one to look after her son, but it was made clear to her

---

[12] See Report of the House of Lords Select Committee on Murder and Life Imprisonment, HL paper 78–1, 1989, p.33, para.108A.

[13] Cmnd. 8932, App.4, p. 320.

that she could not live for more than six months unless the operation was performed.

Case 5. A Chinese pursued for four years the man who had killed his father in Hong Kong, and finally confronted him in a Chinese hostel in England and killed him after a desperate struggle. The offender said that he had committed the crime from motives of filial piety. By Chinese doctrine a son was bound to avenge his father's death.

Case 6. A man killed his wife with an axe. She was an epileptic who also suffered from disseminated sclerosis, and in the last few months her mental state had degenerated into insanity. In a statement to the police he said he had killed her to end her suffering and had then tried to commit suicide but could not bring himself to do so. The crime was evidently due to mental strain.

These cases were drawn from England and Wales and Scotland, and the crimes were committed many years ago. But criminal conduct does not change, and any of these examples could be matched by recent cases. The observation of the Royal Commission remains as true now as it was when made:

there is perhaps no single class of offences that varies so widely in character and in culpability as the class comprising those which may fall within the comprehensive common law definition of murder.[14]

A similar conclusion was strongly expressed in 1993 by an independent committee under the chairmanship of Lord Lane, the former Lord Chief Justice whose experience in these matters is unrivalled in our generation:

It is fundamentally wrong in principle that a judge should be required to pass upon the wife who has been maltreated for years by a brutal husband and eventually kills him, precisely the same sentence as that judge passes upon the ruthless shotgun robber who kills in cold blood. The two cases are extremes: but they help to illustrate that the area of culpability in murder cases is a very wide one.[15]

In *R v Howe* Lord Hailsham of St Marylebone said:

Murder, as every practitioner of the law knows, though often described as one of the utmost heinousness, is not in fact necessarily so, but consists in a whole bundle of offences of vastly differing degrees of culpability, ranging from brutal, cynical and repeated offences like the so-called Moors murders to the almost venial, if objectively immoral, 'mercy killing' of a beloved partner.[16]

If any doubt remains about the unjustifiability of lumping all murders together and treating them all as uniquely heinous, it is surely provided by the relatively recent and very well-known case of Private Lee Clegg. On the facts originally held to be proved at his trial he was guilty of murder. He was said to have

---

[14] Report, 6, para.21.
[15] Report of the Committee on the Penalty for Homicide, commissioned by the Prison Reform Trust, 1993, 20.
[16] [1987] AC 417 at 433.

responded to a threat with an excessive display of violence and he could not escape liability on grounds of self-defence. The result was a life unlawfully taken, and doubtless the victim's family felt as all families feel in such circumstances. I do not suggest that (on the facts then found) no crime was committed or that punishment should not have followed. But he was on any showing a young man of good character, attempting to do his duty in a predicament not of his own making, most unlikely to re-offend. It is a travesty to treat his case or even to appear to treat it as if it were in the same league of criminality as that of a contract killer, or an armed robber who deliberately shoots a police officer or a security guard, or a person who tortures, abuses, and kills children for sadistic or sexual satisfaction.

The contention that any murder, whatever the circumstances, should be regarded as uniquely heinous is also untenable legally. If asked for their understanding of murder, most reasonably well-informed members of the public would, I think, define it as the deliberate taking of a human life, that is, the taking of a human life with the deliberate intention of doing so. The more sophisticated might add 'without lawful excuse', but that addition is irrelevant for present purposes. As lawyers and police officers, however, know, this common understanding is defective. The common law definition of murder covers a case where there is no intention to kill, or even an intention not to kill, provided there is an intention to cause serious bodily injury and death results. The first of my earlier examples illustrates the point. The man who stabbed his brother in the groin plainly intended to cause serious injury; but the summary makes plain that the offender did not wish or intend his brother to die. It was still murder. In practice it is commonplace for the prosecution, in opening a charge of murder, to disclaim expressly any accusation that the defendant intended to kill the deceased. Most cases of murder involve no intention to kill. The absence of an intention to kill does not of course exonerate the offender, since it is serious criminal conduct to intend to injure another, and if one wishes to eliminate any risk that death may result the simple solution is not to cause the injury. But if the absence of an intention to kill does not exonerate, it cannot rationally be held not to mitigate the offence as compared with one where the offender has an intention to kill. It makes no sense to equate the two, by requiring the same sentence to be passed in each case.

It makes even less sense when account is taken of the sister offence of attempted murder. To be guilty of this offence an offender must be shown to have moved beyond the merely exploratory phase, and to have embarked on his endeavour to kill; and, even more significantly, he must be shown to have had the specific intention to kill the victim. An intention to cause serious bodily injury would make him guilty of attempting to cause such injury, or of causing it if the attempt progressed that far. But he would not be guilty of attempted murder in the absence of a proved intention to kill. Yet for attempted murder the maximum sentence of life imprisonment is discretionary, not mandatory. The fact that an offender's conduct has caused a death adds a dimension of seriousness to a case, even if the death is unintended. But in assessing the measure of punishment it is normal and fair to weigh the criminality of an offender's intention, and it is anomalous that a death which is unintended should carry a mandatory sentence of life imprisonment when a result which is intended but not achieved, very probably through no fault of the offender, should leave the judge with the discretion to impose whatever sentence he judges appropriate.

In a House of Lords debate in April 1991 Lord Richard QC, now the Labour Leader of the House of Lords, put the point very clearly and simply:

The argument in favour of change is based upon one simple proposition—that murders vary greatly. They vary from those that are planned and calculated, or are for material gain or from political motives, to those that are committed under severe pressure and in emotional circumstances of great stress, including many domestic murders. As many Members who practise in the courts know, there are many cases in which the killing could hardly be said to be intentional. The intention may have been to cause grievous bodily harm to the individual, but perhaps to the regret of the person causing that harm the individual died.[17]

In an earlier debate Lord Irvine of Lairg QC, now the Lord Chancellor, made the same point with equal force:

A mercy killing is of a different moral order from a sadistic sex-based child murder. Where murder has a much more extended definition so that the mental element is satisfied by an intention to cause serious bodily harm, combined if need be with an awareness of the possibility of death, I would suggest that it is beyond argument that murder embraces such a multitude of diverse sins that the single mandatory life sentence must be inappropriate.[18]

I agree.

A second argument advanced in support of the mandatory life sentence for murder is that to replace the mandatory life sentence with a discretionary maximum sentence of life would erode the distinction between murder and manslaughter, for which life is the discretionary maximum. This is both right and wrong. Legally it is wrong: altering the penalty would not alter the ingredients of the two offences, which would remain distinct as now. But it is right in the sense that, if a judge had discretion in both cases, not all offenders convicted of murder would be sentenced more severely than some offenders convicted of manslaughter. But this is not a possibility to be resisted. Every experienced judge has known cases in which a jury have acquitted a defendant of murder and convicted him of manslaughter in circumstances where the verdict can only be understood as an expression of sympathy; and has also known cases, such as those already summarized, in which the factors mitigating the crime of murder were very strong. It

---

[17] *Hansard*, HL, col. 1566 (18 April 1991).
[18] *Hansard*, HL, col. 521 (6 November 1989).

would make life very simple and easy if it were possible to assert, truly, that every murder was more serious than every manslaughter; unhappily perhaps, the untidy complexity of real life leaves no room for such simplistic notions.

Then it is said that a mandatory sentence of life imprisonment is the only appropriate retributive sentence, meaning the only appropriate punishment, for murder. This has some overtones of the Old Testament doctrine of an eye for an eye, a tooth for a tooth, which may no doubt be a good working rule in a primitive society. But ours is not a primitive society, and the argument could only be sound if all murderers were of roughly equal culpability, which (as already shown) they are not. In any event, the argument could only carry weight if the punishment imposed on all murderers were in practice the same, which it is not. It is hard to see what retributive purpose is served by passing in open court a formulaic sentence which, in the overwhelming majority of cases, bears no relationship to the punishment which the offender will actually undergo.

A more serious argument is that the mandatory life sentence for murder is necessary to protect the public against the risk that an offender who has killed once may, if released, kill again. It is axiomatic that the public should, so far as reasonably practicable, be protected against the risk of unlawful violence, and if the imposition of a mandatory life sentence on convicted murderers were the only way of affording such protection I should regard it as a necessary safeguard. But the argument is not persuasive, for three reasons. First, a mandatory life sentence affords no protection which is not afforded by a discretionary life sentence. As already noted, the primary reason for imposing a discretionary life sentence is apprehension of continuing danger to the public. In the course of dealing with such cases the courts, assisted by medical and other evidence, have acquired considerable expertise in deciding when, in the interests of the public, a life sentence should be imposed. There is no reason to doubt that such a sentence would be imposed in the case of any murderer who was judged to present a continuing threat to the public. Secondly, many—probably most—murders are so much the product of the specific circumstances giving rise to them, being circumstances which never can, or are most unlikely to, recur that the risk of repetition can be effectively discounted. An offender cannot kill an imbecile child, an insane wife, or a long-married brutal husband a second time. No one could reasonably fear that Private Clegg would again kill unlawfully even if he were shown to have killed unlawfully once. Thirdly, it is of course the fact that almost all murderers, although subject to mandatory life sentences, are released after a period of years, provided it is judged safe to release them. There can be no objection to open acknowledgement of this likelihood at the outset, as in the case of almost all discretionary life prisoners.

It has been argued that public confidence in the criminal justice system would be undermined if the penalty for murder became discretionary. Public confidence is plainly a very important aspect of this matter, not something to be taken lightly or taken for granted. But public opinion is the sum of individual opinions, and individual opinions depend on how much individuals know and understand. In this area the level of public knowledge and understanding is very low, for several reasons: the procedures for dealing with mandatory life sentence prisoners have been the subject of constant change over the last 15 years; the procedures are of some complexity; little effort has been made to inform the public exactly how the procedures do work; and the sentence passed by the court is of necessity couched in terms which are, in almost every case, false and do nothing to inform the offender, the relatives of the victim, the media or the public what in practical terms the sentence means.

The first essential pre-condition of public confidence is, surely, that the sentence pronounced by the court should be intelligible, transparent and certain. Those who carry the banner of truth and honesty in sentencing could scarcely challenge that assertion. And the reason is obvious: if, as now, sentence is passed in terms which leave everyone uncertain of all things except one, that the sentence almost certainly does not mean what it says, then rumours may spread and misapprehensions arise as to when the offender may once again be at liberty. A clear statement of what the sentence means by the sentencing court will leave no room for misunderstanding. It is significant that in evidence given to the House of Commons Select Committee in 1994 two bodies representing victims and the bereaved, Victim Support and Support after Murder and Manslaughter, made plain that to those whom they represented the mandatory life sentence was very much less important than certainty as to how long the offender would actually serve in prison before there was any question of release.[19]

Provided that the sentence is clearly and explicitly stated, it seems safe to assume that the second essential pre-condition of public confidence is a broad measure of public acceptance that convicted murderers (in particular those who have committed the most heinous crimes) will serve terms of imprisonment commensurate with their criminality and that dangerous killers will not be let loose to kill again. These are legitimate demands which any acceptable sentencing regime must meet. The public are entitled to expect the most serious murderers to remain in prison for very long terms indeed, perhaps even for the rest of their lives. They are entitled to expect the utmost care to be taken to ensure that those who have killed once will not be freed so long as there is a risk that they may kill again. But the public do not lack a sense of fairness or the power to discriminate: they would not wish Private Clegg (even if guilty as charged) to undergo the same punishment as Fred West; and would much prefer the effect of the sentence passed on each to be spelled out expressly.

If the sentence on a convicted murderer were not a mandatory sentence of life imprisonment but a discretionary maximum of life imprisonment, what I have described as the essential pre-conditions of public confidence would be fully met.

---

[19] Written Response, Victim Support, Dec. 1994; Written Response, Support after Murder and Manslaughter, 18 Nov. 1994.

The sentencing court would either sentence the offender to a determinate term of years, indicating when the offender would become eligible for and entitled to release on parole; or it would impose a life sentence indicating the number of years (real years, not subject to remission) to be served before consideration of release, which would then be subject to a favourable assessment of risk by the Parole Board; or exceptionally it might impose a life sentence, ruling that for purposes of punishment alone the offender should never be released. In each case the sentence would be intelligible, transparent and certain. There would no doubt be cases in which the public would regard sentences passed as, in all the circumstances, excessively severe or unduly lenient, but the usual means of challenge would be open, by the offender in the first case, by the Attorney-General as guardian of the public interest in the other. I can for my part see no acceptable reason why any responsible member of the public should have less confidence in this sentencing regime than in that which operates at present.

Speaking in 1989, with his customary lucidity, Lord Irvine of Lairg QC made this point very clearly:

The mandatory life sentence does not underpin public abhorrence of murder because everyone knows that life does not mean life but on average something less than 10 years. Sentences modulated to the gravity of the individual case would be more likely to achieve the public abhorrence that is desired.[20]

A further argument in favour of the mandatory sentence is that its abolition would present peculiarly difficult sentencing problems for the sentencing judge. It is certainly true that the sentencing of offenders, particularly serious offenders, is an anxious task calling for very considerable skill, insight and judgment. But this is a skill which judges acquire over a professional lifetime and they are after all selected for their qualities of judgment. To decide the right sentence for a murderer is not a task different in kind from deciding the right sentence for a drug baron, a serial rapist, a child abuser, a blackmailer, a kidnapper, a terrorist or an armed robber. Judges are already familiar with discretionary life sentences. And one must, with all appropriate respect for their integrity and professionalism, question whether ministers who serve for a time in the Home Office or the officials who for a time advise them can reasonably be expected to bring any greater skill or judgment to the task. As Lord Lane bluntly put it in the House of Lords:

First, there is no greater difficulty in assessing the proper length of a determinate sentence for murder than there is in doing the same for any other form of serious crime. Secondly, the person in the best position to carry out that task is the one who has heard the evidence; namely the trial judge.[21]

Perhaps I should explain how judges would set about their task. They would, as they now do when making recommendations, work on a benchmark figure

---

[20] *Hansard*, HL, col. 521 (6 November 1989).
[21] *Hansard*, HL, col. 1562 (18 April 1991).

judged to represent the proper term to be served in prison for the unexceptional murder, that is, a murder with no significant aggravating or mitigating features. That benchmark figure would probably be about 14 years, but it might be a bit more or a bit less and it might over time change in the light of experience. It would be increased to take account of aggravating features such as (and I do not attempt to be comprehensive): evidence of a planned, professional, revenge, or contract killing; the killing of a child or a very old or otherwise vulnerable victim; evidence of sadism, gratuitous violence, or sexual maltreatment, humiliation or degradation before the killing; killing for gain, in the course of burglary, robbery, blackmail, or insurance fraud; multiple killings; the killing of a witness or potential witness to defeat the ends of justice; the killing of those doing their public duty, such as police or prison officers; terrorist or politically motivated killings; the use of firearms or other dangerous weapons; a substantial record of gratuitous violence; macabre attempts to dismember or conceal the body. Serious aggravating features of this kind could, depending on the facts, extend the punitive term very greatly. But it would fall to be reduced somewhat if there were mitigating features. Again I do not attempt to be comprehensive. But mitigating features might include such matters as youth; age (where relevant to physical capacity or the likelihood of an offender dying in prison); subnormality or mental abnormality, although not affording a defence of diminished responsibility; provocation (in a non-technical sense), or excessive response to a personal threat; the absence of an intention to kill; spontaneity and lack of premeditation (beyond that necessary to constitute the offence: e.g. a sudden response to family pressure or emotional or other stress); mercy killing; a plea of guilty, if affording hard evidence of remorse or contrition. Features of this kind would shorten the punitive term to be served; but save in very exceptional cases it would remain substantial.

It is then argued that the mandatory life sentence is, or may be, a valuable deterrent. Deterrence, both personal and general, is a recognized objective of punishment and it plainly serves a valuable social objective to impose a sentence which will strongly discourage potential murderers from killing. The deterrent effect of the death penalty was very carefully considered when the abolition and restriction of that penalty were under review, and the Royal Commission of 1949–53, while acknowledging that there might be some deterrent effect, nevertheless pointed out that there were many offenders on whom such effect was limited and concluded that the effect might often be negligible.[22] More recent research reinforces that conclusion.[23] When a potential crime is the product of careful planning and detailed calculation it is reasonable to suppose that, next to certainty of apprehension, the certainty of a very long prison sentence may swing the potential criminal's decision against the commission of the crime and against creating the conditions (such as the carrying of loaded firearms) which

---

[22] Report, 24, para.68.
[23] Hood, *The Death Penalty*, 2nd edn. (1996), 210–12.

may lead to its commission. But many murders, as already emphasized, are not the result of careful planning and detailed calculation. They are the product of sudden anger, drunken fury, obsession, desperation, miscalculation. In such cases the immediate deterrent effect of any penalty must be very small, if it exists at all. It is furthermore important to remember that, in the most serious cases of planned and calculated killing, abolition of the mandatory penalty need not lead, and would in my view be most unlikely to lead, to shorter terms of incarceration. But the length of those terms would be publicly stated; and in that way the deterrent effect of the sentences would in all probability become greater.

In reviewing the arguments for retaining the mandatory life sentence for murder I have so far relied on the summary to be found in the report of the House of Lords Select Committee in 1989.[24] But I should refer to further arguments advanced by the Lord Privy Seal (Lord Waddington QC) on April 18 1991, when the House of Lords debated an amendment to abolish the mandatory life sentence for murder as recommended by the Select Committee. He argued that the change would weaken public confidence in the judiciary.[25] His reason for this, as I infer, was that the public would regard sentences imposed by the judges as too short. He then went on to argue, apparently as an additional argument against the change, that it would lead to the imposition of longer sentences on people guilty of less serious murders.[26] If that were to be the result of the change, one would suppose that public confidence in the judiciary would not in his view be weakened. And since, during a sample 6-month period in 1988, Home Office ministers fixed a punitive term longer than the trial judge had recommended in 63 out of a total of 106 murder cases,[27] one would imagine that the Lord Privy Seal would have welcomed a change that would have led to an increase in terms of imprisonment. Later in his speech, however, the Lord Privy Seal rejected as 'entirely wrong' the Select Committee's prediction that the introduction of a discretionary sentence for murder would lead to a considerable increase in the average length of sentence.[28] The Lord Privy Seal then went on to argue that an offender sentenced to life imprisonment sacrificed his life to the state. When the Criminal Justice Bill of 1991 was debated in the House of Commons the Minister of State at the Home Office expressed a similar view.[29] As Lord Mustill pointed out in *Ex parte Doody*,[30] however, that view of the mandatory life sentence was wholly inconsistent with the regime in fact operated by successive Home Secretaries since 1983.

The Lord Privy Seal also argued that the mandatory life sentence represented an assurance given by Parliament to those nervous about abolishing the capital

---

[24] Report, 33, paras. 108A-114B.
[25] *Hansard,* HL, col. 1578 (18 April 1991).   [26] Ibid.
[27] Lord Windlesham, 'Life Sentences: The Paradox of Indeterminacy', [1989] Crim. LR 244 at 253.
[28] *Hansard,* HL, col. 1583 (18 April 1991).
[29] *Hansard,* HL, cols. 309–310 (16 July 1991).
[30] *R v Secretary of State for the Home Department ex parte Doody* [1994] 1 AC 531 at 557.

penalty. No doubt, as already pointed out, the public wanted to be sure then, and wants to be sure now, that the most serious murderers will be confined for a very long time and not released until, if ever, it is safe to release them. This cannot, however, be a reason for clinging to a sentencing formula which, as pointed out in the House of Lords debate, is known by everyone to be untrue and, which was described as 'a pretence' and 'bogus'.[31]

Later in his speech the Lord Privy Seal, commenting on the difficulty which would face a trial judge in deciding how long an offender should stay in prison for purposes of punishment, observed:

I would suggest to the Committee that in the worst cases of murder it is incredibly difficult to assess the public reaction to the release of a murderer 20, 30 or 40 years on . . . I am not talking about danger to the public now, but I am saying that it is incredibly difficult for anybody to assess now what the public reaction to the release of a terrible murderer will be 20, 30, or 40 years on.[32]

This is, I suggest, a deeply worrying argument. For every crime, however serious, there must (risk apart) be an appropriate punishment, even if different people hold different views of what that punishment is. In deciding what punishment is appropriate, all factors (including the impact of the crime on the mind of the public) should be considered. But the sentence, once imposed, should be final and certain, subject to appeal by the offender, or application by the Attorney-General in the public interest, or retrospective alteration to the very limited extent permitted by statute.[33] What is decided to be appropriate punishment for the crime at the time of sentence cannot become inappropriate because, when that punishment has been undergone, public opinion is hostile to the release of the offender. To accord that role to public opinion—I am tempted to call this the Barabbas argument—is to forget that the reason why civilized democratic societies establish courts of law and appellate procedures is to prevent the fate of individuals, however unpopular they are, being decided by the unreasoned and unstable forces of public clamour. Having heard the Lord Privy Seal's arguments, their Lordships accepted the amendment which he was opposing by 177 votes to 79. The majority included the Lord Chief Justice, the Master of the Rolls, two former Lord Chancellors and one future Lord Chancellor, a former Prime Minister, the former Lord Chief Justice of Northern Ireland, a future leader of the Lords, six Law Lords and two former chairmen of the Parole Board.[34]

In the 1995–6 session of Parliament, the Home Affairs Committee of the House of Commons considered the mandatory life penalty for murder and produced two reports.[35] It recommended that the mandatory life sentence of life

---

[31] *Hansard,* HL, cols. 1563, 1567, 1568, 1578 (18 April 1991).
[32] Ibid., col. 1581.
[33] Supreme Court Act 1981, S. 47(2)-(7).
[34] *Hansard,* HL, cols. 1584-6 (18 April 1991).
[35] First Report of the Home Affairs Committee, HC 111; and Supplementary Report, HC 412.

imprisonment for murder should be retained, but that the responsibility for setting the tariff and for taking decisions on release should be removed from the Home Secretary. While the Committee's reports are of interest and value, I do not think that in reaching the first of these conclusions the Committee relied on arguments to which I have not already made reference. In its first report the Committee found the arguments on the issues to be 'exceptionally finely balanced', and it resolved to take further evidence before coming to a final conclusion.[36]

I have, I hope, touched on all the main arguments in favour of retaining the mandatory sentence for murder. In the course of giving my reasons for rejecting those arguments I have made plain why, in my opinion, a discretionary maximum of life imprisonment should be substituted. I will not repeat those reasons. But perhaps in closing I may emphasize just one of them. As every reasonably informed person knows, our constitutional arrangements reflect no slavish adherence to the doctrine of the separation of powers. But there are some clear and generally respected lines of functional demarcation. One of them is between the formulation of penal policy (including the stipulation of maximum and on rare occasions minimum sentences), which are matters for the executive and Parliament, and the sentencing of criminal defendants, which is a matter for the judiciary. For historical reasons which are easy to understand and reflect no discredit on anyone, this line has, in the sentencing of defendants for murder, become blurred. But the sentencing of criminals is not, despite the contrary suggestion of the then Lord Privy Seal in April 1991,[37] a political matter. It is a job for judges, not politicians or officials. At present, while the judge pronounces a formula which everyone knows to be false, and the Home Secretary voluntarily seeks the recommendations of the trial judge and the Lord Chief Justice, the Home Secretary is in no way bound by those recommendations and the final decision rests with him. If such a system had been operated in Stalin's Soviet Union, Hitler's Germany or Amin's Uganda, we should have been very quick to condemn it as a glaring violation of democratic principle. There is of course no comparison to be drawn between the outrageous abuses of power witnessed in those countries and practice here, but the constitutional point remains. In the House of Lords, Lord Nathan made the point succinctly:

Sentencing is essentially a judicial function which should be exercised in public and be subject to appeal.[38]

The point was also made, clearly and cogently, by Lord Lane's committee in its conclusions:

(6) It is logically and constitutionally wrong to require the distinction between the various types of murder to be decided (and decided behind the scenes) by the Executive as is, generally speaking, the case at present.

---

[36] Para. 101.
[37] *Hansard*, HL, col. 1577 (18 April 1991).   [38] Ibid., col. 1560.

(7) Logically, jurisprudentially and constitutionally, the decision on punishment should be made in open court by the judge who passes sentence. He should be enabled to pass such sentence as is merited by the facts of the particular case, whether a hospital order, a determinate period of imprisonment or, in the type of case which attracts most attention from the media, the wicked 'contract' killings or those for gain, life imprisonment.[39]

This is an argument which has never been effectively answered, for a very simple and compelling reason: there is no effective answer which can be given. Yet resistance to change has so far proved insuperable. Perhaps it will remain so. But we live in a time of change. Old certainties are being questioned, old orthodoxies challenged. The views which I have put forward are not new and not original. But they have the overwhelming support of the Queen's Bench judges, those who sentence murderers up and down the land, week in, week out, and of many experienced and distinguished people whose views I have quoted. I very much hope that a new, open-minded administration will be willing to re-examine the merits of this important question.

[39] Report, 5.

4

*Speech on the Second Reading of the Crime (Sentences) Bill**

My Lords, I am in complete agreement with the noble Baroness and previous speakers in recognising that current levels of crime in this country are a source of acute and proper public concern. I venture to suggest that the judges have cause to feel this concern with particular immediacy since they witness day by day the devastation caused by violence, lawlessness and abuse. We know, perhaps better than anyone, that the victims of crime are not by and large the rich and privileged but the less well to do: the residents of run-down inner city tower blocks and neglected housing estates and those who are in many ways the most vulnerable and defenceless members of society. I hope that your Lordships will give no credence to the subversive lie sometimes heard that the judges are, for some reason, indifferent to the evils of crime.

There are nevertheless three major ingredients of this Bill which cause me and those of my senior colleagues outside this House whom I have consulted profound anxiety. I refer to the proposal to shorten remission and abolish parole for prisoners serving determinate sentences; the proposal to impose automatic life sentences in certain specific cases; and the proposal to impose mandatory minimum sentences on repeat burglars and drug dealers. These provisions are likely to have a profound effect on the lives of those to whom they apply and the administration of criminal justice in this country. That is not in itself an argument against them, but it is necessary to test each of the proposals by asking four questions. Will it be just? Will it serve to reduce levels of crime or increase the protection of society? Will it be cost effective? Will it work in practice? I feel bound to tell your Lordships that in my judgment these measures conspicuously fail to pass all four of those tests.

I begin with parole and remission. As many of your Lordships well know, the existing regime was put in place in 1991 following a far-reaching, careful and respected inquiry by a committee presided over by the noble Lord, Lord Carlisle of Bucklow. It draws a distinction between short term and long term prisoners, the dividing line being a sentence of four years. A short term prisoner is entitled to release on parole, subject to good behaviour, half-way through his sentence. For the whole of the remaining period of the sentence such a prisoner is liable to recall to prison if his conduct gives cause for concern and for the first half of the

* Delivered in the House of Lords Parliamentary Debate on the Second Reading of the Crime (Sentences) Bill (*Hansard*, HL, vol. 577, col. 967 (27 January 1997)).

remaining period he is subject to supervision in the community if he has been sentenced to 12 months or more. A long term prisoner is eligible for the grant of parole by the Parole Board having served half his sentence, and he is entitled to be released, again subject to good behaviour, after two-thirds. Such offenders are also subject to supervision on release and liable to recall until the end of their sentence.

This regime has certain obvious strengths. It is clear and intelligible. It ensures that every day of the sentence pronounced by the court has practical content. It enables offenders to be reintroduced into the community conditionally. It enables decisions on the release of more serious offenders to be based on the experienced judgment of an independent body. It enables offenders whose behaviour in the community causes concern to be recalled quickly and with the minimum legal formality and delay. It avoids the prolonged incarceration of those whom it is judged safe to release. It is a regime that has worked well in practice. The validity of the research that led to its adoption has not been in any way impugned.

One asks why such a system so recently instituted is to be cast aside. The answer is to be found in the slogan 'Honesty in Sentencing'. Your Lordships will react with surprise to the suggestion that a scheme approved by the noble Lord, Lord Carlisle, can be regarded as other than honest in any way. Of course, it is not, as I have tried to demonstrate. If the system has not been understood, that problem can be met by judges explaining the effect of the sentences they pass, which they have not been encouraged to do, or by Ministers seeking to educate the public, which as far as I know they have not attempted to do.

The effect of the new provisions is that prisoners, long or short term, will spend a greater proportion of the sentence pronounced by the court behind bars. That proposal standing alone may not be objectionable, but there are overwhelming disadvantages. First, the period of a sentence that a prisoner will not have to serve will be less clear and predictable than at present. Secondly, the overall period of control by supervision and licence will in all cases be shorter than at present. Thirdly, the invaluable provision for recall during the licence period will be lost. Fourthly, judgment on release of more serious offenders will no longer be made by the Parole Board and prisoners will remain in prison when their continued confinement serves no useful public purpose. Fifthly, the proposals for remission—a maximum of three days a month for those whose behaviour attains the prescribed minimum standard and a maximum of three extra days a month for those whose behaviour has exceeded that standard—will prove incapable of fair operation.

Prisons vary widely in the programmes and facilities that they offer, which become more and more restricted as the prison population rises and the squeeze on the prison budget bites. In many cases it will not be practicable for a prisoner to demonstrate compliance with more than the minimum standard. The decision whether to make an allowance of the additional three days—a decision to be made every two months (six days per two months)—will in practice have to be made by a uniformed landing officer. It would be hard to devise a system more obviously open to corruption or allegations—true or false—of favouritism, inconsistency, racial bias or discrimination, and there will inevitably be a flood of appeals unless the additional days are routinely allowed. Sixthly, research figures—so far as I know, unchallenged—convincingly show that good behaviour in prison is not on its own a reliable indicator of lawful behaviour on release.

It is the intention of the Bill that offenders should not spend longer in prison than they now do. To that end, it is provided in Clause 22 that judges should impose sentences two-thirds of the length of the sentences they would otherwise have passed. If this provision should ever become law, the judges will of course do their best to comply with it. But I have grave fears as to whether they will succeed in doing so. As the noble Lord, Lord Windlesham, has highlighted in volume 3 of his important book, various elements of the mass media have a clear agenda of arousing public disquiet about allegedly lenient sentencing. As a result, judges are frequently and routinely castigated for passing the sentences they do. It requires little imagination to foresee the outcry there will be when a statute, commended to the public as a tough law and order measure, leads to the imposition of sentences one-third shorter than the public and the press are accustomed to hear. This provision also has the effect—apparently unforeseen by the draftsman—of reducing from six months to four the maximum sentence which can be imposed by a magistrates' court, and of revising the maximum sentence of detention on a young person. This is the almost inevitable consequence of ill-considered tinkering with what is, in truth, a complex system.

The slogan 'Honesty in Sentencing' may be new. The underlying idea is not. The principle that an offender should serve the sentence pronounced by the court without reduction was briefly in force following the Penal Servitude Act 1853. It did not work then. This modified version of that principle will achieve nothing of value now. It would be tragic indeed if, 150 years later, we had to learn this lesson again.

I turn to the provisions of Clause 1, requiring the imposition of an automatic life sentence on a second conviction of certain serious sexual and violent offences. Unlike the provisions for remission and parole, this clause addresses a serious penal problem. There is a hard core of offenders sentenced to determinate terms of imprisonment who represent a serious danger to the public on being released. It is appropriate to consider what additional protection can be provided. Unfortunately, the solution contained in Clause 1 is irremediably flawed.

It is a cardinal principle of just sentencing that the penalty should be fashioned to match the gravity of the offence and to take account of the circumstances in which it was committed. Any blanket or scatter-gun approach inevitably leads to injustice in individual cases. Such a result is, I suggest, obvious. But if it is not, it is borne out by authoritative independent research, based on an analysis of those prisoners whom the Parole Board on last review considered to be most dangerous. The research shows that nine out of 10 of these high risk offenders would not be covered by Clause 1, and that one-third of those who would be covered would not be regarded by the Parole Board as dangerous. Your Lordships will be aware that those who perpetrated the tragedies at Hungerford and Dunblane were men with no criminal record. This measure is simply misdirected.

It will also give rise to indefensible anomalies. Commentators have given examples. A man who had sexual intercourse at the age of 16 with a girl of 12 will be automatically sentenced to life imprisonment if, in middle age, he intentionally causes serious injury in the course of a public house brawl. A man convicted as a teenager of wounding with intent to cause serious injury will be automatically sentenced to life imprisonment if, at the age of 50, he returns home drunk and attempts to have intercourse with his wife against her wishes. These are not anomalies of the kind which even the best legal system occasionally produces. They are symptoms of a radically unsound approach.

To some extent, measures of this kind are also self-defeating, for no defendant faced with an automatic life sentence on conviction is likely to plead guilty. This not only means, as evidenced in the United States, a vastly increased workload of contested trials, with all the expense and delay and trauma for vulnerable victims and other witnesses which that involves. It also means that in some cases, perhaps because of intimidation, there will be acquittals, depriving the public in such cases of any protection at all.

These ill results may be in part avoided, but if they are the process of avoidance will itself be deeply objectionable. In the United States, where measures of this kind have been in force for 20 years, experience shows that the effect of taking discretion away from the court is not to destroy it but to transfer it—away from the judge and to prosecutors, defence lawyers and juries. Where on the facts of a particular case the imposition of an automatic penalty offends the conscience of an ordinary person, American prosecutors have charged offences less serious than the facts warranted which attracted no automatic penalty; or pleas of guilty have been offered and accepted to such lesser offences; or juries have convicted of such lesser offences. Sentencing discretion should not be exercised by crown prosecutors, or defence lawyers, or even juries. It should be exercised, as it always has been, by judges.

But what if a judge fails to impose a life sentence in a case covered by Clause 1 where the safety of the public demands that he should? What then? There exists a procedure tailor-made to meet that problem: the power of the Attorney-General to seek to refer sentences to the Criminal Division of the Court of Appeal on the ground that they are unduly lenient, asking for substitution of a more appropriate sentence. The power exists where a determinate sentence has been passed and it is felt that the protection of the public demands an indeterminate life sentence. The proposal in Clause 1 might foster the impression that the Attorney-General had repeatedly made such application in such cases and been denied. That is not so. Neither he nor the Home Office has ever to my knowledge suggested that it is. During the calendar years 1995 and 1996, the Court of Appeal, on references by the Attorney-General, reviewed the cases of 86 offenders in whose cases a life sentence could have been imposed. In only four of those cases did the Attorney-General ask the Court of Appeal to substitute a life sentence. In two cases the court did so, in two it did not. In one other case it did so although it had not been asked. Where such an application is made, it is judged on its merits and an indeterminate sentence substituted where the public interest is shown to demand it. It is open to the Attorney-General to submit that prevailing levels of sentence for a particular offence are too low; in a recent case, the Court of Appeal accepted that submission and increased the level. But such decisions will be made on a case-by-case, and not on a scattergun, basis. If this procedure is for any reason thought to be unsatisfactory—and I know of no reason why it should—consideration should again be given to the reviewable sentence recommended by the Butler Committee 20 years ago.

Thirdly, I would like, if I may, to say something about Clauses 2 and 3 of the Bill; the proposed mandatory minimum sentences for Class A drug dealers and burglars on third conviction. The terms proposed—at current levels, the equivalent of ten and a half years in the one case and four and a half years in the other—do not exceed those which serious professional criminals in these fields would now expect to receive—drug dealers are, indeed, routinely sentenced to very much longer terms.

The vice of these proposals again lies in their indiscriminate, scattergun nature. It is one thing—and a very serious thing—to operate as a large wholesale supplier of heroin or cocaine. It is quite another to buy two ecstasy tablets at a party, one for yourself and another for a friend. Yet both fall within Clause 2 of the Bill. It is one thing—and again a very serious thing—to strip someone's home of its valuable contents, accompanied perhaps by terror to the householder or gratuitous and offensive vandalism. It is quite another to take a gallon of petrol from an outhouse or to reach through an open window and take a pint of milk. Yet both are domestic burglary within Clause 3. A skilful professional burglar who avoids detection until he is brought to book on the same occasion for fifty domestic burglaries or a professional drug dealer eventually tracked down for the first time are not subject to the mandatory penalties. A feckless small-time burglar who is caught each time, or an addict dealing in small quantities at street level, is so subject. Anomalies of this kind are not the stuff of sound lawmaking.

Many of the objections to Clause 1 apply to Clauses 2 and 3 also. There is the same certainty of injustice in individual cases if account cannot be taken of the gravity of the offence, the pattern of offending, the lapse of time between offences and the circumstances of the offender. There is the same risk that prosecutors, defence lawyers and juries will connive at circumvention of the mandatory terms in order to do justice in individual cases. There is the same risk of a sharp increase in the proportion of contested trials, as in California where the rate of trial has increased two and a half times. But there is here an additional vice; it is proposed that the maximum discount from the mandatory minimum penalty should be 20 per cent. That is below the discount now frequently allowed, and well below that where a defendant is willing to give valuable intelligence to the Crown or to spare a victim the trauma of giving evidence.

The current practice of the courts is the result of hard practical experience. If a defendant is to betray a gang of professional burglars, or the members of a powerful drug cartel, putting his own security and that of his family at risk, he needs a generous inducement. No knowledgeable observer could regard 20 per cent. as enough. And there is yet another vice. If these sentences are to be revised upwards, there will be an inevitable upward effect on other sentences, where necessary to maintain differentials or achieve broad comparability. There is bound to be a ripple effect. I apologise for detaining your Lordships for longer than I should—

[Noble Lords: No, no, carry on!]

My Lords, the justification advanced for Clauses 2 and 3, so far as one can gather, is twofold. The first is the principle, christened 'incapacitation' by our American cousins, that so long as a person is in prison he cannot commit crimes. That is of course true. But the effect is very small. Recent Home Office research calculates that a 25 per cent. increase in imprisonment is required to reduce the number of offences by 1 per cent. No adequate justification is to be found here.

The second suggested justification is rested on the deterrent effect of these mandatory penalties. Both general and individual deterrence have an accepted place in sound sentencing, but deterrence cannot justify these mandatory penalties. It is known that only about 3 per cent. of reported crimes lead to convictions, so a rational, calculating criminal would think it worth taking the chance. But criminals are not, in the main, rational and calculating. As the Home Office itself said in 1990:

Deterrence is a principle with much immediate appeal . . . But much crime is committed on impulse, given the opportunity presented by an open window or an unlocked door, and it is committed by offenders who live from moment to moment; their crimes are as impulsive as the rest of their feckless, sad, or pathetic lives. It is unrealistic to construct sentencing arrangements on the assumption that most offenders will weigh up the possibilities in advance and base their conduct on rational calculations.

That informed judgment is reinforced by American experience. Between the early 1980s and December 1995, the heyday of mandatory minimum sentences, the American prison population rose from around 329,000 to nearly 1.6 million. Not, your Lordships may think, a persuasive advertisement for the principle of deterrence.

The Attorney-General's power to refer unduly lenient sentences to the Court of Appeal does not apply to the offences covered by Clauses 2 and 3. If these clauses address a real problem—in my judgment they do not—the solution lies in an extension of the Attorney-General's power. If there is indeed a malignant disease, that is the obvious cure.

It has been suggested that the anomalies I have highlighted in Clauses 1, 2 and 3 and in the maximum discount of 20 per cent. on a plea of guilty, will be met by the repeated qualification based on 'exceptional circumstances'. This argument is based on a misconception. In the closely analogous context of suspended sentences, reflecting the clear meaning of 'exceptional' as a familiar everyday expression and seeking to give effect to the intention of Parliament, the courts have given the word a literal and narrow meaning. It cannot sensibly mean different things in these two contexts. And I must tell your Lordships that to an experienced criminal judge very little will appear to be genuinely exceptional: while the facts of individual cases will be infinitely diverse, the broad patterns of criminal behaviour are in the main as repetitive as the seasons. This qualification contains no route of escape from the vice of these proposals: it simply obliges the judges to choose between emasculating the statute and doing what they regard as injustice.

My Lords, I have almost done. But I would, in closing, urge your Lordships to bear in mind those of our fellow citizens to whom these provisions will in the main apply. They are mostly young, in their late 'teens' or early 20s, and mostly male. They have in very many cases endured extreme deprivation: broken homes; disturbed childhoods; poverty; periods in and out of care; abuse of various kinds; truancy and exclusion from school; unemployment; addiction to alcohol and drugs; and a lack of all those beneficial maturing influences which most of us have been able to take for granted. I do not insult your Lordships by suggesting that these are innocent victims of determinist causes beyond their control. Of course not. But I do suggest that in discharge of our duty to our fellow men we should, instead of spending billions on new prisons, double and redouble existing efforts to identify and treat delinquents at the very earliest sign of delinquency, before—long before—they are sucked into the destructive maw of the penal system.

[Noble Lords: Hear, hear!]

In that way, my Lords, we shall treat the disease and not the symptoms.

In 1910 Mr Winston Churchill, speaking as Home Secretary in another place, drew attention—and I shall not commit the unforgivable sin of quotation—to the need to rehabilitate convicted prisoners in the world of industry, to make tireless efforts to find curative and regenerative processes and to maintain, 'an unfaltering faith that there is a treasure', if only one can find it, in the heart of every man.

That was the thinking—wise, humane and moral—which animated penal thinking in the early years of this century. If, as the century and the millennium slide to a close, our penal thinking is to be judged by the thinking which animates this Bill, then I, for one, will shrink from the judgment of history.

PART IX
MISCELLANEOUS

As the title of this section acknowledges, there is no common theme to the contents. But there are, perhaps, echoes of themes found in some of the earlier sections.

My address to the Centenary Conference of the Bar, the first paper in this section, contains (like the Pilgrim Fathers Lecture in Part VI) some Anglo-American reflections. It also highlights the extraordinary extent to which the just and smooth operation of our legal system depends on the bond of the confidence and trust which exists, or should exist, between the advocate (whether barrister or solicitor) and the judge. This is not, I think, something which the general public fully appreciates.

The second paper returns to the law of tort (touched on in relation to human rights in Part IV) and reintroduces Lord Atkin, (whose judgment in *Liversidge v Anderson* is the subject of a paper in Part V). This paper touches on one of the most baffling and elusive questions in the whole of the law: in what circumstances should one person, not bound to another by any tie of contract or blood, owe that other a duty to take reasonable care for his safety or welfare? There are, yet again, no easy answers.

In Part III the first paper considers the relationship between English law and other legal systems elsewhere. The third paper in this Part touches on the same theme, but from a different angle. In an inaugural lecture sponsored by Trinity College, Oxford, in honour of the college's distinguished alumnus the Earl of Chatham, I consider the future of the common law. My cautious prognosis is that the patient will survive and flourish.

Toynbee Hall is one of the great manifestations of Victorian philanthropy (in the literal meaning of that now somewhat disparaged term). In 1984 it celebrated the centenary of its foundation. In 1998 it celebrated the centenary of its free Legal Advice Centre, originally called its Poor Man's Lawyer Service. In the fourth paper in this Part, a Barnett Lecture given on this 1998 centenary, I look at the history of legal assistance provided for those who cannot afford to pay the fees charged by private lawyers, and consider the proposals then current for reforming the legal aid system as it has existed since 1949.

Lastly in this Part comes the address given at the thanksgiving service for Lord Denning OM, held in Westminster Abbey in June 1999. Born in Whitchurch, Hampshire, the son of a draper, in 1899, Lord Denning served in the First World War, won the highest academic honours in mathematics and law, and was called to the Bar in 1923. He became a judge of the High court in 1944, became a Lord

Justice of Appeal (with remarkable rapidity) in 1948 and in 1957 was elevated to the House of Lords as a Lord of Appeal in Ordinary. In 1962 he returned to the Court of Appeal to succeed a man younger than himself in the ancient office of Master of the Rolls, in which he served with outstanding distinction but not without controversy for over 20 years. He died very shortly after his hundredth birthday. This paper gives a glimpse why he was so widely regarded as one of the truly great men of our time.

1

*Address to the Centenary Conference of the Bar**

I am extremely grateful to the organizers of this Centenary Conference of the Bar for their flattering invitation to me to open it. A glance at the day's programme vividly reminds one of the many points at which modern legal practice touches the life of the society and the wider world in which we live. I am sure that the Conference will prove a memorably rewarding experience.

It is a truism that the century since the Bar Council was established has seen striking changes in the substance of the law, in the structure of the courts, in practice and procedure, in the organization of the legal profession, and in the public's perception of the law, the courts, and legal practitioners. The forthcoming century is unlikely to prove less fertile of change. While prediction is hazardous—particularly about the future—I do not myself think that the forthcoming century will see the disappearance of an independent Bar. But I would like, against a background of impending change, to draw attention to certain features of our system which, I suggest, we should at all cost seek to preserve and enhance and to areas in which we should be the midwives of change.

I do this having enjoyed the privilege, during the vacation, of participating in a week-long exchange with a visiting team of formidably distinguished American judges and practitioners. The British team—I can properly so describe it since it included the Lord President of the Court of Session—was strengthened by the presence and contribution of, among others, Patricia Scotland QC. During the week we discussed a number of topics of common interest. We also visited a number of courts, including the Old Bailey and a London Magistrates' Court, which some of us had not seen in action for some time.

At the Old Bailey we saw a number of trials in progress. In the one which I attended a defendant was accused of raping and indecently assaulting a girl of 15. The defence was that she was a child-prostitute who had consented to intercourse in return for a supply of cocaine. There was at the outset an application that the girl should give evidence behind a screen. The judge heard argument. Authority was cited. He ruled that she should. A screen was erected. The girl was examined in chief. Defence counsel applied for leave to question the girl about her previous history. There was argument. The judge gave leave. Cross-examination began, and was well-advanced when we reluctantly left, two hours after arrival in court.

Our visitors were amazed that the argument and decision of two motions, the direct examination of the main prosecution witness and much of her cross-examination could be accomplished in so short a time. They were loud in their

* Delivered at the Centenary Conference of the Bar on 29 October 1994.

praise of the advocacy they had witnessed. So was I. Not a question too many. Not a question too few. Every question pertinent, well-thought out, and clear. Questions firmly and politely put, with no hint of intimidation or condescension. Argument succinctly and cogently put. Others who visited other courts gained the same favourable impression. This was advocacy at its best. But, as we all know, it is not always so.

This leads me to a simple and obvious point for which I would apologize if I did not regard it as fundamental. I can take it from the Report of Lord Alexander of Weedon's Bar Standards Review Body:

The touchstone for the survival and success of the Bar will be its excellence.

We must all, surely, say Amen to that. The Bar cannot, plainly, rely on restrictive rules to protect it in the face of a public view that high quality services need no protection and low quality services deserve none. Nor, equally plainly, can the Bar rest on its reputation as an elite profession, since the public will be rightly intolerant of pretensions to elitism not fully justified by performance. I would accordingly offer my respectful congratulations to the leadership of the Bar for the steps they are taking to strengthen standards of education, training and professional performance so as to raise every practitioner as nearly as may be to the standards of the best.

The next feature of our system which attracted favourable comment—very favourable comment—was the relationship of mutual respect, understanding, and trust perceived to exist between Bench and Bar. Of course there are occasions when it is the duty of the advocate in performance of his professional duty to stand up to the judge and bluntly oppose some course which the judge has in mind. And there are occasions when a judge may be constrained to rebuke counsel for prolixity, repetition, or even—although never, I think, in my experience— misbehaviour. But by and large, day in day out, the relationship between Bench and Bar is as the Americans perceived it, and we should not take this for granted because it is in my view the most civilised and civilising feature of our system.

It is not of course a necessary feature of any legal system, and it is in some ways a surprising one. For the objectives of counsel and judge in any trial are by no means the same. Counsel's task is to do all that he or she fairly may to achieve a result favourable to the client who is the paymaster. The task of the judge in a jury trial is to enable the jury to arrive at a fair verdict; but that verdict will almost certainly be unwelcome to one party or the other. In a civil trial without a jury the judge's task is to find the right answer; but the right answer will probably be the wrong answer for one party or the other. So the existence of mutual respect, understanding and trust is the more precious because it arises in the context of what is basically an antithetical relationship.

To what do we owe this relationship? It is not enough to attribute it to tradition, since the tradition must be founded on something. I suggest two answers. The first is that historically judges have always been drawn from the ranks of practising advocates. No one who has ever experienced it can quite forget the agony of conducting a weak case for an unreasonable client before a difficult judge. For their part, advocates see judges not as an alien race imported from a different professional planet but as those who have graduated from the Bar to an office traditionally regarded as the culmination of a successful career at the Bar. If that were ever to cease to be so—and there is as yet little sign of it, although the commercial pressures are obvious—it would in my view have the gravest implications for the integrity of our system.

My second answer is to point to the historic collegiate role of the Inns of Court (to which I would add, although necessarily in a more limited way, the role of Bar Messes on circuit). The Inns do provide a forum in which practitioners may meet judges and learn that they are not senile fuddy-duddies living in a different world and judges may appreciate that advocates are not the tiresome people they may sometimes appear. More importantly, the professional fraternity of the Inns has fostered a common ethical culture which has enabled the Bar to function, until recently, with little reliance on written rules and the judiciary to function, until now, with virtually none. The Americans share this perception, for following an earlier exchange they returned home and set up Inns of Court across the United States.

The advent—in my view the welcome advent—of solicitors holding the Higher Courts qualification of course alters the historical picture somewhat. I have a proposal to make. If, as I have suggested, the existence of our present relationship between Bench and Bar derives in significant part from the educative experience of belonging to the Inns as fraternities of past and present advocates, then it seems to me clear that qualified solicitors who so wish—and of course there could be no compulsion—should be accorded membership of the Inns and so given the benefit of this experience. If this proposal sounds revolutionary and subversive of hallowed tradition, then I would recall that up to the second half of the sixteenth-century solicitors and attorneys were members of Inns, and they remained members of the Inns of Chancery until the end. But I would rest my case on pragmatic and not historical grounds. If, as most would think, the Inns confer the benefits I have suggested, the public interest requires that these benefits should be conferred on all practising advocates and not just some of them.

A third feature of our system which attracted very favourable comment was the absence of personal hostility towards each other manifested by opposing counsel. This was again evident at the Old Bailey. No questions in chief were objected to, even leading questions, no doubt because agreement had been reached on the point at which the witness should no longer be led. There was no hint of personal animus. This also is something we take almost for granted. I suggest we should not. I am not at all sure that public respect for our system of government is enhanced by the ritualized unarmed combat routinely televised on Tuesdays and Thursdays. I am even less sure that litigants or the public are edified on the fortunately rare occasions when counsel in a case engage in a personal dog-fight. It certainly does nothing to help the judge or the jury. Nor does intemperate abuse of the other party. As Bishop Hacket observed, 'A strong case can scarce ever be stated too gently.' The effective advocate is not usually he or she who stigmatizes conduct as disgraceful, outrageous, or monstrous but the advocate who describes it as surprising, regrettable, or disappointing.

As a vision of what I devoutly trust is not our future, I cite some exchanges between local counsel drawn to my attention by the Chief Justice of Delaware:

Counsel A to witness: Okay. Do you have any idea why Mr. Oresman was calling that material to your attention?

Counsel B   Don't answer that. How would he know what was going on in Mr Oresman's mind? Don't answer it. Go on to your next question.

Counsel A   No, Joe—

Counsel B   He's not going to answer that. Certify it. I'm going to shut it down if you don't go to your next question.

Counsel A   No. Joe, Joe—

Counsel B   Don't 'Joe' me, asshole. You can ask some questions, but get off of that. I'm tired of you. You could gag a maggot off a meat wagon. Now, we've helped you every way we can.

Counsel A   Let's just take it easy.

Counsel B   No, we're not going to take it easy. Get done with this.

. . . . .

Counsel A   We will go on to the next question. We're not trying to excite anyone.

Counsel B   Come on. Quit talking. Ask the question. Nobody wants to socialize with you.

Counsel A   I'm not trying to socialize. We'll go on to another question. We're continuing the deposition.

Counsel B   Well, go on and shut up.

. . . . .

Counsel A   Are you finished?

Counsel B   I may be and you may be. Now, you want to sit here and talk to me, fine. This deposition is going to be over with. You don't know what you're doing. Obviously someone wrote out a long outline of stuff for you to ask. You have no concept of what you're doing.

. . . . .

Counsel B   You fee makers think you can come here and sit in somebody's office, get your meter running, get your full day's fee by asking stupid questions. Let's go with it.

It is only fair to observe that these exchanges took place on the taking of a deposition and in the absence of the judge, that they were no doubt chosen as an extreme example of the genre and that the Chief Justice was strong in his condemnation of such behaviour. But it remains extraordinary that any professional man taking part in a process of which justice is intended to be the end product could think it appropriate to behave as Counsel B evidently did. It would scarcely be worth mentioning this were it not that there seems to be a developing cult of the mean, hard, no-holds-barred professional litigator. I would only observe that I can imagine no situation, in exchanges between solicitors or in exchanges between counsel, which would justify a departure from ordinary standards of good manners and civilized behaviour.

It would be misleading, and you would be very surprised, if I were to suggest that the appraisal of our system made by these highly qualified American observers was one of undiluted admiration. Perhaps I may mention three areas in which I think they felt, and I certainly feel, that we are lagging.

The first is in the field of case management in civil cases. In the United States, as for instance in Australia, a civil case is assigned to a particular judge at an early stage and that judge is responsible for seeing that case through to a conclusion. When interlocutory decisions have to be made, they may be made by the judge him or her self or by a subordinate judge working in close conjunction with the assigned judge. But the responsibility for managing the case until it is finished rests squarely on the assigned judge, and ability to manage a docket in this way is recognised as a necessary judicial skill in which training is offered. Here, save in relatively few cases of outstanding complexity, there is no such practice. Judges usually encounter a case for the first time when they come to try it, and the summons for directions largely fails to achieve the objectives which its begetters hoped for because the judge or master who conducts it knows little or nothing of the case and is largely confined to choosing between the competing submissions of the parties when contentious issues arise.

Case management is not a panacea for all ills. It has not prevented the American system of discovery becoming even more expensive and burdensome than our own. But I think it could help to alleviate the serious ills of expense and delay which currently dog all common law systems. I do not, however, wish to argue the merits of case management today: it is a substantial subject in its own right; I am conscious of having touched on it rather often before; and there seems now to be a large measure of agreement that movement towards some system of case management (however described) is overdue. Nor do I wish to consider the precise form which any system of case management, if introduced here, might take. We can be confident that Lord Woolf and his working party will make perceptive and workable recommendations, and there is little advantage in seeking to anticipate these. The point I do wish to make is somewhat different. But before coming to it I would like to comment on the other two perceived deficiencies of our system.

American observers are amazed that we continue to allot time for the oral argument of civil appeals on the basis of the time which counsel estimate they will need to argue the appeal. It is of course true that in the House of Lords a carefully drafted written statement of the parties' cases has for many years been required, even though in former times some Law Lords, among them the most distinguished, made a point of not reading these cases before the hearing. It is also true that in recent years the Court of Appeal has required written abstracts of the argument and sought to discourage oral narration of the facts and citation of judgments and documents. But despite this requirement it remains the case, at least in the Civil Division of the Court of Appeal, that counsel's estimates of the time they will need strongly influence, if they do not determine, the time allotted.

Even if this system is accepted as representing the ideal, I do not for my part think it is maintainable. The number of appeals set down each year shows a fairly steady upward trend. The number of applications shows a very steep upward trend. The backlog of unheard appeals increases year by year. The membership of the court has increased from fifteen to thirty over the last two decades, and there may, I hope, be a further increase shortly. But even this may not contain, let alone reduce, current waiting times, in the absence of other steps. It is right that we should be gravely concerned about this, but we should probably not be surprised. It is nearly a century and a half since the Supreme Court of the United States was induced, not by choice but by practical necessity, to limit the time allowed for oral argument. Those limits have since then been progressively reduced. Other American courts have followed, for the same reason.

A moment ago I accepted the hypothesis that our present system of almost unlimited oral argument is ideal. I am far from convinced that is so. The requirement that counsel should summarise their submissions on paper has in my view proved a valuable discipline. A requirement that oral argument should be confined within a tight but reasonable timetable would also, I think, prove a valuable discipline in obliging counsel to winnow out the essential and crucial from the inessential and peripheral. It would also have the beneficial result of deleting from counsel's lexicon two expressions which should never have entered it: one is 'for the sake of completeness', and the other is 'in due course'.

I am fortified in the view I have expressed by two experiences. The first is of attending, with other judges, a training session in what I think was called television awareness, an elementary introduction to what does and does not contribute to the effectiveness of a television appearance. We were all asked to arrive, and did, with a prepared address of 5 or 10 minutes on a subject of our choice, which we then in turn delivered before the cameras and each other. The exercise consisted of progressively condensing and re-delivering these speeches within shorter and shorter time limits, culminating in a slot of 10 seconds, which is (I believe) the maximum sound bite included in the 9 o'clock news. All of us thought that both we and our colleagues were better and more effective in the shorter than in the longer presentation. Now I am not of course suggesting that a complicated point of law (or an adequate introduction to the Centenary Conference of the Bar) can be covered in 10 seconds. But I am suggesting that to distil the point that really matters is greatly to strengthen the effectiveness of the argument. That is, after all, the stock-in-trade of the outstanding advocate.

The second experience is nearer home. It has on occasion proved necessary, because of an impending vacation, reconstitution of the court or some other reason, to impose time limits and allocate the time available to the various parties on the argument of an appeal (probably with a right to deliver supplementary written submissions). Never in my experience has counsel failed to rise to the challenge by tailoring his argument to fit the restricted time allotted. I have never felt that much of value was lost. It can be done, and it seems to me inevitable that it will have increasingly to be done.

The third defect to which I would draw attention is of a different kind. It is our failure, save in the matrimonial/child care field, to exploit the potential of those forms of conciliation and mediation usually lumped together as ADR. Experience elsewhere leaves one in no doubt of the potential effectiveness of these procedures, nor of the expense which can thereby be saved. There appear, unsurprisingly, to be many people and companies in this country who would much prefer to resolve their differences without resort to the costly, protracted and anxious processes of the courts. Yet, subject to the single exception noted, there seems to be little evidence of disputes being resolved in this way, surprisingly since we have been world leaders in the somewhat analogous field of arbitration.

I am not sure where the blockage lies. It may be the result of unfamiliarity with the relevant processes on the part of lawyers when first consulted, or distrust of the unknown. Or it may be due to apprehension that if an unsuccessful resort to mediation has to be followed by legal action the costs overall may be increased. Or it may be that lawyers, engaged to fight a case, hesitate to undermine the client's confidence in them as gladiators by initiating discussion of a negotiated compromise. Or it may be due to the lack of legal aid for mediation, and the absence of any provision for court-annexed mediation. It may, I suppose, but I hope not, be affected by self-interest: if so, I would commend a saying of Abraham Lincoln, himself a notable trial-lawyer:

Discourage litigation. Persuade your neighbours to compromise wherever you can. Point out to them how the nominal winner is often a real loser in fees, expenses and waste of time. As a peacemaker, the lawyer has a superior opportunity of being a good man. There will still be business enough.

Whatever the cause of the blockage, it is in my view important in the interest of the public whom we seek to serve that not only solicitors but barristers also should acquaint themselves with the various processes of ADR and advise resort to them in any promising case. I am pleased to find that in this respect also I echo the Report of Lord Alexander's Bar Standards Review Body.

I have mentioned three suggested defects in our own system. I am not suggesting there are no other defects, but coffee is scheduled for 10 a.m. What the points I have mentioned have in common, however, is this: that if they are to be remedied in what appear to be the obvious ways, some evolutionary development of the role of judges and advocates, and of the relationship between the two, will inevitably be involved.

If any recognizable system of case management is to be introduced, it must mean that cases will to an increasing extent be judge-driven and not, as now, lawyer-driven. This does not mean that parties will not be represented but it does mean that representation will take a somewhat different shape, as in those European countries where there is no trial in the English sense. If oral argument on appeal (or for that matter at first instance) is to be curtailed, it inevitably means that more will turn on written submissions, that judges will spend more time studying documents out of court and less time sitting in it and in all probability that judges will require the help of qualified legal assistants as they do elsewhere. If ADR is to become a practical reality and not, in the main, a literary subject in this country, solicitors and barristers will have to recognize the conciliation of cases out of court, and not only the winning of cases in court, as part of their professional vocation.

No doubt these changes, if they occur, will be unpopular with many, as almost all changes are. They will be criticized as downgrading the role of oral advocacy. They may indeed have that result. But I do not know why we put a higher premium on the spoken than the written word, why a good speech should be entitled to more acclaim than a good article or essay or written submission. The contrary certainly could be argued, since a written argument must be judged on its merit as an argument whereas a speech may be made to seem more cogent than it is by the artifice of the orator.

That is not, however, a point I wish to pursue, nor the point on which I wish to end. The point on which I wish to end is this. If I am right that we are embarking upon (or continuing in) a process of evolutionary change, potentially affecting the roles and relationships of Bench and Bar, it is in the highest degree desirable that we should do so in a co-operative spirit, sensitive to each other's concerns but fully mindful of the needs of society, and above all seeking to preserve and strengthen those features of our system which may fairly be seen as a priceless national asset. It would indeed be tragic if, in the course of seeking to remedy undoubted ills, we were to emulate the man mentioned by Shakespeare who threw a pearl away, richer than all his tribe. We must remember that the ultimate test of any reform is not only its effectiveness in eradicating defects but also its discriminatory preservation of what is good and valuable, of which, in our case, there is much.

2

*Who then in Law is my Neighbour?**

Once upon a time we were all students of law. In my case that was, of course, many years ago, when nightingales sang in New Square and briefs were marked in guineas. For you the experience is more recent. We all of us, I trust, remain students of law still, although we modestly disclaim the title. But when we were all overt, practising students it may be that our experience was somewhat the same.

We struggled, with varying degrees of incomprehension, through various impenetrable fields of law, overreaching interests and shifting trusts, the law of mistake and illegality in contract, larceny by a trick, trespass ab initio, the rolled-up plea and the wilder reaches of the law of evidence. But then we emerged into a wide, open, sunlit upland. This was the law of negligence. And through it ran, limpid, clear and refreshing, the speech of Lord Atkin in *Donoghue v Stevenson*, with its familiar reference to the Good Samaritan. A very distinguished judge recently remarked to me how much he had always disliked this passage—and no doubt it is true that the victim of the mugging could have established no common law duty of care against the priest, the Levite, or the Samaritan. He would have been left to his claim, for what it would have been worth, against the muggers, and to his claim under such Criminal Injuries Compensation Scheme as happened to be in force at the time. But I have always myself felt an affection for the passage: it was readily intelligible; it was simple, avoiding the tendency to over-complicate which is the besetting sin of all but the most luminous legal minds; it was unusually well written; and above all it seemed to make possible the doing of substantial justice.

No one, I think, ever supposed that Lord Atkin's test provided a template which could be simply placed over the facts of a case to determine whether a duty of care existed (independently of contract) or not. But it did provide a bedrock of principle against which new situations could be tested. As Lord Devlin observed in *Hedley Byrne*,

> The real value of *Donoghue v Stevenson* to the argument in this case is that it shows how the law can be developed to solve particular problems. Is the relationship between the parties in this case such that it can be brought within a category giving rise to a special duty?

Perhaps one may also recall two other observations of Lord Devlin in the same speech. First:

---

* Delivered to the Professional Negligence Bar Association on 15 March 1995.

The common law is tolerant of much illogicality especially on the surface; but no system of law can be workable if it has not got logic at the root of it.

And secondly, with reference to the argument that there can be no liability for financial loss caused by negligence in the absence of physical injury:

I am bound to say, my Lords, that I think this to be nonsense. It is not the sort of nonsense that can arise even in the best system of law out of the need to draw nice distinctions between borderline cases. It arises, if it is the law, simply out of a refusal to make sense. The line is not drawn on any intelligible principle. It just happens to be the line which those who have been driven from the extreme assertion that negligent statements in the absence of contractual or fiduciary duty give no cause of action have in the course of their retreat so far reached.

In the *Dorset Yacht* case Lord Reid lent his great authority to the view that Lord Atkin's speech should be treated as applicable to new cases unless there was some reason for rejecting it. I hope you will forgive me if I remind you of the relevant passage:

In later years there has been a steady trend towards regarding the law of negligence as depending on principle so that, when a new point emerges, one should ask not whether it is covered by authority but whether recognised principles apply to it. *Donoghue v Stevenson* [1932] AC 562 may be regarded as a milestone, and the well-known passage in Lord Atkin's speech should I think be regarded as a statement of principle. It is not to be treated as if it were a statutory definition. It will require qualification in new circumstances. But I think that the time has come when we can and should say that it ought to apply unless there is some justification or valid explanation for its exclusion. For example, causing economic loss is a different matter; for one thing, it is often caused by deliberate action. Competition involves traders being entitled to damage their rivals' interests by promoting their own, and there is a long chapter of the law determining in what circumstances owners of land can and in what circumstance they may not use their proprietary rights so as to injure their neighbours. But where negligence is involved the tendency has been to apply principles analogous to those stated by Lord Atkin: cf. *Hedley Byrne & Co. Ltd. v Heller & Partners Ltd.* [1964] AC 465. And when a person has done nothing to put himself in any relationship with another person in distress or with his property mere accidental propinquity does not require him to go to that person's assistance. There may be a moral duty to do so, but it is not practicable to make it a legal duty. And then there are cases, e.g., with regard to landlord and tenant, where the law was settled long ago and neither Parliament nor this House sitting judicially has made any move to alter it. But I can see nothing to prevent our approaching the present case with Lord Atkin's principles in mind.

Then, in *Anns*, Lord Wilberforce (with the unqualified assent of Lord Diplock, Lord Simon of Glaisdale, Lord Salmon and Lord Russell of Killowen) attempted a summary of the law as it then stood in determining whether a duty of care existed or no. I fear I am guilty of excessive quotation, and this passage may now be thought to have no more than an antiquarian interest. But it is relevant to my theme, and no one will have to listen to it many times again:

Through the trilogy of cases in this House—*Donoghue v Stevenson* [1932] AC 562, *Hedley Byrne & Co. Ltd. v Heller & Partners Ltd.* [1964] AC 465, and *Dorset Yacht Co. Ltd. v Home Office* [1970] AC 1004, the position has now been reached that in order to establish that a duty of care arises in a particular situation, it is not necessary to bring the facts of that situation within those of previous situations in which a duty of care has been held to exist. Rather the question has to be approached in two stages. First one has to ask whether, as between the alleged wrongdoer and the person who has suffered damage there is a suffi-cient relationship of proximity or neighbourhood such that, in the reasonable contempla-tion of the former, carelessness on his part may be likely to cause damage to the latter—in which case a prima facie duty of care arises. Secondly, if the first question is answered affirmatively, it is necessary to consider whether there are any considerations which ought to be negative, or to reduce or limit the scope of the duty or the class of person to whom it is owed or the damages to which a breach of it may give rise: see *Dorset Yacht* case [1970] AC 1004, per Lord Reid at p. 1027. Examples of this are *Hedley Byrne's* case [1964] AC 465 where the class of potential plaintiffs was reduced to those shown to have relied upon the correctness of statements made, and *Weller & Co. v Foot and Mouth Disease Research Institute* [1966] 1 QB 569; and (I cite these merely as illustrations, with-out discussion) cases about 'economic loss' where, a duty having been held to exist, the nature of the recoverable damages was limited: see *S.C.M. (United Kingdom) Ltd. v W. J. Whittall & Son Ltd.* [1971] 1 QB 337 and *Spartan Steel & Alloys Ltd. v Martin & Co. (Contractors) Ltd.* [1973] QB 27.

This was, of course, the state of the law when Sir Robert Megarry VC gave his decision in *Ross v Caunters* [1980] Ch. 297, and the judge made express refer-ence to the passages I have quoted from the speeches of Lord Reid and Lord Wilberforce. The facts of that case were very simple. On the instructions of a testator the defendant solicitors prepared a will for execution by the testator. Under this will a residuary bequest was made to Mrs Ross, the plaintiff. The testa-tor signed the will, one of the attesting witnesses being Mr Ross, the plaintiff's husband. The solicitors carelessly failed to advise the testator that spouses of beneficiaries should not be witnesses, and also to observe (on receiving back the signed and attested will) that the spouse of a beneficiary had signed as a witness. The result was that the bequest to Mrs Ross failed, and she sued the solicitors. The defence was that the solicitors owed a duty only to their client, the testator—who would, through his estate, have had a claim for no more than nominal damages—and none to Mrs Ross who, if anyone, was the loser.

Having considered *Robertson v Fleming*, a nineteenth-century Scottish appeal to the House of Lords containing dicta helpful to the solicitor, the Vice-Chancellor said:

Robertson v Fleming was, of course, decided nearly 120 years ago, and some 70 years before *Donoghue v Stevenson* [1932] AC 562. Today, negligence has long been established as an independent tort and not merely a constituent element in certain other torts. Further, it is difficult today to see the logic in the proposition that if A employs B to do an act for the benefit of C, the existence of B's contractual duty to A to do the act with proper care negates any possible duty of B towards C, since B has no contract with C. Why should the existence of a contractual duty to A preclude the existence of any non-contractual duty to others? If one examines the facts of the case before me to discover whether the threefold elements of the tort of negligence exist, a simple answer would be on the following lines. First, the solicitors owed a duty of care to the plaintiff since she was someone within their direct contemplation as a person so closely and directly affected by their acts and omissions in carrying out their client's instructions to provide her with a share of his residue that they could reasonably foresee that she would be likely to be injured by those acts or omissions. Second, there has undoubtedly been a breach of that duty of care; and third, the plaintiff has clearly suffered loss as a direct result of that breach of duty. Accordingly, in the absence of anything to indicate the contrary, the plaintiff's claim should succeed. Such an answer, however, would be far too simple for the volume of case law that has arisen on the subject. It could, no doubt, be called an answer of artless Chancery simplicity; and so in due course I must turn to the authorities.

Not surprisingly, since on any showing the claim was novel, a series of arguments were advanced against the existence of any duty owed by the solicitors to Mrs Ross: they could only be liable to their own client, and such liability lay only in contract and not in tort; if a claim lay for financial loss alone, it could only succeed if it fell strictly within the ambit of *Hedley Byrne*; the beneficiary had suffered no loss, she had merely failed to gain a benefit; reasons of policy militated against any extension of liability to non-clients; failure to receive the testator's intended bounty did not put Mrs Ross in a class deserving of legal protection.

The Vice-Chancellor disposed of all these arguments. He held that a solicitor was not liable to his client only in contract; he could be liable to his client and others for the tort of negligence. He regarded the basis of the solicitor's negligence as most probably a direct application of the principle of *Donoghue v Stevenson*. He said:

A solicitor who is instructed by his client to carry out a transaction that will confer a benefit on an identified third party owes a duty of care towards that third party in carrying out that transaction, in that the third party is a person within his direct contemplation as someone who is likely to be so closely and directly affected by his acts or omissions that he can reasonably foresee that the third party is likely to be injured by those omissions.

It was no bar to the claim that the loss of the beneficiary was purely financial. He found no considerations which sufficed to negate or limit the scope of the solicitors' duty to the beneficiary. Underlying the whole judgment was an acceptance that common justice demanded a remedy from Mrs Ross:

I find it difficult to envisage a fair and reasonable man, seeking to do what is fair and just, who would reach the conclusion that it was right to hold that solicitors whose carelessness deprives an intended beneficiary of the share of a testator's estate that was destined for that beneficiary should be immune from any action by that beneficiary, and should have no liability save for nominal damages due to the testator's estate.

Then the earth moved. A long and familiar series of cases came before the

House of Lords (or the Privy Council) all raising, on different facts, the question whether a defendant owed a plaintiff a duty of care. Did a London Borough with a statutory duty to approve drainage works owe a duty to a building owner if drainage works were constructed otherwise than in accordance with plans previously approved? No. It would not be reasonable or just to impose liability on the local authority when the building owner had relied on and been let down by its own advisers and contractors. Did a shipowner owe a duty of care to a buyer of goods who had not become the owner or acquired a possessory title to the goods? No. It would be contrary to long-established authority to admit such a duty. Did a Housing Executive owe a duty of care to the purchaser of a house if an improvement grant had been used to finance a defective extension of a building? No. The dictates of good sense and the consideration of what was fair and reasonable pointed clearly against the imposition of any duty and it would be contrary to the fitness of things to hold the authority to be under any such duty. Did a financial regulator owe a duty of care to an investor who had lost money in a company the regulator had negligently registered? No. The relationship between the regulator and the investor was not such as to give rise to a duty. Did a police authority owe a duty of care to a murder victim to attempt to apprehend the murderer before he committed the crime? No. There was no special feature of the relationship between the police and the victim which would support such a duty, and the police were in any event immune from actions of this kind. Did a main contractor owe a duty of care to a lessee of a building in relation to defective plasterwork done by a sub-contractor? No. The main contractor had assumed no such duty, and it would be a dangerous course for the common law to embark upon the adoption of novel policies which it saw as instruments of social justice but to which, unlike the legislature, it was unable to set carefully defined limitations. Did an auditor, employed and paid by a company to report to shareholders on the company accounts, and foreseeing that a shareholder might base a decision to buy or sell shares on the accounts, owe a duty of care to the shareholder in preparing the accounts? No. The report was not made to assist shareholders in making investment decisions and there could be liability only where a report was made for the purposes of a particular transaction. Did a local authority, in approving plans for the building of a house, owe a duty of care to a purchaser of the house who had suffered financially as a result of the house proving defective? No. A local authority was under no duty to protect a purchaser against such loss. It was indeed questionable whether a local authority owed a duty to protect a purchaser against personal injury or damage to property other than the house itself. From all these cases it became quite clear that Lord Wilberforce's speech in *Anns* did not provide a reliable ground for deciding whether a duty of care existed or no; that a duty should only be imposed where it was fair, just and reasonable to do so, and that new categories of negligence should be developed incrementally, by analogy with established categories.

The result of the continental drift I have just described of course was that

when, in *White v Jones*, the Court of Appeal came (in effect) to review the
correctness of the Vice-Chancellor's decision in *Ross v Caunters* the world was
a somewhat different place. One might in these circumstances have expected
the judgments to proceed on quite different lines from that of the Vice-
Chancellor 14 years before. The Court of Appeal dismissed the authority of
Robertson v Fleming, as the Vice-Chancellor had done. It found the beneficiary's loss to be an obviously foreseeable result of the solicitor's negligence.
It regarded the relationship between solicitor and beneficiary as sufficiently
proximate to support a duty. Like him it was struck by the obvious mismatch
which arose in a case where one party had a contractual claim but no loss and
a second party had suffered a loss but had no contractual claim. Of the need for
the law to provide a remedy the Court was in no doubt. Lord Justice Nicholls
observed:

Here, a coherent system of law demands that there should be an effective remedy against
the solicitor.

and

The resources of the law must be sufficient to fill what otherwise would be a serious
lacuna.

Lord Justice Farquharson thought there were a number of reasons why a duty
should exist. In Lord Justice Steyn's view there were cogent arguments favour-
ing recognition of a duty, and a coherent law of obligations ought not to render
a solicitor's undoubted responsibility to his client wholly ineffectual. Again a
number of arguments were advanced to show why there could or should be no
duty: the size of the estate would be increased; the beneficiary had no vested
right, but only a spes successionis; the solicitor could not be liable save to his
client and in contract; there could be no liability for pure economic loss in the
absence of reliance; the solicitor would become subject to a conflict between the
interests of competing beneficiaries; problems of limitation would arise; the duty
in tort might not be subject to any limitation of liability in the contract between
solicitor and testator; there might be liability to an indeterminate class. There
was even, it seems, a floodgates argument, no doubt advanced in the belief,
apparently shared by all lawyers, that the effect of opening a floodgate is to
cause a flood and not, as is the case, to prevent one, by releasing water into an
alternative channel. None of these arguments appears to have detained the Court
for very long. It was argued, in reliance on recent House of Lords authority, that
the philosophy of those decisions was inimical to the recognition of a solicitor's
liability for loss negligently caused. If that submission was right, observed Lord
Justice Steyn:

the result is curious. *Murphy* and *Caparo* signalled the retreat from high principle and the
resurgence of pragmatism. It is therefore something of an irony to call in aid *Murphy* and
Caparo for the proposition that *Ross v Caunters* does not fit in with a general theory. And

it is important to bear in mind that *Ross v Caunters* was based not on the analogy of *Hedley Byrne & Co. v Heller & Partners Ltd.* [1964] AC 465, which in the context of negligent misrepresentations requires reliance, but on the general law of negligence, which was first coherently expounded in *Donoghue v Stevenson* [1932] AC 562.

So, despite the changed landscape, it seems that the Court of Appeal in *White v Jones* followed very much the same lines as the Vice-Chancellor had done in *Ross v Caunters*.

As everyone present well knows, the solicitors' appeal to the House of Lords was dismissed by a bare majority of 3 to 2. Lord Goff gave the first and leading speech for the majority. Lord Browne-Wilkinson expressed agreement with Lord Goff's reasons, and in addition gave reasons of his own. Lord Nolan expressed agreement with the reasons of Lord Goff and Lord Browne-Wilkinson, and also gave reasons of his own. Technically, therefore, a majority supported Lord Goff's reasons. But it seems clear that the three members of the majority favoured somewhat different solutions.

Lord Goff acknowledged the conceptual problems to which the appellant solicitors drew attention, and which had caused the Supreme Courts of Australian states to take differing views. But he was impressed, as the Vice-Chancellor and the Court of Appeal had been, by the mismatch between the claimant and the loss and strongly felt that a remedy had to be found if practical justice was to be done. This was a view strongly shared by the other members of the majority.

In his search for a remedy Lord Goff considered two German solutions: the contract with protective effect for third parties, and the doctrine of transferred loss. The first of these solutions, theoretically very much more elegant than our own, is to permit a party for whose benefit a contract is made to sue if the contract is negligently performed so as to deprive him of his intended benefit. The second applies where loss and claim are separated, and permits assignment of the claim to the party who has suffered the loss. Both these solutions plainly attracted Lord Goff, as indeed the doctrine of transferred loss had done in *The Aliakmon*. But he felt bound to reject them, the first because the doctrine of privity of contract was too deeply embedded in English law to be legitimately circumvented, and the second because the lacuna revealed by *The Aliakmon* had required parliamentary plastic surgery to make it good. An alternative solution, by adaptation of the *Albazero* principle, was similarly rejected, since the executors of the will were not the plaintiffs and might not have been willing to be so.

So Lord Goff turned to the tortious solution, holding that an ordinary action in tortious negligence on the lines proposed by the Vice-Chancellor in *Ross v Caunters* was inappropriate because it failed to meet any of the conceptual problems already identified. A straightforward application of *Hedley Byrne* could not in ordinary circumstances give rise to an assumption of responsibility by the testator's solicitor towards an intended beneficiary. But Lord Goff was anxious that a remedy should be found for what he regarded as injustice. He accordingly said:

In my opinion, therefore, your Lordships' House should in cases such as these extend to the intended beneficiary a remedy under the *Hedley Byrne* principle by holding that the assumption of responsibility by the solicitor towards his client should be held in law to extend to the intended beneficiary who (as the solicitor can reasonably foresee) may, as a result of the solicitor's negligence, be deprived of his intended legacy in circumstances in which neither the testator nor his estate will have a remedy against the solicitor.

He added:

Let me emphasize that I can see no injustice in imposing liability upon a negligent solicitor in a case such as the present where, in the absence of a remedy in this form, neither the testator's estate nor the disappointed beneficiary will have a claim for the loss caused by his negligence. This is the injustice which, in my opinion, the judges of this country should address by recognising that cases such as these call for an appropriate remedy, and that the common law is not so sterile as to be incapable of supplying that remedy when it is required.

Lord Browne-Wilkinson agreed that the solicitors were under a duty of care to the plaintiffs arising from an extension of the principle of assumption of responsibility explored in *Hedley Byrne* and traceable back to the fiduciary relationship in issue in *Noctor v Lord Ashburton*. While disclaiming any intention to attempt any comprehensive statement of the law, Lord Browne-Wilkinson said:

The law of England does not impose any general duty of care to avoid negligent misstatements or to avoid causing pure loss even if economic damage to the plaintiff was foreseeable. However, such a duty of care will arise if there is a special relationship between the parties. Although the categories of cases in which such special relationship can be held to exist are not closed, as yet only two categories have been identified, viz. (1) where there is a fiduciary relationship and (2) where the defendant has voluntarily answered a question or tenders skilled advice or services in circumstances where he knows or ought to know that an identified plaintiff will rely on his answers or advice. In both these categories the special relationship is created by the defendant voluntarily assuming to act in the matter by involving himself in the plaintiff's affairs or by choosing to speak. If he does so assume to act or speak he is said to have assumed responsibility for carrying through the matter he has entered upon. In the words of Lord Reid in *Hedley Byrne* [1964] AC 465, 486 he has 'accepted a relationship . . . which requires him to exercise such care as the circumstances require', i.e. although the extent of the duty will vary from category to category, some duty of care arises from the special relationship. Such relationship can arise even though the defendant has acted in the plaintiff's affairs pursuant to a contract with a third party.

He acknowledged, inevitably, that no fiduciary duty was owed by a solicitor to an intended beneficiary, but saw the case as closely analogous to existing categories of special relationship giving rise to a duty of care to prevent economic loss. He accepted that the beneficiary might not rely on the solicitor's actions, but pointed out that where a duty of care flowed from a fiduciary relationship liability was not dependent upon actual reliance by the plaintiff on the defendant's actions but on the fact that, as the fiduciary well knew, the plaintiff's economic wellbeing was dependent upon the proper discharge by the fiduciary of his duty. The solicitor, by accepting instructions, had entered upon, and therefore assumed responsibility for, the task of procuring the execution of a skilfully drawn will knowing that the beneficiary was wholly dependent upon his carefully carrying out his function.

Alone of the majority, Lord Nolan expressed agreement with the judgments of the Court of Appeal. He accepted of course that there was no contact between the disappointed beneficiary and the solicitor, but thought it highly artificial to treat the solicitors' responsibility to the testator as excluding their responsibility to the beneficiary under the law of tort, described it as astonishing if, as a result of their contract with the testator, they owed a duty of care to him alone to the exclusion of the other members of the family, and regarded it as absurd, on the facts, to suggest that the beneficiaries placed no reliance on the solicitors to carry out the instructions given to them.

We have, therefore, a decade of frenetic litigation culminating in a long-considered majority decision of the House of Lords. No one, given the difficulty experienced and the divided opinions expressed here and abroad, can deny the difficulty of these problems. The dissents in *White v Jones* are sufficient evidence of that. But we have, I would suggest, to confront some uncomfortable questions. Is the law clearer than it was when the debate began? Is it easier than it was for professional advisers to tell their clients whether they have a good claim in other than an obvious case or on the prospects of success? Do the judges have clearer guidance on the decision of borderline cases? Is the law fairer, in the sense of discriminating more accurately between cases that call for redress and cases that do not? Perhaps, as the Chinese philosopher replied when asked if he did not think the French Revolution was a good thing, it is too soon to say. The answer may only become clear when a succession of new cases come before the courts for decision. But I have to confess to what, in other legal contexts, is known as a lurking doubt.

The spectre of tort litigation rioting out of control as many would feel it has done across the Atlantic is, I think, a sound policy reason for a cautious approach towards the recognition of new tort claims. But where foreseeability of harm and a relationship of sufficient proximity are clearly established, it seems to me that convincing reasons are needed in most cases to deny a remedy. I wonder if perhaps we are not becoming too reluctant to recognise the existence of duties because judges have been too ready to find breaches. The test of negligence, particularly in a professional context, is after all stated in the authorities in very exacting terms; no one could hope to go through a lifetime of professional practice without making mistakes, probably a number of them; and I wonder if we have always distinguished as carefully as perhaps we should between the sort of mistake that someone really should not make and that which anyone, with the best will in the world, might well make from time to time. The existence of insurance is no doubt part of the reason. Findings of negligence might be more sparingly made if the consequence was to bankrupt the defendant, cost him his home and deprive him of his possessions. But the existence of insurance can scarcely be a reason for denying the existence of a duty of care in appropriate cases.

Nothing could of course be more question-begging than to speak of appropriate cases, because of course the core issue is what cases are appropriate. In a forthcoming article in the Law Quarterly Review Dr Stapleton, well known as a leading authority in this field, will plead for greater clarity in defining the grounds on which a duty claimed to be owed by A to B should be held to be excluded. This would be a step in the right direction. It is all very well to speak of what is fair and reasonable and just and in accordance with the dictates of good sense and the fitness of things but it is not yet clear that these expressions represent much more than a subjective judgment reached ad hoc on the facts of a particular case. It would be a pity if, in our haste to evacuate the high ground of principle staked out in *Donoghue v Stevenson, Dorset Yacht* and *Anns*, we had adopted a pragmatic approach in which principle counted for little and the length of the judicial foot counted for everything.

I have a concern, too, whether the bounds of liability are not becoming too tightly drawn, so as to exclude from the right to recover those who—as some would think—should be compensated. Take Mr Richardson. A motor mechanic and road haulage manager, with some superficial DIY knowledge, he had a growing family and a house which was becoming too small. So he got hold of a local builder who specialised in extensions, and the builder got his jobbing draftsman to draw some plans. These were submitted (after modification) to the local authority for building regulation approval, but were neither approved nor rejected. They were never properly looked at. But the work went ahead as if the plans had been approved, and was inspected from time to time, without discovery of defects later found to be obvious. A year later the defects came to light and were found to represent a danger to the health and safety of Mr Richardson and his family. It was accepted as foreseeable that if the local authority failed to consider with reasonable care the plans submitted for building regulation consent, or failed to exercise reasonable care in making such inspection of the work in progress as it considered necessary, the health or safety of Mr Richardson and his family might be endangered. Their relationship with the local authority was as proximate as could be, since they were living in the house when consent was sought and the local authority knew they were and Mr Richardson dealt with the local authority direct. It was accepted that the requirement of proximity was satisfied. But the Court of Appeal held, with varying degrees of reluctance, that the local authority owed Mr Richardson no duty of care. He was not, in law, their neighbour.

Many, perhaps most, will applaud this result, pointing to the risks of overkill and defensive medicine and to the growing belief that every human mishap must be the fault of someone, somewhere, who must be liable in damages. Others may feel that a law of tort which does not (subject to issues of causation. remoteness, and contributory negligence) compensate the likes of Mr Richardson is falling down on its job. In the final analysis this, like most interesting legal questions, is not purely a legal question, but a wider social, economic, and political question, bearing on the sort of world we want to live in and the sort of society we want to be. That, after all, is where the Good Samaritan came in. Perhaps it is comforting that Lord Atkin's question remains unanswered.

3

*The Future of the Common Law**

In the preface to his novel *Summer Lightning* P. G. Wodehouse acknowledged that there was already in circulation a work by another author bearing the same title. Undeterred, Wodehouse expressed the hope that his own book might be included in any future list of the one hundred best books called *Summer Lightning*.

I must follow his example. For as recently as 1997 Lord Goff of Chieveley, then the senior law lord but, even more grandly, High Steward of this University, delivered a justly acclaimed Wilberforce Lecture on *The Future of the Common Law*, the very topic I have been asked to address. Perhaps the best advice I can give to those interested in this topic is to read his lecture, available in the International and Comparative Law Quarterly.[1] But I have undertaken to address the topic, and *pacta sunt servanda*. So I must content myself by plundering the riches of his lecture from time to time, and expressing the ambitious hope that my lecture may be included in any future list of the hundred best lectures on *The Future of the Common Law*. We can, I think, exclude from the list Professor Jack Beatson's inaugural lecture as Rouse Ball Professor of English Law at Cambridge, entitled *Has the Common Law a Future?*[2] A measure of wistful pessimism is no doubt to be expected in an Oxonian scholar banished to the Fens.

I should like, perhaps perversely, to approach this after-life of the common law by considering its birth, and for that purpose I take as my text a series of four remarkable and interesting lectures delivered at Cambridge in 1968 by Professor R. C. Van Caenegem, Professor of Mediaeval History and Legal History in the University of Ghent. His subject was *The Birth of the English Common Law*.[3] While certain of his detailed conclusions are the subject of continuing debate among mediaeval scholars, as he is the first to acknowledge, the broad thrust of his argument seems, at any rate to an amateur, superannuated historian such as myself, to be highly convincing.

Like most of the important events in the lives of nations, as of men and women, the birth of the common law was the product of time and chance.[4] The Professor (as I shall, for convenience, call him, although conscious that in this of all cities that would not ordinarily be a distinctive reference) attaches particular importance to the conjunction of two events. The first of these was the creation

---

* The Chatham Lecture delivered on 30 October 1998.
[1] (1997), vol. 46, 745.
[2] [1997] CLJ 291.
[3] Published by the Cambridge University Press (2nd edn. 1998).
[4] Ibid. 107.

by the pre-Conquest English kings of a unified English state. As the Professor puts it:

we should certainly not overlook . . . the achievement of old-English kingship in building a unified state. England had learned to live as one country, under one government with a national network of institutions, officials and courts, during those very centuries when elsewhere the Frankish state and its successors were falling apart and their administration disintegrating.[5]

We may perhaps detect an element of hyperbole in the monument to King Alfred at Stowe which describes him as:

> The mildest, justest and most beneficent of kings,
> Who drove out the Danes, scour'd the Seas, promoted Learning,
> Established Juries, crush'd Corruption,
> Guarded Liberty,
> And was the Founder of the English Constitution.

But it was nevertheless true (again I quote the Professor) that:

No European country had a political organization comparable with England, least of all the illiterate duchy of Normandy.[6]

If there is a tendency among some of us to despise the pre-Conquest rulers of England, it is, I think, largely because King Harold had the misfortune to be defeated at Hastings. In that connection it is perhaps relevant to record that Winston Churchill once asked Field Marshal Alexander, conversationally, whether even with modern arms, equipment and means of communication he could pull off the double which eluded Harold, namely defeating an army of invading Norwegians at Stamford Bridge on 25 September 1066 and then marching south to defeat a well-armed force of invading Normans at Hastings on 14 October 1066. The Field Marshal thought hard, and replied that he could not.[7]

The second event was the accession to power, following the battle of Hastings, of Norman and Angevin kings notable for their power, ruthlessness, administrative ability, wealth and, in the case of Henry II, legal genius.[8] Professor Knowles' characterisation of the Conqueror is no doubt apt:

a drastic, hard directness, a metallic lustre of mind, highly coloured and without delicacy of shading, together with a fiery efficiency that easily became brutality.[9]

For all their faults, the Normans showed (again I quote the Professor):

in Normandy, England and Sicily, a truly great gift for administration, state-building and law enforcement which left a lasting mark on the political development of Europe.[10]

---

[5] Ibid. 93.   [6] Ibid. 9.
[7] Ex rel. Lord Caccia, who heard this conversation, to the author.   [8] Op cit. 93.
[9] D. Knowles, 'Archbishop Thomas Becket: a Character Study', *Proceedings of the British Academy*, 35 (1949); *The Historian and Character* (Cambridge 1963), 101.   [10] Op cit. 11.

Lady Stenton wrote that:

it was Henry II with his returnable writs and his carefully built up bench of judges, through his own versatility and that of his great Justiciar, Rannulf de Glanvill, who had started the wheel in perpetual motion which generated the English Common law.[11]

The Professor adds:

The success of the system was remarkable, the enthusiasm of the plaintiffs evident. It resulted from the quality of the professional royal justices: compare the intellectual level and technical standard (only slightly influenced by the revival of Roman Law) of Glanvill's Treatise with some of the helpless compilations of the earlier years of the century; it was also due to the coherence of the system, clearly understood as such in Glanvill, encompassing all free men in the same royal solicitude, and to the combination of royal efficiency with judicial guarantees. There is no doubt that this nascent Common Law owed much of its popularity to the mode of proof that was the heart of the procedure, the jury verdict.[12]

What we call the common law system did not, of course, spring fully armed into life. Many of its roots lay far in the past, and some of its seeds almost certainly germinated in foreign soil. At the time of the Conquest, and a century later, local justices sat in local courts and administered what passed for justice.[13] The royal writ was a creation of the Anglo-Saxon monarchy.[14] Juries were not an institution unique to England,[15] and may have developed from the Carolingian *inquisitio*.[16] Itinerant royal justices were known in the reign of Henry I.[17] These are deep and learned matters, into which the unlearned venture at their peril. But it can, I think, be safely asserted that the achievement of Henry II was to build on and transform the system and the institutions he inherited, in a way and—importantly—at a date unmatched in Europe. I quote the Professor's judgment:

The Common Law of England—so different from the *jus commune* or common learned law of the European universities—is the oldest national law in Europe. It is the oldest body of law that was common to a whole kingdom and administered by a central court with a nation-wide competence in first instance . . .[18] If the modernization of the law came exceptionally early in England, it was also remarkably systematic. The activity of the justices at Westminster and in eyre and the various actions with which they dealt formed a coherent whole and were grasped and described as such. This new law and its judicial apparatus were national and royal. Not local magnates, but the King and his central justices were the bearers of the whole system and its application was nation-wide. This was very unlike the Continent, where local and regional custom reigned supreme and even the central courts judged according to local custom in appeal cases. This modernized law of England was essentially autochthonous, based on known rule and familiar practice. It owed very little to Roman Law . . .[19]

It is time, if not after time, to attempt to identify certain of the dominant

---

[11] *English Justice*, p. 53.   [12] Op cit. 61.   [13] Op cit. 14.
[14] Op cit. 31.   [15] Op cit. 71.   [16] Op cit. 73.
[17] Op cit. 20.   [18] Op cit. 88.   [19] Op cit. 90.

features of this system established, in particular, by Henry II, since several of these features have, as I suggest, endured with remarkable tenacity to the present day.

First, it was a very highly centralised system.[20] This centralisation was achieved, not by suppressing or denying access to local courts (although means were found to control access),[21] but by offering the litigant a superior system and a more efficacious remedy.[22] This was provided by itinerant justices, travelling the country pursuant to royal command, to administer justice locally, and it is impressive that in 1189 no fewer than 35 such justices took to their horses for this purpose,[23] by the Common Bench at Westminster and the Barons of the Exchequer,[24] and by the bench which travelled with the King himself.[25] This last feature was not unimportant: King John, not otherwise universally admired, was a tireless traveller, visiting parts of his kingdom where his predecessors had rarely, if ever, set foot.[26] One undoubted advantage of a judgment given by a royal justice was that it had the power of the state behind it to enforce it. Henry II was possibly, the Professor suggests,[27] the wealthiest ruler in Europe (deriving his wealth, of course, not from England alone but from Normandy and his other continental possessions, which stretched from Flanders to the Pyrenees also), and he did not take kindly to defiance. So we see:

the rise to absolute predominance of the central royal courts under Henry II as the free man's courts of first instance for all the more important and frequent complaints connected with landholding throughout the country.[28]

And land was, at the time, the only foundation of power and standing;[29] almost everyone lived off it and the Professor likens security of possession then to security of employment in our own times.[30] As the Professor puts it:

Royal will and coercion were the historic mainsprings of Common Law actions . . .[31]

Secondly, it is noteworthy that the royal justices, if not rich and powerful to begin with, became so as a result of their role and their close association with the King.[32] They formed one body of 'justices of the lord king'.[33] It was possible to recruit for the bench men of outstanding quality.[34] Few had received any formal education in civil or canon law, but they became real professionals and upon them the development of the common law depended. The training of practitioners mirrored this highly untheoretical approach:

In England lawyers received their training in the Inns of Court, technical colleges where

---

[20] Op cit. 22.   [21] Op cit. 23.   [22] Op cit. 33.
[23] Op cit. 21.   [24] Op cit. 19.   [25] Op cit. 19.
[26] R. V. Turner, *King John*, 1994, 72; W. L. Warren, *King John*, (1978), 130; J. C. Holt, *Magna Carta and Mediaeval Government* (1985), 95.
[27] Op cit. 102.   [28] Op cit. 19.
[29] A. Harding, *A Social History of English Law* (Penguin 1966), 41.
[30] Op cit. 41.   [31] Op cit. 56.   [32] Op cit. 23.
[33] Op cit. 22.   [34] Op cit. 101.

they learned their craft like every medieval craftsman, in contact with practising masters, not in universities at the feet of scholars who were apt to lose themselves in controversy.[35]

Thirdly, I would mention the royal writs, pioneered before the Conquest but greatly developed and improved thereafter. In earlier days those aggrieved, for example by an allegedly wrongful dispossession from land, would approach the King seeking redress,[36] and if he were persuaded to grant it a writ would be issued requiring the complainant to be put back into possession of the land.[37] It was an obvious disadvantage of this procedure, effective though it was, that the issue of the writ followed a one-sided hearing, which gave no opportunity to the allegedly wrongful dispossessor to justify his action; so it naturally happened that arbitrary and unjust orders were made, which a hearing of both sides would have avoided.[38] Not surprisingly, this obvious defect was quickly recognised; and the wording of the writs was altered, not to enjoin a stated outcome but to enjoin that outcome unless the dispossessor could show why he should not surrender the land,[39] or if the complainant could show that he had been wrongfully dispossessed.[40] This process of course called for judicial enquiry, and for proof of the relevant facts. Thus was laid the foundation of the adversarial forensic procedures which we now take so much for granted; and thus early was developed that notion of fairness which is perhaps the most distinctive contribution of the common law to the jurisprudence of the world.

Fourthly, I come to the all-important subject of juries. In classical times legal disputes were resolved by the application of reason, informed by precedent, to the problem at hand. In earlier medieval times reliance was placed not on reason but on faith. It was on faith that God would intervene to condemn the guilty and acquit the innocent that the ordeals of cold water, and hot iron and judicial combat depended. But in the twelfth century these hallowed modes of proof came under criticism in many European countries, including England.[41] One of the reasons for this was religious: it was thought, on scriptural authority, to be wrong to tempt the Lord thy God.[42] There were probably other reasons: in the ordeal of cold water it was thought to be possible to cheat;[43] there are figures to suggest that in the ordeal by hot iron the acquittal rate was such as to dismay any prosecutor,[44] and judicial combat, apparently unknown in Anglo-Saxon England, was not enforced by the Normans on English litigants.[45] In any event, judicial combat favoured those rich enough to engage the best champions, a fact which prompted a merchant guild in Flanders to set up a system of mutual assistance.[46] In Glanvill's view 'justice was seldom arrived at by battle': as the Professor observes, 'a devastating pronouncement on an institution that was supposed to prove where right and wrong lay'. So the need was there for a rational mode of

[35] Op cit. 88.	[36] Op cit. 34.	[37] Op cit. 35.
[38] Op cit. 36.	[39] Op cit. 52.	[40] Op cit. 40.
[41] Op cit. 68	[42] Op cit. 69.	[43] Op cit. 69–70.
[44] Op cit. 68.	[45] Op cit. 65.	[46] Op cit. 70.

proof, of a more secular character, and not open to the objections just noted. The answer was found in the trial jury, which has been at the heart of the common law from the beginning.[47] The availability of such juries in civil and criminal matters became a matter of course before the royal justices[48] and was one of the key reasons why litigants preferred trial before the royal justices to the local alternatives.

Fifthly, I come—not before time, many would say—to what is perhaps the most characteristic feature of the common law: that it is to be found not in codes, treatises, statutes or learned compilations but in the decisions of the judges on the particular facts of particular cases argued before them, and in the body of precedent built up over the years. As Lord Goff put it,

judge-made law is not only a source of law, but an important source of law.[49]

The reason why, from this very early date, England chose to rely on this unsystematic and piecemeal approach to law-making is not, I think, obscure. Because of its precocious development, the English legal system emerged in a centralized and modernised form before Roman law was in a position to exert any profound influence.[50] The materials needed for a systematic reception of Roman law were not available.[51] And when the Roman law breakthrough came, influential of course throughout much of Europe[52] and, later, in Scotland,[53] England was set in its ways and unwilling to change. In that spirit one must read the barons' famous, and highly Euro-sceptical, declaration in 1236: '*Nolumus leges Angliae mutari*'. Earlier, at the time of Glanvill, there was some unease about unwritten laws.[54] But he himself made a robust defence of them, and in addition provided a masterly summary of the infant common law,[55] of which there was at the time no European equivalent.[56]

One last word before I tear myself away from the twelfth century. We all, I think, at any rate the lawyers among us, tend to regard the common law as, in origin, a very English thing, flesh of our flesh, bone of our bone, a product of the peculiar genius of the English people. It is of course true that the English common law was born here, and grew up here. But we must remind ourselves that when the common law was born there were in this country two nations—the French and the English—and the common law was the law of the rich, powerful, dominant French, not of those among the English who, being unfree, were denied access to it.[57] It is significant that, well over a century after the Conquest, Richard I's chancellor could speak no English, much to the annoyance of the people.[58] While the Normans built on the foundations they found, the common law was none the less the creation of an alien invader.

---

[47] Op cit. 71.   [48] Op cit. 79.   [49] Op cit. 48.
[50] Van Caenegem, op cit. 90; and Preface to 2nd edn., p x.
[51] Op cit. 91.   [52] Op cit. 92.   [53] Op cit. 104.
[54] Op cit. 2.   [55] Op cit. 3.   [56] Op cit. 90.
[57] Op cit. 95.   [58] D. Stenton, *English Society*, 269.

Entering at this point a technically rather impressive time machine, I move in an instant from the twelfth century to the present. To what extent can one still discern in the common law of today the characteristic features which I have identified when the common law was born?

We still operate a system which is, by any international standards, extraordinarily centralized. As the Professor observes:

Even today, after the creation of the county courts in 1846 and the Judicature Acts of 1873 and 1875, English judicial organization astounds the continental observer by its highly centralized nature.[59]

In any developed country there must, no doubt, be one final appellate court, such as we have in the Appellate Committee of the House of Lords. What, I suggest, is striking here is that we have one Court of Appeal, one High Court (albeit with specialised divisions), one Crown Court and one County Court. The judges of these courts (other than the Civil Division of the Court of Appeal) sit in more than one place, but wherever they sit the judges are judges of the same court and administer exactly the same law. The old tradition of itinerant justices setting out from London to administer the law in outlying counties, leaving behind a significant *corps* of judges sitting in London, survives. The trumpets which used to greet the red judge on his arrival in the assize town are muted, and the judicial centre of gravity has shifted from Westminster to the Strand, but to a remarkable extent the organisation introduced in the twelfth century remains operational. That such organization is not an inherent feature of a common law system is plain, as a glance at the United States, with its complex system of interlocking courts and jurisdictions, establishes. But it remains a cardinal feature of our system.

It also remains true, despite the best efforts of the popular press and some political spokesmen, that the standing of common law judges in this country and elsewhere remains high. Lord Goff observes:

Our civilian friends marvel at the status of the judge in the common law world.[60]

In this connection he draws attention to the disparity in numbers: something over 1,000 professional judges in this country following a large increase in recent years; 15,000 in Germany since unification, with 123 members of the Federal Supreme Court alone.[61] In part this disparity is explained by our very heavy reliance on non-professional judges, the lay magistrates, and the United States boasts (or is compelled to admit) some 35,000 judges. It seems safe to assert that the relative smallness of the English bench, combined with our traditions of professional practice and our political arrangements, contribute to the respect generally accorded, not necessarily to individual judges, but to the office of judge. The judges' relationship with the crown has of course altered over the centuries:

---

[59] Op cit. 24.   [60] Op cit. 754.   [61] Op cit. 754.

as the monarch has ceased to be the executive, so the judges have ceased to be servants of the executive. But the monarch continues to receive each High Court judge individually on appointment to confer the accolade, and each new Lord Justice kisses the monarch's hand on appointment to the Privy Council: in more than a merely romantic or post-prandial sense the judges continue proudly to regard themselves as Her Majesty's Judges. All this does, I think, tend to distinguish the English judge from his continental counter-part who has, on graduating, chosen to become a judge rather than a practitioner.

Despite proposals for change (to which I shall return) the jury remains the sole mode of trial in cases of serious crime, and also less serious at the option of the accused. In contrast, the civil jury has died, save effectively in cases of defamation, malicious prosecution and false imprisonment,[62] with notably few red-eyed mourners at the graveside. But paradoxically we have continued to conduct civil trials as if the jury box, still physically present in many civil courts, were still occupied. Rules of evidence designed to save the unqualified and the uneducated from error very largely remain in force. And the entrenched tradition of the single continuous trial, the one fateful encounter when all the evidence is presented and all argument deployed, necessary when a jury of twelve had to meet, deliberate and decide in one place at one time, remains the norm. It is a practice not followed in continental Europe. The civil jury, even if largely extinct, continues to rule us from its grave: in our adherence to increasingly anomalous rules of evidence, in our addiction to the single continuous trial and in our insistence that almost the whole case, evidence and argument, be conducted orally.

As the eight centuries which divide us from Henry II have seen the emergence of Parliament, so they have seen the development of statute as a very important source of law. It would no longer be true to describe the law of England as judge-made law. In some fields—tax, social security, labour law, company law, family law are obvious examples—statutory law is dominant. These areas are, although we do not customarily use the word, codified. In some less obvious areas, such as private international law, statutory inroads are also evident.[63] Whether such statutes give effect to our own domestic policy, or to international commitments deriving from the European Union or other international conventions, they represent a formidable body of law, viewed with some jealousy by common lawyers down the centuries.[64] But there remain other important fields, such as contract and tort, in which statutes, although they intrude, do not dominate; there are no comprehensive codes. In yet other fields, such as judicial review and restitution, the role of statute is minimal. In other cases again, such as those involving the continued treatment of irremediably insensate patients[65] or the sterilisation of

---

[62] Supreme Court Act 1981, s. 69.

[63] e.g. The Civil Jurisdiction and Judgments Acts 1982 and 1991, giving effect to the Brussels and Lugano Conventions, and the Contracts (Applicable Law) Act 1990, giving effect to the Rome Convention.   [64] J. Beatson, op cit. 299.

[65] *Airedale NHS Trust v Bland*, [1993] AC 789.

mentally handicapped adults,[66] the judges are almost literally on their own, with no statute to govern and very little in the way of precedent to guide.

I suppose that almost all practitioners and judges have on occasion been driven almost to desperation by the impenetrability of the statutory material they have been called on to interpret, and have been aggravated by the prolixities of parliamentary draftsmanship, and have felt that this or that issue would have been better left to the pragmatic, piecemeal, fact-dependent determination of the courts. But all must recognize that the complexity and range of modern government, the increasing sophistication of legal issues and relationships, the demands of representative democracy, the growth of regulation and the ever-growing interdependence of national communities make it inconceivable and impracticable that the law should depend on the decisions of the judges alone. The extraordinary thing is, in truth, not that statutes should have proliferated but that the tradition of judicial lawmaking should have proved so durable.

From this diet of case law has sprung the characteristic mode of reasoning habitually used by common lawyers, well described by Lord Goff:

Common lawyers tend to proceed by analogy, moving gradually from case to case. We tend to avoid large, abstract, generalisations, preferring limited, temporary, formulations, the principles gradually emerging from concrete cases as they are decided. In other words, we tend to reason *upwards* from the facts of the cases before us, whereas our continental colleagues tend to reason *downwards* from abstract principles embodied in a code. The result is that we tend to think of each case as having a relatively limited effect, a base for future operations as the law develops forwards from case to case—and occasionally backwards if we are modest enough to recognise that perhaps they have gone too far. This method of working can be epitomised in the statement that common lawyers worship at the shrine of the working hypothesis.[67]

Perhaps, in part at least, because of its mongrel origins, the common law has proved an avid importer and a vigorous exporter. A learned author has written:

English law is like a river. The channel widens and deepens as it flows through the course of years and tributaries join in from time to time. It was first fed by the springs of the common law, but the fountain of equity and the wells of the law merchant and ecclesiastical law have increased the waters of the growing current. And upon the tide is borne the ship which is the soul of England.[68]

While this language may strike some as lacking in academic rigour, it does, I think, express an important truth, that the common law has over the centuries proved a shameless snapper-up of well-considered trifles of foreign law, from Rome, France, Germany, the United States and, of course, in more recent times, from the European Community and the European Court of Human Rights in

---

[66] *Re. F (Mental Patient: Sterilisation)*, [1990] 2 AC 1.
[67] Op cit. 753.
[68] H. Potter, *Outline of English Legal History*, 5th edn., A. K. R. Kiralfy (London, 1958), Introd., 1.

Strasbourg. In parallel with these imports, the common law has been exported to British dominions and dependencies all over the world including those, such as India, South Africa and Ceylon in which a different system of law already prevailed. As Lord Goff observes, although the British Empire has fragmented into a Commonwealth of 53 independent states, the common law persists as perhaps the most enduring link between them[69]—as, at any rate arguably, it is with the United States.

So, at last, to the future. It is time to bring out the crystal ball and embark on the hazardous task of prophecy.

The future is likely, I think, to bring increased devolution of legal services, a trend already evident in the establishment of mercantile courts in major provincial centres, sittings by Chancery judges and judges of the Technical and Construction Court outside London, efforts to arrange for some judicial review applications to be heard on circuit and moves (as yet little more than formal) to accord greater recognition to the separate identity of Wales. But this administrative devolution is unlikely, I think, to weaken the strong centralised character of the law itself, which has been such a marked feature of the English common law from the beginning, unless—and this is the wild card—the somewhat limited political devolution now enacted for Wales were to progress to fuller-blooded devolution on the Scottish model, or to an even greater degree of autonomy. In this last event one could, I suppose, see the Welsh common law becoming as distinct from the English as (say) the Australian. But this seems to me improbable, and a similar development in the English regions seems even more improbable.

The power and prestige of the earliest royal justices, derived from their personal relationship with the sovereign, himself the source of all power, have not as already noted survived intact into modern times; and independence of the executive is of course axiomatic. But the high standing still, as I suggest, enjoyed by the common law judge, not least in England, is not something we can take for granted. Lord Goff said:

There are, of course, continuing worries that the high level of fees may deter successful silks from accepting judicial preferment; but the status of the judge, the interest of the work, and the quality of our existing judiciary, still encourage new recruits of distinction to join their ranks. If, however, this delicate balance should be upset, it could be disastrous for the whole future of our legal system. Disaster would also befall us if the close and fruitful relationship between our judges and advocates, upon which we all depend, and which is the envy of other legal systems, should be destroyed.[70]

I share this apprehension, even more strongly voiced by Sir Gerard Brennan, then Chief Justice of Australia, when opening the 30th Australian Legal Convention in Melbourne in September 1997. Having referred to the financial disincentive to

---

[69] Op cit. 746.   [70] Op cit. 757.

acceptance of judicial appointment, operative here as well as in Australia, the Chief Justice continued:

The respect for, and status of, the office of Judge was and, to a great extent, still is an inducement to accept judicial office. But it is clear that intemperate and ill-informed attacks on particular members of the judiciary, the trumpeting of criticism by commentators who have little knowledge of the judicial method and the absence of effective defence of judicial institutions by the political branches of government have damaged that respect and status to some extent. . . . In the present context, the significance of these developments is that it becomes more difficult to attract practitioners who value both their reputation and their privacy.[71]

This is a serious worry. Just as the quality of cabinet government depends on the quality of those who sit in cabinet, and the quality of a health service depends on the quality of the doctors and nurses, so, particularly with a common law system, its quality depends on the quality of those who make, interpret and administer the law. If the bench were to become the refuge of the mediocre, the unambitious, the timid and the unsuccessful, or if the appointment of judges were to be blighted by a search for the safe, the conformist and the representative, I have no doubt that the quality of justice would suffer and respect for the law decline. Happily, the tradition that most of those judged suitable for higher judicial office are found willing, often eager, to serve remains strong. I am concerned, but by no means despondent, about the future.

The boundaries of jury trial in criminal cases will, I feel sure, be subject to continuing pressure in the years ahead. Such pressure is of course already evident in suggestions that serious fraud trials should be conducted without a jury,[72] and that a defendant's right to opt for trial by jury in either-way cases should be curbed.[73] No doubt the boundaries may over time be adjusted, and defendants accused of serious crime might, as elsewhere, be offered the option to choose trial by judge alone. But confidence in the criminal jury is, I think, so deeply rooted in the public mind as to protect it against newer and less democratic modes of trial. In Blackstone's words:

And, however *convenient* these may appear at first . . . yet, let it again be remembered, that delays and little inconveniences in the forms of justice are the price that all free nations must pay for their liberty in more substantial matters; that these inroads upon this sacred bulwark of the nation are fundamentally opposed to the spirit of our constitution; and that, though begun in trifles, the precedent may gradually increase and spread, to the utter disuse of juries in questions of the most momentous concern.[74]

---

[71] Printed text of address, p. 22.

[72] *Juries in Serious Fraud Trials: A Consultation Document*, Home Office Communication Directorate, Feb. 1998.

[73] *Determining Mode of Trial in Either-Way Cases: A Consultation Paper*, The Stationery Office, July 1998.

[74] *Commentaries on the Laws of England*, vol. IV. (John Murray, 1857), 410.

So I have no doubt that jury trial will remain the norm in most cases of serious crime.

I do not foresee any significant attempt to restrict the classes of civil case now tried by jury, particularly since the main defect of such trials—the making of absurdly high awards of damages by juries—has now, as one hopes, been controlled. But I think it inconceivable that we shall witness any revival or extension of the civil jury. Instead, we shall witness a wholesale discarding of rules and procedures which, however necessary in a jury trial, have little or no place in a trial by judge alone. Thus rules on the admissibility of evidence, already widely neglected, will give way to a pragmatic evaluation of what evidence is worth. The tradition of a single continuous trial before a judge coming to the case afresh will yield to a more spasmodic process of issue determination by a judge with continuing responsibility for the case—in-course assessment as opposed to the one glorious (or inglorious) trial of the Oxford Final Honours Schools. Information technology will reduce the need for some personal appearances before the judge. The trend, already very evident, to place increased reliance on written (as opposed to oral) evidence and argument will continue, and gather pace—but not, I devoutly hope, to the exclusion of oral evidence and argument, since I feel sure that the common law trial as we know it is the best means yet found of uncovering dishonesty and many a time and oft a judge who has formed a provisional view on the written argument alters it as a result of oral debate. The door to radical change has been opened by Lord Woolf's far-sighted reforms, and the civil trial of the future will in many ways look and feel different from the model we now know. The challenge is to ensure that the essential virtues of our existing system survive. I think they will.

It seems inevitable that in the future as in the past statutes will increase and multiply. This does not depress me, for three main reasons. First, the accurate and faithful interpretation of a statute, as of a complex commercial agreement, is not a simple, mechanical task below the notice of a judge. It calls for qualities of judgment and insight scarcely less demanding than the application or development of common law principle. The new Human Rights Bill is a striking example. The judges will of course be called upon to construe the European Convention, scheduled to the Bill, taking account of the jurisprudence built up at Strasbourg. But the Convention is expressed in very broad terms, few of them defined. The application of these broad provisions to particular facts is not in my view, as some have suggested, an unjudicial task; it is a task calling for the highest judicial qualities. Secondly, I do not for my part see the relationship between statutes and common law as that between oil and water, flowing next to but separately from each other in separate streams.[75] Just as, in the absence of contrary indications one expects, and for purposes of interpretation assumes,

---

[75] Beatson, op cit. 300.

that statutes reflect the principles of the common law, so it seems to me right that, in determining the issues of policy which so heavily engage the attention of the higher courts, regard should be paid to the policy inherent in any relevantly analogous statute. If (to take a wholly imaginary example) a statute imposed a certain duty of care on osteopaths, and the question arose, in the absence of statute, whether a similar common law duty should be imposed on chiropractors, it would at first blush seem absurd to reach an answer different from that given by the statute. I see no reason why statute and the common law should not feed and refresh each other. Thirdly, it seems to me inevitable, short of a dramatic but unlikely revolution in our parliamentary procedures, that the scope for judicial lawmaking will remain very extensive. The political imperative to honour manifesto commitments and address perceived public problems is likely in the future, as now, to leave little legislative time for the sort of problem with which the courts are often concerned.

For this reason, I do not think we shall witness any wholesale codification of our private law but rather, as now, specific statutes dealing with limited matters such as sale of goods, bills of exchange or consumer credit. While appreciating the benefits which a comprehensive civil code would bring, in terms of accessibility and saving of cost[76] the development of the law to meet contemporary needs would undoubtedly become, if not impossible,[77] at least more difficult. The criminal law cannot, however, be judicially developed without a very high risk of injustice, whether to an existing defendant or to those convicted in the past. In this field if no other the need for certainty and accessibility is overwhelming. It is accordingly depressing to find Professor Beatson writing, with all the authority of a former law commissioner:

it seems reasonably clear now that statutory reform . . . of the criminal law . . . is unlikely to be by codification but will be by statutes correcting particular defects.[78]

Since I regard the absence of a comprehensive criminal code as a critical deficit in the democratic provision of our country, I hope he is wrong. I do not think so ill of our governors as to believe him right.

In describing the future development of the common law itself, here and elsewhere in the world, one is ineluctably drawn into riverine metaphors. It seems clear that the common law will flow not in a single broad channel, like the Nile, but in a mass of smaller channels, like the Nile Delta. In the United States the common law has already developed its own distinctive character. The diminished role of the Judicial Committee of the Privy Council has given a similar freedom to the courts of Australia, Canada, India and elsewhere to develop principles of their own, and Sir Gerard Brennan was able, with justifiable pride, to describe the common law as:

---

[76] R. Goff, op cit. 751.   [77] Op cit. 752.   [78] Beatson, op cit. 301.

the law created and developed at first by English judges and, in more recent times, chiefly by Australian judges . . .[79]

The Privy Council itself, dismissing an appeal from the New Zealand Court of Appeal, has recognized that:

The ability of the common law to adapt itself to the differing circumstances of the countries in which it has taken root, is not a weakness, but one of its great strengths. Were it not so, the common law would not have flourished as it has, with all the common law countries learning from each other.[80]

Sometimes a line of thinking developed elsewhere will be adopted here;[81] sometimes not.[82] Future development will not be uniform but variegated.

But it seems quite clear that the process of 'learning from each other' will not be confined to the common law countries of the world. I have suggested that the common law has, throughout its history, proved a ready importer and a vigorous exporter. There seem to me to be many reasons why this process should not only continue but gather strength: our ever-increasing exposure to the laws and legal thinking of our European neighbours; the law of the European Union, with its reliance on the laws common to the member states; the law of human rights, as developed under the European Convention, the International Covenant on Civil and Political Rights and other international instruments of the same kind; the harmonising effect of international trade and finance in a world of instant communication; our disproportionate involvement in international arbitration; and the increasing globalisation of almost all activity. It will surely be true in the future, as never before, that no island is an island. But as we borrow and domesticize the thinking of others so others will borrow from us, as they already have: the Russians, for example, have embarked on reviving the jury system; the Italians have explored the merits of a more adversarial procedure; the choice of law rules adopted in the Contract (Applicable Law) Act 1990 reflect very clearly our own common law rules.

So, like Lord Goff, my prognosis for the future is cautiously optimistic:[83] I conclude with his words:

Above all, the fundamental ethos of the common law will, I believe, remain intact. The common law has already fathered the idea of the rule of law, surely the most important legal principle in the world. Its underlying philosophy of pragmatism may be unpopular in some quarters; but it may be justified in practical terms and it is, I believe, inbred into our very being, and shared by us with millions of people throughout the world. It can operate as a brake on unbridled idealism; and surely we can see, from the history of the

---

[79] Address on Retirement (21 May 1998), 10.
[80] *Invercargill City Council v Hamilton* [1996] AC 624 at 640.
[81] e.g. *Caparo Industries PLC v Dickman* [1990] 2 AC 605 at 633.
[82] e.g. *Reynolds v Times Newspapers Ltd* [1998] 3 WLR 862 at 907.
[83] Op cit. 759.

twentieth century, how necessary such a brake is for the well-being of all nations. Let us therefore continue to worship at the shrine of the working hypothesis, and continue too to contemplate the great idea with all the caution bred of common sense and our long experience.[84]

---

[84] Op cit. 760.

4

Lecture at Toynbee Hall on the Centenary of its Legal Advice Centre*

On its centenary in 1984, Toynbee Hall was justly acclaimed as the pioneering and imaginative venture it was, a product of that serious, high-minded intelligent and practical concern for others which distinguished so many of the later Victorians. The centenary of the Poor Man's Lawyer at Toynbee Hall—or the Legal Advice Centre as it is now called—is inevitably a lesser event, for it is only one of the services which Toynbee Hall has rendered to the community since its foundation. But like the foundation of Toynbee Hall itself, this service responded to a pressing and unmet social need; it has proved enormously influential; it has been of value to countless people; and it seems likely that in the years ahead, in conditions vastly different from the 1890s, it will continue to be of value. So it must, I think, be appropriate to celebrate this centenary also, and in doing so both to remind ourselves of the past and to ponder the possible shape of the future.

The Poor Man's Lawyer established here 100 years ago was not, it seems, the first of its kind in this country. That accolade belongs to the Mansfield House Settlement in Canning Town, set up in 1890.[1] And even that was anticipated by a number of public-spirited Germans in New York City who in 1887 established the German Law Protection Society, later called The Legal Aid Society of New York.[2] It was not long, however, before the initiative at Mansfield House was repeated here, at Cambridge House in Camberwell and in Manchester.[3] The rationale underlying these schemes was simple and very compelling. As a later author was to put it:

Our law makes access to the Courts dependent on the payment of fees and renders assistance by skilled lawyers in many cases indispensable. Under such a legal system the question of legal aid to those who cannot pay must not be allowed to play a Cinderella part. Its solution decides nothing less than the extent to which the State in which that system is in force is willing to grant legal protection to its subjects. Where there is no legal protection, there is in effect no law. In so far as citizens are precluded from access to the Courts, the rules of the law which they would like to invoke are for them as good as non-existent.[4]

---

* The Barnett Lecture delivered on 11 June 1998 at Toynbee Hall.
[1] R. Egerton, 'Historical Aspects of Legal Aid', 61 LQR (1945) 87 at 92.
[2] W. E. Walz, 'Legal Aid Societies—Their Nature, History, Scope, Methods and Results' (1914) 7 Maine LR 111 at 112.
[3] Egerton, op cit., at 92.
[4] E. J. Cohn, 'Legal Aid for the Poor: A Study in Comparative Law and Legal Reform', 59 LQR (1943) 250 at 251.

For the public whom the Poor Man's Lawyer here at Toynbee Hall sought to serve, there was in effect no law; the rules of law which they would have liked to invoke were indeed for them as good as non-existent—except, of course, when those laws were invoked against them.

One is tempted to observe, with apologies to Laurence Sterne, that they order these matters better in Scotland. The oldest statutory authority on legal aid for the poor, anywhere in the world, appears to be a Scottish Act of 1424[5] which provided that:

If there be any poor creature for default of cunning or means that cannot or may not follow his cause

free legal assistance should be given to him. Under this Act the 'poor creature' would seek admission to the Poor's Roll, which would require him to show both that he was qualified on grounds of poverty and that he had a *probabilis causa litigandi*, in other words a reasonable cause of action.[6] If an applicant showed himself to be qualified on both grounds, then either in the Court of Session or the Sheriff courts counsel and agents would be appointed to act for him free of charge, and no court fees would be payable. If he succeeded, however, and was found to be entitled to expenses, the professional charges of counsel and solicitors and court dues were included in his expenses and on recovery were to be paid to those entitled. The strength of this system, from the client's point of view, was that it gave him advice and assistance well before a trial began. The weakness was that it only applied in litigious matters, civil or criminal, and was unavailable where no court proceedings were in prospect. This omission was made good, just after the founding of the Poor Man's Lawyer here at Toynbee Hall, by the establishment of the Edinburgh Legal Dispensary, which offered a somewhat similar service: four consulting rooms were open every Tuesday evening throughout the year, and lawyers served for a month at a time, giving their services voluntarily.[7] By the mid-1930s the number of petitions to be admitted to the Poor's Roll in the Court of Session and in the Sheriff courts was running at an annual total of just over 200 and just over 2,000 respectively, with the great majority of petitions being accepted.[8] By the same date, the number of those consulting the Edinburgh Legal Dispensary was approaching an annual total of 2,000.[9] From 1929 onwards, facilities for free legal advice were also provided under the auspices of the City of Glasgow Society of Social Service.[10]

An English statute of 1494 purported on its face to give much the same help to indigent litigants as the earlier Scottish Act.[11] It provided:

---

[5] Cohn, op cit., at 253, n.8; 79 Sol. Jo. (1935) 713.
[6] S. Shaw, 'Justice and the Poor. A Plea for Legal Insurance' (1936) SLT 135 at 136.
[7] Ibid.   [8] Ibid., at 142.   [9] Ibid., at 143.
[10] Ibid., at 137.   [11] See Egerton, op cit., at 87.

Every poor person . . . shall have . . . writ or writs . . . according to the nature of their causes, therefore paying nothing to your Highness for the seals of the same, nor to any person for the writing of the same writ or writs; . . . and that the Lord Chancellor shall assign . . . learned counsel and attorneys for the same without any reward taking thereof; and . . . the Justices shall assign to the same poor person or persons counsel learned by their discretion, which shall give their counsel nothing taking for the same; and likewise the Justices shall appoint attorney and attorneys for the same poor person or persons and all other officers requisite . . . which shall do their duties without any reward for their counsel, help and business in the same.[12]

This provision only applied to plaintiffs, (although it was extended to cover defendants also in the Chancery Courts), it only applied to civil proceedings and it did not cover advice or help otherwise than for purposes of litigation. But it was on its face a generous measure. It was, however, deprived of practical effect by the introduction of procedural requirements designed to restrict the flow of causes reaching the court under it. Thus a requirement was introduced to obtain a certificate from counsel on the merits of the case, and a solicitor had to be found who was willing to prepare an affidavit and a case to counsel and thereby run the risk of being chosen by the court to conduct the case free of charge. These requirements were no doubt effective to prevent undeserving cases reaching the court; by the end of the last century they were preventing deserving cases also.[13]

If the position of the poor man needing advice or assistance in the civil field was dire, the position of the criminal defendant was even worse. In the 18th century, the criminal trial was a very amateur affair.[14] Most prosecutions were brought by private individuals in the hope of reward. There were no professional prosecutors. The majority of trials were conducted without lawyers. The defendant had no right to give evidence. And one suspects that many of the judges were extremely arbitrary. The nineteenth century saw a movement towards much greater professionalization. In many cases prosecutors were represented by counsel. And in 1836, after failures in 1821, 1824, 1826, and 1834, a measure was enacted granting defence counsel the right to address the jury on behalf of the accused.[15] This led to a rapid expansion of the Bar, with young barristers conducting defences for a fairly standard fee of 1 guinea per case. But this was a far from nominal sum, well beyond the means of many of those in the dock. In the most serious cases, such as murder, it was the practice for judges to ask barristers to represent defendants without any fee, but this request was rarely if ever made until the trial was on the point of beginning. As the century progressed, the dock brief came into vogue, enabling prisoners to be defended by any barrister robed and in court when the selection was made; but the fee of £1. 3*s*. 6*d*. was again far from nominal and only a minority of prisoners was able to raise such a

[12] Ibid.   [13] Ibid., at 87–8.
[14] See T. Goriely, 'The Development of Criminal Legal Aid in England and Wales' in Young and Wall (eds) *Access to Criminal Justice: Legal Aid, Lawyers and the Defence of Liberty* (1996).
[15] Ibid., at 29.

large amount. The great majority of criminal defendants in trials a century ago were unrepresented. The problem was graphically described by Sir James Stephen in his History of the Criminal Law published in 1883:

> It must be remembered that most persons accused of crime are poor, stupid and helpless. They are often defended by solicitors who confine their exertions to getting a copy of the depositions and endorsing it with the name of some counsel to whom they pay a very small fee, so that even when prisoners are defended by counsel the defence is often extremely imperfect, and consists rather of what occurs at the moment to the solicitor and counsel than of what the man himself would say if he knew how to say it. When a prisoner is undefended his position is often pitiable, even if he has a good case. An ignorant uneducated man has the greatest possible difficulty in collecting his ideas, and seeing the bearing of facts alleged. He is utterly unaccustomed to sustained attention or systematic thought, and it often appears to me as if the proceedings on a trial which to any experienced person appear plain and simple, must pass before the eyes and mind of the prisoner like a dream he cannot grasp.[16]

In 1898 criminal defendants at long last won the right to testify on their own behalf; but this meant that those who chose to exercise that right were exposed to cross-examination by skilful prosecuting counsel, while lacking any advocate to advise them or protect their interests.

Recognizing that the plight of unrepresented poor defendants was scandalous, a group of leading lawyers promoted a Bill in 1903 for their assistance. The Home Office, thinking it difficult to oppose the Bill 'in principle',[17] was reassured that it stood no chance of becoming law.[18] But it did: henceforward magistrates could grant legal aid to prisoners on committal for trial, but only if the prisoner disclosed his defence and showed that he had a proper case to advance. Lawyers would be paid out of local funds. The Poor Prisoners' Defence Act 1903, as the Bill became, proved highly unsuccessful in practice. Most defendants were unaware of it. So were many magistrates, and those who did know of it were reluctant to make orders which would increase the burden on local ratepayers.[19] The Society of Clerks of the Peace regarded the scheme as a means by which villains could escape their just deserts at the public expense.[20] Judges were inclined to think that the rights of prisoners were safe in their hands.[21] The number of cases in which aid was granted was, it seems, extremely low.

So unsuccessful was the Act, and so obvious the need for improvement, that pressure for reform built up. Sir Claude Schuster, the long-serving and highly influential Permanent Secretary to the Lord Chancellor, recorded that he looked upon the move for reform with horror.[22] But something had to be done, and the first response was to appoint a committee to investigate, under the chairmanship of Mr Justice Finlay and with what must have seemed a very safe membership.[23]

---

[16] Quoted by Goriely, op cit., at 32.   [17] Ibid., at 35.   [18] Ibid.
[19] Ibid., at 37.   [20] Ibid.   [21] Ibid.   [22] Ibid., at 38.
[23] Ibid., at 38, n. 63.

The Committee did indeed conclude that the present system in criminal cases worked satisfactorily and that no alterations were urgently or imperatively required.[24] Most prisoners in its view were manifestly so guilty as to leave no room for doubt.[25] But the Committee did recognize some small deficiencies. It did not think that defendants should be precluded from assistance because they failed to disclose their defence, as other defendants would not be obliged to do. Instead, magistrates should have discretion to grant legal aid for jury trial when it was in the interests of justice to do so. In grave charges, such as murder, it was recommended that help should be available at committal. In a few summary trials magistrates should also be able to grant legal aid if it was necessary in the interests of justice by reason of the exceptional circumstances of the case.[26] These proposals were generally well received, save by the Home Office which felt that 'the public should not spend money in helping a guilty man to establish a false defence'.[27] A Private Member's Bill introduced into the House of Commons in 1928, and reintroduced the following year, earned reluctant Home Office support, provided that the Home Office could re-write its provisions. The Home Office regarded it as 'absurd' that steps should be taken to inform defendants of their rights.[28] Thus, with much official hesitation and reluctance, the Poor Prisoners' Defence Act 1930 became law.[29] It removed the requirement that prisoners should disclose their defence on committal, and made legal aid automatic in murder trials. In other cases magistrates were given wide discretion to grant legal aid where the defendants' means were insufficient and it appeared to them to be desirable in the interests of justice. Some help was given in summary trials in exceptional circumstances. And for grave charges or again in exceptional circumstances legal aid could be provided before committal.[30]

Meanwhile a belated attempt was made to improve the lot of poor litigants in the High Court. A scheme was launched in 1925, administered by the Law Society and provincial Law Societies, under which solicitors and barristers gave their services for nothing and free legal aid was in that way afforded to poor persons. The scheme only operated in the High Court, and the vast majority of the cases handled were matrimonial. Having in its first report dealt with legal assistance for poor criminal defendants, Mr Justice Finlay and his Committee moved on to consider legal advice and aid in civil cases. In its final report published in 1928 the Committee lavished praise on the work done by Poor Man's Lawyers, which it described in some detail, and felt that the need of the poor to be advised could be best met by the expansion of such centres.[31] It did not favour giving free legal assistance to poor litigants in the county court, fearing that this would lead to undesirable litigiousness.[32] Nor did it, for a variety of unpersuasive reasons,

---

[24] First Report of the Committee on Legal Aid for the Poor, Cmd. 2638, (1926), para. 22.

[25] Ibid., para. 9.   [26] Ibid., para. 15.   [27] Goriely, op. cit., at 39.

[28] Ibid.   [29] Ibid., at 39–40.   [30] Ibid., at 40.

[31] Cmd. 3016 (1928), para. 9.   [32] Ibid., para. 13.

favour extending the Poor Persons Rules of the High Court to the county court, save where a High Court action assisted in that way was remitted to the county court. In a passage which I think deserves quotation the Committee reported:

It was suggested to us by one witness, whose experience well entitled his evidence to careful consideration, that provision should be made for legal aid being given to all persons insured under the National Health Insurance Acts. This suggestion depends really upon a supposed analogy between medical advice in the case of sickness or accident and legal advice. The analogy is in our opinion infelicitous. It was admitted that the application of the Acts to legal advice would be attended with much difficulty, and that there was an absence of reliable data upon which the finance of such a scheme could be computed. We are convinced that the scheme would, in practice, prove unworkable chiefly because the suggested analogy between medical benefit and the proposed legal benefit does not exist. . . . It is manifestly in the interests of a State that its citizens should be healthy, not that they should be litigious.[33]

It does not seem to have occurred to the Committee that it might be in the interests of a State, and even its duty, to ensure that even its poorest citizens were able to enjoy the protection of the laws by which they were governed. To fill the gap, the Bentham Committee, a charitable organisation, was established in 1929 to conduct cases in the county courts and magistrates' courts in London. The result was not an upsurge of litigiousness.[34]

This, impressionistically described, is the environment in which the Poor Man's Lawyer at Toynbee Hall operated for most of its first half-century of life. A paper read to the Law Society in 1935 described what was, I suspect, a fairly typical picture, although the centre described was not identified.[35] The centre would be open on one evening a week for 2 or 3 hours, during which members of the public would attend and receive free legal advice from members of the Bar and solicitors. The lawyers would have little in the way of a library beyond, perhaps, a book on the Rent Restriction Acts, a book on the Workmen's Compensation Acts, Stone's Justices' Manual and the County Court Practice.[36] The paper continued:

As can be imagined, many of the problems presented to the Poor Man's lawyer have very little to do with the law. Any one equipped with a sympathetic nature and a fund of common-sense could deal with many of the applicants. Some of the cases are most trivial and some of them profoundly tragic. It is common to find cases where advantage has been taken of a person's poverty to attempt to deprive him of his legal rights. No doubt experiences differ in each centre as to the class of cases which preponderates. My own experience has been that what may be called Landlord and Tenant cases head the list, including, of course, a large number of cases arising out of the Rent Restriction Acts. It is surprising how sometimes poor persons have quite a good idea of the law on this subject, though perhaps more often they have an entirely wrong idea which may take some time to dispel.

---

[33] Ibid., paras. 16, 17.   [34] Egerton, op. cit., at 91.
[35] Pritchard, 79 Sol. Jo. (1935) 713 at 714. See also H. W. Samuell, 'An Evening with a Poor Man's Lawyer', *The Conveyancer* (Mar. 1941), 195.   [36] A. L. Pritchard, op. cit., at 714.

Probably the next largest class of cases consist of matrimonial or similar domestic problems, and after that cases of master and servant, including workmen's compensation cases, claims for wrongful dismissal, etc. Many cases arise from hire-purchase agreements usually relating to some luxury article such as a gramophone. In such cases a solicitor giving advice is often placed in a difficulty owing to the fact that the client has not got a copy of the agreement.[37]

Another author recalls:

This applicant had lost most of his clothing and his small amount of furniture had been seriously damaged as a result of a fire in the house where he lived. Was his landlord liable for the damage, which he said amounted to £30, as the fire had occurred through the stupidity and carelessness of a man employed by the landlord to remove a quantity of cardboard boxes from the ground floor or basement of the house, where he worked by the light of an unprotected candle?

The Judge of the Whitechapel County Court said Yes, and assessed the damages at £29, which encouraged the client to return to the P.M.L. with two other clients, fellow tenants of his, with exactly similar claims.[38]

This service offered at Toynbee Hall was very highly regarded in the area. As the centenary history records, when a workman in the Shoreditch County Court pleaded that he had transgressed in ignorance of the law the judge replied: 'Have you never heard of Toynbee Hall? The lawyers there would give you the soundest advice obtainable, and it will cost you nothing.'[39] When one reads in the same volume that among the advisers attending here were those who later became Lord Roskill, Lord Birkett, Mr Justice Talbot, Lord Justice Browne, and Sir Frank Milton, the Chief Metropolitan Stipendiary Magistrate, among other very distinguished lawyers, the quality of the advice given speaks for itself.[40] Whatever reservations one may have about the main thrust of the Finlay Committee's report on civil legal aid, there can be no doubting the justice of the tribute which it paid to the work of Poor Man's Lawyers. By 1928 there were twenty-seven such centres operating in London, several of them at more than one address; and there were in addition another twenty-seven such centres run by the three political parties.[41] Similar schemes were to be found in ten major provincial towns, some but by no means all of these offering representation as well as advice.[42] The business handled by these centres was very considerable. An article published in 1940 recorded that the Poor Man's Lawyers' Association in Birmingham had dealt in 1938 with over 4,000 cases, and Manchester had dealt with almost as many.[43] At Cambridge House in Camberwell about 3,000 persons were advised annually.[44] It, like Toynbee Hall, carried its cases right through to trial, as compared with other London centres which referred those needing action to the Bentham

---

[37] Ibid.   [38] Samuell, op. cit., at 197.
[39] Asa Briggs and Anne Macartney, 'Toynbee Hall—The First Hundred Years' (1984), at 99.
[40] Ibid.   [41] Final Report of Finlay Committee, App. III.
[42] Ibid.
[43] 'The Poor Man's Lawyer', 104 JP & LQR (March 1940), 160.   [44] Ibid.

Committee. Increasingly, however, it was coming to be recognized that this ad hoc response, for all its virtues, could not meet the changing expectations of the public. Partly perhaps this was due to the war, during which each of the three Services set up a department to give free advice to serving personnel.[45] The Law Society itself set up a department with a staff of sixty to conduct divorce cases.[46] When consideration was given to the new and fairer Britain which was to follow the war, the provision of legal assistance to the poor featured in the discussion. And it seems very likely, although unprovable, that impetus was given to the movement for reform by the work of foreign scholars, refugees from fascist oppression, who were able to compare arrangements in this country with those in the countries of continental Europe.[47] The comparison was very much to our disadvantage. One of these scholars, Dr E. J. Cohn, wrote with a clarity and directness which remain compelling:

Legal aid is a service which the modern State owes to its citizens as a matter of principle. It is part of that protection of the citizen's individuality which, in our modern conception of the relation between the citizen and the State, can be claimed by those citizens who are too weak to protect themselves. Just as the modern State tries to protect the poorer classes against the common dangers of life, such as unemployment, disease, old age, social oppression, etc., so it should protect them when legal difficulties arise. Indeed, the case for such protection is stronger than the case for any other form of protection. The State is not responsible for the outbreak of epidemics, for old age or economic crises. But the State is responsible for the law. That law again is made for the protection of all citizens, poor and rich alike. It is therefore the duty of the State to make its machinery work alike for the rich and the poor.[48]

His view was very clear:

Legal aid is not a favour bestowed upon a poor applicant by the members of the Bar. It is— or at least it should by now be—a right granted to him by the State as part of the protection which the State bestows upon its citizens.[49]

In May 1944 Viscount Simon, the Lord Chancellor, wrote to Herbert Morrison, the Home Secretary, informing him that he was setting up a committee under the chairmanship of Lord Rushcliffe to consider the reform of legal aid within the civil courts. In direct contradiction of the views of the Finlay Committee he commented that:

If we make efforts to get a better medical service for people who are ill, had we better not see whether there is anything to be done about better legal advice and assistance for those who have the misfortune to be involved in a legal dispute.[50]

---

[45] Egerton, op. cit., at 93.   [46] Ibid.
[47] Cohn, op. cit., 251, 359; see also L. Loewensohn, 'The Poor Man's Right to Legal Aid—A Comparative View', 61 Scottish LR (1945), 55.
[48] Cohn, op. cit., at 256.   [49] Ibid., at 265.
[50] Goriely, op. cit., at 41.

In May 1945—a month memorable in other ways also—the Rushcliffe Committee reported. It recommended that there should be a salaried advice scheme to provide initial help with both civil and criminal matters, a recommendation not implemented up to now. On the civil side, it recommended a comprehensive scheme in which the State would pay private lawyers to represent poor and middle income litigants before a wide range of courts and tribunals, subject only to their showing a reasonable case to argue.[51] This report was hailed by Dr Cohn as:

a document of first-rate significance for the entire development of English law. Its acceptance will result in a considerable proportion of all Court business being financed by the State.[52]

It was essentially this scheme, as recommended by Rushcliffe, which was in due course enacted as the Legal Aid and Advice Act 1949. On the criminal side Rushcliffe's recommendations were less far reaching, partly because there was less need for reform. Certain changes were, however, recommended, among them, almost as an aside, a recommendation that the costs of criminal legal aid should be borne by taxpayers rather than ratepayers.[53] This recommendation was eventually implemented in 1960, and had a dramatic effect on the generosity of those responsible for granting legal aid to criminal defendants.[54]

The last half century has seen a number of very important developments in this field. I shall make brief reference to some of the more important. First, it has seen a proliferation of tribunals, bodies set up to adjudicate on issues involving a specialized subject-matter, the intention being that proceedings should be conducted with a minimum of formality so as not to disadvantage the unrepresented party. Research shows that this is a result which has proved very hard to achieve.[55] But there are now some seventy-eight tribunals for which the Council on Tribunals is responsible. Secondly, the last half century has seen the rise and multiplication of Citizens' Advice Bureaux offering free advice to members of the public on questions of law and almost anything else. Initially the bureaux were a response to war: within a month of September 1939, 200 had been established, and by 1943 the figure had reached over 1,000.[56] The National Association of Citizens' Advice Bureaux now has over 700 members; between them they receive nearly £60m in central government and local authority funding.[57] Thirdly, there has, since the founding of the first law centre in North Kensington in 1970, been

---

[51] Ibid.

[52] Cohn, 'Legal Aid to the Poor and the Rushcliffe Report', 9 MLR (1946) 58 at 66.

[53] Goriely, op. cit., at 42.

[54] Ibid., at 43.

[55] H. Genn and Y. Genn, 'The Effectiveness of Representation at Tribunals', Report to Lord Chancellor, July 1989.

[56] D. Lovelock, 'Review of the National Association of Citizens' Advice Bureaux', Cmnd. 9139 (Feb. 1984), chap. 4, para. 4.3.

[57] LCD Briefing Paper.

a rapid growth of such centres elsewhere. The Law Centres Federation now has fifty-three members; the Federation and the centres between them received over £13m from public sources during the year 1996/7.[58] At these centres members of the public have been able to obtain advice on matters such as disability, immigration, discrimination, and welfare in which the centres have acquired great expertise.[59] Fourthly, we have seen a very rapid growth of advice agencies. The Federation of Independent Advice Centres has some 800 members,[60] covering fields so various that the Law Society has published a Referral Guide to assist solicitors to refer clients to the appropriate agency. If I mention the Child Poverty Action Group, Shelter, Youth Access, the Money Advice Association, Dial UK (disability information and advice lines) and the Refugee Legal Centre, it is only to illustrate the breadth of the fields which these agencies cover. In the year 1993/94 the Federation and its members received some £74m in public funding, mostly from local government. Fifthly, reference should be made to the growth of Ombudsman schemes. The National Consumer Council has published an A–Z of such schemes in Britain and Ireland. Some of these are very well known. Others, such as the Funeral Ombudsman, are perhaps less so. Almost all these bodies (not all bearing the name Ombudsman) have power to direct or recommend the payment of compensation: the exceptions are the Police Complaints Authorities in England and Wales and Northern Ireland and the Broadcasting Standards Commission. The Press Complaints Commission does not appear in the guide; if it did, it would provide another exception. Sixthly, we have seen the introduction, for the first time in England and Wales, of conditional fees, that is, arrangements which provide for barristers and solicitors to undertake cases on the condition that they receive no fee if the client's case is unsuccessful but an enhanced fee if it succeeds. Such arrangements, made possible by section 58 of the Courts and Legal Services Act 1990, were in 1995 made applicable in proceedings involving personal injury, insolvency and human rights cases in Europe. It is thought that conditional fee agreements may have been made in one or two human rights cases,[61] and in a trickle of insolvency cases;[62] but in the relatively short period (about 30 months) since such agreements have become possible it appears that about 34,000 such agreements have been made in personal injury cases.[63] Seventhly, we have seen the growth of alternative methods of resolving disputes, in particular by mediation and conciliation. A number of bodies, among them the Centre for Dispute Resolution, the Chartered Institute of Arbitrators and Mediation UK, have sponsored such processes. Acceptance of these processes has been disappointingly slow, but progress, if slow, has been steady, and there is increasing recognition, not least among professional lawyers, that such processes have a valuable contribution to make in the resolution of some otherwise

---

[58] Ibid.
[59] See, for example, the Law Centre Federation Annual Report 1996–7.
[60] LCD Briefing Paper.
[61] 'Future Conditional', *Law Society Gazette* (Mar. 1998) 18 at 22.   [62] Ibid.
[63] 'Access to Justice with Conditional Fees', LCD Consultation Paper (Mar. 1998), para. 2.5.

very intractable disputes. Eighthly, mention should be made of work which the Bar and solicitors undertake *pro bono*. Since 1972 the Bar has run its Free Representation Unit, through which Bar students, pupils and young barristers have provided representation for otherwise unrepresented members of the public. In 1996 the unit provided such representation to 1,615 individuals.[64] In May 1996 the Bar established a Pro Bono Unit to co-ordinate the *pro bono* contributions of practising barristers. To date some 800 barristers (including 130 QCs) have joined the register of those ready to offer at least 3 days' advice and assistance each year without charge.[65] Even more recently a number of leading firms of solicitors have launched the Solicitors' Pro Bono Group with a view to co-ordinating the *pro bono* work which solicitors have always done and continue to do on behalf of needy clients up and down the country.[66] This is a field in which other jurisdictions, particularly in the United States and parts of Australia, have moved much more quickly and much more effectively than we have ourselves. Finally, attempts have been made to reform civil procedures so as to reduce delay and expense and make legal proceedings less unaffordable to those of limited means. There can scarcely have been a year during the last half century when some body has not reported on means of achieving that end. But there can be no doubt that the most far-reaching and comprehensive reforms to have been proposed during this long period have been those proposed by Lord Woolf in his two reports on Access to Justice. These proposals have the very clear intention of reducing the cost of proceedings, particularly of smaller actions, so as to make it less grossly disproportionate to the sum in dispute.

Through all these years, the Legal Advice Centre at Toynbee Hall has continued to operate on lines remarkably similar to those on which it began, open on one evening a week, staffed by volunteers and giving help and advice, by no means all of it legal, to the poor and the disadvantaged. Apprehension in the early 1970s that the growth of legal aid might lead to a decline in demand for the Centre's services quickly proved to be ill-founded. As the booklet prepared for this centenary points out, the level of demand has remained very constant: around 1,500 cases were handled in 1973; in 1993 the Centre handled 1,601. The mix of cases has also remained very constant: while problems concerning immigration and the right to buy council properties did not loom large a century ago, other problems—matrimonial and family cases, disputes between landlord and tenant, personal injuries, employment problems and crime—have remained a staple part of the diet. There can be no doubt that the volunteers' services are as valuable today as they have ever been, perhaps, even more so, and it is right that their work, and the support of leading City firms, in particular Linklaters and Paines, should be warmly applauded.

---

[64] 'Access to Justice: A Fair Way Forward', The Bar's Response to the Government's Proposals (Jan. 1998), para. 8.2.   [65] Ibid., para. 8.3.

[66] The Group was formed in November 1996 following a meeting of fifty solicitors from all parts of the country.

Despite all the initiatives I have mentioned, however, and despite the continuing and valuable work done by legal advice centres such as that at Toynbee Hall, there can be no doubt that the main burden of bringing legal advice and representation to those who cannot pay for it has fallen over the last half century on the legal aid scheme, through duty solicitor schemes established in police stations and courts, through the green form scheme providing for initial advice, through assistance by way of representation and through the main legal aid scheme established in 1949 and modified but not fundamentally altered since. Over the past half century the scheme has, to a very great extent, lived up to the ideals of those who conceived and established it: countless people have been enabled by it to assert and defend their rights in a way which they could not otherwise have done. But during the 1990s, the scheme has come under great and growing pressure. In part this has stemmed from recognition that many cases have been brought with the benefit of legal aid which no well-advised client would have thought it prudent to finance from his own resources. But there is nothing new in this: it has been known for years that professional advisers, naturally and properly anxious for their clients to be compensated, are inclined to be more sanguine about the prospects when failure means the loss of a potential benefit rather than the suffering of a substantial actual loss. Partly it has stemmed from recognition of an unfairness inherent in the existing system: a privately funded defendant facing a legally aided plaintiff has a choice between paying his own costs if he wins and both parties' costs if he loses; so he has an obvious incentive to pay the plaintiff something, however unmeritorious the claim, simply to restrict his losses. But this again is nothing new. It has been a feature of the scheme from the beginning, and this element of unfairness has long been recognized. It seems unlikely that these two objections, for all their force, would have led to pressure for a fundamental change of the system but for a third objection of incomparably greater weight: that the system has become hugely and uncontrollably expensive. Net expenditure of £682m in 1990–1 rose within 6 years to more than double, a total of £1477m. Over the period the average cost of actions funded has risen by more than the rate of inflation, while the number of people helped (in the civil and matrimonial fields) has fallen.[67] Some practitioners appear to have been rewarded, out of the public purse, with considerable generosity. The last government attempted to grapple with the problem of rising cost by restricting eligibility for and tightening the administration of legal aid. But these efforts proved unavailing.

The present government were elected to office on a manifesto which contained the following pledge:

Labour will undertake a wide-ranging review both of the reform of the civil justice system and Legal Aid. We will achieve value for money for the tax-payer and the consumer. A

---

[67] Lord Chancellor, speech to Law Society at Cardiff, 18 Oct. 1997; Lord Chancellor, HL Deb. 9 December 1997, cols. 41–2; 'Access to Justice with Conditional Fees' (Mar. 1998), paras. 1.4, 3.3.

community legal service will develop local, regional and national plans for the development of Legal Aid according to the needs and priorities of regions and areas. The key to success will be to promote a partnership between the voluntary sector, the legal profession and the Legal Aid Board.[68]

Indications of the shape which the proposed community legal service may take have so far been given only in very general terms. But it seems very likely that an attempt will be made, with the benefit of new information technology, to build on the existing network of agencies already offering advice and representation.[69] In relation to the reform of legal aid, the government have given very clear indications of their thinking, which has developed somewhat over recent months in the light of representations and discussions. The main thrust of the current proposals, as derived from a consultation paper issued in March 1998 (limited to civil, excluding matrimonial, legal aid), are these:[70]

1. Clients and lawyers will be free to enter into conditional fee agreements in any proceedings other than family and criminal cases.[71]

2. The government will remove, over time as the market for conditional fees and supporting insurance and funding develops, most money and damages claims from the scope of legal aid.[72]

3. The government will remove from the scope of legal aid claims for money or damages arising from disputes about inheritance under a will or an intestacy; matters affecting the administration of a trust or the position of a trustee; matters relating to the position of company directors, restoring a company to the Register or dealing with the position of minority shareholders; matters affecting partnerships; matters before the Lands Tribunal; cases between landowners over a disputed boundary of adjacent property; and cases pursued in the course of a business.[73]

4. The government will concentrate legal aid resources on certain priority areas including

    (*a*) claims arising from people's maintenance, possession, use or enjoyment of their homes;[74]

    (*b*) actions brought to challenge the exercise of power by governmental and other public bodies, including action based on the conduct of bodies such as the police;[75]

    (*c*) the defence of claims, at any rate where there is no counter-claim;[76]

    (*d*) for the time being, and subject to a requirement that cases are handled by

---

[68] New Labour 'Because Britain Deserves Better', (1997), 35.

[69] HL Deb. 9 Dec. 1997, col. 47; Parliamentary Secretary at the LCD, speech to Law Society conference, 29 Apr. 1998. 'Access to Justice with Conditional Fees' (Mar. 1998), para. 1.7. See also NCC Report, 'A Community Legal Service' (Apr. 1998).

[70] 'Access to Justice with Conditional Fees', Mar. 1998.

[71] Ibid., para. 2.7.   [72] Ibid., para. 3.11.   [73] Ibid., para. 3.23.

[74] Ibid., para. 3.12.   [75] Ibid., para. 3.13.   [76] Ibid., para. 3.14.

solicitors with experience in the field, claims based on medical negligence.[77]

5. The government will establish a transitional fund to provide additional or support funding for, or to fund, cases in which the investigative cost or the cost of conducting the action is very high, or in which there is a demonstrable public interest (as in a case concerned with distribution of a pharmaceutical product, or pollution), where the interests of many people are affected and the case is unlikely to be the subject of a conditional fee agreement.[78]

6. The government will reconsider granting assistance with the initial start-up costs of a Contingency Legal Aid Fund as proposed by the Bar, or a Conditional Legal Aid Fund as proposed by the Law Society, if a business case is developed to show that such a fund would be viable.[79]

7. The government will consider taking the necessary reserve powers to allow it to establish a contingency Legal Aid Fund to guard against the possibility that conditional fee agreements do not achieve the results which the government hopes for.[80]

The issue that has emerged, between the Bar and the Law Society on the one side (with impressive support from the Consumers' Association, the National Consumer Council, the Legal Action Group, the Law Centres Federation, the Advice Services Alliance, Liberty, Justice, The Federation of Independent Advice Centres, The Child Poverty Action Group and Shelter) and the government on the other is in some ways surprisingly narrow. No one argues that the system should continue to operate as it currently does. It is accepted, however reluctantly, that the Lord Chancellor is bound by his government's spending limits and there is a welcome for his pledge that overall spending on legal aid will not be reduced.[81] There is fairly general acceptance that legal aid has been used in the past to finance cases which did not deserve support on their merits. Most would agree on the desirability of focusing available resources on areas of greatest need to a greater extent than in the past. There is, however, at present a radical difference of view on the best means of achieving these ends, and the crux of the difference concerns the extension of conditional fee agreements and the corresponding withdrawal of legal aid.

The government's argument is attractively, perhaps even deceptively, simple. It starts from the fact, already mentioned, that upwards of 30,000 personal injury cases have already been funded by conditional fee agreements. In the bulk of these cases the claimant has, on payment of a premium, obtained insurance cover against the possible debt he may incur to his opponent if the action is unsuccess-

---

[77] Ibid., paras. 3.15, 3.16, 3.18.
[79] Ibid., para. 4.11.
[81] HL Deb., 9 Dec. 1997, col. 42.

[78] Ibid., paras. 3.28, 3.30, 3.31, 3.32, 3.25, 3.36.
[80] Ibid., para. 4.12.

ful. As conditional fee agreements become more widely permissible, so (in the government's view) it can be assumed that insurance will become more widely available. The virtue of extending conditional fee agreements, it is argued, is that they require a party's professional advisers personally to back their judgment that a claim has a good chance of success; if they have too little confidence in their own judgment to back it by entering into a conditional fee agreement, then there is no reason (save in special categories of case) why the taxpayer should back it. The government place reliance on a report which indicates that up to now conditional fee agreements have operated fairly and in the client's interest[82] and on discussions which indicate that insurance cover is likely to become increasingly available at reasonable cost.[83]

Opponents of these proposals challenge the government's starting point. The experience of conditional fee agreements in personal injury cases, it is argued, provides no reliable guide to the future, since many of these cases are relatively straightforward, they proved in the past to have a very high rate of success and they have as a result made relatively modest demands on the Legal Aid Fund. The Bar does not, from its own inquiries, accept that insurance cover would become available at reasonable cost in the much wider and more varied range of disputes which it is proposed to exclude from legal aid cover. The Bar therefore disagree, strongly, with the proposal to extend conditional fee agreements and abolish legal aid in money recovery claims. They contend that conditional fee agreements

cannot provide a fair and effective substitute for legal aid for the poor, primarily because of the need for affordable costs insurance, the lack of quality control, ethical dangers and the reduction in plaintiffs' damages.[84]

While accepting the existence of such agreements as one means of access to justice, the Bar regard any general extension of these agreements as premature even if legal aid were preserved in money recovery claims. The Bar, however, oppose the abolition of legal aid for money recovery cases on the ground that this will effectively deny access to justice to the poorest members of society, and for deserving claims. In a response to the Lord Chancellor's consultation paper, *Justice* take the same view.[85] As a constructive counter-suggestion, the Bar (supported by *Justice*) propose a Contingency Legal Aid Fund. Access to this fund would not depend on means but on merit. The Fund would be financed by contributions from successful plaintiffs supported by the Fund, who would pay into the Fund a pre-determined proportion of the sum recovered. Out of the Fund there would be paid the costs of the unsuccessful, costs ordered to be paid in

---

[82] 'Access to Justice with Conditional Fees' (Mar. 1998), para. 2.10; 'The Price of Success Lawyers' Clients and Conditional Fees', Yarrow, Policy Studies Institute (1997).

[83] HL Deb., 9 Dec. 1997, col. 44.

[84] 'Access to Justice: A Fair Way Forward' (Jan. 1998), para. 1.13. And see 'Access to Justice with Conditional Fees—The Bar's Response to the Consultation Paper' (27 Apr. 1998) para. 1.7.

[85] *Justice* Response (April, 1998), para. 5.5.3.

favour of their successful opponents and the administration costs of the Fund. The Bar rely on an expert study which they have commissioned, and which suggests that a Fund run in this way would be financially viable. The Bar argue that such a Fund would avoid most of the undesirable features which would flow from extending conditional fee agreements and abolishing legal aid in most money recovery cases. The Law Society's proposed Conditional Legal Aid Fund is more complicated, and has some features in common both with the government's proposal and with the Bar's.

In their March 1998 consultation paper, the government acknowledge that a Contingency Legal Aid Fund as proposed by the Bar has some advantages,[86] but criticize the scope of the feasibility study on which the Bar has relied and question whether such a Fund would be financially viable, given its initial obligation to repay start-up loans. The root of the government's objection to such a Fund, however, lies in the belief that such a Fund would not work alongside conditional fees,[87] and the government are firm in their view that conditional fees offer the best means of extending legal advice and assistance in the great majority of money recovery cases. It is, however, interesting, and perhaps significant, that the government do not slam the door on the Bar's proposal: they accept that legal aid funds might properly be used to assist in the establishment of a Contingency or Conditional Legal Aid Fund; and they propose to take powers to establish such a Fund if their confidence in conditional fee agreements, and the availability of insurance, prove in the longer term to be ill-founded.[88]

It is perhaps important to bear in mind that the government's present proposals do not affect the availability of legal aid in criminal cases, which on the most recent figures absorbed £355 million out of the total net expenditure of £1216.7 million.[89] While the scales of fees paid for the conduct of such cases is of course open to review, it would indeed be hard for the government to make substantial changes in principle since article 6.3 (*c*) of the European Convention on Human Rights, currently in course of incorporation, provides that:

Every one charged with a criminal offence has the following minimum rights: . . . (c) to defend himself in person or through legal assistance of his own choosing or, if he has not sufficient means to pay for legal assistance, to be given it free when the interests of justice so require.

Nor do the government's present proposals extend to family cases, which on the most recent figures absorbed £392.6 million of the Legal Aid Fund's total expenditure, more than is spent on criminal proceedings.[90] Of this family expenditure, nearly half related to proceedings under the Children Act 1989:[91] while no one would question the prime importance of proceedings relating to the welfare and

---

[86] 'Access to Justice with Conditional Fees' (Mar. 1998), para. 4.5.
[87] Ibid., para. 4.10.   [88] Ibid., paras. 4.11, 4.12.
[89] Annual Report, Legal Aid Board (1996–7), para. 1.12.
[90] Ibid.   [91] Ibid., 78.

upbringing of children, it may well be doubted whether all this money is usefully and prudently spent.

In relation to the main thrust of the government's proposals for the reform of civil legal aid, the argument is a complex and closely reasoned one. One cannot read the well-argued responses to the Government's proposals submitted, for instance, by the Bar, the Personal Injuries Bar Association[92] and Justice without appreciating the difficulties and the potentially fateful consequences of any radical change to the current arrangements. Those of us who have had no contact with insurance interests cannot be other than unsure whether insurance cover will be available in the much wider range of civil proceedings which are suggested as suitable for conditional fee agreements. If such cover is not generally available at reasonable cost, then it seems unlikely that conditional fee agreements will fill the gap left by the withdrawal of legal aid, unless of course we were to modify the rule, taken for granted by lawyers in this country but not in comparable jurisdictions elsewhere or on the Continent of Europe, that the successful party in litigation should recover his reasonable costs against the unsuccessful. For us in judging these proposals, and for the government in implementing their proposed changes, the guiding principle must surely be that so clearly recognized by the founders of the Toynbee Hall Poor Man's Lawyer a century ago and by those who introduced the legal aid scheme half a century later: that the laws of our country exist for the benefit of the poor as well as the rich; that equality before the law is a pretence if some citizens can assert and protect their rights and others cannot; that the rule of law, to be meaningful, must ensure that justice is available to all, irrespective of means. For it is three and a half centuries since Colonel Rainborough so memorably observed, during the Putney Debates of 1648, that 'The poorest he that is in England has a life to live as the greatest he.' That is a precept which underpins not only the Legal Advice Centre but also Toynbee Hall itself, and all that it does.

---

[92] 'The Better Way Ahead—Building on Success' (27 Apr. 1998).

5

*Address at the Service of Thanksgiving for the Rt Hon Lord Denning, OM**

Lord Denning is the best-known and best-loved judge in the whole of our history.

There have over the centuries been judges of strong character, powerful intellect, great learning, courage, wisdom, compassion, eloquence, robust common-sense. All these qualities Lord Denning had in abundance. But he had something more: a unique gift of human warmth which endeared him to everyone who knew him and many who did not.

The story of Lord Denning's upbringing in Whitchurch, with his parents, his sister and his four brothers, has been so vividly and movingly told by him that it is familiar to us all. But one thing in particular is striking. Throughout his long life he remained unfailingly true to the values, beliefs, habits and tastes of his early years. He was a devoted member of the Anglican Church, loving its worship, liturgy and language. He answered to an unbending sense of duty. He had an indefatigable capacity and inexhaustible relish for hard work. He had a love of his country both deep and proud. He had a passionate love of the English countryside, particularly the chalk uplands of North Hampshire and the magical valley of the Test. He felt an instinctive respect for the continuity of our institutions and traditions and for authority, if not always for the authorities. He practised the virtues of thrift, sobriety and plain living. He had an unaffected simplicity of speech and bearing. He believed, profoundly, in the brotherhood of man and the worth of individual human beings. He was contemptuous of 'the fugitive, the trivial and the mean'. The late Victorian principles by which he governed his life are unfashionable today; and it is not perhaps surprising that his lifelong adherence to them should have given ammunition to his critics in a later and more permissive age.

This is not the place and this is not the occasion to attempt any assessment of Lord Denning's legal legacy. But nor, I think, would he wish us to ignore the great work to which, during his now unrepeatable 38-year tenure of high judicial office, he devoted his life. There was little in the law which over that time he did not touch; and little that he touched which he did not adorn. In the vast body of cases which he decided, two chords in particular are dominant. The first is fairness, a term which cannot (I believe) be accurately translated into any other language: fairness in the treatment of the citizen by the state, of the litigant by the judge, of

* Address delivered at Westminster Abbey on 17 June 1999.

the applicant by the tribunal, of the consumer by the supplier, of the tenant by the landlord, of the customer by the bank, of the deserted wife by her husband, of the member by the trade union or the profession, of the patient by the hospital and the doctor, of the party injured by a careless statement or act by the author of the injury. The second chord is freedom: freedom of the press; freedom of the person; freedom of mind and conscience; freedom from executive interference; freedom under the law.

If wrapped in legal jargon, with an occasional dash of Latin, all these things may sound technical and abstruse and remote from the humdrum realities of everyday life. But in his mouth they never did. Lord Denning's judgments were rooted not in discussion of abstract jurisprudential principle but in the vivid experience of recognizable men and women. It was this human dimension, coupled with a distinctive literary style, which gave his judgments their unmistakable and very personal quality. We all have our favourites. I cannot forbear to quote four of his:

Old Peter Beswick was a coal merchant in Eccles, Lancashire. He had no business premises. All he had was a lorry, scales and weights . . .

It happened on 19 April 1964. It was bluebell time in Kent. Mr and Mrs Hinz had been married some ten years, and they had four children, all aged 9 and under. The youngest was one. Mrs Hinz was a remarkable woman . . .

Broadchalke is one of the most pleasing villages in England. Old Herbert Bundy, the defendant, was a farmer there. His home was at Yew Tree Farm. It went back for three hundred years. His family had been there for generations. It was his only asset. But he did a very foolish thing. He mortgaged it to the bank. Up to the very hilt . . .

To some this may appear to be a small matter, but to Mr Harry Hook it is very important. He is a street trader in the Barnsley market. He has been trading there for some six years without any complaint being made against him; but, nevertheless, he has now been banned from trading in the market for life. All because of a trifling incident . . .

The peculiar genius of Lord Denning was perfectly matched to the need of the hour. 'When Tom and I were young', wrote Lord Devlin, 'the law was stagnant'. In Lord Hailsham's words, 'It seemed almost as if Our Lady of the Common Law had gone into a decline . . .' The age of creation appeared to have gone. That of literalists, slavish adherents of precedent and quietist acceptors of the status quo appeared to have succeeded; and the glory of the common law appeared to have been extinguished forever. That the law was aroused from its torpor was not, of course, the work of one court or one judge. The credit must be much more widely shared. But in any roll of the great emancipators Lord Denning would be assured of an honoured place, probably at the head of the list. For he brought a new, adventurous and imaginative vision to bear. He was more concerned with the intention of a statute than with its precise terminology. He was not overly respectful of precedent. He was prepared to entertain unorthodox arguments if they appeared to lead to what he saw as justice. He did not shrink from novelty. 'What is the argument on the other side?' he asked in one case, and answered:

Only this, that no case has been found in which it has been done before. That argument does not appeal to me in the least. If we never do anything which has not been done before, we shall never get anywhere. The law will stand still while the rest of the world goes on: and that will be bad for both.

The secret of his attraction to the legal profession and to the general public was, as Lord Devlin suggested, the belief that he opened the door to the law above the law. He had, to the end, an almost uncanny insight into the thoughts and values of his fellow-countrymen.

To the advocate he was the perfect judge: courteous, unintimidating, open-minded, very quick, self-deprecating, devoid of pomposity. He seemed genuinely interested in every case, however arid; he was warm and encouraging to counsel, particularly the untried. Under his benign but exacting enquiry all advocates gave of their best. Unlike some other judges, he could demolish an argument he judged to be false without needlessly humiliating its author. And for all his interest and patience he was never indecisive; there was never any doubt about who had won.

His longevity could on occasion be a problem. I recall one case in which my argument depended heavily on an observation of Viscount Simon, speaking for a unanimous seven-member House of Lords in 1942. I warmed to my theme. But the Master of the Rolls interrupted. 'Oh', he said, 'but Lord Simon was very sorry he ever said that. He told me so.' But sometimes his encyclopedic knowledge of the cases, or his vivid imagination, would come to the aid of an advocate cowering under the assault of his opponent or of Lord Denning's judicial colleagues. Like all great judges he was of course, on occasion, inconsistent and unpredictable. All depended on his, sometimes very personal, perception of where the merits lay and what justice required. But that made the hearing all the more absorbing. No wonder the Bar loved him. No wonder that his colleagues embarked on so many hazardous journeys under his leadership. No wonder that his exchanges with litigants representing themselves, conducted on his side in his broadest Hampshire burr, were the stuff of legend. No wonder that he inspired such loyalty among those who worked for him.

For five days a week, over a continuous period of more than 20 years, Lord Denning presided in the Master of the Rolls' court, giving the first judgment in every single case, usually as soon as the argument had ended. It was an intellectual, and also a physical, achievement which will never be rivalled. His energy, his interest, and his appetite were unflagging. If the beleaguered advocate were tempted to enquire, at 4 o'clock on a Friday afternoon, whether the court might think it a convenient moment to rise, he would be disappointed.

I have so far said nothing of the private man. His devotion to the memory of his first wife Mary, who died so tragically and so young, is a matter of record. He was a very proud and very affectionate father of Robert, who followed in his footsteps with great distinction to Magdalen College Oxford, and a great patriarch of his extended family. His attachment to his second wife Joan is perhaps best expressed in a letter written on her death after nearly 47 years of married life:

I feel it is really an occasion for thankfulness for a long and happy life—but for me it is all sadness at the loss of her so dear to me.

It would scarcely be possible to list the bodies to which, over the years, he gave his loyalty and lent his energetic support. They would certainly include Magdalen College Oxford, Birkbeck College London, and the University of Buckingham; the Inns of Court, particularly Lincoln's Inn, his parent Inn, and the Law Society; the Lawyers' Christian Fellowship; the Cheshire Homes, Cumberland Lodge and Outpost Emmaus; the Magna Carta Trust, the Public Record Office, the Historical Manuscripts Commission; the Magistrates' Association; the British Institute of International and Comparative Law; the English Association; the National Association of Parish Councils; the National Marriage Guidance Council; the Draper's Company; Queen Elizabeth College, Greenwich; the City of London. But he still found time to arbitrate about sugar cane in Fiji and bananas in Jamaica. He still accepted the Prime Minister's invitation to report on the Profumo Affair, a task accomplished between June and September of 1963; many years later he presided at a dinner in Lincoln's Inn to celebrate the outstanding service of Mr Profumo to Toynbee Hall, an event which testifies to the stature of both men. At an age when most men look for leisure, Lord Denning turned author, publishing books in each of his last four years in office, books valued by those who have them not only for their contents but also for their very personal dedications. And throughout his term as Master of the Rolls he travelled the world, tirelessly and repeatedly, giving lectures and addresses, receiving honorary degrees, making friends and establishing a rapport with the young of five continents which few men of any age have ever enjoyed. To those who expect judges to be cold, formal, bloodless and pedantic he was a revelation. The respect and affection he inspired, particularly in the countries of the Commonwealth, was indeed extraordinary: I recall meeting a Guyanese advocate who practised from Denning Chambers in Georgetown and who had christened his eldest son Alfred Thompson. Last year saw the opening of Denning House in Calgary, Alberta. Many other examples could be given, in this country and round the world. For all these services alone, Her Majesty's appointment to the Order of Merit, unique for a professional judge, would have been well-earned recognition.

We are privileged to remember Lord Denning as an unforgettable human being whose hundredth birthday we recently celebrated with pride and pleasure. But we also remember him as a great judge and it is as a great judge that he will take his place in history. Not all his judgments, of course, will stand the test of time; some, indeed, were cut down in the pride of their youth; others were raked by academic grapeshot. But more, many more, left an indelible imprint on the living law of our country, and the spirit which inspired all these judgments will endure. He saw the law not as a code of rules, but as a collection of human stories, each with a moral; not as a fetter, but as a source of freedom; not as an unwelcome but inescapable response to the ills of society, but as a means of providing that justice upon which good government and social harmony fundamentally depend. He invested the art of the advocate and the role of the judge with a new nobility. He always looked forward, never back. He sought to build, not to pull down. Some well-known lines of Wordsworth provide, I think, an appropriate epitaph:

> Enough, if something from our hands have power
> To live, and act, and serve the future hour;
> And if, as toward the silent tomb we go,
> Through love, through hope, and faith's transcendent dower,
> We feel that we are greater than we know.

Index

Index compiled by Frank Pert